Foundation Accounting

Tutorial

Second edition

NVQ Accounting Units 1 – 4

David Cox

Michael Fardon

osborne BOOKS

Second edition. First edition published 2000.

Published by Osborne Books Limited
Unit 1B Everoak Estate
Bromyard Road
Worcester WR2 5HP
Tel 01905 748071
Email books@osbornebooks.co.uk
Website www.osbornebooks.co.uk

Design by Richard Holt
Cover image from Getty Images

Printed by the Bath Press, Bath

British Library Cataloguing in Publication Data
A catalogue record for this book is available from the British Library

ISBN 1 872962 81 5

Student Activities

4.1 Balance the following accounts at 30 April 2004, bringing down the balances on 1 May:

Dr — Sales Account — Cr

2004		£	2004		£
			1 Apr	Balance b/d	12,555
30 Apr	Bal c/d	17,195	30 Apr	Sales Day Book	4,640
		17,195			17,195
			1 May	Bal b/d	17,195

Dr — Sales Returns Account — Cr

2004		£	2004		£
1 Apr	Balance b/d	527			
30 Apr	Sales Returns Day Book	200	30/4	Bal c/d	727
		727			727
1 May	Bal b/d	727			

Dr — Value Added Tax Account — Cr

2004		£	2004		£
30 Apr	Sales Returns Day Book	35	1 Apr	Balance b/d	1,233
30 Apr	Bal c/d	2010	30 Apr	Sales Day Book	812
		2045			2,045
			1 May	Bal b/d	2010

Dr — T Johnson — Cr

2004		£	2004		£
1 Apr	Balance b/d	496			
5 Apr	Sales	198			
20 Apr	Sales	467			
26 Apr	Sales	302	30 Apr	Bal c/d	1463
		1463			1463
1 May	Bal b/d	1463			

Dr — Doyle Traders — Cr

2004		£	2004		£
1 Apr	Balance b/d	183	14 Apr	Sales Returns	47
8 Apr	Sales	221			
22 Apr	Sales	395	30 Apr	Bal c/d	752
		799			799
1 May	Bal b/d	752			

4.2 You have the following information:

- opening debtor balances at start of month £18,600
- credit sales for month £9,100
- sales returns for month £800

What is the figure for closing debtor balances at the end of the month?

(a) £10,300

(b) £26,900

(c) £27,700

(d) £28,500

Answer (a) or (b) or (c) or (d)

4.3 A friend has recently started work as an accounts clerk for a large electrical wholesalers. He asks you the following questions about control accounts:

- "What are the principles of control accounts?"
- "I've heard it said that control accounts help the management of the business. How is this?"
- "In our double-entry system we have a sales ledger control account in the main ledger, with an account for each debtor kept in the subsidiary (sales) ledger. I thought you told me earlier that debtors' accounts were part of double-entry ..."

Write answers to your friend.

4.4 Prepare a sales ledger control account for the month of June 2004 from the following information:

2004		£
1 Jun	Debit balance brought down	17,491
30 Jun	Credit sales for month	42,591
	Sales returns	1,045
	Payments received from debtors	39,024

Balance the account at 30 June 2004.

4.5 The main ledger of Shire Traders contains the following accounts on 1 February 2004:

sales, balance £5,097.24 credit

sales returns, balance £346.97 debit

Value Added Tax, balance £452.31 credit

The subsidiary (sales) ledger contains the following accounts on 1 February 2004:

Arrow Valley Retailers, balance £826.40 debit

B Brick (Builders) Limited, balance £59.28 debit

Mereford Manufacturing Company, balance £293.49 debit

Redgrove Restorations, balance £724.86 debit

Wyvern Warehouse Limited, balance £108.40 debit

The following transactions, which have been authorised by the accounts supervisor, took place during February 2004:

3 Feb	Sold goods on credit to Arrow Valley Retailers £205.75 + VAT, invoice no 2731
5 Feb	Sold goods on credit to Mereford Manufacturing Company £112.37 + VAT, invoice no 2732
6 Feb	Redgrave Restorations returned goods £85.90 + VAT, credit note no CN127 issued
10 Feb	Sold goods on credit to Wyvern Warehouse Limited £412.96 + VAT, invoice no 2733
12 Feb	Sold goods on credit to Redgrove Restorations £258.21 + VAT, invoice no 2734
17 Feb	Mereford Manufacturing Company returned goods £45.27 + VAT, credit note no CN128 issued
19 Feb	Sold goods on credit to B Brick (Builders) Limited £275.36 + VAT, invoice no 2735
23 Feb	Sold goods on credit to Redgrove Restorations £204.47 + VAT, invoice no 2736
27 Feb	B Brick (Builders) Limited returned goods £28.40 + VAT, credit note no CN129 issued

You are to:

(a) prepare the accounts in the main ledger – including a sales ledger control account – and subsidiary (sales) ledger of Shire Traders and record the balances at 1 February 2004.

(b) enter the above transactions in Shire Traders' sales day book and sales returns day book for February 2004.

(c) from the books of prime entry, record the accounting entries in the main ledger and subsidiary (sales) ledger, balancing all accounts at the month-end (29 February 2004).

(d) reconcile the control account balance with the subsidiary accounts at 1 February and 29 February 2004.

5 Receiving and recording payments

this chapter covers . . .

This chapter explains the different ways in which money is received by an organisation and then sets out the procedures it follows in recording those payments. It covers:

- *receiving money in the form of cash, cheques and similar items, inter-bank transfers and payment by debit and credit card*
- *the legal meaning of cheque crossings and endorsements*
- *checking of the money against covering documentation where appropriate*
- *checking cash, giving change and issuing receipts*
- *recording incoming payments on remittance lists, cash books and cash registers*
- *dealing with problem payments – incorrect cheques, suspicious cards, situations where the money received does not tally with the accompanying documentation*

*This chapter concentrates on the manual recording of receipts. Recording receipts using **computer accounting** is dealt with in Chapter 26.*

NVQ PERFORMANCE CRITERIA COVERED

unit 1: RECORDING INCOME AND RECEIPTS

element 1.2

process receipts

A *check receipts against relevant supporting information*

D *identify unusual features and either resolve or refer to the appropriate person*

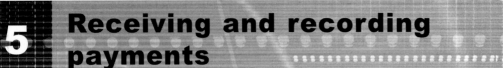

INCOMING PAYMENTS

Payments can be received by an organisation in a variety of ways:

- cash
- cheque
- credit card and debit card transactions (which can be manually or electronically processed)
- direct to the bank by inter-bank transfer: BACS and CHAPS

It depends on the nature and the size of the organisation how the payments are received and processed. In the retail sector, for example, a newsagent will depend to a great extent on cash transactions and the cash register, a large supermarket on the other hand will use electronic tills and accept cash, cheques, and credit and debit card payments.

CASH

Cash is still used for most small transactions, and we are still nowhere near the 'cashless society' which is often talked about.

As far as the organisation accepting payments in cash is concerned, the main disadvantage of cash is the security problem, and there is a risk of receiving forged notes.

receiving payment in cash

For a business receiving sums of money in the form of cash it is necessary for an employee to count the cash received and check it against the amount due. Notes should be checked for forgeries (held against the light or viewed on special machines). Change will need to be given when the exact amount is not tendered (given). For example:

Sale	£3.64
Amount tendered (given) by customer	£10.00
Change to be given	£6.36

The amount of change is the difference between the amount tendered and the amount of the sale. When a cash till is in use, modern types of till will indicate the amount of change to be given after the amount tendered has been entered through the keypad. You will know, from having bought items in shops, that many cashiers count out the change starting with the amount of the sale and working to the amount tendered.

Often when payment is made in cash, a receipt is given: this can take the form of a machine-produced receipt, such as is given in a shop, or a handwritten receipt. Look at these examples:

Receipt		
Everest Sports	←	retailer
15 High St Mereford	←	address
08 10 03 15.07	←	date and time of transaction
Salesperson Tina	←	salesperson
Tennis balls 5.99	←	goods purchased
Shin guards 8.99	←	goods purchased
TOTAL 14.98	←	total due
CASH 20.00	←	£20 (probably a £20 note) given by the customer
CHANGE 5.02	←	change given
Thank you for your custom	←	personal message to help public relations
Please retain this receipt in case of any query	←	advice to retain receipt in case of a problem with the goods
VAT REG 373 2888 11	←	VAT Registration number

a till receipt

ENIGMA MUSIC LIMITED **receipt** **958**

13 High Street, Mereford MR1 2TF
VAT Reg 343 7645 23

Customer *R V Williams* **date** *3 Oct 2003*

'Golden Oldies' by J Moore	*£20.00*
	£20.00
VAT @ 17.5%	*£3.50*
Total	*£23.50*

a hand-written receipt

tills and cash floats

At the end of the day it will be necessary to 'cash up' by balancing the amount of cash held. As most cash tills start each day with a float of cash (to enable change to be given, if necessary, to the first customers), the amount in the till at the end of the day will be:

cash float at start

plus sales made during the day (listed on the till roll)

equals amount of cash held at end of day

a modern electronic till

A cash float will be kept back for the following day, and the surplus will be transferred to the safe for paying into the bank next day. Alternatively, a bank paying-in slip (see the next chapter) might be made out, and the cash, together with the paying-in slip and any cheques received placed in a 'wallet' to be deposited in the bank's night safe (see the next chapter).

A typical calculation would be:

cash float at start	£150.00
plus sales made during the day (listed on the till roll)	£2,608.50
equals amount of cash held at end of day	£2,758.50
less cash float retained for next day	£150.00
amount transferred to safe or bank's night safe	£2,608.50

If the cash in the till does not agree with the total on the till roll, the discrepancy needs investigation. Regular discrepancies for significant amounts, eg £5 or £10, will lead to urgent investigations – there could be pilfering taking place if the till is often short at the end of the day, or it could be caused by poor cashiering – giving the wrong change.

guidelines for cash handling

Those who handle cash in an organisation are responsible for its safekeeping. Cash is often a target for theft – and regrettably not only from people outside the organisation. General security guidelines for looking after cash received will vary according to the size and type of organisation:

- cash should be kept in a cash till or in a cash box which should be kept locked when not in use
- keys should be retained under the control of the cashier
- as little cash as is practically possible should be kept in tills
- cash should be paid into the bank as soon as possible

'topping up' the petty cash

The organisation may also operate a petty cash system for making small payments (see Chapter 16). The cash will be kept in a locked tin and will need to be 'topped up' from time-to-time to what is known as the 'imprest amount'. Care will have to be taken when transferring money from the main cash fund to the petty cash tin: security precautions should be observed and the transaction recorded.

CHEQUES

Cheques are issued by banks to their personal and business account customers. Building societies also issue cheques on current accounts – their customers are mainly personal. Payment by cheque is a common method of payment for all but the smallest amounts. A specimen cheque is shown below (there is more on how to write out a cheque in Chapter 13).

what is a cheque?

A cheque, as used in normal business practice, may be defined as

a written order to the bank (known as the 'drawee') signed by its customer (known as the 'drawer') to pay a specified amount to a specified person (known as the 'payee')

Some organisations – large retail stores, for example – have machines which print out their customers' cheques on the till. A large number of cheques, however, are still written by hand, and great care must be taken both when writing out cheques and also when receiving cheques in payment. The cheques must be examined to ensure that all the details and signatures are correct. The vast majority of cheques are 'crossed' – they have two parallel lines, known as a 'crossing' on the front of the cheque.

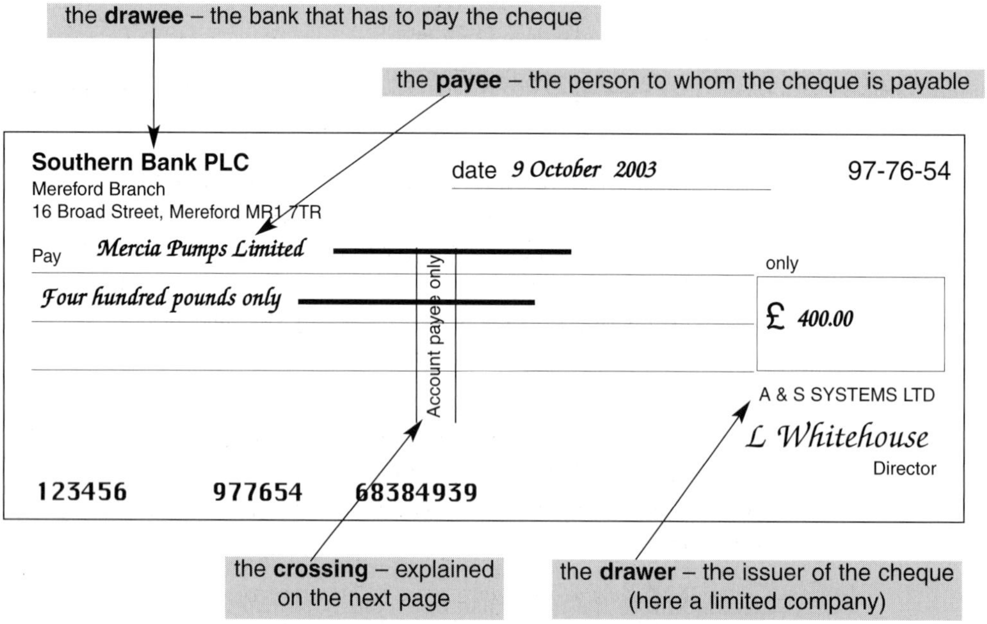

the 'parties' and crossing on a cheque

examining the cheque

If you are receiving payment by cheque, whether it is direct from the customer over the counter or through the post on a remittance advice, there are a number of basic checks to carry out:

- is the cheque signed? – it is invalid if it is not
- is the payee's name correct? – it should be changed and initialled by the drawer (issuer) if it is not
- is the cheque in date? – a cheque becomes out of date ('stale') and invalid after six months; note that if the date is missing, it may be written in
- do the words and figures agree? – the cheque may be returned by the bank if they do not

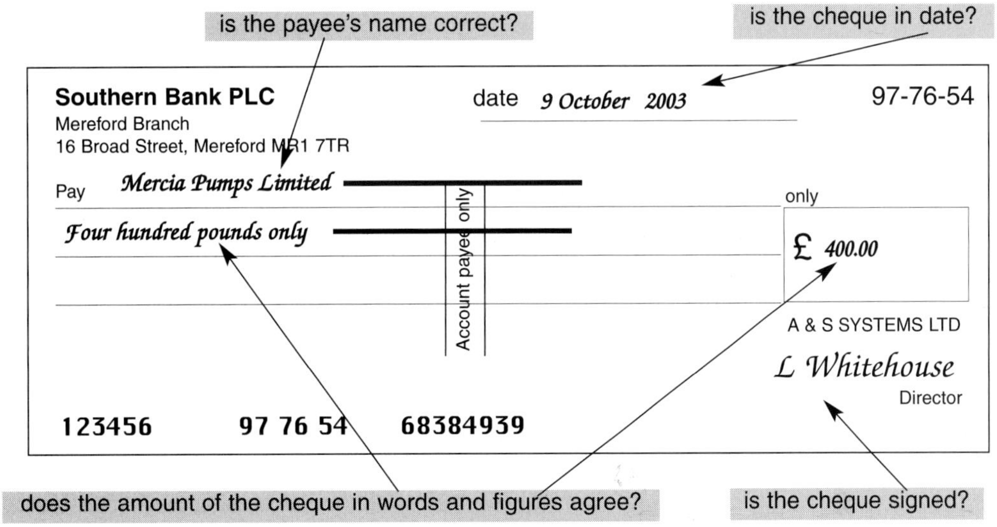

checking the cheque

If the organisation accepting payment by cheque is inefficient and does not carry out these precautions, the cheque concerned may be returned to the organisation's bank after it has been paid in, and the amount of the cheque deducted from the organisation's bank account. If the cheque is issued with a guarantee card, different conditions apply (see page 96).

crossings

Cheques are normally *crossed* – they are printed with two parallel lines across the face of the cheque. Often there are words printed or written in the crossing. If a cheque is not crossed, it is an *open* cheque. Open cheques are very rare.

A crossed cheque may only be paid into a bank account. The crossing says in effect: 'this cheque must be paid into a bank account'.

types of crossing

If you are receiving cheques you will need to know the different types of crossing, as the type of crossing may affect whether or not the cheque can be paid into the organisation's bank account. These are the basic types of crossing:

crossing	***effect***
& co or (two parallel lines)	A *general* crossing – the cheque can be paid into the bank
HSBC Bank Pershore	This crossing is known as a *special* crossing – the cheque can *only* be paid into HSBC Bank in Pershore
account payee	An *account payee* crossing' – this cheque should only be paid into the payee's account

endorsements – a historical note

Traditionally the payee of a cheque was entitled to sign it on the back – *endorse* it – so that it could be passed on to another person who could pay it into his or her bank account and receive payment. This signature on the back was known as an *endorsement,* which means 'written on the back'. Owners of a driving licence with an 'endorsement' may be familiar with this term!

The Cheques Act 1992 has, in effect, made cheque endorsements redundant. The Act states that a cheque which has an 'account payee' or 'a/c payee' crossing is 'not transferable'. This means it cannot change hands after the payee has received it – except, of course, when it is paid into the bank. As most cheques are now crossed 'account payee' the idea of the payee endorsing the cheque has become largely meaningless. Banks generally nowadays *only accept cheques for the account of the payee.*

PAYMENT BY MULTIFUNCTION CARD

Banks issue 'multifunction cards' which combine a number of different services for their customers. These services include:

- giving cash from cash machines in the UK and abroad
- guaranteeing payment of customers' cheques up to a certain amount, usually £100 or (more commonly) £250
- acting as debit cards – enabling customers to make payment without issuing a cheque

Businesses which accept payment from customers using these cards either over the counter, by telephone or through mail order must be familiar with the procedures for accepting payment.

The details shown below describe The Royal Bank of Scotland 'Highline' multifunction card. They also explain how the customer's photograph can be incorporated into the card as an added security measure.

The symbols which are also shown below relate to the functions of the card.

On the pages which follow we describe how businesses deal with:

- the cheque guarantee function
- the debit card function

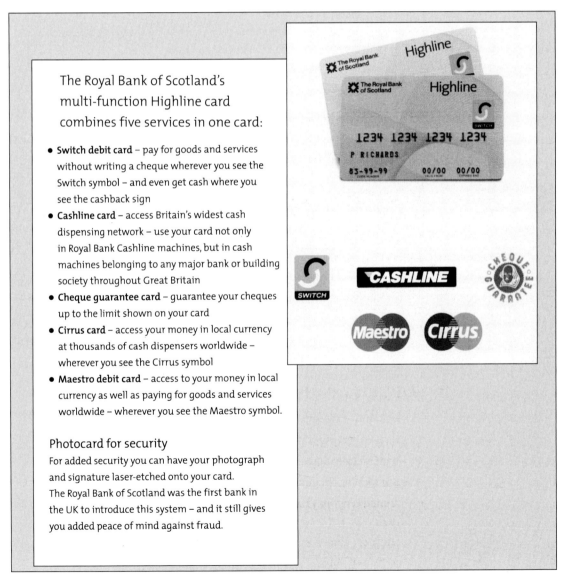

The Royal Bank of Scotland's multi-function Highline card combines five services in one card:

- **Switch debit card** – pay for goods and services without writing a cheque wherever you see the Switch symbol – and even get cash where you see the cashback sign
- **Cashline card** – access Britain's widest cash dispensing network – use your card not only in Royal Bank Cashline machines, but in cash machines belonging to any major bank or building society throughout Great Britain
- **Cheque guarantee card** – guarantee your cheques up to the limit shown on your card
- **Cirrus card** – access your money in local currency at thousands of cash dispensers worldwide – wherever you see the Cirrus symbol
- **Maestro debit card** – access to your money in local currency as well as paying for goods and services worldwide – wherever you see the Maestro symbol.

Photocard for security

For added security you can have your photograph and signature laser-etched onto your card.
The Royal Bank of Scotland was the first bank in the UK to introduce this system – and it still gives you added peace of mind against fraud.

a card used to guarantee cheques

The rules for the use of a multifunction card used to guarantee a customer's cheques may be set out in the agreement form signed when the card is issued, or may be available at the bank. Here are some typical conditions:

> XYZ Bank plc guarantees in any single transaction the payment of one cheque taken from one of its own cheque books for up to £250 provided the cheque is not drawn on the account of a Limited Company, and
>
> (1) The cheque bears the same name and code number as this card.
>
> (2) It is signed, before the expiry of the card, in the United Kingdom of Great Britain and Northern Ireland, the Channel Islands or the Isle of Man in the presence of the payee by the person whose signature appears on this card.
>
> (3) The card number is written on the back of the cheque by the payee.
>
> (4) The card has not been altered or defaced.

receiving payment by cheque and guarantee card

If you have read the guarantee card conditions set out above you will appreciate that when you accept payment by cheque and cheque guarantee card you must take great care that all the conditions are met. If you do not, the purchaser's bank may not 'honour' (pay) the cheque, and your organisation stands to lose the money. Also, because of the large number of stolen and fraudulent cards in circulation, you must be on your guard against suspicious-looking cards and customers. The procedure is therefore as follows:

- if there is a photograph of the customer on the card, check it to make sure that the person in front of you is that customer
- examine the card to make sure it is not defaced – has the photograph or signature been tampered with? – be suspicious if the card is handed to you in a plastic wallet – it may be a forgery
- examine the card for
  - expiry date
  - amount of the guarantee (if it is stated)
  - name agreeing with the name on the cheque
  - bank details agreeing with those on the cheque
- examine the cheque for
  - signature (this should agree with the signature on the card)
  - date
  - payee's name
  - amount in words and figures (they should agree)

- write the card number on the back of the cheque – an essential procedure, adding any other details which your organisation requires (some businesses use a rubber stamp on the back of the cheque to list the required details)

cheque card limits – a common mistake

Bank customers sometimes think that if the cost of the item being purchased is above the cheque guarantee limit, then a number of cheques may be issued and payment is guaranteed. This is not correct – the cheque card guarantee covers only *one cheque per transaction.*

DEBIT CARDS

Debit cards are issued to personal customers by banks and building societies to enable their customers to make payments from their bank accounts by Electronic Funds Transfer (see page 102). *No cheque is written out.*

Debit cards are issued to selected customers of the bank; they enable a payment to be made from the person's bank account electronically. A debit card has the obvious advantages of being quicker to use and more convenient. Examples of debit cards are Barclays' Connect (see below) and Royal Bank of Scotland Highline cards.

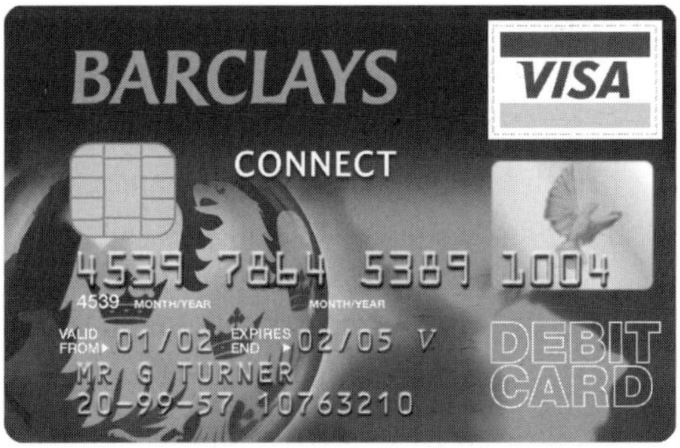

From a seller's point of view, when a customer wishes to pay by debit card in person, the transaction is handled in a similar way to a credit card, (see next page) using either

- a manually completed sales voucher on an imprinter, or, more commonly
- an electronic terminal, either 'standalone' and linked by telephone (used by smaller organisations), or connected to an electronic 'card swipe' till (as in the big supermarkets)

CREDIT CARDS

Credit cards provide a means of obtaining goods and services immediately, but paying for them later. The commonest credit cards used in the UK are from Visa and Mastercard. The card illustrated below is a Visa Barclaycard.

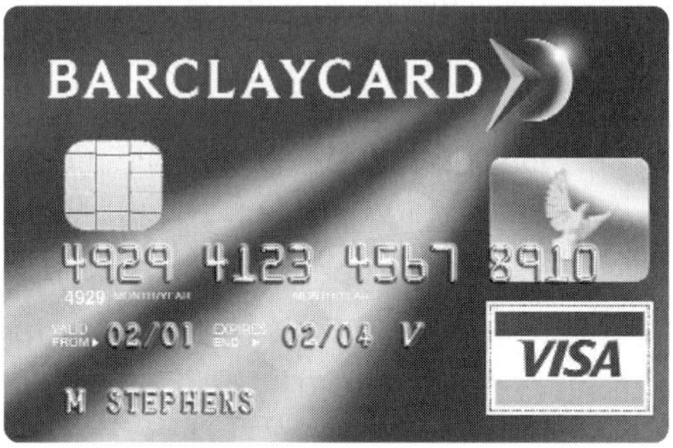

Credit cards are issued, upon application, to customers of banks, building societies, retail chains and an increasingly wide variety of businesses and other organisations, including charities. A credit limit is set on each cardholder's credit card account. Goods and services can be obtained at shops and other outlets having imprinters or computer terminals requiring a customer signature, or a 'Chip and PIN' system, for preparing sales vouchers to record the transaction. Credit cards are also increasingly used for mail order, telephoned and internet sales.

Retailers use a *card merchant* to process all their card payments, and pay a set percentage (up to 5%) of each transaction amount for the use of the credit card facility. An example of a card merchant is Streamline.

Each month a cardholder is sent a statement of the purchases made and can choose to pay off the balance of the account, or to pay part only (subject to a certain minimum amount), carrying forward the remaining balance to next month. Interest is charged on balances owing to the credit card company.

ACCEPTING CARD PAYMENTS – 'OVER THE COUNTER' SALES

A business will have a variety of methods of receiving payment by credit card or debit card by a customer who calls in person:

- a mechanical imprinter machine, which imprints the embossed details from the credit card onto the sales voucher – this method is becoming less common as the electronic terminal (see below) gains popularity
- an electronic till or a terminal for processing the payments – linked to the card merchant by telephone line, requiring a signature or a PIN number

mechanical imprinter machine

The procedure is as follows:

- check any photograph on the card and make sure that the card has not been defaced or tampered with
- check that the card has not expired
- imprint the sales voucher (see illustration below)
- complete the sales voucher with date, details of goods, and total money amount
- the customer signs the imprinted sales voucher, and the signature should be compared with that on the card
- the list of stolen cards is checked
- if the payment is above a certain amount – the *floor limit* (which varies according to the type of business) it will be necessary to telephone the card merchant company to obtain an authorisation code for the transaction to go ahead (see page 102) – the authorisation code is recorded on the sales voucher
- the top copy of the sales voucher is handed to the customer, and the other three copies are retained
- of the three copies of the sales voucher which are retained, the white copy is treated in the same way as a cheque, and is kept in the till and added to the cheques and cash received to give the total sales figure; the other two copies (yellow and blue) are kept in the event of a query in the future
- the white copy of the sales voucher kept in the till is then banked along with the cash and cheques

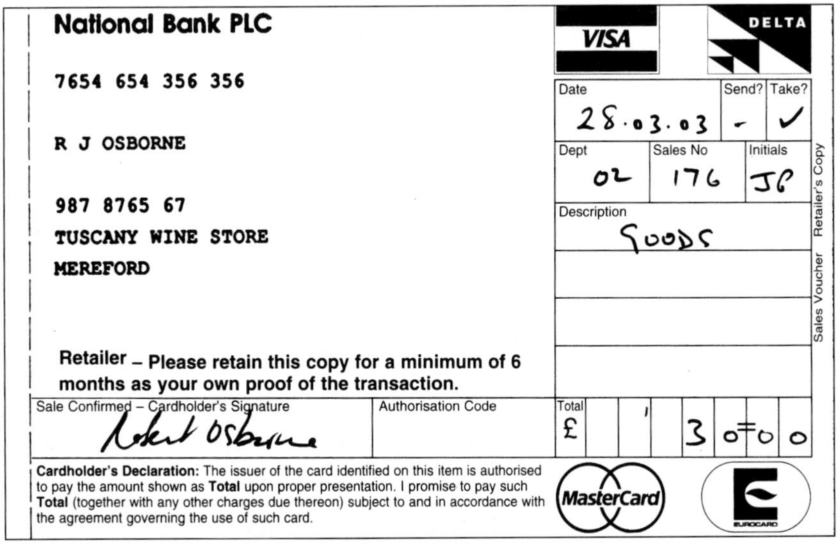
National Bank PLC

7654 654 356 356

R J OSBORNE

987 8765 67

TUSCANY WINE STORE

MEREFORD

Retailer – Please retain this copy for a minimum of 6 months as your own proof of the transaction.

VISA DELTA

Date	Send?	Take?
28.03.03	-	✓

Dept	Sales No	Initials
02	176	JP

Description: GOODS

Sales Voucher Retailer's Copy

Sale Confirmed – Cardholder's Signature: Robert Osborne

Authorisation Code

Total £ 30.00

Cardholder's Declaration: The issuer of the card identified on this item is authorised to pay the amount shown as **Total** upon proper presentation. I promise to pay such **Total** (together with any other charges due thereon) subject to and in accordance with the agreement governing the use of such card.

MasterCard EUROCARD

a credit card sales voucher

credit and debit card sales through a terminal

An electronic terminal can be used for both credit card and debit card transactions. The assistant operating the terminal should:

- in the case of a shop till, put the card through the card reader – this 'captures' the details encoded in the magnetic stripe on the reverse of the card or in the chip embedded in the card
- in the case of a business using a 'standalone' terminal, the details are input manually when the terminal is connected to the card merchant by telephone line
- in both cases, the card merchant's system checks automatically that
  - the card number is valid
  - the card has not been lost or stolen
  - there is enough money (or limit) available to pay for the transaction
- if all is well, each transaction will be allowed to pass through; if it is not, the customer will be asked to pay another way, eg cash!
- if the amount is above the 'floor limit', a telephone call to the card merchant may be required to authorise the transaction (see page 102)
- the till prints a receipt which includes space for the cardholder's signature (which is compared with that on the card) unless it is a 'Chip and PIN' transaction, in which case no signature is required
- the customer is handed the top-copy of the receipt, and the other copy is kept in the event of a query in the future
- the amount of the transaction is automatically debited (deducted)
  - in the case of a credit card from the cardholder's credit card account
  - in the case of a debit card from the cardholder's bank account
- the amount of the transaction is automatically credited (added) to the bank account of the business
- the business will receive a regular schedule of amounts automatically paid into the bank account (see illustration below); this will be checked with the bank statement when it is received

ALBION BANK CARD SERVICES **PAYMENT SUMMARY** 12 March 2003

Debit/credit card batches paid to account Hermes Trading Limited, Albion Bank, Mereford Account 1248934

Date	Type	Amount
05 03 03	Credit Card batch	1356.75
05 03 03	Switch transactions	56.75
07 03 03	Credit Card batch	1756.29
07 03 03	Switch transactions	128.00
09 03 03	Credit Card batch	5634.01
09 03 03	TOTAL FOR WEEK	8931.80

Charges to account 12489341 **Credit card charges** (2.5%) £218.68 **Debit card charges** £5.50

checks when accepting a card on a terminal

There are a number of checks that should be made when accepting payment when operating an electronic terminal. These apply equally to debit cards and to credit cards. You should make sure that:

- the card has an appropriate logo, eg 'Maestro' – you will probably have a list against which you can compare the logo
- the card has a magnetic stripe on the reverse or an embedded chip
- the card has not expired
- the start date on the card is not in the future
- the card holder title is appropriate (eg a card issued to Miss Helen Jones is not used by a man!)
- the signature on the card is consistent and has not been tampered with, unless it is a 'Chip and PIN' card, in which case the PIN number has to be accepted satisfactorily
- the card has not been defaced or mutilated in any way
- any photograph on the card looks like the customer

mail order and telephone sales

Buying goods and services by credit card and debit card over the telephone, and by mail order is very common. When accepting payment by this means, the organisation must exercise the same degree of care as a shop accepting an 'over the counter' transaction. Some organisations will complete the same type of sales voucher used for an 'over the counter' transaction and send the top copy to the customer as a receipt; some organisations will use an electronic terminal, and send a copy of the receipt to the customer. Organisations which have a large volume of transactions will not use vouchers but instead record the details of sales on a Mail Order Schedule, a form which will provide space for recording ten transactions or more.

When accepting payment by credit card by telephone or mail order, the following details must be obtained:

- the card number
- the expiry date of the card
- the issue number and/or start date of any debit card
- the name and initials of the cardholder as shown on the card
- the cardholder's address
- the cardholder's signature (mail order only)

Any authorisation of amounts over the 'floor limit' must be carried out in the normal way. Internet sales are also booming – see page 103.

floor limits and authorisations

As we have seen, it may be necessary from time-to-time for a business accepting a debit or credit card payment to seek authorisation for the transaction from the card merchant company (the company that deals with all the payments). Authorisation can be given over the telephone or in some cases electronically. Authorisation may be needed in a number of situations:

- when the amount of the transaction exceeds the Floor Limit – this limit is a transaction amount set by the card merchant company – it can vary
- the terminal indicates that the card is not valid for some reason or other (it may be out of date)
- when the cashier is suspicious about the signature
- when the cashier is suspicious about the customer
- the terminal indicates that the cashier should contact the card merchant company (it may be a stolen card!)

These authorisations are important because if they are not carried out the business accepting payment may lose the money – it will not be a guaranteed payment. Many retail businesses give rewards to vigilant cashiers who recover a stolen card used by a suspicious customer – who normally runs out of the store when the cashier decides to ask for authorisation!

ELECTRONIC FUNDS TRANSFER AT POINT OF SALE (EFTPOS)

EFT stands for 'Electronic Funds Transfer'. Credit card and debit card transactions which go through an electronic terminal are processed by a system known as *Electronic Funds Transfer at Point Of Sale* (EFTPOS). This allows a retail outlet to debit the bank account or credit card account of the purchaser at the point of sale and, at the same time, to credit the retailer's bank account. Besides removing the need to carry a lot of cash, the system reduces the paperwork of writing out cheques or filling in card vouchers.

Details of the transaction are transmitted electronically by means of a computer link to a central computer either immediately, or, normally, at the end of the day.

The benefits of EFTPOS to a retail business are:

- greater efficiency, with less time taken by customers to make payment
- reduced queuing time
- less cash to handle (giving fewer security risks)
- guaranteed payment once acceptance has been made

INTERNET PAYMENT TRANSACTIONS

Businesses which have on-line facilities for selling their products from their websites carry out these sales on a 'remote control' basis. They do not deal with these customers personally. The customers order and pay for the goods on-line using a credit or debit card and all the business has to do is to despatch the goods (eg an on-line shop) or provide the service (eg a holiday company). The money is credited (added) directly to the bank account of the business.

The business will receive a schedule of the payments received which it can check against its bank statement.

The buying public is naturally concerned about the security of this system. Stories abound of people hacking into shop and bank websites and obtaining names and credit card numbers and then going on spending sprees. Businesses setting up on-line selling facilities have to ensure that the security of the system is as watertight as it can be. Software companies are constantly working to improve levels of security and methods of encoding data ('encryption') so that payment details – including card numbers – remain secret.

The mechanics of how the payment from an internet purchase reaches the bank account of the seller is explained in detail on page 128.

PAYABLE ORDERS

Sometimes a business will receive documents similar to cheques as a means of payment. These *payable orders* include

- *Postal orders* – money orders purchased from the Post Office, often used by people who do not have bank accounts and who wish to send money through the post.
- *Bank drafts* – these are cheques issued by a *bank* and are as good as cash. They are bank cheques so they will not 'bounce' – the bank is both drawer (issuer) and drawee (the bank that pays). Drafts are often used by people wanting to pay large amounts, eg for a house or car purchase.
- *Building society cheques* – these work on the same principle as bank drafts, except that the drawer (issuer) is a building society and the drawee (the organisation who has to make payment) is a bank. Like bank drafts, they are often accepted for large purchases.

If you receive payment in the form of a postal order, bank draft or building society cheque, it can be paid into the bank account like a cheque.

CHECKING PAYMENTS AGAINST DOCUMENTATION

It is important that incoming payments received from customers are checked against any documentation that the supplier receives. This is to ensure that the correct amount is received and that no future disputes can arise – for example "We sent you £450, that's what it says on our advice" … "No you didn't, you only sent us £405, that's what it shows on your account."

The most common type of document which advises the amount of a payment is a *remittance advice* (see page 244 for an explanation of this document).

Payments from customers can be received either through the post, or through the bank as inter-bank transfers. A remittance advice will be issued in both instances by the person paying.

postal payments

Any cheque received through the post should be checked carefully against the accompanying remittance advice, which can be

- a special form prepared by the person paying, setting out the amount of the cheque, the date and the item(s) the cheque is covering, or
- a tear-off slip sent with the statement of account by the seller; often the items being paid are ticked off by the buyer, but the amount of the cheque may not be written down

In both cases (and particularly the second) the organisation receiving payment *must* check that the total of the items being paid less any credit due equals the amount of the cheque. Failure to carry out this simple check could cause problems later on if there is a discrepancy. Any differences should be marked on the remittance advice which is then normally queried with the customer by telephone.

inter-bank transfers – BACS

An increasing number of payments are now made automatically from bank account to bank account, normally on the instructions of the payer, through the BACS system (BACS stands for Bankers Automated Clearing Services). As no cheque is issued, payment is made more quickly and more cheaply. The problem of how the seller is to *know* that payment is made is solved by the buyer sending a BACS advice – essentially a remittance advice for a BACS payment.

BACS payments are made in a number of situations:

- by customers who buy from a business regularly, settling up invoices
- by people paying standing orders (a regular payment) – the BACS payment is originated by the person sending the money

- by people paying direct debits – a regular payment from bank account to bank account where the payment is originated by the business receiving the money

The organisation receiving payment will have to check each advice carefully against the bank statement when it arrives to ensure that the correct amount has been received. In the case of the direct debit, the business receiving the money has also originated the transfer, so the bank statement will be checked against the payment schedule produced internally by the business.

Examples of remittance advices are shown below.

TO

REMITTANCE ADVICE

FROM

Cool Socks Limited
Unit 45 Elgar Estate,
Broadfield, BR7 4ER

Trends
4 Friar Street
Broadfield
BR1 3RF
Tel 01908 761234 Fax 01908 761987
VAT REG GB 0745 8383 56

Account 3993 **6 November 2003**

date	your reference	our reference	payment amount
01 10 03	INVOICE 787923	47609	277.30
10 10 03	CREDIT NOTE 12157	47609	(27.73)

CHEQUE TOTAL 249.57

remittance advice sent with a cheque payment

BACS REMITTANCE ADVICE

FROM: Trends
4 Friar Street
Broadfield BR1 3RF

TO
Cool Socks Limited
Unit 45 Elgar Estate, Broadfield, BR7 4ER

06 11 03

Your ref	Our ref		Amount
787923	47609	BACS TRANSFER	249.57

TOTAL 249.57

THIS HAS BEEN PAID BY BACS CREDIT TRANSFER DIRECTLY INTO YOUR BANK ACCOUNT AT ALBION BANK NO 11451226 SORT CODE 90 47 17

remittance advice sent to advise of a BACS payment

RECORDING MONEY RECEIVED

The individual amounts of money received should be recorded by the organisation. The *way* in which they are recorded will depend on the way in which they are received. The fact that the amounts are recorded will help security by discouraging employees from being tempted to raid the till and steal money.

cash tills

Money received over a counter is likely to be recorded on a cash till tally roll or electronic till memory – the totals on the till roll or memory can then be checked with the actual money received, ready for paying into the bank. The security of cash tills is tightly controlled: they are operated by a security key and any transfer of change is recorded. The more modern cash registers (supermarket tills, for example) are linked to a central computer and automatically change the stock level records as items are sold.

remittance lists (postal items)

Cheques and other money received may be recorded manually on a *remittance list*. 'Remittance list' just means a list of what you have been sent. It can record items received through the post by a business, or it can be used at the counter of old-fashioned shops instead of a cash register. A remittance list for items received through the post is likely to include columns for the date, sender, the nature of the 'remittance' amount, and, as a security measure, the signature of the person opening the post.

date	sender	remittance	amount	signature
12.3.03	*Travers Toys Ltd*	*cheque*	*234.50*	*G Palmer*
12.3.03	*Grampian Traders*	*bank draft*	*10,500.00*	*G Palmer*
12.3.03	Mrs D Dodds	cash	14.50	R Patel
12.3.03	*Mercia Foods*	*cheque*	*450.00*	*G Palmer*

example of a remittance list for items received through the post

remittance lists/cash received lists

A remittance list is also used to record payments received over the counter. It is an old-fashioned method, but it serves its purpose very well. The person at the till will record each sale as it occurs; the cash and cheques are likely to be kept in a locked cash box, as there is no cash register. The total of the remittance list (or *cash received list*) should be agreed with the takings at the end of each day.

The items can either be written on a separate piece of paper or they may be entered in a book. The example below shows the sales made by a second-hand bookshop during the course of day.

FOLIO BOOKS	takings for *22 January 2003*	
Milton, Paradise Lost, 1793	*cash*	*£45.00*
Hardy, Mayor of Casterbridge, 1896	*cheque*	*£65.00*
Graham Greene, The End of the Affair	*cash*	*£1.75*
Punch selections	*cheque*	*£25.00*
T S Eliot, 4 Quartets	*cheque*	*£12.50*
Haynes, Worcester within the Walls	*cheque*	*£14.95*
Culpeper, Tudor Remedies	*cash*	*£4.95*
W English, Alvechurch - a History	*cheque*	*£9.95*
TOTAL CASH		*£51.70*
TOTAL CHEQUES		*£127.40*
Total Takings		*£179.10*

example of a remittance list for items received over the counter

cash book

The cash book is the central record of money amounts received and paid out by the organisation either in the form of cash, or as items passed through the bank account. All the receipts referred to in this chapter will eventually pass through the cash book. It will be dealt with in detail in Chapter 7.

Chapter Summary

- Incoming payments can be received in a number of ways: cash, cheque, credit and debit card, inter-bank transfer from BACS and internet sales.
- Receipts are often issued for cash payments; either till receipts or handwritten receipts.
- Cash in a till will be counted up at the end of each day; the amount should equal the takings for the day plus any 'float' held in the till.
- Cheques should be examined carefully when taken in payment, either over the counter or through the post. Normally they are crossed, and should only be paid into the account of the payee.
- Cheques received over the counter are normally only accepted with a bank multi-function card which has a cheque guarantee. When this occurs, the card and the cheque should be carefully inspected together.
- Debit cards are commonly accepted as a means of payment in place of cash or cheques. They are processed either with a mechanical imprinter or alternatively using an electronic terminal.
- Payment can also be accepted by credit card – here the seller has to generate a paper sales voucher, either with a mechanical imprinter or alternatively using an electronic terminal. A credit card enables payment to be made to the credit card company by the buyer at a later date.
- If a business uses an electronic terminal, the money will be transferred electronically from the customer's bank account or credit card account to the business bank account. This system is known as EFTPOS (Electronic Funds Transfer at Point Of Sale).
- Sales transactions over the Internet are processed under secure conditions and the money transferred automatically to the seller's bank account.
- When payments are evidenced by documentation such as a remittance advice, the payment should be checked against the documentation. Payment in this case can be by cheque or by inter-bank transfer.
- When money is received it should be recorded, both for security purposes and also as part of the operation of the accounting system. Forms of recording include the cash till roll, remittance lists and the cash book.

Key Terms

cash float — the amount of cash kept in a till at the end of the day to provide change when the till is next used

cheque — a written order to the bank, signed by its customer, instructing it to pay a specified amount to a specified person

drawer of a cheque — the person who signs the front of the cheque – the customer from whose account the money is to be paid

drawee of a cheque — the bank which has to make payment – its name and address normally appears at the top of the cheque

payee of a cheque — the person to whom the cheque is payable – normally specified on the first line of the cheque amount

cheque crossing — two parallel lines on the front of a cheque, with or without writing in them – they mean that the cheque has to be paid into a bank account

'account payee' crossing — two parallel lines on the face of the cheque with the words 'account payee' between them – the cheque cannot be endorsed over – it must be paid into the account of the payee

bank guarantee card — a plastic card issued by a bank to its customer which will guarantee payment of its customer's cheque up to a certain limit

debit card — a plastic card which enables customers to make payment for purchases without having to write out a cheque – payment is made electronically from the bank account straightaway

credit card — a plastic card issued by a credit card company which enables customers to make purchases and pay for them at a later date

EFTPOS — Electronic Funds Transfer at Point Of Sale – the electronic transfer of payments between the bank accounts of buyer and seller which is originated at a till

BACS — BACS stands for Bankers Automated Clearing Services, a body (owned by the banks) which organises computer payments between bank accounts

remittance advice — a document sent to the recipient of a payment, advising that a payment is being made

remittance list — also known as a 'cash received list' – a record of money amounts received, either through the post, or over the counter

cash book — the central record kept by a business of cash and bank transactions

Student Activities

5.1 You operate the cash till at the firm where you work. The following are the sales for one day:

		Amount of sale £	*Notes and/or coin tendered*		
Customer	1	8.50	£10 note	1-50	£1 50p
	2	3.30	£10 note	6-70	£5 £1 50p 20p
	3	2.51	£5 note	2-49	£2 2×20 5p 2×2p
	4	1.79	£5 note	3-21	£2 £1 20p 1p
	5	0.34	£1 coin	0-66	50p 10p 5p 1p
	6	6.22	£10 note	3-78	£2 £1 50p 20p 5p 2p
	7	12.76	£20 note	7-24	£5 £2 20p 2×2p
	8	1.42	two £1 coins	0-58	50p 5p 2p 1p
	9	6.54	£10 note	3-46	£2 £1 2×20p 5p 1p
	10	3.08	£5 note	1-92	£1 50p 2×20p 2p

Calculate

(a) the amount of change to be given to each customer

(b) the notes and/or coins that will be given in change, using the minimum number possible

5.2 If the cash till in activity 1 had a float of £28.71 at the start of the day, how much cash should be held in the till after the sales from activity 1 had been made? Present your answer in the following form:

	£
cash float at start	28.71
plus sales made during the day	46-46
equals amount of cash held at end of day	75-17

5.3 You work as a shop counter assistant at New Era Lighting. You make a number of sales during the day (use today's date) which require the completion of a handwritten receipt. Complete the receipts set out on the next page. Include VAT on all purchases at the current rate. All prices quoted here are catalogue prices and exclude VAT.

(a) 2 flexilamps @ £13.99, 2 60w candlelight bulbs @ 85p, to Mr George Ohm

NEW ERA LIGHTING **977**
17 High Street Mereford MR1 2TF
VAT reg 141 7645 23

CASH RECEIPT

Customer: Mr George Ohm date: 27/9/05

2 x Flexilamp @ £13-99	£27-98
2 x Candlelight bulbs @ £0-85	£1-70
	29-68
VAT	£5-19
TOTAL	£34-87

(b) 1 standard lamp @ £149.95, 1 3amp plug @ 99p, to Mr Alex Bell

NEW ERA LIGHTING **978**
17 High Street Mereford MR1 2TF
VAT reg 141 7645 23

CASH RECEIPT

Customer: Mr Alex Bell date: 27/9/05

1 Standard Lamp @ £149-95	£149-95
1 3amp plug @ £0-99	£0-99
	150-94
VAT	£26-41
TOTAL	£177-35

(c) 2 external Georgian lamps @ £35.99, to Tom Edison

NEW ERA LIGHTING **979**
17 High Street Mereford MR1 2TF
VAT reg 141 7645 23

CASH RECEIPT

Customer: Tom Edison date: 27/9/05

2 External Georgain Lamps @ £35-99	£71-98
	£71-98
VAT	£12-59
TOTAL	£84-57

5.4 Examine the cheque shown below and state who is

(a) the drawer G BROWN A+S SYSTEMS LTD THE ACCOUNT FROM WHICH THE MONEY IS DRAWN.

(b) the drawee SOUTHERN BANK PLC THE BANK WHICH CARRIES OUT THE PAYMENT

(c) the payee ELECTRON GAMES WHO WILL BE PAID

In each case, explain what the term means.

Southern Bank PLC
Mereford Branch
16 Broad Street, Mereford MR1 7TR

date *9 October 2003*

97-76-54

Pay *Electron Games Limited* only

Three hundred pounds only

Account payee only

£ *300.00*

A & S SYSTEMS LTD

G Brown

Director

762511 977654 68384939

5.5 What difference does a crossing on a cheque make to the payee?

Has to be paid into a bank account

5.6 What are the following cheque crossings called, and what do they mean?:

(a) General — Must be paid into Bank Acc

(b) Barclays Bank, Hanover Square — Special — Must be paid into B/Acc at Barclays Bank Hanover Square

(c) & co — General – Must be paid into B Acc

(d) account payee — Account payee crossing — Paid into payee bank account only

5.7 Henry Enfield is the payee of a cheque for £100 which has the following crossing:

account payee

What would you do if Sandra Lobb sent you the cheque for £100 in payment of an outstanding invoice on her acount. She says 'Henry has endorsed the cheque over to me – so all you have to do is to pay it into your bank account and it will be OK.' Give reasons for your answer.

Pay Sandra Lobb
Henry Enfield

Contact Sandra Say this is no longer possible / Send cheque back

Harry Enfield only person who can pay in cheque + writes new cheque to you

5.8 List three checks a cashier should make to a cheque when receiving it in the post for payment of an outstanding invoice.

Signed | In date | Words + figures agree

5.9 List three checks a cashier should make when accepting a cheque over the counter when the cheque is supported by a bank guarantee card.

Card is Valid / Card is OK / Within guarantee amount

5.10 List three checks a cashier should make when accepting a credit card payment over the counter.

Card is in Date / Card OK / Within Floor limit

5.11 What should a cashier do if the amount of a purchase being made by a customer (£500) exceeds the cheque guarantee amount of £250 on the customer's card? *Ask if other method of payment*

 (a) Refuse to allow the purchase to go ahead.

 (b) Ask for two cheques for £250, all dated differently. ✗

 (c) Ask the customer to use the credit card which the cashier has spotted in the customer's card wallet.

 (d) Request the customer to go and get a bank draft for £500.

Choose *one* answer.

5.12 If a credit card purchase exceeds the shop's floor limit, it should be refused. True or false?

FALSE — REFER IT.

5.13 The advantage to a shop of accepting payment by debit card is that

 (a) All cheques are automatically guaranteed.

 (b) There is no cheque.

 (c) The cheque is automatically debited to the customer' bank account.

 (d) The signature on the cheque is automatically verified.

Choose *one* answer.

5.14 EFT stands for:

 (a) Electronic Foreign Transfer

 (b) Electronic Financial Transaction

 (c) Electronic Funds Till

 (d) Electronic Funds Transfer

Choose *one* answer.

5.15 List three advantages to a shop of using EFTPOS.

Immediate payment Computerised
No cheques or cash

5.16 (a) Who is the drawer and the drawee of a bank draft? *The Bank is Both*

 (b) Give examples of two transactions for which a bank draft would be suitable.

CAR PURCHASE or HOUSE PURCHASE

5.17 Give two examples of situations where a remittance list would be used.

To RECORD CHEQUES REC'D IN POST
To RECORD CASH RECEIVED OVER THE COUNTER

6 Paying into the bank

this chapter covers . . .

This chapter explains the relationship between banks and their customers and sets out the procedures for paying money into the bank. The chapter covers the areas of:

- *the legal relationship between the bank and its customers*
- *banking services available to customers*
- *the bank clearing system*
- *paying money into the bank using paying-in slips*
- *banking documents, including sales voucher summaries and statements*
- *security procedures used when handling cash*

NVQ PERFORMANCE CRITERIA COVERED

unit 1: RECORDING INCOME AND RECEIPTS

element 1.2

process receipts

C prepare paying-in documents and reconcile to relevant records

KNOWLEDGE AND UNDERSTANDING COVERAGE

7 the use of banking documentation

8 automated payments

19 credit card procedures

20 methods of handling and storing money, including the security aspects

27 banking and personal security procedures

BANKS AND CUSTOMERS

By way of introduction we will look briefly at the legal background to the bank and customer relationship, the main types of accounts offered by banks to their personal and business customers, and the bank clearing system.

a legal relationship

It is important to appreciate when studying and practising banking procedures that there is a distinct *legal relationship* between a bank and its customer. Normally this relationship does not give much cause for concern; it is only when something goes wrong – for example when a bank pays a cheque which its customer has stopped – that the legal relationship becomes particularly important.

bank and customer contract

In law there is said to be a *contract* between the customer and the bank. A contract may be defined as:

a legally binding agreement which is recognised in a court of law

You may wonder why a contract between a bank and a customer is important in business dealings. The answer is that the bank/customer contract means that the customer has certain rights and duties to perform, including keeping the bank account in credit (not overdrawn, unless by arrangement) and taking care when writing out cheques so that they cannot be altered by a fraudster.

If the customer fails in any of these duties and the bank loses a substantial amount of money, it has the right in law under the contract to take the customer to court to recover its money.

Similarly, the bank has certain rights and duties to perform under the contract, and if it fails to do so and the customer suffers a loss (money or reputation), the customer can take the bank to court. Examples of the bank's duties include:

- paying the customer's cheques when there is sufficient money in the account
- keeping details of the customer's account secret
- sending statements of account to the customer

Clearly a customer will not take a bank to court if a statement is not sent out! But it may do so if the bank by mistake fails to pay a business cheque issued to a supplier, and the supplier cuts off supplies to the business. This could bankrupt the customer and is a clear *breach of the contract* between the bank and the customer. For further details of the theory of contract see Chapter 9.

BANK/CUSTOMER RELATIONSHIPS

There are a number of different bank/customer relationships:

debtor and creditor

This terminology relates to whether or not the customer has any money in the bank. Remember that:

debtor = a person who owes money

creditor = a person to whom you owe money

Therefore:

customer has money in bank:	*customer = creditor (is owed money)* *bank = debtor (owes money)*
customer is borrowing:	*customer = debtor (owes money)* *bank = creditor (is owed money)*

This may seem complicated, but if you think it through, it is logical.

mortgagor and mortgagee

If the customer has a mortgage with the bank (a mortgage is a legal document which secures a loan), the customer is a *mortgagor* and the bank is a *mortgagee.*

bailor and bailee

If the customer deposits valuable items in the bank's safe, the customer is a *bailor* and the bank a *bailee.*

principal and agent

If the customer uses the bank to carry out a transaction, eg to arrange an insurance policy, to sell shares, then the customer is known as the *principal* and the bank the *agent.* Note that the word 'agent' is also used in 'travel agent' and 'estate agent' – businesses that arrange travel and property deals.

TYPES OF ACCOUNT

There are three main types of accounts offered by banks to its customers:

- current account/overdraft
- deposit (savings) account
- loan accounts

current account/overdraft

With this type of account a customer is issued with a cheque book and card and may make use of most of the services of the bank. Bank customers use a current account as a 'working account' into which receipts are paid and out of which expenses are paid by means of cheques and automated computer payments. Many current accounts now pay interest.

An **overdraft** is borrowing from the bank on a current account.

If a business thinks that it will need an overdraft, it should contact the bank and seek agreement for an overdraft 'facility' up to a certain limit for a specified time. Interest will be charged on overdrawn balances and an arrangement/renewal fee is normally payable.

deposit account

A deposit account is used for savings by personal customers, or excess money held by a business, and interest is paid by the bank. Current account facilities such as cheque books, standing orders, direct debits, and overdrafts are not normally allowed on deposit accounts for business customers. Notice of withdrawal may need to be given to the bank. Other types of account may need a longer period of notice of withdrawal, perhaps one month or three months.

Many business customers have both a current and a deposit account. A business can use a deposit account as a temporary 'home' for surplus money, where it can earn interest. When the money is needed it can be transferred on request to the firm's current account.

loan accounts

Whereas an overdraft is a means of borrowing on an ordinary current account and will cover day-to-day running (*revenue*) expenses of the business, loan accounts are long-term loans for items of *capital* expenditure, eg machinery and new projects. Different banks will offer different types of loan account. Some typical examples include:

business loan

A loan for three to ten years to cover large items of expense such as new plant, premises expansion, a new project.

commercial mortgage

A loan for up to twenty five years to cover the purchase of property (the business equivalent of a 'home loan' mortgage to an individual).

CHEQUE CLEARING

Every working day each bank branch receives cheques paid in by customers. These cheques take a defined time to 'clear'. The term to 'clear' means that the cheque must have passed to the bank of the issuer of the cheque for payment before the money amount of the cheque – the amount paid in – can be used by the customer. The clearance times are normally:

- cheques paid in and issued by customers of the same branch – same day clearance
- cheques paid in by customers of other banks and branches – three working days' clearance

This means that if you are given a cheque by someone who has an account at your branch and you pay it in on Monday, you can draw against it, ie you can use the money on the account, on Monday, the same day. This assumes, of course, that the cheque does not 'bounce'. On the other hand, if you are given a cheque which is issued by someone who banks at another bank (or another branch of your bank), then if you pay it in on Monday, you will have to wait ~~three~~ working days, ie until Wednesday before the cheque is cleared, and you can use the money.

Now (5)

The reason for this delay is that the cheque will have to be sent to London for sorting. This long and expensive process, required by a law dating back to the nineteenth century, is illustrated on the next page. In this case Enigma Cafe, which banks at HSBC Bank in Malvern pays a cheque for £500 to their supplier, Broadheath Bakers, who then pay it into their bank, Barclays Bank in Worcester. The diagram follows the two hundred and fifty mile journey of the cheque. The two bank branches, incidentally, are seven miles apart.

new developments in cheque clearing

Not surprisingly, the expense of operating this centuries-old clearing system has led banks to experiment with sending scanned images of cheques for clearance rather than the actual bits of paper. These experiments are currently under way, but for the time being, the old-fashioned clearing continues.

special clearance

Sometimes you may need to know quickly whether or not a cheque will be paid, for example, if you sell goods for £5,000 to an unknown buyer. The banks offer a special clearance service, known as a Special Presentation, where for a fee (around £10) a bank will send a cheque to the issuer's branch (or service centre) by first class post, and then telephone the following day to establish whether or not the cheque will be paid.

Now 5 Days

bank cheque clearing system

day 1 — Barclays Bank, Worcester branch — cheque for £500 paid into the account of Broadheath Bakers

↓ sent by courier to London ↓

day 2 — Barclays Bank Clearing Department, London — cheques sorted into banks

↓ delivery van ↓

Central Clearing House, London — cheques sorted into banks

↓ delivery van ↓

Day 3 — HSBC Bank Service Centre ~~Clearing Department, London~~ — HSBC Service Centre ~~cheques sorted into HSBC branches~~

↓ sent by courier to Malvern ↓

~~day 3~~ — HSBC Bank, Malvern Branch — cheque paid and £500 deducted from the account of Enigma Cafe

~~day 3~~ — Barclays Bank, Worcester branch — cheque for £500 is now cleared and may be drawn against (ie the money may be used)

Day 4 Cleared for Fete – Can be drawn against at managers discretion. Not available at cashpoint.

Day 5 Cleared For Debit/Credit Cards etc

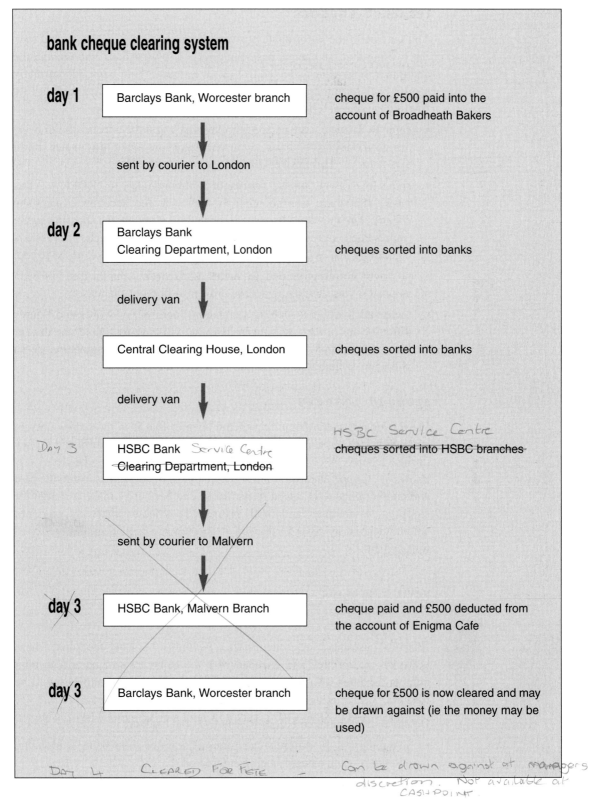

> **study note**
> Returned cheques will no longer be examined, but they are explained here as they are important background knowledge.

returned cheques

You may be in the unfortunate position of having paid in a cheque and then discovering that the cheque has been returned to your bank *unpaid*, and the amount of the cheque deducted from your account. Your bank will normally send it back to you by post. You will receive it five days after paying it in. It will have one of a number of answers written along the top:

- **refer to drawer** – the person who has given you the cheque (the drawer) has no money in the bank – you will have to contact him or her for an explanation! This answer is often abbreviated to 'RD'
- **refer to drawer, please represent** – (abbreviated to 'RDPR') – this means that there was not enough money in the account to meet the cheque, but that the cheque has been sent through the clearing again (represented) in the hope that it will be paid when it reaches the issuers bank (note that in this case the cheque will *not* be sent back to the payee)
- **payment countermanded by order of drawer** – the cheque has been stopped – you should contact the drawer to find out the reason
- **technical problems** such as a signature required, or words and figures differ, or out of date, will mean that you will have to contact the drawer for a new cheque (if the reason is out of date), or a signature, or an alteration (which will have to be signed by the drawer)

stopped cheques

We mentioned at the beginning of the chapter that it is the bank's duty in contract law to pay a customer's cheque as long as there is sufficient money in the account. A customer may order a bank not to pay a cheque; this is known as *stopping* a cheque. This often happens if a cheque is lost in the post and another cheque is issued in its place. The bank may make a charge for stopping a cheque, and will return the cheque marked 'payment countermanded by order of drawer' if and when it is paid in and presented for payment.

PAYING-IN SLIPS

Business customers are issued with a *paying-in* book by the bank. These books are pre-printed and encoded with the customer's name and account number together with details of the bank branch where the money will be paid in.

Details to be completed before paying in at the bank are:

- a summary of the different categories of notes or coins being paid in, the amount of each category being entered on the slip

- amounts and details of cheques being paid in, usually entered on the reverse of the slip, with the total entered on the front
- the cash and cheques being paid in are totalled to give the amount being paid in
- the counterfoil is completed (some counterfoils do not require the breakdown of cash)
- the person paying-in will sign the slip and get it checked in the office

A completed paying-in slip (with counterfoil) is illustrated below.

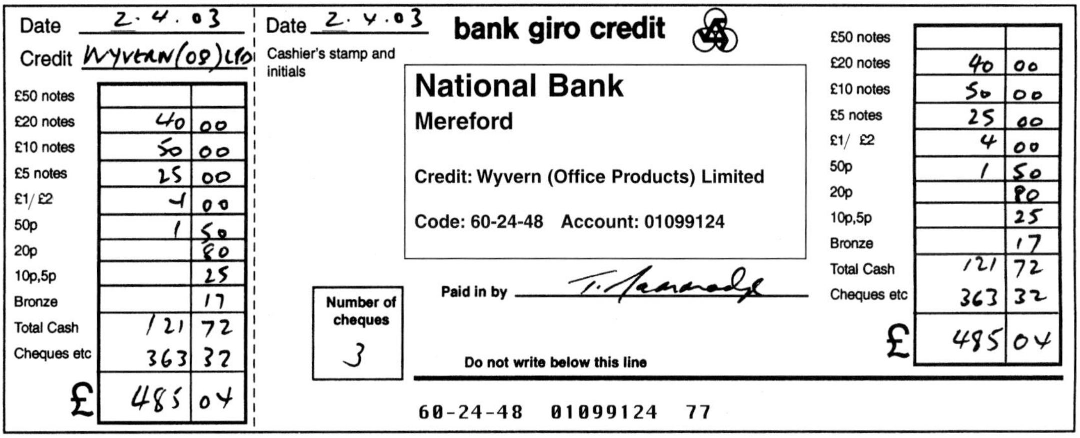

Date 2.4.03	Date 2.4.03	bank giro credit		£50 notes		
Credit WYVERN (OP) LTD	Cashier's stamp and initials			£20 notes	40	00
£50 notes		**National Bank**		£10 notes	50	00
£20 notes 40 00		Mereford		£5 notes	25	00
£10 notes 50 00				£1/ £2	4	00
£5 notes 25 00		Credit: Wyvern (Office Products) Limited		50p	1	50
£1/ £2 4 00				20p		80
50p 1 50		Code: 60-24-48 Account: 01099124		10p,5p		25
20p 80				Bronze		17
10p,5p 25			Paid in by T.	Total Cash	121	72
Bronze 17	Number of cheques			Cheques etc	363	32
Total Cash 121 72	3	Do not write below this line		£	485	04
Cheques etc 363 32						
£ 485 04		60-24-48 01099124 77				

paying-in slip and counterfoil (front)

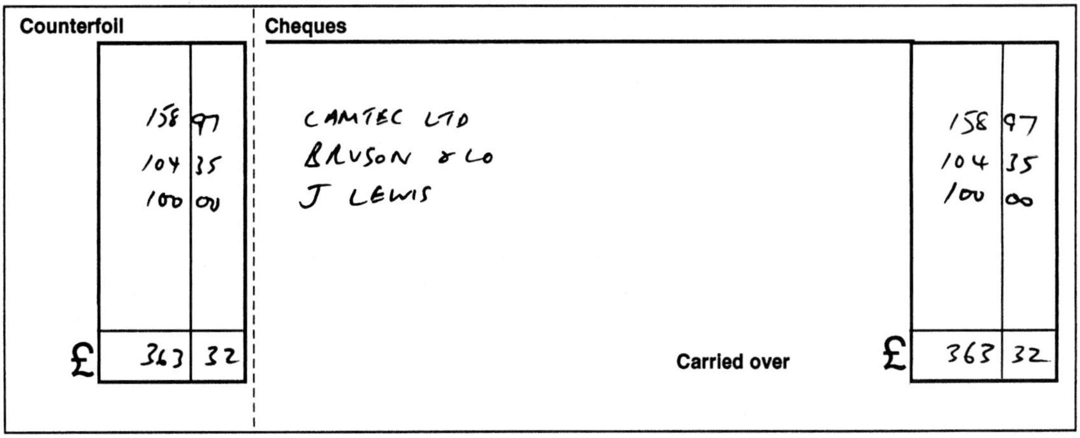

Counterfoil		Cheques			
	158 97	CAMTEC LTD		158 97	
	104 35	BRUSON & CO		104 35	
	100 00	J LEWIS		100 00	
£	363 32		**Carried over**	£ 363	32

paying-in slip and counterfoil (back)

PROCEDURES FOR PAYING IN

the accounting process

Cash and cheques paid in at the bank will normally have been received by the business as cash sales and on remittance advices from debtors, and so form part of the accounting process. We will see how they are entered in the cash book in Chapter 7.

preparing the cash

The notes should be counted, checked and sorted so that they all face the same way, but should be kept separate. Defaced (damaged) notes, and notes from Scotland and Northern Ireland are normally accepted by banks. Coins should normally be sorted into denominations, eg £2, £1, 50p and so on, and placed in plastic money bags.

preparing the cheques

The cheques must first be examined carefully for any irregularities, such as

- **signatures** – has the drawer (issuer) signed the cheque?
- **payee** – if the name on the payee line is not the same as the name of the account into which it is being paid, the cheque will not be accepted
- **crossings** – if the cheque has the 'account payee' wording in the crossing and your organisation is not the payee, it will not be possible to pay it in (Cheques Act 1992) – see also 'payee' above
- **date** – is it out of date (over six months old)? is it post-dated? – if so, it cannot be paid in (but note that you can fill in a missing date and pay in the cheque)
- **words and figures** – do they agree?

The details of the cheques – the amounts and the customer names – may then be listed on the back of the paying-in slip, as in the illustration on the previous page.

If the volume of cheques paid in is very large, there will not be room on the paying-in slip, so the cheque details may be listed on a separate schedule. Some banks accept instead a calculator tally-roll listing the amounts, the number of cheques, and the total money amount transferred to the front of the paying-in slip.

The important point is that the organisation paying in the cheques must keep a record of the cheque details in case of future queries, and in the unfortunate event of any of the cheques 'bouncing' – ie being returned unpaid.

reconciliation with the financial records

It is important that the paying-in slips are reconciled with the relevant financial and accounting records before the slips are taken to the bank. For example, the total of the paying-in slip should be agreed with the subtotal of receipts shown in the cash book (see page 141). Further reconciliations could be carried out between the cheque total and the remittance list and the cash total with the total taken from the cash tills. These reconciliations will highlight any errors – either in the records or on the paying-in slip.

paying in at the bank

At the bank the completed paying-in book is handed to the bank cashier together with the notes, coins, and cheques. The cashier counts the cash, ticks off the cheques and, if everything is correct, receipt stamps and initials the paying-in slip and counterfoil. The slip is retained by the bank for the amount to be credited to the account-holder, while the paying-in book is handed back, complete with the receipted counterfoil. A business paying-in book is sometimes larger than the paying-in slip illustrated, and sometimes there is a carbon copy which acts as a counterfoil.

security measures for cash handling – night safes

Care must be taken when taking large amounts of cash to the bank. If possible two staff members should visit the bank. If the amount is very large, for instance the takings from a department store, a security firm may be employed to carry the cash. If the cash is received by an organisation over the weekend or, late in the day, it may be placed in a special wallet and lodged in the bank's *night safe* – a small lockable door leading to a safe in the wall of the bank.

When a business pays in money to the bank, it will record the amount in its own records, called the cash book (see Chapter 7).

card voucher clearing – card merchant services

As we saw in the last chapter, the sales voucher is the basic document produced when a debit card and a credit card transaction are processed manually (see the illustration on page 99). The sales voucher may be produced as a result of an 'over the counter' sale or from a mail order or telephone sale. The details recorded on it will enable the card company to charge the amount to their customer's bank account (debit card transaction) or credit card account. The voucher like a cheque, is paid in at the bank and sent to the card company and 'cleared'.

Although there are a number of different card companies – Mastercard and Visa for example – the normal practice is for the organisation accepting payment to sign an agreement with a separate company – a card merchant –

which will accept all vouchers from cards issued by different companies. For example, a customer of The Royal Bank of Scotland may sign an agreement with a company called Streamline (owned by The Royal Bank of Scotland) and accept payment by Mastercard and Visa and other cards.

The customer will pay in all credit card vouchers on the one paying-in slip and schedule (see below) at the The Royal Bank of Scotland or NatWest (owned by The Royal Bank of Scotland). The bank will pass them to Streamline, which will then process them by sending them to the issuing card company (Mastercard or Visa, for example). Streamline is only one of a number of 'card merchant' companies which will process credit card sales vouchers.

The customer paying in the vouchers is charged a set percentage fee – usually between 2% and 5% – of the total sales amount. Some debit card transactions, Switch for example, are charged at a flat amount 'item charge'.

preparing card sales vouchers for paying-in

The vouchers are paid in after completion of a three-part Retailer Summary, illustrated below and on the next page. In this case three sales vouchers are listed on the back of the summary.

	£	p	
1	12	50	
2	10	00	
3	8	00	
4			
5			
6			
7			
8			
9			
10			
11			
12			
13			
14			
15			
16			
17			
18			
19			
20			
Total	30	50	Carried Overleaf

retailer sales voucher summary – back

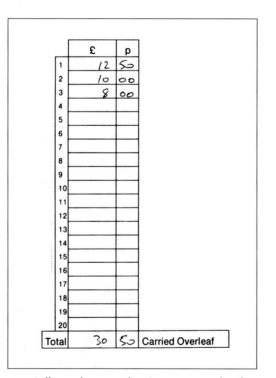

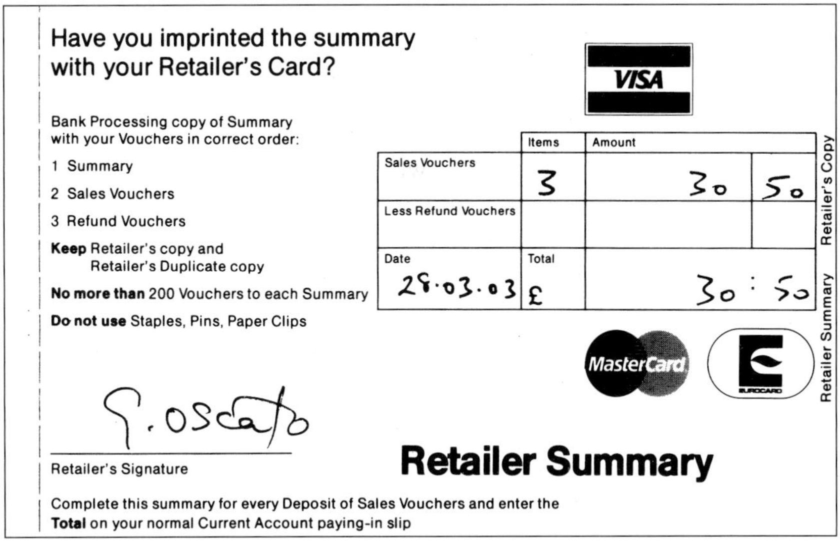

Have you imprinted the summary with your Retailer's Card?

VISA

Bank Processing copy of Summary with your Vouchers in correct order:

1 Summary

2 Sales Vouchers

3 Refund Vouchers

Keep Retailer's copy and Retailer's Duplicate copy

No more than 200 Vouchers to each Summary

Do not use Staples, Pins, Paper Clips

	Items	Amount	
Sales Vouchers	3	30	50
Less Refund Vouchers			
Date 28.03.03	Total £	30	50

Retailer's Copy

Retailer Summary

MasterCard

EUROCARD

Retailer's Signature

Retailer Summary

Complete this summary for every Deposit of Sales Vouchers and enter the **Total** on your normal Current Account paying-in slip

retailer sales voucher summary – front

The procedure for listing credit card sales vouchers on the retailer's summary is as follows:

- the summary is imprinted with details of the retailer using a plastic card – the Retailer's Card – supplied with the imprinter machine
- the amounts of the sales vouchers are listed on the reverse of the summary and totalled
- the total is carried forward to the front of the summary
- any refund vouchers are listed on the front of the summary
- the summary is dated, signed and totalled
- the summary is separated into its three copies – the top two are retained by the organisation and the bottom copy (the processing copy) is placed in front of the sales vouchers
- the processing copy and sales and any refund vouchers are placed in a transparent envelope and are paid into the bank on a paying-in slip, the total from the summary listed as a single item on the paying-in slip

Organisations which accept sales by mail and telephone may use schedules rather than sales vouchers for recording and listing the credit card transactions. The procedure for paying-in for these organisations is exactly the same, except that the totals of the schedule(s) are listed on the back of the Retailer Summary rather than the individual amounts of the sales vouchers as described above.

THE IMPORTANCE OF PAYING IN PROMPTLY

Organisations are well aware that problems can arise if money is not banked promptly and safely.

theft

Cash is tempting to a thief, and it must be remembered that many instances of theft are carried out by employees of an organisation rather than by criminals with tights over their heads. An organisation will therefore have a security policy, for example:

- cash and cheques being paid in will be kept under lock and key at the place of work, normally in a cash box, under the control of the cashier
- amounts received through the post or over the counter are recorded on remittance lists or on a cash register (or equivalent) as an additional security measure – money, once it is recorded, will be missed when stolen
- larger organisations will have a system of spot checking (internal audit) to identify any theft by employees
- arranging for cash and cheques to be taken to the bank by security firm (appropriate for large businesses)
- arranging for Friday and weekend takings of cash to be lodged in the bank's night safe
- making arrangements for payroll – the organisation will have to arrange the pick up of cash from the bank, using employees or a security firm

timescale – security and cashflow

Organisations will also have a policy for the prompt paying of money into the bank, for two main reasons – *security* and *cashflow.* Money kept on the premises is a security risk: the longer it remains there, the more likely it is that it will be stolen. Also, money not paid in is money that is not available for paying cheques and other items from the organisation's bank account: *cashflow* will be restricted. For example, it may be that the business is borrowing money on overdraft – it could save paying interest if money is banked promptly: a cheque for £50,000 lying around in the office for a week could cost the business around £50 in interest!

procedures

Because of these factors an organisation will draw up procedures for banking money. These will include the security measures mentioned above and also set timescales for paying in money, eg twice a week, one visit to coincide with the collection of the payroll cash (often a Friday). If you work in an accounts office, you will be familiar with these procedures.

confidentiality

If you work for an organisation, the importance of confidentiality will have been impressed on you. Confidentiality basically means not telling outsiders about the internal workings of your place of work. Important aspects of this include not talking to outsiders about your customers, not disclosing secret details of your products, and most importantly to this area of your studies, not disclosing your security arrangements for handling of money. Imagine the consequences of telling a group of friends in the pub that the firm's wages are collected from the bank every Friday at 10.00 in the morning.

AUTOMATED PAYMENTS INTO THE BANK

So far in this chapter we have looked at how a business pays into the bank manually, ie paying in on a paying-in slip. Many payments nowadays come into the bank account by computer transfer from other banks. The business will know about these payments because:

- it will receive notification either through the post or by email
- the payments will appear on the bank statement (see page 130)

A business will enter details of cash and cheque payments in the accounts when the money is received. Payments received electronically must also be entered in the accounts when notification is received and checked in due course against the bank statement. The diagram below shows the variety of payments that can be received. The mechanics of *making* these payments are covered in Chapter 13.

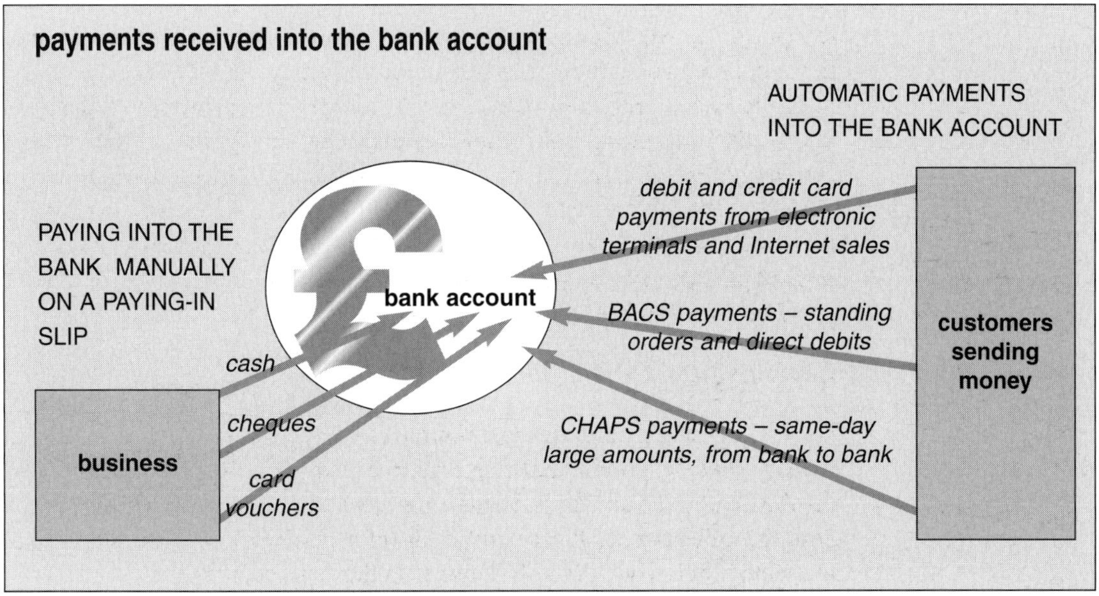

PAYMENTS THROUGH THE INTERNET

the process

If a business has an internet shopping facility, its customers order and pay for goods or services online using a credit or debit card and the money is credited direct to the bank account of the business. The business will receive a schedule of the payments received which it can check against its bank statement.

The diagram below shows the procedure adopted for this process. There is nothing significantly different from other payment systems about the way the system works – it is merely another way of providing a shopping outlet to customers with debit cards and credit cards.

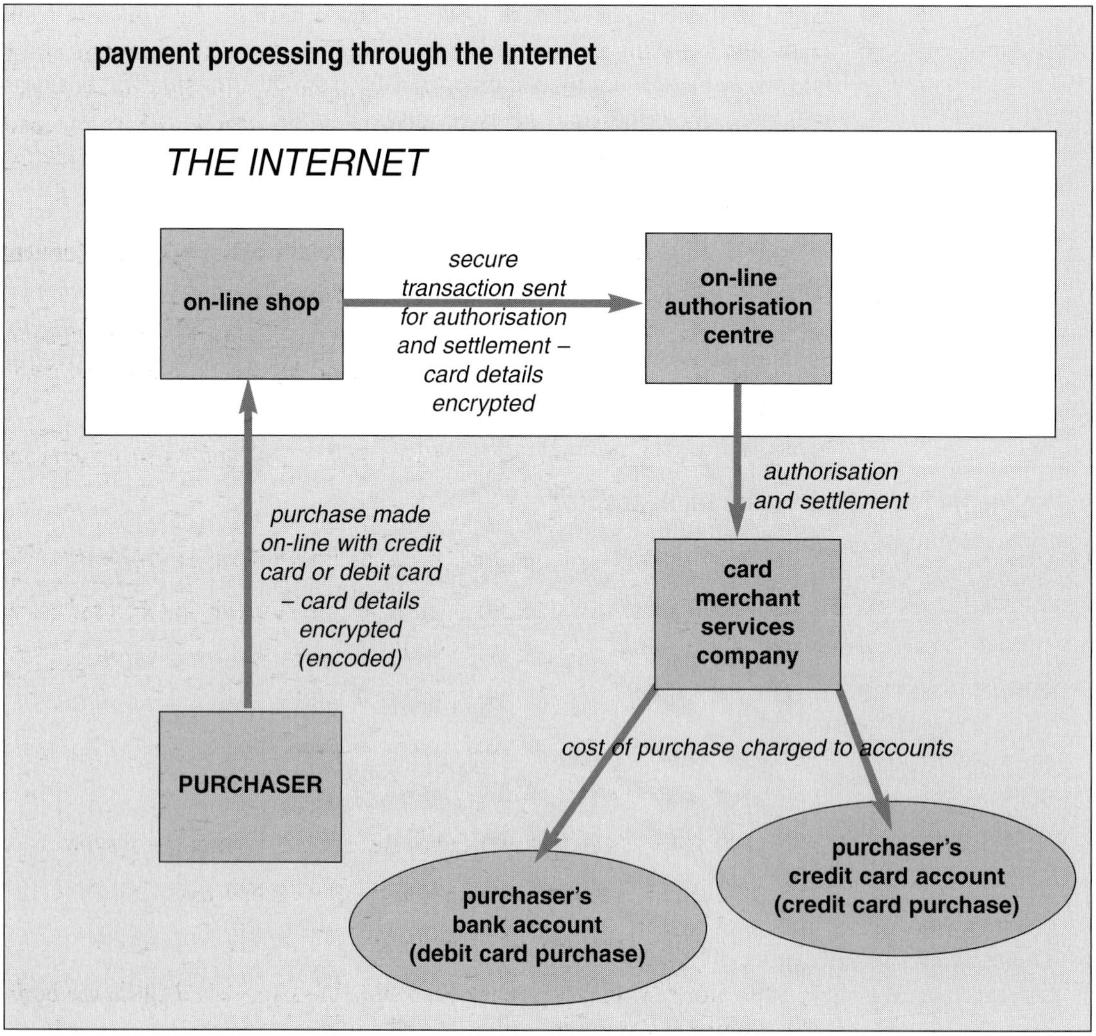

As we noted in the last chapter, the buying public is concerned about the security of giving their names, addresses and card numbers on-line. Businesses setting up selling facilities on-line have to ensure that the security of the system is ensured by using software which encodes the data (data 'encryption') so that payment details remain secret.

This security is no different *in principle* from the security measures adopted by businesses which accept debit and credit card payments over the counter, ie to keep any records of customers and their card numbers under lock and key and not to throw copies of sales vouchers (with card numbers on) in the bin where they can be found by people committing frauds.

BANK STATEMENTS

At regular intervals the bank sends out statements of account to its customers. A business current account with many items passing through it may have weekly statements, while a less active account or a deposit account may have monthly or even quarterly statements.

A bank statement is a summary showing:

- the balance at the beginning of the statement – 'balance brought forward'
- amounts paid into (credited to) the account
- amounts paid out of (debited to) the account – eg cheques issued, cheques returned 'unpaid', bank charges and standing orders and direct debits (automatic computer payments)

The balance of the account is shown after each transaction. A specimen bank statement is shown on the next page.

a note on debits, credits and bank accounts

You should be aware of the fact that the terms 'credit' and 'debit' mean different things to banks and their customers.

In the double-entry system of a business customer

debit = money received

credit = money paid out

Banks see things from the opposite angle. To their accounting system:

debit = money paid out from a customer's account

credit = money paid into a customer's account

In other words a credit to a bank account is the same as a debit in the books of a customer. Think about it!

Albion Bank plc
7 The Avenue, Broadfield, BR1 2AJ

Account title Trends

Account number 11719512
Statement 85

Date	Details	Payments	Receipts	Balance
2003				
3 Nov	Balance brought down			1,678.90 CR
10 Nov	Credit 109626		1,427.85	3,106.75 CR
10 Nov	238628	249.57		2,857.18 CR
11 Nov	238629	50.00		2,807.18 CR
13 Nov	POS Switch		67.45	2,874.63 CR
17 Nov	Credit 109627		100.00	2,974.63 CR
17 Nov	Albionet Card Services POS 2824242		500.00	3,474.63 CR
21 Nov	238630	783.90		2,690.73 CR
24 Nov	238626	127.00		2,563.73 CR
24 Nov	Albionet Netsales 43182639		1,006.70	3,570.43 CR
25 Nov	BACS ORLANDO 37646		162.30	3,732.73 CR
25 Nov	DD Westmid Gas	167.50		3,565.23 CR
27 Nov	238634	421.80		3,143.43 CR
27 Nov	DD RT Telecom	96.50		3,046.93 CR
28 Nov	Bank charges	87.50		2,959.43 CR

checking the bank statement for payments received

You will see from the specimen bank statement shown above that the balance of the account is followed each time by the abbreviation 'CR'. This means that the customer has a credit balance, ie has money in the bank. The abbreviation 'DR' would indicates a debit balance – an overdraft, ie the customer would owe the bank money and be a 'debtor' of the bank.

Note the following payments that have been received during the month:

- on 10 and 17 November the business has paid in on a paying-in slip
- on 13 November payment is received from debit card transactions
- on 17 November payment is received from credit card transactions
- on 24 November payment is received from Internet sales
- on 25 November payment is received via the BACS electronic transfer system – possibly a customer settling up an invoice

When a bank statement is received it should be checked and compared with the firm's record of bank receipts and payments – the cash book – and a bank reconciliation statement prepared (see Chapter 19).

Chapter Summary

- The legal relationship between a bank and its customer can take a number of forms: debtor and creditor, mortgagor and mortgagee, bailor and baliee, principal and agent.
- Banks offer a wide range of accounts: current accounts (including overdraft) deposit accounts and loan accounts.
- When a cheque is paid into a bank it normally takes three days to clear. When a cheque is cleared the person who has paid it in can draw on the money.
- A cheque can be returned unpaid ('bounce') for a number of reasons, eg 'refer to drawer' – which means there is no money in the drawer's bank account.
- Organisations pay money into their bank account on a paying-in slip which lists the cash and cheques paid in and totals the amounts.
- Cash and cheques must be checked and listed before they are paid in.
- Credit and debit card vouchers may also be paid into the bank account on a retailer summary form which lists all of the vouchers.
- Organisations should set up procedures to ensure that cash, cheques and card vouchers are kept safely on the premises and in transit to the bank.
- Money should be paid into the bank as soon as possible, both for security reasons and also to help the cashflow of the organisation.
- Automated payments – BACS, CHAPS and card payments processed electronically over-the-counter and through the Internet are also received into the bank account and will be advised to the business.
- Businesses should keep records of automatically processed card payments secure for security reasons – card numbers are valuable to thieves.
- Bank statements are sent regularly to customers and should be checked on receipt for manual and automatically processed payments received.
- To a bank, money paid in is a 'credit' and money paid out is a 'debit.'

Key Terms

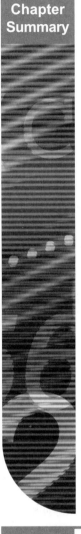

contract	a legally binding agreement which is recognised in a court of law
mortgagor/mortgagee	when a mortgage is signed the borrower is the mortgagor and the bank the mortgagee
bailor/bailee	when a customer deposits items of value for safe keeping with a bank the customer is the bailor and the bank the bailee
principal/agent	when a customer asks the bank to carry out something on its behalf (eg arrange insurance) the customer is the principal and the bank the agent
cheque clearing	a system used by the banks to clear cheques paid in – the process takes three working days

paying-in slip	a paper slip listing cash and cheques paid into a bank
retailer summary	a form listing credit card sales vouchers paid into a bank account
night safe	a wallet or bag containing cash and cheques lodged with a bank (when it is closed) through an opening in the wall of the bank – used by shops and clubs banking their takings
card merchant	a company which handles all the payments by debit card and credit card received by a business over-the-counter or through the Internet
encryption	the encoding for security reasons of debit and credit card details sent over the Internet
BACS	Bankers Automated Clearing Services – used for sending computer payments from bank to bank
CHAPS	Clearing House Automated Payment System – used for sending same-day high value payments
bank statement	a document sent by the bank to its customer setting out transactions on the bank account

Student Activities

6.1 State two duties of a bank to its customer.

Pay cheques if in funds
Send regular statement of account

6.2 State two duties of a customer to the bank.

Keep in credit unless overdraft agreed
Write cheques properly

6.3 If a customer has an overdraft with a bank, the customer is a creditor of the bank. True or false?

6.4 If a customer has a credit balance with a bank, the customer is a debtor of the bank. True or false?

6.5 Write out and complete the following sentences:

(a) When a customer signs a mortgage to the bank, the customer is a *mortgagor* and the bank is a *mortgagee*.

(a) When a customer deposits items of value with a bank, the bank is a *bailee* and the customer is a *bailor*.

(c) A bank that arranges an insurance policy for a customer is known as an *Agent*.

6.6 What type of bank account would be appropriate in the following circumstances?

(a) A business needs finance for the purchase of a new machine (capital expenditure). *Bank loan*

(b) A business needs finance for day-to-day expenses (revenue expenditure). *Current Acc*

(c) A business needs an account which will pay interest on a large sum of money. *Deposit acc*

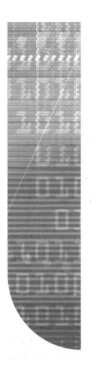

6.7 A business receives a large cheque from a customer for a purchase, but wants to make sure that the cheque will be paid before releasing the goods. The business bank account is at HSBC Bank, Holborn Circus and the cheque bears the name of Barclays Bank, Finsbury Circus. How long will it take to obtain clearance

(a) through the normal bank clearing system? *5 Days*

(b) by means of special clearance? *Next Day.*

Would it make any difference if the cheque bore the name of HSBC Bank, Holborn Circus? *Yes Same Day*

6.8 The cheque in Activity 7 is unfortunately returned unpaid. The answer on the cheque is 'Refer to Drawer, please Represent'. What are the implications of this for the business? Would the situation be any different if the answer on the cheque had been 'Refer to Drawer'?
Done by Bank – Company would be informed + may check customer. Refer to Drawer – Need to contact Co

6.9 State two advantages to the customer of using a night safe. *Gets large amounts of cash off premises / Reduces security risk.*

6.10 State two reasons why cash should not be kept on the business premises for a long period of time. *Increases risk of theft + may be paying interest. CASHFLOW*

6.11 State whether the following entries are debits or credits – from the viewpoint of the bank:

(a) an amount paid into a bank account *CREDIT*

(b) an amount paid out of the bank account *DEBIT*

6.12 The firm you work for is Eveshore Traders Ltd., which has a bank account at Barclays Bank, Eveshore. You are required to prepare the paying-in slip (below) and counterfoil (see next page) as at today's date. The cheques are to be listed on the back of the paying-in slip. The items to be banked are:

Cash	*Cheques*	
two £20 notes	£20.00	Maytree Enterprises
five £10 notes	£18.50	Bakewell Catering
eight £5 notes	£75.25	Henderson & Co
two £1 coins	£68.95	Musgrave Fine Art
six 50p coins		
four 10p coins	*182–70*	
two 2p coins	*2 1 1*	

Date *28/9/05*	Date *28/9/05*	**bank giro credit**		£50 notes		
Credit *EVESHORE TRADERS*	Cashier's stamp and initials			£20 notes	*40*	*—*
£50 notes		**Code no** 20 23 88		£10 notes	*50*	*—*
£20 notes	*40* *—*	**Bank** BARCLAYS		£5 notes	*40*	*—*
£10 notes	*50* *–*	**Branch** EVESHORE		£1 **£2**	*2*	*—*
£5 notes	*40* *—*			50p	*3*	*—*
£1 **£2**	*2* *—*	EVESHORE TRADERS LTD		20p		
50p	*3* *—*	Credit		10p,5p	*0* *40*	
20p		Account No. 90003174		Bronze	*0* *04*	
10p,5p	*0* *40*			Total Cash	*135* *44*	
Bronze	*0* *04*	Paid in by *CPBower*		Cheques etc	*182* *70*	
Total Cash	*135* *44*	Number of cheques				
Cheques etc	*182* *70*	*4*	Do not write below this line	£	*318* *14*	
£	*318* *14*	20-23-88 90003174 77

Counterfoil			Cheques		
	20	–	MATTRESS ENTERPRISES	20	–
	18	50	BAKEWELL CATERING	18	50
	75	25	HENDERSON + CO	75	25
	68	95	MUSGRAVE FINE ART	68	95
£	182	70	**Carried over** £	182	70

6.13 The firm you work for is Buxton Fine Wines, which has a bank account at Western Bank, Grantminster. Using today's date you are required to prepare the Retailers Summary and paying-in slip for ten credit card sales vouchers and a refund voucher. The documents are shown below and on the next page. The items to be banked are:

Sales vouchers	£45.60	£56.85
	£10.00	£56.00
	£15.50	£45.00
	£25.99	£49.50
	£67.50	£25.00
Refund voucher	£13.50	

Date 28/9/05

Credit BUXTON FINE WINES

£50 notes		
£20 notes		
£10 notes		
£5 notes		
£1 £2		
50p		
20p		
10p,5p		
Bronze		
Total Cash	–	
Cheques etc	383	44
£	383	44

Date 28/9/05

Cashier's stamp and initials

bank giro credit

Code no 47 21 95

Bank WESTERN

Branch GRANTMINSTER

Credit BUXTON FINE WINES

Account No. 87163729

Number of cheques 1

Paid in by CPBond

Do not write below this line

47 21 95 87163729 77

£50 notes		
£20 notes		
£10 notes		
£5 notes		
£1 £2		
50p		
20p		
10p,5p		
Bronze		
Total Cash	–	
Cheques etc	383	44
£	383	44

	£	p
1	45	60
2	10	00
3	15	50
4	25	99
5	67	50
6	56	85
7	56	00
8	45	00
9	49	50
10	25	00
11		
12		
13		
14		
15		
16		
17		
18		
19		
20		
Total	396	94

Carried Overleaf

53 1

Have you imprinted the summary with your Retailer's Card?

VISA

Bank Processing copy of Summary with your Vouchers in correct order:

1 Summary

2 Sales Vouchers

3 Refund Vouchers

Keep Retailer's copy and Retailer's Duplicate copy

No more than 200 Vouchers to each Summary

Do not use Staples, Pins, Paper Clips

	Items	Amount	
Sales Vouchers	10	396	94
Less Refund Vouchers	1	13	50
Date 28/9/05	Total £	383:44	

Retailer's Copy

Retailer Summary

MasterCard

EUROCARD

C P Bowes

Retailer's Signature

Retailer Summary

Complete this summary for every Deposit of Sales Vouchers and enter the **Total** on your normal Current Account paying-in slip

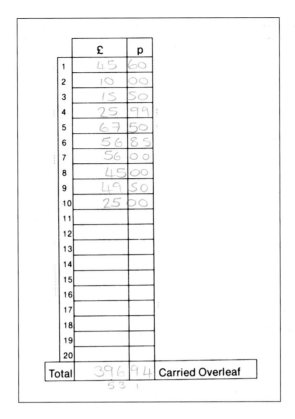

7 Cash book – recording receipts

this chapter covers . . .

In this chapter we look at the way in which the cash book records money received in the form of cash, cheques and other bank transfers.

The cash book is used to record the money side of book-keeping transactions and is part of the double-entry system.

This chapter focuses on the receipts (debit) side of the cash book; we will see also how the opposite credit entry is recorded in debtors' and other accounts.

NVQ PERFORMANCE CRITERIA COVERED

unit 1: RECORDING INCOME AND RECEIPTS

element 1.2

process receipts

B *enter receipts in appropriate accounting records*

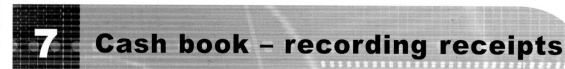

THE CASH BOOK IN THE ACCOUNTING SYSTEM

For most businesses, accounting for cash – including both bank and cash transactions – takes place in the cash books which comprise:

- *cash book,* for receipts and payments in cash and through the bank (cheques and BACS transfers)
- *petty cash book* (see Chapter 16), for low-value expense payments

The cash books combine the roles of books of prime entry and double-entry book-keeping. Cash books are:

- books of prime entry for cash and bank transactions
- double-entry accounts for cash and bank accounts

In this chapter we look at how the cash book is used to record receipts; the recording of payments made through the cash book is covered in Chapter 15; petty cash payments are dealt with in Chapter 16.

USES OF THE CASH BOOK

The cash book brings together the cash and bank transactions of a business. Thus it is used to record the money side of book-keeping transactions such as:

- cash transactions
  - all receipts in cash
  - most payments for cash, except for low-value expense payments (which are paid through petty cash book: see Chapter 16)
- bank transactions
  - all receipts through the bank (including the payment of cash into the bank)
  - all payments through the bank (including the withdrawal of cash from the bank)

Note that receipts are dealt with in this chapter, whilst payments are considered in Chapter 15.

The cash book is usually controlled by a cashier who:

- records receipts and payments through the bank and in cash
- makes cash payments, and prepares cheques and other bank transfers for signature by those authorised to sign
- pays cash and cheques received into the bank
- has control over the firm's cash, in a cash till or cash box

- issues cash to the petty cashier who operates the firm's petty cash book (see Chapter 16)
- checks the accuracy of the cash and bank balances at regular intervals

It is important to note that transactions passing through the cash book must be supported by documentary evidence. In this way an audit trail is established which provides a link that can be checked and followed through the accounting system:

- prime document
- book of prime entry
- double-entry accounts

Such an audit trail is required both as a security feature within the business (to help to ensure that false and fraudulent transactions cannot be made), and also for taxation purposes – both for Value Added Tax and for the Inland Revenue.

The cashier has an important role to play within the accounting function of a business – most business activities will, at some point, involve cash or cheque transactions. Thus the cash book and the cashier are at the hub of the accounting system. In particular, the cashier is responsible for:

- issuing receipts for cash (and sometimes cheques) received
- making authorised payments in cash, and by cheque and other bank transfers against documents received (such as invoices and statements) showing the amounts due
- checking expenses claims (see Chapter 15) and seeking authorisation before making payment

With so many transactions passing through the cash book, accounting procedures must include:

- accuracy – in writing up the cash book, in cash handling, and in ensuring that payments are made only against correct documents and appropriate authorisation
- security – of cash and cheque books, correct authorisation of payments
- confidentiality – that all cash/bank transactions, including cash and bank balances, are kept confidential

If the cashier has any queries about any transactions, he or she should refer them to the accounts supervisor.

RECORDING RECEIPTS – LAYOUT OF THE CASH BOOK

In this chapter we focus on the debit side of the cash book, which is used for recording receipts. The credit side of the cash book – used for recording payments is covered in Chapter 15.

A cash book can be set out in a variety of formats to suit the requirements of a particular business. One format that can be used is a columnar cash book incorporating several money columns. An example of the receipts side of a three-column cash book (with three money columns) is shown below:

Debit		**Cash Book: Receipts**			**CBR**
Date	Details	Folio	Discount allowed	Cash	Bank
			£	£	£

points to note

- The cash book receipts (CBR) is the debit side (the payments side is the credit side – see Chapter 15); thus the cash book is part of the double-entry system.
- The cash book shown here has separate money columns for cash receipts and for bank receipts, eg cheques, BACS transfers received. Note that the cash column does not always appear in the cash book – it is most often used by businesses, such as shops, which have a high volume of cash receipts. Many businesses use a cash book which just has a bank column to record receipts such as cheques, BACS transfers and any cash received – all paid straight into the bank. Whatever the format of the cash book, the basic principles will remain the same.
- A third money column is used to record any settlement (cash) discount allowed to customers (that is, an allowance offered to customers for quick settlement of the amount due, eg 2% discount for settlement within seven days).
- As the cash book is part of the double-entry system, each entry on the receipts side (the debit side) of the cash and bank columns must have an opposite entry on the credit side of another account elsewhere.
- The discount allowed column is not part of the double-entry system – it is used in the cash book as a listing device or memorandum column. We will see later in this chapter how amounts from this column are transferred into the double-entry system.

Case Study

SEVERN TRADING COMPANY – CASH BOOK RECEIPTS

situation

The cashier at the firm for which you work, Severn Trading Company, is away on a training course this week. You are required, in her absence, to take over as cashier. The following receipts are to be entered into the firm's three column cash book:

2004	
5 Apr	Balances at start of week: cash £300, bank £1,550
5 Apr	Cash sales £235 (including VAT of £35)
6 Apr	Received a cheque from S Wright, a debtor, for £98 – we have allowed her £2 settlement discount
6 Apr	Received a bank giro credit from Peter Singh Limited, a debtor, for £205 (no settlement discount)
7 Apr	J Jones settles her account of £80, by cheque, after deducting 5% settlement discount
7 Apr	Cash sales £94 (including VAT of £14), a cheque received
9 Apr	Received a cheque for £45 from D Whiteman Limited in full settlement of the account of £48
9 Apr	Received a monthly standing order payment for £110 from Natasha Lloyd and Co, a debtor (no settlement discount)

Note: all cheques are banked on the day of receipt

solution

The receipts side of the cash book records these transactions as shown below:

Debit		**Cash Book: Receipts**			**CBR 24**
Date	Details	Folio	Discount allowed	Cash	Bank
2004			£	£	£
5 Apr	Balances brought down			300	1,550
5 Apr	Sales	ML 4001/2200		235	
6 Apr	S Wright	SL 295	2		98
6 Apr	Peter Singh Limited (CR)	SL 147			205
7 Apr	J Jones	SL 86	4		76
7 Apr	Sales	ML 4001/2200			94
9 Apr	D Whiteman Limited	SL 278	3		45
9 Apr	Natasha Lloyd and Co (SO)	SL 121			110
			9	535	2,178

notes

- The cash book receipts page is numbered – here 'CBR 24'.
- The cash book forms a part of the double-entry book-keeping system. The receipts side of the cash book records the debit entry for cash and bank transactions – in the section which follows we shall see how the credit entry for each transaction is recorded in order to complete double-entry. (The discount allowed column is not part of double-entry – we will see how it is transferred into the accounts in the next section.)
- The balances brought down on 5 April are the amounts of cash held and the amount of money in the bank account as shown by the cash book at the beginning of the week. The cash book, like other accounts, is balanced at regular intervals – eg weekly or monthly – and we shall look at how it is balanced in Chapter 19.
- The folio column has been completed to show in which division of the ledger and to which account number(s) the opposite book-keeping entry appears:

  ML = main ledger

  SL = sales ledger, ie subsidiary (sales) ledger
- Where receipts have been transferred direct into the bank account, for example here on 6 April by bank giro credit and on 9 April by standing order, the transactions have been indicated – this information will help when the firm's bank statement is received (see page 385).
- Where two or more cheques are banked on the same day and on the same paying-in slip, it is possible to sub-total the cash book in order to show that the cheques total on the paying-in slip agrees with the sub-total of the cash book. This is a very useful checking device.
- For cash sales, the amount of cash (or cheques) received and recorded in the cash book includes VAT; when recording the entries to be shown on the credit side of the accounts, we need to distinguish between the sales amount and VAT – see the section which follows. This is the reason why two main ledger account numbers are shown in the folio column against cash sales – the first number refers to sales account, the second to VAT account.
- The money columns of the cash book have been sub-totalled – this helps as we take information forward into other accounts within the double-entry system, and also when we balance the cash book (see Chapter 19).

COMPLETING DOUBLE-ENTRY TRANSACTIONS

We have seen how the debit side of the cash book is used to record receipts in the form of cash or through the bank account. In this section we look at how to complete the double-entry accounts for

- cash sales
- receipts from debtors

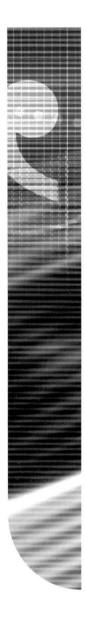

recording cash sales

By 'cash sales' we mean where a customer buys goods or services and pays immediately either in cash or by cheque (or other payment method such as BACS, debit card, credit card). The double-entry book-keeping entries are:

- payment received in cash
  - *debit* cash column of the cash book
  - *credit* sales account (or *credit* cash sales account – some businesses prefer to separate cash sales from credit sales)
  - *credit* VAT account (with the amount of VAT)
- payment received by cheque (or other banking payment method)
  - *debit* bank column of the cash book
  - *credit* sales account (or *credit* cash sales account)
  - *credit* VAT account

The credit entries from the Case Study for the cash sales transactions of 5 April and 7 April are recorded in the double-entry accounts as follows:

MAIN LEDGER

Dr **Sales Account** (account no 4001) Cr

2004	£	2004			£
		5 Apr	Cash	CBR 24	200
		7 Apr	Bank	CBR 24	80

Dr **Value Added Tax Account** (account no 2200) Cr

2004	£	2004			£
		5 Apr	Cash	CBR 24	35
		7 Apr	Bank	CBR 24	14

recording receipts from debtors

When customers (debtors) pay for goods or services that have been sold to them on credit, the method of payment is:

- either by cheque, or other payment method such as BACS, debit card, credit card
- or, less commonly, in cash

The double-entry book-keeping entries are:

- payment received by cheque (or other banking method)
  - *debit* bank column of the cash book
  - *credit* sales ledger control account (in the main ledger)
  - and a credit to the debtor's account in the subsidiary (sales) ledger
- payment received in cash
  - *debit* cash column of the cash book
  - *credit* sales ledger control account (in the main ledger)
  - and a credit to the debtor's account in the subsidiary (sales) ledger

As well as the credit to sales ledger control account, remember that a credit must be recorded on the debtor's account in the subsidiary (sales) ledger. Note that no entry is needed in VAT account as it will have been made when the credit sale was recorded in the accounting system (see Chapter 3).

Where cash discount allowed for prompt settlement has been taken by the debtor, ie settlement discount has reduced the amount of the payment, entries must be made in the double-entry system as follows:

- *debit* discount allowed account (in the main ledger)
- *credit* sales ledger control account (in the main ledger)
- and a credit to the debtor's account in the subsidiary (sales) ledger

The credit entries from the Case Study for the receipts from debtors are as follows, starting with the subsidiary (sales) ledger. It is suggested that you 'tick back' each transaction.

Note: for illustrative purposes an amount for sales has been debited to each debtor's account (with the cross-reference to SDB 98).

SUBSIDIARY (SALES) LEDGER

Dr **S Wright** (account no 295) Cr

2004			£	2004			£
15 Mar	Sales	SDB 98	100	6 Apr	Bank	CBR 24	98
				6 Apr	Discount Allowed	ML 6501	2

Dr **Peter Singh Limited** (account no 147) Cr

2004			£	2004			£
15 Mar	Sales	SDB 98	400	6 Apr	Bank	CBR 24	205

Dr		J Jones (account no 86)			Cr
2004		£	2004		£
15 Mar	Sales SDB 98	80	7 Apr	Bank CBR 24	76
			7 Apr	Discount Allowed ML 6501	4

Dr		D Whiteman Limited (account no 278)			Cr
2004		£	2004		£
15 Mar	Sales SDB 98	48	9 Apr	Bank CBR 24	45
			9 Apr	Discount Allowed ML 6501	3

Dr		Natasha Lloyd and Co (account no 121)			Cr
2004		£	2004		£
15 Mar	Sales SDB 98	350	9 Apr	Bank CBR 24	110

Notes:

- In the above accounts amounts for sales have been shown for illustrative purposes – see Chapter 3, which covers accounting for sales.
- In order to complete double-entry book-keeping, discount allowed amounts, which have been credited to the debtors' accounts, must also be debited to discount allowed account in the main ledger (the discount column in the cash book is not part of the double-entry system, but is a memorandum column only). The account is completed by entering the total of the discount column from the cash book, as follows:

MAIN LEDGER

Dr		Discount Allowed Account (account no 6501)			Cr
2004		£	2004		£
9 Apr	Cash Book CBR 24	9			

- Sales ledger control account (see below) is credited with the amount of discount allowed.
- Once the total of discount allowed has been taken from the cash book, the discount column 'starts again' (ie the amount of £9, above, for this week will not be included in next week's transfer).
- Sales ledger control account is written up as follows at 9 April (the end of the week):

MAIN LEDGER

Dr		**Sales Ledger Control Account** (account no 6001)			Cr
2004		£	2004		£
15 Mar	Sales SDB 98	*978	9 Apr	Bank CBR 24	**534
			9 Apr	Discount Allowed ML 6501	9

* As the sales day book is not shown here, the sales figure is the total of the debits to the subsidiary debtors' accounts, ie £100 + £400 + £80 + £48 + £350.

** The total bank receipts of £534 comprises cheques and bank transfers from debtors, ie £98 + £205 + £76 + £45 + £110 (the amount does not include receipts from cash sales). Later in this chapter – page 151 – we will see how an analysed cash book can be used to obtain more easily the total of receipts from debtors.

treatment of VAT – cash sales and credit sales

Remember the terminology:

cash sales = *sales where payment (whether in cash, by cheque or debit/credit card) is received straightaway*

credit sales = *sales where payment (whether in cash, by cheque or debit/credit card) is received from the debtor at a later date*

When carrying out the book-keeping entries for receipts from cash sales and receipts from debtors, the treatment of VAT is quite different. It is important to bear these differences in mind. Remember:

The double-entry for a payment received from **cash sales** is:

- *debit* bank column of the cash book (or cash column if it is used)
- *credit* sales account
- *credit* VAT account (with the amount of VAT)

The double-entry for a payment received from **credit sales** (ie from a debtor):

- *debit* bank column of the cash book
- *credit* sales ledger control account (in the main ledger)

There is no entry for VAT here because the VAT has already been accounted for when the sale was first made (see Chapter 3). The entries would then have been: *debit* debtor account and *credit* sales account and *credit* VAT account.

The diagram on the next page illustrates the book-keeping entries for the receipts from sales, which have been described in this section of the chapter.

book-keeping entries for receipts from sales

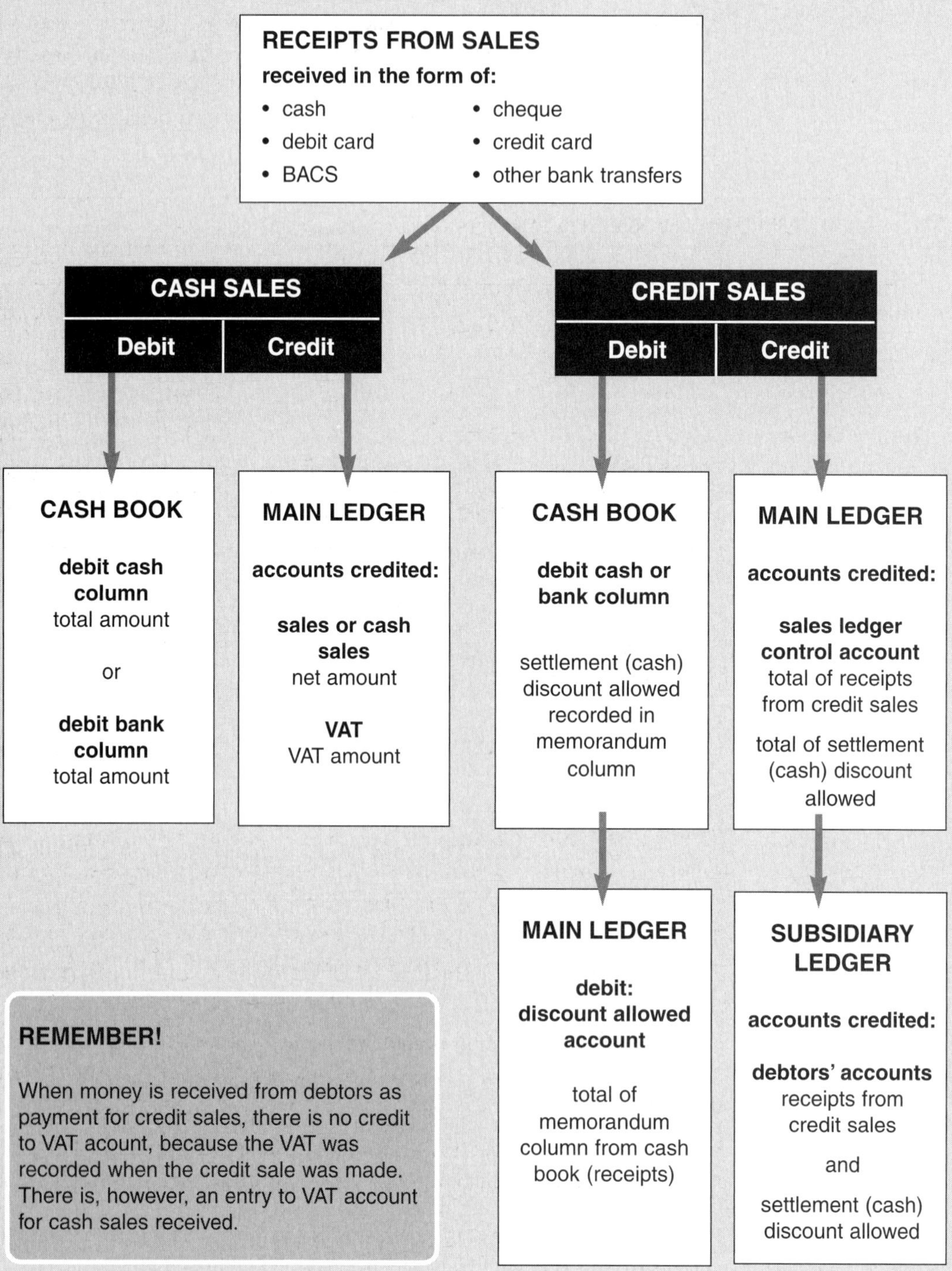

REMEMBER!

When money is received from debtors as payment for credit sales, there is no credit to VAT acount, because the VAT was recorded when the credit sale was made. There is, however, an entry to VAT account for cash sales received.

BATCH CONTROL SYSTEMS

Where businesses have a large number of receipts – from cash sales and/or from debtors – they often use batched data entry in order to enter such transactions into the accounts in one 'run'. As we have seen previously in Chapter 3, a batch of transactions for a day, week or month is pre-listed on a batch control form; the example shown below is for a batch of cheques received from debtors:

Batch Control: cheques received from debtors

Customer			Debit	Debit	Credit
Date	Account No	Name	Discount allowed	Bank	Debtors control
2004			£	£	£
6 Apr	SL 295	S Wright	2.00	98.00	100.00
7 Apr	SL 86	J Jones	4.00	76.00	80.00
7 Apr	SL 278	D Whiteman Ltd	3.00	45.00	48.00
		Check list totals	9.00	219.00	228.00

Prepared by	*Neil Ford*	Date	*9 Apr 2004*
Checked by	*Barbara Smith*	Date	*9 Apr 2004*
Posted by	*Dan Ryan*	Date	*9 Apr 2004*

Note that receipts from customers by BACS and other bank transfers have not been shown on the batch control form – only cheques received are listed. A business that has a lot of cash sales or receives large numbers of payments from customers by BACS or other methods – such as credit and debit cards – will use batch control systems for each type of receipt. As always, in accounting, businesses adapt systems to suit their own circumstances.

Totals are taken from the batch control form and transferred to sales ledger control account. It is probably better practice to credit the two separate amounts, ie £9.00 and £219.00, rather than the total credit of £228.00.

Payments received by methods other than by cheque – such as BACS, debit card and credit card receipts – will also be credited to sales ledger control account.

THE CASH BOOK IN THE ACCOUNTING SYSTEM

The cash book performs two functions within the accounting system:

- it is the book of prime entry for cash/bank transactions
- it forms part of the double-entry system

For the receipts side of the cash book these functions are illustrated in the diagram which follows:

CASH AND BANK RECEIPTS

PRIME DOCUMENTS

- receipts issued
- bank paying-in slips
- BACS and other bank transfers received
- debit and credit card vouchers

↓

BOOK OF PRIME ENTRY
AND DOUBLE-ENTRY BOOK-KEEPING

DEBIT cash book receipts

↓

DOUBLE-ENTRY BOOK-KEEPING

either

- CREDIT sales ledger control account (money received), and debtors' accounts in the subsidiary (sales) ledger

or

- CREDIT other account, eg sales account (for cash sales), VAT account (for VAT on cash sales)

CASH BOOK INCORPORATING VAT

A cash book can be adapted to suit the needs of a business – already we have seen how a cash book incorporates a memorandum column for settlement discount. Another common layout uses a money column for VAT, as shown in the Case Study which follows. The VAT column acts as a memorandum column and, at the end of the week or month, is transferred to VAT account.

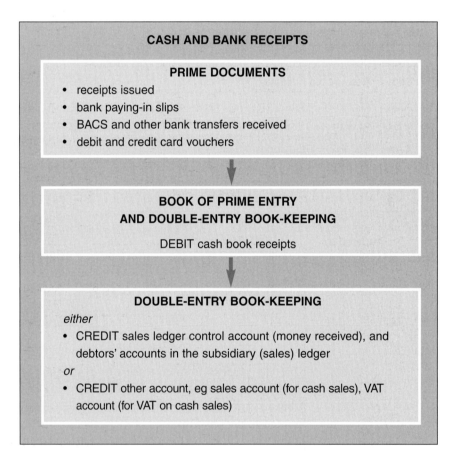

Case Study

CASH BOOK INCORPORATING VAT

situation

On Monday 7 June 2004, the cash book of Eveshore Growers showed a balance of £248 in the bank. Receipts for the week were:

7 June Received a cheque for £470 from a debtor, Sisco Systems

7 June Cash sales of £282, including Value Added Tax, paid direct into the bank

8 June Received a cheque for £230 from a debtor, P Leech, who was settling his account balance of £235 after deducting £5 settlement discount

9 June Cash sales of £423, including Value Added Tax, paid for by cheque

The rate of Value Added Tax is 17.5%.
All cheques are banked on the day of receipt.

As cashier to Eveshore Growers, you are to:

- write up page 54 of the receipts side of the cash book for the week commencing 7 June 2004, using separate columns for discount, VAT and bank (note that no cash column is required in this cash book – all cash is paid straight into the bank)
- sub-total the cash book at 11 June 2004
- explain how the totals for the discount and VAT columns will be entered in the main ledger of Eveshore Growers

solution

Debit			**Cash Book: Receipts**		**CBR 54**
Date	Details	Folio	Discount allowed	VAT	Bank
2004			£	£	£
7 Jun	Balance brought down				248
7 Jun	Sisco Systems	SL			470
7 Jun	Sales	ML		42	282
8 Jun	P Leech	SL	5		230
9 Jun	Sales	ML		63	423
			5	105	1,653

Notes:

- The folio columns have been completed as follows (account numbers have not been shown)

  ML = main ledger

  SL = sales ledger, ie subsidiary (sales) ledger

- For transactions involving sales ledger (eg Sisco Systems), no amount for VAT is shown in the VAT column. This is because VAT has been charged on invoices issued and was recorded in the VAT account (through the sales day book) when the sale was made.
- VAT on cash sales and other transactions is recorded in the VAT analysis column.
- Receipts from debtors (eg Sisco Systems) are credited to sales ledger control account in the main ledger, and to the debtors' accounts in the subsidiary (sales) ledger.

The discount and VAT columns:

- discount allowed column – the total of £5 will be debited to discount allowed account in the main ledger, credited to sales ledger control account in the main ledger and to P Leech's account in the subsidiary (sales) ledger
- VAT column – the total of £105 will be credited to VAT account in the main ledger (alternatively the individual amounts of £42 and £63 could be credited)

Note that, in the cash book, the discount allowed and VAT columns 'start again' from zero after the totals have been transferred to the main ledger accounts.

ANALYSED CASH BOOK

Many businesses use an analysed cash book to provide more information. An analysed cash book divides receipts (and payments – see Chapter 15) between a number of categories.

Receipts could be divided between:

- the main sections of a business, such as (1) furniture, and (2) carpets, for a home furnishing shop
- (1) discount allowed, (2) Value Added Tax (where a business is registered for VAT), (3) cash sales, (4) sales ledger, ie receipts from debtors, (5) sundry receipts

A business will use whatever analysis columns suit it best: the cash book should be adapted to meet the needs of the business in the best possible way.

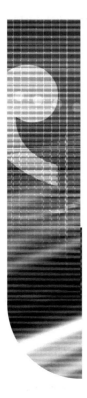

Case Study

ANALYSED CASH BOOK

situation

Wyvern Auto Spares Limited sells car parts to local garages and to members of the public. The company is registered for Value Added Tax.

The business uses a cash book which analyses receipts as follows:

RECEIPTS

- discount allowed
- VAT
- cash sales
- sales ledger, ie subsidiary (sales) ledger
- sundry receipts

The following receipts transactions are to be entered on page 31 of the receipts side of the cash book for the first week of December 2004:

6 Dec	Balances from previous week: cash £255, bank £875
6 Dec	Sales for cash £240 + VAT
7 Dec	A debtor, Main Street Garage, settles an invoice for £195, paying by cheque
7 Dec	Sales for cash £200 + VAT
9 Dec	A debtor, A45 Service Station, settles an invoice for £240, paying £235 by cheque and receiving £5 discount for prompt settlement
9 Dec	Sales £320 + VAT, received by cheque
10 Dec	Sales for cash £200 + VAT

The rate of Value Added Tax is 17.5%. All cheques are banked on the day of receipt.

solution

Debit **Cash Book: Receipts** **CBR 31**

Date	Details	Folio	Cash	Bank	Discount allowed	VAT	Cash sales	Sales ledger	Sundry
2004			£	£	£	£	£	£	£
6 Dec	Balances brought down		255	875					
6 Dec	Sales	ML	282			42	240		
7 Dec	Main Street Garage	SL		195				195	
7 Dec	Sales	ML	235			35	200		
9 Dec	A45 Service Station	SL		235	5			235	
9 Dec	Sales	ML		376		56	320		
10 Dec	Sales	ML	235			35	200		
			1,007	1,681	5	168	960	430	–

notes

- The receipts side of the cash book analyses each receipt between a number of headings. A business will adapt the cash book and use whatever analysis columns suit it best for its receipts.
- References to the ledger sections have been shown in the folio column.
- For transactions involving sales ledger, no amount for VAT is shown in the VAT columns. This is because VAT has been charged on invoices issued and was recorded in the VAT account (through the sales day book) when the sale was made.
- The columns are sub-totalled at the end of the week and the totals of the analysis columns are transferred to other accounts as follows:
  - discount allowed column total of £5 is debited to discount allowed account in the main ledger and credited to sales ledger control account in the main ledger
  - Value Added Tax column, the total of £168 is credited to VAT account in the main ledger
  - cash sales column, the total of £960 is credited to sales account (or cash sales account) in the main ledger
  - sales ledger column, the total of £430 is credited to sales ledger control account in the main ledger
- Individual amounts of receipts from debtors and discount allowed are credited to debtors' accounts in the subsidiary (sales) ledger
- Sundry receipts are dealt with individually by crediting the appropriate account (eg capital, loan, income): see section below

OTHER RECEIPTS

In addition to receipts from debtors and from cash sales, the debit side of the cash book is used to record other receipts of the business. These include:

- capital introduced by the owner(s)
- loans made to the business, such as a bank loan, or from a relative or friend
- income, such as rent received, commission received

We will look at further aspects of these transactions in more detail in Chapter 17 and see how they fit into the double-entry system. For the moment we will see how they are recorded in the double-entry system of cash book and ledger accounts:

- capital introduced
  - *debit* cash book
  - *credit* capital account

  The owner of the business pays in capital (or more capital) in the form of cash or a cheque.

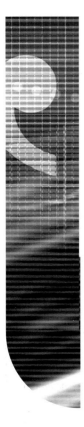

- loans received
  - *debit* cash book
  - *credit* loan account, eg bank loan, loan from J Smith

  The amount of the loan is received in the cash book, by cheque or through the bank.
- income received
  - *debit* cash book
  - *credit* income account (using the appropriate account, eg rent received, commission received)

  Business income, other than from sales, may be received in the form of cash, a cheque or by bank transfer.

example transactions

2004

16 Jun	The owner of the business pays in additional capital of £1,000, by cheque
17 Jun	Received a loan of £500, by cheque, from A Friend (no VAT)
18 Jun	Rent received from tenant, £150 by cheque (no VAT)

The cash book (receipts) records these transactions as follows:

Debit		**Cash Book: Receipts**			**CBR 10**
Date	Details	Folio	Discount allowed	Cash	Bank
2004			£	£	£
16 Jun	Capital	ML			1,000
17 Jun	Loan: A Friend	ML			500
18 Jun	Rent received	ML			150

The credit entries are shown in the main ledger (in which all of these accounts are contained) as follows:

MAIN LEDGER

Dr		**Capital Account**	Cr
2004	£	2004	£
		16 Jun Bank CBR 10	1,000

Dr		**Loan Account: A Friend**	Cr
2004	£	2004	£
		17 Jun Bank CBR 10	500

Dr		**Rent Received Account**	Cr
2004	£	2004	£
		18 Jun Bank CBR 10	150

Chapter Summary

- The cash book records receipts (debits) for cash and credit transactions.
- The basic layout for a cash book (receipts) includes a money column for bank transactions, together with a column for discount allowed. Cash books for businesses which receive substantial amounts of cash (eg shops) may have a further money column to record cash (notes and coins) transactions.
- Another common cash book layout incorporates a VAT column.
- An analysed cash book is used to provide more information: it divides receipts between a number of categories.

Key Terms

cash book	records bank (and in some cases cash) transactions; it combines the roles of book of prime entry and double-entry book-keeping
columnar cash book	commonly-used layout for cash books which incorporates several money columns, eg for settlement discount, VAT, cash, bank
analysed cash book	cash book which divides receipts (and payments) between a number of categories, eg the main sections of the business

Student Activities

7.1 The cash book is:

(a) a prime document

(b) a book of prime entry only

(c) part of double-entry book-keeping only

(d) combines book of prime entry and double-entry book-keeping

Answer (a) or (b) or (c) or (d)

7.2 You work as the cashier for Wyvern Publishing, a company which publishes a wide range of travel and historical books. As cashier, your main responsibility is for the firm's cash book.

Explain to a friend what your job involves and the qualities required of a cashier.

· recording receipts to bank   make payment into bank
- making payments from bank - preparing cheques + RA.
· checking statements   checking expense claims.
- paying money to petty cash when required   accuracy/confidentiality/security

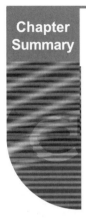

7.3 The following are the receipts transactions of Metro Trading Company for August 2004:

1 Aug	Balances from previous month: cash £276, bank £4,928
3 Aug	Received a cheque from a debtor, Wild & Sons Limited, £398
6 Aug	Sales for cash, £160 + VAT
16 Aug	Received a cheque for £1,755 from A Lewis Limited in full settlement of their account of £1,775
18 Aug	Sales for cash, £240 + VAT
20 Aug	Received a cheque for £261 from Harvey & Sons Limited, a debtor
23 Aug	Received a loan of £750 from the bank (no VAT)
24 Aug	Sales £400 + VAT, received half in cash, and half by cheque
26 Aug	Rent received from tenant, £100 in cash (no VAT)
27 Aug	Received a cheque for £595 from Wild & Sons Limited in full settlement of their account of £610

The rate of Value Added Tax is 17.5%

All cheques are banked on the day of receipt

Account numbers are to be used – see below

You are to:

- Enter the above receipts on page 45 of the three column cash book of Metro Trading Company. This cash book has columns for discount allowed, cash and bank.
- Sub-total the money columns at 31 August.
- Show the entries to be made in the following accounts:

  subsidiary (sales) ledger

  Wild & Sons Limited (account no 843)

  A Lewis Limited (account no 531)

  Harvey & Sons Limited (account no 467)

  main ledger

  sales ledger control account (account no 6001)

  discount allowed account (account no 6501)

  bank loan (account no 2210)

  rent received account (account no 4951)

  sales account (account no 4001)

  VAT account (account no 2200)

7.4 The following are the receipts transactions of Johnson Brothers for April 2004:

1 Apr	Balance at bank from previous month, £718
8 Apr	J Bowen, a debtor, settles an invoice for £90, paying £85 by cheque and receiving £5 discount for prompt settlement
9 Apr	Cash sales £470 (including Value Added Tax) received by cheque
12 Apr	Rent received from tenant, £250 by cheque (no VAT)

16 Apr	Cash sales of £94 (including Value Added Tax) received by cheque
19 Apr	Received a cheque for £575 from J Burrows, a debtor, in full settlement of an invoice for £600
20 Apr	Cash sales of £188 (including Value Added Tax) paid direct into the bank
26 Apr	Received a cheque for £245 from Wilson Limited, a debtor, in full settlement of an invoice for £255

The rate of Value Added Tax is 17.5%

All cash and cheques are banked on the day of receipt

Account numbers are to be used – see below

You are to:

- Enter the above receipts on page 88 of the cash book of Johnson Brothers. The cash book has columns for date, details, discount allowed, VAT and bank.
- Sub-total the money columns at 30 April.
- Show the entries to be made in the following accounts:

  subsidiary (sales) ledger

  J Bowen (account no 117)

  J Burrows (account no 125)

  Wilson Limited (account no 855)

  main ledger

  sales ledger control account (account no 6001)

  discount allowed account (account no 6501)

  rent received account (account no 4951)

  sales account (account no 4001)

  VAT account (account no 2200)

7.5 David Lewis runs a shop selling carpets to the public on cash terms and also to a few trade customers – such as carpet fitters – on credit terms. His business is registered for VAT.

He uses an analysed cash book which has columns for:

- bank
- discount allowed
- VAT
- sales
- sales ledger
- sundry

The following transactions take place during the week commencing 17 May 2004:

17 May	Balance at bank from previous week, £825.30
17 May	Sales £534.62 (including VAT), cheque received
17 May	Rent received from tenant of flat above the shop, £255.50 by cheque (no VAT)
18 May	Sales £164.50 (including VAT), cash received and paid direct into the bank
18 May	A debtor, T Jarvis, settles an invoice for £157.50, paying £155.00 by cheque, £2.50 discount being allowed for prompt settlement
19 May	David Lewis' brother, Terry, makes a loan to the business of £500.00 by cheque (no VAT)

19 May	Sales £752.00 (including VAT), cheque received
20 May	Sales £264.37 (including VAT), cash received and paid direct into the bank
21 May	David Lewis pays in additional capital of £1,000.00 by cheque (no VAT)
21 May	A debtor, Wyvern District Council, settles an invoice for £565.45, paying £560.45 by cheque and receiving £5.00 discount for prompt settlement

The rate of Value Added Tax is 17.5%

All cash and cheques are banked on the day of receipt

Account numbers are to be used – see below

You are to:

- Enter the above receipts on page 96 of the cash book of David Lewis (VAT amounts should be rounded down to the nearest penny).
- Sub-total the money columns at 21 May.
- Show the entries to be made in the following accounts:

  subsidiary (sales) ledger

  T Jarvis (account no 497)

  Wyvern District Council (account no 924)

  main ledger

  capital account (account no 3005)

  sales ledger control account (account no 6001)

  discount allowed account (account no 6501)

  loan account: T Lewis (account no 2220)

  rent received account (account no 4951)

  sales account (account no 4001)

  VAT account (account no 2200)

7.6 Prepare a sales ledger control account for the month of December 2004 from the following information:

2004		£
1 Dec	Debit balances brought down	38,643
31 Dec	Credit sales for month	45,419
	Sales returns	3,210
	Payments received from debtors	43,987
	Settlement discount allowed	695

Balance the account at 31 December 2004.

8 Communicating with customers

this chapter covers . . .

This chapter explains the importance of polite and effective handling of communications between a business and its customers. It covers:

- *the need for politeness – adopting the right mental attitude*
- *the need for effectiveness – choosing the right means of communication and expressing the facts accurately and in an appropriate way*
- *an illustration of the wide variety of business communication formats*
- *practical examples of how those formats are used*
- *the different forms of written communication – notes, letters and memoranda*

NVQ PERFORMANCE CRITERIA COVERED

unit 1: RECORDING INCOME AND RECEIPTS

element 1.1: process documents relating to goods and services supplied

G *communicate politely and effectively with customers regarding accounts, using the relevant information from the aged debtors analysis*

COMMUNICATING WITH CUSTOMERS

Your course requires that you communicate with your customers (the people to whom you sell) **politely** and **effectively**.

In other words, you are pleasant and respectful in your communication and you transfer the necessary message accurately and within the correct timescale. These principles are often set out in an organisation's 'customer charter' scheme or will form part of a general 'quality' policy adopted by a business.

Politeness involves putting the other person first, no matter how stupid or arrogant that person might be – politeness is your mental attitude – it may come naturally, or it may not!

Effectivness of communication, on the other hand, is less easy to achieve. It means:

- choosing the right means of communication
- getting your facts right
- being able to express those facts in the appropriate way

Effectiveness is a skill that has to be learned over a period of time.

Over the next few pages we will look at the different types of communication used internally in an organisation and externally with customers. You will need to study these; they will feature not only in the Case Study at the end of the chapter, but also in the last two chapters of the book which deal with communicating management information. First however, we give some examples of situations relating to customers which will require your communication skills.

examples of customer communications

The types of situation which might arise include:

- answering a customer enquiry about an invoice – eg the terms
- sending a customer a copy of a document which has gone astray
- sending back a customer's cheque with a missing signature
- chasing up debts from customers who are slow in paying – the aged debtor analysis is the central document for this process

aged debtor analysis

An *aged debtors analysis* is a summary of amounts owed by customers (debtors), analysed into columns showing how long the amounts have been outstanding. It shows a business which customers are slow in paying up. It enables a business to decide which customers to chase for payment.

An aged debtors analysis can either be drawn up manually, or it can be printed out as a report from a computer accounting package. An example of a computer printed aged debtors analysis is shown and explained below.

Pronto Supplies Limited

Aged Debtors Analysis (Summary)

Page: 1

A/C	Name	Crd Limit	Turnover	Balance	Current	Period 1	Period 2	Period 3	Older
CH001	Charisma Design	5,000.00	2,416.00	18.80	18.80	0.00	0.00	0.00	0.00
CR001	Crowmatic Limited	5,000.00	3,334.00	117.50	117.50	0.00	0.00	0.00	0.00
DB001	David Boossey	5,000.00	3,400.00	235.00	235.00	0.00	0.00	0.00	0.00
FE001	French Emporium	10,000.00	5,960.00	470.00	470.00	0.00	0.00	0.00	0.00
JB001	John Butler & Associates	10,000.00	6,020.00	611.00	611.00	0.00	0.00	0.00	0.00
JG001	Jo Green Systems	5,000.00	3,728.00	310.20	310.20	0.00	0.00	0.00	0.00
KD001	Kay Denz	10,000.00	6,620.00	6,641.00	141.00	6,500.00	0.00	0.00	0.00
LG001	L Garr & Co	15,000.00	8,680.00	211.50	211.50	0.00	0.00	0.00	0.00
PT001	Prism Trading Limited	5,000.00	2,906.00	376.00	376.00	0.00	0.00	0.00	0.00
	Totals:		43,064.00	8,991.00	2,491.00	6,500.00	0.00	0.00	0.00

the account code

the account name

the credit limit – the maximum amount of credit allowed

turnover – the total of the sales made to the customer

balance – the amount owed by the customer

current – invoices issued in the last 30 days

the periods are months - they show how long amounts invoiced have been outstanding:

- period 1 is 30 to 59 days
- period 2 is 60 to 89 days
- period 3 is 90 to 119 days
- 'older' is 120 days or more

The aged debtor analysis is normally produced at the end of each month when the statements go out. From this report the business decides which customers it is going to chase up, and how. It may send a letter or an email, it may telephone the customer and put them on the spot.

In the next section we will look at some of these methods of communication used by a business.

THE MEMORANDUM

format

The memorandum (plural memoranda) is a formal written note used for internal communication within an organisation. It may be word-processed or handwritten, and will often be produced in a number of copies which can be circulated as necessary. A memorandum may be sent by email within an organisation. A memorandum can be used for situations such as:

- giving instructions
- requesting information

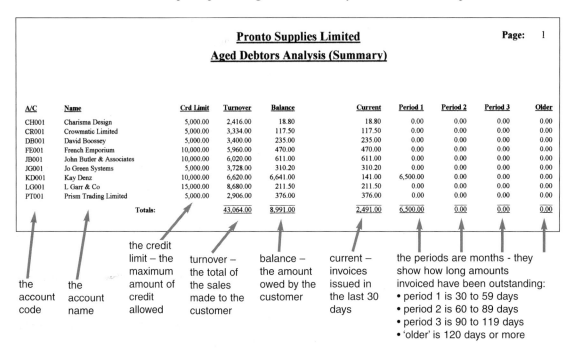

- making suggestions
- recording of opinions
- confirming telephone conversations

A memorandum is normally pre-printed by the organisation with all the headings in place, and can be half page or full page in size.

elements of the memorandum

'to' and 'from'	the name and job title of the sender and the recipient are entered in full, and the formal phrases you find on letters, eg 'Dear......' and 'Yours ....' are not necessary
copies to	memoranda are sometimes sent to a number of people; the recipients will be indicated in this section of the document
subject	the subject matter of the memorandum must be stated concisely
text	the message of the memorandum should be clear and concise
signature	a memorandum can be signed, initialled, or even – as is often the case – left blank
enclosures	if material is circulated with the memorandum, the abbreviation 'enc' or 'encl' should be used

MEMORANDUM

To John Stone, Accounts Supervisor

From Tim Blake, Sales Manager **Ref** TB/AC/1098

Copies to n/a **Date** 23 June 2003

Subject Bad payers

Please can you let me have an updated list of our customers who exceed their credit period and pay late.

I need to give this list to the sales reps so that they will not be tempted to extend credit any further to these customers.

Thank you.

a completed memorandum relating to customer accounts

THE NOTE

One of the most common forms of communication within an organisation is the *note.* This can be:

- an informal written note, passing on a message or an instruction
- a telephone message (some organisations use preprinted telephone message pads)

The important elements of a written note are

- the name of the person who is sending the note
- the name of the person who is to receive the note
- the time and date that the note is written
- a clearly stated message
- a clear indication of any action to be taken as a result of the message

Examine the examples set out below and see how they contain all these elements.

To Tim Blackstock,
Order Processing

Please remember to allow PDT Ltd an extra 10% trade discount on invoices this month.

John Tregennick, Sales
03.04.03 10.30

TELEPHONE MESSAGE

TO Karin Schmidt, Accounts
FROM H Khan, Sales
DATE 22 April 2003
TIME 12.30

Please ring Jim Stoat at RF Electronics - he is complaining that they have not received a credit note for returned damaged stock (order ref 823423).

Please treat urgently - he is not very happy!

HK

THE FAX

The fax (short for 'facsimile') enables you to transmit electronically an exact copy of the details on a sheet of paper. This can either be done on a computer or on a fax machine. If you use a fax machine you feed the sheet into the machine, dial up the recipient on the inbuilt telephone pad and transmit the document down the line. The machine at the other end will print out an exact copy of the original document.

The fax can be used within an organisation or for external contact with a customer. You normally send a 'fax header' first sheet (see illustration below) and then feed in any further pages/documents as required.

The fax is very useful for sending copies of documents. A frequent excuse given by people who are slow at paying is "I can't pay because I don't seem to have the original invoice". This can be replied to with 'No problem! We can fax you a copy. What is your fax number?' Look at the example below.

Winterborn Electronics Limited

Unit 4 Everoak Estate, Bromyard Road
St Johns, Worcester WR2 5HN
tel 01905 748043 fax 01905 748911

facsimile transmission header

To: Jamie Milne, Accounts Office, Zippo Computers

Fax number: 01350 525504

Number of pages including this header: 2 Date: 17 October 2003

message

Invoice 24375

Further to our recent telephone conversation I am faxing you a copy of invoice 24375 which is now overdue.

I shall be grateful if you will arrange for the £4,678.50 owing to be paid to us as soon as possible.

R Pound

Credit Controller

THE EMAIL

Email is the sending and receiving of electronic messages by means of computer. Emails can be

- external – communications with customers through the Internet, or
- internal – through a network of computers in the business – an intranet

Emails can be sent quickly and cheaply within the UK and overseas.

When someone wants to check an email account, it is necessary to log in. A list of messages is displayed. The user can read them or delete them. When a message is read, it is easy to reply to it. The original message re-appears and comments can be added to the original. If a message is of interest to someone else, it can be forwarded. Computer files – eg spreadsheets – can also be sent by email as 'attachments'.

When composing an email, a screen such as the one illustrated below is used.

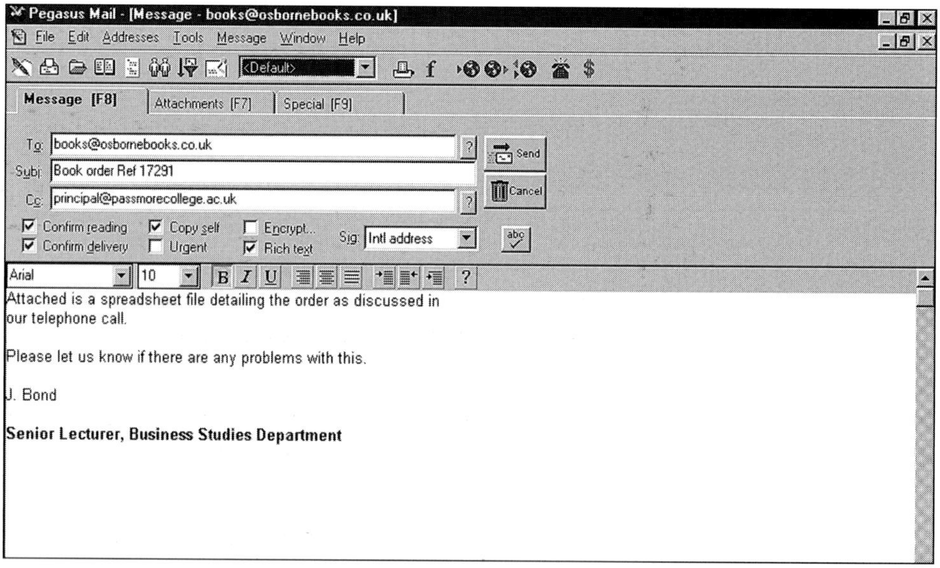

It can be seen that there is:

- space for the message
- a place to type in the email address of where the email has to go
- a box to summarise the content of the email – useful so that the person reading a message list knows which ones are the most important
- a CC (carbon copy) box so that a copy of the email can be sent to anyone else who needs to know about the message

THE 'HOUSE STYLE' LETTER

When you deal with business letters you will see that the appearance and format of each letter is in a uniform 'house' style, a style which identifies that business, and is common to all letters that it sends. The letter will normally be on standard printed stationery showing the name, address and details of the business, and will be set out with headings, paragraphs, signatures – the 'elements' of the letter – in a uniform way.

There are a number of different ways of setting out the text of a letter. The most of common of these – the 'fully blocked' style is illustrated and explained on the next two pages.

characteristics of a fully blocked letter

- the most commonly used style of letter
- all the lines start at the left margin
- the use of open punctuation, ie there is no punctuation, except in the main body of the letter, which uses normal punctuation
- paragraphs are divided by a space, and are not indented
- a fully blocked letter is easy to type as all the lines are set uniformly to the left margin

elements of the letter

The explanations which follow refer to the illustration of the letter on page 167.

printed letterhead The name and address of the business is normally pre-printed, and must be up-to-date.

reference The reference on the letter illustrated – DH/SB/69 – is a standard format

- DH (Derek Hunt), the writer
- SB (Sally Burgess), the secretary
- 69, the number of the file where Mr Smart's correspondence is kept

If you need to quote the reference of a letter to which you are replying, the references will be quoted as follows: Your ref TR/FG/45 Our ref DH/SB/69.

date The date is typed in date (number), month (word), year (number) order.

recipient The name and address of the person to whom the letter is sent. This section of the letter may be displayed in the window of a window envelope, so it is essential that it is accurate.

salutation 'Dear Sir. . . Dear Madam' – if you know the person's name and title (ie Mr, Mrs, Miss, Ms) use it, but check that it is correct – a misspelt name or an incorrect title will ruin an otherwise competent letter.

heading The heading sets out the subject matter of the letter – it will concentrate the reader's mind.

body The body of the letter is an area where the message of the letter is set out. The text must be

- laid out in short precise paragraphs and short clear sentences
- start with a point of reference (eg referring to an invoice)
- set out the message in a logical sequence
- be written in plain English – but avoid 'slang' expressions and, equally, avoid 'posh' words
- finish with a clear indication of the next step to be taken (eg please telephone, please arrange appointment, please buy our products, please pay our invoice)

complimentary close The complimentary close (signing off phrase) must be consistent with the salutation:

'Dear Sir/Dear Madam' followed by 'Yours faithfully'

'Dear Mr Sutton/Dear Ms Jones' followed by 'Yours sincerely'.

name and job title It is essential for the reader to know the name of the person who sent the letter, and that person's job title, because a reply will need to be addressed to a specific person.

enclosures If there are enclosures with the letter, the abbreviation 'enc' or 'encl' is used at the bottom of the letter.

the 'house style' letter

Wyvern Motor Supplies
107 High Street
Mereford
MR1 9SZ
Tel 01605 675365 Fax 01605 765576

reference	Ref DH/SB/69
date	15 December 2003
name and address of recipient	Purchasing Department Osborne Car Accessories 17 Pump Street Mereford MR6 7ER
salutation	Dear Sir
heading	<u>Invoice 8288 £10,589.50</u>
body of the letter	We note from our records that we have not yet received payment of our invoice 8288 dated 15 September 2003. Our up-to-date statement of account is enclosed, together with a copy of the invoice. Our payment terms are strictly 30 days from the date of the invoice. We shall be grateful if you will settle the £10,589.50 without further delay. We look forward to receiving your cheque.
complimentary close	Yours faithfully
signature	*D M Hunt*
name and job title	Derek Hunt Accounts Manager
enclosures	enc

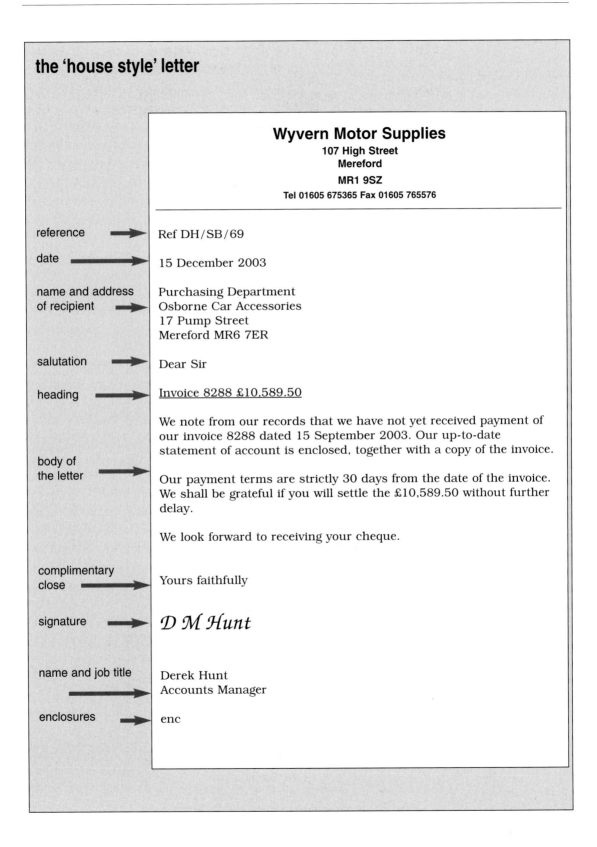

TYPES OF BUSINESS LETTER

Different types of business letter require different treatment. We will look at four situations and in each case give an example of how the text of the letter might read:

- dealing with queries and providing information
- chasing a debt

dealing with queries and providing information

The body of a letter providing information in answer to an enquiry will be structured in a number of stages:

1 Refer to the original enquiry, eg 'Further to your telephone enquiry/visit/letter' and give the enquiry a date … 'of 1 April.'

2 Provide the information, either in the text, or by enclosing promotional literature, eg a catalogue.

3 Finish the text of the letter on a positive note or 'selling' note, eg 'Please let us know if we can be of further help' … 'We look forward to your order' … 'If you wish to order the goods, please contact Mr Eden in our Sales Department, telephone 01908 384983.'

Here is an extract from a letter following a telephone enquiry to a bathroom centre. Note that the text is not particularly lengthy, but is polite and to the point. It follows the three stages set out above.

Dear Mr Knott

Shower Enclosures

Thank you for your telephone enquiry of today.

I am pleased to enclose a brochure and price list for the Niagara range of shower enclosures.

If you require further information, please do not hesitate to give me a call.

Yours sincerely

J Waterman

J Waterman
Sales Manager

a letter chasing a debt

This type of letter is used by an accounts department or by a sole trader chasing up overdue invoices. Often the letter will be a 'set' letter, already formatted on the computer. There may be a number of set letters on file: a gentle reminder, a firm reminder, a threat of legal action and a formal demand. Each letter is set out in a number of stages:

1. Details of the amount owing is clearly stated: the amount itself and the date of the original invoice(s). Sometimes a copy invoice(s) will be included in the letter to avoid the common problem of the customer claiming that the original invoice has been lost!

   Mention will often be made of the fact that statements of account have also been sent.

2. The terms of the invoice will be stated and the fact that the terms have not been complied with will be stressed.
3. Payment will be firmly requested – often a time limit will be stated.
4. Sometimes it may be necessary to threaten what will happen if the money is not received, eg 'If we do not receive settlement by this date we regret we will have no alternative but to place the matter in the hands of our solicitors.'

The text of a chaser letter for a long overdue invoice is shown below. Study the text and then read the Case Study which follows.

30 April 2003

Dear Mr Khan

<u>Invoice 23846 £1,250</u>

We note from our records that invoice 23846 (copy enclosed)for £1,250, dated 8 January 2003, has not yet been settled.

The terms of this invoice were strictly 30 days and therefore it is well overdue.

We shall be grateful if you will kindly settle this amount by return of post.

Yours sincerely

N Wakefield

N Wakefield
Accounts Manager

Case Study

VALLEYMORE FOODS

situation

Valleymore Foods Limited produces a variety of foodstuffs – pies, desserts, ready-made meals – which are sold frozen to its customers, who include supermarkets, pubs and local shops.

You work in the Accounts Department of Valleymore Foods and spend some of your time answering customer queries and debt chasing.

This Case Study illustrates some of the more common tasks you have to undertake.

situation 1: a customer overpays

You receive a telephone message on your voicemail from Sid Parks, owner of 'The Pig and Whistle', a local pub which you supply with snack meals.

> *"Hello there. I have just received my monthly statement of account from you. The balance should be back down to zero, but in fact it is showing a credit balance of £40. Does this mean that you owe me money? If so, can you let me have a refund? Perhaps you can let me know. Bye."*

You look into the ledgers and find that Sid's last cheque to you was for £155 rather than the £115 owing on the account. He has overpaid by £40. You speak to Ivor Penny, your Customer Accounts Manager, who agrees that you can issue him with a refund cheque. He asks you to write a covering letter for his signature.

Valleymore Foods Limited

Martley Road, St Gregorys, MR2 5GT

Tel 01908 675234 Fax 01908 675332 email foods@valleymore.com

Mr S Parks
The Pig and Whistle
The Green
Clitteridge
MR4 9YH

3 July 2003

Dear Mr Parks

Account 29847

Further to your recent telephone message left with us we have pleasure in enclosing our cheque for £40. This represents the balance of your account with us. The account had gone into credit because the last settlement cheque you issued was for £155 rather than the £115 owing.

Yours sincerely

Ivor Penny
Customer Accounts Manager

situation 2: an unsigned customer cheque

You receive a cheque through the post from a customer Totley Limited. Unfortunately the cheque is unsigned. Your Manager says that you will have to send it back to the customer with a request for the customer to sign it ...

Accounts Department
Totley Limited
Unit 17 Deepend Estate
Bath
BA2 3BR

4 July 2003

Dear Sirs

Account 28761

I enclose your cheque 564132 for £12,349.50 which was received in our office today. Unfortunately the cheque has not been signed. I shall be grateful if you will arrange for it to be signed by the appropriate signatories and returned to us as soon as possible.

Yours faithfully

Ivor Penny
Customer Accounts Manager

situation 3: a missing credit note

You receive an email from Tredco Limited. The text reads:

'We have received your July statement today. It lists a credit note for £1,876.50 which we cannot trace. Please can you let us have a copy.'

You refer it to your Manager who suggests you fax the document with a suitable fax header message...

facsimile transmission header

To: Asaf Patel, Accounts Office, Tredco Limited
Fax number: 01350 525504
Number of pages including this header: 2 Date: 4 July 2003

message

Credit Note 8732
Further to your email of 3 July I am faxing you a copy of credit note 8732 for £1,876.50.

R U Shaw

Sales Ledger,
Accounts Department

situation 4: dealing with the aged debtors analysis

Every month you print out from the computer an aged debtors analysis which lists all your sales ledger customers, their balances, credit limits and the length of time invoices have been outstanding. It is an important document in the credit control process – it highlights customers who are not paying up on time.

Every month you have to send out standard chaser letters to late payers. Some letters are polite reminders, others are stronger in their terms.

An extract from this month's aged debtors analysis is shown below.

VALLEYMORE FOODS LIMITED   AGED DEBTORS ANALYSIS   JULY 2003

Account	Turnover	Credit Limit	Balance	up to 30 days	30 - 59 days	60 - 89 days	90 days & over
Thamesco Trading	370.00	1000.00	164.50	164.50	0.00	0.00	0.00
J Singh	320.00	750.00	376.00	376.00	0.00	0.00	0.00
Maxwell Foods	1730.00	2000.00	1632.75	799.00	833.75	0.00	0.00
Premier Chef Trading	2025.00	2000.00	1926.88	380.00	0.00	1046.88	500.00
H Dunlittle	425.00	750.00	499.38	499.38	0.00	0.00	0.00
TOTALS	4870.00		4599.51	2218.88	833.75	1046.88	500.00

Valleymore Foods Limited gives a standard 30 days credit to its sales ledger customers. You have been given a number of tasks.

Task 1

You have been asked to send 'Letter A' (a polite reminder) to any customers who have not settled within 60 days.

Task 2

You have been asked to send 'Letter B' (a firm reminder) to any customer who is exceeding 60 days.

These letters are to be signed by Ann Dover, the Credit Controller.

The aged debtor analysis shows that Maxwell Foods are due Letter A and Premier Chef Trading are due Letter B.

The letters are as shown on the next page.

Task 1
Letter A

Valleymore Foods Limited

Martley Road, St Gregorys, MR2 5GT
Tel 01908 675234 Fax 01908 675332 email foods@valleymore.com

The Manager, Accounts Department
Maxwell Foods Limited
Parsons Road
Farmborough
SY3 7YH

4 August 2003

Dear Sir

Account 29613

We note from our records that we have not yet received settlement of due invoices totalling £833.75. Our invoice terms are strictly 30 days and these items are now overdue.

We shall be grateful if you will kindly settle this amount by return of post.

Yours faithfully

Ann Dover
Credit Controller

Task 2
Letter B

Valleymore Foods Limited

Martley Road, St Gregorys, MR2 5GT
Tel 01908 675234 Fax 01908 675332 email foods@valleymore.com

Accounts Manager
Premier Chef Trading
78 High Road
Brimley
BR6 5GF

4 August 2003

Dear Sir

Account 28745

Further to our previous reminders we still have not received settlement of the overdue invoices on your account. We shall be grateful if you will kindly forward us your cheque for £1546.88. If this amount has not been received at this address within seven working days we will have no alternative but to place the matter in the hands of our solicitors.

Yours faithfully

Ann Dover
Credit Controller

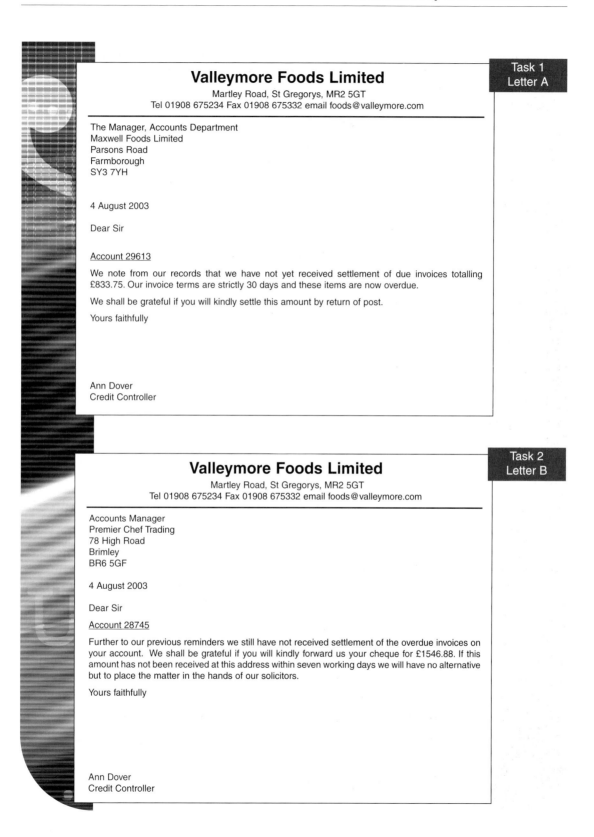

Chapter Summary

- Businesses need to communicate regularly with their customers, including organisations that buy on credit.
- The communications should be both polite and effective – they should use the appropriate format and the appropriate wording and be sent within the appropriate timescale.
- Common reasons for communicating are replying to queries and chasing overdue debts.
- There are a number of different forms of written communication which are used both within an organisation and also when dealing with outsiders.
- The memorandum is a formal written note used within an organisation; it may be typed, word processed or handwritten. Memoranda may also be sent by internal email. Examples of its use include giving information, asking for information, giving instructions and recording data and opinions.
- Informal written notes are also widely used for communicating information. It is important that they record the date and time of writing. They range from informal scribbled messages to the pre-printed telephone message.
- The fax can be used for internal or external communications. It is useful for sending copy documents and also for more informal communications.
- The email is a fast and convenient form of communication both for external (internet) use and internal (intranet) networks. Files can be sent by email.
- The written letter, sent by post or by fax, is still a widely used form of business communication. Letters can be used for a variety of purposes in the context of accounting, including giving information and chasing debts.

Key Terms

aged debtors analysis	a regular report scheduling all the sales ledger customers, their balances, limits and length of time their invoices have been outstanding
memorandum	a formal written communication used internally within an organisation
fax	short for 'facsimile' – an electronic transmission of an exact image
email	an electronic message sent from one computer to another
Internet	a world-wide network of interlinked computers
intranet	a linked network of computers within an organisation
attachment	a digital file (text or image, for example) which is sent with an email
house style letter	a letter produced by a business in a style which has been adopted as standard by the business

Student Activities

In these exercises you may have to make up names, addresses and dates. Unless your tutor states otherwise, make these up as you think appropriate.

8.1 You receive a cheque through the post from a sales ledger customer. The words and figures are different. The words say 'five hundred and fifty pounds' and the figures '£500'. The amount should be £550. Write the text of a suitable letter to the customer.

8.2 One of your sales ledger customers, Adrian Duffe Associates, is well known in your Accounts Department as a bad payer. When telephoned recently about the non-payment of invoices, the assistant said 'We don't seem to have received these invoices. Are you sure they are ours?' You check your records and find that the invoices were sent to Adrian Duffe Associates with the goods. How would you deal with this problem?

8.3 You are an Accounts Supervisor and you need to circulate to all the Sales Managers in the business a list of the customers who are more than 2 months behind in settling their accounts. These customers should be referred to the Accounts Manager before any further credit sales are made. You are to write a suitable memorandum, using your own name and today's date.

Note: you do not need to produce the list (which has been produced on your computer).

8.4 Draft a letter chasing up an overdue invoice. The letter is a 'gentle' reminder and follows previous statements of account. Complete the letter with details of a specimen invoice. The letter is for signature by your Accounts Manager.

8.5 You are an Accounts Supervisor in the Accounts Department of Janus Fabrics. You receive the following email message from your Customer Services Department on 1 April:

'Mrs Joan Pearce of Lizard Designs telephoned. She is furious. She placed an urgent customer order for 25 square metres of Roma velvet curtain fabric, colour burgundy, and has only received 15 square metres. I have sent a further 10 square metres today. Please write to her – she is a valued customer and needs to be kept happy.'

You check your records and find that on her purchase order (no 6234) the figure '25' could be read as '15' because the first digit is indistinct. Write her a suitable letter, using your own name and today's date. Her address is Lizard Designs, 13 Regency Passage, Mereford, MR2 6DA.

9 Businesses and the law

this chapter covers . . .

This chapter explains how businesses are affected by the law – both by contract law and by statute law (Acts of Parliament). The chapter covers:

- *the agreement in a contract – the offer and the acceptance*
- *the bargain in a contract – the need for both parties to provide something (known as 'consideration')*
- *the need for both sides to a contract to intend it to be legally binding*
- *breach of contract – what to do when things go wrong*
- *protection given in statute law when someone purchases goods or services*
- *the implications for businesses of the Data Protection Act*
- *the legal reasons for retaining documents*

NVQ KNOWLEDGE AND UNDERSTANDING COVERAGE

unit 1: RECORDING INCOME AND RECEIPTS
unit 2: MAKING AND RECORDING PAYMENTS

2 basic law relating to contract law and Sale of Goods Act

3 document retention policies

*6 cheques, including crossings and endorserments**

10 basic law relating to data protection

**Note: the legal requirements relating to cheques, cheque crossings and endorsements are covered in full on pages 92 to 94.*

A CONTRACT DEFINED

Part of your course involves the understanding of the legal framework which enables buying and selling to take place and which states what can happen if there is a dispute. The agreement between the parties is known as a *contract.*

what is a contract?

a contract is a legally binding agreement enforceable in a court of law

Contracts, which may be in writing, or by word of mouth (oral), are agreements between two parties. Examples include:

- a written contract which you sign if you buy a house
- a written contract for a loan agreement if you borrow money
- a written contract of employment
- an oral contract if you buy goods in a shop
- an oral contract if you order goods over the telephone
- an oral contract if you hire a decorator to paint your house

In each case somebody does something for which some kind of payment is made. A contract is *an agreement with legal consequences* because if the work done is not satisfactory, or if the payment is not made, the wronged party can take the other person to court for *breach of contract.*

You may rightly wonder how all this affects you in the workplace. The answer is that the principles of contract affect any person carrying out normal business activities. For example if you quote an incorrect price to a customer, they may be able to hold your business to that price, under the terms of the contract of sale. If you fail to finish a job for a customer, they may be able to go to court to obtain a court order for your business to complete the work under the contract.

the three elements of contract

There are three elements which are common and essential to all contracts:

agreement – an offer and an acceptance

bargain – some value (consideration) passes

intention to create legal relations – the agreement is commercial

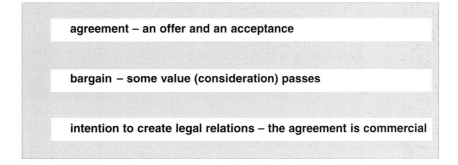

THE AGREEMENT - OFFER AND ACCEPTANCE

the offer

A firm and clear offer must be made either to a single party, a group, or to the world at large. In a famous legal case in 1893, a manufacturer of medicines (the Carbolic Smoke Ball Company) advertised a patented smoke ball and promised to pay a £100 reward to any person who contracted a specified illness having used the ball three times a day for two weeks. A Mrs Carlill used the ball for eight weeks and still contracted 'flu. She claimed her £100, the company refused, and she had to take the matter to the court which ruled that she should be granted her £100, as the offer of £100 had been to the "whole world" and needed no communicated acceptance from Mrs Carlill. It formed part of a valid contract which the company had to honour. Note that this is *not* the same situation as an *advertised price* which is not an offer but information which will enable a purchase – the contract – to be made (see below).

invitation to treat

An offer is quite different from an *invitation to treat* which is an invitation for a person to make an offer. Goods on supermarket shelves are an invitation for a customer to take them to the checkout where that customer can offer to purchase them at the price indicated at the checkout, which is where the contract takes place. That is the reason why shop tills indicate the price for each item, normally on an illuminated display; it is also the reason why a shop is not obliged to sell the goods at the price shown on the shelves.

practical example – invitation to treat

problem

Basil sees a holiday advertised in the local paper for £50. He telephones the travel company which tells him that the figure is a printing error – it should have been £500. Basil is angry and insists on booking his week in Menorca for £50. The problem is, does a contract exist on the basis of the £50 quoted?

answer

Basil has no rights here. There is no contract because the £50 quoted is only *an invitation to treat*, an invitation for Basil to make an agreement for booking the holiday. The company will clearly not agree to £50 for a week in Menorca!

termination of an offer

An offer may only be accepted while it is still open for acceptance. An offer may be terminated in the following circumstances:

- the time limit (if there is one) expires; if there is no time limit the offer lapses after a reasonable period of time
- the offeror – the person making the offer – may revoke (cancel) the offer
- an offer may be rejected by the making of a counter-offer; for instance, if you offer your car for sale for £1,500 and someone offers you £1,350, that is a counter-offer
- by acceptance or rejection of the offer

acceptance of an offer

Acceptance of an offer must be firm and unambiguous; it may be in spoken words, written form or even implied by action. Acceptance cannot be assumed from silence on the part of the person to whom the offer is made. For instance, if you say "I offer you my car for £1,500; if I have not heard from you within a week I will assume the deal is done", there is no acceptance. The offeree may go on holiday, or forget it even happened. Acceptance must also be *unconditional.* Any new term introduced – "I will agree to buy your car as long as the wing is resprayed" – amounts to a counter-offer (see above) and revokes the original offer.

practical example – conditional acceptance

problem

Basil works for Martley Garden Centre and has recently sent a quotation for a fountain to Mrs Waters: the cost will be £250.00 plus VAT and the fountain will have to be ordered from an outside supplier. Mrs Waters writes back saying she wants to accept the price, but the fountain must be delivered before the end of the month. Is there a valid contract between Mrs Waters and the garden centre?

answer

No. There is no contract because the acceptance has been conditional. *Acceptance must be unconditional.* Any new term introduced amounts to a counter-offer: "I will pay £250 plus VAT if the fountain is delivered by the end of the month".

The term "subject to contract", often seen on estate agents' boards, means that the terms of the offer to the offeree are agreeable, but have not been finally accepted. The two parties involved have agreed to draw up a formal contract for signature at a later date. There is no binding contract at this point.

communication of acceptance

The rules relating to communication of acceptance are largely dictated by what is required by the offer:

- the acceptance must normally be communicated to the person making the offer
- if the offer requires acceptance by a specific means (letter/fax/verbal message) then that means must be used

the postal rule

An acceptance by post is effective as long as the letter of acceptance is correctly addressed, correctly stamped and actually posted.

The time of acceptance is when the letter is posted (not when it is received). Given that letters may be delayed or lost in the post, this rule may seem unjust to the offeror! The postal rule only applies to an acceptance, it does not apply to a posted offer which must reach the offeree.

practical example – acceptance by post

problem

On 1 April Cotheridge Conifers telephones Basil at Martley Garden Centre to offer a job lot of 150 Leylandii trees at a knock-down price of £1.50 each. Basil needs time to think about this and says he will drop a line in the post. On 3 April he posts a reply to Cotheridge Conifers accepting the offer and placing an order for the trees. On 5 April the order is received. The question is, what is the date on which the contract was formed?

answer

3 April. The postal rule states that the date of posting of an acceptance of an offer is the effective date of the contract.

THE BARGAIN: CONSIDERATION

definition of consideration

A valid contract involves a bargain, a passing of value, known in law as consideration. If a business buys goods there is a two way process involved:

- the supplier promises to deliver the goods
- the buyer agrees to pay for them

The parties involved are:

- the promisor, the supplier that promises to supply the goods
- the promisee, the buyer who has to make payment

The consideration here is the payment, the price paid for the service provided. The principle is simple in itself, but there are a number of rules which relate to consideration.

consideration must be sufficient

Consideration must by law be sufficient. This means that:

- it must have value, although the value need not be adequate in some eyes; for example, you could sell this book for 5p; many would consider the amount to be inadequate, but the 5p still has value and is therefore consideration
- it must be sufficient, ie it must be in return for the promise; money due for some other reason or obligation is not sufficient consideration

consideration must move from the promisee

This legal phrase means, in effect, that the person who is promised goods or a service must themselves provide payment if the promise is to be enforceable as a contract. If you buy goods, you must make the payment. If someone else pays for you (an unlikely event!) you cannot take the supplier to court if the goods do not arrive.

consideration cannot be past

This legal phrase means that the consideration should not precede the promise. If you mend someone's car without any mention of payment, and the car owner the following week promises to give you £5, and subsequently refuses to pay you, there is no contract. The promise of payment followed the good turn done, consideration (the repair) was past as it had taken place the previous week.

practical example – consideration

problem

Basil promises to cut down some trees for a friend free of charge one weekend. Unfortunately Basil cuts down the wrong trees. His friend is very upset and says he will sue Basil. Can he? Is there a contract?

answer

No. There is no contract because there is no consideration – no money has been paid. Basil has made a mistake but he cannot be sued.

THE INTENTION TO CREATE LEGAL RELATIONS

A contract is an agreement involving consideration which the parties intend to be legally binding. In other words the parties entering a contract can reasonably expect the agreement to be enforced in a court of law if the necessity arises. The law assumes:

- commercial agreements are intended to be legally binding
- social and domestic arrangements are not intended to be legally binding

In short, if a person enters a contract to buy your car and then, without reason, refuses to pay for it, you can take him or her to court. If you ask a friend out for the evening, promising to take him or her out for a meal, and your friend doesn't turn up, you can not take court action. The sale of a car involves the intention to create legal relations, the invitation out does not.

BREACH OF CONTRACT

A contract normally contains certain terms which must be fulfilled as part of the agreement. If a person breaks one of those terms, that person is in *breach of contract.* For example, if a supplier undertakes to supply goods, it must send the goods on the due date, and in turn expects the goods to be paid for by a certain time. If the customer does not pay, he or she is in breach of contract and may be taken to court for damages (money compensation).

Contract terms may be classified as follows:

express terms	explicitly stated terms which are binding on both parties to the contract
conditions	fundamental terms of the contract which, if broken, will enable the injured party to reject the contract and to go to court to sue for damages
warranties	minor terms which if broken can be cause for an action for damages for loss suffered; the contract, however, remains in force
implied terms	terms which are not stated, but which are implied by trade custom or by law; for instance, goods sold should be of "satisfactory quality", in accordance with the Sale of Goods Act

In short:

- express terms are written into the contract; implied terms are not
- conditions are important terms, warranties are less important

practical example – breach of contract

problem

Martley Garden Centre orders 1500 flower arrangements from a London wholesale supplier for delivery two days before Mothers Day. Unfortunately, because of a transport strike they arrive during the week following Mothers Day. Martley Garden Centre threatens to sue the supplier. Is the garden centre within its rights to do so?

answer

There is a clear breach of contract – the delivery date is a term of the contract and has not been met. Martley Garden Centre could sue.

SELLING AND STATUTE LAW

Statute law is law set down in an Act of Parliament.

There are a number of statutes which govern the way in which goods and services are sold, and they obviously affect the way in which businesses operate. The principal statutes are the Trades Descriptions Act, the Sale of Goods Act and the Unfair Contract Terms Act.

Trades Descriptions Act

The Trades Descriptions Act makes it a criminal offence:

- to make false statements about goods offered for sale
- to make misleading statements about services

Examples of offences therefore include:

- stating that a car for sale has clocked up 15,000 miles, when in fact the figure is 25,000 miles
- making a misleading statement about the price of goods, eg saying 'Now only £49.95, was £99.95' when it has only ever sold for £69.95
- making a misleading statement about a service, eg 'our dry cleaning is guaranteed to remove every stain' when it does not, or 'our apartments are within easy reach of the sea' when they are fifteen miles away

Sale of Goods Act

This Act states that you are entitled to expect any goods that you buy from a shop to be:

of 'satisfactory quality'

This means they must meet the standard that a 'reasonable' person would expect given the description and the price.

'fit for the purpose'

The goods must do what they are supposed to do, or what the shop claims they can do: an umbrella should keep the rain out, a watch should keep accurate time.

'as described'

The goods must be what they are claimed to be: a 'leather coat' must be made of leather, a 'stereo TV' must provide stereo sound.

If any of these three conditions is not met, the purchaser is entitled to a full or a part refund, depending on how soon the fault appears, how serious it is and how quickly the matter is taken up. Note also the following practical points:

- the buyer can accept a replacement, but can also insist on a refund if a replacement is not wanted
- the buyer does not have to accept a credit note for spending on other purchases
- a shop is not entitled to put up a notice saying "No Refunds!"

practical example – Sale of Goods Act

problem

Jason buys a watering can from Martley Garden Centre but finds that it leaks. He returns it to the Garden Centre, asking for a refund. The sales assistant refuses, pointing to a sign on the counter which states "No refunds given!" What is Jason's position?

answer

Jason *is* entitled to a refund. The Sale of Goods Act clearly states that goods must be of 'satisfactory quality'. The shop has no right to try and avoid statute law.

Unfair Contract Terms Act

Any organisation that tries to insist on *unfair* terms (eg in small print on the back of a sales contract) may be in breach of the Unfair Contract Terms Act. This would protect, for example, holidaymakers who are not put up in the hotel they booked because the small print stated that the holiday company had the right to move them to another resort. This would be seen as an 'unfair term' and would enable the holidaymaker to seek compensation. In short, a business cannot 'contract out' through the small print.

DATA PROTECTION LEGISLATION

data

Businesses inevitably keep records of their customers and suppliers on file – either manually – a card index system, for example – or, more likely, on computer file. This is 'personal data'. In the normal course of business this poses no problem to the person whose details are kept on file. But what if those details are passed into the hands of a third party and those details are wrong? Think about the following examples:

- a credit reference agency gives a bad credit reference on Mrs A Jones who is applying to a shop for finance on some new furniture – in fact they have got their files mixed up and are reporting on a different Mrs A Jones who had been to court for non-payment of debt – as a consequence the first Mrs Jones is unlikely to get finance for her furniture
- Trader A is asked to give a trade reference on one of its customers, Trader B; Trader A gets his files muddled up and gives a poor reference which results in Trader B being refused credit by the business asking for the reference

Clearly these two 'individuals', a consumer and a trader, need protection for their personal data. This is provided by the Data Protection Act.

Data Protection Act

The Data Protection Act (1998) which came into force on 1 March 2000 establishes rules for the processing of personal data. It follows the guidelines of an EC Directive and brings the UK in line with European legal principles. The Act applies to:

- a filing system of records held on **computer** – eg a computer database of customer names, addresses, telephone numbers, sales details
- a **manual** set of accessible records – eg a card index file system of customer details

Data protection is regulated by the Data Protection Commission.

There are certain terms which are defined by the Act:

personal data	information which relates to an individual
data subject	the individual whose information is stored
data controller	the person in the organisation who is responsible for the processing of the data
recipient	the person who receives the data

the eight principles of 'good information handling'

All organisations which process personal data should register with the Data Protection Commission. Their 'data controllers' should follow the eight guiding principles set out in the Data Protection Act. These principles require that personal data is handled properly. They state that personal data must be:

1. fairly and lawfully processed
2. processed for limited purposes
3. adequate, relevant and not excessive
4. accurate
5. not kept for longer than is necessary
6. processed in line with the data subject's rights
7. kept securely
8. not transferred to countries outside the European Union unless it is adequately protected in those countries

right of access

People have the legal right to know what personal details about them is held by an organisation. They should apply in writing for a copy of the personal data held on file by the organisation; they may have to pay a fee.

implications for confidentiality

We have already seen throughout this book the need for confidentiality in business dealings. The Data Protection Act reinforces this duty. A business should not without permission reveal:

- information about one customer to another customer
- information about its employees

implications for storage and retention of data

Business records are normally stored for at least six years (and a minimum of three years for payroll data). The Data Protection Act reinforces the requirement that personal data is kept securely and that it should be accurate. There are a number of legal reasons why financial data (which will include personal data) should be kept for this period of time:

- accounting records should be kept so that they can be inspected by the Inland Revenue if required (if there is a tax inspection)
- accounting records should be kept so that they can be inspected by HM Customs & Excise if required (if there is a VAT inspection)
- accounting records should be kept for at least six years in case they are needed as evidence in any legal action

Chapter Summary

- A contract is an agreement between two people ('parties') with legal consequences – if something goes wrong with the agreement, the matter can go to court if necessary.
- A contract contains three elements: an agreement made between two parties, a bargain struck involving each party giving up something of value, and an intention that the agreement is a legal one.
- A contract involves an offer being made and accepted. An offer may be made to an individual, a group of people or to everyone. For a contract to exist, an offer must be accepted clearly and without any conditions attached.
- The bargain in a contract – the passing of something of value – must involve both parties and must follow the contract.
- The intention behind a contract should be to form a legal agreement; arrangements such as 'doing someone a favour' do not form a contract.
- If one of the parties breaks the terms of a contract – eg does not pay, does not do the work required – the matter can be taken to court as a breach of contract, either for damages (money compensation) or to ensure the work is done.
- Statute law (laws passed in Parliament) protects buyers of goods and services. Examples include the Trades Descriptions Act and the Sale of Goods Act.
- The Data Protection Act (1998) ensures that data held by organisations on computer or in manual records is handled properly. There are eight principles set out in the Act. They state that personal data must be:
  1. fairly and lawfully processed
  2. processed for limited purposes
  3. adequate, relevant and not excessive
  4. accurate
  5. not kept for longer than is necessary
  6. processed in line with the data subject's rights
  7. kept securely
  8. not transferred to countries outside the European Union unless it is adequately protected in those countries
- Accounting data (and all other business records) should kept confidential and should be retained for at least six years in case of legal actions being taken (a minimum of three years for tax investigations).

Key Terms

contract	a legally binding agreement enforceable in a court of law
parties	the people directly involved in a contract
consideration	value which is passed between the parties to a contract, eg money, doing a job
invitation to treat	an invitation for someone to make an offer, eg priced goods on a shop shelf
subject to contract	the stage reached when the terms of an offer are said to be acceptable but the final agreement has not been finalised
postal rule	if an acceptance of an offer is made by post, the contract comes into being when the acceptance is correctly posted
breach of contract	the situation where one of the parties to a contract breaks one or more of the terms of the contract
damages	money compensation awarded in a court of law
personal data	information which relates to an individual held by an organisation on computer or manual file
data subject	the individual whose information is stored
data controller	the person in the organisation who is responsible for the processing of the data
recipient	the person who receives the data
right of access	the legal right of the individual to request a copy of the personal data held by an organisation

Student Activities

9.1 Write down a sentence defining a contract – use your own words.

9.2 State the three elements of a contract, writing down a sentence describing each of the three elements.

9.3 State in each of the following situations whether a contract exists. In each case give reasons for your answer.

(a) You order goods over the phone and agree a price but do not issue a purchase order.

(b) You order goods by sending a signed purchase order by fax to the supplier who then despatches them.

(c) You do a job for someone free of charge and as a favour. She later gives you £10 but then complains that the job has not been done properly.

(d) You do a job for a friend and agree a price, but after you have done the job he refuses to pay you.

9.4 You go to a local DIY store and see a power drill on the shelves with a price sticker of £39.95. You think it is a good buy and take it to the till. The cashier says that the price is now £49.95; the lower price was for a special offer that has now expired. Is the cashier right to insist on charging the higher price or can you insist that the contract is based on the lower price being the offer price? Give *legal reasons* for your answer.

9.5 You fill in an order form for some stationery. The order form is contained in the catalogue sent to you by the supplier. At the bottom of the form you write in red "We are only placing this order on the basis that we will receive the goods by 4 April." The order form says "Allow 28 days for delivery." The date is 15 March. Is this a valid acceptance of the offer for sale made by the stationery company in its catalogue?

9.6 You telephone for a mail order catalogue on 15 March, complete the order form on 16 March and post the order form on 17 March. It is received by the mail order company on 19 March. On what date is the contract formed?

9.7 You buy a word processor from Zenith Office Supplies. Unfortunately the machine will not work – it appears to be damaged. You take it back to Zenith. The salesman says "Sorry - nothing we can do – you will have to get in touch with the manufacturer!" Is he right? What is the legal position?

9.8 You buy an office chair from Summit Office Furniture. It is advertised as having an adjustable back. When you get it back to your office, you find it does not. You telephone the supplier to complain and are told "Sorry we can't change it – you saw what it was like when you picked it up." Is the supplier right?

9.9 The Data Protection Act only covers personal data held on computer file. True or false?

9.10 State the eight principles set out in the Data Protection Act which ensure that personal data is handled properly.

9.11 Financial records should be retained by a business for:

(a) a minimum of six months

(b) a minimum of twelve months

(c) a minimum of six years

(d) a maximum of six years

Answer (a), (b), (c), or (d)

10 Documents for goods and services received

this chapter covers . . .

In Chapter 2 we looked at the selling of goods and services from the point of view of the supplier. This chapter examines the transactions from the point of view of the purchaser and describes the procedures and documents involved. The chapter covers the areas of:

- *the use of business documents – purchase order, invoice, delivery note, goods received note, returns note, credit note, statement, remittance advice*
- *the checking of the supplier's documents against the purchaser's documents*
- *the calculation of document totals, including discounts and VAT*
- *the coding and filing of documents*
- *the checking and authorisation of documents and dealing with discrepancies*

This chapter explains the manual completion of documents. Processing purchase transactions using ***computer accounting*** *is dealt with in Chapter 27.*

NVQ PERFORMANCE CRITERIA COVERED

unit 2: MAKING AND RECORDING PAYMENTS

element 2.1

process documents relating to goods and services received

A *check suppliers' invoices and credit notes against relevant documents for validity*

B *check calculations on suppliers' invoices and credit notes for accuracy*

C *identify and deduct available discounts*

D *correctly code invoices and credit notes*

G *identify discrepancies and either resolve or refer to the appropriate person if outside own authority*

H *communicate appropriately with suppliers regarding accounts*

BUSINESS DOCUMENTS – THE PURCHASER'S POINT OF VIEW

When a business *sells* goods and services its main concern is that it provides what has been ordered and that it gets paid on time. When a business, on the other hand, *orders* goods and services it will want to ensure that:

- the correct goods and services are provided
- they are provided on time
- they are charged at the right price

Businesses vary in the way they achieve this. The normal procedure is for the purchaser to accumulate on file – normally stapled together – a series of documents which will be checked against each other as they are produced or come into the office, eg copy purchase order, delivery note, invoice, a copy of any returns note, any credit note, statement, and so on. These will often be kept in a 'pending invoices' file until payment is finally made, when they will go into a 'paid invoices' file. The diagram below shows this flow of documents.

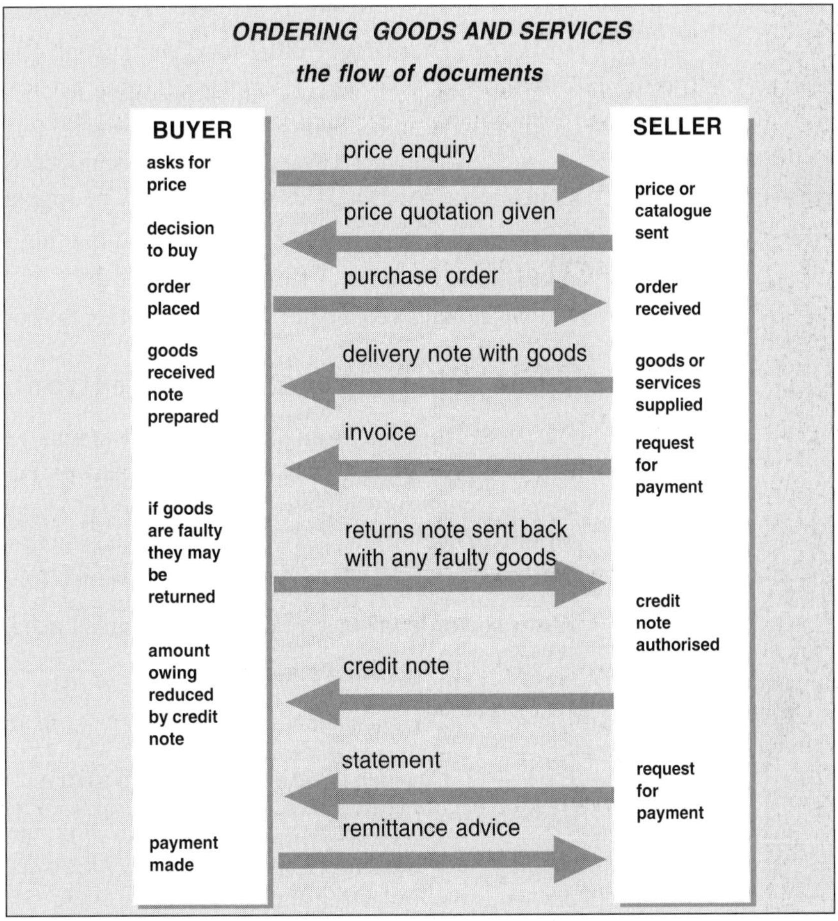

ORDERING PROCEDURES

the traditional method

The diagram on the previous page shows the traditional method of ordering goods and services: a paper purchase order is issued, the goods (or services) are delivered (or provided) and an invoice is sent which is eventually paid by cheque. There are of course, many variations on this procedure, particularly with the introduction of e-commerce where buying and selling and settlement takes place on-line.

In this book and in your studies the emphasis is on the traditional method of ordering and paying because the principles of this method underlie all the other methods. You should however be aware of the other methods as you may encounter some of them in your day-to-day work.

other ordering methods – paper based

Businesses can order goods and services in a variety of other ways:

- filling in a catalogue order form and posting off a cheque with the order
- telephoning a company which is selling to you for the first time to ask them to issue you with a 'pro-forma invoice' for the goods or service you need; when you receive this invoice document, you will send it back with a cheque and the goods or service will be supplied by return
- faxing off a catalogue order form and quoting the company credit card details
- telephoning a catalogue order and quoting the company credit card details

other ordering methods – electronically based

Businesses are increasing turning to Internet retailers for purchases of goods and services, eg computers. Ordering goods or services from an Internet site is very straightforward: all you need to do is to get on-line, place your order on one of the virtual 'shopping malls' and quote the company credit card details.

Electronic ordering has produced terms which need some explanation:

- EDI (Electronic Data Interchange)
- e-commerce

EDI – electronic data interchange

This a method of connecting businesses by computer link so that documents such as purchase orders and invoices can be electronically generated and payments made electronically when they are due. The EDI system should *not* be confused with the Internet, which is basically an uncontrolled electronic free-for-all. EDI has been running for many years, the electronic links are private and secure; the system is expensive to set up. A number of supermarkets have adopted EDI: the supermarket is the 'hub' of the system and its suppliers are on 'spokes'. Look at the diagram below.

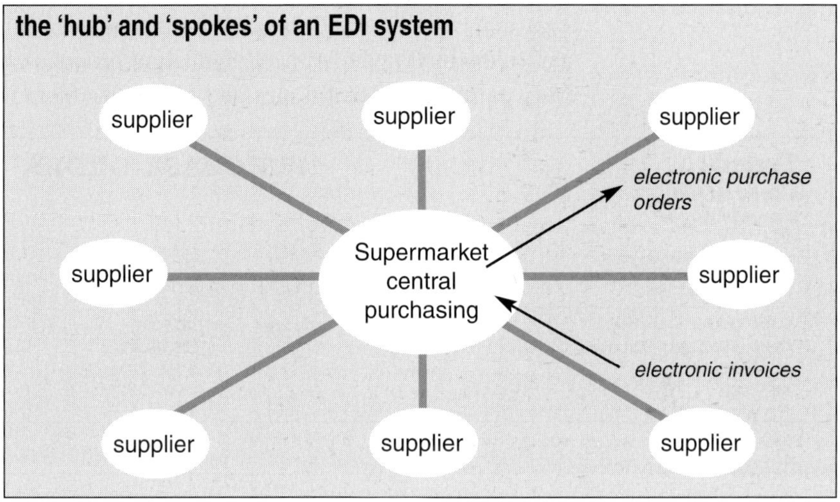

e-commerce

E-commerce is a loose term which is short for 'electronic commerce'. It covers selling and buying on the Internet, both business-to-business and business-to-customer. We have already seen in Chapter 6 how Internet sales receipts are tracked onto the bank account. The screen extract here shows a book for sale on the on-line shop at www.osbornebooks.co.uk

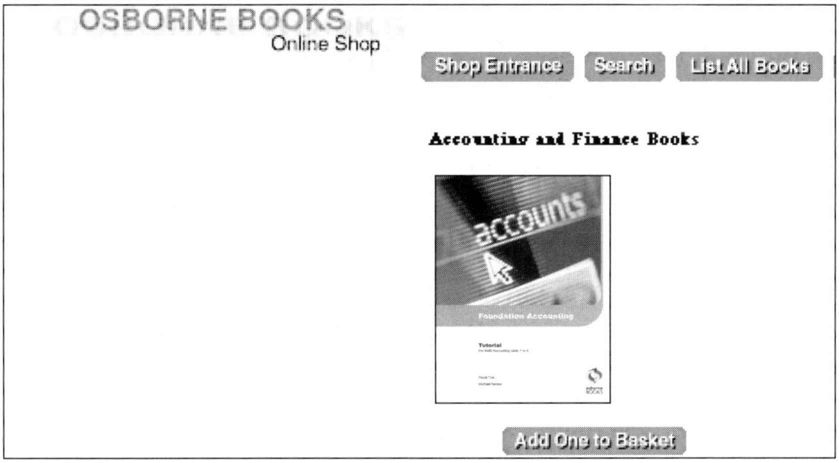

In the rest of this chapter we will look at the traditional method of ordering goods and services which is most likely to feature in your exams and skills tests.

AUTHORISATION OF PURCHASE ORDERS

A purchaser, once the price of the product(s) has been agreed, normally issues a *purchase order*. It is essential that this purchase order is *authorised* by the appropriate person. This authority is shown on the document in the form of a signature and date. Some businesses will insist that more senior staff in the buying department sign larger orders. A business keeps a copy of every purchase order it issues and often files them in numerical order (each order has a numerical code). The purchase order from the Case Study in the last chapter is shown here.

Trends
4 Friar Street
Broadfield
BR1 3RF
Tel 01908 761234 Fax 01908 761987
VAT REG GB 0745 8383 56

PURCHASE ORDER

Cool Socks Limited,
Unit 45 Elgar Estate,
Broadfield,
BR7 4ER

purchase order no **47609**
date **25 09 03**

product code	quantity	description
45B	**100 pairs**	**Blue Toebar socks**

AUTHORISED signature *D Signer* date *25 Sept 03*

It should be noted that a business may not *always* issue a purchase order: if the order is small, or if the buyer knows the seller well, the order may be made by telephone.

CHECKS AND CONTROLS: PURCHASES

When an organisation purchases goods, it is important that the accounting system includes checks and controls to ensure that:

- the correct goods have been received in an acceptable condition
- the correct terms and price have been applied
- the goods are paid for once only (paying for goods twice does occur!)

The three main documents involved in the checking process are the *purchase order* (a copy of which will be kept by the purchaser), the *delivery note* and the *invoice,* received from the seller.

You should note that some organisations use an internal document known as a *goods received note* on which the buyer records the receipt of the goods and the details set out on the delivery note or advice note sent by the supplier. Most businesses, however, rely on the delivery note as a record of the goods received, and we will concentrate on this document here.

CHECKING INVOICE, DELIVERY NOTE AND PURCHASE ORDER

The checking process involves two separate procedures carried out in the Accounts Department:

- checking the three documents – the invoice, delivery note and copy purchase order – with each other
- checking the calculations on the invoice

We will deal with these in separate stages, starting with the checking of the three documents:

check 1 – goods received and delivery note

When the goods are received they should be checked against the delivery note – the quantities should be counted and the condition of the goods checked. Any discrepancies or damage should be notified immediately to the supplier, usually on a *discrepancy note*, so that replacements can be sent or the buyer credited with the value of the missing or damaged goods (ie the bill reduced by the issue of a credit note).

check 2 – delivery note and purchase order

The delivery note should then be checked in the Accounts Department against a copy of the original purchase order. The illustration on the next page shows the details that should be checked:

- catalogue number (ie the supplier's catalogue) – has the right type of goods been delivered?
- quantity – has the right number been delivered?
- specifications – are the goods delivered to the same specifications as those ordered
- purchase order reference number – do the goods relate to the purchase order being examined?

If all is in order, the delivery note will be filed with the copy purchase order under the purchase order reference number, ready for checking against the invoice when it arrives.

check 3 – invoice, delivery note and purchase order

When the invoice arrives from the supplier, it should be checked against the delivery note and the purchase order (which should be filed together). The specific points to look at are:

- *invoice and delivery note*
  Are the details of the goods on the invoice and delivery note the same? The product code, description and quantity of the goods should agree.

- *invoice and purchase order*
  Has the correct price been charged? The unit price quoted by the supplier or obtained from the supplier's catalogue will be stated on the purchase order, and should agree with the unit price stated on the invoice. If there is a difference, it should be queried with the supplier.

student task

Look at the invoice below and the purchase order and delivery note on the next page. They all relate to the same transaction. Can you spot any discrepancies? The answers are set out at the bottom of the page.

INVOICE

Stourford Office Supplies

Unit 12, Avon Industrial Estate, Stourford, SF5 6TD
Tel 01807 765434 Fax 01807 765123 Email stourford@stourford.co.uk
VAT Reg GB 0745 4001 76

invoice to

Martley Machine Rental Limited
67 Broadgreen Road
Martley
MR6 7TR

deliver to

as above

invoice no	**652771**
account	**MAR435**
your reference	**47780**
date/tax point	**31 03 03**

product code	description	quantity	price	unit	total	discount %	net
3564748 (49) P Code diff	**80gsm white Supalaser** 100gsm	**15**	**3.50** 4.00	**ream**	**52.00** 52.50 60.00	**0.00** For 3.5	**52.00**

goods total	**52.00**
VAT	DEDUCTED **9.01**
TOTAL	**42.99**

terms
Net monthly
Carriage paid
E & OE

The purchase order and delivery note agree, but the invoice has a number of discrepancies:

- the order reference differs (47700 and 47780)
- the product code differs (3564749 and 3564748)
- the product description differs (100 gsm and 80 gsm)
- the price differs (£4.00 and £3.50 per ream)

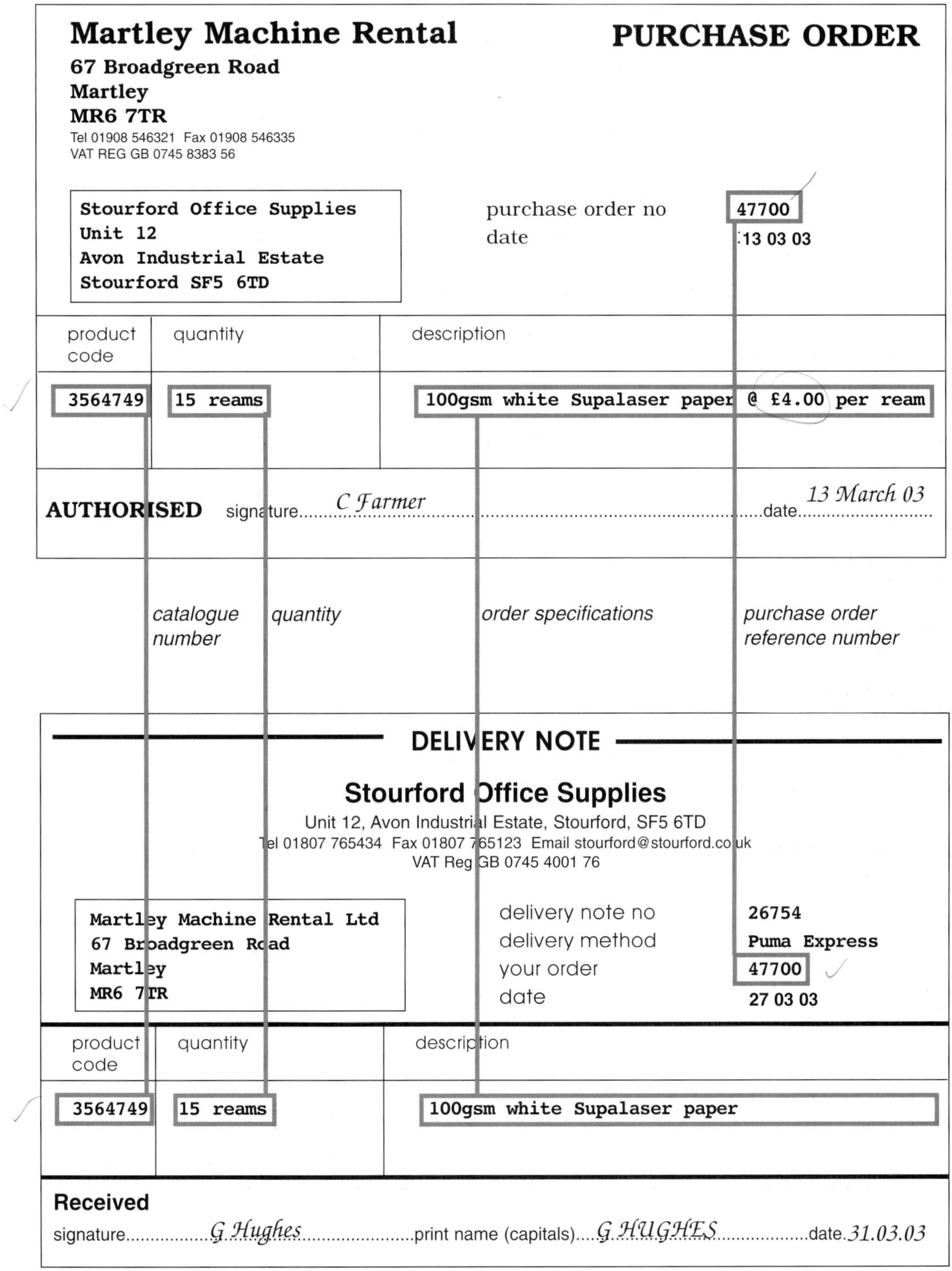

Martley Machine Rental **PURCHASE ORDER**

67 Broadgreen Road
Martley
MR6 7TR
Tel 01908 546321 Fax 01908 546335
VAT REG GB 0745 8383 56

Stourford Office Supplies
Unit 12
Avon Industrial Estate
Stourford SF5 6TD

purchase order no 47700
date 13 03 03

product code	quantity	description
3564749	15 reams	100gsm white Supalaser paper @ £4.00 per ream

AUTHORISED signature *C Farmer* date *13 March 03*

catalogue number | *quantity* | *order specifications* | *purchase order reference number*

DELIVERY NOTE

Stourford Office Supplies
Unit 12, Avon Industrial Estate, Stourford, SF5 6TD
Tel 01807 765434 Fax 01807 765123 Email stourford@stourford.co.uk
VAT Reg GB 0745 4001 76

Martley Machine Rental Ltd
67 Broadgreen Road
Martley
MR6 7TR

delivery note no 26754
delivery method Puma Express
your order 47700
date 27 03 03

product code	quantity	description
3564749	15 reams	100gsm white Supalaser paper

Received
signature *G Hughes* print name (capitals) *G HUGHES* date *31.03.03*

details to check on the purchase order and delivery note

CHECKING THE CALCULATIONS ON THE INVOICE

Another important step is for the Accounts Department to check the calculations on the invoice. If any one of these calculations is incorrect, the final total will be wrong, and the invoice will have to be queried with the supplier, so accurate checking is essential. The checks to be made are:

quantity x unit price The quantity of the items multiplied by the unit price must be correct. The result – the total price or *price extension* – is used for the calculation of any trade discount applicable.

trade or bulk discount Any trade or bulk discount – allowances given to approved customers or for bulk purchases – must be deducted from the total price worked out. Trade or bulk discount is calculated as a percentage of the total price, eg a trade discount of 20% on a total price of £150 is calculated

$$£150 \times \frac{20}{100} = £30$$

The net price charged (before VAT) is therefore

£150 – £30 = £120 = net total

settlement discount Any settlement (cash) discount – an allowance sometimes given for quick payment – is deducted from the net total before VAT is calculated. Settlement discount, when it is offered, is usually included as one of the terms at the bottom of the invoice. It is not normally deducted from the invoice total, so it will be up to the buyer to settle early and to adjust the invoice total down.

VAT Value Added Tax is currently charged at 17.5%. To calculate VAT, the total after the deduction of any settlement discount is treated as follows

$$\text{Total} \times \frac{17.5}{100} = \text{VAT amount}$$

If you are using a calculator, all you need to do is to multiply the total by 0.175 to give the VAT, which is then added to the total.

Remember that any fractions of a penny are ignored. For example if the total price is £55.75, the VAT will be:

£55.75 x 0.175 = £9.75625

£9.75625 then loses the last three digits – the fraction of a penny – to become £9.75.

For the purpose of your studies you must assume that the calculations on all invoices must be checked. In practice, invoicing programs perform the calculations automatically, and in principle should be correct.

Now check the calculations on the invoice on page 196. You should be able to detect a large number of errors:

- quantity x unit price should be £52.50, not £52.00
- the VAT is wrongly calculated £52.00 x 0.175 = £9.10, not £9.01 (it would be £9.18 on £52.50)
- the VAT has been deducted instead of added: the total should be £52.50 + £9.18 = £61.68

AUTHORISING THE INVOICE FOR PAYMENT

In most organisations checked invoices are passed to the person in the Accounts Department who deals with making payments to suppliers. First, however, an invoice will have to be *authorised* for payment. It will then, as long as no credit notes are due, be paid after the statement arrives and the date for payment is reached. Clearly only correct invoices can be passed forward for payment. Invoices with errors will need to be queried with the supplier.

When an invoice is checked and found to be correct, the person carrying out the check will usually mark the document and authorise it for payment. This authorisation can take a number of forms:

- the checker can initial and date the invoice, and tick it or write 'pay' as an authorisation
- the organisation may have a special rubber stamp which can be used in the authorisation process (see next page) – this stamp may also allow provide space for details such as the cost code (see page 489) and the allocation of an internal reference number which can be entered in the purchases day book and used for internal filing purposes

This procedure of authorisation obviously helps the efficiency of the organisation:

- only authorised invoices will be passed forward in the Accounts Department for entry into the purchases day book and double-entry accounts (see Chapter 11); each invoice will be attached to the copy purchase order and will eventually be paid when the due date comes

- the checker's initials will be there in case of any future query on the invoice, eg an undetected error

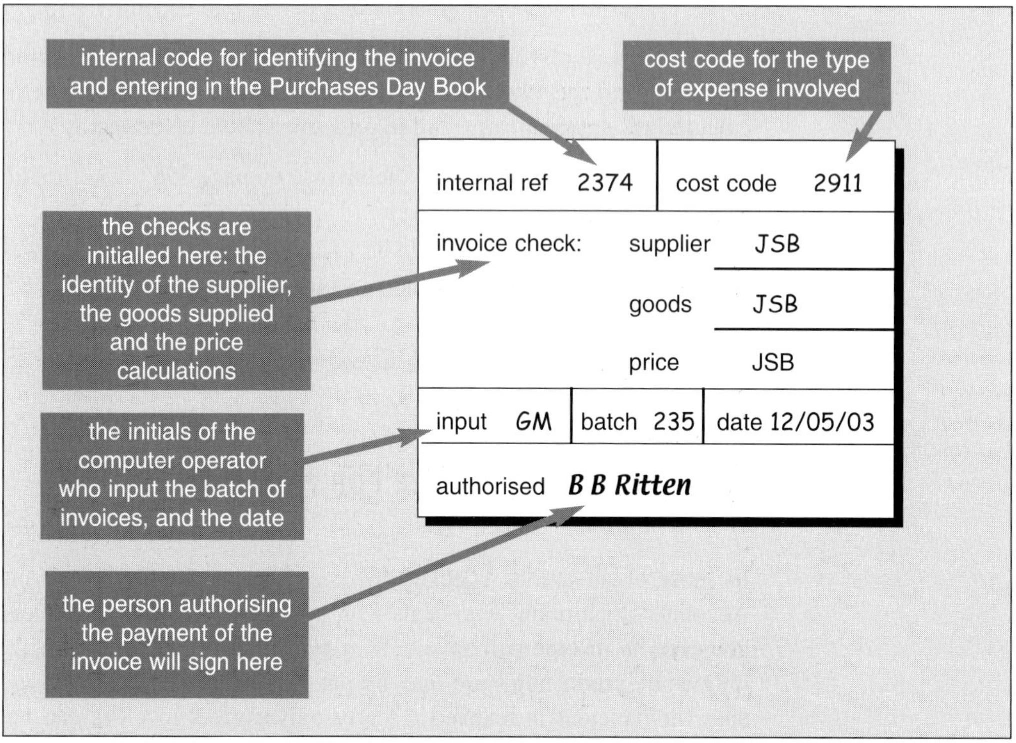

authorisation stamp placed on an invoice received for checking

GOODS RECEIVED NOTES (GRNS)

As mentioned earlier in the chapter some purchasers use a document known as a *goods received note* (GRN). This is essentially a checklist on which is recorded the name of the supplier and details of the goods ordered. As the goods are received and are checked in, the GRN is ticked and initialled to indicate that the right quantity and description of goods has been received. The GRN forms part of the payment authorisation process: only when a completed and correct GRN is approved by the Accounts Department can the relevant invoice be paid. As you will see, the GRN fulfils the same checking function as the entries on the invoice authorisation stamp shown above.

Shown on the next page is the goods received note relating to the Case Study in the last chapter in which the shop 'Trends' ordered some fashion socks from Cool Socks Limited. Note that the receipt of the 100 pairs of socks has been recorded, and also the fact that 10 pairs are damaged.

Trends **GOODS RECEIVED NOTE**

Supplier

Cool Socks Limited,
Unit 45 Elgar Estate,
Broadfield,
BR7 4ER

GRN no 1871
date 06 10 03

quantity	description	order number
100 pairs	Blue Toebar socks	47609

carrier Lynx Parcels consignment no 8479347

received by *V Williams* checked by *R Patel*

condition of goods (please tick and comment)		copies to
	good condition damaged ✓ (10 pairs) shortages	Buyer ✓ Accounts ✓ Stockroom ✓

RETURNS

As you can see from the goods received note above, a purchaser will sometimes have to return faulty or incorrect goods and request a credit note from the seller to reduce the amount owed. Note that a purchaser should *never* for this reason change figures on an invoice – this would cause havoc with the accounting records! When the goods are sent back – the socks in the Case Study – they will be accompanied by a *returns note.*

When the goods are received back by the seller and checked, a *credit note* will be issued to reduce the amount owing. This is illustrated on the next page.

Trends **RETURNS NOTE**

4 Friar Street
Broadfield
BR1 3RF
Tel 01908 761234 Fax 01908 761987
VAT REG GB 0745 8383 56

Cool Socks Limited,
Unit 45 Elgar Estate,
Broadfield,
BR7 4ER

returns note no 2384
date 08 10 03

product code	quantity	description
45B	10 pairs	Blue Toebar socks

REASON FOR RETURN: *faulty goods, credit requested*

SIGNATURE *R SINGH* DATE *10 10 03*

CREDIT NOTE

COOL SOCKS LIMITED

Unit 45 Elgar Estate, Broadfield, BR7 4ER
Tel 01908 765314 Fax 01908 765951 Email toni@cool.u-net.com
VAT REG GB 0745 4672 76

to

Trends
4 Friar Street
Broadfield
BR1 3RF

credit note no	12157
account	3993
your reference	47609
our invoice	787923
date/tax point	13 10 03

product code	description	quantity	price	unit	total	discount %	net
45B	Blue Toebar socks	10	2.36	pair	23.60	0.00	23.60

Reason for credit
10 pairs of socks received damaged
(Your returns note no. R/N 2384)

GOODS TOTAL	23.60
VAT	4.13
TOTAL	27.73

CHECKING THE CREDIT NOTE

When the credit note is received by the purchaser it will have to be checked carefully to make sure that the quantity of goods, the price, discount and VAT are correctly calculated. If it is correct, the document will be entered into the purchases returns day book and double-entry accounts (see Chapter 11) and then filed with (stapled to) the appropriate copy purchase order, delivery note, invoice and copy returns note, awaiting the arrival of the statement.

PAYING SUPPLIERS' INVOICES

resolving discrepancies

Before an invoice can be authorised for payment, any problems and discrepancies must be resolved. These may be simple problems, which can be resolved at the level at which you are working:

- calculation errors on the invoice which can be put right by requesting the issue of a correct invoice (the incorrect invoice must never be corrected by the organisation to which it is issued)
- duplicated invoices – a duplicate can be disregarded and returned

Other issues may need to be referred to a supervisor before the invoice can be paid, for example:

- the goods or the services have not been supplied – they will have to be chased up by someone elsewhere in the organisation
- an incorrect discount will have to be referred internally so that the problem can be taken up at a higher level with the seller

The guidelines suggested here are not 'cast in stone'. The relative size of the business paying the invoice will dictate what will and will not need referring. A small office is likely to give more decision-making authority to junior employees. Larger businesses are more likely to require referrals.

paying the invoice

There are two common ways of setting up a system for paying invoices:

1. Many businesses pay on receipt of a statement, not on receipt of the invoice. As most statements tend to go out at the end of the month, paying of invoices often then becomes a monthly routine. In this case payments due can be put on diary for a set day of the month, eg the 27th.
2. Some businesses will pay invoices after the maximum number of days allowed – normally 30 days. In this case a diary system will be set up and the checked/authorised invoices filed in payment date order.

MAKING PAYMENT – REMITTANCE ADVICES

The cycle of documents is completed by the issue of a remittance advice by the supplier when payment is made. Payment can either be made by *cheque* or by *electronic transfer* through the bank using a system known as BACS (Bankers Automated Clearing Services). A remittance advice will be issued for both types of transfer.

REMITTANCE ADVICE

TO
Cool Socks Limited
Unit 45 Elgar Estate,
Broadfield, BR7 4ER

FROM
Trends
4 Friar Street
Broadfield
BR1 3RF
Tel 01908 761234 Fax 01908 761987
VAT REG GB 0745 8383 56

Account 3993 6 November 2003

date	your reference	our reference	payment amount
01 10 03	INVOICE 787923	47609	277.30
10 10 03	CREDIT NOTE 12157	47609	(27.73)
		CHEQUE TOTAL	249.57

a remittance advice sent with a cheque payment

Chapter Summary

- Traditionally, a business placing an order will request the goods or services by means of a paper document – a purchase order. There then follows a 'flow' of paper documents, concluding with payment.
- Although electronic methods of ordering through e-commerce and EDI have become more common, the same traditional principles apply; it is just that the documents are on-screen rather than paper-based.
- A business purchasing goods or services will need to ensure that the right goods have been supplied, at the right price, before payment is made.
- When the goods arrive they should be checked against the delivery note which accompanies the goods. The delivery note is then checked against the purchase order and attached to it.
- Some businesses will prepare a goods received note to check off the goods when they arrive and to record any subsequent returns.
- When the invoice arrives it will be checked against the purchase order and delivery note and attached to the documents.
- The calculations and terms on the invoice will be checked carefully, particularly if it is not a computerised invoice.
- If any goods have to be returned they will be sent back with a returns note.
- Any credit notes issued to the purchaser (including any for returned goods) will have to be checked carefully on receipt.
- When the invoice and any relevant credit notes have been found to be correct the invoice can be authorised for payment.
- Authorised invoices are filed in a diary system until the appropriate payment date (normally after receipt of a statement).
- Payment is normally advised to the seller by means of a remittance advice.

Key Terms

EDI	Electronic Data Interchange is an electronic system of ordering goods and services using secure private computer links
e-commerce	buying and selling on the Internet – business to business and business to customer
purchase order	a document issued and authorised by the buyer of goods and services, sent to the seller, indicating the goods or services required
delivery note	a document listing and accompanying the goods sent to the purchaser
goods received note	a document sometimes used by purchasers to record receipt of stock and any returns made
invoice	a document issued by the seller of goods or services to the purchaser indicating the amount owing and the required payment date

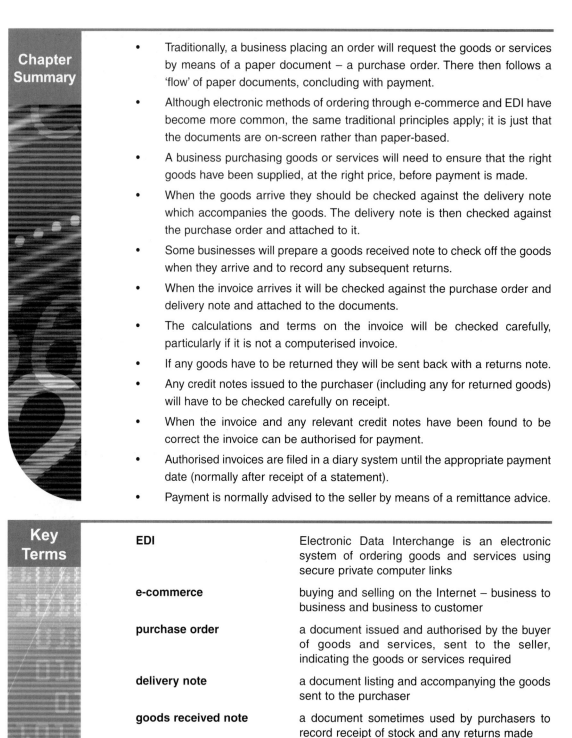

returns note a document sent with goods returned by the purchaser to the seller, requesting credit

credit note a document issued by the seller of the goods or services reducing the amount owed by the buyer

statement a document issued by the seller to the buyer summarising invoices and credit notes issued and payments received

remittance advice a document sent by the purchaser to the seller advising the amount and date of payment of money due

Student Activities

10.1 What type of business document would normally be used when goods are bought on credit

(a) to order the goods from the seller? PURCHASE ORDER

(b) to accompany goods sent from the seller? DELIVERY NOTE

(c) to record the receipt and any return of goods at the buyer's premises? RECEIVED GOODS NOTE / RETURNS NOTE

(d) to advise the seller of the amount of money being paid on account? REMITTANCE ADVICE

(e) to advise the buyer in the first instance of the amount of money due on an order? INVOICE

(f) to accompany faulty goods sent back by the buyer? RETURNS NOTE

10.2 An unsigned purchase order is sent out to a supplier. What is likely to happen to it, and why?

~~TO~~ RETURNED TO PURCHASER FOR AUTHORISATION.

10.3 Which documents would normally be checked by the buyer against the purchase order? Answer (a) or (b) or (c) or (d).

(a) the delivery note and the returns note

(b) the invoice and the returns note

(c) the goods received note and the remittance advice

(d) the delivery note and the invoice

(d)

10.4 What is the difference between a returns note and a credit note?

RETURNS NOTE – RETURNED WITH THE GOODS DETAILS GOODS RETURNED

CREDIT NOTE – NOTIFIES MONEY TO BE CREDITED.

10.5 What would be the problem if the seller of goods accidentally forgot to include the normal trade discount on an invoice to a regular customer? What should the customer do?

INVOICE WOULD BE WRONG. TOO HIGH – CUSTOMER SHOULD REQUEST CREDIT NOTE OR REPLACEMENT INVOICE.

10.6 Eduservice, an educational consultancy business, ordered some computer disks from Compusupply Limited on purchase order 53659 for courses it runs at Itec College in Broadfield. The goods were delivered to the Eduservice office at 45 The Ridings, Broadfield on 3 February.

You work in the Eduservice office as an administrative assistant. Part of your job is to deal with all the documents, including the accounting work.

You have today (5 February 2003) received an invoice from Compusupply. You are not happy with the service you are receiving from this company and are thinking of going elsewhere for a supplier.

Shown below and on the next page are:

- a list of Compusupply customer trade discounts (for information purposes)
- the original purchase order
- the invoice you receive

You are to write a letter to Compusupply setting out the errors that have been made. Address the letter to the Sales Manager and sign it with your own name as an administrative assistant. The date is 5 February 2003.

Compusupply – Customer discounts and credit limits (extracts)

Customer	*Trade discount (%)*	*Credit limit (£)*
Donmar Estates	15	12,000
Dugdale, E	10	5,000
Easifit Ltd	15	10,000
Eduservice	15	12,500
Estima Designs	10	5,000

EDUSERVICE

45 The Ridings
Broadfield
BR2 3TR
Tel 01908 333691

PURCHASE ORDER

TO

Compusupply Limited
Unit 17 Elgar Estate,
Broadfield, BR7 4ER

purchase order no 53659

date 27 January 2003

product code	quantity	description
4573	10 disks	Zap 100MB Storage disks @ £95 per box of 10

Authorised signature *J Wales* date *27.1.03*

INVOICE

COMPUSUPPLY LIMITED
Unit 17 Elgar Estate, Broadfield, BR7 4ER
Tel 01908 765756 Fax 01908 765777 Email rob@compusupply.u-net.com
VAT Reg GB 0745 4689 13

invoice to

Eduservice
45 The Ridings
Broadfield
BR2 3TR

invoice no	20424
account	242
your reference	53659
date/tax point	30.01.2003

deliver to

J Wales
Itec College
Fairacre
Broadfield BR5 7YT

NOT DELIVERED TO THIS ADDRESS

product code	description	quantity	price	unit	total	discount %	net
4574	Zap 200MB Storage disk	10	125.00	box (10)	125.00	10	112.50
PRODUCT CODE INCORRECT	WRONG GOODS + PRICE				95-00	Discount incorrect 15% 15%	80-75 14-13 94-88

goods total	112.50
VAT	19.68
TOTAL	132.18

terms
Net monthly
Carriage paid
E & OE

Goods being returned for credit

10.7 You work for J Hudson & Partners, a wholesaler. You are an accounts assistant and one of your tasks is to process payments to suppliers. The business normally pays on the second and last Friday of each month. In September 2003 these Fridays fall on the 12th and 26th. The company takes full advantage of the credit terms offered by its suppliers.

J Hudson & Partners has recently been having problems with its supplier RMC Import Agency, which supplies on 30 day terms. Orders have been delivered late and wrong goods have been supplied. As a result J Hudson & Partners withheld the July payment until a credit note for £568.00 was received in respect of wrong goods supplied.

The credit note finally arrived on 22 August 2003.

It is 29 August and you have been told that you can now process a payment to RMC Import Agency. The statement is shown below.

You are to calculate the amount owing and complete the remittance advice and cheque shown on the next page. You will not sign the cheque, as it has to be authorised and signed by John Hudson.

STATEMENT OF ACCOUNT

RMC Import Agency
56 Russell Court
London
WC1A 2MS
Tel 0207 764098 Fax 01207 764083 Email mail@rmc.com
VAT Reg GB 0748 4872 99

TO

J Hudson & Partners
45 Helby Road
Mereford
MR1 4FG

account 2941

date 26 August 2003

date	details	debit £	credit £	balance £
2003				
1 Aug	Balance b/f			3,650.00
8 Aug	Invoice 23721	1,200.00		4,850.00
11 Aug	Invoice 23788	1,945.00		6,795.00
22 Aug	Invoice 23921	4,560.00		11,355.00
20 Aug	Credit note 3525		568.00	10,787.00

To pay 6227

TOTAL **£** 10,787.00

REMITTANCE ADVICE

TO

RMC Import Agency
56, Russell Court
LONDON
WC1A 2MS

FROM

J Hudson & Partners
45 Helby Road
Mereford
MR1 4FG
Tel 01908 761276 Fax 01908 761998
VAT REG GB 0745 8383 01

Account: 2941 **Date:** 29 Aug 2003

date	your reference	our reference	payment amount
1 Aug	Balance @ 1 Aug		3,650 - 00
8 Aug	Invoice 23721		1,200 - 00
11 Aug	Invoice 23788		1,945 - 00
20 Aug	Credit Note 3525		(568 - 00)

CHEQUE TOTAL 6,227 - 00

Southern Bank PLC
Mereford Branch
16 Broad Street, Mereford MR1 7TR

date 29th August 2003 97-76-54

Pay RMC Import Agency only
Six thousand, two hundred and twenty seven pounds only

Account payee only

£ 6,227-00

J HUDSON & PARTNERS

989451 97 76 54 87453219

11 Accounting for credit purchases and purchases returns

this chapter covers . . .

In this chapter we apply the principles of the accounting system to credit purchases and purchases returns.

We shall see how the prime documents for credit purchases (purchases invoices) and purchases returns (credit notes) are entered in the books of prime entry (purchases day book and purchases returns day book).

The information is then transferred from the day books into the ledger accounts of the double-entry system.

NVQ PERFORMANCE CRITERIA COVERED

unit 2: MAKING AND RECORDING PAYMENTS

element 2.1

process documents relating to goods and services received

E *correctly enter invoices and credit notes into books of prime entry according to organisational procedures*

F *enter invoices and credit notes in the appropriate ledgers*

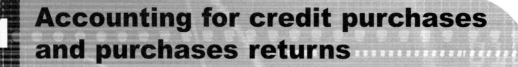

ACCOUNTING FOR CREDIT PURCHASES TRANSACTIONS

This chapter focuses on credit purchases transactions; the recording of transactions for *cash purchases* will be covered when we study the payments side of the cash book in Chapter 15.

In accounting, the term 'purchases' has a specific meaning:

the purchase of goods with the intention that they should be resold at a profit

Thus an office stationery shop will record as purchases those items – such as photocopier paper, ring binders – which it buys in with the intention of resale at a profit. Other items purchased in connection with the running of the business – eg buildings, shop fittings – are recorded not as purchases but, instead, are accounted for against the name of the item, ie buildings, shop fittings.

The accounting system for credit purchases starts its recording process from prime documents – these comprise:

- purchases invoices
- credit notes received

The diagram which follows shows the order in which the accounting records are prepared for credit purchases transactions.

accounting for credit purchases transactions

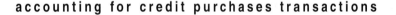

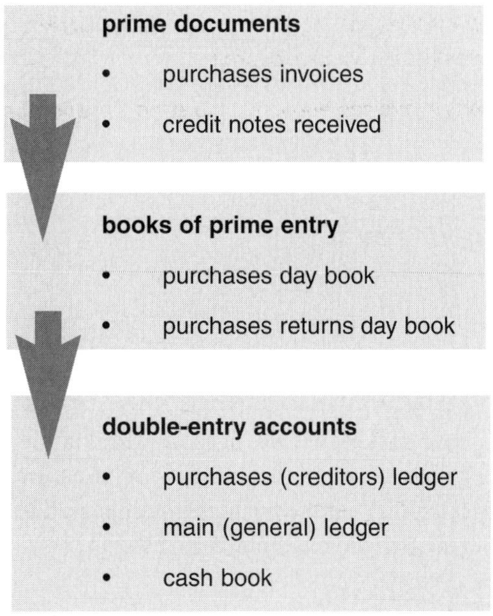

We will now look in more detail at the use of the books of prime entry and the double-entry system for credit purchases. These are very similar to the system already used for credit sales in Chapter 3 and you may wish to refer to the sections of Chapter 3 which cover books of prime entry (pages 50 - 52), the double-entry system (pages 52 - 55), and methods of coding in accounting systems (pages 55 - 56).

ACCOUNTING SYSTEM FOR CREDIT PURCHASES

The accounting system for credit purchases fits together in the following way:

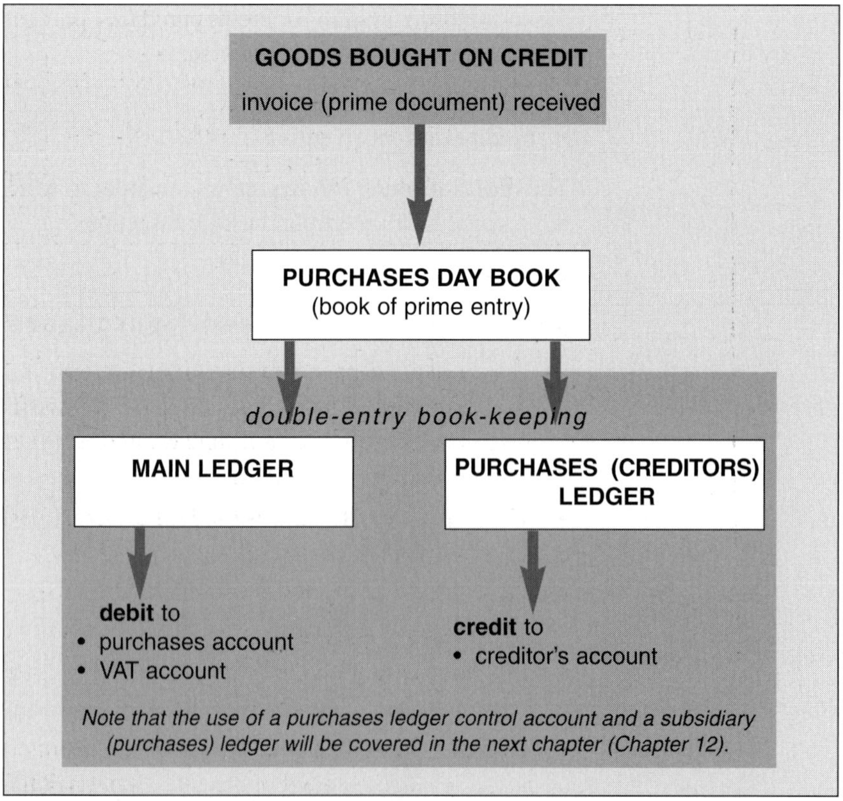

We shall now look in more detail at the purchases day book and the double-entry accounts for credit purchases. In the examples which follow we will assume that the business is registered for Value Added Tax. The rate of VAT used in the example is 17.5%.

PURCHASES DAY BOOK

The purchases day book is a collection point for accounting information on the credit purchases of a business and is set out in the following way (with sample entries shown):

Purchases Day Book						**PDB 57**
Date	Supplier	Invoice No	Folio	Total	VAT*	Net
2004				£	£	£
5 Jan	P Bond Ltd	1234	PL 125	94.00	14.00	80.00
9 Jan	D Webster	A373	PL 730	141.00	21.00	120.00
16 Jan	P Bond Ltd	1247	PL 125	47.00	7.00	40.00
20 Jan	Sanders & Sons	5691	PL 495	188.00	28.00	160.00
31 Jan	Totals for month			470.00	70.00	400.00

* VAT = 17.5 per cent

Notes:

- The purchases day book is prepared from purchases invoices received from suppliers. The invoice number used is either that of the supplier's invoice (as above) or is a unique number given to each invoice by the buyer's accounts department.
- The reference 'PDB 57' is used for cross-referencing to the book-keeping system: here it indicates that this is page 57 of the purchases day book.
- The *folio* column is also used for cross-referencing purposes: 'PL' refers to Purchases Ledger, followed by the account number.
- The *total* column records the amount of each invoice, ie after VAT has been included.
- The day book is totalled at appropriate intervals – daily, weekly or monthly – and the total of the *net* column will tell the business the amount of credit purchases for the period.
- When control accounts (see Chapter 12) are in use, the total for the month from the 'total' column from the purchases day book is entered into the purchases ledger control account.

Thus, to write up the purchases day book, we take the purchases invoices –

that have been checked and authorised (see pages 198-200) – for the period and enter the details:

- date of invoice
- name of supplier
- purchase invoice number, using either the supplier's invoice number, or a unique number given to each invoice by the buyer's accounts department
- cross-reference to the supplier's account number in the purchases ledger, eg 'PL 125'
- enter the total amount of the invoice into the 'total' column
- enter the VAT amount shown on the invoice – don't be concerned with any adjustments to the VAT for the effect of any settlement discounts, simply record the VAT amount shown
- enter the net amount of the invoice (often described as 'goods or services total'), before VAT is added

DOUBLE-ENTRY BOOK-KEEPING FOR CREDIT PURCHASES

After the purchases day book has been written up and totalled, the information from it is transferred into the double-entry system. The accounts in the purchases ledger and main ledger to record the transactions from the purchases day book seen earlier are as follows:

PURCHASES (CREDITORS) LEDGER

Dr **P Bond Limited** (account no 125) Cr

2004		£	2004		£
			5 Jan	Purchases PDB 57	94
			16 Jan	Purchases PDB 57	47

Dr **Sanders & Sons** (account no 495) Cr

2004		£	2004		£
			20 Jan	Purchases PDB 57	188

Dr **D Webster** (account no 730) Cr

2004		£	2004		£
			9 Jan	Purchases PDB 57	141

MAIN LEDGER

Dr		**Purchases Account** (account no 5001)		Cr
2004		£	2004	£
31 Jan	Purchases Day Book PDB 57	400		

Dr		**Value Added Tax Account** (account no 2200)		Cr
2004		£	2004	£
31 Jan	Purchases Day Book PDB 57	70		

Note that from the purchases day book:

- the amounts from the total column *for each separate purchase* have been credited to the accounts of the suppliers, ie the business owes to each creditor the amounts shown
- the total of the VAT column, £70, has been debited to VAT account (which has gained value)
- the total of the net column, £400, has been debited to purchases account (ie the account which has gained value)
- the folio column in the day book gives a cross-reference to the creditors' accounts in the purchases ledger (PL)
- each entry in the purchases ledger and main ledger is cross-referenced back to the page number of the purchases day book; here the reference is to 'PDB 57'.

ACCOUNTING SYSTEM FOR PURCHASES RETURNS

Purchases returns (or returns out) are when goods previously bought on credit are returned by the business to its suppliers. A credit note (see page 202) is requested and, when received, it is entered in the accounting system to reduce the amount owing to the creditor.

The accounting procedures for purchases returns involve:

- *prime documents* – credit notes received from suppliers
- *book of prime entry* – purchases returns day book
- *double-entry accounts* – purchases ledger (accounts for each creditor) and main ledger (purchases returns account, which records the total of credit notes received, and Value Added Tax account, which records the VAT amount of purchases returns)

The accounting system for purchases returns is summarised as follows:

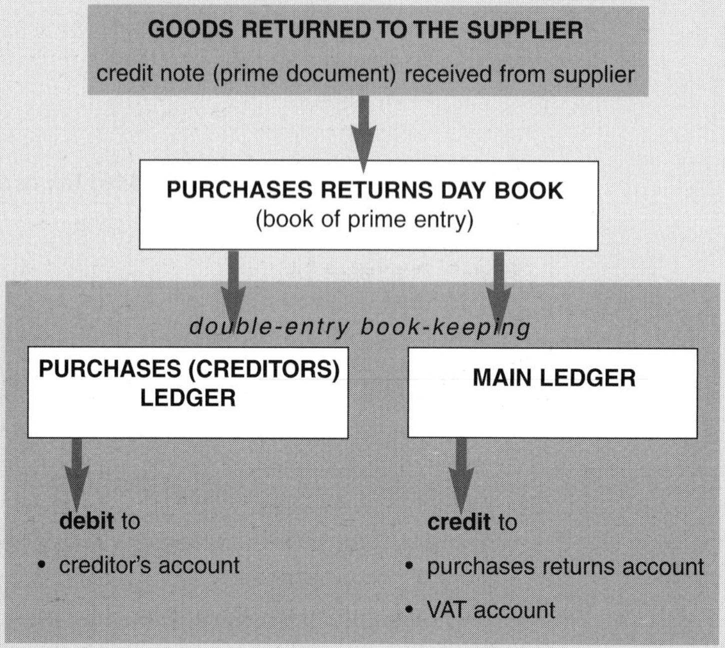

Note that the use of a purchases ledger control account and a subsidiary (purchases) ledger will be covered in the next chapter (Chapter 12).

We shall now look in more detail at the purchases returns day book and the double-entry accounts for purchases returns. Note that the business is registered for Value Added Tax.

PURCHASES RETURNS DAY BOOK

The purchases returns day book uses virtually the same layout as the purchases day book seen earlier in this chapter. It operates in a similar way, storing up information about purchases returns until such time as a transfer is made into the double-entry accounts system. The prime documents for purchases returns day book are credit notes received from suppliers.

example transactions

2004

20 Jan Returned goods, £40 + VAT to D Webster, credit note no 123 received

27 Jan Returned goods, £80 + VAT to Sanders & Sons, credit note no 406 received

The purchases returns day book is written up as follows:

Purchases Returns Day Book						PRDB 3
Date	Supplier	Credit Note No	Folio	Total	VAT*	Net
2004				£	£	£
20 Jan	D Webster	123	PL 730	47.00	7.00	40.00
27 Jan	Sanders & Sons	406	PL 495	94.00	14.00	80.00
31 Jan	Totals for month			141.00	21.00	120.00

* VAT = 17.5 per cent

Notes:

- The purchases returns day book is prepared from credit notes received from suppliers. The credit note number used is either that of the supplier's credit note (as above) or is a unique number given to each credit note by the buyer's accounts department.
- The day book is totalled at appropriate intervals – weekly or monthly.
- The VAT-inclusive amounts from the total column are debited to the creditors' personal accounts in the purchases ledger.
- The total of the VAT column is transferred to the credit of the VAT account in the main ledger.
- The total of the net column tells the business the amount of purchases returns for the period. This amount is transferred to the credit of purchases returns account in the main ledger.
- The total column records the amount of each credit note received, ie after VAT has been included. When control accounts (see Chapter 12) are in use, the total for the month of the 'total' column is entered into the purchases ledger control account.

DOUBLE-ENTRY BOOK-KEEPING FOR PURCHASES RETURNS

After the purchases returns day book has been written up and totalled, the information from it is transferred into the double-entry system. The accounts in the purchases ledger and main ledger to record the transactions from the above purchases returns day book (including any other transactions already recorded on these accounts) are:

PURCHASES (CREDITORS) LEDGER

Dr		**Sanders & Sons** (account no 495)			Cr
2004		£	2004		£
27 Jan	Purchases Returns PRDB 3	94	20 Jan	Purchases PDB 57	188

Dr		**D Webster** (account no 730)			Cr
2004		£	2004		£
20 Jan	Purchases Returns PRDB 3	47	9 Jan	Purchases PDB 57	141

MAIN LEDGER

Dr		**Purchases Returns Account** (account no 5010)			Cr
2004		£	2004		£
			31 Jan	Purchases Returns Day Book PRDB 3	120

Dr		**Value Added Tax Account** (account no 2200)			Cr
2004		£	2004		£
31 Jan	Purchases Day Book PDB 57	70	31 Jan	Purchases Returns Day Book PRDB 3	21

THE USE OF ANALYSED PURCHASES DAY BOOKS

Businesses use analysed day books whenever they wish to analyse purchases and purchases returns between different categories of purchases:

- goods for resale, perhaps split between types of goods, eg in a clothes shop between ladies wear and mens wear
- other items of expenditure, eg bills for expenses, such as telephone, electricity etc

An example of an analysed purchases day book is shown below.

Purchases Day Book									PDB 86
Date	Supplier	Invoice ref.	Folio	Total	VAT*	Net	Ladies wear	Mens wear	Other expenses
2004				£	£	£	£	£	£
2 Sep	Fashions Limited	1401	PL 87	129.25	19.25	110.00	50.00	60.00	–
4 Sep	Eastern Telephones	1402	PL 61	175.66	26.16	149.50	–	–	149.50
8 Sep	Mercian Models	1403	PL 102	301.74	44.94	256.80	256.80	–	–
12 Sep	Media Advertising	1404	PL 92	528.75	78.75	450.00	–	–	450.00
15 Sep	Style Limited	1405	PL 379	432.87	64.47	368.40	218.20	150.20	–
19 Sep	Wyvern Motors	1406	PL 423	149.81	22.31	127.50	–	–	127.50
26 Sep	Denim Traders	1407	PL 45	322.36	48.01	274.35	65.50	208.85	–
30 Sep	Totals for month			2,040.44	303.89	1,736.55	590.50	419.05	727.00

* VAT = 17.5 per cent

Analysed purchases day books and purchases returns day books can be adapted to suit the particular needs of a business. Thus there is not a standard way in which to present the books of prime entry – the needs of the user are all important. By using analysed day books, the owner of the business can see how much has been bought for each of the different categories of purchases.

Notes:

- Each purchases invoice has been given a unique number (starting at 1401) by the buyer's accounts department
- The references in the folio column are to the 'PL' (Purchase Ledger) and supplier's account number
- The analysis columns – here ladies wear, mens wear and other expenses – show the amount of purchases net of VAT (ie before VAT is added)
- The analysis columns analyse the net amount – by category of expenditure – from purchases invoices

BATCH CONTROL SYSTEMS

As we have seen with sales ledger (page 63), many firms use batch control systems in place of day books. Batched data entry for purchases enables a computer operator to enter a series of, say, purchases invoices without the need to keep changing from one area of the computer program to another. The pre-list is prepared on a batch control form such as that shown below for a batch of purchases invoices:

Batch Control: purchases invoices

Supplier		Invoice		Total	VAT*	Net
Account No	Name	Date	No	£	£	£
		2004				
PL 125	P Bond Ltd	5 Jan	1234	94.00	14.00	80.00
PL 730	D Webster	9 Jan	A373	141.00	21.00	120.00
PL 125	P Bond Ltd	16 Jan	1247	47.00	7.00	40.00
PL 495	Sanders & Sons	20 Jan	5691	188.00	28.00	160.00
		Check list totals		470.00	70.00	400.00

Prepared by	*Keith Moore*	Date	*31 Jan 2004*
Checked by	Karen Abrahall	Date	31 Jan 2004
Posted by	*Clare McGougan*	Date	*31 Jan 2004*

* VAT = 17.5 per cent

The purchases invoice batch form is completed from invoices which have been received and checked.

The transactions are then entered into the purchases ledger section of the computer accounting program. The computer screen shows the total money amount of purchases invoices and this is compared with the check list total from the purchases invoices batch control form; if there is a discrepancy, the error must be located and corrected.

Where a business uses control accounts (see Chapter 12), the total from the batch control form for purchases invoices is recorded in the purchases ledger control account.

Case Study

WYVERN TRADERS

To bring together the material covered in this chapter, we will look at a comprehensive Case Study which makes use of

- **books of prime entry**
  - purchases day book
  - purchases returns day book
- **double-entry accounts**
  - purchases (creditors) ledger
  - main ledger

The Case Study also includes a diagram (page 224) which summarises the procedures for recording credit purchases and purchases returns transactions in the accounting system.

situation

Wyvern Traders is a wholesaler of stationery and office equipment. The business is registered for VAT. The following are the credit purchases and purchases returns transactions for April 2004:

2004	
1 Apr	Bought goods from Midland Supplies, £120.00 + VAT, their invoice no 12486
9 Apr	Returned goods to Midland Supplies, £20.00 + VAT, credit note no 104 received
14 Apr	Bought goods from National Stationery, £60.00 +VAT, their invoice no A184
28 Apr	Bought goods from Swan Equipment, £160.00 + VAT, their invoice no P102
30 Apr	Returned goods to Swan Equipment, £40.00 + VAT, credit note no X102 received

The day books and double-entry accounts are illustrated on the next two pages: arrows indicate the transfers from the day books to the individual accounts. Note that some accounts have been repeated on both pages in order to show, on the same page, the accounts relating to a particular day book: in practice a business would keep all the transactions together in one account.

The diagram on page 224 summarises the material we have studied in this chapters. It shows the procedures for recording transactions in the accounting system for

- credit purchases
- purchases returns

Purchases Day Book

PDB 19

Date	Supplier	Invoice No	Folio	Total	VAT	Net
2004				£ p	£ p	£ p
1 Apr	Midland Supplies	12486	PL 45	141 00	21 00	120 00
14 Apr	National Stationery	A184	PL 67	70 50	10 50	60 00
28 Apr	Swan Equipment	P102	PL 112	188 00	28 00	160 00
30 Apr	Totals for month			399 50	59 50	340 00

PURCHASES (CREDITORS) LEDGER

Dr **Midland Supplies** (account no 45) Cr

Date	Details	£ p	Date	Details	£ p
2004			2004 1 Apr	Purchases PDB 19	141 00

Dr **National Stationery** (account no 67) Cr

Date	Details	£ p	Date	Details	£ p
2004			2004 14 Apr	Purchases PDB 19	70 50

Dr **Swan Equipment** (account no 112) Cr

Date	Details	£ p	Date	Details	£ p
2004			2004 28 Apr	Purchases PDB 19	188 00

MAIN LEDGER

Dr **Value Added Tax Account** (account no 2200) Cr

Date	Details	£ p	Date	Details	£ p
2004 30 Apr	Purchases Day Book PDB 19	59 50	2004		

Dr **Purchases Account** (account no 5001) Cr

Date	Details	£ p	Date	Details	£ p
2004 30 Apr	Purchases Day Book PDB 19	340 00	2004		

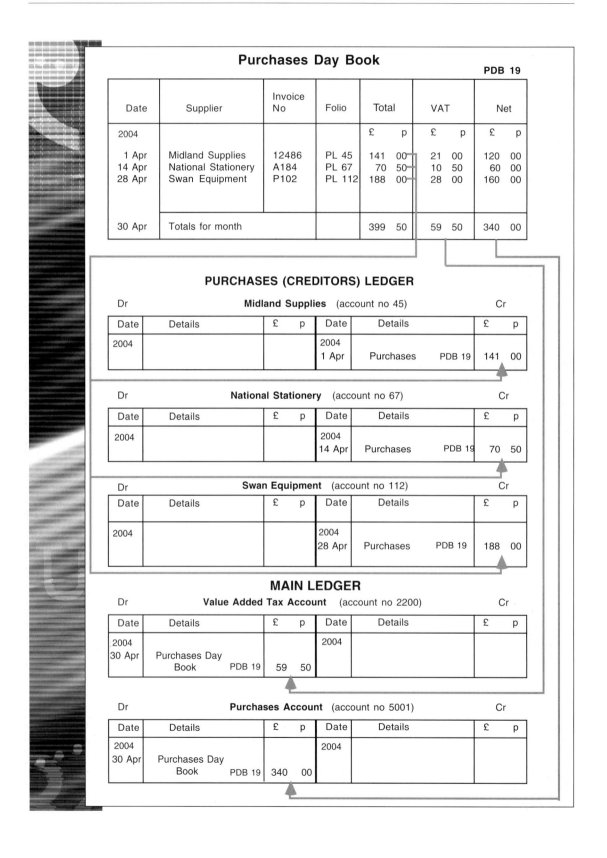

Purchases Returns Day Book

PRDB 7

Date	Supplier	Credit Note No	Folio	Total	VAT	Net
2004				£ p	£ p	£ p
9 Apr	Midland Supplies	104	PL 45	23 50	3 50	20 00
30 Apr	Swan Equipment	X102	PL 112	47 00	7 00	40 00
30 Apr	Totals for month			70 50	10 50	60 00

PURCHASES (CREDITORS) LEDGER

Dr **Midland Supplies** (account no 45) Cr

Date	Details	£ p	Date	Details	£ p
2004			2004		
9 Apr	Purchases Returns PRDB 7	23 50	1 Apr	Purchases PDB 19	141 00*

Dr **Swan Equipment** (account no 112) Cr

Date	Details	£ p	Date	Details	£ p
2004			2004		
30 Apr	Purchases Returns PRDB 7	47 00	28 Apr	Purchases PDB 19	188 00*

MAIN LEDGER

Dr **Value Added Tax Account** (account no 2200) Cr

Date	Details	£ p	Date	Details	£ p
2004			2004		
30 Apr	Purchases Day Book PDB19	59 50*	30 Apr	Purchases Returns Day Book PRDB 7	10 50

Dr **Purchases Returns Account** (account no 112) Cr

Date	Details	£ p	Date	Details	£ p
2004			2004		
			30 Apr	Purchases Returns Day Book PRDB 7	60 00

* transactions entered previously

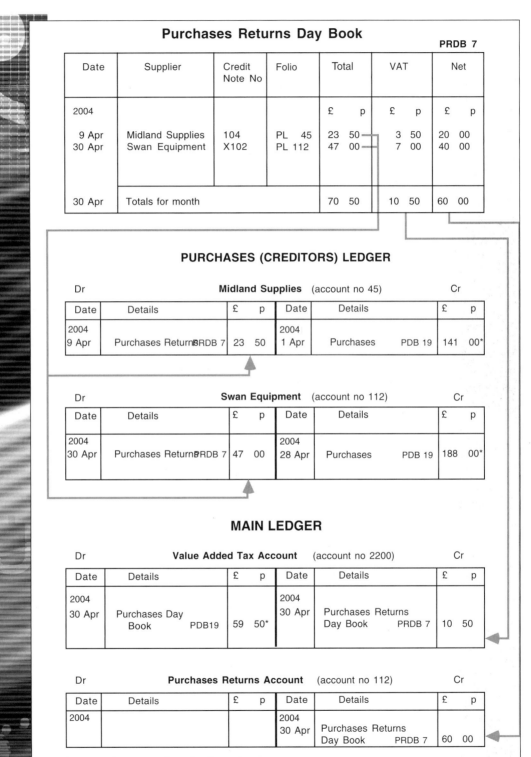

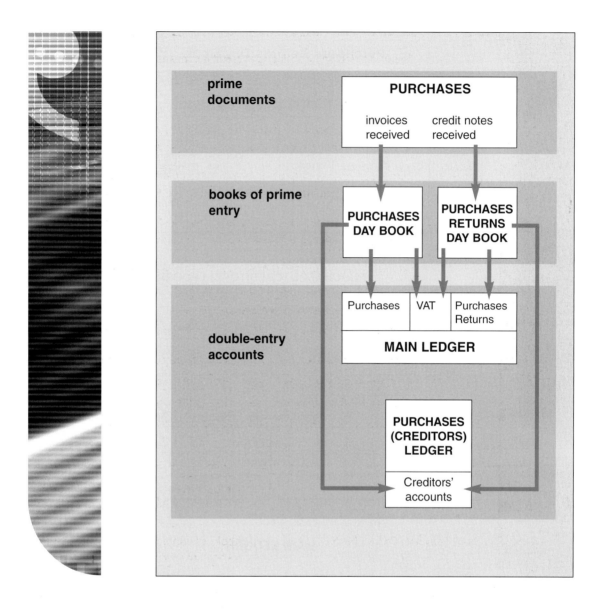

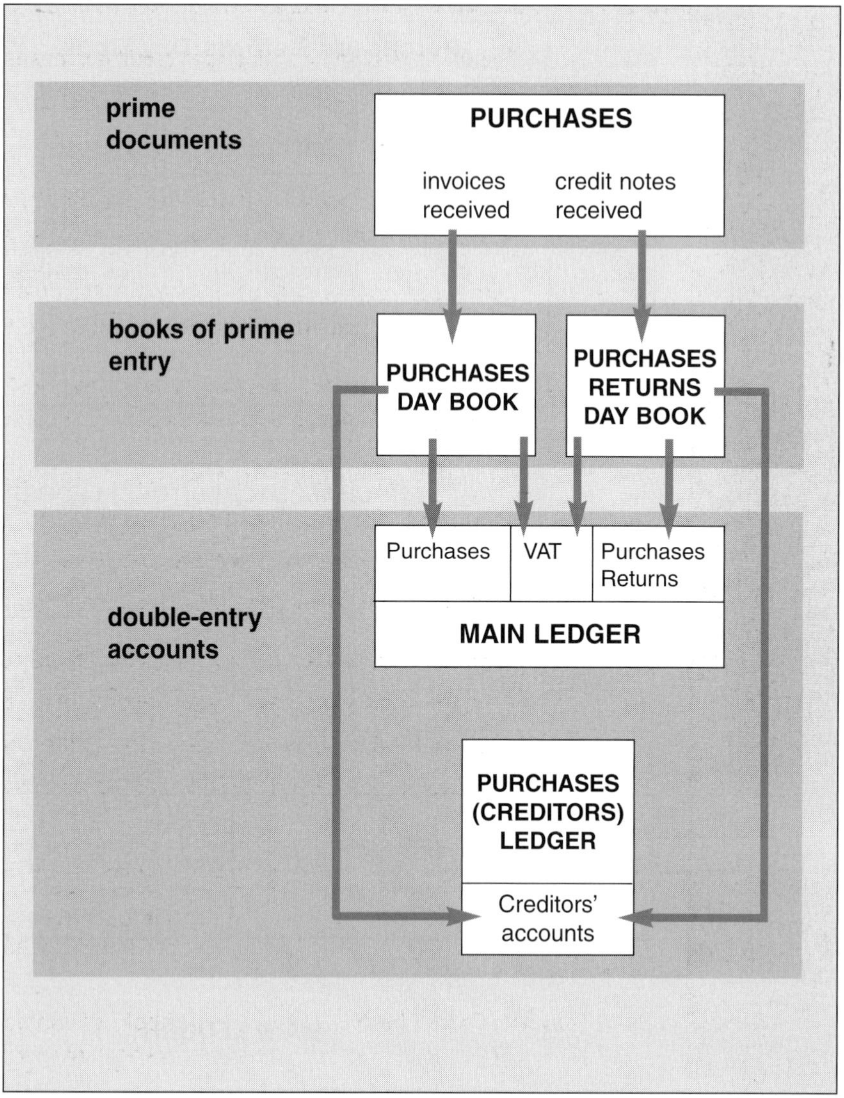

BALANCING ACCOUNTS

Where there is more than one transaction on an account, it is necessary to balance the account at regular intervals – often monthly, sometimes more often.

We have already seen how to balance accounts in Chapter 4, and the technique is summarised at the beginning of the next chapter.

Chapter Summary

- The prime documents relating to credit purchases are:
  - purchases invoices
  - credit notes received
- Purchases day book is the book of prime entry for credit purchases. It is prepared from purchases invoices received from suppliers.
- Purchases returns day book is the book of prime entry for purchases returns. It is prepared from credit notes received from suppliers.
- Analysed purchases day books are used when a business wishes to analyse its purchases between different categories of expenditure.
- Recording credit purchases in the double-entry system uses:
  - prime documents, purchases invoices
  - book of prime entry, purchases day book
  - double-entry accounts, purchases ledger and main ledger
- Recording purchases returns in the double-entry system uses:
  - prime documents, credit notes received from suppliers
  - book of prime entry, purchases returns day book
  - double-entry accounts, purchases ledger and main ledger

Key Terms

purchases	the purchase of goods with the intention that they should be resold at a profit
purchases day book	book of prime entry prepared from purchases invoices
purchases returns	goods purchased on credit which are returned to the supplier
purchases returns day book	book of prime entry prepared from credit notes received from suppliers
analysed purchases day book	day book which incorporates analysis columns between different categories of expenditure
purchases (creditors) ledger	division of the ledger which contains the accounts of the firm's creditors (suppliers)

Student Activities

11.1 Which one of the following is in the right order?

(a) purchases returns day book; credit note issued; purchases returns account; creditor's account

(b) purchases returns account; creditor's account; purchases returns day book; credit note issued

(c) purchases returns day book; purchases returns account; creditor's account; credit note issued

(d) credit note issued; purchases returns day book; purchases returns account; creditor's account

Answer (a) or (b) or (c) or (d) (d)

11.2 Explain in note format:

(a) the principles of recording a credit purchases transaction in the accounting system

(b) the principles of recording a purchases returns transaction in the accounting system

In the Activities which follow, the rate of Value Added Tax is to be calculated at the current rate (17.5% at the time of writing). When calculating VAT amounts, you should ignore fractions of a penny, ie round down to a whole penny.

For Activities 11.3 and 11.4 use a cross-referencing system incorporating the following:

- *purchases day book* – *PDB 36*

  purchases returns day book – *PRDB 11*
- *purchases ledger account numbers*
  - *AMC Enterprises* – *account no 520*
  - *S Green* – *account no 574*
  - *I Johnstone* – *account no 604*
  - *Mercia Manufacturing* – *account no 627*
  - *L Murphy* – *account no 659*
  - *Severn Supplies* – *account no 721*
- *main ledger accounts*
  - *purchases account* – *account no 5001*
  - *purchases returns account* – *account no 5010*
  - *Value Added Tax account* – *account no 2200*

11.3 During April 2004, Wyvern Wholesalers had the following credit transactions:

2004	
2 Apr	Bought goods from Severn Supplies £250 + VAT, invoice no 6789
5 Apr	Bought goods from I Johnstone £210 + VAT, invoice no A241
9 Apr	Bought goods from L Murphy £185 + VAT, invoice no 2456
15 Apr	Bought goods from Mercia Manufacturing £180 + VAT, invoice no X457
19 Apr	Bought goods from AMC Enterprises £345 + VAT, invoice no AMC 456
26 Apr	Bought goods from S Green £395 + VAT, invoice no 2846

You are to:

(a) enter the above transactions in Wyvern Wholesaler's purchases day book for April 2004

(b) record the accounting entries in Wyvern Wholesaler's purchases ledger and main ledger

11.4 The following are the purchases returns of Wyvern Wholesalers for April 2004. They are to be:

(a) entered in the purchases returns day book for April 2004

(b) recorded in the purchases ledger and main ledger (use the ledgers already prepared in the answer to Activity 11.3)

2004	
7 Apr	Returned goods to Severn Supplies £50 + VAT, credit note no CN225 received
14 Apr	Returned goods to L Murphy £80 + VAT, credit note no X456 received
21 Apr	Returned goods to AMC Enterprises £125 + VAT, credit note no C3921 received
29 Apr	Returned goods to S Green £68 + VAT, credit note no CN/SG247 received

11.5 Jason Smythe owns a business selling furniture and carpets. During April 2004 he received the following invoices from his suppliers:

2004	
2 Apr	Invoice for furniture from T Table Limited for £1,247.50 + VAT
7 Apr	Invoice for carpets from Eastern Imports for £796.80 + VAT
9 Apr	Invoice for carpets from Minster Carpets Limited for £1,875.24 + VAT
14 Apr	Invoice for furniture from Pegasus Limited for £498.13 + VAT
16 Apr	Invoice for carpets from United Carpets Limited for £476.22 + VAT
21 Apr	Invoice for furniture from Gerrard Furniture for £831.49 + VAT
23 Apr	Invoice for furniture from T Table Limited for £648.90 + VAT
28 Apr	Invoice for carpets from Eastern Imports for £1,297.31 + VAT

You are to:

(a) give each invoice a unique number – Jason tells you to start with number 2750

(b) enter the above transactions into page 21 of the *analysed* purchases day book including columns for VAT, net, furniture, and carpets

(b) total the day book at 30 April 2004

Notes:

- folio entries are *not* required.
- entries in the purchases ledger and main ledger are *not* required

12 Balancing accounts and control account for purchases

this chapter covers . . .

In the previous chapter we saw how to record credit purchases and purchases returns transactions in the ledger accounts of the double-entry system. In this chapter we will develop the double-entry system by using purchases ledger control account in the main ledger with the individual creditors' accounts being held in the subsidiary (purchases) ledger.

Before looking at the use of purchases ledger control account we need to recap on how to balance accounts. This topic has been covered already in Chapter 4 (when we were dealing with Unit 1 of NVQ in Accounting); however, it is also specifically referred to in the Knowledge and Understanding for Unit 2, so it is important to check out your skills again.

NVQ PERFORMANCE CRITERIA COVERED

unit 2: MAKING AND RECORDING PAYMENTS

element 2.1

process documents relating to goods and services received

F enter invoices and credit notes in the appropriate ledgers

KNOWLEDGE AND UNDERSTANDING COVERAGE

ACCOUNTING METHODS

5 double entry book-keeping, including balancing accounts

BALANCING ACCOUNTS – A RECAP

It is important for you to acquire the skill of balancing accounts for your NVQ Accounting Unit 2. This topic has been covered already in Chapter 4 (pages 73 - 76) and you might want to refer back to the practical steps involved in balancing accounts.

The objective of balancing accounts is to show the running total of the account to date, for example:

- the amount of purchases made
- the amount of purchases returns
- the amount owing to each creditor
- the amount of VAT due to or from HM Customs & Excise

Set out below is an example of a creditor's account which has been balanced at the month-end:

Dr		**Phoenix Traders**			Cr
2004		£	2004		£
13 Sep	Purchases Returns	50	1 Sep	Balance b/d	530
28 Sep	Purchases Returns	100	8 Sep	Purchases	260
30 Sep	Balance c/d	810	21 Sep	Purchases	170
		960			960
			1 Oct	Balance b/d	810

The four steps to balancing the above account are:

Step 1: in pencil, total the entries in the debit and credit money columns – here they are £150 on the debit side, and £960 on the credit side.

Step 2: calculate the difference between the two amounts in Step 1 – here it is £960 – £150 = £810; enter this amount on the side with the smaller total, using the date of balancing (here 30 September) and the description 'Balance c/d'.

Step 3: total both sides of the account (here £960) and bold – underline or double-underline each total; make sure that the two totals are on the same line on each side of the account

Step 4: complete double-entry book-keeping by recording an equal but opposite entry to the balance c/d; this is entered on the first available line below the totals 'boxes' and is described as 'balance b/d'; the date shown is usually recorded as the next day after 'balance c/d' (here it is 1 October).

FURTHER EXAMPLES OF BALANCING ACCOUNTS

ARJ Limited

Dr					Cr
2004		£	2004		£
30 Apr	Balance c/d	880	1 Apr	Balance b/d	360
			6 Apr	Purchases	170
			14 Apr	Purchases	200
			22 Apr	Purchases	150
		880			880
			1 May	Balance b/d	880

The above creditor's account has transactions on one side only, but is still balanced in the same way. This account shows that, according to the accounting records, ARJ Limited is owed £880, ie is a creditor of the business.

Harper and Company

Dr					Cr
2004		£	2004		£
3 Sep	Purchases Returns	280	1 Sep	Balance b/d	280
20 Sep	Purchases Returns	110	13 Sep	Purchases	110
		390			390

This creditor's account has a 'nil' balance after the transactions for September have taken place. The two sides of the account are totalled and, as both debit and credit side are the same amount, there is nothing further to do, apart from entering the bold- or double-underlined total.

Purchases Returns Account

Dr					Cr
2004		£	2004		£
			31 Jan	Purchases Returns Day Book	120

This account has just the one transaction and, in practice, there is no need to balance it. It should be clear that the account has a credit balance of £120 which is the amount of purchases returns for what is probably the first month of a new financial year.

Dr		D Patel			Cr
2004		£	2004		£
6 Dec	Purchases Returns	120	1 Dec	Balance b/d	120

This creditor's account has a 'nil' balance, with just one transaction on each side. All that is needed here is to bold- or double-underline the amount on both sides.

PURCHASES LEDGER CONTROL ACCOUNT

The previous chapter looked at the basics of the double-entry book-keeping system for credit purchases and purchases returns. This system uses a main ledger – which contains the accounts for purchases, purchases returns, and VAT – and a purchases ledger which contains the accounts of the creditors from whom the business has bought goods on credit terms. As we did with credit sales, we are now going to develop the book-keeping system by introducing a control account: here it is the purchases ledger control account which fits in with the book-keeping for credit purchases and purchases returns.

The concept of control accounts has been discussed earlier (pages 76-79), so here we will focus on the layout of the purchases ledger control account.

The set-out of a purchases ledger control account (also known as creditors control account) is shown below. The layout is explained on the next page. Note that some of the items have not yet been covered – they will be dealt with in later chapters.

Dr	Purchases Ledger Control Account		Cr
	£		£
Cash/cheques paid to creditors		Balance b/d	
Settlement (cash) discount received		Credit purchases	
Purchases returns		Interest charged by creditors	
Set-off/contra entries			
Balance c/d			
		Balance b/d	

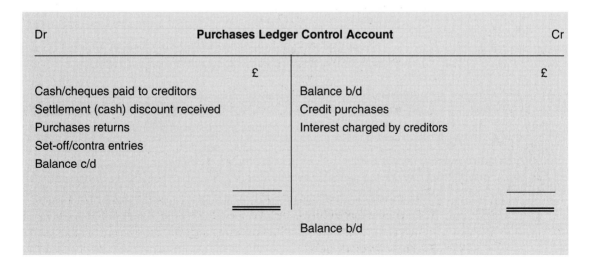

balance b/d

The figure for balance b/d on the credit side of the control account represents the total of the balances of the individual creditors' accounts in the purchases ledger. This principle is illustrated in the diagram on the next page.

Note that it is possible for a creditor's account to have a debit balance, instead of the usual credit balance – for example, if the creditor has been overpaid. Most accounting systems 'net off' any such debit balances against the credit balances to give an overall figure for creditors.

credit purchases

Only credit purchases – and not cash purchases – are entered in the control account. However, the total purchases of the business will comprise both credit and cash purchases.

interest charged by creditors

If a creditor charges interest because of slow payment, this must be recorded on both the creditor's account and the control account. The supervisor might well enquire of the creditor why and how the interest has been calculated.

set-off/contra entries

See page 234.

reconciliation of purchases ledger control account

The diagram on the next page shows how a purchases ledger control account acts as a totals account for the creditors of a business. Reconciliation (agreement) of the balances on the purchases ledger control account and subsidiary accounts is made as follows:

Reconciliation of purchases ledger control account

	1 January 2004	*31 January 2004*
	£	£
F Francis	100	200
G Gold	200	350
H Harris	300	500
I Ingram	400	900
Purchases ledger control account	1,000	1,950

Any discrepancy should be investigated immediately and the error(s) traced.

Dr — Purchases Ledger Control Account — Cr

2004		£	2004		£
31 Jan	Purchases returns	150	1 Jan	Balance b/d	1,000
31 Jan	Bank	594	31 Jan	Purchases	1,700
31 Jan	Discount received	6			
31 Jan	Balance c/d	1,950			
		2,700			2,700
			1 Feb	Balance b/d	1,950

SUBSIDIARY (PURCHASES) LEDGER

Dr — F Francis — Cr

2004		£	2004		£
16 Jan	Bank*	98	1 Jan	Balance b/d	100
16 Jan	Discount received*	2	2 Jan	Purchases	200
31 Jan	Balance c/d	200			
		300			300
			1 Feb	Balance b/d	200

Dr — G Gold — Cr

2004		£	2004		£
15 Jan	Purchases returns	50	1 Jan	Balance b/d	200
28 Jan	Bank*	100	9 Jan	Purchases	300
31 Jan	Balance c/d	350			
		500			500
			1 Feb	Balance b/d	350

Dr — H Harris — Cr

2004		£	2004		£
28 Jan	Purchases returns	100	1 Jan	Balance b/d	300
30 Jan	Bank*	200	16 Jan	Purchases	500
31 Jan	Balance c/d	500			
		800			800
			1 Feb	Balance b/d	500

Dr — I Ingram — Cr

2004		£	2004		£
22 Jan	Bank*	196	1 Jan	Balance b/d	400
22 Jan	Discount received*	4	27 Jan	Purchases	700
31 Jan	Balance c/d	900			
		1,100			1,100
			1 Feb	Balance b/d	900

Note that the book-keeping transactions for 'bank' and 'discount received' will be explained fully in Chapter 15.

SET-OFF/CONTRA ENTRIES

These entries occur when the same person or business has an account in both subsidiary ledgers – sales ledger and purchases ledger – ie they are both buying from, and selling to, the business whose accounts we are preparing. For example, M Patel Limited has the following accounts in the subsidiary sales and purchases ledgers:

SUBSIDIARY (SALES) LEDGER

Dr	**A Smith**		Cr
	£		£
Balance b/d	200		

SUBSIDIARY (PURCHASES) LEDGER

Dr	**A Smith**		Cr
	£		£
		Balance b/d	300

From these accounts we can see that:

- A Smith owes M Patel Limited £200 (sales ledger)
- M Patel Limited owes A Smith £300 (purchases ledger)

To save each having to write out a cheque to send to the other, it is possible (with A Smith's agreement) to set-off one account against the other, so that they can settle their net indebtedness with one cheque. The book-keeping entries in M Patel's books will be:

– *debit* A Smith (purchases ledger) £200

– *credit* A Smith (sales ledger) £200

The accounts will now appear as:

SUBSIDIARY (SALES) LEDGER

Dr	**A Smith**		Cr
	£		£
Balance b/d	200	Set-off: purchases ledger	200

SUBSIDIARY (PURCHASES) LEDGER

Dr	A Smith		Cr
	£		£
Set-off: sales ledger	200	Balance b/d	300

The net result is that M Patel Limited owes A Smith £100. The important point to note is that, because transactions have been recorded in the subsidiary accounts, an entry needs to be made in the two control accounts:

– *debit* purchases ledger control account

– *credit* sales ledger control account

Set-off transactions should be appropriately documented and authorised. The book of prime entry for set-off transactions is the journal (see Chapter 20).

INFORMATION SOURCES FOR PURCHASES LEDGER CONTROL ACCOUNT

Control accounts use totals (remember that their other name is totals accounts) for the week, month, quarter or year – depending on what time period is decided upon by the business. The totals for purchases ledger control account come from a number of sources in the accounting system:

- total credit purchases (including VAT) – from the 'total' column of the purchases day book
- total purchases returns (including VAT) – from the 'total' column of the purchases returns day book
- total cash/cheques paid to creditors – from the cash book (see Chapter 15)
- total settlement discount received – from the discount received column of the cash book (see Chapter 15), or from discount received account

CONTROL ACCOUNTS AS AN AID TO MANAGEMENT

As we have already seen in Chapter 4, control accounts provide important information for the manager of a business. For example, from purchases ledger control account, the manager can find out quickly the figure for creditors without having to go through the subsidiary (purchases) ledger and add up the balances of the individual creditors' accounts. With a computer accounting system control accounts can be printed out at any time.

Other benefits of control accounts include:

- fraud is made more difficult because fraudulent transactions have to be entered in both the control account and the subsidiary account
- locating errors is made easier because the control account is able to demonstrate the arithmetical accuracy of the subsidiary accounts which it controls

PURCHASES LEDGER CONTROL ACCOUNT AND BOOK-KEEPING

The usual way of using control accounts is to incorporate them into the double-entry book-keeping system. This means that purchases ledger control account is in the main ledger while the individual accounts of creditors are held as subsidiary accounts in the subsidiary (purchases) ledger.

The diagram on the opposite page illustrates this.

From time-to-time, the balances of the subsidiary accounts are agreed with the balance of the control account, and any discrepancies investigated. When a purchases ledger control account is in use and journal entries are made (eg for correction of errors – see Chapter 21), transactions involving creditors' accounts must be recorded in

- the purchases ledger control account in the main ledger
- the subsidiary (purchases) ledger

the role of control accounts

Now that we have studied the two control accounts for purchases ledger and sales ledger, it is worth taking a few moments to confirm the position of control accounts in relation to double-entry book-keeping.

The way in which we have used control accounts (and also the usual way in which you will find them in Skills Tests and Examinations) is for the control accounts to be part of double-entry book-keeping. Thus, when we look at the trial balance (in Chapter 21), it is the balance of the control account that is used to give us the trial balance figures for debtors and creditors. As control accounts are part of double-entry book-keeping – in the main ledger – then it follows that the subsidiary ledgers for purchases and sales are not part of double-entry book-keeping. Nevertheless, the subsidiary ledgers are important because they tell us the balances of each individual debtor and creditor account. Also, it is good accounting practice to reconcile (agree) the balance of each control account to its subsidiary ledger balances at regular intervals.

- **Purchases ledger control account incorporated into the double-entry book-keeping system**
- **Creditors' accounts in the subsidiary (purchases) ledger**

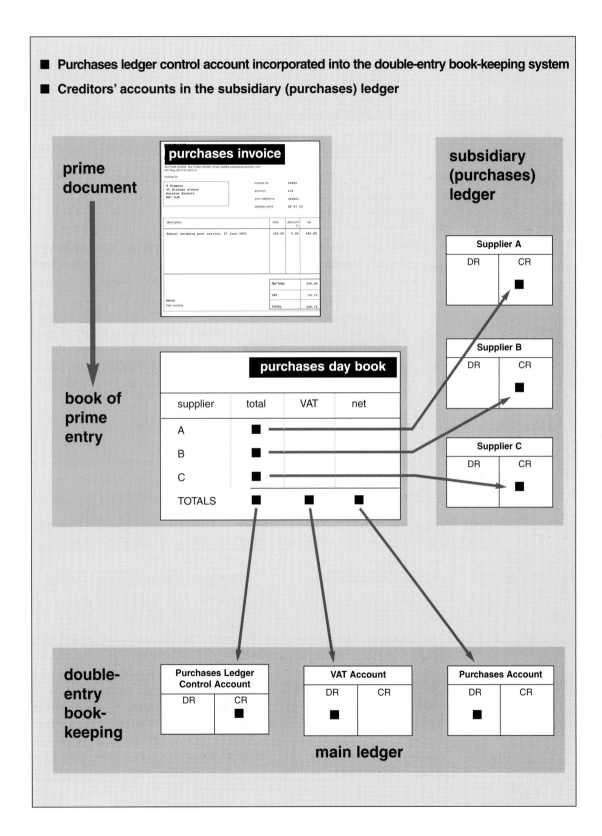

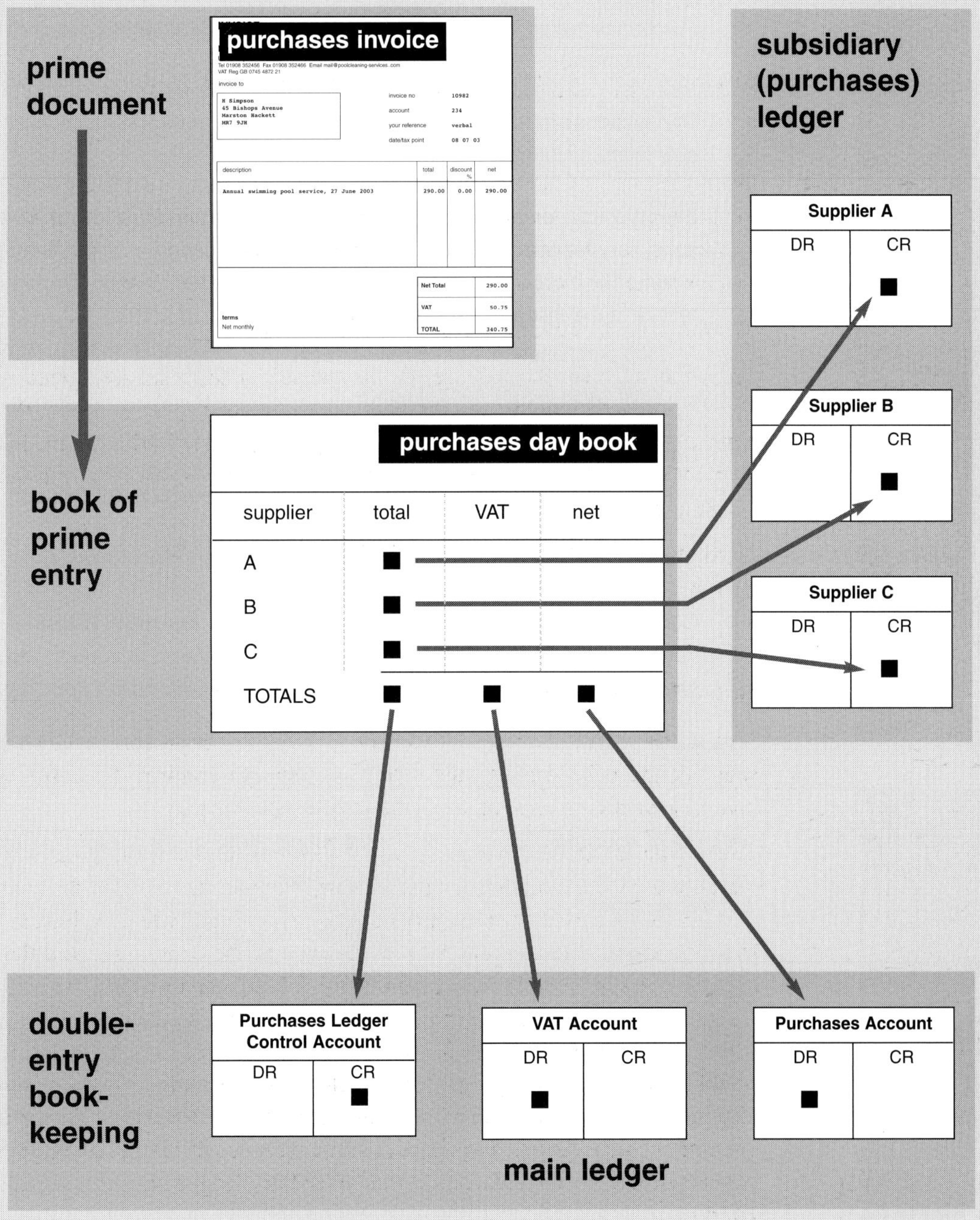

Chapter Summary

- The traditional 'T' account needs to be balanced at regular intervals – often the month-end.
- The 'balance b/d' is the account balance at the start of the next period.
- Purchases ledger control account acts as a totals account for the creditors of a business.
- Transactions are recorded on the same side of the control account as on the subsidiary accounts.
- Set-off/contra entries occur when one person has an account in both subsidiary ledgers – sales ledger and purchases ledger – and it is agreed to set-off one balance against the other to leave a net balance. This usually results in the following control account entries:
  - *debit* purchases ledger control account
  - *credit* sales ledger control account
- Control accounts are an aid to management:
  - they give up-to-date information on the total of creditors (or debtors)
  - by making fraud more difficult
  - in helping to locate errors
- Control accounts are normally incorporated into the main ledger of the double-entry book-keeping system. The subsidiary accounts, eg for creditors, are in a separate subsidiary ledger – subsidiary (purchases) ledger.

Key Terms

balance of account	the running total of the account to date
control account	a 'master' account which controls a number of subsidiary accounts
purchases ledger control account	account which acts as a totals account for the creditors of a business
set-off/contra entries	where balances in the subsidiary (sales) ledger and the subsidiary (purchases) ledger are to be set-off against one another

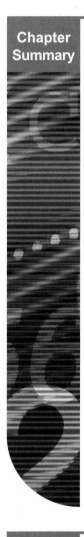

Student Activities

12.1 Balance the following accounts at 30 November 2004, bringing down the balance on 1 December:

Dr		**Purchases Account**			Cr
2004			£	2004	£
1 Nov	Balance b/d		64,287		
30 Nov	Purchases Day Book		6,720	*30 Nov Bal c/d*	*71,007*
			71,007		*71,007*
	1 Dec Bal b/d		*71,007*		

Dr		**Purchases Returns Account**			Cr
2004			£	2004	£
				1 Nov Balance b/d	1,349
				30 Nov Purchases Returns Day Book	160
30 Nov	*Bal c/d*		*1509*		*1509*
			1509		*1509*
				1 Dec Bal b/d	

Dr		**Value Added Tax Account**			Cr
2004			£	2004	£
30 Nov	Purchases Day Book		1,176	1 Nov Balance b/d	644
				30 Nov Purchases Returns Day Book	28
				30 Nov Bal c/d	*504*
			1,176		*1,176*
1 Dec Bal b/d			*504*		

Dr		**Ryan and Company**			Cr
2004			£	2004	£
				1 Nov Balance b/d	348
				4 Nov Purchases	427
				19 Nov Purchases	311
30 Nov	*Bal c/d*		*1342*	24 Nov Purchases	256
			1342		*1342*
				1 Dec Bal b/d	*1342*

Dr		**Murray Limited**			Cr
2004			£	2004	£
1 Nov	Balance b/d		15	8 Nov Purchases	230
11 Nov	Purchases Returns		42	16 Nov Purchases	315
				24 Nov Purchases	171
30 Nov	*Bal c/d*		*659*		*716*
			716		*716*
				1 Dec Bal b/d	*659*

12.2 You have the following information:

- opening creditor balances at start of month £15,300 *CR*
- credit purchases for month £8,100 *CR*
- purchases returns for month £200 *Dr*

What is the figure for closing creditor balances at the end of the month?

(a) £7,000

(b) £7,400

(c) £23,200

(d) £23,600

Answer (a) or (b) or (c) or (d)

12.3 Prepare a purchases ledger control account for the month of April 2004 from the following information:

DR PLCA CR

2004			£
1 Apr	Credit balance brought down	*CR*	14,275
30 Apr	Credit purchases for month	*CR*	36,592
	Purchases returns	*Dr.*	653
	Payments made to creditors	*Dr*	31,074
	Transfer of credit balances to sales ledger		597

1/4 Bal b/d 14,275
30/4 PRDB 653 30/4 Purch DB 36,59
Pay 31,074

The creditors figure at 30 April is to be entered as the balancing figure.

12.4 The main ledger of Rowcester Traders contains the following accounts on 1 February 2004:

purchases, balance £4,397.21 debit

purchases returns, balance £456.29 credit

Value Added Tax, balance £524.86 credit

The subsidiary (purchases) ledger contains the following accounts on 1 February 2004:

Apple Supplies Limited, balance £1,843.22 credit

Beatty Brothers, £51.47 debit

J Johnson, £675.38 credit

Myford Limited, balance £478.29 credit

Newtown Equipment Limited, balance £684.86 credit

W Wright, balance £987.20 credit

The following transactions, which have been authorised by the accounts supervisor took place during February 2004 (note that Rowcester Traders gives each invoice and credit note received its own unique number):

3 Feb	Bought goods on credit from Apple Supplies Limited £1,027.98 + VAT, invoice no 6434
5 Feb	Bought goods on credit from Beatty Brothers £150.68 + VAT, invoice no 6435
6 Feb	Bought goods on credit from J Johnson £328.22 + VAT, invoice no 6436
10 Feb	Returned goods to Apple Supplies Limited £157.20 + VAT, credit note no 145
14 Feb	Bought goods on credit from W Wright £476.38 + VAT, invoice no 6437
17 Feb	Returned goods to Newtown Equipment Limited £105.68 + VAT, credit note no 146
24 Feb	Bought goods on credit from Apple Supplies Limited £849.36 + VAT, invoice no 6438
27 Feb	Transfer of debit balance of £154.27 in the subsidiary (sales) ledger to Myford Limited's account in the subsidiary (purchases) ledger

You are to:

(a) prepare the accounts in the main ledger – including a purchases ledger control account – and subsidiary (purchases) ledger of Rowcester Traders and record the balances at 1 February

(b) enter the above purchase invoices and credit notes in Rowcester Traders' purchases day book and purchases returns day book for February 2004

(c) from the books of prime entry, record the accounting entries – together with the set-off – in the main ledger and subsidiary (purchases) ledger, balancing all accounts at the month-end

(d) reconcile the control account balance with the subsidiary accounts at 1 February and 29 February 2004

13 Making payments

this chapter covers . . .

This chapter explains the different ways in which payments are prepared and made by an organisation; it sets out the procedures followed to make sure that all payments are authorised and that confidentiality is maintained. The chapter covers the areas of:

- *making payments by cheque*
- *making payments by inter-bank transfer: giro credits, CHAPS and BACS (computer) payments such as standing orders, direct debits and autopay systems*

Two other forms of making payment are covered by separate chapters:

- *payroll payments and accounting records are explained in Chapter 14.*
- *petty cash payments and accounting records are explained in Chapter 16.*

The recording of payments in the accounting records is covered in Chapter 15.

This chapter explains the manual completion of documents. Processing payment transactions using ***computer accounting*** *is dealt with in Chapter 28.*

NVQ PERFORMANCE CRITERIA COVERED

unit 2: MAKING AND RECORDING PAYMENTS

element 2.2: process payments

A *calculate payments from relevant documentation*

B *schedule payments and obtain authorisation*

C *use the appropriate payment method and timescale, in accordance with organisational procedures*

E *identify queries and resolve or refer to the appropriate person*

F *ensure security and confidentiality is maintained according to organisational requirements*

OUTGOING PAYMENTS

If you work for an organisation, you will readily appreciate that there are different types of payments involved; some will involve the issue of cheques or cash, some will involve paying money from the organisation's bank account direct to the recipient's bank account, other will involve paying wages and salaries. Here are some typical examples of these different forms of payment:

issue of cheques

- paying suppliers by cheque for goods and services against invoices and statements
- paying for 'one-off' items of *capital* expenditure, eg a computer system
- paying bills (*revenue* expenditure) by cheque and bank giro credit
- making small one-off 'cash' purchases

paying through the bank account

- paying wages
- paying regular suppliers for goods and services
- paying bills, for example business rates

PAYING TRADE SUPPLIERS

internal procedures

Each business or organisation will have its own policies and regulations laid down to ensure that payments to suppliers of goods and services are only made when the goods and services have been received as ordered. A supplier of goods and services is therefore paid when:

- the documents relating to the transaction – the purchase order, delivery note (or goods received note) and invoice have been checked against each other (they are normally filed together)
- any credit due, eg for returned goods, has been received in the form of a credit note
- all discounts, whether *settlement (cash) discount* (for early payment) or *trade discount* or *bulk discount* have been identified and allowed for
- the payment has received the necessary authorisation – often in the form of a supervisor's initials on the invoice, or a rubber stamp

timescales – when to pay?

Each business or organisation will also have its own policies and regulations dictating *when* payment is to be made.

payment on invoice – diary system

Businesses or organisations often pay strictly according to the *due date of the invoice*. Each invoice (and all the accompanying documentation), when it is received will be marked with the due date of payment – eg 30 days after the invoice issue date – and placed in a diary system. With this system a business may make individual payments to different suppliers on any number of days of the month. The system is best suited to small businesses which do not have too many payments to make.

payment runs – based on statements

Another widely adopted system is for suppliers to be paid regularly on the basis of the monthly statement issued rather than in response to individual invoices. A business using this system will set up *payment runs* – ie days on which payments will be made during the month. This might be once a month on the last day of the month, or it could be on the second and last Friday of the month – it is up to the business to decide. On each payment run date the supplier statements will be examined and outstanding items paid (unless they are disputed). This system is easy to manage, particularly if the payments are computerised (see below) as only a limited number of payment runs are needed each month to originate either computer-printed cheques or BACS (inter-bank) payments.

payment schedule and remittance advices

We have already seen that the remittance advice tells the supplier what is being paid, either:

- by *cheque,* in which case the remittance advice accompanies the payment, or
- by *BACS* (inter-bank computer payment), in which case the remittance advice is sent separately by post, fax, or by e-mail

If your job is to make payments and prepare remittance advices, you will probably have a *schedule* of payments to work from, with the payment amount already decided upon and authorised by a supervisor.

paying by cheque

If you are paying a supplier you should attach the cheque to the remittance advice. This may be a tear-off slip attached to the supplier's statement of account, or it may be a standard form used within your organisation. An example of the latter is illustrated on the next page and an example of a cheque on page 246. You should note that the following details are shown:

- the date of the payment
- the amount of the cheque
- the details – ie the reference number ('your reference') and date – of the invoice(s) being paid
- the details (reference number and date) of any credit notes deducted
- the purchaser's order number ('our reference')
- the account number of the buyer (from the sales ledger of the seller)

In addition the remittance advice may show further details such as the cheque number and the amount of any settlement (cash) discount deducted for early settlement (there is none in the illustration).

REMITTANCE ADVICE

TO
Cool Socks Limited
Unit 45 Elgar Estate,
Broadfield, BR7 4ER

FROM
Trends
4 Friar Street
Broadfield
BR1 3RF
Tel 01908 761234 Fax 01908 761987
VAT REG GB 0745 8383 56

Account 3993 31 October 2003

date	your reference	our reference	payment amount
01 10 03	INVOICE 787923	47609	277.30
10 10 03	CREDIT NOTE 12157	47609	(27.73)
		CHEQUE TOTAL	249.57

a remittance advice accompanying a cheque payment

payment of suppliers by BACS

The use of BACS, the inter-bank computer payment system, will be dealt with in detail later in the chapter. All BACS payments must be communicated to the supplier by means of a posted, faxed, or emailed remittance advice, otherwise the supplier will not know that payment has been made until the bank statement is received, and even then it may be difficult to identify the origin of the payment. If the supplier does not know payment has been received, he or she may start chasing up the debt, which could prove embarrassing!

A BACS remittance advice is illustrated on page 105.

ISSUING OF CHEQUES

Cheques may be either completed manually, or printed out on a computer printer.

When writing out (using ink, not pencil) or typing out the cheque you should take care to complete the

- correct date
- name of the payee (person receiving the money)
- amount in words
- amount in figures (which should be the same!)
- authorised signature (it may be your signature, it may be that of a supervisor or manager)
- counterfoil (date, amount, payee)

No room should be left on the cheque for possible fraudulent additions or alterations; any blank spaces should be ruled through. If any errors are made when you are writing out the cheque, they should be corrected and an authorised signature placed close to the alteration in order to tell the bank that it is an approved correction.

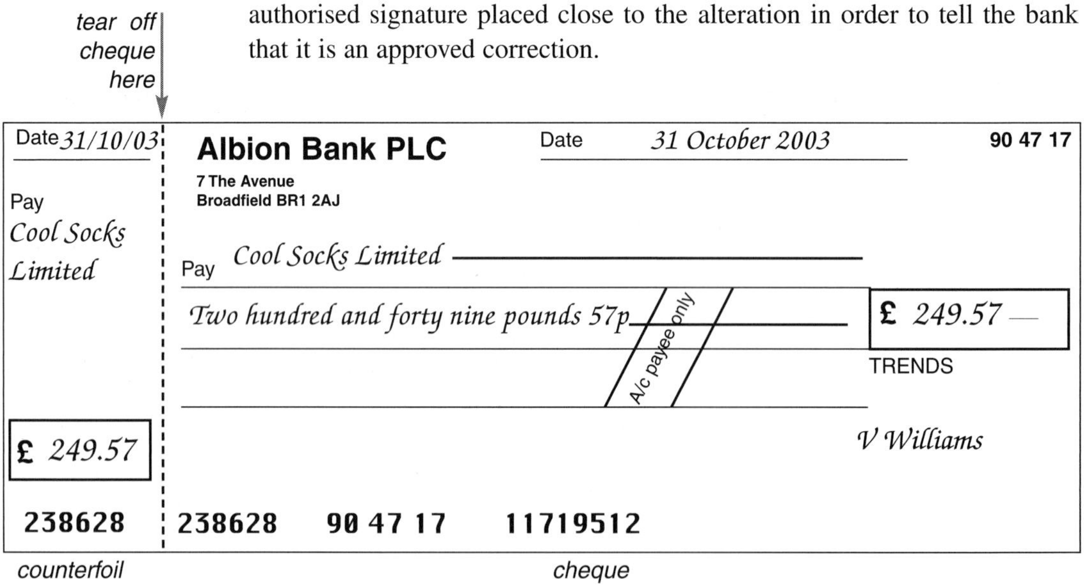
tear off cheque here
Date 31/10/03
Pay
Cool Socks Limited
£ 249.57
238628
Albion Bank PLC
7 The Avenue
Broadfield BR1 2AJ
Date 31 October 2003
90 47 17
Pay Cool Socks Limited
Two hundred and forty nine pounds 57p
A/c payee only
£ 249.57
TRENDS
V Williams
238628 90 47 17 11719512
counterfoil
cheque

Computer cheque printing is increasingly used by organisations which use computer accounting programs with a purchase ledger facility. The computer will automatically indicate payments that are due and, subject to authorisation, print out the remittance advice and cheque together, ready for posting. Clearly the computer involved must be closely controlled – and probably password protected – in order to prevent unauthorised access and fraudulent payments.

PAYING FOR 'ONE-OFF' ITEMS – CHEQUE REQUISITION FORMS

So far we have looked at the payment of trade suppliers who supply on a regular basis for the normal activities of an organisation, eg merchants who supply potatoes for crisps manufacturers. The procedure for the issue of cheques in this case is reasonably straightforward. There will be times, however, when a cheque is needed for a 'one-off' purpose, for example:

- purchase of an item of equipment, authorised by the organisation
- reimbursement of 'out-of-pocket' expenses incurred by an employee
- payment of a pro-forma invoice (a pro-forma invoice is a request for payment to be made before the supply of the goods or services – contrast this with a normal invoice when payment follows supply)

The normal procedure in these cases is the completion of a cheque requisition form by the person who needs the cheque, as shown below.

Mercia Pumps Limited
CHEQUE REQUISITION FORM

Required by **Tom Paget** Department **Marketing**

CHEQUE DETAILS

date for cheque **31 March 2003**

payable to **Media Promotions Limited**

amount £ **360.00**

despatch to (if applicable) **Media Promotions Limited, 145 High Street, Mereford, MR1 3TF**

reason **Advert in trade journal** nominal code **7556**

DOCUMENTATION

invoice attached/~~to follow~~ **invoice 24516**

receipt attached/to follow

other

AUTHORISATION *Andrew Wimbush, Marketing Director* date *31 March 2003*

a cheque requisition form

Note the following details on the cheque requisition form:

- the cheque has been ordered by Tom Paget, but is to be sent direct to Media Promotions Limited
- the requisition is authorised by Andrew Wimbush, the Marketing Director
- the invoice is attached
- the nominal ledger code is included – this is the category of expense for which an account is maintained in the computer accounting system of the business – 7556 is the computer account number for 'advertising account'; if the business did not have a computer accounting system the name of the account in the main ledger – 'advertising' – would be entered

CONTROL AND AUTHORISATION OF PAYMENTS

spending limits

In order to avoid fraud or unchecked spending within an organisation, all payments must be controlled and authorised. We have seen that incoming invoices must normally be stamped, and signed or initialled by an authorised person before being passed for payment. This is part of an overall system whereby no payment can be made without the necessary authority. The system will vary from organisation to organisation, but the following elements will be usually be found:

- the larger the payment, the more senior the person who needs to authorise it; often each level of management has a money limit imposed – for example a new vehicle will need to be authorised by senior management
- when an item of expenditure is authorised, the person giving their authority will sign or initial and date the supporting document, eg an invoice, a cheque requisition form

cheque signatures

While an organisation will have an internal system of signing for and authorising expenditure, it will also have a written agreement with the bank – a bank mandate – which will set out who can sign cheques. A limited company or partnership may, for example, allow one director or partner to sign cheques up to £5,000, but will require two to sign cheques in excess of £5,000. It is common to have a number of different signatories to allow for partners and directors going on holiday, going sick and being otherwise unavailable for signing cheques.

cash payments and wages

Most organisations will keep a cash float – petty cash – to allow for small everyday items of expenditure such as taxi fares and coffee for customer reception. The operation of the petty cash system is strictly controlled and documented, and will be dealt with in Chapter 16. Organisations are also likely to use cash, cheques and/or BACS for the payment of wages; this will be dealt with in the next chapter.

PAYING BY BANK GIRO CREDIT

We have already seen in Chapter 6 how money can be paid into a bank account by means of a bank paying-in slip. So far we have looked at an organisation which pays in at its own branch, and receives the money in the account on the same day. The banking system also allows for a *bank giro credit* to be paid in at one branch and processed through a three day clearing system (like the cheque clearing system) to another bank or branch. The bank credit clearing system is widely used for:

- paying bills (electricity, gas, telephone)
- settling credit card accounts

The preprinted bank giro credit is usually a tear-off slip at the bottom of a bill. The person or business paying the bill will fill in:

- the amount of the payment
- the date that the payment is being made at the bank
- in some cases the signature of the person paying in the credit at the bank

The bill is then taken to the bank and paid in, together with a cheque for the appropriate amount. A water bill is shown below.

It should be noted that the practice of a business using blank giro credits for 'one-off' payments or for paying suppliers and wages has now largely been discontinued, because of the amount of fraud that was taking place.

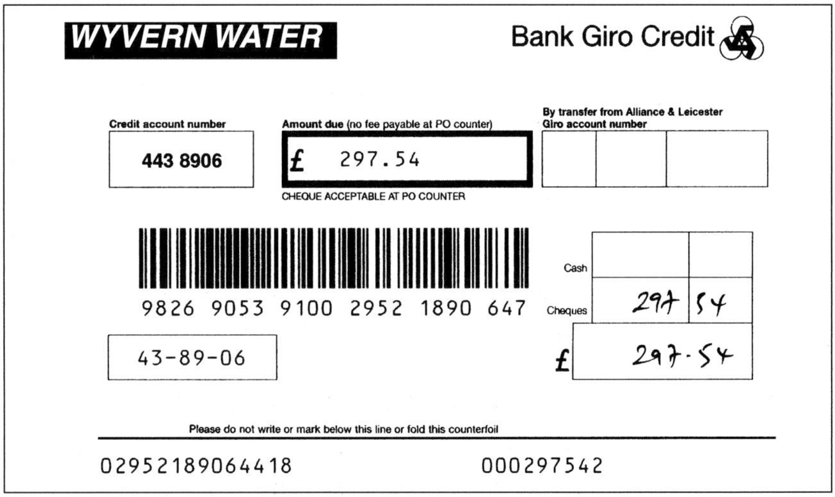
WYVERN WATER

Bank Giro Credit

Credit account number: 443 8906

Amount due (no fee payable at PO counter): £ 297.54

CHEQUE ACCEPTABLE AT PO COUNTER

By transfer from Alliance & Leicester Giro account number

9826 9053 9100 2952 1890 647

43-89-06

Cash

Cheques 297 54

£ 297.54

Please do not write or mark below this line or fold this counterfoil

02952189064418 000297542

BACS PAYMENTS

Bankers Automated Clearing Services (BACS) is a computer transfer payment system owned by the banks. It is widely used for regular payments such as insurance premiums, settlement of trade debts, wages and salaries. BACS is a cheap and efficient means of payment because, instead of a piece of paper having to be prepared and despatched, the transfer is set up on a computer file and transferred between the banks' computers – the payment goes direct from account to account.

The payment cycle is three working days. If a business wants its suppliers or employees to have the money in their accounts on Friday, the money must leave the employer's account on Wednesday. The payment instructions will need to be received by the end of Wednesday, so the accounts department will need to observe this deadline.

STANDING ORDER

The business that needs to make regular payments, eg a loan repayment, completes a written authority (a mandate – see below) instructing the bank what payments to make, to whom, and when. The bank then sets up the instructions on its computer, and the payments are made automatically by computer link on the due dates.

STANDING ORDER MANDATE

To National Bank

Address 45 High Street, Hightown, HT1 7FG

PLEASE PAY TO

Bank Western Branch Radstock Sort code 33 09 87

Beneficiary Mendip Loan Brokers Account number 29384729

The sum of £ 100.00 Amount in words one hundred pounds only

Date of first payment 1 April 2003 Frequency of payment 1st monthly

Until 1 March 2008 Reference FTL294231

Account to be debited Janus Limited Account number 22472434

SIGNATURE(S) *Archie Rice*

If it is a business which is setting up the standing order, it is important that the mandate form is signed by a person (or persons) authorised to do so – it will often be the person(s) authorised to sign cheques.

BACS 'autopay' systems

Businesses often need to make regular payments of variable amounts, for example:

- paying wages on pay day
- making payments to established suppliers at the end of each month

The banks have established a BACS system whereby they set up standing orders to these regular beneficiaries. This has now superseded the practice of completing *blank* bank giro credits for making payments in bulk.

setting up an 'autopay' system

To set up an 'autopay' system the bank needs written instructions from the customer before the amounts can be deducted from the account. What it does, in effect, is to set up a series of standing orders.

The details needed by the bank are:

- the name of the 'beneficiary' – the organisation or person that is to receive the money, eg supplier, employee, insurance company, hire purchase company, etc
- the details of the beneficiary's bank:
  - bank branch
  - sort code number
  - bank account number
- a unique reference number for each beneficiary which is used each time payment is to be made

operating an 'autopay' system

At the end of each month, for example, the accounts department will draw up a list of the suppliers to be paid and a payroll schedule (see the next chapter). Clearly these details will need careful checking and authorisation before instructions are given to the bank. All the business has to do each time payment is to be made is to complete and send to the bank a schedule setting out the payment date, the people who are to receive the money and the amounts. The bank will then process these details through its computers, and payments will be made automatically via the BACS system on the due date. The details may be sent in by post, fax, telephone, or more commonly these days by online instructions.

Case Study

PAYING SUPPLIERS BY 'AUTOPAY'

City Traders is a shop based in Mereford. In an attempt to cut administrative costs the Accounts Department has decided to pay suppliers through the BACS system. The bank has suggested its AutoCredit System. City Traders has supplied the banking details (sort code and account number) of its suppliers in advance for the bank to put in its own computer. City Traders then writes the monthly payment details on the bank schedule shown below, which is faxed to the bank by Wednesday 24 September. The suppliers will be paid on Friday 26 September.

Mercian Bank PLC
AutoCredit Schedule

Bank branch......Mereford......

Originator name..City Traders......reference...07246......

Date ..24-9-03

Branch	*Account no*	*Name*	*Payee no*	*Amount*
45-45-62	10386394	Trendsetters	234	250.00
56-67-23	22347342	FitMan Delivery Co	344	129.76
40-47-07	42472411	Jamesons Ltd	634	450.67
76-87-44	56944491	John Proctor	123	409.79
33-00-77	23442413	Red Skin Company	264	305.78
59-99-01	46244703	Tatters Ltd	197	560.85
		PAYMENT TOTAL		2106.85

Please make the above payments to reach the payees on ....26-9-03.......(date)

Please debit account no......87620261.......with the sum of £...2106.85......

authorised signature.....*J.Craig*......

DIRECT DEBIT

The direct debit system is useful for organisations such as insurance companies that receive a large number of variable payments:

- direct debits can be used for either fixed and variable amounts and/or where the time intervals between payments vary
- it is the receiver (beneficiary) of the payment who prepares the computer instructions that request the payer's bank account for payment through the banking system; a direct debit is like a standing order operating backwards

paper-based direct debit instructions

The traditional procedure for setting up a direct debit was for the customer making payment to complete and sign a written authority (mandate) prepared by the beneficiary (the person getting the money, eg an insurance company); this was then returned to the beneficiary (eg the insurance company). The payment details were then posted off to the beneficiary's bank so that the computer instructions could be set up. The original form was then returned to the payer's bank. An example of a direct debit mandate is shown below.

DIRECT Debit

Tradesure Insurance Company
PO Box 134, Helliford, HL9 6TY

Originator's Identification Number 914208

Reference (to be completed by Tradesure Insurance) 03924540234

Please complete the details and return this form to Tradesure Insurance

name and address of bank/building society

National Bank plc
Market Street
Netherway
MR7 9YT

account name

Grecian Travel Services

instructions to bank/building society

- I instruct you to pay direct debits from my account at the request of Tradesure Insurance Company.
- The amounts are variable and may be debited on various dates.
- I understand that Tradesure Insurance Company may change the amounts and dates after giving me prior notice.
- I will inform the bank/building society if I wish to cancel this instruction.
- I understand that of any direct debit is paid which breaks the terms of this instruction, the bank/building society will make a refund.

account number	sort code	signature(s)	date
10318736	76 54 29	M Callapolos	1 April 2003

problems with paper-based direct debits

As you can see, setting up a paper-based direct debit was a protracted and expensive process, open to error and delay. As a consequence the decision was taken by BACS to allow the direct debit payment instructions to be sent electronically by a system known as AUDDIS (Automated Direct Debit Instruction Service).

AUDDIS – the paperless direct debit

A customer wanting to set up a direct debit through AUDDIS (Automated Direct Debit Instruction Service) does not have to sign anything. The instructions (including bank account number, account name and bank sort code) can be provided by the customer over the telephone or on-line over the internet (see screen details below).

This is useful, for example, if a business wants to arrange finance for an item purchased and needs to set up repayments straightaway. A business subscribing to a service can also give similar repayment instructions – nothing need be in writing.

The organisation setting up the 'paperless' direct debit can then enter the details (the amounts, dates, paying bank) into its computer system and send them electronically to the bank making the payments.

an internet screen for accepting AUDDIS instructions

COMPANY CREDIT CARDS, BANK DRAFTS AND CHAPS

company credit cards

Many organisations, particularly those which employ travelling sales representatives, set up a company credit card scheme. This convenient and useful scheme allows company representatives to have credit cards for paying expenses related to the company's business, eg rail tickets, accommodation and food. The credit card bill is settled by the company which is then able to monitor the expenses incurred by its employees.

bank drafts

An organisation may have to make a large purchase – for example new vehicles – and be asked to pay by bank draft. A bank draft is a bank cheque, a guaranteed means of payment which is as good as cash, but without the security risks. In legal terms the bank is both drawer (issuer) and drawee (issuing bank) of the cheque.

CHAPS

The CHAPS (Clearing House Automated Payments System) payment system is for high value payment sent by the banks through their computer networks. It is used extensively by solicitors when they are arranging the purchase and sale of property for their clients. Businesses use it for high value, same day, transfers.

A similar system exists for making payments abroad through the banks' computer network. The banks provide forms for setting up these payments which are sometimes known as IMT's (International Money Transfers).

ONLINE BANKING

With the growth of the use of the internet, many banks are encouraging their customers to manage their payments online. Electronic banking schemes such as Hexagon from HSBC allow customers:

- to get balances and view past transactions
- to make payments from one account to another
- to set up standing orders
- to make CHAPS and international payments

This makes day-to-day management of the finances of a business much simpler. The bank accounts can be monitored 24 hours a day, and greater control can be exercised over payments and receipts.

Chapter Summary

- Outgoing payments made by an organisation include payments to suppliers, payment of bills, cash payments, 'one-off' items and wages.
- Before paying a supplier an organisation must see that all procedures and timescales are observed.
- Businesses often pay suppliers at the end of the month, they pay on receipt of the statement rather than in response to individual invoices.
- When making payment by cheque or by BACS a business will normally send the supplier a remittance advice.
- Care must be taken when issuing cheques to ensure that the details are correct and that no room is left on the cheque for fraudulent alterations.
- If an employee needs a cheque for a 'one-off' payment, he or she will need to have a cheque requisition form completed and authorised.
- The issue of cheques should be strictly controlled through a system of signing 'limits'; normally the larger the amount, the more senior the signatory and the greater number of signatures.
- Payments may be made through the inter-bank transfer system either in paper form or through computer links.
- Bank giro credits, which take three working days to reach their destination account, are preprinted and are used for paying bills and settling credit card accounts.
- Bank computer-based payments are made through Bankers Automated Clearing Services (BACS). These also take three working days to clear.
- A standing order is authorised by the customer in writing and instructs the bank to make regular BACS payments to the beneficiary.
- If a business needs to send a number of BACS payments on a regular basis but with differing amounts each time – eg when paying regular suppliers – it can ask the bank to set up an 'autopay' system. All it needs to do each month is to complete a bank schedule listing the amounts due and the accounts to which they have to be sent.
- A direct debit is authorised by the customer in writing, over the telephone or the internet and instructs the bank to allow the beneficiary to take sums of money through the BACS from the customer's bank account.
- Other methods of payment include:
  - company credit cards for use by employees for expenses
  - bank drafts (bank cheques which are 'as good as cash')
  - CHAPS (computer inter-bank same day payments, usually for large amounts)
- The growth of internet banking has given businesses greater control and flexibility over making payments, and at the same time has allowed them to monitor their bank accounts more closely.

Key Terms

remittance advice	a document sent by the buyer to the supplier to advise the details of payment being made
cheque requisition form	an internal form which is completed and authorised when a cheque needs to be issued, normally for a 'one-off' payment
bank giro credit	a paper slip (used largely for paying bills) which passes through the bank clearing system to the bank of the organisation receiving payment
BACS	the BACS system (Bankers Automated Clearing Services) passes payments through the banking system by computer transfer
beneficiary	the person or organisation who gets the money placed in his/her bank account
standing order	a BACS payment where the person paying the money sets up a regular series of payments through his/her bank
direct debit	A BACS payment where the person paying the money authorises the supplier's bank to take money from their bank account
AUDDIS	AUDDIS (Automated Direct Debit Instruction Service) allows the customer to authorise a direct debit by telephone or on-line and the beneficiary to send those instructions electronically to the payer's bank
autopay system	a system whereby periodic payments can be made to a number of suppliers through the BACS system – the payer completes a schedule setting out the amounts and beneficiaries and passes it to the bank
company credit card	a credit card – in the name of the company – issued to a company employee and used for paying expenses
bank draft	a cheque issued by a bank (and drawn on the bank) purchased by a customer as a payment which is 'as good as cash'
CHAPS	a CHAPS payment (CHAPS = Clearing House Automated Payments System) is a high-value same-day inter-bank computer payment – often used for vehicle and property purchase payments

Student Activities

13.1 The BACS remittance advice is normally attached to the cheque sent in settlement of an account. True or false? *BACS system does not involve cheques* *BACS RA would be sent to person whose acc. # is*

13.2 Why should a cheque not be completed in pencil? *Could be altered fraudulently*

13.3 A cheque requisition form is used for which *one* of the following purposes?

(a) ordering a new cheque book

(b) stopping a cheque

(c) providing specimen signatures to the bank

(d) requesting a cheque within an organisation

13.4 Explain why a partnership or limited company business has to sign a bank mandate. *To authorise signatories for the account?*

13.5 (a) What is the difference between a standing order and a direct debit? *SO set up by bank a/c holder to DD set up by company requiring payment*
State whether a standing order or a direct debit is the better method for the following payments, and why: *SO for set amount DD can vary.*

(b) A repayment of a fixed loan: £125 per month for five years *SO won't change*

(c) A monthly insurance premium which is likely to increase over the years. *DD*

13.6 Name two commonly-used methods suitable for making high value 'one-off' payments:

(a) a paper-based payment *BANK DRAFT*

(b) a computer-based payment *CHAPS Bank to Bank same day transfer*

13.7 Company credit cards are a popular means of making payment.

(a) State one advantage to the employee of the company credit card. *Doesn't have to use own money*

(b) State one advantage to the employer of the company credit card. *Doesn't have to keep petty cash*

For the remainder of the Activities in this chapter you are to take the role of an assistant in the Accounts Department of Nimrod Drainage Limited (a VAT-registered company). Part of your day's work is the preparation of remittance advices and cheques for payments to suppliers. You are not required to sign the cheques. The date is 30 April 2003.

13.8 Your supervisor, Ivor Cash, hands you a list of authorised invoices from Jaeger Building Supplies to pay this month. Calculate the amount of the cheque you will have to make out to send with the remittance advice. You do not need to complete any documents. The date is 30 April 2003.

invoice date	payment terms	invoice total (£)	
31 March	30 days	125.89	*125-89*
2 April	30 days	14,658.95	*14,658-95*
3 April	2.5% cash discount for settlement within 7 days	345.50	*345-50*
9 April	30 days	125.00	*125-00*

15255-34

13.9 Your Supervisor hands you a statement from Mercia Wholesalers, Unit 12 Riverside Industrial Park, Mereford MR2 7GH, with a note, indicating the following invoices to be paid, and a credit note to be set off against payment:

Invoice 8765 dated 12 March 2003, your order number 5517, £765.25

Invoice 8823 dated 2 April 2003, your order number 5792, £3,567.80

Credit note CN 3420 dated 25 April 2003 (your ref R/N 5168), £250.00

Complete the remittance advice and cheque set out below. Note that the total of the credit note should be shown in the money column in brackets, indicating that it is a deduction from the payment.

TO

Mercia Wholesaler
Unit 12 Riverside Industrial Park
Mereford
MR2 7GH

REMITTANCE ADVICE

FROM

Nimrod Drainage
Unit 6, Riverside Park
Mereford
MR4 5TF
Tel 01908 761200 Fax 01908 761900
VAT REG GB 0745 8383 46

Cheque no. 000451 **Date** 30 April 2003

date	your reference	our reference	payment amount
12.3.03	Invoice 8765	5517	765-25
2.4.03	Invoice 8823	5792	3,567-80
25.4.03	Credit Note 3420	R/N 5168	(250-00)
		CHEQUE TOTAL	4,083-05

Date 30/4/03

Nimrod

Drainage

£4,083-05

National Bank PLC
Mereford Branch
10 Cathedral Street, Mereford, MR1 5DE

Date 30 April 2003

35 09 75

Pay Nimrod Drainage only

Four thousand and eighty-three pounds 05p

A/c payee only

£4,083-05

NIMROD DRAINAGE LIMITED
Director Director

000451 000451 35 09 75 12034875

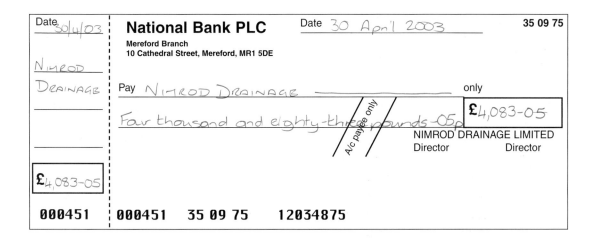

13.10 As an accounts assistant at Nimrod Drainage Limited you have to process the documentation for a wide variety of payments to employees, suppliers and for other business expenses such as one-off purchases, travel costs and bills.

What method of payment would you <u>normally</u> expect to use for the following:

(a) paying wages BACS AUTOPAY

(b) paying the electricity bill which is sent to the business quarterly DD

(c) buying a new car for the Managing Director BANK DRAFT OR CHAPS

(d) paying travelling expenses for sales representatives CREDIT CARD

(e) sending £200,000 to a firm of solicitors for the purchase of new premises
BANK DRAFT / CHAPS

13.11 You have just started work as an accounts assistant and are not authorised to sign cheques or other payment instructions.

The date is 30 April 2003. Your supervisor, Ivor Cash, hands you two documents (shown on the next page):

- a blank standing order form provided by the bank
- a direct debit instruction received from Tradesure Insurance Company

He is in rather a rush and asks you to process the two documents, and to return them to the appropriate address with a compliments slip. He also leaves you a piece of paper with written instructions:

> Note from: Ivor 30 April 2003
>
> Hire Purchase Payments
>
> 12 monthly instalments of £350 to Broadbent Finance from 15 May 2003, under reference BE/6637.
>
> Bank details Barclays, Eveshore, 30 98 15, Account 72627161.
> Debit our Account 12034875

You are to:

(a) complete the forms as required (look at a Nimrod Drainage cheque for your banking details)

(b) state to which address you will send them

(c) comment on any other procedure which you may have to carry out before sending off the forms

STANDING ORDER MANDATE

To NATIONAL Bank

Address MEREFORD BRANCH, 10, CATHEDRAL STREET, MEREFORD, MR1 5DE

PLEASE PAY TO

Bank BARCLAYS Branch EVESHORE Sort code 30 98 15

Beneficiary BROADBENT FINANCE Account number 72627161

The sum of £ 350 Amount in words Three hundred + fifty pounds

Date of first payment 15 May 2003 Frequency of payment Monthly

Until 15 April 2004 Reference BE/6637

Account to be debited NIMROD DRAINAGE Account number 12034875

SIGNATURE(S) ....

.... date 30/4/03

POST TO NATIONAL BANK

DIRECT Debit

Tradesure Insurance Company

PO Box 134, Helliford, HL9 6TY

Originator's Identification Number 914208

Reference (to be completed by Tradesure Insurance) 03924540234

Please complete the details and return this form to Tradesure Insurance

name and address of bank/building society

NATIONAL BANK
10, CATHEDRAL STREET
MEREFORD
MR1 5DE

account name

NIMROD DRAINAGE

instructions to bank/building society

- I instruct you to pay direct debits from my account at the request of Tradesure Insurance Company.
- The amounts are variable and may be debited on various dates.
- I understand that Tradesure Insurance Company may change the amounts and dates after giving me prior notice.
- I will inform the bank/building society if I wish to cancel this instruction.
- I understand that if any direct debit is paid which breaks the terms of this instruction, the bank/building society will make a refund.

account number	sort code	signature(s)	date
12034875	35 09 75		30/4/03

POST TO TRADESURE INS.
GET THEM SIGNED!

14 Payroll payments

this chapter covers . . .

This chapter looks in detail at the completion of the documentation involved in preparing and authorising payroll payments. It also looks at the different ways in which payroll payments can be made. The chapter includes:

- *an overview of the way in which wages and salaries are calculated*
- *an explanation of tax codes and the compulsory and voluntary deductions made from pay*
- *an explanation of the completion of payslips*
- *practical illustrations of the documentation used when making payroll payments*
- *examples of the double-entry accounting entries used when making payroll payments*

NVQ PERFORMANCE CRITERIA COVERED

unit 2: MAKING AND RECORDING PAYMENTS

element 2.2: process payments

A *calculate payments from relevant documentation*

B *schedule payments and obtain authorisation*

C *use the appropriate payment method and timescale, in accordance with organisational procedures*

D *enter payments into accounting records*

E *identify queries and resolve or refer to the appropriate person*

F *ensure security and confidentiality is maintained according to organisational requirements*

WHAT IS PAYROLL?

payroll

Payroll is a system set up by an individual or an organisation employing people which:

- records the personal details of the employees
- records wages or salaries together with any other payments due to them
- arranges for the money to be paid
- calculates appropriate deductions to be made, eg income tax, National Insurance Contributions, student loan repayments
- arranges for the deductions to be paid to the appropriate authority, eg income tax and National Insurance Contributions to the Inland Revenue

It goes without saying that a payroll system must be *accurate* and be kept *confidential.* Employees need to be paid the right amount and they need to be sure that the details of their pay are not circulated to all their colleagues.

manual and computer records

Payroll records may either be maintained manually (on paper) or on a computer-based system. There are a number of commercially available computer systems such as Sage. If a computer system is used it is essential that it has been approved by the Inland Revenue. You can normally assume that commercially available systems have been approved for use.

Any payroll system – manual or computer-based – must meet the needs of:

- the organisation's internal record keeping – its accounting system and employee records
- the employees – paying them promptly and accurately
- outside agencies to which returns have to be made, eg the Inland Revenue

Payroll records should be kept for a minimum of three years after the end of the year of a tax assessment; some organisations keep them for longer periods, eg six years. They should be filed in an organised way as they may be needed not only by the organisation but also by external auditors. They may also be the subject of inspection by the Inland Revenue.

the need for accuracy

The accuracy of the payroll records is essential. Staff must be paid for work done and external authorities such as the Inland Revenue must be paid the correct amount. Input of information into the payroll system (eg hours worked, rates of pay) must be carefully checked and authorised.

the need for security

The system must be organised to minimise the risk of information being corrupted or interfered with. Practical considerations include:

- information must not be processed without authorisation
- information must be checked, whether held manually or input into a computer system
- duties must be separated where possible – different people should carry out the various stages of payroll processing – if just one person did everything, carrying out fraud would become easier

When computers are used, care must be taken that data does not fall into the wrong hands. Practical precautions include:

- ensuring that the payroll program has been exited when the computer is unattended, eg lunchtimes, so that passers-by cannot see confidential data
- changing computer passwords regularly (and not writing them down where they can be seen!)

TYPES OF INCOME

salaries and wages – gross and net pay

An annual **salary** is agreed between employer and employee and a proportionate amount is usually paid in weekly or monthly amounts.

Wages are normally paid weekly. A payment rate for each hour worked is agreed and the employee will be paid for the number of hours worked.

Gross pay is the total amount earned by an employee. It is the basic wage or salary plus any additional payments such as overtime and bonuses.

Net pay is the amount the employee receives after the employer has made tax deductions and voluntary deductions such as pensions.

overtime

Overtime is any time worked beyond what is normal for the working day, or time worked on a day not normally worked. Overtime can be worked by salaried staff and also 'wages' staff.

shift allowances

Shift allowances are extra payments given to staff who work unsocial hours because of the demands of shift working. For example a production worker who works from 12 noon to 8pm may be paid an extra £1 per hour for 6pm to 8pm, or he/she may receive an fixed payment of, say, £10 a week.

bonus payments

A *bonus scheme* is an incentive to employees to reach and exceed set targets, or to save time. For example, an employer may fix the amount of work to be completed in a certain time; if the work target is exceeded, bonus payments will be paid. The bonus payment will be paid either individually to each employee based on his or her performance, or paid as an average bonus to every employee based on the amount by which the target has been exceeded. The bonus, often referred to as a 'productivity bonus', can be paid either as a specific amount of money or as a percentage of the basic pay.

commission

Commission payments are normally made to employees engaged in selling goods or services. A salesperson receives commission on the sales that are made during a specific period. The commission is usually paid as a percentage of the total sales made. Commission could be paid in addition to a basic salary, or instead of a salary.

output-related pay: piece rate payments

Piece rate payment is another form of incentive to employees to work more quickly. The employer will agree a rate of pay for each article produced or operation completed and the employees will be paid only for the work that they have completed. Normally, however, there is an agreement between employer and employees that a minimum wage will be paid regardless of the work completed. An agreement of this nature is to provide the employee with a wage when the employer cannot provide work.

authorisation process – records of attendance

An essential part of the payroll process is that all amounts due must be *authorised* before payment. In order to regularise the authorisation process it is important that all work done must be *documented* accurately and in line with the guidelines set down by the organisation. For staff paid on a time basis, a record of attendance must be kept. Employees' attendance records take a number of different forms which include the following:

- *time book* – a simple 'signing in' book into which is entered the time of arrival and departure and the signature of the employee
- *clock cards* – a card used in conjunction with a time 'clock' – the employee inserts his or her card when arriving and leaving from work
- *time sheets* – records used by employees who work away from the premises
- *'swipe card'* – a card which records the hours on a computer activated by the employee 'swiping' the card through a reader

When you are preparing payroll payment sheets you will need to ensure that the records of attendance – whatever form they may take – have been extracted accurately and suitably authorised.

TAX CREDITS

Another form of income which passes through the payroll process is not part of earnings but a form of State benefit known as a *tax credit*. There are two types of benefit which now appear in the 'wage packet' as tax credits:

- Working Families' Tax Credit (WFTC)
- Disabled Person's Tax Credit (DPTC)

This money which is paid to employees does not come out of the employer's pocket (that would hardly be fair!) but comes from a reduction in the amount of tax which the employer collects from employees and pays to the Inland Revenue. This is why it is called a 'tax credit'.

For example, if an employer pays out £450 in tax credits to employees in a month and owes the Inland Revenue £4,120 in income tax and National Insurance Contributions for that month, the employer will only be out of pocket by £4,120:

money paid by employer in tax credits to employees	£450
money due to Inland Revenue for tax collected	£4,120
less tax credit allowed	(£450)
net amount paid (the same as the tax bill)	£4,120

You will not have to calculate tax credits as part of your course, but you may well see it on documentation – for example on Sage computer payroll payslips – along with Statutory Sick Pay and Statutory Maternity Pay which employers are obliged by law to pay to employees.

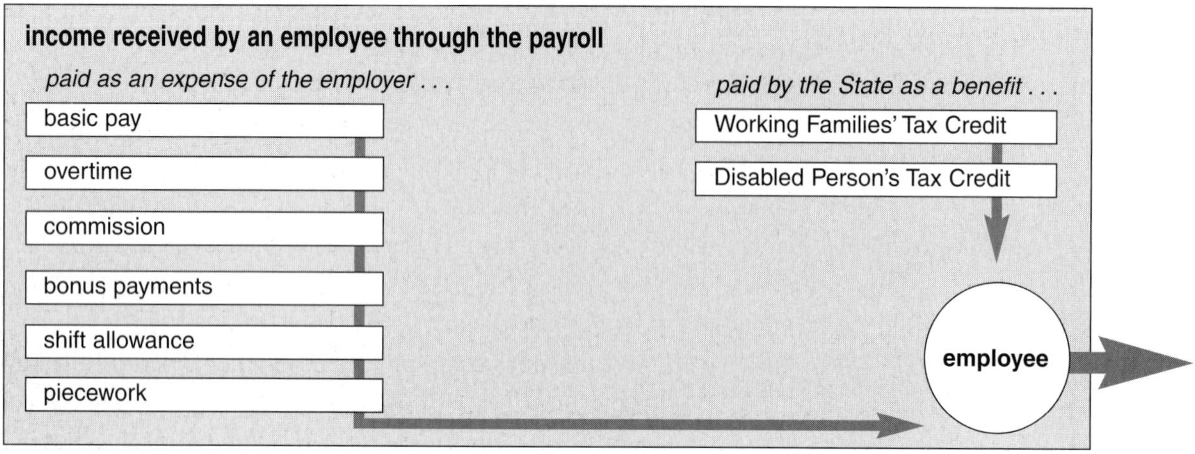

DEDUCTIONS FROM PAY

There are a number of deductions an employer is likely to make from gross pay. Some are *compulsory* and some are *voluntary.*

compulsory deductions from gross pay

An employer must deduct two government taxes as and when they are due:

- income tax
- National Insurance Contributions

Student Loan repayments may also be made from gross pay. If an employee used to be a student and took out a loan under the government scheme when studying, that loan will have to be repaid from earnings. When the student gets a job, the Inland Revenue will issue a notice to the employer with all the details so that deductions can then be made.

voluntary deductions

An employer may deduct the following at the request of the employee:

- payments to charity by means of a Payroll Giving scheme – deducted *before* the tax calculations are made (not shown above)
- pensions (superannuation) scheme payments, stakeholder pensions
- union fees (not shown above)
- SAYE (Save as You Earn) Sharesave Schemes for employees who wish to buy shares in the company that employs them
- payments to lottery syndicates in the workplace
- repayment of loans from employers

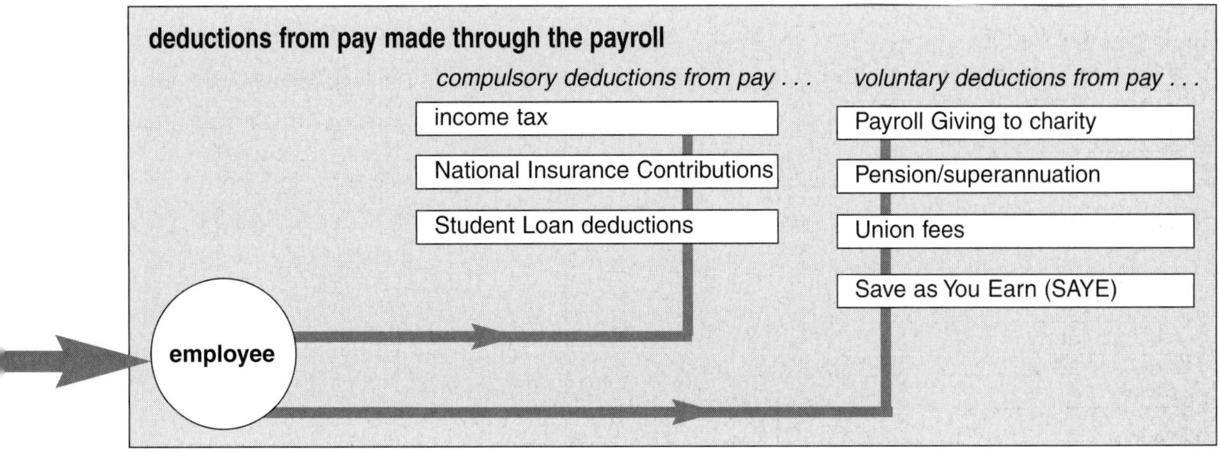

PAY AS YOU EARN – PAYE

what is PAYE?

Pay As You Earn, abbreviated and commonly referred to as *PAYE,* is the arrangement whereby an employer deducts income tax and National Insurance from an employee's gross pay on each pay day. This money is paid to the Inland Revenue by the employer who effectively *collects* the tax for the government. This is quite different from the regulations which apply to a self-employed person who has to settle up personally with the Inland Revenue, normally with a payment every six months.

the tax year

PAYE operates whether the employee is paid weekly, monthly or for any other time period. The income tax and National Insurance collected is normally paid to the Inland Revenue monthly, but can be paid quarterly if the amounts are low.

Tax calculations are based on amounts due on earnings during the course of a 'tax' year – which is *not* the same as a calendar year. The tax year runs from April 6 in one year to April 5 in the next year. The tax year April 6 2003 to April 5 2004, for example, is referred to as the '03/04' tax year.

The tax year is divided into numbered tax 'weeks' and 'months.' These are:

Week	Period	Month	Period
1	6 April to 12 April	1	6 April to 5 May
2	13 April to 19 April	2	6 May to 5 June
3	20 April to 26 April	3	6 June to 5 July
4	27 April to 3 May	4	6 July to 5 August
5	4 May to 10 May	5	6 August to 5 September
6	11 May to 17 May	6	6 September to 5 October
7	18 May to 24 May	7	6 October to 5 November
8	25 May to 31 May	8	6 November to 5 December
9	1 June to 7 June	9	6 December to 5 January
10	8 June to 14 June	10	6 January to 5 February
11	15 June to 21 June	11	6 February to 5 March
12	22 June to 28 June	12	6 March to 5 April
	and so on . . .		

cumulative pay and tax

Any pay day – whether the employee is paid weekly or monthly – will therefore fall in a given tax week or tax month. This is important to appreciate because tax calculations are carried out by reference to the appropriate tax week or month. Calculation of tax through the PAYE system is normally carried out in what is known as a *cumulative* way, ie an employer works out how much tax an employee has to pay using the totals of pay and tax deducted *since the start of the tax year* (April 6). If the payroll is processed manually, sets of tax tables produced by the Inland Revenue, will be used. You do not need to study these for your course.

Note that National Insurance, unlike income tax, is not cumulative.

tax allowances

Income tax is a tax on the income received by an individual. 'Income' for tax purposes means wages and salaries, tips, bonuses, and benefits such as a company car.

Employees do not, fortunately, have to pay tax on all their income. In order to help the lower paid, the Government gives a *tax allowance* known as the *personal allowance*, an amount which can be earned during the tax year on which no tax is paid at all. This tax-free income is known as *Free Pay*.

The amount of the personal allowance varies, depending on factors such as whether employees are over a certain age. Additional *tax allowances* are also available for items such as the purchase of special work clothing.

taxable income

Income which *is* liable to tax is known as *taxable income*. Taxable income is calculated by deducting the tax allowances (eg the personal allowance) from gross income. For any tax year therefore:

Taxable income = gross income minus the tax allowance

The basic personal allowance, for example, for the tax year 2003/2004 is £4,615. With this allowance only income above £4,615 will be taxed.

TAX CODES AND TAX RATES

calculation of the tax code

How does the employer know what allowances have been given to the employee and how much tax to deduct? The Inland Revenue gives each employee a *tax code*, a number which is used by the employer to calculate the taxable pay. The tax code incorporates all the tax allowances, including the personal allowance, and is quoted *less the final digit*. The tax code for someone with a basic personal allowance in the 03/04 year would be 461L, ie £4,615 less the final digit plus the letter 'L'. There are also other tax codes such as BR (Basic Rate) and K codes (a negative personal allowance).

income tax rates

The personal allowances and income tax rates used during a tax year are fixed in the government's previous *Budget.* The Budget – which also sets duties on various items including drink and cigarettes – is usually announced before the beginning of the tax year and receives wide coverage in the media.

There are three rates of income tax applicable to various 'slices' of taxable income.

The figures quoted here (relating to payroll) apply to the 2003/2004 tax year.

- *Starting Rate Tax*: 10%, charged on the first £1,960 of taxable income
- *Basic Rate Tax*: 22%, charged on the remaining taxable income up to £30,500, ie on the next £28,540
- *Higher Rate Tax*: 40%, charged on taxable income over £30,500

If, therefore, you are fortunate to receive more than £30,500 of taxable income, you pay income tax at 10% on the first £1,960 and 22% on £28,540 and 40% on the excess.

Take for example an accounts assistant earning £15,000 a year and a finance director earning £40,000. How much tax do they have to pay during the tax year, and at what rates?

Assume they both receive the basic personal allowance. The calculations (rounded to the nearest £ for simplicity) are as follows:

		accounts assistant		**finance director**
		nearest £		*nearest £*
Gross pay		15,000		40,000
Less personal allowance		4,615		4,615
Taxable pay		10,385		35,385
Income tax @ 10%	1,960 @ 10% =	196	1,960 @ 10% =	196
Income tax @ 22%	8,425 @ 22% =	1,854	28,540 @ 22% =	6,279
Income tax @ 40%		nil	4,885 @ 40% =	1,954
TOTAL INCOME TAX		2,050		8,429

NATIONAL INSURANCE

National Insurance Contributions (NIC) are also deducted by the employer under the PAYE system. All employees, except those under 16 and those over 60 (females) and over 65 (males) are liable to pay National Insurance. In this explanation we refer to the Not Contracted Out Class 1 contributions which are deducted in most payroll systems.

The system described below came into effect on 6 April 2003.

National Insurance is payable *by both employer and employee* once an employee's earnings have reached a certain amount known as the *Earnings Threshold.* This threshold is £89 a week (or £385 a month, or £4,615 a year) in the 2003/04 tax year. The National Insurance payments – once these limits have been reached – are as follows:

employer National Insurance is paid by the employer at a fixed percentage rate (12.8%) on *all earnings* over the Earnings Threshold (ie over £89 a week) – this includes earnings over the Upper Earnings Limit.

employee National Insurance is paid at a fixed percentage rate (11%) up to a maximum amount known as the *Upper Earnings Limit* (£595 a week in the 03/04 tax year). Employees then also pay National Insurance at 1% on any earnings over the Upper Earnings Limit.

The diagram below illustrates the National Insurance Contributions paid by employer and employee in the case of an employee earning £700 a week, ie an amount greater than the Upper Earnings Limit. Note the extra 1% paid by the employee on earnings over the Upper Earnings Limit.

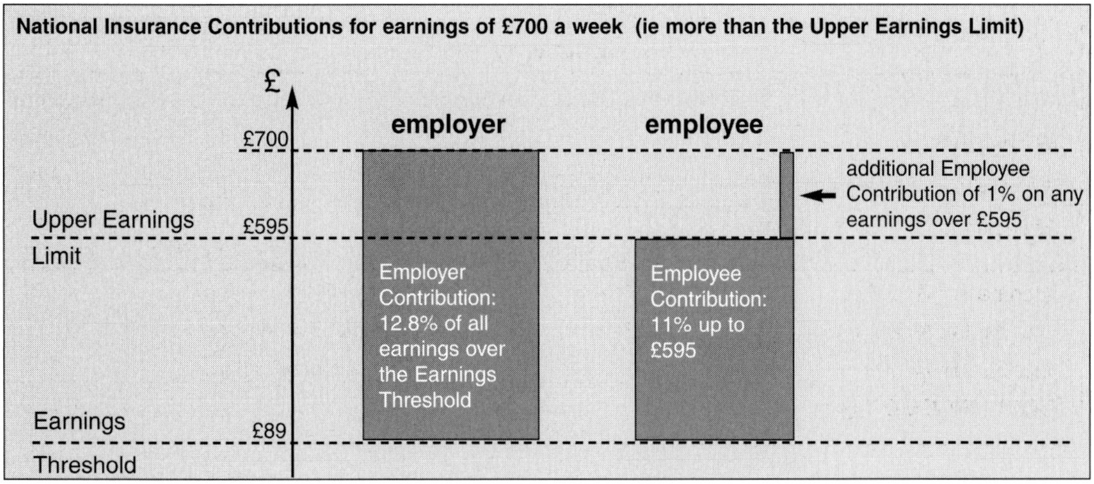

THE PAYSLIP

Employees must by law be given a *payslip* showing gross pay and the deductions made to arrive at net pay. There is no set format for a payslip. Some organisations will write or type out the details on a printed form, other organisations may use a computer payroll program which will calculate all the figures and automatically print out the payslip. A typical payslip for an employee paid monthly is shown below.

OSBORNE ELECTRONICS			**Pay Advice**	June 2003
payments			**deductions**	
		£		£
Basic pay		918.75	Income tax	132.87
Overtime		100.00	National Insurance	70.80
Bonus		20.00	Pension	32.08
TOTAL GROSS PAY		1038.75	Student Loan deduction	20.00
			TOTAL DEDUCTIONS	255.75
Gross pay to date		3427.88		
			TOTAL NET PAY	783.00
Date	**Employee**	**Code**	Income tax to date	467.00
30.06.03	J Smithers	461L	National insurance to date	244.00

details on the payslip

As noted above, there is no set format for a payslip. The details that will normally be found – if appropriate – are:

essential details	**optional details**
employer name	tax code
employee name	payroll number
gross pay	National Insurance number
statutory sick pay	method of payment
statutory maternity pay	
tax credits	
deductions made, eg	
– tax for the period	
– tax and NI to date	
– NI for the period	
– Student Loan deductions	
– employee's pension payment	
net pay	

scheduling to deadlines

Weekly pay is normally paid on a Friday and monthly pay at or towards the end of the month. It is essential that timescales are observed for making sure that employees are paid promptly and provided with a payslip at the same time. The larger the organisation, very often the longer the lead time, particularly if the system is computerised. You may therefore sometimes find a delay in the payment of overtime – extra hours worked in January may be paid in February, particularly if the overtime has to be authorised first.

providing information to employees

Employees may query payslips if they are not happy with them. For example you may be asked:

> *"Please check my overtime; I am sure I did more hours than that."*
>
> *"What has happened to my pay rise?"*

You will see from this that many of the queries will have to be referred elsewhere – to the Human Resources Department in the case of a larger organisation, or to the boss in the case of a small business. Some queries you may be able to deal with yourself, others may need to be referred to a supervisor or manager. Remember always that the information will be highly confidential.

where do the figures come from? – payroll analysis

If your job is to prepare payslips, you will need to know where the figures come from. The income and deduction figures we have explained so far are brought together on a **payroll analysis**. If the business operates a manual payroll this will be a printed form which you will have to fill in with details of income and deductions taken from special Inland Revenue working sheets known as P11s. If you operate a computer payroll system, the computer does all the work for you, including the payslips. Study the form and payslip on the next two pages and see how the figures on the payslip are compiled.

payroll checking and authorisation

The payroll analysis and payslips will only be accurate as long as the information provided is correct, for example:

- the amount of gross pay – including any overtime, commission, or bonus
- the tax code applied
- the employee's identity (it has not been unknown for the right pay to go to the wrong person!)

It is essential therefore that all these payroll details are checked thoroughly and authorised before processing. Again, remember that the information you are dealing with is highly confidential.

Case Study

OSBORNE ELECTRONICS – WEEKLY PAYROLL

OSBORNE ELECTRONICS **payroll analysis sheet** **tax year ..../..........** **week/month..........**

employee reference	employee name	Earnings				Deductions				Employer's National Insurance Contributions	Employer's Pension Contributions	Net Pay
		Basic £	Overtime £	Bonus £	Total Gross Pay £	Income Tax £	National Insurance £	Pension Contributions £	Total Deductions £	£	£	£
2345	W Rowberry	205.00	25.00	15.00	245.00	35.00	19.50	10.25	64.75	24.50	10.25	180.25
2346	M Richardson	205.00	10.00	15.00	230.00	32.50	18.00	10.25	60.75	23.05	10.25	169.25
2347	D Stanbury	205.00	25.00	15.00	245.00	35.00	19.50	-	54.50	24.50	-	190.50
2348	D Payne	205.00	25.00	15.00	245.00	35.00	19.50	-	54.50	24.50	-	190.50
2349	K Peters	205.00	10.00	15.00	230.00	32.50	18.00	10.25	60.75	23.05	10.25	169.25
2350	O Robinson	205.00	25.00	15.00	245.00	35.00	19.50	10.25	64.75	24.50	10.25	180.25
TOTALS		1230.00	120.00	90.00	1440.00	205.00	114.00	41.00	360.00	144.10	41.00	1080.00

situation

Osborne Electronics is a small manufacturing company which has six employees on a weekly payroll. Each Friday a payroll analysis sheet (see opposite page) is completed by the payroll clerk. The figures for this analysis are taken from the P11 deduction working sheet for each employee, except for the pension details which are kept in a separate file in the accounts office.

Before the payslips can be prepared, the payroll analysis has to be checked for accuracy and authorised by the Accounts Supervisor. The checks that have to be carried out are as follows:

gross pay the total of the columns (at the bottom of the form):

basic + overtime + bonus = total gross pay

This should equal the sum of the items in the total gross pay column.

total deductions the total of the columns (at the bottom of the form):

income tax + NI + pension = total deductions

This should equal the sum of the items in the total deductions column.

net pay the total of the columns (at the bottom of the form):

total gross pay – total deductions = net pay

This should equal the sum of the items in the net pay column.

When the payroll analysis has been checked and authorised, the payslips can be prepared, checked and authorised. The payslip for O Robinson is shown below. Note that the cumulative ('to date') figures are not included on the payroll analysis – they will be picked up from the P11 deduction working sheet.

OSBORNE ELECRONICS		**Pay Advice**	Week No ....
payments	£	**deductions**	£
Basic pay	205.00	Income tax	35.00
Overtime	25.00	National Insurance	19.50
Bonus	15.00	Pension	10.25
TOTAL GROSS PAY	245.00	Student Loan deduction	0.00
		TOTAL DEDUCTIONS	64.75
Gross pay to date	3500.00	TOTAL NET PAY	180.25
Date / **Employee** / **Code**		Income tax to date	450.00
..../.../......... / O Robinson / 461L		National insurance to date	245.00

what else needs to be done?

All that now remains to be done is to pay the wages, pay the Inland Revenue the tax and NI collected, pay the pension company the money due and make the necessary entries in the accounting records of the business.

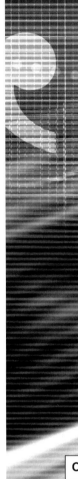

PAYING WAGES BY CASH

Calculating the net pay is the first part of the payroll process. The wages or salaries then have to be paid. There are a number of different ways of paying:

- by cash
- issuing a cheque
- direct to an account by electronic transfer (BACS)

We will deal with each of these in turn.

cash and the need for security

The traditional way of paying wages is by cash, and it is still popular despite the increasing number of people with bank accounts. An employer paying wages in cash can either sub-contract the work to a security firm which will make up the wage packets, or it can be completed by the company's own staff. Preparing wage packets involves collecting sufficient notes and coins from the bank to make up the exact amount for each pay packet.

It is normal practice to telephone the bank in advance to tell them the exact denominations of notes and coins needed. Organisations using online banking services can give these instructions electronically. Employees collecting wages cash from the bank are a obvious target for armed robbery, so common security measures include using two people to collect the money, and for them to vary the route from the bank.

The cash is placed inside a wage packet marked with the name and pay reference or clock number of the employee. Details showing how the payment is made up and the deductions that have been made are provided to each employee. These details can be shown on a separate pay slip or written on the wage packet itself. The office in which this is carried out should be kept secure – for obvious reasons. Employees should sign for the cash wages when they are received.

The total number of notes and coins needed from the bank is worked out on a form known as a *cash analysis*. An important internal security check for the employer is to ensure that the total of the cash analysis is the same as the amount of the cheque given to the bank to cover the wages. A typical cash analysis is illustrated on the next page.

why pay cash wages?

There are a number of reasons why wages are still paid in cash:

- employees like cash in hand
- some employees may not have bank accounts

cash analysis for week ending......................

name	£50	£20	£10	£5	£2	£1	50p	20p	10p	5p	2p	1p	total
W Rowberry	1	2	1		2			2		1			104.45
D Stanbury	1	1	1		1	1	1	1	1				83.80
K Peters		2		1	1		1		2		1		47.72
O Robinson	2	2	1	1	1	1		2		1		1	158.46
M Richardson	1	1	2	1			1	1		1	1	1	95.78
NUMBER	5	8	5	3	5	2	3	6	3	3	2	2	
TOTAL (£.p)	250.00	160.00	50.00	15.00	10.00	2.00	1.50	1.20	0.30	0.15	0.04	0.02	490.21

a cash analysis

PAYMENT OF WAGES BY CHEQUE

Another traditional method of payment of wages and salaries is the issue of cheques. This avoids the complexities and security problems involved in the paying of cash wages.

The employee can either cash the cheque at the employer's bank, or, more commonly, pay it into a bank or building society account.

manual and computerised systems

If the employer uses a *manual* payroll system this will involve the person doing the payroll writing out individual cheques made payable to each employee for the net pay earned. This cheque will then be enclosed with the payslip in a sealed envelope.

If a *computerised* payroll system is used, it will commonly print out the payment cheque for each employee, together with the payslip (which may be physically attached to the cheque).

issue of pay cheques – manual payroll

A number of security and authorisation procedures need to be followed:

- the cheques need to be kept in a secure place
- the cheques have to be written out carefully – the details (name, date, words and figures) have to be checked carefully against the payroll analysis
- the cheques have to be signed by the required number of authorised signatories (some cheques may be rubber stamped with signatures by authorised staff, or be passed through a 'cheque signing' machine)
- additional controls can include:
  - checking the cheque amounts against the payslips
  - adding up the cheque amounts on a tally-roll calculator and agreeing the total with the payroll analysis total for employees paid by cheque

Although the security risk is not as great as it is with handling cash wages, employers who pay employees by cheque need to ensure that internal checks exist to prevent staff from fraudulently altering amounts on cheques.

A typical pay cheque is illustrated at the top of the opposite page. Note that:

- the words and figures agree
- lines are drawn after the payee's name and the amount in words – this is to deter fraud
- the cheque is signed by two authorised signatories – directors of the company

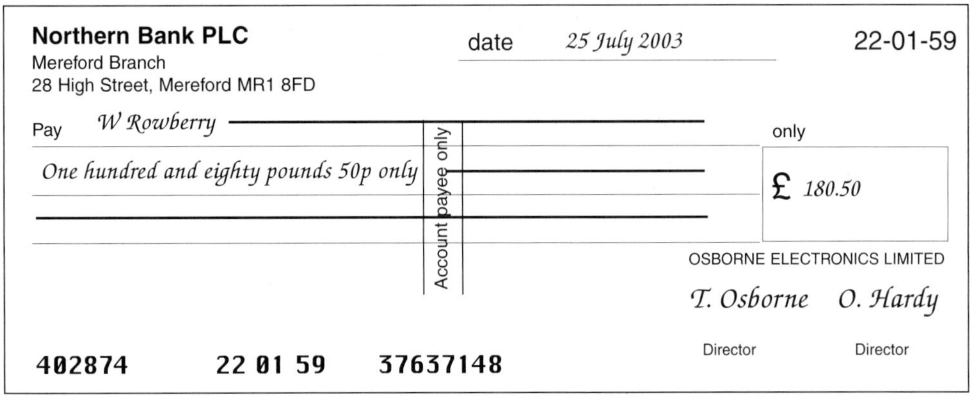
Northern Bank PLC
Mereford Branch
28 High Street, Mereford MR1 8FD

date *25 July 2003*

22-01-59

Pay *W Rowberry*

One hundred and eighty pounds 50p only

Account payee only

only

£ *180.50*

OSBORNE ELECTRONICS LIMITED

T. Osborne *O. Hardy*

Director Director

402874 22 01 59 37637148

a typical pay cheque

BACS PAYMENTS AND PAYROLL

We saw in the last chapter that the Bankers Automated Clearing Services (BACS) is a computer transfer payment system owned by the banks. It is widely used for regular payments such as

- insurance premiums
- settlement of trade debts
- paying wages and salaries

BACS is a cheap and efficient means of payment because, instead of a piece of paper having to be prepared and despatched, the transfer is set up on a computer file and transferred between the banks' computers – the payment goes direct from account to account.

Sometimes the organisation *receiving* the money, such as an insurance company, will set up the computer data itself for the BACS system to process – this is a *direct debit.*

Sometimes the organisation *sending* the money will set up the computer data, or will get the bank to set it up. When an organisation wants to send a group of payments to different beneficiaries – such as employees – it will set up *automated credits* using the BACS system.

The payment cycle is three working days. If an organisation is paying its wages through BACS and wants its employees to have their money on account on Friday, the money must leave the employer's account on Wednesday. The payment instructions will need to be received by the end of Wednesday, so the payroll department will need to observe this deadline.

PROCESSING PAYROLL THROUGH BACS

Payment of wages and salaries through the BACS system can be made in two different ways:

1 **direct dealing with BACS**

The organisation paying the wages and salaries sets up the data on computer file *itself* and sends the data on disk (or direct on-line) to BACS – this is often the system used by large organisations which have thousands of wages and salary payments to make each week and month. With this system, the organisation's bank is not directly involved, except to the extent that the total of all the payments will be debited (deducted) from the organisation's bank account.

2 **bank 'automated credit' systems**

The principle of this system is that the organisation provides the data to its *bank,* which then sets up the computer transfers.

When an organisation sets up this 'automated credit' system in the first place it will have to provide the banking details of the employees so that the bank can input them into its computer. These details are:

- the name of the employee
- the bank sort code
- the account number

Once these details have been provided to the bank, the bank will allocate a reference number to each payee/employee. This reference is the 'payee number' shown on the schedule on the opposite page.

When each payroll date approaches, the payment details are written on a schedule (see opposite page) and sent or faxed to the bank, which then inputs them into its own computer. Organisations with online banking facilities can set up the payroll details over the internet.

Inevitably, an organisation will want to change the employee details from time-to-time: employees will leave and new staff will be taken on. Amendments can easily be made to the employee records set up on the bank computer. Banks provide amendment forms which enable records to be deleted and new ones added.

It is important to appreciate that if you are operating an automated credits system, every instruction to the bank is authorised by an authorised signature, which must be obtained if the instructions are to be validated.

You should also note that this 'automated credit' system is very useful for *smaller* organisations, not only for payroll but also for making payments to suppliers (see page 252).

Case Study

WAGES BY BACS AUTOMATED CREDIT

City Insurance is an insurance broking firm, based in Mereford. In an attempt to cut administrative costs the Finance Manager has decided to pay employees through the BACS system. The bank has suggested its AutoCredit System. City Insurance has supplied the banking details (sort code and account number) of its employees in advance for the bank to put in its own computer. The weekly pay details are then written on the schedule shown below by City Insurance and faxed to the bank on Wednesday 24 September. The employees will be paid on Friday 26 September.

Northern Bank PLC
AutoCredit System

Bank branch...Mereford...

Originator name...City Insurance Co...reference...07246...

Date...24-9-03...

Branch	*Account no*	*Name*	*Payee no*	*Amount*
45-45-62	10386394	Smithson H	347	250.00
56-67-23	22347342	Smith M	456	129.76
40-47-07	42472411	Olivier L	209	450.67
76-87-44	56944491	O'Casey S	492	409.79
33-00-77	23442413	French W	385	305.78
59-99-01	46244703	Jones R	546	560.85
		PAYMENT TOTAL		2106.85

Please make the above payments to reach the payees on ...26-9-03...(date)

Please debit account no...37637927...with the sum of £...2106.85...

authorised signature...*S. Laurel*...

procedures for the schedule

Note that:

- the employer has a reference – 07246 – which is quoted on all instructions
- each employee also a reference number, which is also quoted on all instructions
- the form is totalled to provide the amount which will be taken from the employer's bank account
- the form is signed by an authorised signatory within the organisation – the data cannot be processed without this signature
- it is common for a form of this type to be in two parts: the bank is given the top copy, and the bottom copy is retained by the organisation making payment

It is essential therefore that before the schedule is handed to the bank it is carefully checked for accuracy. The net pay amounts must tally with the figures on the payroll analysis and the authorised signature must be present.

BACS: CONFIDENTIALITY AND SECURITY

confidentiality

Payroll records should be kept confidential. If a person works on payroll and has access to colleagues' pay details, they will undoubtedly be very interesting, but on no account should they be revealed to anyone else, inside or outside the organisation. The only body which will require pay details is the Inland Revenue, as we will see in the next chapter.

security

We have already seen that cash and cheques must be kept securely in order to deter theft. Security measures must also be taken when computer payments are sent. Common frauds include:

- the sending of bogus BACS payments to an employee's account
- changing the totals of a large number of payments by a few pence in the hope that the changes will not be noticed – the total difference will then be diverted to an account to which the employee can gain access

These dangers can be overcome by exercising care and caution:

- the individual 'code' issued by BACS to an organisation – without which no payments can be made – should be restricted to a limited number of employees
- payment amounts on the BACS records should be carefully checked against the originals – in the Case Study the net pay amounts were checked against the payroll analysis

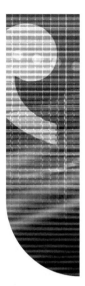

PAYMENTS TO THE INLAND REVENUE

Organisations operating PAYE collect income tax and National Insurance Contributions each time the payroll is run. This money must then be paid to the Inland Revenue. For most organisations this means a monthly payment sent within fourteen days of the end of the tax month, using a P30B payslip (bank giro credit). As the tax month ends on the 5th, this means that the money must by sent by the 19th. For example, the January income tax and National Insurance Contributions collected must be sent by 19 February. The payments will comprise:

- income tax collected from employees
- employees' and employer's National Insurance Contributions
- less any money reclaimable from the Inland Revenue (eg tax credits)

The data for these payments is first calculated for individual employees on the P11 deductions working sheet and may then be transferred to a yellow summary sheet P32 and then to the P30B giro credit for the appropriate month in the payslip booklet (this is a chequebook-sized book of bank giro credits used for paying the money to the Inland Revenue). The giro credit is normally paid into the bank with a covering cheque.

Now look at the diagram below which summarises the month-end procedure for a small business with three employees. Examples of the documents involved are shown on the next page.

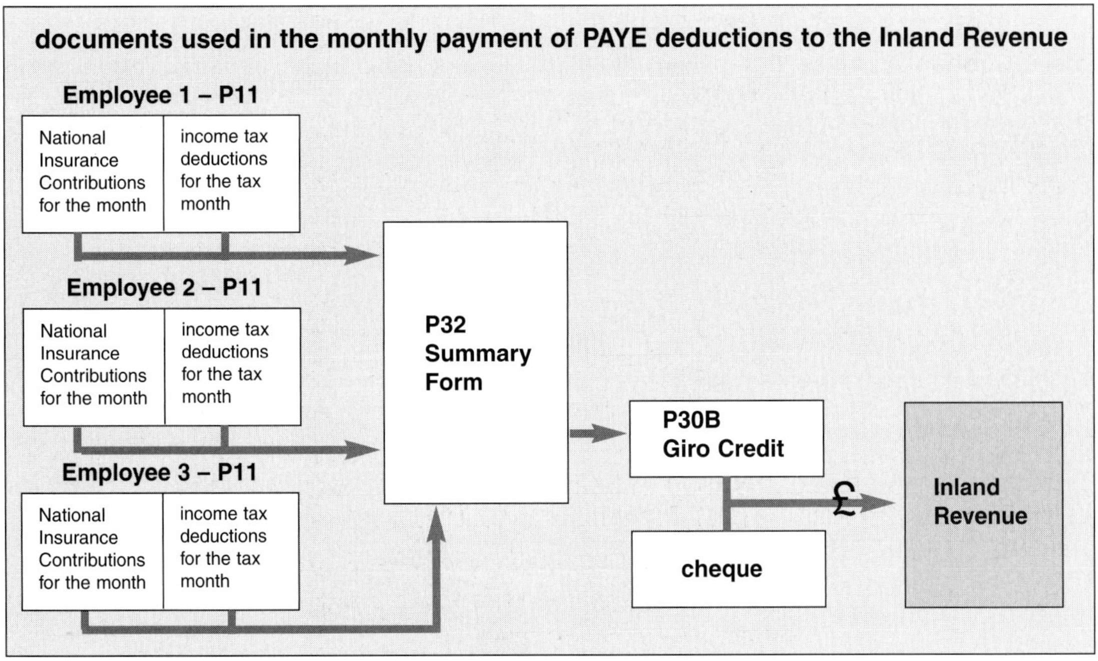

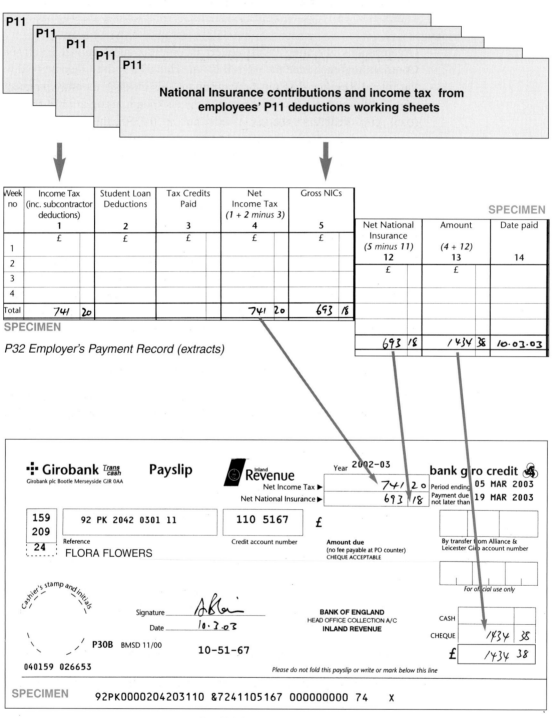

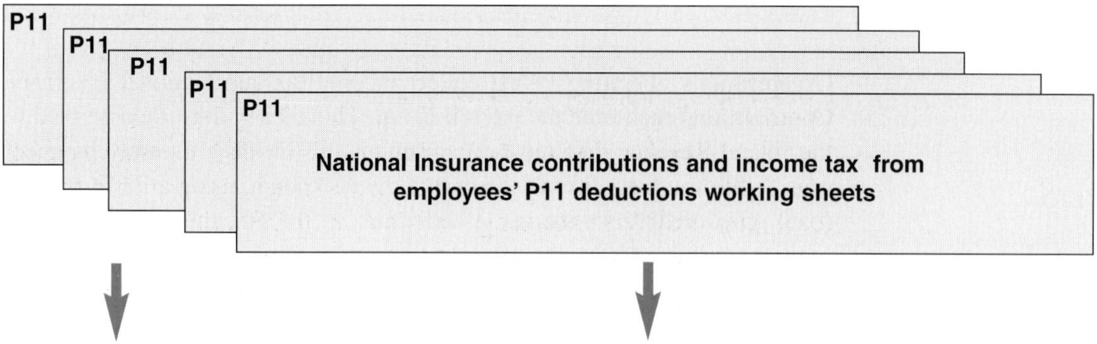

Week no	Income Tax (inc. subcontractor deductions) 1	Student Loan Deductions 2	Tax Credits Paid 3	Net Income Tax (1 + 2 minus 3) 4	Gross NICs 5
	£	£	£	£	£
1					
2					
3					
4					
Total	741 20			741 20	693 18

SPECIMEN

Net National Insurance (5 minus 11) 12	Amount (4 + 12) 13	Date paid 14
£	£	
693 18	1434 38	10.03.03

SPECIMEN

P32 Employer's Payment Record (extracts)

Girobank Trans cash
Girobank plc Bootle Merseyside GIR 0AA

Payslip

Inland Revenue

Year 2002-03

Net Income Tax ▶ 741 20

Net National Insurance ▶ 693 18

bank giro credit

Period ending 05 MAR 2003

Payment due not later than 19 MAR 2003

159
209
24

92 PK 2042 0301 11

Reference

FLORA FLOWERS

110 5167

Credit account number

£

Amount due (no fee payable at PO counter) CHEQUE ACCEPTABLE

By transfer from Alliance & Leicester Giro account number

For official use only

Cashier's stamp and initials

Signature

Date 10.3.03

P30B BMSD 11/00

10-51-67

BANK OF ENGLAND
HEAD OFFICE COLLECTION A/C
INLAND REVENUE

CASH

CHEQUE 1434 38

£ 1434 38

040159 026653

Please do not fold this payslip or write or mark below this line

SPECIMEN 92PK0000204203110 &7241105167 000000000 74 X

P30B Inland Revenue Payslip

PAYROLL AND THE DOUBLE-ENTRY ACCOUNTING SYSTEM

types of accounting system

Payroll accounting systems will either be paper-based, or computerised. Many 'off-the-shelf' payroll accounting packages are now available, such as the widely-used Sage programs. In this chapter, however, we will use a paper-based system to illustrate the accounting entries generated by the operation of payroll so that you will understand the double-entry principles involved.

types of accounts used

Wages and salaries are a major *expense* for any organisation, but remember that the net pay received by employees is not the same as the *gross pay*, the expense to the employer. The wages and salaries expenses figure that appears in the trial balance of the organisation – the expenses that the employer will have to pay – will be the result of a number of adjustments:

- calculated in the payroll process
- entered in the double-entry accounts of the organisation

There is no 'hard-and-fast' rule which states what accounts have to be set up. The accounts used in this chapter are fairly typical, but you may well find that practice varies from organisation to organisation. The main accounts to be used will be:

- in the cash book (for bank transactions)
- in the main (general) ledger (expenses)

The types of transaction which need entering in the accounts include:

- income tax collected by the employer under PAYE and paid to the Inland Revenue by the 19th of the month *after* the payroll has been processed
- employees' National Insurance Contributions collected by the employer under PAYE and paid to the Inland Revenue by the 19th of the month *after* the payroll has been processed
- employer's National Insurance Contributions paid to the Inland Revenue
- employees' pension contributions deducted from employees' pay and paid to pension funds
- pension contributions provided by the *employer* and paid to pension funds

The double-entry accounts commonly used include:

Bank this is in the cash book and records:

- payment of cash wages, wages cheques and BACS wages transfers – ie the *net pay* of employees
- payment of cheques to outside agencies, eg the monthly payment of deductions to the Inland Revenue and payments to pension funds

Wages & Salaries this is in the main ledger and records:

- employees' *gross pay*
- employer's National Insurance Contributions
- employer's pension contributions (if there are any)

– in short, it is the employer's *expense* account for paying employees

Inland Revenue this is in the main ledger and records amounts payable to the Inland Revenue (PAYE deductions)

Pension Fund this is in the main ledger and records amounts payable to external pension funds: the employer's and employees' contributions as appropriate (with some schemes the employer and employee make a contribution, with others it is just the employee that contributes)

A common practice is to put all the entries through a Wages and Salaries Control account.

wages and salaries control account

You may already have studied the *control accounts* used by businesses for purchases and sales. They are covered in Chapters 4 and 12 of this book.

A *control account* is a 'master' account which 'controls' a number of other subsidiary ledger accounts. It is used to record the total of transactions passing through the subsidiary accounts. The balance of the control account should always be equal to the total balances of the subsidiary accounts.

For example, the sales ledger *control account* will give the total of the debtors of an organisation and the purchases ledger *control account* will give the total of the creditors. This provides useful information for the management: they will be able to see how much the business is owed by its customers and the amount it owes to its suppliers.

A *wages and salaries control account* is also a master account: all the entries to the various accounts set up to deal with payroll transactions pass through the control account.

The diagram below shows the structure of the control account and subsidiary accounts. Note that the bank account is not shown here – it is involved in many of the transactions, as we will see in the Case Study which follows, but it is not strictly speaking 'subsidiary'.

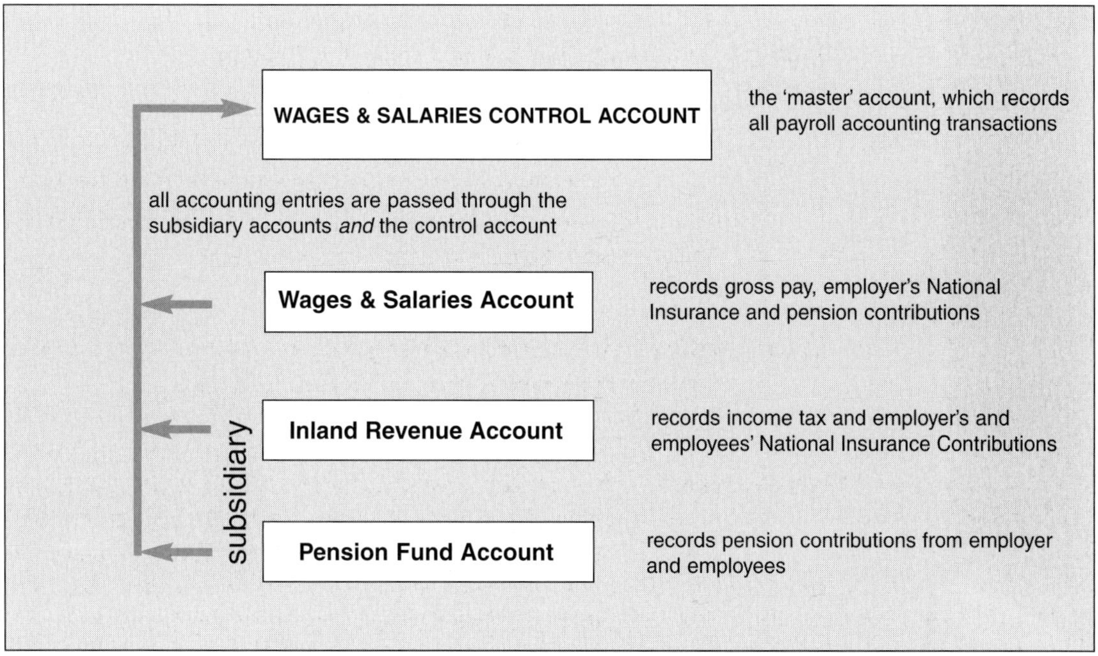

Wages & Salaries control account and subsidiary accounts

Case Study

FLUFFIES: WAGES & SALARIES CONTROL ACCOUNT

Fluffies is a small knitwear business employing five staff. It operates a monthly payroll which is run on the last day of the month. Payroll figures for November 2003 are:

gross pay	£5,500
net pay received by employees	£3,875
income tax deducted by PAYE	£900
NIC (employees' contribution)	£450
NIC (employer's contribution)	£550
pension: paid by the employees by deduction from pay	£275
pension: employer's contribution	£275

What are the payments that are due, and to whom are they payable?

payments due to the Inland Revenue

Income tax deducted from employees' pay	£900	
Employees' National Insurance Contributions	£450	
Employer's National Insurance Contributions	£550	
		£1,900

payments due to the pension fund, Allied Life PLC

Employees' contributions, deducted from pay	£275	
Employer's contributions	£275	
		£550

payments due to the employees

Gross pay	£5,500	
less		
Income tax	£900	
National Insurance	£450	
Pension contributions	£275	
Net pay due		£3,875

payments total	£6,325

These four amounts, shown here in the right-hand column, are recorded in the payroll records and have to be entered into the ledger accounts. This is done as follows:

Step 1

Transfer the total of the payments (here £6,325) to Wages & Salaries Account (this is the cost to the employer) and to Wages & Salaries Control Account

debit Wages & Salaries Account
credit Wages & Salaries Control Account

Dr		Wages & Salaries Account			Cr
2003		£	2003		£
30 Nov	Wages & salaries Control Account	6,325			

Dr		Wages & Salaries Control Account			Cr
2003		£	2003		£
			30 Nov	Wages & salaries	6,325

You will see that this total agrees with the *total monthly payroll expense to the business*: gross pay (£5,500) *plus* employer's National Insurance (£550) *plus* employer's pension contribution (£275) *equals* £6,325.

Step 2
Make entries for the payment of wages (the net pay paid from the bank)

debit Wages & Salaries Control Account
credit Bank Account

Dr		Wages & Salaries Control Account			Cr
2003		£	2003		£
30 Nov	Bank	3,875	30 Nov	Wages & salaries	6,325

Dr		Bank Account			Cr
2003		£	2003		£
			30 Nov	Wages & Salaries Control Account	3,875

Step 3
Transfer the amount due to the Inland Revenue to the Inland Revenue Account

debit Wages & Salaries Control Account
credit Inland Revenue Account (which will become a 'creditor' account until the amount is paid in December and 'clears' the account back to zero)

The 'amount due' is £1,900 and comprises income tax (£900) and National Insurance contributions (employer's [£550] and employees' [£450]).

Dr		Wages & Salaries Control Account			Cr
2003		£	2003		£
30 Nov	Bank	3,875	30 Nov	Wages & salaries	6,325
30 Nov	Inland Revenue	1,900			

Dr	Inland Revenue Account		Cr
2003	£	2003	£
		30 Nov Wages & Salaries Control Account	1,900

Step 4

Transfer the amount due to the pension fund, Allied Life PLC

The amount due is £550 (employer's contribution £275, employee's contribution £275)

debit Wages & Salaries Control Account
credit Pension Fund Account (which will become a 'creditor' account until the amount is paid in December and 'clears' the account back to zero)

Dr	Wages & Salaries Control Account				Cr
2003		£	2003		£
30 Nov	Bank	3,875	30 Nov	Wages & salaries	6,325
30 Nov	Inland Revenue	1,900			
30 Nov	Pension Fund	550			
		6,325			6,325

Dr	Pension Fund Account		Cr
2003	£	2003	£
		30 Nov Wages & Salaries Control Account	550

conclusion

You will see from the double-entry book-keeping entries shown above that the Wages & Salaries Control Account acts as a 'master' account for all the payroll accounting transactions carried out each time the payroll is run. At the end of the process the control account balance reverts to zero – you will see above that the total of both sides after the pension fund transfer is £6,325 – ie the balance is nil.

The double-entry book-keeping also shows:

- *Wages & Salaries Account:* the cumulative cost during the year of paying the employees – this includes the gross pay, employer's National Insurance and any pension contributions paid by the employer; this is the figure that will appear in the organisation's profit statement – it is the expense borne by the employer
- in the *Inland Revenue Account* and *Pension Fund Account* any amounts owing – for example at the end of the month before payments are passed to these agencies – these will be *creditor* accounts

Chapter Summary

- Payroll records – which are highly confidential – must be maintained accurately and securely.
- Employees' income from the employer, which may be termed 'wages' or 'salary' can be made up of a number of elements: basic pay, overtime, shift allowance, bonus payments, commission, piece rate.
- The payroll is also used to pay certain forms of State benefit – Working Families' Tax Credit and Disabled Person's Tax Credit.
- Compulsory deductions from gross pay include income tax, National Insurance Contributions and any Student Loan repayments which are due to be made.
- Voluntary deductions from gross pay include Payroll Giving schemes, pensions (superannuation), Union fees, and Save as You Earn (SAYE) Sharesave schemes.
- The tax year runs from 6 April in one year until 5 April in the next and is divided into numbered tax weeks and tax months.
- Employees are given tax allowances – amounts of earnings which are free of tax. Taxable income is income on which tax has to be paid; it is gross income less the total tax allowance.
- The tax allowance of an employee is notified by the Inland Revenue by means of a tax code – the amount of the tax allowance less the final digit.
- Income tax is charged in three 'bands': Starting Rate, Basic Rate and Higher Rate tax. It is calculated and charged cumulatively – on the basis of how much tax is due by each employee since the beginning of the tax year.
- National Insurance is a tax on earnings paid by employers and employees – it is worked out on a percentage basis but is not cumulative, ie it is worked out each week or month and does not relate to the previous period.
- National Insurance is only payable once an employee's pay has reached a certain weekly or monthly money amount – the Earnings Threshold.
- All income items and deductions are shown on the employee's payslip together with 'year-to-date' figures.
- Each time the payroll is run the figures needed for the payslips and the payments that have to be made are drawn up on a payroll analysis form.
- Wages can be paid in cash, by cheque or by BACS. The breakdown of notes and coins for cash wages is calculated on a cash analysis form.
- Payments of income tax and National Insurance Contributions to the Inland Revenue are made on a P30B bank giro credit form.
- Payroll transactions are recorded in the double-entry accounting records of the business – normally using a control account to record the total of transactions passing through the accounts involved in payroll.

Key Terms

gross pay	the total amount earned by an employee
net pay	the total amount earned by an employee less deductions, ie what the employee 'gets'
tax credit	a form of State benefit paid through the payroll and reclaimable by the employer
overtime	extra time worked by an employee, often at a higher rate of pay
shift allowance	an extra allowance paid for working a shift with unsocial hours
bonus payment	an extra 'bonus' payment normally calculated as a percentage of sales
commission	a payment which is calculated as a percentage of sales – a normal part of the payment package
piece rate payment	a payment which is based on the number of items processed by the employee
income tax	a tax, based on the level of an employee's income, collected by the Inland Revenue
National Insurance	(NI) – a tax based on an employee's earnings, collected by the Inland Revenue on behalf of the Department of Social Security
PAYE	Pay As You Earn is a cumulative tax collection system operated by employers on behalf of the Inland Revenue
tax allowance	an amount of income earned by an employee on which tax does not have to be paid
tax code	a numeric code (plus a letter) which enables the employer to calculate the amount of tax due – it is the tax allowance less the final digit
taxable income	the income earned by an employee which is subject to income tax (gross income minus the tax allowance)
payslip	a document given to the employee when the payroll is run, setting out income and deductions
payroll analysis sheet	a summary sheet showing all the figures produced when payroll is processed – useful as a cross-checking device for accuracy of figures
cash analysis	a form setting out the details of notes and coin needed from the bank by an employer when paying wages in cash
P30B	a bank giro credit issued by the Inland Revenue – used for paying income tax and NI collected
control account	a double-entry account which acts as a 'master' account for other 'subsidiary' accounts

Student Activities

14.1 What is the difference between

(a) gross pay and net pay

(b) overtime and shift allowance

(c) bonus payments and piece rate payments

(d) a time book and a time sheet

(e) a clock card and a swipe card

14.2 Calculate the *weekly* gross pay of the following employees:

	employee	*annual salary*
(a)	J Smith	£6,500
(b)	I Rose	£9,360
(c)	R Pellerini	£11,440
(d)	N Mutt	£6,760
(e)	R Singh	£7,800

14.3 Calculate the following employees' gross wages for the week, assuming that they are paid at an hourly rate of £6 for the first 40 hours and time-and-a-half for hours in excess of 40.

	Employee	*Hours worked during week*
(a)	Helen Marsh	35
(b)	Derek Hall	42
(c)	Eddie Bristow	48
(d)	Dilip Patel	50
(e)	Roger Draper	39

14.4 There are seven employees on your hospital payroll, each with a tax allowance of £4615. Their annual earnings are:

(a)	N Doskopi	£6,000
(b)	Ivor Payne	£11,000
(c)	N Trails	£14,000
(d)	L Bowe	£18,000
(e)	N Emmer	£27,000
(f)	Ray D Oligist	£40,000
(g)	Anne S Thettick	£60,000

Calculate (to the nearest p) the amount of income tax each employee will have to pay.
Use the tax rates and tax bands shown in this chapter (page 270) for Starting Rate Tax, Basic Rate Tax and Higher Rate Tax.

14.5 The payslip below shows a number of income items and deductions. Study it carefully.

OSBORNE ELECRONICS			Pay Advice	June 2003
payments			**deductions**	
	£			£
Basic pay	918.75		Income tax	132.87
Overtime	100.00		National Insurance	70.80
Bonus	20.00		Pension	32.08
TOTAL GROSS PAY	1038.75		Student Loan deduction	0.00
			TOTAL DEDUCTIONS	235.75
Gross pay to date	3427.88			
			TOTAL NET PAY	803.00
Date	**Employee**	**Code**	Income tax to date	467.00
30.06.00	J Smithers	461L	National insurance to date	244.00

(a) Write short explanatory notes on the income items (including any cumulative items).

(b) Write short explanatory notes on the deduction items (including any cumulative items). Identify in your notes the compulsory deductions and the voluntary deductions.

(c) What does the code 461L mean? *Means allowed to earn £4615 before paying tax*

(d) What is the meaning of 'TOTAL GROSS PAY' and 'TOTAL NET PAY'? *EARNED BY EMPLOYEE* *PAID TO EMPLOYEE AFTER DEDUCT.*

(e) Why is there an entry for 'Student Loan deduction'? Why do you think the entry is zero? *SOME EMPLOYEES HAVE TO PAY BACK S L's* *DIDN'T HAVE A STUDENT LOAN OR*

(f) What item of payroll, which the employer will have to deal with, does *not* appear on the payslip? *HAS PAID IT OFF*
EMPLOYERS NI CONTRIBUTION or *EMPLOYER PENSION CONTRIB*

14.6 Using the National Insurance Contribution rates quoted in this chapter (page 271), calculate the separate amounts payable by the employer *and* the employee for the following weekly-paid employees at a garage: *EMPLOYER 12.8% OVER 89* *EMPLOYEE 11% OVER 89 - 595* *1% >595*

	employee	weekly pay (£)	EMPLOYER	EMPLOYEE	
(a)	Alf Romeo	50.00	0	0	
(b)	Mike Rarr	95.00	0.77 +	0.66	= 1-43
(c)	Sue Barrew	250.00	20-61 +	17-71	= 38-32
(d)	S Tate-Carr	700.00	78-21 +	55-66+ 1-05	= 134-92
(e)	Portia Carrera	900.00	103-81 +	55-66+ 3-05	= 162-52

14.7 Using the Payroll Analysis sheet on page 274 draw up payslips for the first five employees. A blank payslip is shown on the next page.

All employees have a tax code of 461L. The week is week 17 of the tax year. You do not need to quote the employee reference number for the purposes of this exercise.

The P11 deduction working sheets show the following cumulative figures (these include week 17's figures shown on the payroll analysis form):

employee	*gross pay to date*	*income tax to date*	*National Insurance to date*
	£	£	£
W Rowberry	3,650.00	489.00	256.50
M Richardson	3,500.00	450.00	245.00
D Stanbury	3,120.00	410.00	203.50
D Payne	3,400.00	423.50	225.60
K Peters	3,510.00	490.00	260.50

OSBORNE ELECTRONICS		**Pay Advice**	**Week**
payments		**deductions**	
	£		£
Basic pay		Income tax	
Overtime		National Insurance	
Bonus		Pension	
TOTAL GROSS PAY		Student Loan deduction	
Gross pay to date		TOTAL DEDUCTIONS	
Employee	**Tax Code**	TOTAL NET PAY	
		Income tax to date	
		National insurance to date	

14.8 Refer again to the Payroll Analysis sheet on page 274. Also, look at the example P30B on page 284. You have been asked to complete a giro credit P30B for the four weeks ending week 17. The total figures for the three previous weeks are:

week	*income tax*	*National Insurance (employee)*	*National Insurance (employer)*
	£	£	£
14	205.50	115.00	125.00
15	227.00	120.50	132.00
16	210.75	118.50	128.00
17	205.00	114.00	144.10

What are the money amounts that you will enter on the P30B? Income Tax = 848-25
NIC = 997-10

14.9 The six staff on the payroll of Osborne Electronics are paid in cash. The net pay of the staff for Week 8 is as follows:

W Rowberry	£211.56	M Richardson	£189.74
D Stanbury	£206.83	D Payne	£196.75
K Peters	£178.89	O Robinson	£183.69

You are to complete a cash analysis for the six employees. The format of the cash analysis can be found on page 277. The highest value notes and coins should be used, but no more than two £50 notes should be included in any pay packet.

14.10 What method of payment would you recommend for the payroll systems of the following businesses? Give reasons in each case.

(a) a fully computerised insurance company with 1,200 staff on its books

(b) a firm of solicitors with fifteen employees but no computers, apart from word processors

(c) a sole trader builder who employs two workers who do not have bank accounts

Your choice should be based on the cheapest and most convenient alternative. Choose from: cash wages, cheque payment, automated credit (manually completed schedule for BACS input by the bank), direct BACS (tape/disk).

The following data will form the basis for multiple-choice questions 14.11 to 14.13. In each case, choose one option from (a) to (d)

The payroll system of Home Fires Limited has recorded the following totals for the month of July:

gross pay	£350,780
income tax deducted by PAYE	£69,500
NIC (employees' contribution)	£31,450
NIC (employer's contribution)	£35,085
pension: paid by the employees by deduction from pay	£7,500
pension: employer's contribution	£7,500

14.11 The total payment to the Inland Revenue for the month will be

(a) £100,950

(b) £104,585

(c) £15,000

(d) £136,035

14.12 The total wages & salaries expense to the employer will be

(a) £350,780

(b) £462,865

(c) £393,365

(d) £308,195

14.13 The total net pay to employees will be

(a) £242,330

(b) £249,830

(c) £389,730

(d) £350,780

14.14 Pegasus Limited has recorded the following payroll totals for the month of October:

gross pay	£101,500
income tax deducted by PAYE	£20,500
NIC (employees' contribution)	£9,860
NIC (employer's contribution)	£10,150
pension: employer's contribution (non-contributory pension)	£7,500

(a) Calculate the total payroll cost to the employer £119,150 ✓

(b) Calculate the payment due to the Inland Revenue £40,510 ✓

(c) Calculate the net pay due to employees £71,140 ✓

(d) Draw up double-entry accounts for Wages & Salaries, Inland Revenue, Pension Fund, Bank, and Wages & Salaries Control and enter the relevant entries. Assume a nil opening balance for each account. You do not need to balance the accounts.

14.15 Jasons Wool Shop has recorded the following payroll totals for the month of October:

gross pay	£50,000
income tax deducted by PAYE	£11,110
NIC (employees' contribution)	£4,985
NIC (employer's contribution)	£5,010
pension: paid by the employees by deduction from pay	£1,100
pension: employer's contribution	£1,100

(a) Calculate the total payroll cost to the employer £56,110 ✓

(b) Calculate the payment due to the Inland Revenue £21,105 ✓

(c) Calculate the amount due to the Pension Fund £2,200 ✓

(d) Calculate the net pay due to employees £32,805 ✓

(e) Draw up double-entry accounts for Wages & Salaries, Inland Revenue, Pension Fund, Bank, and Wages & Salaries Control and enter the relevant entries. Assume a nil opening balance for each account. You do not need to balance the accounts.

WAGES + SALARIES CONTROL

NET PAY	71,140	WAGES EXP (GP)	101,500	
NIC (EMPLOYEE)	9,860	WAGES EXP (NIC)	10,150	
NIC (EMPLOYER)	10,150	WAGES EXP (PENSION)	7,500	
PAYE	20,500			
PENSION	7,500			
	119,150		119,150	

WAGES + SALARIES

WCA (GP)	101,500
WCA (NIC)	10,150
WCA (PENS)	7,500

INLAND REVENUE

WCA (PAYE)	20,500
WCA (NIC EMEE)	9,860
WCA (NIC EMR)	10,150

PENSION FUND

WCA (PENSION)	7500

BANK

WCA (PAY)	71,140

15 Cash book – recording payments

this chapter covers . . .

In this chapter we examine the way in which the cash book records payments in the form of cash, cheques and other bank transfers.

As well as recording the money side of book-keeping transactions, the cash book is part of the double-entry system. This chapter focuses on the payments (credit) side of the cash book and we will see also how the opposite debit entry is recorded in creditors' and other accounts.

Also in this chapter we explain the authorisation and payment of expenses claims – a task which is often carried out by a firm's cashier.

NVQ PERFORMANCE CRITERIA COVERED

unit 2: MAKING AND RECORDING PAYMENTS

element 2.2

process payments

D *enter payments into accounting records*

F *ensure security and confidentiality is maintained according to organisational requirements*

USES OF THE CASH BOOK

The payments (credit) side of the cash book brings together:

- cash transactions – most payments for cash, except for low-value expense payments (which are paid through petty cash book – see next chapter)
- bank transactions – all payments through the bank (including the withdrawal of cash from the bank)

We have already seen in Chapter 7 (which dealt with the receipts side of the cash book) how the cash books – ie cash book and petty cash book – combine the roles of books of prime entry and double-entry book-keeping.

Cash books are:

- books of prime entry for cash and bank transactions
- double-entry accounts for cash and bank accounts

RECORDING PAYMENTS – LAYOUT OF THE CASH BOOK

The payments (credit) side of the cash book can be set out in a variety of formats to suit the requirements of a particular business. The columnar cash book is a format which incorporates several money columns. An example of the payments side of a three-column cash book (with three money columns) is shown below:

Credit		**Cash Book: Payments**			**CBP**
Date	Details	Folio	Discount received	Cash	Bank
			£	£	£

This is an almost identical layout to that already seen in Chapter 7, page 139. The only differences are that:

- the cash book payments (CBP) is the credit side
- discount received column relates to any settlement or cash discount received by the firm in respect of prompt payments made to creditors

Remember that a business can set out its cash book in the format that best suits its requirements. As we saw in Chapter 7, not all businesses use a cash column. This is most commonly used by businesses that have a high volume of cash transactions (see Case Study below).

book-keeping and the cash book

As the cash book is part of the double-entry system, each entry on the payments side (the credit side) of the cash and bank columns must have an opposite entry on the debit side of another account elsewhere. Note that the discount received column is not part of the double-entry system – it is used in the cash book as a listing device or memorandum column (we will see later in this chapter how amounts from this column are transferred into the double-entry system).

Case Study

SEVERN TRADING COMPANY – CASH BOOK PAYMENTS

situation

The cashier at the firm for which you work, Severn Trading Company, is away on a course this week. You are required, in her absence, to take over as cashier. The following payments are to be entered into the firm's cash book, which has columns for discount received, cash payments and bank:

2004

5 Apr Paid E Lee & Son, a creditor, £160 by cheque no 101261

6 Apr Paid Hayes Limited, a creditor, £200 by standing order

6 Apr Paid S Crane, a creditor, £145 by cheque no 101262 – he has allowed £5 settlement discount

7 Apr Cash purchases £94 (including VAT of £14)

8 Apr Cash purchases £282 (including VAT of £42), paid for by cheque no 101263

9 Apr Paid cheque no 101264 for £70 to S Ford, a creditor, in full settlement of our account of £75

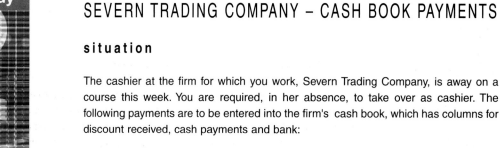

solution

Credit	Cash Book: Payments					CBP 24
Date	Details		Folio	Discount received	Cash	Bank
				£	£	£
2004						
5 Apr	E Lee & Co	101261	PL 804			160
6 Apr	Hayes Limited	SO	PL 752			200
6 Apr	S Crane	101262	PL 610	5		145
7 Apr	Purchases		ML 5001/ 2200		94	
8 Apr	Purchases	101263	ML 5001/ 2200			282
9 Apr	S Ford	101264	PL 698	5		70
				10	94	857

notes

- The cash book payments page is numbered – here 'CBP 24'.

- The cash book forms a part of the double-entry book-keeping system. The payments side of the cash book records the credit entry for cash and bank transactions – in the section which follows we shall see how the debit entry for each transaction is recorded to complete double-entry. (The discount received column is not part of double-entry – we will see how it is transferred into the accounts in the next section.)

- The details column includes a note of the cheque number of each cheque drawn, together with standing orders and direct debits – this information will help when the firm's bank statement is received.

- The folio column has been completed to show in which division of the ledger and to which account number(s) the opposite book-keeping entry appears:

  ML = main ledger

  PL = purchases ledger, ie subsidiary (purchases) ledger

- For cash purchases, the amount of cash (or cheques) paid and recorded in the cash book includes VAT; when recording the debit entries we need to distinguish between the purchases amount and VAT – see the section which follows. This is the reason why two main ledger account numbers are shown in the folio column against cash purchases – the first number refers to purchases account, the second to VAT account.

- The money columns of the cash book have been sub-totalled – this helps as we take information forward into other accounts within the double-entry system, and also when we balance the cash book (see Chapter 19).

COMPLETING DOUBLE-ENTRY TRANSACTIONS

The Case Study has shown us how the credit side of the cash book is used to record payments in the form of cash or through the bank account. In this section we look at how to complete double-entry accounts for:

- cash purchases
- payments made to creditors
- contra entries

recording cash purchases

By 'cash purchases' we mean the purchase of goods (with the intention that they should be resold at a profit) from a supplier, with payment made immediately either in cash or by cheque (or other payment method such as BACS, debit card, credit card). The double-entry book-keeping entries are:

- payment made in cash
  - *debit* purchases account
  - *debit* VAT account (with the amount of VAT)
  - *credit* cash column of the cash book
- payment made by cheque (or other banking payment method)
  - *debit* purchases account
  - *debit* VAT account
  - *credit* bank column of the cash book

The debit entries from the Case Study for the cash purchases transactions of 7 April and 8 April are recorded in the double-entry accounts as follows:

MAIN LEDGER

Dr **Purchases Account** (account no 5001) Cr

2004			£	2004	£
7 Apr	Cash	CBP 24	80		
8 Apr	Bank	CBP 24	240		

Dr **Value Added Tax Account** (account no 2200) Cr

2004			£	2004	£
7 Apr	Cash	CBP 24	14		
8 Apr	Bank	CBP 24	42		

recording payments to creditors

When payment is made to creditors for goods that have been bought from them on credit, the method of payment is:

- either by cheque, or other payment method such as BACS, debit card, credit card
- or, less commonly, in cash

The double-entry book-keeping entries are:

- payment made by cheque (or other banking method)
  - *debit* purchases ledger control account (in the main ledger)
  - *credit* bank column of the cash book
  - and a debit to the creditor's account in the subsidiary (purchases) ledger
- payment made in cash
  - *debit* purchases ledger control account (in the main ledger)
  - *credit* cash column of the cash book
  - and a debit to the creditor's account in the subsidiary (purchases) ledger

As well as the debit to purchases ledger control account, remember that a debit must be recorded on the creditors account in the subsidiary (purchases) ledger. No entry is needed in VAT account when payment is made to creditors – the VAT entry will have been made when the credit purchase was recorded in the accounting system (see Chapter 11).

When cash discount for prompt settlement has been received from the creditor, ie settlement discount has reduced the amount of the payment, entries must be made in the double-entry system as follows:

- *debit* purchases ledger control account
- *credit* discount received account (in the main ledger)
- and a debit to the creditor's account in the subsidiary (purchases) ledger

The debit entries from the Case Study for the payments to creditors are as follows, starting with the subsidiary (purchases) ledger. It is suggested that you 'tick back' each transaction.

Note: for illustrative purposes an amount for purchases has been credited to each creditor's account (with the cross-reference to PDB 67).

SUBSIDIARY (PURCHASES) LEDGER

Dr				**E Lee & Co** (account no 804)			Cr
2004			£	2004			£
5 Apr	Bank	CBP 24	160	22 Mar	Purchases	PDB 67	300

Dr		**Hayes Limited** (account no 752)					Cr
2004			£	2004			£
6 Apr	Bank	CBP 24	200	22 Mar	Purchases	PDB 67	540

Dr		**S Crane** (account no 610)					Cr
2004			£	2004			£
6 Apr	Bank	CBP 24	145	22 Mar	Purchases	PDB 67	150
6 Apr	Discount Received	ML 6502	5				

Dr		**S Ford** (account no 698)					Cr
2004			£	2004			£
9 Apr	Bank	CBP 24	70	22 Mar	Purchases	PDB 67	75
9 Apr	Discount Received	ML 6502	5				

Notes:

- Amounts for purchases have been shown in the above accounts for illustrative purposes – see Chapter 11, which covers accounting for purchases
- In order to complete double-entry book-keeping, discount received amounts, which have been debited to the creditors' accounts, must also be credited to discount received account in the main ledger (the discount column in the cash book is not part of the double-entry system, but is a memorandum column only). The account is completed by entering the total of the discount column from the cash book, as follows:

MAIN LEDGER

Dr	**Discount Received Account** (account no 6502)					Cr
2004	£	2004				£
		9 Apr	Cash Book		CBP 24	10

- Purchases ledger control account (see below) is credited with the amount of discount received.
- Once the total of discount received has been taken from the cash book, the discount column 'starts again' (ie the amount of £10, above, for this week will not be included in next week's transfer).

- Purchases ledger control account is written up as follows at 9 April (the end of the week):

MAIN LEDGER

Dr	**Purchases Ledger Control Account** (account no 6002)						Cr
2004			£	2004			£
9 Apr	Bank	CBP 24	**575	22 Mar	Purchases	PDB67	*1,065
9 Apr	Discount Received	ML6502	10				

* As the purchases day book is not shown here, the purchases figure is the total of the credits to the subsidiary creditors' accounts, ie £300 + £540 + £150 + £75.

** the total bank receipts of £575 comprises cheques and bank transfers to creditors, ie £160 + £200 + £145 + £70 (the amount does not include payments for cash purchases, here £282). Later in this chapter – page 311– we will see how an analysed cash book can be used to obtain more easily the total of payments to creditors.

treatment of VAT – cash and credit purchases

When carrying out the book-keeping entries for payments for cash purchases and payments to creditors, the treatment of VAT is quite different. It is important to bear these differences in mind. Remember:

The double-entry for a payment made for **cash purchases** is:

- *debit* purchases account
- *debit* VAT account (with the amount of VAT)
- *credit* bank column of the cash book (or cash column if it is used)

The double-entry for a payment made for a **credit purchase** (ie to a creditor) is :

- *debit* purchases ledger control account (in the main ledger)
- *credit* bank column of the cash book

There is no entry for VAT here because the VAT has already been accounted for when the purchase was first made (see Chapter 11). The entries will then have been: *debit* purchases account, *debit* VAT account and *credit* creditor's account

The diagram on the next page illustrates the book-keeping entries for the payments for purchases, as described in this section of the chapter.

book-keeping entries for payments for purchases

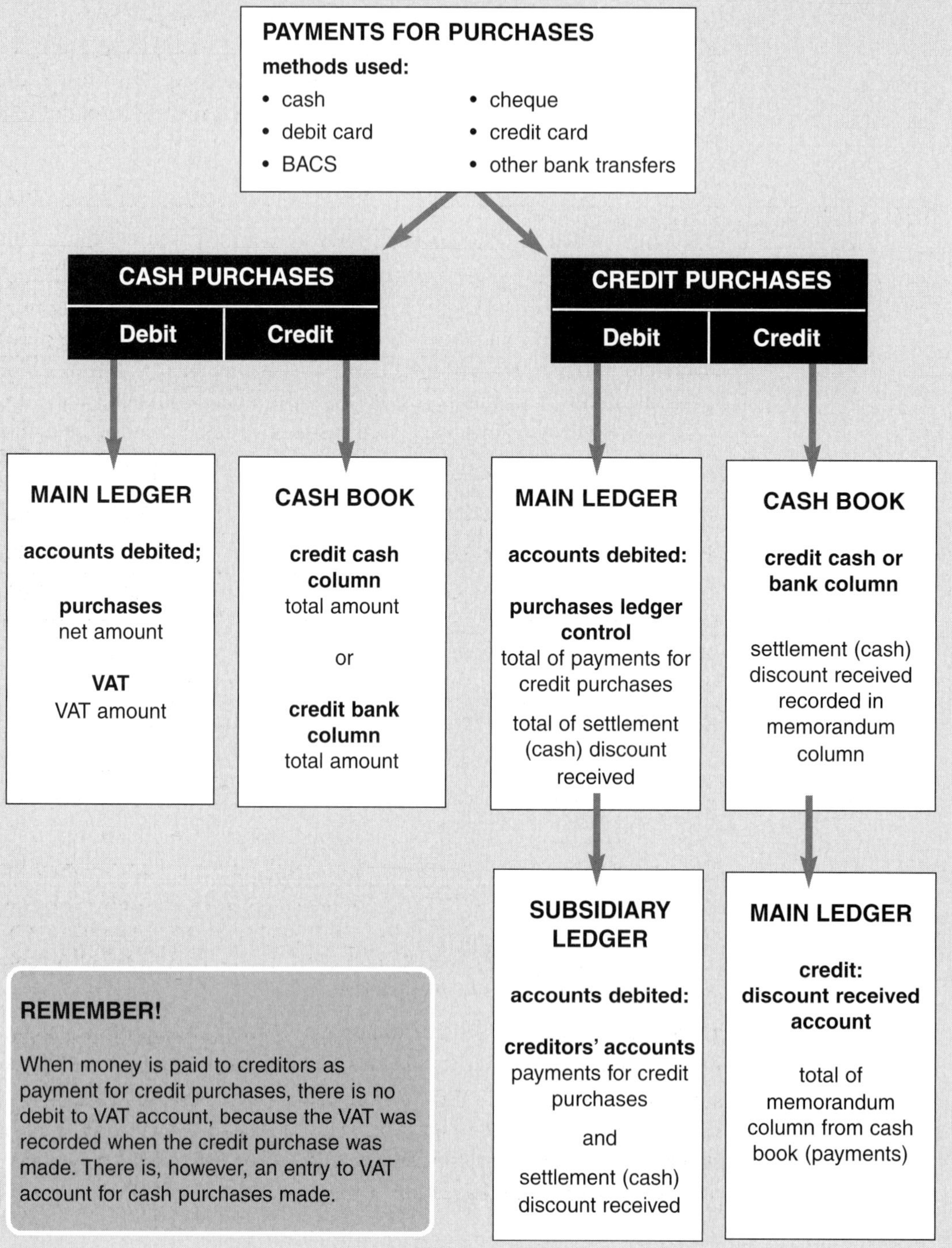

REMEMBER!

When money is paid to creditors as payment for credit purchases, there is no debit to VAT account, because the VAT was recorded when the credit purchase was made. There is, however, an entry to VAT account for cash purchases made.

BATCH CONTROL SYSTEMS

Businesses that have a large number of payments to creditors will often use batched data entry in order to enter such transactions into the accounts in one 'run'. As we have seen previously in Chapter 11 (page 220), a batch of transactions for a day, week or month is pre-listed on a batch control form, for example:

Batch Control: cheques paid to creditors

Supplier				Debit	Credit	Credit
Date	Account no	Name	Cheque no	Creditors control	Bank	Discount received
				£	£	£
2004						
5 Apr	PL 804	E Lee & Co	101261	160.00	160.00	–
6 Apr	PL 610	S Crane	101262	150.00	145.00	5.00
9 Apr	PL 698	S Ford	101265	75.00	70.00	5.00
			Check list totals	385.00	375.00	10.00

Prepared by	Neil Ford	Date	9 Apr 2004
Checked by	*Barbara Smith*	Date	*9 Apr 2004*
Posted by	*Dan Ryan*	Date	*9 Apr 2004*

Note that payments to suppliers by bank credit and by standing order have not been shown on the batch control form – only cheques paid are listed. Where a business has large numbers of payments – using methods such as bank credit, standing order, credit and debit cards – it can use batch control systems for each type of payment.

Totals are taken from the batch control form and transferred to purchases ledger control account – it is probably better practice to debit the two separate amounts, ie £375.00 and £10.00, rather than the total debit of £385.00. Payments made other than by cheque – such as bank transfers, standing orders and debit/credit card payments will also be debited to purchases ledger control account.

THE CASH BOOK IN THE ACCOUNTING SYSTEM

The cash book performs two functions within the accounting system:

- it is the book of prime entry for cash/bank transactions
- it forms part of the double-entry system

For the payments side of the cash book these functions are illustrated below:

CASH AND BANK PAYMENTS

PRIME DOCUMENTS

- receipts
- cheque book counterfoils
- BACS and other bank transfers made
- debit and credit card vouchers

↓

BOOK OF PRIME ENTRY
AND DOUBLE-ENTRY BOOK-KEEPING

CREDIT cash book payments

↓

DOUBLE-ENTRY BOOK-KEEPING

either

- DEBIT purchases ledger control account (money paid), and creditors' accounts in the subsidiary (purchases) ledger

or

- DEBIT other account, eg purchases account (for cash purchases), VAT account (for VAT on cash purchases)

CASH BOOK – ALTERNATIVE LAYOUTS

A cash book can be adapted to suit the needs of a business – earlier in this chapter we have seen how a three-column cash book incorporates a memorandum column for settlement discount. Two further layouts often used are:

- a cash book which incorporates a money column for VAT
- an analysed cash book which divides both receipts (see Chapter 7) and payments between a number of categories; for example payments could

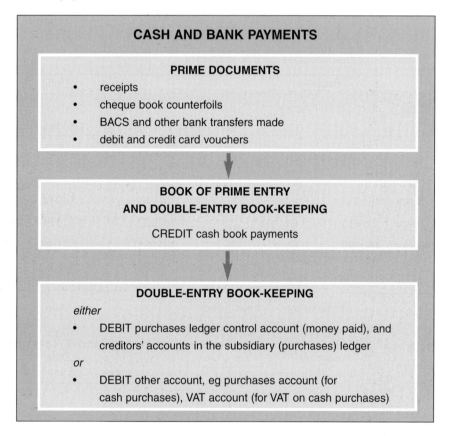

be divided between:

- the main sections of a business, eg, for an audio/video shop, (1) compact discs, (2) video tapes, and (3) DVDs
- (1) discount received, (2) Value Added Tax, (3) cash purchases (4) purchases ledger, ie payments to creditors, (5) sundry payments

Examples of these further cash book layouts are shown in the two Case Studies which follow: the first is for a cash book which incorporates a VAT column, the second is for an analysed cash book.

CASH BOOK INCORPORATING VAT

situation

The following payments transactions are to be recorded in the cash book of Eveshore Growers for the week commencing Monday, 7 June 2004. Assume the VAT rate is 17.5%. The cash book has columns for discount received, VAT and bank.

7 Jun	Paid £235 by cheque to a creditor, Brooklyn Traders
7 Jun	Paid insurance premium of £130 by cheque (no Value Added Tax)
8 Jun	Paid for office stationery by cheque £47, including Value Added Tax
8 Jun	Paid an invoice for £100 from A–Z Supplies, a creditor, by cheque after deducting £5 cash discount
9 Jun	Cash purchase of £188, including Value Added Tax, paid for by cheque
9 Jun	Paid wages of £305, by cheque.

As cashier to Eveshore Growers, you are to:

- write up page 54 of the payments side of the book for the week commencing 7 June 2004, using separate columns for discount, VAT and bank (note that no cash column is required in this cash book)
- sub-total the cash book at 11 June 2004
- explain how the totals for the discount and VAT columns will be entered in the main ledger of Eveshore Growers

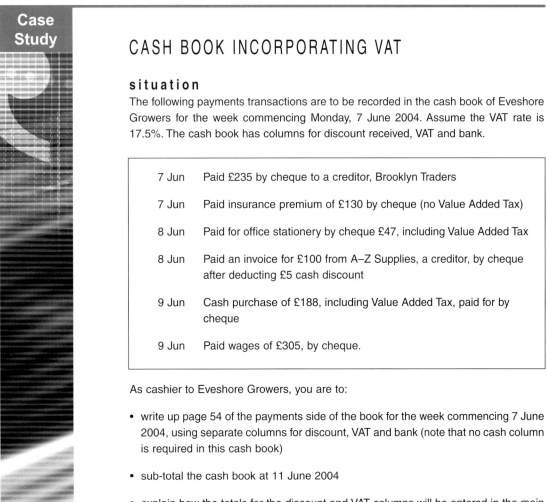

solution

Credit		Cash Book: Payments			CBP 54
Date	Details	Folio	Discount received	VAT	Bank
2004			£	£	£
7 Jun	Brooklyn Traders	PL			235
7 Jun	Insurance	ML			130
8 Jun	Office stationery	ML		7	47
8 Jun	A-Z Supplies	PL	5		95
9 Jun	Purchases	ML		28	188
9 Jun	Wages	ML			305
			5	35	1,000

notes:

- The folio columns have been completed as follows (account numbers not shown):

  ML = main ledger

  PL = purchases ledger, ie subsidiary (purchases) ledger

- For transactions involving purchases ledger (eg Brooklyn Traders), no amount for VAT is shown in the VAT columns. This is because VAT has been charged on invoices received and was recorded in the VAT account (through the purchases day book) when the purchase was made.
- VAT on cash purchases, and other transactions, is recorded in the VAT analysis column.
- Payments to creditors (eg Brooklyn Traders) are debited to purchases ledger control account in the main ledger, and to the creditors' accounts in the subsidiary (purchases) ledger.

The discount and VAT columns:

- discount received column – the total of £5 will be credited to discount received account in the main ledger, debited to purchases ledger control account in the main ledger and to the account of A-Z Supplies in the subsidiary (purchases) ledger
- VAT column – the total of £35 will be debited to VAT account in the main ledger (alternatively the individual amounts of £7 and £28 could be debited)

Note that, in the cash book, the discount received and VAT columns 'start again' from zero after the totals have been transferred to the main ledger accounts.

Case Study

ANALYSED CASH BOOK

situation

Wyvern Auto Spares Limited buys car parts from manufacturers. The company is registered for VAT. The business uses a cash book which analyses payments as follows:

PAYMENTS

- discount received
- VAT
- cash purchases
- purchases ledger, ie subsidiary (purchases) ledger
- sundry payments

The following payments transactions are to be entered on page 31 of the payments side of the cash book for the first week of December 2004:

6 Dec	Purchases for cash, £120 + VAT
6 Dec	Paid £235 by cheque to a creditor, Wyvern Electronics
7 Dec	Paid rent on premises, £325 (no VAT) by cheque
7 Dec	Paid an invoice for £250 from Boxhall Supplies Limited (a creditor) by cheque for £240, £10 discount being received for prompt settlement
8 Dec	Paid for office stationery in cash, £40 + VAT
9 Dec	Paid for urgently needed spares in cash, £80 + VAT
9 Dec	Paid an invoice for £155 from Vord Supplies (a creditor) by cheque for £150, £5 discount being received for prompt settlement
10 Dec	Paid wages £385 in cash

The rate of Value Added Tax is 17.5%

solution

Credit				Cash Book: Payments					CBP 31
Date	Details	Folio	Cash	Bank	Discount received	VAT	Cash purchases	Purchases ledger	Sundry
2004			£	£	£	£	£	£	£
6 Dec	Purchases	ML	141			21	120		
6 Dec	Wyvern Electronics	PL		235				235	
7 Dec	Rent paid	ML		325					325
7 Dec	Boxhall Supplies Limited	PL		240	10			240	
8 Dec	Office stationery	ML	47			7			40
9 Dec	Purchases	ML	94			14	80		
9 Dec	Vord Supplies	PL		150	5			150	
10 Dec	Wages	ML	385						385
			667	950	15	42	200	625	750

notes

- The payments side of the cash book analyses each payment between a number of headings. A business will adapt the cash book and use whatever analysis columns suit it best for its payments.
- References to the ledger sections have been shown in the folio column.
- For transactions involving purchases ledger, no amount for VAT is shown in the VAT columns. This is because VAT has been charged on invoices received and was recorded in the VAT account (through the purchases day book) when the purchase was made.
- The columns are sub-totalled at the end of the week and the totals of the analysis columns are transferred to other accounts as follows:
  - discount received column total of £15 is credited to discount received account in the main ledger and debited to purchases ledger control account in the main ledger
  - Value Added Tax column, the total of £42 is debited to VAT account in the main ledger
  - cash purchases column total of £200 is debited to purchases account in the main ledger
  - purchases ledger column, the total of £625 is debited to purchases ledger control account in the main ledger
- Individual amounts of payments to creditors and discount received are debited to creditors' accounts in the subsidiary (purchases) ledger.
- Sundry payments are dealt with individually by debiting the appropriate account (eg rent paid, office stationery, wages): see section below.

OTHER PAYMENTS

In addition to payments to creditors and for cash purchases, the credit side of the cash book is used to record other payments of the business. These include:

- drawings withdrawn from the business by the owner
- loan repayments made by the business to the loan provider
- expenses of running the business, such as wages, telephone
- purchase of fixed assets (items bought for use in the business on a semi-permanent basis, eg buildings, vehicles, office equipment)

Each of these will be considered in further detail in Chapter 17 where we will see where they fit into the double-entry system. For the moment we will see how they are recorded in the double-entry system of cash book and ledger accounts:

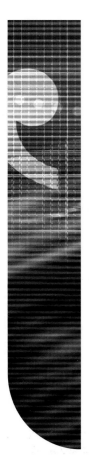

- **owner's drawings**
  - *debit* drawings account
  - *credit* cash book

  The owner of the business withdraws money from the business in the form of cash or a cheque.

- **loan repayments**
  - *debit* loan account
  - *credit* cash book

  The amount of the loan repayment is recorded in cash book.

- **business expenses**
  - *debit* expenses account (using the appropriate account, eg wages account, telephone expenses account)
  - *credit* cash book

  Business expenses are paid either in the form of cash or through the bank. Also note that low-value business expenses are often paid in cash through the petty cash book – see next chapter.

- **purchase of fixed assets**
  - *debit* fixed asset account (using the appropriate account, eg buildings account, vehicles account, office equipment account)
  - *credit* cash book

  The amount of the cost of fixed assets purchased is paid from cash book.

example transactions:

2004

16 Jun	The owner of the business draws £100 from the bank for own use
17 Jun	Made a loan repayment of £750 by direct debit to MBC Bank (no VAT)
18 Jun	Paid telephone bill of £282 (including VAT) by cheque
21 Jun	Bought new computer for use in the office, £1,175 (including VAT) paid by cheque

The cash book (payments) records these transactions as follows:

Credit		Cash Book: Payments			CBP 10
Date	Details	Folio	Discount received	Cash	Bank
2004			£	£	£
16 Jun	Drawings	ML			100
17 Jun	Loan: MBC Bank	ML			750
18 Jun	Telephone expenses	ML			282
21 Jun	Computer	ML			1,175

Note: alternative layouts of the cash book (payments) could be used; in particular, a layout incorporating the VAT column is especially useful on the payments side.

The debit entries are shown in the main ledger (which contains all of these accounts) as follows:

MAIN LEDGER

Dr		Drawings Account			Cr
2004			£	2004	£
16 Jun	Bank	CBP 10	100		

Dr		Loan Account : MBC Bank			Cr
2004			£	2004	£
17 Jun	Bank	CBP 10	750		

Dr		Telephone Expenses Account			Cr
2004			£	2004	£
18 Jun	Bank	CBP 10	240		

Dr		Value Added Tax Account			Cr
2004			£	2004	£
1 Jun	Bank	CBP 10	42		
21 Jun	Bank	CBP 10	175		

Dr			Computer Account		Cr
2004			£	2004	£
21 Jun	Bank	CBP 10	1,000		

PETTY CASH BOOK

Petty cash book is another type of cash book; it is used for low-value expenses payments made in cash. A particular benefit of the use of a petty cash book is that it takes a lot of small transactions away from the main cashier and reduces the number of transactions passing through the cash book.

We shall look in detail at petty cash book in the next chapter.

EXPENSES CLAIMS

A further duty of the cashier (or the petty cashier – see Chapter 16) is the checking of *expenses claims.*

Often an employee is required to pay for expenses incurred on behalf of the business or organisation, and then to claim back the amount already paid from the business. Typically, expenses which can be reclaimed include:

- Travel, eg rail, bus, air and taxi fares, mileage allowance where a private car, motorbike or cycle has been used. (Note that the costs of travel to and from work are not paid, except under special circumstances, eg the burglar alarm goes off in the middle of the night and the police request the presence of the keyholder).
- Hotel bills, including meals.
- Subsistence allowance – to cover the costs of working away from the normal place of employment, often paid at a daily rate.
- Other expenses, eg part of the employee's domestic telephone bill.

A business will establish the terms under which it will reimburse an employee. For example, travel claims might have to be at the cheapest form of travel, such as a bus, even if the employee uses his/her private car; first-class travel is likely to be available only to senior employees. Before refunding expenses, the business will usually require proof of the expense, eg a receipt, or the travel ticket.

claims procedure

At regular intervals – perhaps monthly – an employee will be required to submit an expenses claim (see next page). The procedure is likely to be:

- Employee completes and signs expenses claim form.
- Receipts for the expenses are attached to the expenses claim form.
- The form is passed to the employee's manager or section head for authorisation.
- The form is then sent to the accounts department where the amounts will be checked against the company's policies. The calculations on the form will also be checked. The various expenses will then be coded for the appropriate main ledger account, eg travel expenses, telephone expenses, etc. The book-keeping will be:

  – *debit* appropriate expense account (in the main ledger)

  – *credit* cash book payments (cash or bank column, as appropriate)
- The amount will either be paid direct to the employee in cash, by cheque or BACS (small amounts can be paid out of petty cash – see Chapter 16), or the employee's pay will be credited and the amount paid at the next payroll run.
- The firm's main ledger expenses accounts will be debited with the cost. Where an expense includes VAT, a VAT-registered business will debit the appropriate expense account with the net amount of the expense, and debit the VAT to VAT account; in this way, the business claims back the VAT paid on the expense.

income tax and expenses

Most expenses are wholly incurred on behalf of the business or organisation. As such, their reimbursement does not form a part of the employee's salary, and is not subject to income tax. However, some expenses incurred are only partly used on behalf of the business, the other part is a benefit to the employee. Examples include the provision of a company car, or payment of the employee's telephone bill.

The Inland Revenue lays down guidelines which, depending on the circumstances, state the employee's liability for income tax, together with the employee's and employer's liability for National Insurance Contributions.

WYVERN TRADERS LIMITED

EXPENSES CLAIM FOR THE MONTH ENDING ....

Name:

Department:

							OFFICE USE ONLY	
Date	Item	Travelling £	Subsistence £	Entertaining £	Miscellaneous £	Total £	VAT £	Net £
	Total							

Signed:

Date:

Authorised by:

Date:

expenses claim form

Chapter Summary

- The cash book records payments (double-entry credits) made through the bank.
- The basic layout for a cash book (payments) includes a money column for bank transactions, together with a column for discount received. Cash books for businesses which deal with substantial amounts of cash may have a further money column to record cash transactions.
- Another common cash book layout incorporates a VAT column.
- An analysed cash book is used to provide more information: it divides payments between a number of categories.
- The cashier may be responsible for checking expenses claims.

Key Terms

cash book records both cash and bank transactions; combines the roles of book of prime entry and double-entry book-keeping

columnar cash book commonly-used layout for cash books which incorporates several money columns, eg for settlement discount, VAT, cash, bank

analysed cash book cash book which divides payments (and receipts) between a number of categories, eg the main sections of the business

expenses claims forms used by employees to claim back expenses paid by the employee but incurred on behalf of the business or organisation

Student Activities

15.1 The cash book records:

(a) receipts and payments in cash only

(b) receipts and payments through the bank only

(c) all receipts and payments both in cash and through the bank

(d) receipts and payments both in cash (except for low-value expense payments) and through the bank

Answer (a) or (b) or (c) or (d)

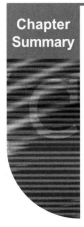

15.2 The following are the payments transactions of Trevellas Traders for February 2004:

3 Feb	Paid G Wheaton, a creditor, £195 by cheque no 101359
5 Feb	Paid A Aznar, a creditor, cheque no 101360 for £390 in full settlement of a debt of £400
10 Feb	Paid wages in cash, £370
12 Feb	Paid Singh Limited, a creditor, cheque no 101361 for £570 in full settlement of a debt of £585
17 Feb	Paid telephone account £155 in cash
19 Feb	Paid Farr and Company, a creditor, cheque no 101362 for £220 in full settlement of a debt of £230
27 Feb	Paid rent £160 by standing order

You are to:

- Enter the above payments on page 22 of the three column cash book (which has columns for discount received, cash, and bank) of Trevellas Traders.
- Sub-total the money columns at 29 February.

Note: entries in the subsidiary (purchases) ledger and main ledger are *not* required.

15.3 The following are the payments transactions of Metro Trading Company for August 2004:

2 Aug	Cash purchases paid for in cash, £80 + VAT
5 Aug	Paid T Hall Limited a cheque for £541 in full settlement of a debt of £565
9 Aug	Paid wages in cash, £254 (no VAT)
17 Aug	Paid F Jarvis £457 by cheque
18 Aug	The owner of the business withdraws £200 in cash for own use
19 Aug	Paid rent by cheque, £275 (no VAT)
20 Aug	Paid wages in cash, £436 (no VAT)
24 Aug	Paid J Jones a cheque for £628 in full settlement of a debt of £661
27 Aug	Cash purchases paid for by cheque, £200 + VAT
27 Aug	Paid salaries by cheque, £2,043 (no VAT)
30 Aug	Paid telephone account by cheque, £282 (including VAT)
30 Aug	Bought office equipment, paying by cheque, £600 + VAT

The rate of Value Added Tax is 17.5%.

Account numbers are to be used – see the next page.

You are to:

- Enter the above payments on page 45 of the three column cash book of Metro Trading Company. The cash book has columns for discount received, cash and bank.
- Sub-total the money columns at 31 August.

- Show the entries to be made in the following accounts:

  subsidiary (purchases) ledger

  T Hall Limited (account no 451)

  F Jarvis (account no 510)

  J Jones (account no 643)

  main ledger

  purchases ledger control account (account no 6002)

  discount received account (account no 6502)

  drawings account (account no 7005)

  office equipment account (account no 750)

  purchases account (account no 5001)

  rent paid account (account no 6950)

  telephone expenses account (account no 6212)

  VAT account (account no 2200)

  wages and salaries account (account no 7750)

15.4 The following are the payments transactions of Johnson Brothers for April 2004:

2 Apr	Cash purchases of £47 (including VAT) paid by cheque
2 Apr	Paid travelling expenses of £65 (no VAT) by cheque
5 Apr	Paid the telephone bill of £235 (including VAT) by cheque
6 Apr	Loan repayment of £500 made to ABC Bank by direct debit (no VAT)
9 Apr	The owners of the business withdrew £600 by cheque for own use
13 Apr	Paid an invoice for £190 from M Hughes (a creditor) by cheque for £180, £10 being received for prompt settlement
15 Apr	Bought office stationery £80 + VAT, paying by cheque
16 Apr	Cash purchases of £94 (including VAT) paid by cheque
19 Apr	Bought office equipment, paying by cheque, £400 + VAT
26 Apr	Paid a cheque for £245 to Wilson Limited, a creditor, in full settlement of an invoice for £255
27 Apr	Cash purchases of £120 + VAT, paid by cheque
29 Apr	Paid wages, £350 (no VAT) by cheque
30 Apr	Paid a cheque for £560 to Lucinda Luz, a creditor, in full settlement of an invoice for £580

The rate of Value Added Tax is 17.5%

Account numbers are to be used – see below.

You are to:

- Enter the above payments on page 88 of the cash book of Johnson Brothers, using columns for date, details, discount received, VAT and bank.
- Sub-total the money columns at 30 April.
- Show the entries to be made in the following accounts:

  subsidiary (purchases) ledger

  M Hughes (account no 498)

  Wilson Limited (account no 752)

  Lucinda Luz (account no 601)

  main ledger

  purchases ledger control account (account no 6002)

  discount received account (account no 6502)

  drawings account (account no 7005)

  loan account: ABC Bank (account no 2250)

  office equipment account (account no 750)

  office stationery account (account no 6384)

  purchases account (account no 5001)

  telephone expenses account (account no 6212)

  travelling expenses account (account no 6330)

  VAT account (account no 2200)

  wages and salaries account (account no 7750)

15.5 David Lewis runs a shop selling carpets. He buys his carpets direct from the manufacturers, who allow him credit terms. His business is registered for VAT.

He uses an analysed cash book which has columns for:

- bank
- discount received
- VAT
- purchases
- purchases ledger
- sundry

The following transactions take place during the week commencing 17 May 2004:

17 May	Cash purchases of £75.70 + VAT paid by cheque
17 May	Paid telephone bill of £238.90 (including VAT) by cheque
18 May	Loan repayment of £250.00 made to Wyvern Finance by direct debit (no VAT)
18 May	Paid shop rent by cheque, £255.50 (no VAT)
19 May	Cash purchases of £100.00 (including VAT) paid by cheque

19 May	Paid an invoice for £368.20 from Terry Carpets Limited (a creditor) by cheque for £363.55 and receiving £4.65 discount for prompt settlement
19 May	Paid for stationery by cheque, £28.20 (including VAT)
20 May	David Lewis draws £100.00 from the bank, by cheque, for his own use
20 May	Bought shop fittings £265.00 + VAT, paying by cheque
21 May	Paid an invoice for £295.80 from Longlife Carpets Limited (a creditor), paying £291.50 by cheque, £4.30 discount being received for prompt settlement
21 May	Paid wages, £314.20 by cheque (no VAT)
21 May	Paid a cheque to Trade Supplies (a creditor) for £145.50 in full settlement of an invoice for £149.00

The rate of Value Added Tax is 17.5%

Account numbers are to be used – see below.

You are to:

- Enter the above payments on page 96 of the analysed cash book of David Lewis (VAT amounts should be rounded down to the nearest penny).
- Sub-total the money columns at 21 May.
- Show the entries to be made in the following accounts:

subsidiary (purchases) ledger

Terry Carpets Limited (account no 721)

Longlife Carpets Limited (account no 624)

Trade Supplies (account no 784)

main ledger

purchases ledger control account (account no 6002)

discount received account (account no 6502)

drawings account (account no 7005)

loan account: Wyvern Finance (account no 2270)

purchases account (account no 5001)

shop fittings account (account no 740)

shop rent account (account no 6345)

stationery account (account no 6382)

telephone expenses account (account no 6212)

VAT account (account no 2200)

wages and salaries account (account no 7750)

15.6 Prepare a purchases ledger control account for the month of April 2004 from the following information:

2004		£
1 Apr	Purchases ledger balances	14,275
30 Apr	Credit purchases for month	36,592
	Purchases returns	653
	Payments made to creditors	31,074
	Settlement discount received	1,048
	Transfer of credit balances to sales ledger	597

The creditors figure at 30 April is to be entered as the balancing figure.

16 Petty cash book

this chapter covers . . .

A petty cash book is used to record low-value cash payments for various small purchases and expenses incurred by a business or other organisation.

An amount of cash is handed by the cashier to a member of staff, the petty cashier, who:

- *is responsible for security of the petty cash money*
- *makes cash payments against authorised petty cash vouchers*
- *records the payments made, and analyses them, in a petty cash book*

Towards the end of the chapter we will see how a petty cash book is balanced, and the way in which it fits into the double-entry book-keeping system.

NVQ PERFORMANCE CRITERIA COVERED

unit 2: MAKING AND RECORDING PAYMENTS

element 2.2

process payments

A *calculate payments from relevant documentation*

B *schedule payments and obtain authorisation*

D *enter payments into accounting records*

E *identify queries and resolve or refer to the appropriate person*

F *ensure security and confidentiality is maintained according to organisational requirements*

THE PETTY CASH PROCEDURE

The petty cash book is used to record low-value cash payments for purchases and expenses – such as small items of stationery, postages – items which it would not be appropriate to enter in the cash book. Instead, an amount of cash is handed by the cashier to a member of staff, the petty cashier, who is responsible for all aspects of the control of petty cash, principally:

- security of the petty cash money
- making cash payments against authorised petty cash vouchers
- recording the payments made, and analysing them, in a petty cash book

In order to operate the petty cash system, the petty cashier needs the following:

- a *petty cash book* in which to record and analyse transactions
- a *lockable cash box* in which to keep the money
- a stock of blank *petty cash vouchers* (see page 329) for claims on petty cash to be made
- a *lockable desk drawer* in which to keep these items

making a claim

As an employee you are most likely to encounter the petty cash system when making claims for money for small purchases you have made. Before studying the form-filling procedures in detail, read the summary of a typical petty cash transaction set out below:

your supervisor asks you to go and buy a box of computer disks from an office supplies shop

↓

you go to the shop and buy the computer disks; having paid for them, you retain the receipt (for £5.50) which you hand to the petty cashier on your return to the office

↓

the petty cashier authorises a petty cash voucher which contains details of the purchase

↓

the petty cashier gives you £5.50 in cash

↓

the petty cashier attaches the receipt to the petty cash voucher and enters the details in the petty cash book

WHAT ITEMS CAN BE PASSED THROUGH PETTY CASH BOOK?

Petty cash is used to make small cash payments for purchases and expenses incurred by the business. Examples of the type of payments made from petty cash include:

- stationery items
- small items of office supplies
- casual wages
- window cleaning
- bus, rail and taxi fares (incurred on behalf of the business)
- meals and drinks (incurred on behalf of the business)
- postages
- tips and donations

Petty cash should not be used to pay for private expenses of employees, eg tea, coffee, and milk, unless the business has agreed these in advance.

All payments made through petty cash must be supported by relevant documentation. Such documentation includes:

- receipt from a shop
- post office receipt for postage
- rail or bus ticket
- restaurant bill
- receipt from taxi company
- receipt from window cleaning firm

The petty cashier is usually able to authorise petty cash transactions up to a maximum value – for example, up to £25 for any one expense item is a common figure. Larger amounts can often be paid from petty cash provided the expense is authorised by the accounts supervisor.

Case Study

TYAX ENGINEERING LTD: PETTY CASH EXPENSES

situation

You work in the accounts office of Tyax Engineering Limited. One of your duties is that of petty cashier; you are able to authorise transactions up to £25. Which of the following expenses would you allow to be paid out of petty cash?

- envelopes for use in the office, £2.50
- postage on an urgent parcel of engineering parts, £3.75
- bus fare to work claimed by secretary, £1.20
- car mileage to work of office manager called in late at night when the burglar alarm went off (false alarm!), £5.50

- tea and coffee for use in the office, £3.70
- office window cleaning, £2.80
- plant bought for reception area, £5.50
- computer disks, £35.00
- donation to local charity by the business, £5.00
- meal allowance paid to a member of staff required to work during the lunch hour, £3.50

Note: you may assume that all expenses are supported by relevant documentation, such as receipt from a shop, post office etc.

solution

For most expenses it is clear whether or not they can be drawn from petty cash. However, there are points to consider for some of the expenses.

Envelopes	pay from petty cash
Postage	pay from petty cash
Bus fare to work	this is a personal expense and cannot be drawn from petty cash
Car mileage	travel to work is a personal expense, as seen with the previous item; however, as this expense was a special journey in the middle of the night in order to resolve a business problem, it can be paid from petty cash
Tea and coffee	this is a personal expense of employees and cannot normally be paid out of petty cash; however, if the ingredients were used to make drinks for official visitors and customers, it can be paid from petty cash
Window cleaning	pay from petty cash
Plant	pay from petty cash (but plants for the general office cannot be bought with the company's money)
Computer disks	this is a business expense but, in view of the amount (above the authorised limit of the petty cashier) it should be referred to the supervisor or manager for authorisation
Donation	pay from petty cash, subject to authorisation by supervisor
Meal allowance	pay from petty cash, provided that it is company policy to make an allowance in these circumstances

Notes to the Case Study

- If the petty cashier is unable to resolve whether or not an expense can be paid from petty cash, the item should be referred to the accounts supervisor for a decision.
- Before payments can be made for petty cash expenses, they must be:
  - within the authorisation limit of the petty cashier (for example, £25 maximum for any one expense item)

  - supported by documentary evidence, such as a receipt or a rail/bus ticket
  - authorised by the petty cashier, or referred to the appropriate supervisor or manager

- Some businesses allow amounts above the authorisation limit of the petty cashier to be paid from petty cash provided that the expense is authorised by the accounts supervisor.

THE IMPREST METHOD

Most petty cash books operate using the imprest method. With this method the petty cashier starts each week (or month) with a certain amount of money – the imprest amount. As payments are made during the week (or month) the amount of money will reduce and, at the end of the period, the cash will be made up by the main cashier to the imprest amount. For example:

Started week with imprest amount	£100.00
Total of petty cash amounts paid out during week	£80.50
Cash held at end of week	£19.50
Amount drawn from cashier to restore imprest amount	£80.50
Cash at start of next week, ie imprest amount	£100.00

If, at any time, the imprest amount proves to be insufficient, further amounts of cash can be drawn from the cashier. Also, from time-to-time, it may be necessary to increase the imprest amount so that regular shortfalls of petty cash are avoided.

THE NON-IMPREST METHOD

Where a petty cash book is *not* kept on the imprest method, the petty cashier has a float of cash which is replenished by the cashier whenever it runs low. Thus, unlike the imprest method where the cash float is replenished at regular intervals eg weekly or monthly, the float of the non-imprest method is 'topped up' only as and when required.

PETTY CASH VOUCHER

Payments out of petty cash are made only against correct documentation – usually a petty cash voucher (see next page). Petty cash vouchers are completed as follows:

- details and amount of expenditure

- signature of the person making the claim and receiving the money
- signature of the person authorising the payment to be made – usually the petty cashier for amounts within the authorisation limit; larger amounts will be authorised by the accounts supervisor or manager
- additionally, most petty cash vouchers are numbered, so that they can be controlled, the number being entered in the petty cash book
- relevant documentation, such as a receipt from a shop or post office etc, should be attached to the petty cash voucher

petty cash voucher Number *807*

date *8 October 2004*

description	amount £	p
C5 Envelopes	*2*	*35*
Photocopier paper	*4*	*70*
	7	*05*

signature *T Harris*

authorised *R Singh*

Petty cash vouchers are the *prime documents* for the petty cash book.

LAYOUT OF A PETTY CASH BOOK

Petty cash book is usually set out as follows:

Receipts	Date	Details	Voucher No	Total Payment	Analysis columns				
					VAT	Postages	Stationery	Travel	Ledger
£				£	£	£	£	£	£

The layout shows that:

- receipts from the main cashier are entered in the column on the extreme left
- there are columns for the date and details of all receipts and payments

- there is a column for the petty cash voucher number
- the total payment (ie the amount paid out on each petty cash voucher) is in the next column
- then follow the analysis columns which analyse each transaction entered in the 'total payment' column (note that VAT may need to be calculated – see below)

A business or organisation will use whatever analysis columns are most suitable for it and, indeed, there may be more columns than shown in the example. It is important that expenses are analysed to the correct columns so that the contents show a true picture of petty cash expenditure.

PETTY CASH AND VAT

Value Added Tax is charged by VAT-registered businesses on their taxable supplies. Therefore, there will often be VAT included as part of the expense paid out of petty cash. However, not all expenses will have been subject to VAT. There are four possible circumstances:

- VAT has been charged at the standard rate
- VAT has not been charged because the supplier is not VAT-registered
- the zero rate of VAT applies, eg food and drink (but not meals which are standard-rated), books, newspapers, transport (but not taxis and hire cars)
- the supplies are exempt (eg financial services, postal services)

Often the indication of the supplier's VAT registration number on a receipt or invoice will tell you that VAT has been charged at the standard rate.

Where VAT has been charged, the amount of tax might be indicated separately on the receipt or invoice. However, for small money amounts it is quite usual for a total to be shown without indicating the amount of VAT. An example of a receipt which does not show the VAT content is illustrated below. The receipt is for a box of envelopes purchased from Wyvern Stationers. It shows:

- the name and address of the retailer
- the date and time of the transaction
- the VAT registration number of the retailer
- the price of the item – £4.70
- the amount of money given – a £10 note
- the amount of change given – £5.30

	Wyvern Stationers
	25 High St Mereford
	08 10 04 16.07
	VAT Reg 454 7106 34
Salesperson Rashid	
Stationery	**4.70**
TOTAL	**4.70**
CASH	**10.00**
CHANGE	**5.30**

What it does not show, however, is the VAT content of the purchase price – it only shows the price after the VAT has been added on.

How do we calculate purchase price before the VAT is added on?

The formula, with VAT at 17.5%, is:

price including VAT ÷ 1.175 = price before VAT is added on

in this case …

£4.70 ÷ 1.175 = £4.00 = price before VAT is added on

The VAT content is therefore

£4.70 less £4.00 = 70p

Here £0.70 will be entered in the VAT column in the petty cash book, £4.00 in the appropriate expense column, and the full £4.70 in the total payment column.

Remember when calculating VAT amounts that fractions of a penny are ignored, ie the tax is rounded *down* to a whole penny.

Case Study

WYVERN TRADERS: PETTY CASH BOOK

situation

You work in the accounts office of Wyvern Traders. One of your tasks is to keep the petty cash book, which is operated on the imprest method. There are a number of transactions which you have authorised (all transactions, unless otherwise indicated, include VAT at 17.5%) to be entered for the week on page 30 of the petty cash book:

2004	
5 Apr	Started the week with an imprest amount of £50.00
5 Apr	Paid stationery £3.76 on voucher no 47
5 Apr	Paid taxi fare £2.82 on voucher no 48
6 Apr	Paid postages £0.75 (no VAT) on voucher no 49
7 Apr	Paid taxi fare £4.70 on voucher no 50
7 Apr	Paid J Jones, a creditor, £6.00 (no VAT shown in petty cash book – amount will be on VAT account already) on voucher no 51
8 Apr	Paid stationery £3.76 on voucher no 52
8 Apr	Paid postages £2.85 (no VAT) on voucher no 53
9 Apr	Paid taxi fare £6.11 on voucher no 54

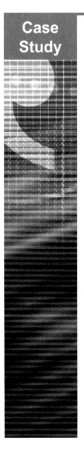

solution

The petty cash book is written up as follows:

Petty Cash Book									PCB 30
						Analysis columns			
Receipts	Date	Details	Voucher No	Total Payment	VAT	Postages	Stationery	Travel	Ledger
£	2004			£	£	£	£	£	£
50.00	5 Apr	Balance b/d							
	5 Apr	Stationery	47	3.76	0.56		3.20		
	5 Apr	Taxi fare	48	2.82	0.42			2.40	
	6 Apr	Postages	49	0.75		0.75			
	7 Apr	Taxi fare	50	4.70	0.70			4.00	
	7 Apr	J Jones	51	6.00					6.00
	8 Apr	Stationery	52	3.76	0.56		3.20		
	8 Apr	Postages	53	2.85		2.85			
	9 Apr	Taxi fare	54	6.11	0.91			5.20	
				30.75	3.15	3.60	6.40	11.60	6.00

Notes to the Case Study

Each page of the petty cash book is numbered – here 'PCB 30' – this helps with cross-referencing in the accounts system.

- For each petty cash item, the analysis columns add up to the amount shown in the 'total payment' column
- The totals of the analysis columns add up to the total payment
- The petty cashier will give the firm's book-keeper a posting sheet (see page 335) giving details of the total of each analysis column so that the amounts can be recorded in the double-entry accounts system
- Total payments are £30.75 and, as the petty cash book is kept using the imprest method, this is the amount of cash which will need to be drawn from the cashier in order to restore the imprest
- We shall see how the petty cash book is balanced in the next section (below).

BALANCING PETTY CASH BOOK

A petty cash book is balanced by comparing the receipts and payments columns – just like other double-entry accounts. Where a petty cash book is operated using the imprest method, a further receipt will be the amount of cash received from the main cashier to restore the imprest amount – this is equal to the total paid out during the week.

The following shows how the petty cash book seen in the Case Study above is balanced at the end of the week:

Petty Cash Book										PCB 30
Receipts	Date	Details	Voucher No	Total Payment	Analysis columns					
					VAT	Postages	Stationery	Travel	Ledger	
£	2004			£	£	£	£	£	£	
50.00	5 Apr	Balance b/d								
	5 Apr	Stationery	47	3.76	0.56		3.20			
	5 Apr	Taxi fare	48	2.82	0.42			2.40		
	6 Apr	Postages	49	0.75		0.75				
	7 Apr	Taxi fare	50	4.70	0.70			4.00		
	7 Apr	J Jones	51	6.00					6.00	
	8 Apr	Stationery	52	3.76	0.56		3.20			
	8 Apr	Postages	53	2.85		2.85				
	9 Apr	Taxi fare	54	6.11	0.91			5.20		
				30.75	3.15	3.60	6.40	11.60	6.00	
30.75	9 Apr	Cash received								
	9 Apr	Balance c/d		50.00						
80.75				80.75						
50.00	9 Apr	Balance b/d								

Note that, here, the imprest amount has been restored at the end of the week and before the petty cash book has been balanced. An alternative method, depending on the policy of the company, is to balance the petty cash book *before* restoring the imprest amount – in the above example, this will give a balance brought down on 9 April of £19.25 (ie £50.00 minus £30.75); the money received from the cashier (£30.75) will then be recorded in the receipts column.

Where the petty cash book is operated *not* using the imprest method, it is balanced at regular intervals by comparing the receipts and payments columns. Whenever cash is received from the cashier, it is recorded in the receipts column.

The petty cashier prepares a posting sheet giving details of the total of each analysis column so that the amounts can then be recorded in the double-entry system by the book-keeper.

PETTY CASH AND THE ACCOUNTING SYSTEM

Petty cash book has two uses within the accounting system:

- it acts as a book of prime entry for low value expense payments
- it is part of the double-entry system

Petty cash book, as well as being a book of prime entry, is usually incorporated into the double-entry system, as is shown in the diagram below.

petty cash payments

PRIME DOCUMENT

petty cash voucher for low-value expense payments

↓

BOOK OF PRIME ENTRY AND DOUBLE-ENTRY BOOK-KEEPING

CREDIT petty cash book payments

↓

DOUBLE-ENTRY BOOK-KEEPING

- DEBIT VAT account with total of VAT column

and

- DEBIT appropriate expense account with total of each analysis column

Note: if payments are made to creditors through petty cash book (eg to J Jones in the Case Study on page 331), the debits will be to:

– *purchases ledger control account in the main ledger*
– *creditor's account in the subsidiary (purchases) ledger*

The double-entry book-keeping entries from petty cash book are either posted direct to the main ledger accounts – VAT account and expenses accounts – or often a posting sheet (see below) is used.

At regular intervals – weekly or monthly – the petty cashier prepares a posting sheet which gives the firm's book-keeper details of the totals from the analysis columns of the petty cash book. The posting sheet for the transactions from the Case Study is as follows:

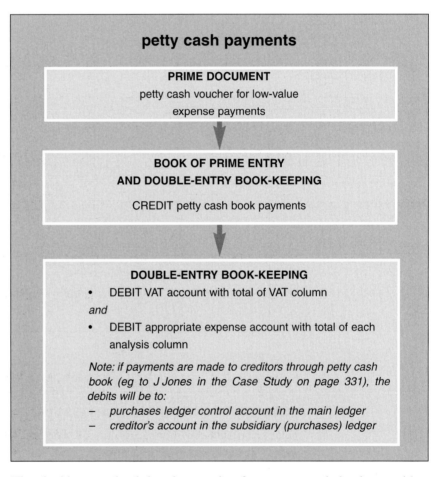

WYVERN TRADERS

Posting sheet: Petty Cash

account name	account number	debit	credit	reference
		£	£	
VAT	ML 2200	3.15		PCB 30
Postages	ML 6348	3.60		PCB 30
Stationery	ML 7290	6.40		PCB 30
Travel expenses	ML 7755	11.60		PCB 30
Purchases ledger control	ML 6002	6.00		PCB 30
Bank	CBP		30.75	PCB 30
TOTAL		30.75	30.75	

Prepared by	*Jane Watkins*	Date	*9 April 2004*
Checked by	*Natalie Wilson*	Date	*9 April 2004*
Posted by	Mark Hopwood	Date	9 April 2004

The posting sheet shows:

- *debits* to VAT and expenses accounts in the main ledger in respect of the total of each analysis column
- *debits* in respect of the ledger column amounts (eg J Jones in the Case Study) to:
  - purchases ledger control account
  - subsidiary (purchases) ledger
- *credit* to bank account, being the total amount of expenses paid from petty cash during the period and the amount that will need to be withdrawn from the bank in order to restore the imprest amount of petty cash

From the Case Study, above, and posting sheet, main ledger accounts will be written up as follows at the end of the week (9 April):

MAIN LEDGER

Dr **Value Added Tax Account** (account no 2200) Cr

2004		£	2004		£
9 Apr	Petty cash book PCB 30	3.15			

Dr	**Postages Account** (account no 6348)		Cr	
2004		£	2004	£
9 Apr	Petty cash book PCB 30	3.60		

Dr	**Stationery Account** (account no 7290)		Cr	
2004		£	2004	£
9 Apr	Petty cash book PCB 30	6.40		

Dr	**Travel Expenses Account** (account no 7755)		Cr	
2004		£	2004	£
9 Apr	Petty cash book PCB 30	11.60		

Dr	**Purchases Ledger Control Account** (account no 6002)		Cr	
2004		£	2004	£
9 Apr	Petty cash book PCB 30	*6.00		

* this transaction will also be debited to the account of the creditor – here J Jones – in the subsidiary (purchases) ledger.

To restore the imprest amount (or to top-up petty cash when the non-imprest method is used), the petty cashier will complete a cheque requisition form either for the cash itself, or for a cheque made payable to cash. The petty cashier will take the cheque to the bank and obtain the cash. An example of a cheque requisition is shown below:

CHEQUE REQUISITION	
Amount	*£30.75*
Payee	*Cash*
Date	*9 April 2004*
Details	*Reimbursement of petty cash*
Signature	*Jane Watkins, petty cashier*
Authorised by	*Natalie Wilson, supervisor*
Cheque no	*017234*

cheque requisition form

The double-entry book-keeping entries to record this reimbursement are:

- *debit* petty cash book
- *credit* cash book, ie the payments side

For example, the amount of £30.75 cash received when balancing the petty cash book seen earlier (page 333) is recorded in the cash book as follows:

Credit		**Cash Book: Payments**			**CBP**
Date	Details	Folio	Discount received	Cash	Bank
2004			£	£	£
9 Apr	Petty cash book 017234	PCB 30			30.75

After this reimbursement, the imprest amount is restored and petty cash book has a balance brought down of £50.00 on 9 April. The petty cash book is now ready for next week's transactions.

CONTROL OF PETTY CASH

The petty cashier is usually responsible to the accounts supervisor for control of the petty cash and for correct recording of authorised petty cash transactions.

Most businesses and organisations set out in writing the procedures to be followed by the petty cashier. This is of benefit not only for the petty cashier to know the extent of his or her duties, but also to help the person who takes over at holiday or other times.

The main procedures for the operation and control of petty cash are:

- On taking over, the petty cashier should check that the petty cash book has been balanced and that the amount of cash held agrees with the balance shown in the book. If there is any discrepancy, this should be referred to the accounts supervisor immediately.
- When the petty cash book is kept under the imprest method, ensure that each week is started with the imprest amount of cash which has been agreed with the accounts supervisor.

- The petty cash is to be kept securely in a locked cash book, and control kept of the keys.
- Petty cash vouchers (in number order) are to be provided on request.
- Petty cash is paid out against correctly completed petty cash vouchers after checking that:
  - the voucher is signed by the person receiving the money
  - the voucher is signed by the person authorising payment (a list of authorised signatories will be provided)
  - a receipt (or other supporting evidence) is attached to the petty cash voucher, and that receipt and petty cash voucher are for the same amount
  - the amount being claimed is within the authorised limit of the petty cashier
- The petty cash book is written up (to include calculation of VAT amounts when appropriate); it is important that the petty cash book is accurate.
- Completed petty cash vouchers are stored safely – filed in numerical order. The vouchers will need to be kept for at least six years. They may be needed by the auditors or in the event of other queries. Completed petty cash books will also need to be retained.
- A surprise check of petty cash will be made by the accounts supervisor – at any one time the cash held plus amounts of petty cash vouchers should equal the imprest amount.
- At the end of each week (or month) the petty cash book is to be balanced.
- Details of the totals of each analysis column are given to the book-keeper – usually on a posting sheet – so that the amount of each expense can be entered into the double-entry system.
- Where the imprest method is used, an amount of cash is drawn from the cashier equal to the amount of payments made, in order to restore the imprest amount.
- The petty cash book and cash in hand are to be presented to the accounts supervisor for checking.
- Any discrepancies are to be dealt with promptly; these may include:
  - petty cash claims that have not been authorised
  - insufficient supporting evidence (eg receipt) attached to the petty cash voucher
  - amounts being claimed which exceed the authorised limit of the petty cashier
  - a receipt and petty cash voucher total differing – the matter should be queried with the person who made the purchase
  - a difference between the totals of the analysis columns and the total payments column in the petty cash book – check the addition of the

columns, the figures against the vouchers, the VAT calculations (does the VAT plus the analysis column amount equal the total payment amount?)
  - a difference between the cash in the petty cash box and the balance shown in the petty cash book – if this is not an arithmetic difference it may be a case of theft, and should be reported promptly to the accounts supervisor
  - where discrepancies and queries cannot be resolved, they should be referred to the accounts supervisor
- All aspects of petty cash are confidential and should not be discussed with others.

SUPPLEMENTARY NOTE ON PETTY CASH CONTROL ACCOUNT

This chapter has explained how petty cash book forms part of the double-entry system, The *disadvantage* of this procedure is that petty cash book, from which the postings are made, may have many transactions, and so could contain errors. As the balance of petty cash book is used whenever a trial balance (covered in Chapter 21) is prepared, any error in the petty cash book balancing could 'feed through' into the trial balance and cause problems.

An alternative procedure is to treat petty cash book as a subsidiary ledger, with a *petty cash control account* in the main ledger as part of double-entry – shown on right-hand side of the diagram below. The *advantage* here is that petty cash book – the subsidiary ledger – will be reconciled (agreed) with petty cash control account, in the main ledger (reconciliation is explained on pages 412-414). With this method, errors should be found and corrected before a trial balance is prepared, as it is the balance of petty cash control account rather than the petty cash book totals that is used in the trial balance.

petty cash: alternative methods of book-keeping

petty cash book as part of double-entry book-keeping	**using a petty cash control account**
DOUBLE-ENTRY BOOK-KEEPING:	**DOUBLE-ENTRY BOOK-KEEPING:**
• petty cash book totals • VAT and expense accounts	• petty cash control account • VAT and expense accounts
	SUBSIDIARY LEDGER
	• petty cash book

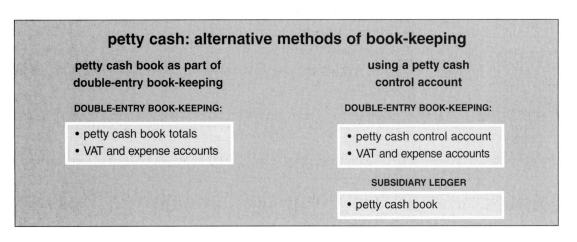

The format of petty cash control account, using figures from the petty cash book seen earlier (page 333) is as follows:

Dr	**Petty Cash Control Account** (account no 925)					Cr
2004			£	2004		£
5 Apr	Balance b/d		50.00	9 Apr	Petty cash book PCB 30	30.75
9 Apr	Cash book	CBP	30.75	9 Apr	Balance c/d	50.00
			80.75			80.75
9 Apr	Balance b/d		50.00			

Notes:

- The debit 'balance b/d' on 5 April is the same as the opening balance in petty cash book – see page 333. For a petty cash book using the imprest method, as here, this is the imprest amount.
- The credit entry for 'petty cash book PCB 30' on 9 April is the total of the analysis columns (VAT and expenses) from petty cash book. These amounts are debited to their respective accounts in the main ledger as already seen as pages 335 and 336.
- The debit entry for 'cash book CBP' on 9 April is the reimbursement of petty cash in order to restore the imprest amount. The cheque requisition for this is shown on page 336.
- Finally, the 'balance c/d' on 9 April (and also brought down) is the new balance on petty cash book, ready for next week's transactions.

important tutor note: Petty cash control account (pages 339-340) should be ignored for the purposes of NVQ Accounting Unit 2 assessment, but it is required for NVQ Accounting Unit 3 (see page 409). It is introduced in this chapter to show the different ways in which a petty cash book can be fitted into the double-entry book-keeping system.

Chapter Summary

- The petty cash book records payments for a variety of low-value business expenses. It is both a book of prime entry and is usually incorporated into the double-entry system.
- The person responsible for maintaining the petty cash book is the petty cashier, who is responsible for security.
- Payment can only be made from the petty cash book against correct documentation – usually a petty cash voucher, which must be signed by the person authorising payment.
- Where a business is registered for Value Added Tax, it must record VAT amounts paid on petty cash purchases in a separate column in the petty cash book.

- When petty cash book is a subsidiary account, petty cash control account is used as the main ledger account.
- At regular intervals – weekly or monthly – the petty cash book will be balanced; the total of each analysis column will be debited to the relevant account in the main ledger, and the cashier will restore the imprest amount of cash.

Key Terms

petty cash book	book of prime entry usually incorporated into the double-entry system; used for low-value cash payments for business expenses
petty cashier	person responsible for the petty cash system
imprest method	where the money held in the petty cash float is restored to the same amount for the beginning of each week or month
non-imprest method	where the petty cashier has a float of cash which is replenished by the cashier whenever it runs low
petty cash voucher	prime document used to claim amounts from petty cash
petty cash control account	main ledger account used when petty cash book is a subsidiary ledger; it shows the total payments made by the petty cashier during the week or month, and records receipts of cash from the cash book

Student Activities

16.1 Most petty cash books operate using the imprest method. This means that:

(a) the petty cashier draws money from the main cashier as and when required

(b) the main cashier has to authorise each petty cash payment

(c) a copy has to be kept of each petty cash voucher

(d) the petty cashier starts each week or month with a fixed amount of money

Answer (a) or (b) or (c) or (d)

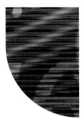

16.2 You work as an accounts clerk in the office of Temeside Printers Limited. One of your duties is that of petty cashier; you are able to authorise transactions up to £30 each. Which of the following expenses will you allow to be paid out of petty cash?

- (a) postage on a parcel of printing sent to a customer, £3.85 ✓
- (b) a rubber date stamp bought for use in the office, £4.60 ✓
- (c) rail fare to work claimed by the office manager's secretary, £2.50 ✗
- (d) donation to charity, £5.00 *if authorised*
- (e) tea and coffee for use by office staff, £5.50 ✗
- (f) mileage allowance claimed by works foreman who had to visit a customer, £4.80 *if autho*
- (g) meal allowance paid to assistant who had to work her lunch hour, £4.00 *only if auth*
- (h) window cleaning, £3.50 ✓
- (i) purchase of shelving for the office, £55.00 *(refer to supervisor) as above £30*
- (j) taxi fare claimed for delivering an urgent parcel of printing to a customer, £6.25 ✓

Note: you may assume that all expenses are supported by relevant documentation.

Explain any expenses that you will refer to the accounts supervisor.

16.3 As petty cashier, prepare petty cash vouchers under today's date for signature by the person making the claim. You are able to authorise payments up to £10.00 each. A blank voucher is shown below. Alternatively you can download blank documents from www.osbornebooks.co.uk

- £4.45 claimed by Jayne Smith for postage (no VAT) on an urgent parcel of spare parts sent to a customer, Evelode Supplies Limited.
- ✓ £2.35, including VAT, claimed by Tanya Howard for air mail envelopes bought for use in the office.
- £8.60, including VAT, claimed by Toni Wyatt for a taxi fare used on a business visit to a customer, Jasper Limited.

Number the vouchers, beginning with number 851

What documentation will you require to be attached to each voucher?

petty cash voucher No. *852*

date

description	amount (£)	
Air Mail Envelopes	*2*	*00*
	2	*00*
VAT	*0*	*35*
	2	*35*

signature ....

authorised *CBowe* ....

16.4 The business for which you work is registered for VAT. The following petty cash amounts include VAT at 17.5% and you are required to calculate the amount that will be shown in the VAT column and the appropriate expense column (remember that VAT amounts should be rounded down to the nearest penny):

		VAT	Expense
(a)	£9.40	1-40	8-00
(b)	£4.70	0-70	4-00
(c)	£2.35	0-35	2-00
(d)	£2.45	0-36	2-09
(e)	£5.60	0-83	4-77
(f)	£3.47	0-51	2-96
(g)	£8.75	1-30	7-45
(h)	94p	0-14	0-80
(i)	99p	0-14	0-85
(j)	£9.41	1-40	8-01

16.5 The petty cashier of the company where you work as an accounts assistant is away on holiday. The accounts supervisor asks you to balance the petty cash book at 31 August. The petty cash book uses the imprest method and the imprest amount is £75.00.

You are to:

- restore the imprest amount of petty cash to £75.00, making appropriate entries in the petty cash book
- balance the petty cash book at 31 August 2004 and bring down the balances on 1 September

Petty Cash Book

Receipts	Date	Details	Voucher No	Total Payment	VAT	Analysis columns: Postages	Travel	Meals	Office Sundries
£	2004			£	£	£	£	£	£
75.00	1 Aug	Balance b/d							
	4 Aug	Postages	223	7.20		7.20			
	6 Aug	Travel expenses	224	4.50			4.50		
	9 Aug	Postages	225	2.54		2.54			
	12 Aug	Envelopes	226	4.70	0.70				4.00
	13 Aug	Window cleaning	227	7.05	1.05				6.00
	17 Aug	Taxi fare	228	7.52	1.12		6.40		
	20 Aug	Postages	229	8.56		8.56			
	23 Aug	Meals	230	6.35				6.35	
	27 Aug	Envelopes	231	6.58	0.98				5.60
				55.00	3.85	18.30	10.90	6.35	15.60
55.00	31 Aug	Bank							
	31 Aug	Balance c/d		75.00					
130.00				130.00					
75.00	1 Sep	Balance b/d							

16.6 On returning from holiday, you are told to take charge of the petty cash book of Carr Trading. This is kept using the imprest method, the float being £75.00 at the beginning of each month. Analysis columns are used for VAT, travel, postages, stationery, meals, and miscellaneous.

There are a number of transactions for the month which you authorise (all transactions, unless otherwise indicated, include VAT at 17.5%). You are to enter the transactions for the month on page 42 of the petty cash book.

2004	
1 Aug	Balance of cash £75.00
4 Aug	Voucher no 39: taxi fare £3.80
6 Aug	Voucher no 40: parcel postage £2.35 (no VAT)
9 Aug	Voucher no 41: pencils £1.26
11 Aug	Voucher no 42: travel expenses £5.46 (no VAT)
12 Aug	Voucher no 43: window cleaner £8.50 (no VAT)
16 Aug	Voucher no 44: large envelopes £2.45
18 Aug	Voucher no 45: donation to charity £5 (no VAT)
19 Aug	Voucher no 46: rail fare £5.60 (no VAT); meal allowance £5.00 (no VAT)
20 Aug	Voucher no 47: recorded delivery postage £0.75 (no VAT)
23 Aug	Voucher no 48: roll of packing tape £1.50
25 Aug	Voucher no 49: excess postage paid £0.55 (no VAT)
27 Aug	Voucher no 50: taxi fare £5.40

You are to:

- Total the analysis columns and prepare a posting sheet which shows the entries to be recorded in the main ledger at the end of the month, on 31 August. Account numbers need not be shown.
- Restore the imprest amount of petty cash book to £75.00 by transfer from the cash book.
- Balance the petty cash book at 31 August 2004 and bring down the balance on 1 September.

16.7 Prepare a petty cash book for Tyax Systems Limited with analysis columns for VAT, postages, travel, meals, and sundry office expenses. Enter the following authorised transactions for the week on page 18 of the petty cash book. The voucher amounts include VAT at 17.5% unless indicated.

2004	
7 June	Balance of cash £100.00
7 June	Postages £6.35 (no VAT), voucher no 123
8 June	Travel expenses £3.25 (no VAT), voucher no 124
8 June	Postages £1.28 (no VAT), voucher no 125
9 June	Envelopes £4.54, voucher no 126
9 June	Window cleaning £5.50, voucher no 127
10 June	Taxi fare £4.56, meals £10.85, voucher no 128
10 June	Postages £8.56 (no VAT), packing materials £3.25, voucher no 129
10 June	Taxi fare £4.50, meals £7.45, voucher no 130
11 June	Marker pens £2.55, envelopes £3.80, voucher no 131

You are to:

- Total the analysis columns and prepare a posting sheet which shows the entries to be recorded in the main ledger at the end of the week, on 11 June. Account numbers need not be shown.
- Restore the amount of petty cash to £100.00 by transfer from the cash book.
- Balance the petty cash book and bring down the balance at 11 June 2004.

17 Further aspects of double-entry accounts

this chapter covers . . .

So far we have studied the principles of double-entry book-keeping and applied them to transactions for sales, purchases, returns, receipts and payments.

In this chapter, we examine in detail the double-entry aspects of a number of transactions (some of which we have seen briefly in earlier chapters):

- *capital*
- *fixed assets*
- *expenses*
- *income*
- *drawings*
- *loans*
- *stock*
- *bad debts written off*

The importance of the distinction between capital expenditure and revenue expenditure is discussed later in the chapter. Firstly though, we study in detail the division of the ledger, and the types of accounts found in the book-keeping system.

NVQ PERFORMANCE CRITERIA COVERED

unit 2: MAKING AND RECORDING PAYMENTS

element 2.2

process payments

D payments are entered into accounting records

DIVISION OF THE LEDGER

In previous chapters we have already made use of the division of the ledger, whereby separate ledgers are kept, each containing different classes of account. The ledger of a business is usually divided into four sections:

- *subsidiary (sales) ledger*, containing the accounts of the firm's debtors (customers)
- *subsidiary (purchases) ledger*, containing the accounts of the firm's creditors (suppliers)
- *cash book*, containing bank and cash records of the receipts and payments of the business
- *main ledger*, containing all other accounts

When computers are used for accounting, the physical ledger books do not exist. However, the principles of manual and computerised accounting are the same, and the term 'ledgers' is used in computer accounting systems. Accounting software is available for each of the ledgers mentioned above, usually combined into one integrated computer program. The four divisions of the ledger are illustrated in full on the next page.

TYPES OF ACCOUNT

Within a book-keeping system there are different types of accounts: a distinction is made between personal and impersonal accounts. Personal accounts are in the names of people or businesses, eg the accounts for debtors and creditors. Impersonal accounts are non-personal accounts; these are usually divided between real accounts, which represent things such as cash, bank balance, computers, motor vehicles, machinery, etc, and nominal accounts, which record income and expenses such as sales, purchases, wages, etc. The diagram below distinguishes between the different types of account.

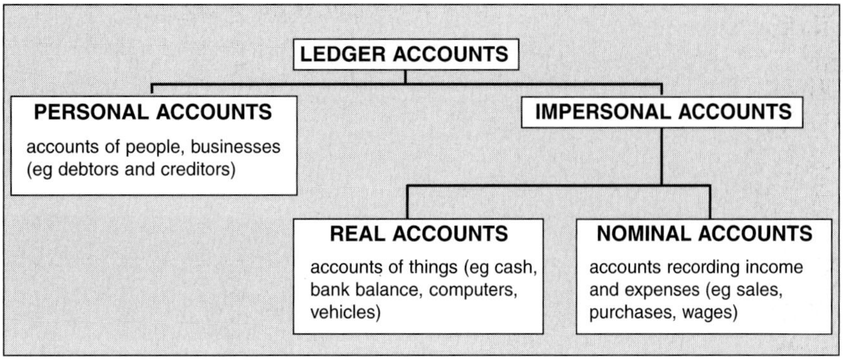

DIVISION OF THE LEDGER

subsidiary (sales) ledger

Subsidiary (sales) ledger contains the accounts of debtors, and records:

- sales made on credit to customers of the business
- sales returns by customers
- payments received from customers
- cash discount allowed for prompt settlement

Cash sales are not recorded in this ledger.

Subsidiary (sales) ledger contains an account for each debtor and records the transactions with that debtor. The total of the subsidiary (sales) ledger account balances should agree with the balance of sales ledger control account in the main ledger.

subsidiary (purchases) ledger

Subsidiary (purchases) ledger contains the accounts of creditors, and records:

- purchases made on credit from suppliers of the business
- purchases returns made by the business
- payments made to suppliers
- cash discount received for prompt settlement

Cash purchases are not recorded in this ledger.

Subsidiary (purchases) ledger contains an account for each creditor and records the transactions with that creditor. The total of the subsidiary (purchases) ledger account balances should agree with the balance of purchases ledger control account in the main ledger.

cash books

The cash books comprise:

- Cash Book
  - records all transactions for bank account and cash account
  - cash book is also often used for listing the amounts of settlement (cash) discount received and allowed, and for recording Value Added Tax
- Petty Cash Book
  - records low-value cash payments too small to be entered in the cash book

main ledger

The main ledger contains the other accounts of the business:

- Nominal Accounts
  - sales account (cash and credit sales)
  - purchases account (cash and credit purchases)
  - sales returns, purchases returns
  - expenses and income
  - loan
  - capital, drawings
  - Value Added Tax (where the business is VAT-registered)
- Real Accounts
  - fixed assets, eg premises, computers, motor vehicles
  - other assets, eg cash, bank balance, stock
  - control accounts, eg sales ledger, purchases ledger

In previous chapters we have used accounts to record transactions for purchases, sales, returns, receipts and payments. In order to complete our study of double-entry accounts at NVQ level 2 we will look in detail at a number of transactions (some of which have been seen briefly in earlier chapters):

- capital
- fixed assets
- expenses
- income
- drawings
- loans
- stock
- bad debts written off

Note that aspects of Value Added Tax (VAT) are considered later in the chapter (pages 354-355).

CAPITAL ACCOUNT

Capital is the amount of money invested in the business by the owner (or owners). The amount is owed by the business to the owner, although it is unlikely to be repaid immediately as then the business would be unable to operate. A capital account is used to record the amount(s) paid into the business; the book-keeping entries are:

- **capital introduced**
  - *debit* cash book (bank or cash columns as appropriate)
  - *credit* capital account

The dual aspect (see page 54) of this transaction is that cash book (bank or cash columns) has gained value and has been debited; capital account records a liability (to the owner) and is credited. Remember that book-keeping entries look at transactions from the point of view of the business or organisation.

The introduction of capital into a business is often the very first transaction to be entered into the accounts.

Sometimes capital is introduced into the business in forms other than in cash or by cheque. For example, the owner might transfer property or other fixed assets (see below) into the business as capital; the book-keeping entries are:

- *debit* property account (or other account as appropriate)
- *credit* capital account

FIXED ASSETS

Fixed assets are items purchased by a business for use on a permanent or semi-permanent basis. Examples are buildings, machinery, motor vehicles and office equipment. All of these are bought by a business with the intention that they will be used for some time in the business. When a business buys fixed assets, the expenditure is referred to as *capital expenditure* (don't confuse the word capital here with the owner's capital). Capital expenditure means that items have been bought for use in the business for some years to come. By contrast, revenue expenditure is where the items bought will be used by the business quite quickly. For example, the purchase of a car is capital expenditure, while the cost of petrol or diesel for the car is revenue expenditure. The importance of distinguishing between capital and revenue expenditure is discussed on pages 365-366.

When fixed assets are bought, a separate account for each type of fixed asset is used, eg buildings account, machinery account, motor vehicles account, etc. The book-keeping entries are:

- **purchase of a fixed asset**
  - *debit* fixed asset account (using the appropriate account)
  - *credit* cash book (bank or cash column, as appropriate)

Here the fixed asset account, which has gained value, is debited. The account which has given value – cash book (bank or cash column) – is credited.

Sometimes fixed assets are returned to the supplier because they do not work, or are unsuitable. When the returns transaction has been agreed with the supplier it will be recorded in the accounts as:

- **return of unsuitable fixed assets**
  - *debit* cash book* (bank or cash column, as appropriate)
  - *credit* fixed asset account (using the appropriate account)
  - * assuming that a bank/cash payment is received for the return

As you will see, such a transaction is the opposite of the original purchase.

Often fixed assets are bought on credit terms (rather than immediate payment by cheque or in cash). The book-keeping entries are:

- **purchase of a fixed asset on credit**
  - *debit* fixed asset account
  - *credit* creditor's account

The creditor's account shows the amount the business owes, which will be subsequently paid by cheque or in cash.

EXPENSES

Businesses and other organisations pay various running expenses, such as rent, wages, electricity, telephone, vehicle running expenses, etc. These day-to-day expenses are referred to as *revenue expenditure*. A separate account is used in the accounting system for each main class of revenue expenditure, eg rent account, wages account, etc.

The book-keeping entries are:

- **payment of an expense**
  - *debit* expense account (using the appropriate account)
  - *credit* cash book (bank or cash column as appropriate)

Here the expense account is debited because the business has gained value – for example, with rent paid the business has had the use of the premises for a certain time. The account which gives value, cash book (bank or cash column), is credited.

Often with expenses, there may be a period of credit allowed. For example, the electricity bill may be received today stating that payment is to be made by the end of the month. The business will treat the electricity supplier as a creditor and makes the following accounting entries:

- *debit* electricity account
- *credit* creditor's subsidiary account (in the name of the electricity supplier)

When payment is due it can then be made through the cash book as follows:

- *debit* creditor's subsidiary account (electricity supplier)
- *credit* cash book

Also, entries will need to be made in the purchases ledger control account in the main ledger.

INCOME

From time-to-time a business or organisation may receive amounts of income apart from its normal sales income.

Examples of such 'other income' include rent received, commission received, or fees received. These are recorded in separate accounts for each category of income, eg rent received account, commission received account. The book-keeping entries are:

- **receipt of income**
  - *debit* cash book (bank or cash column as appropriate)
  - *credit* income account (using the appropriate account)

The account which has gained value, cash book, is debited; the account which has given value, eg rent received, is credited.

OWNER'S DRAWINGS

Drawings is the term used when the owner takes money, in cash or by cheque (or sometimes goods), from the business for personal use. A drawings account is used to record such amounts; the book-keeping entries for withdrawal of money are:

- **owner's drawings**
  - *debit* drawings account
  - *credit* cash book (bank or cash column)

When the owner of the business takes some of the goods in which the business trades for his or her own use, the book-keeping entries are:

- *debit* drawings account
- *credit* purchases account

Note that where a business is VAT-registered, VAT must be accounted for on goods taken by the owner.

LOANS

When a business or organisation receives a loan, eg from a relative or the bank, it is the cash account or bank account which gains value, while a loan account (in the name of the lender) records the liability.

- **loan received**
  - *debit* cash book (bank or cash column)
  - *credit* loan account (in name of the lender)

Interest paid to the lender is recorded by means of an expenses account called loan interest paid account. Repayment of the loan, or part of the loan by instalments, is recorded in the accounts as:

- **loan repayment**
  - *debit* loan account
  - *credit* cash book (bank or cash column)

STOCK

We have seen in earlier chapters how businesses use separate purchases and sales accounts to record when the goods in which they trade are bought and sold. The reason for using separate accounts for purchases and sales is because there is usually a difference between the buying price and the selling price – the latter is higher and gives the business its profit. At least once a year, however, a business values the stock it has on the shelves of the shop, for example, or in the warehouse (the techniques of stock valuation are covered at NVQ level 3). As stock is an asset of a business, the valuation is debited to stock account; the credit transaction is to trading account (part of the profit and loss account) where it is used to assist in the calculation of profit.

To summarise, stock account is used only when the stock of a business is valued – at least once a year at the end of the financial year. The book-keeping entries to record the valuation in the accounts are:

- **stock valuation**
  - *debit* stock account
  - *credit* trading account (part of the profit and loss account)

Thus at the start of each financial year there will, for most businesses, be a debit balance on stock account representing the value of stock held.

BAD DEBTS WRITTEN OFF

A bad debt is a debt owing to a business or organisation which it considers will never be paid.

One of the problems of selling goods and services on credit terms is that, from time-to-time, some customers will not pay. As a consequence, the balances of such accounts have to be written off when they become uncollectable. This happens when all reasonable efforts to recover the amount owing have been exhausted, ie statements and letters have been sent to the debtor requesting payment, and legal action – where appropriate – or the threat of legal action has failed to obtain payment.

In writing off a debtor's account as bad, the business is bearing the cost of the amount due. The debtor's account is closed and the amount (or amounts, where a number of accounts are dealt with in this way) is debited to bad debts written off account. This account stores up the amounts of account balances written off during the year (in much the same way as an expense account).

The book-keeping transactions are:

- **bad debt written off**
  - *debit* bad debts written off account
  - *credit* sales ledger control account, and also credit the debtor's subsidiary account in the subsidiary (sales) ledger

VAT AND DOUBLE-ENTRY ACCOUNTS

When a business is registered for Value Added Tax it is able to claim back VAT paid on purchases of goods, fixed assets, and expenses. At the same time it must charge VAT whenever it supplies goods and services (except for zero-rated and exempt goods and services).

We have already seen in previous chapters how VAT is dealt with for purchases, sales and returns. When a business buys, for example, fixed assets it will enter the amount of VAT direct to the debit side of VAT account.

example transaction

On 16 April 2004, Acme Supplies Limited, a company which is registered for Value Added Tax, buys a new computer at a cost of £600 + VAT (at 17.5%) of £105, paying by cheque.

This is recorded in the double-entry accounts as:

Dr		Computer Account			Cr
2004		£	2004		£
16 Apr	Bank	600			

Dr		Value Added Tax Account			Cr
2004		£	2004		£
16 Apr	Bank	105			

Credit		Cash Book: Payments			CBP
Date	Details	Folio	Discount received	Cash	Bank
2004			£	£	£
16 Apr	Computer				705

The Value Added Tax account in the main ledger records:

Value Added Tax Account

Debits (input tax)	*Credits (output tax)*
VAT on purchases	VAT on sales and/or services
VAT on purchases of fixed assets (except cars)	VAT on the sale of fixed assets
VAT on expenses	VAT on other income
VAT on sales returns	VAT on purchases returns

Not all goods and services purchased can be assumed to include VAT: as well as zero-rated and exempt goods, the supplier might be a business which is not registered for VAT.

VAT relief on bad debts

A VAT-registered business can reclaim VAT originally charged on debts which are now being written off. However, in order to claim relief, *the debt must be more than six months overdue*, ie more than six months from the date the payment was originally due – a sale made on 30 day terms on 1 January would be due for payment on 31 January; if this sale is written off as a bad debt, VAT relief would be available after 31 July.

businesses not registered for VAT

Where businesses and other organisations are not registered for Value Added Tax, they cannot reclaim VAT paid on purchases, fixed assets and expenses, nor can they charge VAT when they supply goods and services.

Thus, for a non-registered business, expenses which include VAT are entered in the accounts at the full invoice value.

PRIME DOCUMENTS AND BOOKS OF PRIME ENTRY

The types of transactions that we have looked at in this chapter follow the pattern that we have seen earlier:

prime document

↓

book of prime entry

↓

double-entry accounts

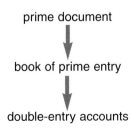

prime documents

For each of the transactions we have seen, there will be a prime document. These include:

- *purchase of fixed assets* – receipt or invoice from supplier
- *expenses* – receipt or invoice from supplier
- *income* – copy of receipt or invoice issued to a tenant for rent received, or a statement showing amount of commission earned
- *loans* – details of loan agreement, statement of interest paid, receipts for loan repayments
- *capital introduced* – copy of receipt for the money, or memorandum showing how much capital is being introduced
- *owner's drawings* – receipt signed by the owner, or note showing amount of withdrawal
- *stock* – stock-taking sheets and records
- *bad debt written off* – note or memorandum from accounts supervisor to write off debts

The type of prime document will vary from transaction to transaction. For external transactions (ie those involving outsiders) there will usually be some form of receipt, or invoice, or other document. For internal transactions (ie those taking place within the business, including with the owner), there will be more reliance on notes or memorandums.

books of prime entry: regular transactions

For routine day-to-day transactions which pass through the cash book, such as payment of expenses, the cash book forms *both* the book of prime entry *and* one of the double-entry accounts. Income transactions involving the cash book, if routine in nature, are dealt with in the same way, ie no separate book of prime entry is needed.

Where a period of credit is received from expenses suppliers, the bill is listed in an analysed purchases day book as the book of prime entry and the supplier is recorded in the accounts as a creditor. The purchases day book is easily adapted to give appropriate analysis as shown below with sample transactions.

Purchases Day Book							PDB 49
Date	Supplier	Invoice No	Folio	Total	VAT	Purchases	Expenses
2004				£	£	£	£
13 May	Western Electricity	400791	PL 779	235.00	35.00		200.00
14 May	P Bond	1479	PL 125	94.00	14.00	80.00	

books of prime entry: non-regular transactions

For non-regular transactions – such as the introduction of capital to the business, purchase of fixed assets, raising a loan, valuation of stock, writing off bad debts – the book of prime entry is called the *journal*. Like the day books that we have seen in earlier chapters, the journal is used to list transactions before they are recorded in the double-entry accounts.

An example journal entry for the introduction of capital is as follows:

Date	Details	Folio	Dr	Cr
2004			£	£
1 Jul	Bank account	CBR	20,000	
	Capital account	ML		20,000
	Opening capital introduced			

Notes:

- journal entries are prepared from authorised prime documents (which are stored securely for possible future reference)
- the names of the accounts to be debited and credited in the book-keeping system are written in the details column; in a journal entry it is customary to show the debit transaction first
- the money amounts of the debit and credit entries are stated in the appropriate columns
- a journal entry always balances, ie the debit entry is equal to the credit entry
- it is usual to include a brief narrative explaining why the transaction is being carried out

- each journal entry is complete in itself and is ruled off to separate it from the next entry
- journal entries are dealt with in more detail in Chapter 20

Case Study

DOUBLE-ENTRY ACCOUNTS – GALAXY MEDIA

situation

You are the book-keeper to Galaxy Media, which has just been started by its owner Henry Stardust. The business is an agency which supplies actors and actresses to advertising agencies. The business is registered for Value Added Tax

The transactions for the first month of trading, May 2004, are listed below:

2004

3 May	Started in business with capital of £5,000, a cheque from Henry Stardust paid into the business bank account
7 May	Paid rent for the office, £500 (no VAT) by cheque
10 May	Bought office equipment for £2,000 + VAT, paying by cheque
12 May	Received a loan of £1,000 (no VAT) from Mike Way by cheque
14 May	Received commission of £200 + VAT by cheque
17 May	Received electricity bill of £80 + VAT from Western Electric to be paid by 31 May
18 May	Withdrew £100 from the bank for own use (drawings)
21 May	Returned some of the office equipment (unsuitable) for £400 + VAT, a refund cheque being received
28 May	Paid Western Electric the amount due

Show how the above transactions will be recorded in the double-entry accounts of Galaxy Media. Books of prime entry and account numbers need not be shown.

solution

The double-entry accounts for May 2004 will be entered as follows:

CASH BOOK

Debit		**Cash Book: Receipts**			**CBR**
Date	Details	Folio	Discount allowed	Cash	Bank
2004			£	£	£
3 May	Capital				5,000
12 May	Loan: M Way				1,000
14 May	Commission received				235
21 May	Office equipment				470

Credit	Cash Book: Payments				CBP
Date	Details	Folio	Discount received	Cash	Bank
2004			£	£	£
7 May	Rent paid				500
10 May	Office equipment				2,350
18 May	Drawings				100
28 May	Western Electric				94

MAIN LEDGER

Capital Account

Dr					Cr
2004		£	2004		£
			3 May	Bank	5,000

Rent Paid Account

Dr					Cr
2004		£	2004		£
7 May	Bank	500			

Office Equipment Account

Dr					Cr
2004		£	2004		£
10 May	Bank	2,000	21 May	Bank	400

Value Added Tax Account

Dr					Cr
2004		£	2004		£
10 May	Bank	350	14 May	Bank	35
17 May	Western Electric	14	21 May	Bank	70

Loan Account: M Way

Dr					Cr
2004		£	2004		£
			12 May	Bank	1,000

Commission Received Account

Dr					Cr
2004		£	2004		£
			14 May	Bank	200

Purchases Ledger Control Account

Dr					Cr
2004		£	2004		£
28 May	Bank	94	17 May	Electricity	80
			17 May	VAT	14

Electricity Account

Dr					Cr
2004		£	2004		£
17 May	Western Electric	80			

Drawings Account

Dr					Cr
2004		£	2004		£
18 May	Bank	100			

SUBSIDIARY (PURCHASES) LEDGER

Western Electric

Dr					Cr
2004		£	2004		£
28 May	Bank	94	17 May	Electricity	80
			17 May	VAT	14

Notes:

- Account numbers have not been used here for cross referencing
- The book of prime entry for each transaction is as follows:
  - capital introduced, book of prime entry is the *journal*
  - rent paid, book of prime entry is the *cash book*
  - purchase of office equipment, *journal*
  - loan received, *journal or cash book*
  - commission received, *cash book*
  - electricity bill, *analysed purchases day book*
  - drawings, *journal or cash book*
  - office equipment returned, *journal*
  - payment of electricity bill, *cash book*

Remember that:

- cash book is the book of prime entry for regular transactions
- journal is the book of prime entry for non-regular transactions
- analysed purchases day book is the book of prime entry for expenses where credit is received

A list of the double-entry accounting entries for the transactions shown in this Case Study is illustrated in the form of a posting sheet on page 364.

Case Study

WRITING OFF A BAD DEBT – DON'S DINER

situation

You work as a sales ledger clerk in the accounts department of Severn Catering Supplies Limited. The company, which is VAT-registered, sells kitchen equipment to hotels and restaurants throughout the country. The company's terms of trade are for payment within 30 days of invoice date.

It is December 2004 and the accounts supervisor, Sue Robinson, has been reviewing the debtors' accounts in the subsidiary (sales) ledger before the end of the financial year on 31 December. She has been looking at the following account:

Dr	**Don's Diner** (account no 258)		Cr
2004	£	2004	£
5 Jan Sales	47		

Monthly statements of account and 'chaser' letters have been sent to this debtor – the last letter was dated 28 September and was returned marked 'gone away, not known at this address'.

solution

The accounts supervisor has decided that it is time to write off the account of Don's Diner as a bad debt. The debt outstanding is £47 and it is not worthwhile taking legal action for such an amount. You are given the following memo which authorises you to go ahead with the write off:

MEMORANDUM

TO: Sales Ledger Accounts Clerk

FROM: Accounts Supervisor

DATE: 10 December 2004

SUBJECT: DON'S DINER

Please write off the balance of this account as a bad debt – we have done all we can to collect the amount. As we charged VAT on the original invoice, do not forget to reclaim VAT when writing off the balance.

Thanks

Sue

Sue Robinson

prime document

The memo acts as the authorised prime document for this accounting transaction.

book of prime entry

The book of prime entry for this non-regular transaction is the journal. The journal entry to write off the account of Don's Diner is as follows:

Date	Details	Folio	Dr	Cr
2004			£	£
10 Dec	Bad debts written off account	ML 7000	40	
	Value Added Tax account	ML 2200	7	
	Sales ledger control account	ML 6001		47
	Balance of subsidiary (sales) ledger account of Don's Diner written off as a bad debt, as per memo from accounts supervisor dated 10 December 2004		47	47

Note: journal entries are dealt with in more detail in Chapter 20.

double-entry accounts

The account of Don's Diner is closed off as follows:

SUBSIDIARY (SALES) LEDGER

Dr **Don's Diner** (account no 258) Cr

2004	£	2004	£
5 Jan Sales	47	10 Dec Bad debts written off	40
		10 Dec Value Added Tax	7
	47		47

The balance net of VAT, ie £40, is transferred to the debit of bad debts written off account, (together with any other accounts being written off). The VAT amount, ie £7, (VAT at 17.5%) is transferred to the debit of VAT account.

MAIN LEDGER

Dr **Bad Debts Written Off Account** (no 7000) Cr

2004	£	2004	£
10 Dec Don's Diner	40		

Dr **Value Added Tax Account** (no 2200) Cr

2004	£	2004	£
10 Dec Don's Diner	7		

Dr		Sales Ledger Control	Account (no 6001)		Cr
2004		£	2004		£
			10 Dec	Bad debts written off	40
			10 Dec	Value Added Tax	7

Thus the account of Don's Diner is now closed and no further goods will be supplied to this customer on credit terms. To summarise writing off a bad debt:

- *prime document* – memo or other authority from accounts supervisor
- *book of prime entry* – the journal
- *double-entry accounts* (for a VAT-registered business claiming VAT relief)
  - *debit* bad debts written off account with the amount of the bad debt, net of VAT
  - *debit* Value Added Tax account with the VAT part of the debt
  - *credit* sales ledger control account with the amount of the bad debt and the VAT relief, and also credit the debtor's account in the subsidiary (sales) ledger

Remember that the debt must be more than six months overdue before VAT relief can be claimed.

THE USE OF POSTING SHEETS

In a large business or organisation, the various aspects of the accounting function will be allocated to a number of staff. For example, to look more closely at the recording and payment of credit purchases:

- one person may be involved in checking invoices received
- another person may prepare the purchases day book
- another may pass invoices or statements received for payment
- another may prepare remittance advices and cheques for sending to creditors
- another may keep the double-entry accounts up-to-date

These job allocations are given as an example only – as always, it is for the business to organise its accounting function to suit its needs. The essential point, though, is that in a larger business several people may be involved in just one area of record keeping, such as purchases, sales, etc. (In a small business, all of these tasks and more would, most likely, be carried out by just one person.)

One feature of a large business is that use may be made of a posting sheet. This lists transactions that are to be entered (or posted) into the double-entry accounts and will be prepared by a member of the accounts department. For example, a posting sheet for the transactions of Galaxy Media (see case Study, page 358) is prepared as follows:

Posting Sheet			
Account	**Folio**	**Debit** £	**Credit** £
Bank	CBR	5,000	
Capital	ML		5,000
Rent paid	ML	500	
Bank	CBP		500
Office equipment	ML	2,000	
VAT	ML	350	
Bank	CBP		2,350
Bank	CBR	1,000	
Loan: M Way	ML		1,000
Bank	CBR	235	
Commission received	ML		200
VAT	ML		35
Electricity	ML	80	
VAT	ML	14	
Purchases ledger control (West. Electric)	ML		94
Drawings	ML	100	
Bank	CBP		100
Bank	CBR	470	
Office equipment	ML		400
VAT	ML		70
Purchases ledger control (West. Electric)	ML	94	
Bank	CBP		94
TOTALS		9,843	9,843

Prepared by	J Jarvis	Date	31 May 2004
Checked by	N Wilson	Date	31 May 2004
Posted by	S Ahmed	Date	31 May 2004

Notes:

- The posting sheet can be designed in any format to suit the needs of the business.
- It can be used for one day's transactions, or for longer periods such as a week or a month – much depends on the number of transactions to be recorded.
- Essential information includes:
  - name of account
  - folio, usually together with the account number
  - amount of debit entry
  - amount of credit entry
- The posting sheet is totalled – this shows that the money amounts of debit entries are equal to credit entries.

- The name of the person preparing the posting sheet is stated with the date, together with the person checking it and the date.
- The name of the person posting the transactions to the firm's double-entry accounts, together with the date, is given.

CAPITAL EXPENDITURE AND REVENUE EXPENDITURE

In the double-entry book-keeping system, it is important to distinguish between **capital expenditure** and **revenue expenditure**.

capital expenditure

Capital expenditure can be defined as expenditure incurred on the purchase, alteration or improvement of fixed assets. For example, the purchase of a car for use in the business or organisation is capital expenditure. Included in capital expenditure are such costs as:

- delivery of fixed assets
- installation of fixed assets
- improvement (but not repair) of fixed assets
- legal costs of buying property

revenue expenditure

Revenue expenditure is expenditure incurred on running expenses. For example, the cost of petrol or diesel for the car (above) is revenue expenditure. Included in revenue expenditure are the costs of:

- maintenance and repair of fixed assets
- administration
- selling and distributing the goods or products in which the business or organisation trades

capital expenditure and revenue expenditure – the differences

In the accounting system, it is important to classify correctly capital expenditure and revenue expenditure. An error at the double-entry book-keeping stage will give problems later on when the profit and loss statement and balance sheet (both of these are covered at NVQ level 3) are prepared. For example, if the cost of the car was shown as an expense instead of as a fixed asset, the profit and loss account would show a much lower profit (or even record a net loss), while the balance sheet would not show the car as a fixed asset – clearly this is incorrect as the business or organisation owns the asset.

Study the following examples: they show the differences between capital expenditure and revenue expenditure.

- **£30,000 cost of building an extension to the factory, which includes £1,000 for repairs to the existing factory**
  - capital expenditure £29,000
  - revenue expenditure £1,000 (because it is for repairs to an existing fixed asset)

- **a plot of land has been bought for £20,000, the legal costs are £750**
  - capital expenditure £20,750 (the legal costs are included in the capital expenditure, because they are the cost of acquiring the fixed asset, ie the legal costs are 'capitalised')

- **the business' own employees are used to install a new air conditioning system: wages £1,000, materials £1,500**
  - capital expenditure £2,500 (an addition to the property); note that, in cases such as this, revenue expenditure, ie wages and materials purchases, will need to be reduced to allow for the transfer to capital expenditure

- **own employees used to repair and redecorate the premises: wages £500, materials £750**
  - revenue expenditure £1,250 (repairs and redecoration are running expenses)

- **purchase of a new machine £10,000, payment for installation and setting up £250**
  - capital expenditure, £10,250 (costs of installation of a fixed asset are capitalised)

Only by allocating capital expenditure and revenue expenditure correctly in the accounting system can the profit and loss account and balance sheet reflect accurately the financial state of the business.

Chapter Summary

- Ledger accounts are classified between:
  - personal accounts
  - impersonal accounts (which are further classified between real accounts and nominal accounts)
- Entries in the cash book are:
  - debit money in
  - credit money out
- Other accounts are opened in the book-keeping system for:
  - capital
  - fixed assets
  - expenses
  - income
  - drawings
  - loans
  - stock
  - bad debts written off
- Posting sheets are used to list transactions to be entered in the double-entry accounts.
- Expenditure is classified between capital expenditure and revenue expenditure.

Key Terms

personal accounts	accounts in the names of people or businesses, eg the accounts for debtors and creditors
impersonal accounts	non-personal accounts, usually divided between real accounts and nominal accounts
real accounts	accounts which represent things, such as cash, bank balance, computers, motor vehicles, machinery
nominal accounts	accounts which record income and expenses, such as sales, purchases, wages

capital account — records the amount of money invested in the business by the owner (or owners)

fixed assets — items purchased by a business for use on a permanent or semi-permanent basis, such as buildings, machinery, motor vehicles, office equipment

expenses — the running expenses of a business, such as rent, wages, electricity, telephone, vehicle running expenses

drawings — amount of money taken by the owner in cash, or by cheque (or sometimes goods), from the business for personal use

stock account — an asset of the business, stock is valued usually at the end of the financial year and the amount is debited to stock account

bad debt — a debt owing to a business or organisation which it considers will never be paid

bad debts written off account — the account to which the amounts of account balances written off as bad are transferred

journal — book of prime entry for non-regular transactions

posting sheets — a list of transactions to be entered in the double-entry accounts

capital expenditure — expenditure incurred on the purchase, alteration or improvement of fixed assets

revenue expenditure — expenditure incurred on running expenses

Student Activities

17.1 Subsidiary (sales) ledger contains:

(a) creditors' accounts

(b) sales account

(c) debtors' accounts

(d) sales returns account

Answer (a) or (b) or (c) or (d)

17.2 Which one of the following is not a division of the ledger?

(a) main ledger

(b) sales account

(c) subsidiary (sales) ledger

(d) cash book

Answer (a) or (b) or (c) or (d)

17.3 A friend has recently set up in business. To help him, you have written up the first month's double-entry accounts. Your friend asks you to reply to the following points:

- "I bought a computer, but you've shown it on the debit side. Surely it must go on the credit side? You must be wrong."
- "Why is the transaction for my capital on the credit side of capital account. I've paid in capital, so surely this is the account which has gained value?"

Write your answer to your friend.

17.4 James Anderson set up in business on 1 March 2004 and registered for Value Added Tax. During the first month he has kept the cash book up-to-date as follows:

Debit		**Cash Book: Receipts**		**CBR**
Date	Details	Folio	Discount allowed	Bank
2004			£	£
1 Mar	Capital			7,500
15 Mar	Bank loan			2,500
19 Mar	Commission received*			141

Credit		Cash Book: Payments		CBP
Date	Details	Folio	Discount received	Bank
2004			£	£
5 Mar	Computer*			2,350
8 Mar	Rent paid			500
12 Mar	Wages			425
23 Mar	Drawings			200
26 Mar	Wages			380
29 Mar	Van*			5,875

The items with asterisks (*) include Value Added Tax.

James Anderson has not got around to the other double-entry accounts.

You are to draw up the other accounts for James Anderson, and to make the appropriate entries.

Notes:

- Use the current rate of Value Added Tax (17.5% at the time of writing)
- Account numbers need not be used
- Separate books of prime entry need not be shown

17.5 The following are the business transactions of Tony Long, who is registered for Value Added Tax, for the month of May 2004:

3 May	Started a business with capital of £6,000 in the bank
4 May	Bought a machine* for £2,350, paying by cheque
7 May	Bought office equipment* for £2,820, paying by cheque
10 May	Paid rent £350, by cheque
13 May	Obtained a loan of £1,000 from a friend, Lucy Warner, and paid her cheque into the bank
14 May	Paid wages £250, by cheque
18 May	Commission received* £188, by cheque
21 May	Drawings £85, by cheque
28 May	Paid wages £135, by cheque

The items with asterisks (*) include Value Added Tax

You are to:

(a) write up Tony Long's cash book receipts and cash book payments (his cash book has a bank column and no cash column)

(b) complete the double-entry book-keeping transactions

Notes:

- Use the current rate of Value Added Tax (17.5% at the time of writing)
- Account numbers need not be used
- Separate books of prime entry need not be shown

17.6 Enter the following transactions into the double-entry book-keeping accounts of Jean Lacey, who is registered for Value Added Tax. Include a cash book with a column for bank.

2004

2 Aug	Started in business with capital of £5,000 in the bank
3 Aug	Bought a computer for £1,800 + VAT, paying by cheque
6 Aug	Paid rent £100, by cheque
10 Aug	Received commission £200 + VAT, by cheque
13 Aug	Bought office fittings £2,000 + VAT, paying by cheque
16 Aug	Received a loan £1,000, by cheque from a friend, Sally Orton
17 Aug	Drawings £100, by cheque
20 Aug	Returned some of the office fittings (unsuitable) and received a refund cheque of £240 + VAT
24 Aug	Received commission £160 + VAT, by cheque
27 Aug	Made a loan repayment to Sally Orton of £150, by cheque

Notes:

- Use the current rate of Value Added Tax (17.5% at the time of writing)
- Account numbers need not be used
- Separate books of prime entry need not be shown

17.7 You work as an assistant in the accounts department of Fleet Sales Limited, a VAT-registered company.

The subsidiary (sales) ledger includes the following account:

Dr	**Dailey Trading Company** (account no 754)				Cr
2004		£	2004		£
15 Jan	Sales	94			

Monthly statements of account and 'chaser' letters have been sent to this debtor – the last letter was dated 10 September 2004 and was returned marked 'gone away, not known at this address'.

Today, 29 November 2004, the accounts supervisor gives you the following memo:

MEMORANDUM

TO: Sales Ledger Accounts Clerk

FROM: Accounts Supervisor

DATE: 29 November 2004

SUBJECT: DAILEY TRADING COMPANY

Please write off the balance of this account as a bad debt – we have done all we can to collect the amount. As we charged VAT on the original invoice, do not forget to reclaim VAT when writing off the balance.

Thanks.

Lucinda

Lucinda Luz

You are to show:

- the journal entry made on 29 November
- the transactions on Dailey Trading Company's account in the subsidiary (sales) ledger
- bad debts written off account in the main ledger
- VAT account in the main ledger
- sales ledger control account in the main ledger

Note: account numbers need not be used

17.8 Classify the following costs as either *capital expenditure* or as *revenue expenditure*

(a) purchase of vehicles CAPITAL

(b) rent paid on premises REVENUE

(c) wages and salaries REVENUE

(d) legal fees relating to the purchase of property CAPITAL

(e) redecoration of the office REVENUE

(f) installation of air-conditioning in the office CAPITAL

(g) wages of own employees used to build extension to the stockroom CAPITAL

(h) installation and setting up of a new machine CAPITAL

18 Communicating with suppliers

this chapter covers . . .

This chapter explains how a business communicates with its suppliers. It covers:

- *oral communication – face-to-face and telephone communication*
- *the different forms of written communication – notes, letters, emails*

The format of the various forms of communication have already been covered in Chapter 8, 'Communicating with Customers'. If you have not read this earlier chapter you are advised to do so before starting this one.

NVQ PERFORMANCE CRITERIA COVERED

unit 2: MAKING AND RECORDING PAYMENTS

element 2.1: process documents relating to goods and services received

H communicate appropriately with suppliers regarding accounts

COMMUNICATING WITH SUPPLIERS

We have already seen in Chapter 8 'Communicating with Customers' that your course requires that you communicate politely and effectively with people to whom you sell goods or services.

Although in many organisations, 'customer care' is generally given more emphasis than dealing with suppliers, you should bear in mind that the principle of dealing politely and efficiently applies equally to customers and to suppliers.

raising queries with suppliers

Suppliers sell goods and services to the organisation or business for which you work. They may supply on credit or on a cash basis. They may supply materials and stock or they may provide services such as computer maintenance or 24 hour courier delivery. Most communications with suppliers involve queries such as:

- when are the goods arriving?
- when will the service be provided?
- problems with the delivery of incorrect goods
- the wrong amount charged
- an incorrect discount on an invoice
- a credit note which has not been sent

When situations such as this arise, there are various channels of communication that can be used:

oral communications

These are communications by word of mouth. In other words, if you have a simple query, the most efficient way of contacting the supplier may be by telephone or by speaking to the supplier face-to-face. The message can be delivered quickly and an appropriate response received.

If you are unfortunate enough to deal with a supplier that has a telephone system which plays you classical music for fifteen minutes and then connects you to a voicemail, you may have to leave a message. This is a skill which requires concentration and mastery of the facts that you want to communicate.

written communications

Written communications have been dealt with in detail in Chapter 8 'Communicating with Customers' (pages 158 to 175). It would be a good idea to read these pages again to remind yourself of the wide range of means of written communication available. The main methods used when dealing with suppliers are:

- **letter** – used for formal communications, eg complaints, asking for an increase in a credit limit, asking for an increase in trade discount
- **fax** – used for more informal requests, eg sending a purchase order, asking for a copy of an invoice or statement, sending a copy of a incorrrect document from the supplier
- **email** – used increasingly for sending orders, raising queries about delivery dates, notifying the supplier about shortages in delivery (not enough goods sent), damaged stock, requesting permission to return goods

Case Study

VALLEYMORE FOODS LIMITED

situation

Valleymore Foods Limited produces a variety of foodstuffs – pies, desserts, and ready-made meals. You work in the Accounts Department of the company and spend some of your time dealing with supplier queries relating to prices, financial documents and purchase ledger accounts. Your name is Patsy Cornish.

This Case Study shows some of the queries and tasks you had to deal with in one working day and provides examples of how you dealt with them.

queries and tasks

1. Your supervisor, Sue Flay, asks you to telephone Tasty Fillings Limited who have overcharged you on their invoice 29841 dated 1 July 2003. They have charged £1.10 per kilo for mixed fruit filling rather than £1.05, the price on the last consignment. You get through to their Sales Department, but have to leave a message on a voicemail.
2. Later in the day you receive an email from the Tasty Fillings Sales Department stating that £1.10 is the latest price quoted on their website, and so the invoice is correct. You are to write a note to your supervisor, passing on this message.
3. You are checking invoice 8745 received from Tropical Fruits for 50 kilos of passion fruit purée. The price on the invoice is 80p per kilo, but they have entered £80 in the total column and added on VAT of £14. You refer the mistake to your supervisor, Sue Flay, who suggests you send them an email asking for a new invoice.
4. You sent a purchase order to Wessex Meats for 100 kilos of lambs kidneys ten days ago, but have not received the goods. You telephone their Sales Office but they say the purchase order has not arrived; they ask you to fax a copy.
5. Sue Flay has been looking through the supplier discounts your company is given. She asks you to draft the text of a letter asking Tasty Fillings Limited for an increase in trade discount from 15% to 25% in view of the increased business you have given them over the last twelve months.

1 voicemail message

'Hello. This is Patsy Cornish from Valleymore Foods calling at 10.30 on Friday morning. We notice that on your invoice 29841, the mixed fruit filling is charged at £1.10 per kilo rather than at £1.05, which is what we were charged last time. Please can you look into this for me and get back to me on 01908 675234. Thank you.'

2 the internal note

To Sue Flay

4 July 2003 14.10

Re Tasty Fillings Invoice 29841

Tasty Fillings say that the price of the mixed fruit filling has gone up to £1.10 since we last ordered. Their website is showing £1.10 a kilo and so I guess we will have to accept the invoice.

Patsy Cornish

3 the email request

To: accounts@tropicalfruits.com
From: accounts@valleymorefoods.com
Time: 4 July 2003 14.55.23
Subject: your invoice 8745

We note that we have been charged £80 instead of £40 (excluding VAT) for 50 kilos of passion fruit purée on invoice 8745. Please can you issue a new invoice for this consignment. Many thanks.

Regards
Patsy Cornish
Accounts (Purchase Ledger), Valleymore Foods Limited

4 the faxed document

facsimile transmission header

To: Josie, Sales Office, Wessex Meats
Fax number: 01475 333692
Number of pages including this header: 2 Date: 4 July 2003

message

Purchase Order 12124

Further to our telephone conversation today we are faxing our Purchase Order for lambs kidneys. As the original order appears to have been lost in the post we shall be grateful if you will kindly treat this order as very urgent. Many thanks.

Patsy Cornish, Accounts (Purchase Ledger)

5 the formal letter

Valleymore Foods Limited

Martley Road, St Gregorys, MR2 5GT
Tel 01908 675234 Fax 01908 675332 email foods@valleymore.com

Accounts Manager, Sales Ledger
Tasty Fillings Limited
Unit 12 Moor Park
Newcastle
NE4 7YT

3 July 2003

Dear Sir

Trade Discount

We have been reviewing our records and note that the total of our purchases made from your company increased by 50% during the last twelve months to a total of £56,750. You currently give us 15% trade discount. We shall be grateful if you would kindly consider increasing this rate to 25% in view of the increased business we have given you.

I look forward to hearing from you.

Yours faithfully

Lionel Edger, Accounts Manager

Chapter Summary

- Businesses need to communicate regularly with their suppliers, who provide goods and services on credit and on a cash basis.
- Communications can be oral – face-to-face meetings and telephone conversations.
- Communications can be also be written – emails, faxes, letters.
- The choice of communication method will depend on the context and the urgency of the message. Typical communications are enquiries, complaints and requests.

Note: there are no Key Terms in this chapter. All the relevant terms are defined in Chapter 8, page 174.

Student Activities

In these four activities you work as an Accounts Assistant for Omnisupplies Limited, an office furniture wholesaler. Use your own name and the current date and make up any other details, such as addresses, which may be needed in each activity.

18.1 Omnisupplies Limited, an office furniture wholesaler, has received delivery of an order placed with Parker Hill Limited for five luxury office chairs in burgundy cloth, catalogue code 2982B. When you receive the invoice (No 24622) you notice that the order code is 2982GL. This code is for the same type of chair, but in green leather. The leather chairs cost £75 more than the cloth-covered chairs and this extra cost has substantially increased the amount of the invoice.

When you telephone the Accounts Department of Parker Hill, the supplier, you are asked to leave a message on voicemail. Write down the script of the message that you would leave.

18.2 You receive an invoice (No 3241) from one of your suppliers, Clifton Trading Company, clifton@cliftontrading.co.uk. You are normally given a 2.5% settlement (cash) discount and a 20% trade discount, but these are not included on this invoice. Write the text of an email pointing this out, as you want to settle the invoice as soon as possible to take advantage of the discount. The goods total before any discounts is £500, plus VAT.

18.3 You receive a statement of account from one of your suppliers, Mordern Stationery, which still operates a manual accounting system and has been known to make mistakes in the past. The statement does not show a credit note for £345.00, reference 2346, received from the company in the last month. Your supervisor suggests faxing the document to Mordern Stationery. Write a suitable fax message to Mordern Stationery explaining why you are faxing the credit note.

18.4 Your supervisor is not happy with the level of discount you are given by Regal Supplies. They give you 10% and the normal level of discount in the trade is at least 20%. Last year you placed £25,000 worth of orders with them. Your supervisor is seriously considering taking the business elsewhere. You are to draft a polite letter for your Accounts Manager's signature, asking for a review of the discounts that Regal Supplies give you. The letter should be addressed to the Accounts Manager.

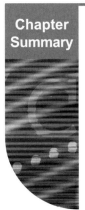

19 Balancing the cash book and bank reconciliation

this chapter covers . . .

In previous chapters we have looked at the receipts side of the cash book (Chapter 7) and at the payments side (Chapter 15). In this chapter we see how cash book is totalled and balanced at the end of the week or month in order to give a figure for cash and bank balances.

We then see what to do when the bank statement is received:

- *the comparison of individual items on the bank statement and in the bank columns of the cash book*
- *the identification of discrepancies*

Using the discrepancies, a bank reconciliation statement can be prepared. This provides a link between the balance shown on the bank statement and the balance at bank shown in the cash book of the book-keeping system. The bank reconciliation statement forms part of the check and control process of book-keeping – the regular checking of the bank statement balance against the cash book balance.

NVQ PERFORMANCE CRITERIA COVERED

unit 3: PREPARING LEDGER BALANCES AND AN INITIAL TRIAL BALANCE

element 3.1

balance bank transactions

A *record details from the relevant primary documentation in the cash book and ledgers*

B *correctly calculate totals and balances of receipts and payments*

C *compare individual items on the bank statement and in the cash book for accuracy*

D *identify discrepancies and prepare a bank reconciliation statement*

BALANCING THE CASH BOOK

The cash book is the ledger for cash and bank transactions and, like other accounts, needs to be balanced at regular intervals.

As we have seen in earlier chapters, the debit (receipts) and credit (payments) sides of the cash book include columns for bank transactions; other columns – such as discount allowed, discount received, Value Added Tax and cash transactions – may also be incorporated.

Remember that a business adapts its cash book layout to suit its needs. If a business does not deal much in cash, it is unlikely to have a cash column. This will help the book-keeper, as it will make balancing much easier!

Shown below and on the top of the next page are the receipts and payments pages from a sample cash book with columns for bank, cash, and discounts allowed and received. If you want to refresh your memory about these two sides of the cash book, they are covered in Chapters 7 and 15 respectively.

In handwritten book-keeping systems the debit (receipts) side forms the left-hand page of cash book, while the credit (payments) side is detailed on the right-hand page. If you look at the bottom of the next page you will see that the debit and credit columns can be put side-by-side to form the full cash book. In this illustration the columns are balanced after the week's transactions.

Debit		Cash Book: Receipts			CBR 24
Date	Details	Folio	Discount allowed	Cash	Bank
2004			£	£	£
5 Apr	Balances brought down			300	1,550
5 Apr	Sales	ML 4001/ 2200		235	
6 Apr	S Wright	SL 295	2		98
6 Apr	Peter Singh Limited (CR)	SL 147			205
7 Apr	J Jones	SL 86	4		76
7 Apr	Sales	ML 4001/ 2200			94
9 Apr	D Whiteman Limited	SL 278	3		45
9 Apr	Natasha Lloyd and Co (SO)	SL 121			110
			9	535	2,178

cash book: debit side

Credit			Cash Book: Payments			CBP 24
Date	Details		Folio	Discount received	Cash	Bank
2004				£	£	£
5 Apr	E Lee & Co	101261	PL 804			160
6 Apr	Hayes Limited	SO	PL 752			200
6 Apr	S Crane	101262	PL 610	5		145
7 Apr	Purchases		ML 5001/ 2200		94	
8 Apr	Purchases	101264	ML 5001/ 2200			282
9 Apr	S Ford		PL 698	5		70
				10	94	857

cash book: credit side

cash book: receipts side (debits) **cash book: payments side (credits)**

Dr				Cash Book							Cr
Date	Details	Folio	Discount allowed	Cash	Bank	Date	Details	Folio	Discount received	Cash	Bank
2004			£	£	£	2004			£	£	£
5 Apr	Balances b/d			300	1,550	5 Apr	E Lee & Co				160
5 Apr	Sales			235		6 Apr	Hayes Ltd (SO)				200
6 Apr	S Wright		2		98	6 Apr	S Crane		5		145
6 Apr	Peter Singh Ltd (CR)				205	7 Apr	Purchases			94	
						8 Apr	Purchases				282
7 Apr	J Jones		4		76	9 Apr	S Ford		5		70
7 Apr	Sales				94						
9 Apr	D Whiteman Ltd		3		45						
9 Apr	Natasha Lloyd and Co (SO)				110						
			9	535	2,178				10	94	857
						11 Apr	Balances c/d			441	1,321
			9	535	2,178				10	535	2,178
12 Apr	Balances b/d			441	1,321						

full cash book: debit and credit sides combined

Note that in the 'side-by-side' cash book at the bottom of the previous page, details from the folio columns and cheque numbers have not been shown (they are shown in the separate debit and credit sections seen earlier).

The cash and bank columns are balanced using the sub-totals, as follows:

- for the cash columns compare the two subtotals, ie £535 and £94
- deduct the lower figure from the higher (here payments from receipts) to give the balance of cash remaining (£535 – £94 = £441)
- the higher total is recorded at the bottom of both cash columns in a totals 'box' (£535)
- the balance of cash remaining (£441) is entered as a balancing item above the totals box (on the credit side), and is brought down underneath the total on the debit side as the opening balance for next week (£441)
- the two bank columns are dealt with in the same way (£2,178 – £857 = £1,321)

Notice that, in the cash book shown above, the cash and bank balances have been brought down on the debit side. It may happen that the balance at bank is brought down on the credit side: this occurs when payments exceed receipts, and indicates a bank overdraft. It is very important to appreciate that the bank columns of the cash book represent the firm's own records of bank transactions and the balance at bank – the bank statement may well show different figures (see the next page).

At the end of the month, each discount column is totalled separately – no attempt should be made to balance them. At this point, amounts recorded in the columns and the totals are not part of the double-entry system. However, the two totals are transferred to the double-entry system as follows:

- the total on the debit side (£9 in the example above) is debited to discount allowed account in the main ledger (see Chapter 7, page 144)
- the total on the credit side (£10 in the example) is credited to discount received account, also in the main ledger (see Chapter 15, page 304)

The opposite book-keeping entries will have been entered already in the debtors' and creditors' accounts respectively – see Chapters 7 and 15.

CHECKING THE CASH BOOK

As the cash book forms such an integral part of a firm's book-keeping system, it is essential that balances are calculated correctly at regular intervals, eg weekly or monthly – depending on the needs of the business. How can the cash book be checked for accuracy?

cash columns

To check the cash columns is easy. It is simply a matter of counting the cash in the cash till or box, and agreeing it with the balance shown by the cash book. In the example above there should be £441 in the firm's cash till at 11 April 2004. If the cash cannot be agreed in this way, the difference needs to be investigated urgently and any discrepancy referred to the accounts supervisor or other appropriate person.

bank columns

How are these to be checked? We could, perhaps, enquire at the bank and ask for the balance at the end of each week or month, or we could arrange for a bank statement to be sent to us at the end of each week or month. However, the balance of the account at the bank may well not agree with that shown by the bank columns of the cash book.

The reasons why the cash book and bank statement may differ are because there are:

- timing differences caused by
  - unpresented cheques
  - outstanding lodgements
- updating items for the cash book

We will now look at these two differences in the section which follows.

RECEIVING THE BANK STATEMENT

When the bank statement is received it must be matched or compared with the cash book in order to identify any differences or discrepancies. These are:

- timing differences
- updating items for the cash book

timing differences

The two main timing differences or discrepancies between the bank columns of the cash book and the bank statement are:

- *unpresented cheques*, ie cheques drawn, not yet recorded on the bank statement
- *outstanding lodgements*, ie amounts paid into the bank, not yet recorded on the bank statement

The first of these – unpresented cheques – is caused because, when a cheque is written out, it is immediately entered on the payments side of the cash book, even though it may be some days before the cheque passes through the bank clearing system and is recorded on the bank statement. Therefore, for a few days at least, the cash book shows a lower balance than the bank statement in respect of this cheque. When the cheque is recorded on the bank statement, the difference will disappear. We have looked at only one cheque here, but a business will often be issuing many cheques each day, and the difference between the cash book balance and the bank statement balance may be considerable.

With the second timing difference – outstanding lodgements – the firm's cashier will record a receipt in the cash book as he or she prepares the bank paying-in slip. However, the receipt may not be recorded by the bank on the bank statement for a day or so, particularly if it is paid in late in the day (when the bank will put it into the next day's work), or if it is paid in at a bank branch other than the one at which the account is maintained. Until the receipt is recorded by the bank the cash book will show a higher bank account balance than the bank statement. Once the receipt is entered on the bank statement, the difference will disappear.

For these two timing differences the cash book must *not be altered* because, as we have seen, they will correct themselves on the bank statement as time goes by.

updating the cash book

Besides the timing differences described above, there may be other discrepancies between the bank columns of the cash book and the bank statement, and *these do need to be entered* in the cash book to bring it up-to-date. For example, the bank might make an automatic standing order payment on behalf of a business – such an item is correctly debited by the bank, and it might be that the bank statement acts as a reminder to the business cashier of the payment: it should then be entered in the cash book.

Examples of items that show in the bank statement and need to be entered in the cash book include:

receipts

- standing order and BACS (Bankers' Automated Clearing Services) receipts credited by the bank, eg payments from debtors (customers)
- bank giro credit (credit transfer) amounts received by the bank, eg payments from debtors (customers)
- dividend amounts received by the bank
- interest credited by the bank

payments

- standing order and direct debit payments
- bank charges and interest
- unpaid cheques debited by the bank (ie cheques from debtors paid in by the business which have 'bounced' and are returned by the bank marked 'refer to drawer')

For each of these items, the cashier needs to check to see if they have been entered in the cash book; if not, they need to be recorded (provided that the bank has not made an error). If the bank has made an error, it must be notified as soon as possible and the incorrect transactions reversed by the bank in its own accounting records.

THE BANK RECONCILIATION STATEMENT

This forms the link between the balances shown in the bank statement and the cash book.

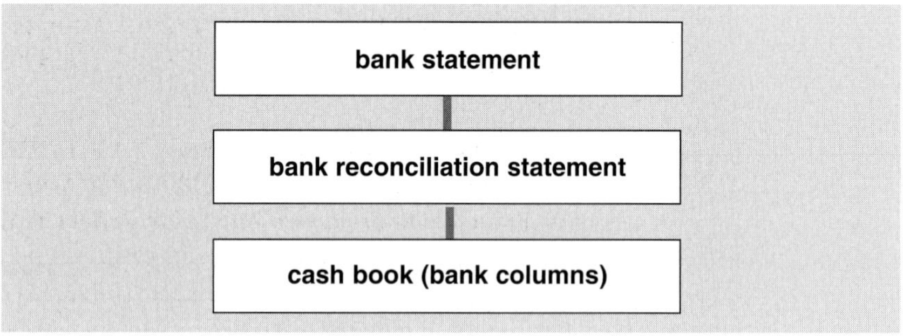

Upon receipt of a bank statement, reconciliation of the two balances is carried out in the following way:

- tick off the items that appear in both cash book and bank statement
- the unticked items on the bank statement are entered into the bank columns of the cash book to bring it up-to-date (provided none are errors made by the bank)
- the bank columns of the cash book are now balanced to find the revised figure
- the remaining unticked items from the cash book will be the timing differences
- the timing differences are used to prepare the bank reconciliation statement, which takes the following format (with example figures):

XYZ TRADING LIMITED

Bank Reconciliation Statement as at 31 October 2004

		£	£
Balance at bank as per bank statement			245
Less: unpresented cheques			
J Lewis	cheque no 0012378	60	
ABC Limited	cheque no 0012392	100	
Eastern Oil Company	cheque no 0012407	80	
			240
			5
Add: outstanding lodgements		220	
		300	
			520
Balance at bank as per cash book			525

notes:

- The layout shown above starts from the bank statement balance, and works towards the cash book balance. A common variation of this layout is to start with the cash book balance and to work towards the bank statement balance (see page 391).
- If a bank overdraft is involved, brackets should be used around the numbers to indicate this for the bank statement or cash book balance. The timing differences are still added or deducted, as appropriate.
- Once the bank reconciliation statement agrees, it should be filed because it proves that the bank statement and cash book were reconciled at a particular date. If, next time it is prepared, it fails to agree, the previous statement is proof that reconciliation was reached at that time.

Case Study

BANK RECONCILIATION STATEMENT

situation

The cashier of Severn Trading Company has written up the firm's cash book for the month of February 2004, as shown on the next page.

Note that the cheque number is shown against payments.

Dr		**Cash Book**					Cr
Date 2004	Details	Cash £	Bank £	Date 2004	Details	Cash £	Bank £
2 Feb	Balances b/d	250.75	1,340.50	3 Feb	Appleton Ltd 123456		675.25
6 Feb	A Abbott		208.50	5 Feb	Wages	58.60	
10 Feb	Sales	145.25		12 Feb	Rent 123457		125.00
16 Feb	Sales		278.30	17 Feb	D Smith & Co 123458		421.80
20 Feb	Sales	204.35		24 Feb	Stationery	75.50	
23 Feb	D Richards Ltd		162.30	25 Feb	G Christie 123459		797.55
26 Feb	Sales		353.95		Balances c/d	466.25	586.25
27 Feb	P Paul Ltd		262.30				
		600.35	2,605.85			600.35	2,605.85
	Balances b/d	466.25	586.25				

The cash balance of £466.25 shown by the cash columns at the month-end has been agreed with the cash held in the firm's cash box. The bank statement for February 2004 has just been received:

National Bank plc

Branch Bartown

TITLE OF ACCOUNT Severn Trading Company

ACCOUNT NUMBER 67812318

STATEMENT NUMBER 45

DATE	PARTICULARS	PAYMENTS	RECEIPTS	BALANCE
2004		£	£	£
2 Feb	Balance brought forward			1340.50 Cr
7 Feb	Credit		208.50	1549.00 Cr
10 Feb	Cheque 123456	675.25		873.75 Cr
17 Feb	Credit		278.30	1152.05 Cr
17 Feb	Cheque 123457	125.00		1027.05 Cr
24 Feb	Credit		162.30	1189.35 Cr
24 Feb	BACS J Jarvis Ltd		100.00	1289.35 Cr
26 Feb	Cheque 123458	421.80		867.55 Cr
26 Feb	Direct debit A-Z Finance	150.00		717.55 Cr
27 Feb	Credit		353.95	1071.50 Cr
27 Feb	Bank charges	10.00		1061.50 Cr

solution

Note that the bank statement is prepared from the bank's viewpoint: thus a credit balance shows that the customer is a creditor of the bank, ie the bank owes the balance to the customer. In the customer's own cash book, the bank is shown as a debit balance, ie an asset.

As the month-end balance at bank shown by the cash book, £586.25, is not the same as that shown by the bank statement, £1,061.50, it is necessary to compare individual items in the cash book and on the bank statement for accuracy. The steps are:

1 Tick off the items that appear in both cash book and bank statement.

2 The unticked items on the bank statement are entered into the bank columns of the cash book to bring it up-to-date. These are:
   - receipt 24 Feb BACS credit, J Jarvis Limited £100.00
   - payments 26 Feb Direct debit, A-Z Finance £150.00
     27 Feb Bank Charges, £10.00

   In double-entry book-keeping, the other part of the transaction will need to be recorded in the accounts.

3 The cash book is now balanced to find the revised balance:

Dr — Cash Book (bank columns) — Cr

2004		£	2004		£
	Balance b/d	586.25	26 Feb	A-Z Finance	150.00
24 Feb	J Jarvis Ltd	100.00	27 Feb	Bank Charges	10.00
			29 Feb	Balance c/d	526.25
		686.25			686.25
1 Mar	Balance b/d	526.25			

4 The remaining unticked items from the cash book are:
   - receipt 27 Feb – P Paul Limited £262.30
   - payment 25 Feb – G Christie (cheque no 123459) £797.55

   These items are timing differences, which should appear on next month's bank statement. They will be used in the bank reconciliation statement.

5 The bank reconciliation statement is now prepared, starting with the bank statement balance of £1,061.50 and using the unticked items from the cash book which were noted above.

SEVERN TRADING COMPANY
Bank Reconciliation Statement as at 29 February 2004

	£
Balance at bank as per bank statement	1,061.50
Less: unpresented cheque, no 123459	797.55
	263.95
Add: outstanding lodgement, P Paul Limited	262.30
Balance at bank as per cash book	526.25

This statement has been produced which starts with the bank statement balance, and finishes with the amended balance from the cash book, ie the two figures are reconciled.

notes on the case study

- The *unpresented cheque* is deducted from the bank statement balance because, until it is recorded by the bank, the bank statement shows a higher balance than the cash book.
- The *outstanding lodgement* is added to the bank statement balance because, until it is recorded by the bank, the bank statement shows a lower balance than the cash book.

PREPARING A BANK RECONCILIATION STATEMENT

In order to help you with the Student Activities at the end of the chapter, here is a step-by-step summary of the procedure. Reconciliation of the bank statement balance with that shown in the cash book should be carried out in the following way:

1 From the bank columns of the cash book tick off, in both cash book and bank statement, the receipts that appear in both.

2 From the bank columns of the cash book tick off, in both cash book and bank statement, the payments that appear in both.

3 Identify the items that are unticked on the bank statement and enter them in the cash book on the debit or credit side, as appropriate. (If, however, the bank has made a mistake and debited or credited an amount in error, this should not be entered in the cash book, but should be notified to the bank for them to make the correction. The amount will need to be entered on the bank reconciliation statement.)

4 The bank columns of the cash book are now balanced to find the up-to-date balance.

5 Start the bank reconciliation statement with the final balance figure shown on the bank statement.

6 In the bank reconciliation statement *deduct* the unticked payments shown in the cash book – these will be unpresented cheques.

7 In the bank reconciliation statement, *add* the unticked receipts shown in the cash book – these are outstanding lodgements.

8 The resultant money amount on the bank reconciliation statement is the balance at bank as per the cash book.

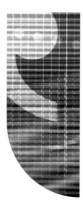

The layout which is often used for the bank reconciliation statement is that shown on page 387. The layout starts with the bank statement balance and finishes with the cash book balance. However, there is no reason why it should not commence with the cash book balance and finish with the bank statement balance: with this layout it is necessary to:

- *add* unpresented cheques
- *deduct* outstanding lodgements

The bank reconciliation statement of Severn Trading Company (see page 389) would then appear as:

SEVERN TRADING COMPANY
Bank Reconciliation Statement as at 29 February 2004

	£
Balance at bank as per cash book	526.25
Add: unpresented cheque, no 123459	797.55
	1,323.80
Less: outstanding lodgement, P Paul Limited	262.30
Balance at bank as per bank statement	1,061.50

DEALING WITH UNUSUAL ITEMS ON BANK STATEMENTS

The following are some of the unusual features that may occur on bank statements. As with other accounting discrepancies, where they cannot be resolved they should be referred to a supervisor for guidance.

out-of-date cheques

These are cheques that are more than six months old. The bank will not pay such cheques, so they can be written back in the cash book, ie debit cash book (and credit the other double-entry account involved).

returned cheques

A cheque received by a business is entered as a receipt in the cash book and then paid into the bank, but it *may be returned* by the drawer's (issuer's) bank to the payee's bank because:

- the drawer (the issuer) has stopped it
- the drawer has no money (the cheque may be returned 'refer to drawer') – ie the cheque has 'bounced'

A cheque returned in this way should be entered in the book-keeping system:

- as a payment in the cash book on the *credit* side
- as a *debit* to the account of the drawer of the cheque in the subsidiary (sales) ledger (if it is a credit sale), and also a *debit* to sales ledger control account

On the other hand, if the business itself stops a cheque, the cheque drawn by the business will have been entered as a payment in the cash book (a *credit*). It should now be entered as

- a receipt on the *debit* side
- a *credit to* the account of the payee, most probably in the subsidiary (purchases) ledger (if it is a credit purchase), and also a *credit* to purchases ledger control account

bank errors

Errors made by the bank can include:

- A cheque debited to the bank account which has not been drawn by the business – look for a cheque number on the bank statement that is different from the current cheque series: care, though, as it could be a cheque from an old cheque book.
- A BACS payment (or other credit) shown on the bank statement for which the business is not the correct recipient. If in doubt, the bank will be able to give further details of the sender of the credit.
- Standing orders and direct debits paid at the wrong time or for the wrong amounts. A copy of all standing order and direct debit mandates sent to the bank should be kept by the business for reference purposes.

When an error is found, it should be queried immediately with the bank. The item and amount should not be entered in the firm's cash book until the issue has been resolved.

bank charges and interest

From time-to-time the bank will debit business customers' accounts with an amount for:

- service charges, ie the cost of operating the bank account
- interest, ie the borrowing cost when the business is overdrawn

Banks usually notify customers in writing before debiting the account.

IMPORTANCE OF BANK RECONCILIATION STATEMENTS

1 A bank reconciliation statement forms an important part of the check and control process of the accounting system. When you prepare it the transactions in the bank columns of the cash book are compared with those recorded on the bank statement. In this way, any errors in the cash book or bank statement will be found and can be corrected (or advised to the bank, if the bank statement is wrong).

2 The bank statement is an independent accounting record, therefore it will assist in deterring fraud by providing a means of verifying the cash book balance.

3 By writing the cash book up-to-date, the business has an amended figure for the bank balance to be shown in the trial balance (see Chapter 21).

4 It is good business practice to prepare a bank reconciliation statement each time a bank statement is received. The reconciliation statement should be prepared as quickly as possible so that any discrepancies – either with the bank statement or in the firm's cash book – can be resolved. Many firms will specify to their accounting staff the timescales for preparing bank reconciliation statements – as a guideline, if the bank statement is received weekly, then the reconciliation statement should be prepared within five working days.

Chapter Summary

- Cash book is balanced at regular intervals – often at the month-end – in order to give a figure for cash and bank balances.

- A bank reconciliation statement is used as part of the check and control process of the accounting system to agree the balance shown by the bank statement with that shown by the bank columns of the cash book.

- Certain differences between the two are timing differences. The main timing differences are:
  - unpresented cheques
  - outstanding lodgements

  These differences will be corrected by time and, most probably, will be recorded on the next bank statement.

- Certain differences appearing on the bank statement need to be entered in the cash book to bring it up-to-date. These include:

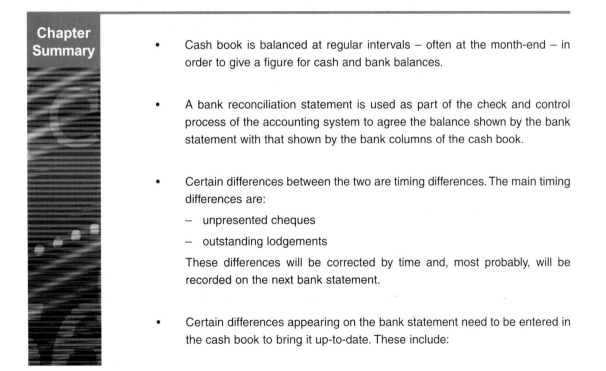

Receipts
- standing order and BACS receipts credited by the bank
- bank giro credit amounts received by the bank
- dividend amounts received by the bank
- interest credited by the bank

Payments
- standing order and direct debit payments
- bank charges and interest
- unpaid cheques debited by the bank

- The bank reconciliation statement makes use of the timing differences.
- Once prepared, a bank reconciliation statement is proof that the bank statement and the cash book (bank columns) were agreed at a particular date.

Key Terms

balance of account	the total of the account to date
bank reconciliation statement	forms the link between the balances shown in the bank statement and the cash book
timing differences	discrepancies between the bank statement and the cash book that will be corrected over time, such as unpresented cheques and outstanding lodgements
unpresented cheques	cheques drawn, but not yet recorded on the bank statement
outstanding lodgements	amounts paid into the bank, but not yet recorded on the bank statement

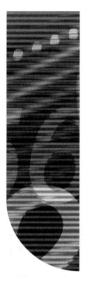

Student Activities

19.1 The cashier of the company where you work as an accounts assistant has asked you to balance the cash book at 31 August. You are aware that the company has a bank overdraft facility of £2,500.

The cash book is as follows:

Dr					Cash Book						Cr
Date	Details	Folio	Discount allowed	Cash	Bank	Date	Details	Folio	Discount received	Cash	Bank
2004			£	£	£	2004			£	£	£
1 Aug	Balances b/d			325	925	6 Aug	Crane & Co		35		845
4 Aug	S Quesne		2		98	12 Aug	Wages			275	
17 Aug	J Ahmed		4	76		16 Aug	T Lewis		15		285
23 Aug	D Lloyd		3		45	27 Aug	S Ford		5	70	
	Balance c/d				62		Balance c/d			56	
			9	401	1130				55	401	1130
1 Sep	Balance b/d			56		1 Sep	Balance b/d				62

You are to:

- balance the cash book at 31 August 2004 and bring down the balances on 1 September
- explain the meaning of the cash and bank balances brought down in the cash book on 1 September

19.2 When preparing a bank reconciliation statement, which one of the following is a timing difference?

(a) unpresented cheques

(b) direct debit payments

(c) bank charges and interest

(d) BACS receipts

Answer (a) or (b) or (c) or (d)

19.3 A firm's bank statement shows a balance of £400. Unpresented cheques total £350; outstanding lodgements total £200. What is the balance at bank shown by the cash book?

(a) £100

(b) £200

(c) £250

(d) £400

Answer (a) or (b) or (c) or (d)

Add lodge 400
200
600
– payments 350
250

19.4 The bank columns of Tom Reid's cash book for December 2004 are as follows:

2004	*Receipts*	£	2004	*Payments*		£
1 Dec	Balance b/d	280	9 Dec	W Smith	345123	40
13 Dec	P Jones	30	13 Dec	Rent	345124	50
17 Dec	H Homer	72	16 Dec	Wages	345125	85
29 Dec	J Hill	13	20 Dec	B Kay	345126	20
			31 Dec	Balance c/d		200
		395				395
1 Jan	Balance b/d	200				

He then received his bank statement which showed the following transactions for December 2004:

BANK STATEMENT		Payments	Receipts	Balance
2004		£	£	£
1 Dec	Balance brought forward			280 CR
13 Dec	Credit		30	310 CR
15 Dec	Cheque no 345123	40		270 CR
17 Dec	Cheque no 345124	50		220 CR
22 Dec	Credit		72	292 CR
23 Dec	Cheque no 345125	85		207 CR

You are to prepare a bank reconciliation statement which agrees the bank statement balance with the cash book balance.

BANK RECON AT 31 DEC

BANK STATEMENT BALANCE	207-00
Add o/s lodgements	13-00
	220-00
Less o/s payments	20-00
CORRECTED CASH BOOK BALANCE	200-00

19.5 The bank columns of P Gerrard's cash book for January 2004 are as follows:

2004	*Receipts*	£	2004	*Payments*		£
1 Jan	Balance b/d	800.50	2 Jan	A Arthur Ltd	001351	100.00
6 Jan	J Baker	495.60	9 Jan	C Curtis	001352	398.50
30 Jan	G Shotton Ltd	335.75	13 Jan	Donald & Co	001353	229.70
			14 Jan	Bryant & Sons	001354	312.00
			23 Jan	P Reid	001355	176.50

He received his bank statement which showed the following transactions for January 2004:

BANK STATEMENT		Payments	Receipts	Balance
2004		£	£	£
1 Jan	Balance brought forward			800.50 CR
6 Jan	Cheque no 001351	100.00		700.50 CR
6 Jan	Credit		495.60	1,196.10 CR
13 Jan	BACS credit: T K Supplies		716.50	1,912.60 CR
20 Jan	Cheque no 001352	398.50		1,514.10 CR
23 Jan	Direct debit: Omni Finance	207.95		1,306.15 CR
26 Jan	Cheque no 001353	229.70		1,076.45 CR

You are to:

(a) check the items on the bank statement against the items in the cash book and update the cash book accordingly; total the cash book and show the balance carried down at 31 January 2004

(b) prepare a bank reconciliation statement at 31 January 2004 which agrees the bank statement balance with the cash book balance

13 Jan	BACS T K Supplies	716-50	23 Jan	Omni Finance DD	207-95
			31 Jan	Balance c/d	923-70
		2348-35			2348-35
31 Jan	Balance b/d	923-70			

19.6 The bank columns of Jane Doyle's cash book for May 2004 are as follows:

2004	*Receipts*	£	2004	*Payments*		£
1 May	Balance b/d	300	3 May	P Stone	867714	28
7 May	Cash	162	14 May	Alpha Ltd	867715	50
17 May	C Brewster	89	28 May	E Deakin	867716	110
27 May	Cash	60	17 May	A-Z Inc	SO	25
28 May	Cash	40	31 May	Bank Charges		10
			31 May	Balance c/d		428
		651				651

She received her bank statement which showed the following transactions for May 2004:

1 June Balance b/d 428

BANK STATEMENT		Payments	Receipts	Balance
2004		£	£	£
1 May	Balance brought forward			300 CR
5 May	Cheque no 867714	28		272 CR
7 May	Credit		162	434 CR
17 May	Standing order: A-Z Insurance	25		409 CR
19 May	Credit		89	498 CR
20 May	Cheque no 867715	50		448 CR
26 May	Credit		60	508 CR
31 May	Bank Charges	10		498 CR

You are to:

(a) write the cash book up-to-date at 31 May 2004, and show the balance carried down

(b) prepare a bank reconciliation statement at 31 May 2004 which agrees the bank statement balance with the cash book balance

Bank Reconciliation as at 31 May 2004

Balance from Bank Statement	498
Add Outstanding lodge	40
	538
Less Out. payments	110
Corrected Cash Book balance	428

19.7 On 4 June Milestone Motors received a bank statement which showed the following transactions for May 2004:

BANK STATEMENT		Paid out	Paid in	Balance
2004		£	£	£
1 May	Balance brought forward			3,652 C
10 May	Cheque no 451762	751		2,901 C
11 May	Cheque no 451763	268		2,633 C
13 May	Cheque no 451765	1,045		1,588 C
14 May	BACS credit: Perran Taxis		2,596	4,184 C
18 May	Direct debit: Wyvern Council	198		3,986 C
20 May	Direct debit: A1 Insurance	1,005		2,981 C
25 May	Direct debit: Okaro and Company	254		2,727 C
25 May	Bank charges	20		2,707 C
D = Debit C = Credit				

The cash book of Milestone Motors as at 31 May 2004 is shown below:

CASH BOOK

Date	Details	Bank	Date	Cheque no	Details	Bank
2004		£	2004			£
1 May	Balance b/f	3,652	4 May	451762	Smith and Company	751
26 May	J Ackland	832	4 May	451763	Bryant Limited	268
28 May	Stamp Limited	1,119	7 May	451764	Curtis Cars	1,895
14 May	Perran Taxis	2596	7 May	451765	Parts Supplies	1,045
			18 May	DD	Wyvern Council	198
			20 May	DD	A1 Ins	1,005
			25 May	DD	Okaro + Co	254
			25 May		Charges	20
			31 May		Balance c/d	2763
		8199				8199

You are to:

(a) check the items on the bank statement against the items in the cash book

(b) update the cash book as needed

(c) total the cash book and show clearly the balance carried down at 31 May and brought down at 1 June

(d) prepare a bank reconciliation statement at 31 May 2004 which agrees the bank statement balance with the cash book balance

Bank Rec as at 31 May 2004

Bank Statement Balance		2,707
Add o/s lodge	832	
	1119	
		4658
Less o/s pay		(1895)
Corrected Cash Book Balance		2763

20 Using the journal and reconciling control accounts

this chapter covers . . .

The journal is the book of prime entry for non-regular transactions, eg purchase of fixed assets on credit, correction of errors, writing off bad debts. The journal – like the other day books (journals) that we have seen – is used to list transactions before they are entered into the double-entry system.

We have already seen how accounts are totalled and balanced at regular intervals – this is an important part of the process towards producing an initial trial balance, which provides a check on the double-entry book-keeping.

As a part of the checking process, we focus in this chapter on the use of control accounts – where a main ledger account controls a number of subsidiary accounts. We review the use of sales ledger and purchases ledger control accounts, petty cash control account, and control accounts for non-trade debtors – such as rent received. The reconciliation of the control account with the total of the subsidiary ledger provides an important check of the book-keeping process.

NVQ PERFORMANCE CRITERIA COVERED

unit 3: PREPARING LEDGER BALANCES AND AN INITIAL TRIAL BALANCE

element 2

prepare ledger balances and control accounts

A *make and record authorised adjustments*

B *total relevant accounts in the main ledger*

C *reconcile control accounts with the totals of the balance in the subsidiary ledger*

D *reconcile petty cash control account with cash in hand and subsidiary records*

E *identify discrepancies arising from the reconciliation of control accounts and either resolve or refer to the appropriate person*

F *ensure documentation is stored securely and in line with the organisation's confidentiality requirements*

USE OF THE JOURNAL

The journal completes the accounting system by providing the book of prime entry for non-regular transactions which are not recorded in any other book of prime entry. The categories of such non-regular transactions include:

- opening entries
- purchase and sale of fixed assets on credit
- correction of errors
- other non-regular transactions or adjustments

The reasons for using a journal are:

- to provide a book of prime entry for non-regular transactions
- to eliminate the need for remembering why non-regular transactions were put through the accounts – the journal acts as a notebook
- to reduce the risk of fraud, by making it difficult for unauthorised transactions to be entered in the accounting system
- to reduce the risk of errors, by listing the transactions that are to be put into the double-entry accounts
- to ensure that entries can be traced back to an authorised prime document, providing an audit trail for non-regular transactions (note that documentation is stored securely for future reference, but only for access to authorised personnel, in order to maintain confidentiality)

THE JOURNAL – A BOOK OF PRIME ENTRY

The journal is a book of prime entry; it is not, therefore, part of the double-entry book-keeping system. The journal is used to list the transactions that are to be put through the accounts. The accounting system for non-regular transactions is as follows:

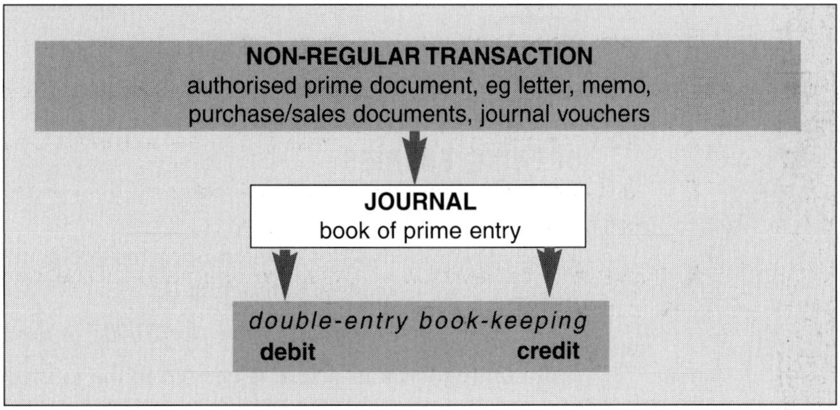

Look at the way the journal is set out with a sample transaction, and then read the notes that follow:

Date	Details	Folio	Dr	Cr
2004			£	£
1 Jul	Bank account	CBR	20,000	
	Capital account	ML		20,000
	Opening capital introduced			

Notes:

- journal entries are prepared from authorised prime documents (which are stored securely for possible future reference)
- the names of the accounts to be debited and credited in the book-keeping system are written in the details column; it is customary to show the debit transaction first
- the money amount of each debit and credit is stated in the appropriate column
- the folio column cross-references to the division of the ledger where each account is found (it can also include an account number)
- a journal entry always balances, ie debit and credit entries are for the same amount or total
- it is usual to include a brief narrative explaining why the transaction is being carried out, and making reference to the prime document whenever possible (in Skills Tests and Examinations you should always include a narrative unless specifically told otherwise)
- each journal entry is complete in itself and is ruled off to separate it from the next entry

Remember that, when a business uses control accounts which are incorporated into the double-entry accounts, the transactions from the journal involving sales ledger and purchases ledger must be recorded in the respective control accounts *and* in the subsidiary accounts for debtors or creditors.

OPENING ENTRIES

These are the transactions which open the accounts of a new business. For example, a first business transaction is:

1 Jan 2004 Started in business with £10,000 in the bank

This non-regular transaction is entered in the journal as follows:

Date	Details	Folio	Dr	Cr
2004			£	£
1 Jan	Bank account	CBR	10,000	
	Capital account	ML		10,000
	Opening capital introduced			

After the journal entry has been made, the transaction can be recorded in the double-entry accounts.

Here is another opening entries transaction to be recorded in the journal:

1 Feb 2004 *Started in business with cash £100, bank £5,000, stock £1,000, machinery £2,500, creditors £850*

The journal entry is:

Date	Details	Folio	Dr	Cr
2004			£	£
1 Feb	Cash account	CBR	100	
	Bank account	CBR	5,000	
	Stock account	ML	1,000	
	Machinery account	ML	2,500	
	Purchases ledger control account	ML		850
	Capital account*	ML		7,750
			8,600	8,600
	Assets and liabilities at the start of business			

* Assets – liabilities = capital

Notes:

- capital is, in this example, the balancing figure, ie assets minus liabilities
- the journal is the book of prime entry for all opening entries, including cash and bank; however the normal book of prime entry for other cash/bank transactions is the cash book
- the amounts for the journal entry will now need to be recorded in the double-entry accounts, and in the subsidiary (purchases) ledger

PURCHASE AND SALE OF FIXED ASSETS ON CREDIT

The purchase and sale of fixed assets are non-regular business transactions which are recorded in the journal as the book of prime entry. Only *credit* transactions are entered in the journal (because cash/bank transactions are recorded in the cash book as the book of prime entry). However, a business (or a Skills Test/Examination question) may choose to journalise cash entries: strictly, though, this is incorrect as two books of prime entry are being used.

15 Apr 2004 *Bought a machine for £1,000 plus VAT (at 17.5%) on credit from Machinery Supplies Limited, purchase order no 2341.*

Date	Details	Folio	Dr	Cr
2004			£	£
15 Apr	Machinery account	ML	1,000	
	VAT account	ML	175	
	Purchases ledger control account*	ML		1,175
	Purchase of machine from creditor, Machinery Supplies Limited: order 2341		1,175	1,175

20 May 2004 *Car sold for £2,500 on credit to Wyvern Motors Limited (no VAT chargeable).*

Date	Details	Folio	Dr	Cr
2004			£	£
20 May	Sales ledger control account*	ML	2,500	
	Car account	ML		2,500
	Sale of car, registration Y787 KAB, to debtor Wyvern Motors Limited			

* Instead of entering the above two transactions in the subsidiary purchases and sales ledgers, an alternative treatment would be to open main ledger accounts for the creditor and the debtor. This would avoid confusion with trade creditors and trade debtors in the subsidiary ledgers.

OTHER TRANSFERS

Any other non-regular transactions need to be recorded in the journal. Examples of such transactions include:

- correction of errors – this topic is covered in the next chapter.
- bad debts written off
- expenses charged to owner's drawings
- goods for the owner's use

bad debts written off

We have already seen, in Chapter 17, the double-entry book-keeping entries to write off a debtor's account:

– *debit* bad debts written off account
– *debit* Value Added Tax account (if VAT relief is available)
– *credit* sales ledger control account (and credit the account of the debtor in the subsidiary ledger)

15 Dec 2004 *Write off the account of Don's Diner which has a balance of £47, as a bad debt (VAT relief is available)*

The journal entry is:

Date	Details	Folio	Dr	Cr
2004			£	£
15 Dec	Bad debts written off account	ML	40	
	Value Added Tax account	ML	7	
	Sales ledger control account	ML		47
			47	47
	Balance of subsidiary (sales) ledger account of Don's Diner written off as a bad debt, as per memo from accounts supervisor dated 10 December 2004			

expenses charged to the owner's drawings

Sometimes the owner of a business uses business facilities for private use, eg telephone, or car. The owner will agree that part of the expense shall be charged to him or her as drawings, while the other part represents a business expense. The book-keeping entry to record the adjustment is:
– *debit* drawings account
– *credit* expense account, eg telephone

31 Dec 2004 *The balance of telephone account is £600; of this, one-quarter is the estimated cost of the owner's private usage*

The journal entry to show the transfer of private usage is:

Date	Details	Folio	Dr	Cr
2004			£	£
31 Dec	Drawings account	ML	150	
	Telephone account	ML		150
	Transfer of private use to drawings account			

goods for the owner's use

When the owner of a business takes some of the goods in which the business trades for his or her own use, the double-entry book-keeping is:

– *debit* drawings account
– *credit* purchases account

15 Oct 2004 Owner of the business takes goods for own use, £105

The journal entry is:

Date	Details	Folio	Dr	Cr
2004			£	£
15 Oct	Drawings account	ML	105	
	Purchases account	ML		105
	Goods taken for owner's use			

Note: where a business is VAT-registered, VAT must be accounted for on goods taken by the owner.

BALANCING ACCOUNTS

The topic of balancing accounts has been studied already in Chapters 4 and 12. We have seen that accounts are totalled and balanced at regular intervals – often at the end of each month – in order to show the amounts, for example:

- owing to each creditor
- owing by each debtor
- of sales
- of purchases
- of sales returns
- of purchases returns
- of expenses incurred by the business or organisation
- of fixed assets – eg premises, machinery – owned by the business or organisation
- of capital and drawings of the owner of the business
- of other liabilities, eg loans

At this point you may wish to look again at the processes involved in balancing accounts. These are covered on pages 73-76 and 229-231. Remember that, when accounts are produced using a computer accounting system, there is no need to balance each account – the balance is calculated automatically after each transaction.

Balancing accounts is an important part of the process towards producing an initial trial balance (see Chapter 21). The initial trial balance uses the balances of accounts in order to provide a check on the double-entry book-keeping. In this chapter we will see how this checking process can be started by focusing on the reconciliation of control accounts with the totals of the balances in the subsidiary ledger.

CONTROL ACCOUNTS

The use of control accounts has been incorporated into all but the earliest transactions we have seen for recording receipts and payments. The idea behind control accounts is that a main ledger account controls a number of subsidiary accounts. This is illustrated by the sales ledger control account, as follows:

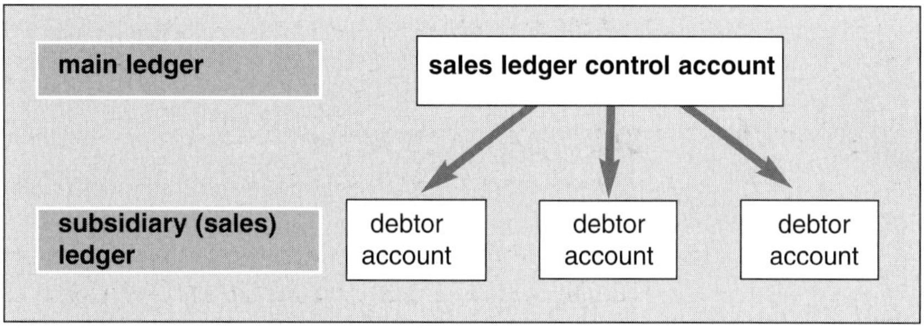

Clearly there can be almost any number of subsidiary accounts under a control account. However, if the number of subsidiary accounts was to become very large, it might be appropriate to divide the accounts between another (or more) control accounts, eg sales ledger control A-K, sales ledger control L-Z.

The principle of control accounts is that they record – usually in the form of totals – the amounts of transactions passing through the subsidiary accounts. For example, if sales for the week to three credit customers were £100, £200 and £300 the individual accounts in the subsidiary ledger will be debited with the separate amounts, while sales ledger control account will be debited with the total credit sales of £600. Taking this principle further, if the total of the opening balances for subsidiary accounts is known, together with the total of amounts increasing these balances, and the total of amounts decreasing these balances, then the total of the closing balances for the subsidiary accounts can be calculated. for example:

	£
Total of opening balances	50,000
Add increases	10,000
	60,000
Less decreases	12,000
Total of closing balances	48,000

TYPES OF CONTROL ACCOUNT

sales ledger control account

This control account has been studied already in Chapter 4 (pages 79-81). The diagram on the previous page shows the link between sales ledger control account in the main ledger and the debtors' accounts in the subsidiary (sales) ledger. An example of sales ledger control account is as follows:

Sales Ledger Control Account

Dr			Cr		
2004		£	2004		£
1 Jan	Balance b/d	500	31 Jan	Bank	443
31 Jan	Sales	700	31 Jan	Discount allowed	7
			31 Jan	Sales returns	70
			31 Jan	Balance c/d	680
		1,200			1,200
1 Feb	Balance b/d	680			

purchases ledger control account

This control account – which has been studied already in Chapter 12 (pages 231-233) – can be illustrated diagrammatically as follows:

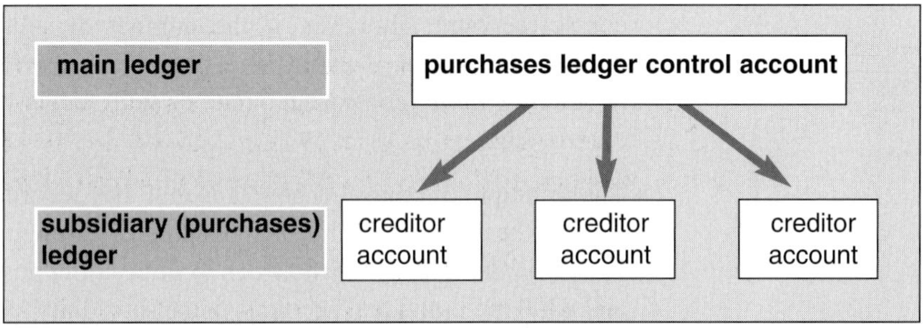

Note the link between purchases ledger control account in the main ledger and the creditors accounts in the subsidiary (purchases) ledger. An example of purchases ledger control account is as follows:

Purchases Ledger Control Account

Dr			Cr		
2004		£	2004		£
31 Jan	Purchases returns	150	1 Jan	Balance b/d	1,000
31 Jan	Bank	594	31 Jan	Purchases	1,700
31 Jan	Discount received	6			
31 Jan	Balance c/d	1,950			
		2,700			2,700
			1 Feb	Balance b/d	1,950

petty cash control account

This control account – which has been explained already in Chapter 16 (pages 337-338) – can be illustrated diagrammatically as follows:

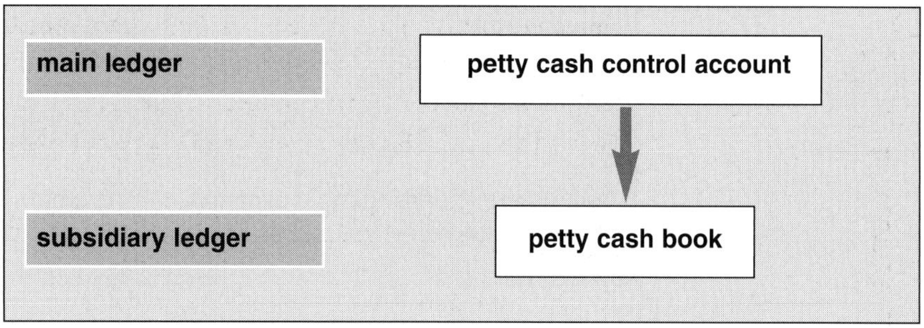

An example of petty cash control account is as follows:

Dr		Petty Cash Control Account			Cr
2004		£	2004		£
5 Apr	Balance b/d	50.00	9 Apr	Petty cash book	30.75
9 Apr	Cash book	30.75	9 Apr	Balance c/d	50.00
		80.75			80.75
9 Apr	Balance b/d	50.00			

Note that, above, the credit entry on 9 April for £30.75 is the total for the period of payments (including VAT) made out of petty cash. The debit entry on 9 April for £30.75 reimburses the petty cashier from the cash book for the amount paid out, so restoring the float of petty cash to £50.00.

other control accounts

An important principle of the accounting system is that it must adapt to the changing needs of the business or organisation which it serves. Accordingly, other types of control accounts can be used where there are a number of accounts – for example, for non-trade debtors – which can be grouped together in a subsidiary ledger. As always, the control account records – usually in the form of totals – amounts of transactions which take place in the subsidiary accounts.

An example of a non-trade debtors control account is where an office or a shop rents out space which is surplus to its requirements to a number of tenants. It will need to keep accounting records of the rent which each tenant is due to pay, together with the amounts of their payments. In other words, the business has an account for each tenant, just like a debtor, except that, here, the tenants are non-trade debtors. In its accounting system, the shop will have a control account for rent receivable in the main ledger, and a subsidiary account for each tenant in a subsidiary (non-trade debtors) ledger. This is illustrated as follows:

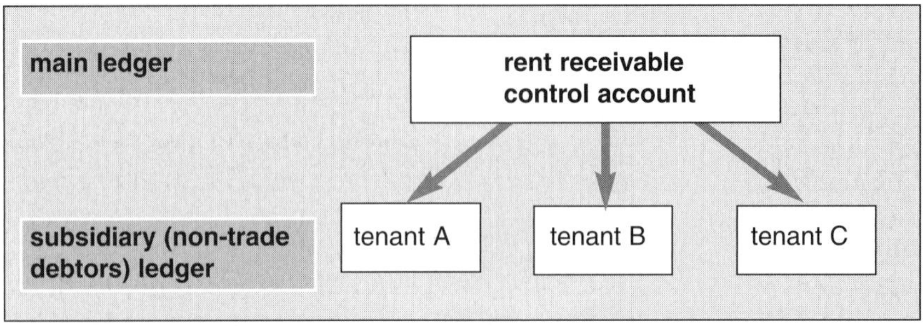

The operations of a rent receivable control account is demonstrated in the Case Study below.

Case Study

RENT RECEIVABLE CONTROL ACCOUNT: PERRAN PLANTS LIMITED

situation

Perran Plants Limited owns a large out-of-town garden centre, selling trees and plants, garden equipment and materials, and aquatics. Part of its land is surplus to the requirements of the garden centre at the moment and it rents this out to three tenants – a builder, Archie Adams, a gardener, Bill Bryce, and a garage, Milestone Motors. Each tenant uses the land for storage purposes – building materials, garden materials and customers' cars awaiting collection.

The rent paid each month by the tenants is:

	£
Archie Adams	300
Bill Bryce	200
Milestone Motors	500

Note that rent of land is exempt from VAT.

In the accounting system of Perran Plants there is a rent receivable control account in the main ledger, and an account for each tenant in a subsidiary (non-trade debtors) ledger.

At 1 February 2004, all tenants had paid the rent due and there are nil balances on the control account and in the subsidiary ledger. The following are the transactions for the month:

16 Feb	Rent due for the month (see amounts above)
19 Feb	Cheque for £250 received from Milestone Motors
20 Feb	Cheque for £300 received from Archie Adams
24 Feb	£200 cash received from Bill Bryce
27 Feb	£100 cash received from Milestone Motors

As an accounts assistant you are to show how these transactions will be recorded in the double-entry book-keeping of Perran Plants.

solution

MAIN LEDGER

Dr — Rent Receivable Control Account — Cr

2004		£	2004		£
16 Feb	Rent receivable	1,000	29 Feb	Cash book	850
			29 Feb	Balance c/d	150
		1,000			1,000
1 Mar	Balance b/d	150			

SUBSIDIARY (NON-TRADE DEBTORS) LEDGER

Dr — Archie Adams — Cr

2004		£	2004		£
16 Feb	Rent receivable	300	20 Feb	Cash book	300

Dr — Bill Bryce — Cr

2004		£	2004		£
16 Feb	Rent receivable	200	24 Feb	Cash book	200

Dr — Milestone Motors — Cr

2004		£	2004		£
16 Feb	Rent receivable	500	19 Feb	Cash book	250
			27 Feb	Cash book	100
			29 Feb	Balance c/d	150
		500			500
1 Mar	Balance b/d	150			

Notes:

- The debit balance brought down on the control account is represented by the subsidiary ledger account of Milestone Motors, which is a debtor for rent of £150.
- In the control account, the debit entry for rent receivable of £1,000 has an opposite entry in rent receivable account (shown on the next page).

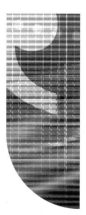

MAIN LEDGER

Dr		Rent Receivable Account			Cr
2004		£	2004		£
			16 Feb	Rent receivable control account	1,000

This account is an income account, the total of which for the year will be included as income on the profit and loss account.

- In conclusion, the non-trade debtors control account – here for rent receivable – is the main ledger account, with accounts for each non-trade debtor being held in a subsidiary ledger.

RECONCILING CONTROL ACCOUNTS

One of the advantages of using control accounts is that, for each control account in the main ledger, there are a number (often a large number) of accounts in the subsidiary ledger. Thus the main ledger is not cluttered up with the accounts of individual debtors and creditors – this is illustrated by the diagram below which shows three accounts in the main ledger representing a total of seven accounts in the subsidiary ledgers. (In practice, the subsidiary ledgers are likely to contain many more accounts than are shown here.)

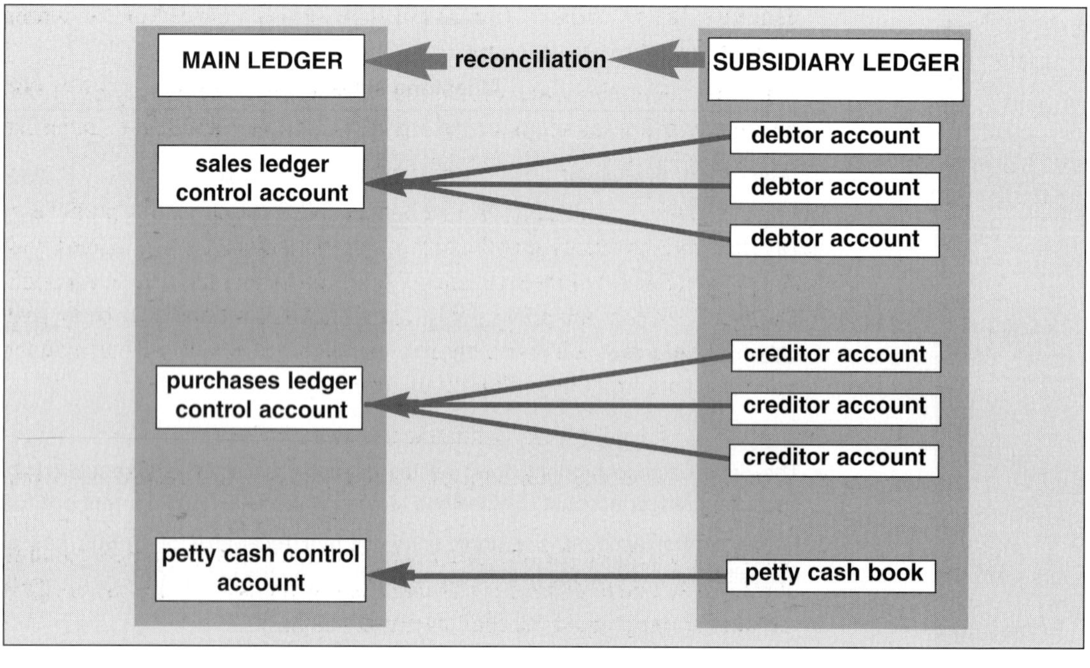

From time-to-time, the book-keeper is able to check that the balance of the control account is the same as the total of the balances of the individual subsidiary accounts which it controls. This reconciliation process is carried out by a listing similar to the following example:

Reconciliation of sales ledger control account

	1 January 2004	*31 January 2004*
	£	£
A Ackroyd	100	150
B Barnes	200	200
C Cox	50	180
D Douglas	150	150
Sales ledger control account	500	680

The sales ledger control account illustrated earlier in this chapter (page 408) shows how the reconciliation has been made with the balance on the control account at the beginning and end of the month. It is for the user of the accounting system to decide how often to reconcile the control account with the subsidiary accounts – weekly, monthly, quarterly or annually.

Any discrepancy between control account and subsidiary ledger should be investigated immediately and the error(s) traced. Discrepancies for sales ledger and purchases ledger control accounts can include:

- errors in the double-entry book-keeping, particularly in the subsidiary ledger, eg transactions not recorded, transactions recorded on the wrong side of the subsidiary account
- errors in calculating or recording the balance, eg a discrepancy of £1,000 in the reconciliation might be caused by a balance of £500 being recorded as debit when it should in fact be credit

With petty cash control account (see pages 337-338), the main purpose of reconciliation is to ensure that the balance of the control account agrees with both a physical count of the cash and with the balance of the petty cash book. (Note that, between balancing dates, cash held plus amounts of petty cash vouchers should reconcile with the imprest amount – which will also be the balance showing on petty cash control account.)

Discrepancies for petty cash control account can include:

- errors in recording transactions, eg transactions not recorded, wrong amounts
- difference between the analysis columns and the total payments column, particularly where there are VAT calculations (does VAT plus the analysis column amount equal the total payment amount?)

- difference between the cash held and the balance of the petty cash book; if this cannot be resolved, it may be a case of theft, and should be reported promptly to the accounts supervisor

Where discrepancies and queries cannot be resolved, they should be referred to the accounts supervisor or other appropriate person.

Case Study

RECONCILING PURCHASES LEDGER CONTROL ACCOUNT: AGGIESURF LIMITED

situation

Aggiesurf Limited sells a range of high quality clothes and accessories which are popular for wear (on dry land) with both surfers and non-surfers. The company buys from manufacturers – some of which are abroad – and sells to specialist surfing shops and other retailers in the popular surfing areas, particularly the south west of England. You work as an accounts assistant for Aggiesurf Limited. Today the accounts supervisor has asked you to reconcile the purchases ledger control account with the total of the subsidiary (purchases) ledger accounts. The information which follows is available to you.

Entries recorded in the subsidiary (purchases) ledger in July 2004:

	£
Balance of creditors at 1 July 2004	47,100
Goods purchased on credit	26,325
Payments to creditors	29,650
Discount received	800
Goods returned to suppliers	1,300

The following balances were in the subsidiary (purchases) ledger at 31 July 2004:

	£	
Wyvern Manufacturing Company	9,150	credit
Clothes by Design Limited	8,975	credit
Mereford Textiles	12,320	credit
Lazydays and Company	4,680	credit
Beachwear Limited	500	debit*
Sunglass Manufacturing Company	2,890	credit
Carrick and Company	3,160	credit

**Note that the balance of Beachwear Limited is debit*

solution

The first thing to do is to prepare a purchases ledger control account for July 2004 from the details above. The account is balanced at 31 July to show the balance carried down to next month.

Dr	Purchases Ledger Control Account				Cr
2004		£	2004		£
31 Jul	Bank	29,650	1 Jul	Balance b/d	47,100
31 Jul	Discount received	800	31 Jul	Purchases	26,325
31 Jul	Purchases returns	1,300			
31 Jul	Balance c/d	41,675			
		73,425			73,425
			1 Aug	Balance b/d	41,675

Reconciliation of the purchases ledger control account with the total of the subsidiary ledger is as follows:

	£
Purchases ledger control account balance as at 31 July 2004	41,675
Total of subsidiary (purchases) ledger accounts at 31 July 2004*	40,675
Difference	1,000

* see previous page: £9,150 + £8,975 + £12,320 + £4,680 – £500 + £2,890 + £3,160

As a discrepancy of £1,000 has been identified, you must either resolve it or refer it to the appropriate person – here the accounts supervisor. It is possible that there has been an error in posting transactions to the accounts and the debit balance of £500 for Beachwear Limited may in fact be a credit balance – this needs to be investigated.

Chapter Summary

- The journal is used to list non-regular transactions.
- The journal is a book of prime entry – it is not a double-entry account.
- Journal entries are prepared from authorised prime documents, which are stored securely for possible future reference.
- The journal is used for:
  - opening entries
  - purchase and sale of fixed assets on credit
  - correction of errors
  - other transfers
- Accounts are totalled and balanced at regular intervals – an important part of the process towards producing an initial trial balance.

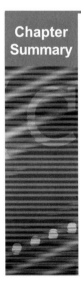

- The idea behind control accounts is that a main ledger account controls a number of subsidiary accounts.
- The main control accounts used in the accounting system are:
  - sales ledger control account
  - purchases ledger control account
  - petty cash control account
  - non-trade debtors control account, eg for rent receivable
- At regular intervals control accounts are reconciled with the totals of the balances in the subsidiary ledger – any discrepancy should be investigated immediately and the error(s) traced.

Key Terms

journal	the book of prime entry for non-regular transactions
opening entries	the transactions which open the accounts of a new business
goods for the owner's use	goods taken by the owner of a business for personal use
sales ledger control account	main ledger account which controls the subsidiary (sales) ledger
purchases ledger control account	main ledger account which controls the subsidiary (purchases) ledger
petty cash control account	main ledger account which controls the petty cash book
non-trade debtors control account	main ledger account which controls the subsidiary (non-trade debtors) ledger – eg rent receivable from tenants
reconciliation of control accounts	process of agreeing the balance of the control account with the total of the balances in the subsidiary ledger

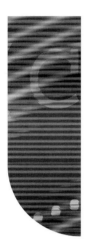

Student Activities

20.1 Which one of the following will not be recorded in the journal?

(a) credit purchase of a fixed asset

(b) cash sale of goods

(c) write off of a bad debt

(d) expenses charged to owner's drawings

Answer (a) or (b) or (c) or (d)

20.2 Which business transaction goes with which book of prime entry?

business transaction	*book of prime entry*
• credit sale of a fixed asset	• petty cash book
• credit purchase of goods from a supplier	• sales day book
• returned credit purchases to the supplier	• purchases day book
• customer returns goods sold on credit	• sales returns day book
• cheque received from a debtor	• purchases returns day book
• credit sale of goods to a customer	• journal
• expense paid out of petty cash	• cash book

20.3 Henry Lewis is setting up the book-keeping system for his new business, which sells office stationery. He decides to use the following books of prime entry:

- Journal
- Sales Day Book
- Purchases Day Book
- Sales Returns Day Book
- Purchases Returns Day Book
- Cash Book

His book-keeping system comprises a main ledger, with a subsidiary (sales) ledger and a subsidiary (purchases) ledger.

The following business transactions take place:

(a) He receives an invoice from Temeside Traders for £956 for goods supplied on credit.

(b) He issues an invoice to Malvern Models for £176 of goods.

(c) He buys a computer for use in his business for £2,000 on credit from A-Z Computers Limited.

(d) He issues a credit note to Johnson Brothers for £55 of goods.

(e) A debtor, Melanie Fisher, settles the balance of her account, £107, by cheque.

(f) He makes cash sales of £25.

(g) Henry Lewis withdraws cash £100 for his own use.

(h) He pays a creditor, Stationery Supplies Limited, the balance of the account, £298, by cheque.

(i) A debtor, Jim Bowen, with an account balance of £35 is to be written off as a bad debt.

(j) A credit note for £80 is received from a creditor, Ian Johnson.

You are to take each business transaction in turn and state:

- the name of the book of prime entry
- the name of the account to be debited
- the name of the account to be credited

Note: VAT is to be ignored.

20.4 You work as an accounts assistant for Chapelporth Limited. The company manufactures kitchen units which are sold on credit to DIY chains, kitchen and cookware shops, and kitchen fitters.

Today the accounts supervisor has asked you to reconcile the sales ledger control account with the total of the subsidiary (sales) ledger. The information which follows is available to you.

Summary of transactions with credit customers in March 2004:

	£
Balance of debtors at 1 March 2004	142,830
Credit sales	105,350
Money received from credit customers	97,247
Discount allowed	840
Sales returns from credit customers	2,890
Bad debt written off	250

The following balances were shown in the subsidiary (sales) ledger at 31 March 2004:

	£	
Q & B Group plc	50,118	debit
House Base Stores plc	35,297	debit
Vickes Limited	37,386	debit
Perran Mills Limited	10,943	debit
Portreath Home and Garden	250	debit
Bradley and Company	9,651	debit
Towan Traders	3,558	debit

You are to:

(a) Prepare a sales ledger control account for March 2004 from the details above. The account is to be balanced at 31 March 2004 to show the balance carried down to next month.

(b) Reconcile the sales ledger control account with the total of the subsidiary ledger in the format shown on the next page.

	£
Sales ledger control account balance as at 31 March 2004	
Total of subsidiary (sales) ledger accounts as at 31 March 2004	
Difference	

(c) If there is a difference calculated in (b) above, what do you think might have caused it?

20.5 The following entries were recorded in the subsidiary (purchases) ledger of Trevaunance Limited during the month of October 2004:

	£
Balance of creditors at 1 October 2004	35,105
Goods purchased on credit	23,294
Paid creditors	28,070
Discount received	430
Goods returned to suppliers	1,270

The following balances were in the subsidiary (purchases) ledger at 31 October 2004:

	£	
C Morgan	3,852	credit
Raven and Company	5,631	credit
Newbeach plc	10,854	credit
Hawke Supplies	350	debit
Packet Traders	752	credit
Durning Limited	4,175	credit
TR Limited	3,015	credit

You are to:

(a) Prepare a purchases ledger control account for October 2004 from the details above. The account is to be balanced at 31 October 2004 to show the balance carried down to next month.

(b) Reconcile the purchases ledger control account with the total of the subsidiary ledger in the following format:

	£
Purchases ledger control account balance as at 31 October 2004	
Total of subsidiary (purchases) ledger accounts as at 31 October 2004	
Difference	

(c) If there is a difference calculated in (b) above, what do you think might have caused it?

20.6 Jennings and Company keeps a petty cash control account in the main ledger and the petty cash book is the subsidiary account. Petty cash book is kept on the imprest method, and the imprest amount is £250.

In April 2004, £176 was spent from pettty cash and, at the end of the month, the imprest amount was restored from the bank.

You are to:

(a) Enter the transactions for April 2004 into the petty cash control account below, showing clearly the balance carried down.

Dr			**Petty Cash Control Account**	Cr
2004		£	2004	£
1 Apr	Balance b/d	250		

(b) State *one* other check you would carry out to ensure that the petty cash book is correct.

20.7 Mereford Stores Limited owns large retail premises in the centre of town. The top floor of the building is rented out to three tenants – a firm of accountants, Archibald and Company, a firm of solicitors, Marshall and Perry, and a firm of surveyors, Okaro and Associates. The rent paid each month by the tenants is:

	£
Archibald and Company	800 ✓
Marshall and Perry	700 ✓
Okaro and Associates	500 ✓

Note that rent is exempt from VAT.

In the accounting system of Mereford Stores, there is a rent receivable control account in the main ledger, and an account for each tenant in a subsidiary (non-trade debtors) ledger.

At 1 April 2004, Archibald and Company owed £250 rent from March; the rent for the other two tenants was fully paid. The following are the transactions for April 2004:

6 Apr	Cheque received from Archibald and Company
22 Apr	Rent due for the month (see amounts above)
23 Apr	Cheque for £700 received from Marshall and Perry
26 Apr	Cheque for £200 received from Okaro and Associates
28 Apr	Cheque for £500 received from Archibald and Company
30 Apr	Cheque for £200 received from Okaro and Associates

You are to show how these transactions will be recorded in the double-entry book-keeping of Mereford Stores Limited. Balance the accounts at 30 April 2004, showing clearly the balance brought down.

20.8 Newell Limited rents out part of its property to four tenants. In the main ledger it has a rent receivable control account; the subsidiary (non-trade debtors) ledger contains accounts in the name of each of its tenants.

The following is a summary of rent receivable activities during the month of October 2004:

	£	
Balance of non-trade debtors at 1 October	350	debit
Rent receivable for the month	2,400	
Money received from tenants	2,300	
Journal credit to correct an error	150	

The following closing balances were in the subsidiary (non-trade debtors) ledger on 31 October 2004:

	£	
Aggie Supplies	50	debit
Kempthorne and Company	175	debit
Towan Traders	75	debit
Zelah Limited	150	debit

You are to:

(a) Prepare a rent receivable control account for October 2004 from the details above. Show clearly the balance carried down at 31 October 2004, and brought down at 1 November 2004.

(b) Reconcile the rent receivable control account with the total of the subsidiary ledger in the following format:

	£
Rent receivable control account balance as at 31 October 2004	
Total of subsidiary (non-trade debtors) ledger accounts as at 31 October 2004	
Difference	

(c) If there is a difference calculated in (b) above, what do you think might have caused it?

21 Initial trial balance and correction of errors

this chapter covers . . .

We have already seen how it is necessary to balance the traditional form of account (the 'T' account) from time-to-time, according to the needs of the business. In this chapter we list the balance of each account from the ledger, distinguishing between those accounts which have debit balances and those which have credit balances. The total of these two lists forms the initial trial balance which, if it balances, proves that the accounting records are arithmetically correct.

A trial balance does not prove the complete accuracy of the accounting records and there may well be errors. These fall into two groups:

- *errors not shown by a trial balance*
- *errors shown by a trial balance*

In this chapter, we look at the types of errors within each of these groups and, when they are found, we explain how to correct them using journal entries.

Note that this chapter shows how to extract a trial balance ***manually****. In Chapters 25 to 28, when we deal with* ***computer accounting****, you will see how the computer prints out a trial balance automatically as a report, thus saving much time and trouble.*

NVQ PERFORMANCE CRITERIA COVERED

unit 3: PREPARING LEDGER BALANCES AND AN INITIAL TRIAL BALANCE

element 3.3

draft an initial trial balance

A *prepare the draft initial trial balance in line with the organisation's policies and procedures*

B *identify discrepancies in the balancing process*

C *identify reasons for imbalance and rectify them*

D *balance the trial balance*

BALANCING THE ACCOUNTS

Before an initial trial balance can be extracted, it is necessary to balance each account in the main ledger, together with the cash book. The balance brought down needs to be calculated correctly and shown on the correct side of the account. It is the balance brought down figure that is used in the initial trial balance.

Before going to the initial trial balance stage it is important to check that control accounts reconcile to their respective subsidiary ledgers. This then demonstrates the arithmetical accuracy of a subsidiary ledger section – although there still could be a number of errors (which we will look at later in this chapter).

Before moving on to the extraction of an initial trial balance, do make sure that you are able to balance accounts accurately – please refer back to Chapters 4 and 12 if you wish to review this process.

EXTRACTING AN INITIAL TRIAL BALANCE

The book-keeper extracts an initial trial balance from the accounting records in order to check the arithmetical accuracy of the double-entry book-keeping, ie that the debit entries equal the credit entries.

A trial balance is a list of the balances of every account from the ledger, distinguishing between those accounts which have debit balances and those which have credit balances.

A trial balance is extracted at regular intervals – often at the end of each month – and the balances are set out in two totalled columns, a debit column and a credit column.

Read the three bullet point notes set out below and refer at the same time to the example trial balance shown on the next page.

- The debit and credit columns are totalled and the totals should agree. In this way the trial balance proves that the accounting records are arithmetically correct. (But note that a trial balance does not prove the complete accuracy of the accounting records – see page 426.)
- The balance for each account listed in the trial balance is the amount brought down after the accounts have been balanced.
- As well as the name of each account, it is quite usual to show in the trial balance the account number. Most accounting systems give numbers to accounts and these can be listed in a separate 'folio' or 'reference' column. For sake of simplicity these details are not shown here.

Trial balance of Ace Suppliers as at 31 January 2004

	Dr	Cr
	£	£
Name of account		
Purchases	7,500	
Sales		16,000
Sales returns	250	
Purchases returns		500
Sales ledger control	1,550	
Purchases ledger control		900
Rent paid	1,000	
Wages	1,500	
Heating and lighting	1,250	
Office equipment	5,000	
Machinery	7,500	
Stock at 1 Jan 2004	2,500	
Cash	500	
Bank	4,550	
Value Added Tax		1,200
J Williams: loan		7,000
Capital		10,000
Drawings	2,500	
	35,600	35,600

DEBIT AND CREDIT BALANCES – GUIDELINES

Certain accounts always have a debit balance, while others always have a credit balance. You should already know these, but the lists set out below will act as a revision guide, and will also help in your understanding of trial balances.

Debit balances include:

- cash account and petty cash account
- purchases account
- sales returns account
- fixed asset accounts, eg premises, motor vehicles, machinery, office equipment, etc
- stock account – the stock valuation at the beginning of the year
- expenses accounts, eg wages, telephone, rent paid, etc

- drawings account
- sales ledger control account

Credit balances include:

- sales account
- purchases returns account
- income accounts, eg rent received, commission received, fees received
- capital account
- loan account
- purchases ledger control account

Notes:

- Bank account can be either debit or credit – it will be debit when the business has money in the bank, and credit when it is overdrawn.
- Value Added Tax account can be either debit or credit – it will be debit when VAT is due to the business and credit when the business owes VAT to HM Customs & Excise.

IF THE INITIAL TRIAL BALANCE DOESN'T BALANCE . . .

If the initial trial balance fails to balance, ie the two totals are different, there is an error (or errors):

- *either* in the addition of the trial balance
- *and/or* in the double-entry book-keeping

The accounts supervisor needs to be informed if the trial balance does not balance; he or she will give guidance as to what is to be done.

The procedure for finding the error(s) is as follows:

- check the addition of the trial balance
- check that the balance of each account has been correctly entered in the trial balance, and under the correct heading, ie debit or credit
- check that the balance of every account in the ledger has been included in the trial balance
- check the calculation of the balance on each account
- calculate the amount that the trial balance is wrong, and then look in the accounts for a transaction for this amount: if one is found, check that the double-entry book-keeping has been carried out correctly

- halve the amount by which the trial balance is wrong, and look for a transaction for this amount: if it is found, check the double-entry book-keeping
- if the amount by which the trial balance is wrong is divisible by nine, then the error may be a reversal of figures, eg £65 entered as £56, or £45 entered as £54
- if the trial balance is wrong by a round amount, eg £10, £100, £1,000, the error is likely to be in the calculation of the account balances
- if the error(s) is still not found, it is necessary to check the book-keeping transactions since the date of the last trial balance, by going back to the prime documents and books of prime entry

ERRORS NOT SHOWN BY A TRIAL BALANCE

As mentioned earlier, a trial balance does not prove the complete accuracy of the accounting records.

There are six types of errors that are not shown by a trial balance. These are explained below.

1 error of omission

Here a business transaction has been completely omitted from the accounting records, ie both the debit and credit entries have not been made.

2 reversal of entries

With this error, the debit and credit entries have been made in the accounts but on the wrong side of the two accounts concerned. For example, a cash sale has been entered wrongly as debit sales account, credit cash account. (This should have been entered as a debit to cash account, and a credit to sales account.)

3 mispost/error of commission

Here, a transaction is entered to the wrong person's account. For example, a sale of goods on credit to A T Hughes has been entered as debit to A J Hughes' account, credit sales account. Double-entry book-keeping has been completed and the sales ledger control account will reconcile with the subsidiary (sales) ledger. However, when A J Hughes receives a statement of account, he or she will soon complain about being debited with goods not ordered or received.

4 error of principle

This is when a transaction has been entered in the wrong type of account. For example, the cost of fuel for vehicles has been entered as debit motor vehicles account, credit bank account. The error is that motor vehicles account represents fixed assets, and the transaction should have been debited to the expense account for motor vehicle running expenses.

5 error of original entry (or transcription)

Here, the correct accounts have been used, and the correct sides: what is wrong is that the amount has been entered incorrectly in both accounts. This could be caused by a 'bad figure' on an invoice or a cheque, or it could be caused by a 'reversal of figures', eg an amount of £45 being entered in both accounts as £54. Note that both debit and credit entries need to be made incorrectly for the trial balance still to balance; if one entry has been made incorrectly and the other is correct, then the error will be shown.

6 compensating error

This is where two errors cancel each other out. For example, if the balance of purchases account is calculated wrongly at £10 too much, and a similar error has occurred in calculating the balance of sales account, then the two errors will compensate each other, and the trial balance will not show the errors.

Correction of errors is covered fully later in this chapter (pages 428-433).

IMPORTANCE OF THE TRIAL BALANCE

A business will extract a trial balance on a regular basis to check the arithmetic accuracy of the book-keeping. However, the trial balance is also used as the starting point in the production of the financial statements (or final accounts) of a business. These are produced once a year (often more frequently) and comprise:

- profit and loss account
- balance sheet

The final accounts show the owner(s) how profitable the business has been, what the business owns, and how the business is financed. The preparation of final accounts is an important aspect of accountancy. Final accounts are covered in later NVQ levels. For the moment, we can say that extraction of a trial balance is an important exercise in the accounting process: it proves the book-keeper's accuracy, and also lists the account balances which form the basis for the final accounts of a business.

CORRECTION OF ERRORS

In any book-keeping system there is always the possibility of an error. Ways to avoid errors, or ways to reveal them sooner, include:

- division of the accounting function between a number of people, so that no one person is responsible for all aspects of a business transaction
- regular circulation of statements of account to debtors, who will check the transactions on their accounts and advise any discrepancies
- checking of statements of account received from creditors against the accounting records
- extraction of a trial balance at regular intervals
- the checking of bank statements and preparing bank reconciliation statements
- checking cash and petty cash balances against cash held
- the use of control accounts
- the use of a dedicated computer accounting program

Despite all of these, errors will still occur from time-to-time and, in this section, we will look at:

- correction of errors not shown by a trial balance
- correction of errors shown by a trial balance, using a suspense account

CORRECTION OF ERRORS NOT SHOWN BY A TRIAL BALANCE

Earlier in this chapter we listed the types of errors in a book-keeping system that are not revealed by a trial balance. These are:

- error of omission
- reversal of entries
- mispost/error of commission
- error of principle
- error of original entry (or transcription)
- compensating error

Although these errors are not shown by a trial balance, they are likely to come to light if the procedures suggested in the previous section, above, are followed. For example, a debtor will soon let you know if their account has been debited with goods they did not buy.

When an error is found, it needs to be corrected by means of a journal entry which shows the book-keeping entries that have been passed. Remember that all journal entries are prepared from authorised prime documents – these could take the form of a memorandum or email from the accounts supervisor; such documents, together with any other paperwork, should be stored securely for possible future reference.

We will now look at an example of each of the errors not shown by a trial balance, and will see how it is corrected by means of a journal entry.

hint!

A practical hint which may help in correcting errors is to write out the double-entry accounts as they appear with the error; then write in the correcting entries and see if the result has achieved what was intended.

error of omission

Credit sale of goods, £200 plus VAT (at 17.5%) on invoice 4967 to H Jarvis completely omitted from the accounting system; the error is corrected on 12 May 2004

Date	Details	Folio	Dr	Cr
2004			£	£
12 May	Sales ledger control	ML	235	
	Sales	ML		200
	VAT	ML		35
			235	235
	Invoice 4967 omitted from accounts: in the subsidiary (sales) ledger – debit H Jarvis £235			

This type of error can happen in a very small business – often where the book-keeping is done by one person. For example, an invoice, when produced, is 'lost' down the back of a filing cabinet. Where a computer accounting system is used, it should be impossible for this error to occur. Also, if documents are numbered serially, then none should be mislaid.

reversal of entries

A payment, on 3 May 2004 by cheque for £50 to a creditor, S Wright (receipt no 93459), has been debited in the cash book and credited to purchases ledger control account; this is corrected on 12 May 2004

Date	Details	Folio	Dr	Cr
2004			£	£
12 May	Purchases ledger control	ML	50	
	Bank	CBP		50
	Purchases ledger control	ML	50	
	Bank	CBP		50
			100	100
	Correction of £50 reversal of entries (receipt no 93459): in the subsidiary (purchases) ledger			
	– debit S Wright £50			
	– debit S Wright £50			

To correct this type of error it is best to reverse the entries that have been made incorrectly (the first two journal entries), and then to put through the correct entries. Although it will correct the error, it is wrong to debit £100 to purchases ledger control account and to credit £100 to bank account. This is because there was never a transaction for this amount – the original transaction was for £50.

As noted earlier, it is often an idea to write out the accounts, complete with the error, and then to write in the correcting entries. As an example, the two accounts involved in this last error are shown with the error made on 3 May, and the corrections made on 12 May indicated by the shading:

Dr		**Purchases Ledger Control Account**			Cr
2004		£	2004		£
12 May	Bank	50	3 May	Bank	50
12 May	Bank	50			

Dr		**Cash Book** (bank columns)			Cr
2004		£	2004		£
3 May	S Wright	50	12 May	S Wright	50
			12 May	S Wright	50

The accounts now show a net debit transaction of £50 on purchases ledger control account, and a net credit transaction of £50 on bank account, which is how this payment to a creditor should have been recorded in the first place.

mispost/error of commission

Credit sales of £47, including VAT (at 17.5%) on invoice no 321 have been debited to the account of J Adams, instead of the account of J Adams Ltd; the error is corrected on 17 May 2004

Date	Details	Folio	Dr	Cr
2004			£	£
17 May	Sales ledger control	ML	47	
	Sales ledger control	ML		47
	Correction of mispost (invoice 321): in the subsidiary (sales) ledger – debit J Adams Limited £47 – credit J Adams £47			

This type of error can be avoided, to some extent, by the use of account numbers, and by persuading the customer to quote the account number or reference on each transaction. All computer accounting systems use numbers/references to identify accounts, but it is still possible to post a transaction to the wrong account.

error of principle

The cost of diesel fuel, £30 (excluding VAT) on receipt no 34535, has been debited to vehicles account; the error is corrected on 20 May 2004

Date	Details	Folio	Dr	Cr
2004			£	£
20 May	Vehicle running expenses	ML	30	
	Vehicles	ML		30
	Correction of error: receipt 34535			

This type of error is similar to a mispost except that, instead of the wrong person's account being used, it is the wrong class of account.

In the above example, the vehicle running costs must be kept separate from the cost of the asset (the vehicle), otherwise the expense and asset accounts will be incorrect, leading to profit for the year being overstated and the fixed asset being shown in the balance sheet at too high a figure.

error of original entry (or transcription)

Postages of £45 paid by cheque entered in the accounts as £54; the error is corrected on 27 May 2004

Date	Details	Folio	Dr	Cr
2004			£	£
27 May	Bank	CBP	54	
	Postages	ML		54
	Postages	ML	45	
	Bank	CBP		45
			99	99
	Correction of error: postages of £45 entered into the accounts as £54			

This error could have been corrected by debiting bank and crediting postages with £9, being the difference between the two amounts. However, there was no original transaction for this amount, and it is better to reverse the wrong transaction and put through the correct one. A reversal of figures either has a difference of nine (as above), or an amount divisible by nine. An error of original entry can also be a 'bad' figure on a cheque or an invoice, entered wrongly into both accounts.

compensating error

Rates account is overcast (ie it is overadded) by £100; sales account is also overcast by the same amount; the error is corrected on 31 May 2004

Date	Details	Folio	Dr	Cr
2004			£	£
31 May	Sales	ML	100	
	Rates	ML		100
	Correction of overcast on rates account and sales account			

Here, an account with a debit balance – rates – has been overcast; this is compensated by an overcast on an account with a credit balance – sales. There are several permutations on this theme, eg two debit balances, one overcast, one undercast; a debit balance undercast, a credit balance undercast.

important notes to remember

We have just looked at several journal entries in connection with the correction of errors. Remember:

- The journal is the book of prime entry for non-regular transactions. The journal entries must then be recorded in the book-keeping system.
- For all the journal entries shown above which involve sales ledger or purchases ledger, we have assumed that control accounts are used, which are incorporated into the main ledger of the accounting system; remember that the transactions must also be recorded in the appropriate subsidiary ledger – subsidiary (sales) ledger or subsidiary (purchases) ledger.

TRIAL BALANCE ERRORS: USE OF SUSPENSE ACCOUNT

There are many types of errors which are revealed by a trial balance:

- omission of one part of the double-entry transaction
- recording two debits or two credits for a transaction
- recording a different amount for a transaction on the debit side from the credit side
- errors in the calculation of balances (not compensated by other errors)
- error in transferring the balance of an account to the trial balance
- error of addition in the trial balance

When errors are shown, the trial balance is 'balanced' by recording the difference in a suspense account, as shown in the Case Study below.

Case Study

SUSPENSE ACCOUNT: TEMESIDE TRADERS:

situation

The book-keeper of Temeside Traders is unable to balance the trial balance on 31 December 2004. As the error or errors cannot be found quickly, the trial balance is balanced by recording the difference in a suspense account:

	Dr	Cr
	£	£
Trial balance totals	100,000	99,850
Suspense account		150
	100,000	100,000

A suspense account is opened in the main ledger with, in this case, a credit balance of £150:

Dr		Suspense Account		Cr
2004	£	2004		£
		31 Dec	Trial balance difference	150

A detailed examination of the book-keeping system is now made in order to find the errors. As errors are found, they are corrected by means of a journal entry. The journal entries will balance, with one part of the entry being either a debit or credit to suspense account. In this way, the balance on suspense account is eliminated by book-keeping transactions. Using the above suspense account, the following errors are found and corrected on 14 January 2005:

- sales account is undercast by £100
- a payment to a creditor, A Wilson, for £65, has been recorded in the bank as £56
- telephone expenses of £55 have not been entered in the expenses account
- stationery expenses £48 have been debited to both the stationery account and the bank account

These errors are corrected by journal entries shown below. Note that the journal narrative includes details of cheque numbers and dates taken from the records of the business.

Date	Details	Folio	Dr	Cr
2005			£	£
14 Jan	Suspense account	ML	100	
	Sales account	ML		100
	Undercast on 23 December 2004 now corrected			
14 Jan	Bank account	CBR	56	
	Suspense account	ML		56
	Suspense account	ML	65	
	Bank account	CBP		65
			121	121
	Payment to A Wilson for £65 (cheque no 783726) on 30 December 2004 entered in bank as £56 in error			
14 Jan	Telephone expenses account	ML	55	
	Suspense account	ML		55
	Omission of entry in expenses account: paid by cheque no 783734			
14 Jan	Suspense account	ML	48	
	Bank account	CBP		48
	Suspense account	ML	48	
	Bank account	CBP		48
			96	96
	Correction of error: payment by cheque no 783736 debited in error to bank account			

After these journal entries have been recorded in the accounts, suspense account appears as:

Dr		Suspense Account			Cr
2005		£	2004		£
14 Jan	Sales	100	31 Dec	Trial balance difference	150
14 Jan	Bank	65	2005		
14 Jan	Bank	48	14 Jan	Bank	56
14 Jan	Bank	48	14 Jan	Telephone expenses	55
		261			261

Thus all the errors have now been found, and suspense account has a nil balance.

Chapter Summary

- Taking the balance of each account in the ledger, an initial trial balance can be extracted.
- A trial balance does not prove the complete accuracy of the accounting records; errors not shown by a trial balance are:
  - error of omission
  - reversal of entries
  - mispost/error of commission
  - error of principle
  - error of original entry
  - compensating error
- Errors shown by a trial balance include: omission of one part of the book-keeping transaction, recording two debits/credits for a transaction, recording different amounts in the two accounts, calculating balances incorrectly, transferring wrong balances to the trial balance.
- Correction of errors is always a difficult topic to put into practice: it tests knowledge of book-keeping procedures and it is all too easy to make the error worse than it was in the first place! The secret of dealing with this topic well is to write down – in account format – what has gone wrong. It should then be relatively easy to see what has to be done to put the error right.
- All errors are non-regular transactions and need to be corrected by means of a journal entry: the book-keeper then records the correcting transactions in the accounts.
- When error(s) are shown by a trial balance, the amount of the error is placed in a suspense account. As the errors are found, journal entries are made which 'clear out' the suspense account.

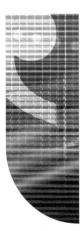

Key Terms

trial balance	list of the balances of every account from the ledger, distinguishing between those accounts which have debit balances and those which have credit balances
error of omission	business transaction completely omitted from the accounting records
reversal of entries	debit and credit entries made on the wrong side of the accounts
mispost/error of commission	transaction entered to the wrong person's account
error of principle	transaction entered in the wrong type of account
error of original entry	wrong amount entered incorrectly in accounts
compensating error	where two errors cancel each other
suspense account	account in which is placed the amount of an error shown by the initial trial balance, pending further investigation

Student Activities

21.1 Which one of the following accounts always has a debit balance?

(a) capital account

(b) purchases account

(c) sales account

(d) purchases returns account

Answer (a) or (b) or (c) or (d)

21.2 Which one of the following accounts always has a credit balance?

(a) sales returns account

(b) premises account

(c) capital account

(d) wages account

Answer (a) or (b) or (c) or (d)

21.3 Andrew Jarvis started in business on 1 April 2004.

During the month he had the following transactions:

2004	
1 Apr	Paid £1,000 into business bank account as opening capital
2 Apr	Bought goods for resale, paying by cheque, £255
5 Apr	Paid for advertising by cheque, £60
7 Apr	Sold goods, £195, a cheque being received
8 Apr	Paid rent by cheque, £125
9 Apr	Sold goods, £248, a cheque being received
12 Apr	Drawings £100 by cheque
14 Apr	Bought goods for resale, paying by cheque, £240
16 Apr	Received a loan from J Couchman, £1,000 by cheque
19 Apr	Sold goods, £220, a cheque being received
21 Apr	Bought shop fittings, £1,250, paying by cheque
23 Apr	Bought goods for resale, paying by cheque, £180
26 Apr	Paid for advertising by cheque, £90
28 Apr	Sold goods, £312, a cheque being received
29 Apr	Paid rent by cheque, £125
30 Apr	Drawings £125 by cheque

You are to:

(a) record the transactions in his cash book (which has a money column for bank only)

(b) record the transactions in his other double-entry accounts

(c) balance all the accounts that have more than one transaction at 30 April 2004

(d) draw up a trial balance at 30 April 2004

Notes:

- *day books are not required*
- *Andrew Jarvis is not registered for VAT*

21.4 Produce the trial balance of Jane Greenwell as at 29 February 2004. She has omitted to open a capital account. You are to fill in the missing figure in order to balance the trial balance.

	£
Bank overdraft	1,250
Purchases	850
Cash	48
Sales	1,940
Purchases returns	144
Creditors	1,442
Equipment	2,704
Van	3,200
Stock at 1 Jan 2004	1,210
Sales returns	90
Debtors	1,174
Wages	1,500
Capital	?

21.5 The following errors have been made in the accounting records of Beacon Traders:

(a) An entry for a credit purchase has been made in purchases and VAT accounts, but has been omitted from purchases ledger control account.

(b) A sales invoice has been omitted from all accounting records.

(c) A purchases invoice has been entered to the account of B Ryan instead of D Ryan.

(d) The amount of VAT on a sales invoice has been calculated incorrectly.

You are to state which of these errors will cause an imbalance in the trial balance.

21.6 An amount has been entered into the book-keeping system as £65 instead of £56. The error is called:

(a) compensating error

(b) mispost

(c) error of principle

(d) error of original entry

Answer (a) or (b) or (c) or (d)

21.7 A trial balance fails to agree by £75 and the difference is placed to a suspense account. Later it is found that a credit sale for this amount has not been entered in the sales account. Which one of the following journal entries is correct?

(a) debit suspense account £75; credit sales account £75

(b) debit suspense account £150; credit sales account £150

(c) debit sales account £75; credit suspense account £75

(d) credit sales account £75

Answer (a) or (b) or (c) or (d)

21.8 The following errors have been made in the main ledger of Mereford Manufacturing:

(a) £100 has been debited to rent paid account instead of to rates account.

(b) Sales returns have been entered into the accounting records as £96 instead of the correct amount of £69. (Note: ignore VAT)

(c) A debtor, Zelah Stores, has ceased trading. The amount outstanding on the account of £200 plus VAT has been written off as a bad debt in the subsidiary (sales) ledger, but no entries have been made in the main ledger.

(d) Purchases returns of £175 have been debited to purchases returns account and credited to purchases ledger control account.

(e) Diesel fuel for vehicles of £45 has been debited to vehicles account. (Note: ignore VAT)

You are to record the journal entries to correct the errors shown above in the main ledger (narratives are not required).

21.9 The trial balance of Thomas Wilson balanced. However, a number of errors have been found in the book-keeping system:

(a) Credit sale of £150 to J Rigby has not been entered in the accounts.

(b) A payment by cheque for £125 to H Price Limited, a creditor, has been recorded in the account of H Prince.

(c) The cost of a new delivery van, £10,000, has been entered to vehicle expenses account.

(d) Postages of £55, paid by cheque, have been entered on the wrong sides of both accounts.

(e) Both purchases account and purchases returns account have been undercast by £100.

(f) A payment for £89 from L Johnson, a debtor, has been entered in the accounts as £98.

You are to take each error in turn and:

- state the type of error
- show the correcting journal entry

Note: VAT is to be ignored.

21.10 Jeremy Johnson extracts a trial balance from his book-keeping records on 30 September 2004. Unfortunately the trial balance fails to balance and the difference, £19 debit, is placed to a suspense account pending further investigation.

The following errors are later found:

(a) A cheque payment of £85 for office expenses has been entered in the cash book but no entry has been made in the office expenses account.

(b) A payment for photocopying of £87 by cheque has been correctly entered in the cash book, but is shown as £78 in the photocopying account.

(c) Sales returns account has been overcast by £100.

(d) Commission received of £25 has been entered twice in the account.

You are to:

- make journal entries to correct the errors
- show the suspense account after the errors have been corrected

Note: VAT is to be ignored.

21.11 You work as an accounts assistant for Durning Supplies. The accounts supervisor hands you the company's trial balance as at 29 February 2004 (see below). Unfortunately the trial balance did not balance and the accounts supervisor has placed the difference in a suspense account until the error(s) can be found.

Trial balance as at 29 February 2004

	Dr	Cr
	£	£
Purchases	122,500	
Sales		239,850
Rent paid	5,220	
Wages	96,310	
Office equipment	6,000	
Machinery	12,000	
Heating and lighting	3,510	
Telephone expenses	2,054	
Stock at 1 March 2003	24,740	
Bank	8,230	
Sales ledger control	22,840	
Purchases ledger control		15,680
Value Added Tax		5,320
Capital		58,500
Drawings	15,900	
Suspense	46	
	319,350	319,350

The accounts supervisor asks you to investigate the difference and to prepare journal entries to correct the error(s). During investigations, you find the following errors:

(a) Sales account has been overcast by £100.

(b) Rent paid of £205 has been entered twice in the account.

(c) A payment for telephone expenses of £56 has been correctly entered in the cash book, but is shown as £65 in telephone expenses account.

(d) A payment for heating of £160 has been entered in the cash book but no entry has been made in the heating and lighting account.

You are to:

- make journal entries to correct the errors (narratives are not required)
- show the suspense account after the errors has been corrected
- rewrite the trial balance after correcting the errors

Note: VAT is to be ignored.

22 Using the trial balance

this chapter covers . . .

This chapter links together the books of prime entry, the double-entry accounts system and the trial balance.

It shows how the accounting system operates and illustrates this by means of two fully-worked Case Studies, one for credit purchases (page 448) and one for credit sales (page 456).

NVQ PERFORMANCE CRITERIA COVERED

unit 3: PREPARING LEDGER BALANCES AND AN INITIAL TRIAL BALANCE

element 3.3

draft an initial trial balance

A *prepare the draft initial trial balance in line with the organisation's policies and procedures*

B *identify discrepancies in the balancing process*

C *identify reasons for imbalance and rectify them*

D *balance the trial balance*

THE ACCOUNTING SYSTEM

As we have seen so far, businesses need to record financial transactions for practical reasons:

- they need to quantify transactions such as purchases, sales, expenses
- they need to present the figures in a meaningful way in order to measure the success of the business or organisation

The accounting system can be complex and this chapter seeks to summarise and bring together the key elements that we have studied so far. The process of accounting follows a number of distinct stages which are illustrated in the diagram on the next page.

The rest of this chapter summarises the stages of the accounting system and brings together all that we have seen so far. Included in the chapter are two fully-worked Case Studies which illustrate, firstly, accounting for credit purchases (page 448) and, secondly, accounting for credit sales (page 456); the Case Studies incorporate the use of control accounts, together with some journal entries.

PRIME DOCUMENTS

Business transactions generate documents, and we have already studied the key documents in depth in Chapters 2 and 10.

sale and purchase of goods and services

When a business or organisation buys or sells goods or services the seller prepares an invoice stating

- the amount owing
- when it should be paid
- details of the goods sold or service provided

cash sales and credit sales – debtors and creditors

An invoice is prepared by the seller for

- **cash sales** – where payment is immediate, whether in cash, by cheque, by debit card or by credit card (Note that not all cash sales will require an invoice to be prepared by the seller – shops, for instance, normally issue a receipt for the amount paid.)
- **credit sales** – where payment is to be made at a later date (often 30 days later)

the accounting system

PRIME DOCUMENTS invoices – issued and received credit notes – issued and received bank paying-in slips cheques issued BACS documents	***sources of accounting information***
BOOKS OF PRIME ENTRY day books journal cash books (also used in double-entry – see below)	***gathering and summarising accounting information***
DOUBLE-ENTRY ACCOUNTS **main ledger** - 'nominal' accounts for sales, purchases, expenses, capital, loans etc, and control accounts - 'real' accounts for items, eg fixed assets **cash books** - cash book for cash and bank transactions - petty cash book **subsidiary ledgers** - for sales ledger, purchases ledger, petty cash and non-trade debtors	***recording the dual aspect of accounting transactions in the ledgers of the accounting system***
TRIAL BALANCE a summary of the balances of all the accounts at the end of the accounting period	***arithmetic checking of double-entry book-keeping***
FINANCIAL STATEMENTS* • profit and loss account • balance sheet	***account which measures the profit (or loss) for an accounting period*** ***statement of assets, liabilities and capital at the end of an accounting period***

* *the topic of financial statements is covered fully at NVQ levels 3 & 4*

A debtor is a person who owes you money when you sell on credit.

A creditor is a person to whom you owe money when you buy on credit.

return of goods – the credit note

If the buyer returns goods which are bought on credit (they may be faulty or incorrect) the seller will prepare a credit note (see page 32 for an example) which is sent to the buyer, reducing the amount of money owed. The credit note, like the invoice, states the money amount and the goods or services to which it relates.

banking transactions

Businesses and organisations, like anyone else with a bank account, need to pay in money, and draw out cash and make payments. Paying-in slips, cheques and BACS transfers are used frequently in business as prime documents for bank account transactions. 'BACS' stands for Bankers Automated Clearing Services, which provide electronic transfer of amounts from one bank account to another.

RECORDING OF TRANSACTIONS

Many businesses and organisations issue and receive large quantities of invoices, credit notes and banking documents, and it is useful for them to list these in summary form. These summaries are known as books of prime entry.

The books of prime entry include:

- **sales day book** – a list of credit sales made, compiled from invoices issued
- **purchases day book** – a list of credit purchases made, compiled from invoices received
- **sales returns day book** – a list of 'returns in', ie goods returned by credit customers, compiled from credit notes issued
- **purchases returns day book** – a list of 'returns out', ie goods returned to credit suppliers, compiled from credit notes received
- **cash book** – the business' record of the cash and bank transactions compiled from receipts, paying-in slips, cheques and BACS documents
- **petty cash book** – a record of low-value purchases, compiled from petty cash vouchers
- **journal** – a record of non-regular transactions, which are not recorded in any other book of prime entry

The books of prime entry provide the information for the double-entry book-keeping system.

DOUBLE-ENTRY ACCOUNTS: THE LEDGER

The basis of the accounting system is the double-entry book-keeping system which is embodied in a series of records known as the ledger. This is divided into a number of separate accounts.

double-entry book-keeping

Double-entry book-keeping involves making two entries in the accounts for each transaction. With a manual accounting system the two entries are made by hand; with a computer accounting system one entry is made on the keyboard, and the computer operator indicates to the machine where the other entry is to be made by means of a code.

accounts

The sources for the entries are the books of prime entry. The ledger into which the entries are made is normally a bound book (in a non-computerised system) divided into separate accounts, eg a separate account for sales, purchases, each type of business expense, each debtor, each creditor, and so on. Each account will be given a specific name, and a number for reference purposes (or input code, with a computer system).

division of the ledger

Because of the large number of accounts involved, the ledger is traditionally divided into a number of sections. These same sections are used in computer accounting systems.

- **Cash book** – comprising cash account and bank account; also a petty cash book (which may be a subsidiary ledger) for low-value purchases. Note that cash books are also books of prime entry.
- **Main ledger** – the remainder of the accounts: nominal accounts, eg sales, purchases, expenses, real accounts for items owned by the business, and control accounts.
- **Subsidiary ledgers** – for sales ledger, purchases ledger, petty cash, and non-trade debtors.

INITIAL TRIAL BALANCE

The initial trial balance lists the balances of all the double-entry accounts, distinguishing between those with debit balances and those with credit balances. The total of the debit and credit columns should be equal, which means that the trial balance 'balances'.

An initial trial balance is prepared or extracted (from the double-entry accounts) at regular intervals – weekly, fortnightly or monthly – depending on the requirements of the business or organisation. One will always be prepared at the end of the financial year, which may vary between businesses and organisations – although 31 December (end of the calendar year) and 31 March (near the end of the tax year) are popular. The heading of a trial balance gives the name of the business or organisation whose accounts have been listed and the date it was extracted, eg 'as at 31 December 2004'.

Whilst the trial balance acts as an arithmetic check on the double-entry book-keeping, there can still be a number of errors within the accounts system. As we have seen in Chapter 21, there may be:

- errors not shown by a trial balance
- errors shown by a trial balance

As well as being a check on the book-keeping, the trial balance is a valuable source of information used to help in the preparation of financial statements.

FINANCIAL STATEMENTS

The financial statements or 'final accounts' comprise:

- profit and loss account, which shows the profit (or loss) for an accounting period such as a year
- balance sheet, which lists the assets, liabilities and capital at the end of the accounting period

Financial statements are covered fully at NVQ levels 3 and 4.

CASE STUDIES

To conclude this part of the book and to bring together the book-keeping system, there now follow two case studies, based on a common scenario:

- **Case Study 1** (on the next page) focuses on accounting for credit purchases, commencing with the books of prime entry – purchases day book and purchases returns day book – together with some aspects of cash book. The Case Study comprises entry of opening balances into accounts, recording of transactions from the day books and cash book, balancing accounts and transfer of balances (including additional balances) to a trial balance. The debit and credit columns of the trial balance are then totalled and shown to be equal.
- **Case Study 2** (on page 456) focuses on accounting for credit sales. As well as the books of prime entry – sales day book and sales returns day book –

it includes aspects of cash book and journal entries. Opening balances are entered into the accounts, transactions are recorded from the day books, and cash book and journal, and the accounts are then balanced. The balances are transferred (together with additional balances) to a trial balance, the debit and credit columns of which are totalled and shown to be equal.

Case Study

WYVERN NURSERIES – ACCOUNTING FOR CREDIT PURCHASES

situation

You work as an accounts assistant for Wyvern Nurseries.

The company runs a garden centre in Wyvern, and buys in plants and other garden and leisure products from suppliers. At its nurseries it grows the 'specialist' range of plants which are also sold to shops and other garden centres in the area. Wyvern Nurseries is registered for VAT.

Your job in the accounts department is principally concerned with the subsidiary purchases and sales ledgers and also with aspects of the main ledger. Main ledger contains purchases ledger and sales ledger control accounts, which form part of the double-entry. Individual accounts of creditors and debtors are kept in subsidiary ledgers.

Today is 1 May 2004 and you are working on the subsidiary (purchases) ledger and main ledger sections of the accounting system.

Books of prime entry

Day books have been written up by a colleague (the rate of VAT is 17.5%) as follows:

Purchases Day Book

Date	Details	Invoice No	Total	VAT	Purchases	Stationery
2004			£	£	£	£
1 May	Garden Supplies Ltd	5439	470	70	400	
1 May	Woodcraft & Co	A471	705	105	600	
1 May	Office Direct	9579	235	35		200
1 May	Pershore Pots	754	329	49	280	
1 May	Pete's Plants	427	188	28	160	
1 May	Garden Supplies Ltd	5459	376	56	320	
	TOTALS		2,303	343	1,760	200

Purchases Returns Day Book						
Date	Details	Credit Note No	Total	VAT	Purchases returns	Stationery returns
2004			£	£	£	£
1 May	Garden Supplies Ltd	CN194	94	14	80	
1 May	Office Direct	C4571	47	7		40
1 May	Pershore Pots	CN761	141	21	120	
	TOTALS		282	42	200	40

Account balances

The following accounts are relevant and the balances shown are at the start of the day on 1 May 2004:

	£
Credit suppliers:	
Garden Supplies Limited	13,254
Office Direct	5,729
Pershore Pots	1,068
Pete's Plants	2,901
Woodcraft & Co	2,784
Purchases ledger control	25,736
Purchases	325,172
Purchases returns	4,850
Stationery	1,379
Discount received	454
VAT (credit balance)	6,274
Cash	260
Bank (debit balance)	14,170

Include a reconciliation of the balance of purchases ledger control account with the subsidiary accounts.

Cash book: payments

Payments made on 1 May 2004 are to be entered into the accounts:

	Total	*VAT*	*Net*
	£	£	£
• Pete's Plants (paid by cheque)	354		
• Woodcraft & Co (paid by cheque) (in full settlement of a debt of £1,800)	1,750		
• Stationery (paid by cheque)	94	14	80

Trial balance

After writing up the double-entry accounts you are asked to prepare a trial balance at the close of business on 1 May 2004. The following account balances are to be incorporated (there have been no transactions on these accounts on 1 May):

	£
Sales ledger control	62,851
Sales	735,450
Sales returns	6,020
Discount allowed	475
General expenses	73,284
Wages and salaries	119,477
Bank charges	354
Bad debts written off	496
Equipment and vehicles	194,646
Stock at 1 Jan 2004	55,270
Capital	100,000
Drawings	18,910

solution

Tutorial note: the layout of the accounts used in this and the following Case Study is very similar to that often found in Skills Tests and Examinations.

Subsidiary (purchases) ledger

This contains the creditors' accounts and is written up in the following steps:

- enter the opening balances
- enter the amounts from purchases day book (using the total figure)
- enter the amounts from purchases returns day book (using the total figure)
- record the amounts of payments from the cash book, including any settlement (cash) discount received

The accounts are balanced and the balances carried down on 1 May 2004. The balances are then brought down on 2 May 2004.

SUBSIDIARY (PURCHASES) LEDGER

Garden Supplies Limited

Date	Details	Amount	Date	Details	Amount
2004		£	2004		£
1 May	Purchases returns	94	1 May	Balance b/d	13,254
1 May	Balance c/d	14,006	1 May	Purchases	470
			1 May	Purchases	376
		14,100			14,100
			2 May	Balance b/d	14,006

Office Direct

Date	Details	Amount	Date	Details	Amount
2004		£	2004		£
1 May	Stationery returns	47	1 May	Balance b/d	5,729
1 May	Balance c/d	5,917	1 May	Stationery	235
		5,964			5,964
			2 May	Balance b/d	5,917

Pershore Pots

Date	Details	Amount	Date	Details	Amount
2004		£	2004		£
1 May	Purchases returns	141	1 May	Balance b/d	1,068
1 May	Balance c/d	1,256	1 May	Purchases	329
		1,397			1,397
			2 May	Balance b/d	1,256

Pete's Plants

Date	Details	Amount	Date	Details	Amount
2004		£	2004		£
1 May	Bank	354	1 May	Balance b/d	2,901
1 May	Balance c/d	2,735	1 May	Purchases	188
		3,089			3,089
			2 May	Balance b/d	2,735

Woodcraft & Co

Date	Details	Amount	Date	Details	Amount
2004		£	2004		£
1 May	Bank	1,750	1 May	Balance b/d	2,784
1 May	Discount received	50	1 May	Purchases	705
1 May	Balance c/d	1,689			
		3,489			3,489
			2 May	Balance b/d	1,689

Reconciliation of purchases ledger control account

	1 May 2004	2 May 2004
	£	£
Garden Supplies Limited	13,254	14,006
Office Direct	5,729	5,917
Pershore Pots	1,068	1,256
Pete's Plants	2,901	2,735
Woodcraft & Co	2,784	1,689
Purchases ledger control account (see below)	25,736	25,603

Main ledger

Main ledger contains all the other accounts of the business, except for cash book (see below). Purchases ledger control account is included in main ledger and records the same transactions as have been entered in the subsidiary (purchases) ledger accounts.

Amounts are transferred to main ledger from purchases day book, purchases returns day book and cash book.

MAIN LEDGER

Purchases Ledger Control Account

Date	Details	Amount	Date	Details	Amount
2004		£	2004		£
1 May	Purchases Returns Day Book	282	1 May	Balance b/d	25,736
1 May	Bank	*2,104	1 May	Purchases Day Book	2,303
1 May	Discount received	50			
1 May	Balance c/d	25,603			
		28,039			28,039
			2 May	Balance b/d	25,603

* £354 + £1,750

Purchases Account

Date	Details	Amount	Date	Details	Amount
2004		£	2004		£
1 May	Balance b/d	325,172	1 May	Balance c/d	326,932
1 May	Purchases Day Book	1,760			
		326,932			326,932
2 May	Balance b/d	326,932			

Purchases Returns Account

Date	Details	Amount	Date	Details	Amount
2004		£	2004		£
1 May	Balance c/d	5,050	1 May	Balance b/d	4,850
			1 May	Purchases Returns Day Book	200
		5,050			5,050
			2 May	Balance b/d	5,050

Stationery Account

Date	Details	Amount	Date	Details	Amount
2004		£	2004		£
1 May	Balance b/d	1,379	1 May	Purchases Returns Day Book	*40
1 May	Purchases Day Book	200			
1 May	Bank	80	2 May	Balance c/d	1,619
		1,659			1,659
2 May	Balance b/d	1,619			

* This returns item could, alternatively, be credited to a stationery returns account

Discount Received Account

Date	Details	Amount	Date	Details	Amount
2004		£	2004		£
1 May	Balance c/d	504	1 May	Balance b/d	454
			1 May	Cash Book	50
		504			504
			2 May	Balance b/d	504

Value Added Tax Account

Date	Details	Amount	Date	Details	Amount
2004		£	2004		£
1 May	Purchases Day Book	343	1 May	Balance b/d	6,274
1 May	Cash Book	14	1 May	Purchases Returns Day Book	42
1 May	Balance c/d	5,959			
		6,316			6,316
			2 May	Balance b/d	5,959

Tutorial note: only the main ledger accounts with transactions on 1 May have been shown here.

Cash book

Cash book contains both cash and bank account. It performs two functions:

- book of prime entry for cash and bank transactions
- part of the double-entry accounts system

CASH BOOK

Date	Details	Discount allowed	Cash	Bank	Date	Details	Discount received	Cash	Bank
2004		£	£	£	2004		£	£	£
1 May	Balances b/d		260	14,170	1 May	Pete's Plants			354
					1 May	Woodcraft & Co	50		1,750
					1 May	Stationery			94*
					1 May	Balances c/d		260	11,972
		–	260	14,170			50	260	14,170
2 May	Balances b/d		260	11,972					

* £80 stationery + £14 VAT

Trial balance

The balance of each account in the double-entry system is listed according to whether it is debit or credit.

Wyvern Nurseries

Trial balance as at 1 May 2004

	Dr	Cr
	£	£
Name of account		
Purchases ledger control		25,603
Purchases	326,932	
Purchases returns		5,050
Stationery	1,619	
Discount received		504
Value Added Tax		5,959
Cash	260	
Bank	11,972	
Sales ledger control	62,851	
Sales		735,450
Sales returns	6,020	
Discount allowed	475	
General expenses	73,284	
Wales and salaries	119,477	
Bank charges	354	
Bad debts written off	496	
Equipment and vehicles	194,646	
Stock at 1 Jan 2004	55,270	
Capital		100,000
Drawings	18,910	
	872,566	872,566

Tutorial notes to the trial balance:

- debit balances include cash, purchases, sales returns, sales ledger control, expenses, fixed assets, stock, drawings
- credit balances include sales, purchases returns, purchases ledger control, income, capital, loans
- bank account can be either debit or credit – debit when there is money in the bank, credit when overdrawn
- VAT account can be either debit or credit – debit when VAT is due to the business, credit when the business owes money to HM Customs and Excise
- a trial balance which balances is not proof of the complete accuracy of the accounting records

Case Study

WYVERN NURSERIES – ACCOUNTING FOR CREDIT SALES

This Case Study is a continuation of the Case Study on the previous eight pages. You work as an accounts assistant for Wyvern Nurseries. The scenario is set out in full at the beginning of the Case Study on page 448.

situation

Today is 2 May 2004 and you are working on the subsidiary (sales) ledger and main ledger sections of the accounting system.

Books of prime entry

Day books have been written up by a colleague (the rate of VAT is 17.5%) as follows:

Sales Day Book

Date	Details	Invoice No	Total	VAT	Net
2004			£	£	£
2 May	Beeching and Sons	SI9075	658	98	560
2 May	The Potting Shed	SI9076	188	28	160
2 May	Beech Ltd	SI9077	282	42	240
2 May	Tranter & Co	SI9078	1,222	182	1,040
2 May	The Potting Shed	SI9079	141	21	120
2 May	Green Fingers Ltd	SI9080	423	63	360
	TOTALS		2,914	434	2,480

Sales Returns Day Book

Date	Details	Credit Note No	Total	VAT	Net
2004			£	£	£
2 May	Tranter & Co	CN454	141	21	120
2 May	Green Fingers Ltd	CN455	94	14	80
	TOTALS		235	35	200

Cash book

The cash book has been written up and balanced by a colleague as follows:

CASH BOOK									
Date	Details	Discount allowed	Cash	Bank	Date	Details	Discount received	Cash	Bank
2004		£	£	£	2004		£	£	£
2 May	Balances b/d		260	11,972	2 May	Vehicle purchase*			5,000
2 May	Beech Ltd	50		950	2 May	Bank charges**			28
2 May	Tranter & Co			357	2 May	Drawings			100
2 May	The Potting Shed			596	2 May	Balances c/d		260	8,747
		50	260	13,875			–	260	13,875
3 May	Balances b/d		260	8,747					

* the vehicle purchased was a secondhand car – no VAT to reclaim on cars

** no VAT on bank charges

Journal transactions

The accounts supervisor asks you to make journal entries for the following:

- the subsidiary (sales) ledger account balance in the name of AB Garden Services is to be written off as a bad debt, you are told that VAT relief is available on this debt
- vehicle insurance of £1,550 has been recorded in the equipment and vehicles account instead of general expenses account

Once the journal entries have been checked by the supervisor, they are to be recorded in the double-entry system.

Account balances

The following accounts are relevant and the balances shown are at the start of the day on 2 May 2004:

	£
Credit customers:	
AB Garden Services	47
Beech Limited	12,367
Beeching and Sons	15,847
Green Fingers Limited	11,236
The Potting Shed	15,596
Tranter & Co	7,758
Sales ledger control	62,851
Sales	735,450
Sales returns	6,020
Discount allowed	475
VAT (credit balance)	5,959
General expenses	73,284
Bank charges	354

Bad debts written off	496
Equipment and vehicles	194,646
Drawings	18,910

Include a reconciliation of the balance of sales ledger control account with the subsidiary accounts.

Trial balance

After writing up the double-entry accounts you are asked to prepare a trial balance at the close of business on 2 May 2004. The following balances are to be incorporated (there have been no transactions on these accounts on 2 May):

	£
Purchases ledger control	25,603
Purchases	326,932
Purchases returns	5,050
Stationery	1,619
Discount received	504
Wages and salaries	119,477
Stock at 1 Jan 2004	55,270
Capital	100,000

solution

Journal transactions

The journal entries are as follows:

JOURNAL			
Date	Details	Debit	Credit
2004		£	£
2 May	Bad debts written off account	40	
	Value Added Tax account	7	
	Sales ledger control account		47
		47	47
	Balance of subsidiary (sales) ledger account of AB Garden Services written off as a bad debt on instructions of the accounts supervisor		
2 May	General expenses account	1,550	
	Equipment and vehicles account		1,550
	Correction of error of principle on ...		

The journal entries are checked by the supervisor and then recorded in the double-entry system.

Subsidiary (sales) ledger

This contains the debtors' accounts and is written up in the following steps:

- enter the opening balances
- enter the total amounts from sales day book
- enter the total amounts from sales returns day book
- record the amounts of receipts from cash book, including any settlement (cash) discount allowed
- record the journal entry which relates to sales ledger accounts

The accounts are balanced and the balances are carried down on 2 May 2004. The balances are then brought down on 3 May 2004.

SUBSIDIARY (SALES) LEDGER

AB Garden Services

Date	Details	Amount	Date	Details	Amount
2004		£	2004		£
2 May	Balance b/d	47	2 May	Bad debts written off	40
			2 May	Value Added Tax	7
		47			47

Beech Limited

Date	Details	Amount	Date	Details	Amount
2004		£	2004		£
2 May	Balance b/d	12,367	2 May	Bank	950
2 May	Sales	282	2 May	Discount allowed	50
			2 May	Balance c/d	11,649
		12,649			12,649
3 May	Balance b/d	11,649			

Beeching and Sons

Date	Details	Amount	Date	Details	Amount
2004		£	2004		£
2 May	Balance b/d	15,847	2 May	Balance c/d	16,505
2 May	Sales	658			
		16,505			16,505
3 May	Balance b/d	16,505			

Green Fingers Limited

Date	Details	Amount	Date	Details	Amount
2004		£	2004		£
2 May	Balance b/d	11,236	2 May	Sales returns	94
2 May	Sales	423	2 May	Balance c/d	11,565
		11,659			11,659
3 May	Balance b/d	11,565			

The Potting Shed

Date	Details	Amount	Date	Details	Amount
2004		£	2004		£
2 May	Balance b/d	15,596	2 May	Bank	596
2 May	Sales	188	2 May	Balance c/d	15,329
2 May	Sales	141			
		15,925			15,925
3 May	Balance b/d	15,329			

Tranter & Co

Date	Details	Amount	Date	Details	Amount
2004		£	2004		£
2 May	Balance b/d	7,758	2 May	Sales returns	141
2 May	Sales	1,222	2 May	Bank	357
			2 May	Balance c/d	8,482
		8,980			8,980
3 May	Balance b/d	8,482			

Reconciliation of sales ledger control account

	2 May 2004	3 May 2004
	£	£
AB Garden Services	47	–
Beech Limited	12,367	11,649
Beeching and Sons	15,847	16,505
Green Fingers Limited	11,236	11,565
The Potting Shed	15,596	15,329
Tranter & Co	7,758	8,482
Sales ledger control account (see next page)	62,851	63,530

Main ledger

Main ledger contains all the other double-entry accounts, except for cash book (see below). Sales ledger control account is included in main ledger and records the same transactions as have been entered in the subsidiary (sales) ledger accounts.

Amounts are transferred to main ledger from sales day book, sales returns day book, the journal and cash book.

MAIN LEDGER

Sales Ledger Control Account

Date	Details	Amount	Date	Details	Amount
2004		£	2004		£
2 May	Balance b/d	62,851	2 May	Sales Rets Day Book	235
2 May	Sales Day Book	2,914	2 May	Bank	*1,903
			2 May	Discount allowed	50
			2 May	Bad debt written off	40
			2 May	Value Added Tax	7
			2 May	Balance c/d	63,530
		65,765			65,765
3 May	Balance b/d	63,530			

* £950 + £357 + £596

Sales Account

Date	Details	Amount	Date	Details	Amount
2004		£	2004		£
2 May	Balance c/d	737,930	2 May	Balance b/d	735,450
			2 May	Sales Day Book	2,480
		737,930			737,930
			3 May	Balance b/d	737,930

Sales Returns Account

Date	Details	Amount	Date	Details	Amount
2004		£	2004		£
2 May	Balance b/d	6,020	2 May	Balance c/d	6,220
2 May	Sales Returns Day Book	200			
		6,220			6,220
3 May	Balance b/d	6,220			

Discount Allowed Account

Date	Details	Amount	Date	Details	Amount
2004		£	2004		£
2 May	Balance b/d	475	2 May	Balance c/d	525
2 May	Cash Book	50			
		525			525
3 May	Balance b/d	525			

Value Added Tax Account

Date	Details	Amount	Date	Details	Amount
2004		£	2004		£
2 May	Sales Rets Day Book	35	2 May	Balance b/d	5,959
2 May	AB Garden Services	7	2 May	Sales Day Book	434
2 May	Balance c/d	6,351			
		6,393			6,393
			3 May	Balance b/d	6,351

General Expenses Account

Date	Details	Amount	Date	Details	Amount
2004		£	2004		£
2 May	Balance b/d	73,284	2 May	Balance c/d	74,834
2 May	Equipment and vehicles	1,550			
		74,834			74,834
3 May	Balance b/d	74,834			

Bank Charges Account

Date	Details	Amount	Date	Details	Amount
2004		£	2004		£
2 May	Balance b/d	354	2 May	Balance c/d	382
2 May	Bank	28			
		382			382
3 May	Balance b/d	382			

Bad Debts Written Off Account

Date	Details	Amount	Date	Details	Amount
2004		£	2004		£
2 May	Balance b/d	496	2 May	Balance c/d	536
2 May	AB Garden Services	40			
		536			536
3 May	Balance b/d	536			

Equipment and Vehicles Account

Date	Details	Amount	Date	Details	Amount
2004		£	2004		£
2 May	Balance b/d	194,646	2 May	General expenses	1,550
2 May	Bank	5,000	2 May	Balance c/d	198,096
		199,646			199,646
3 May	Balance b/d	198,096			

Drawings Account

Date	Details	Amount	Date	Details	Amount
2004		£	2004		£
2 May	Balance b/d	18,910	2 May	Balance c/d	19,010
2 May	Bank	100			
		19,010			19,010
3 May	Balance b/d	19,010			

Trial balance

The balance of each account in the double-entry system is listed according to whether it is debit or credit.

Wyvern Nurseries
Trial balance as at 2 May 2004

	Dr	Cr
Name of account		
Purchases ledger control		25,603
Purchases	326,932	
Purchases returns		5,050
Stationery	1,619	
Discount received		504
Value Added Tax		6,351
Cash	260	
Bank	8,747	
Sales ledger control	63,530	
Sales		737,930
Sales returns	6,220	
Discount allowed	525	
General expenses	74,834	
Wages and salaries	119,477	
Bank charges	382	
Bad debts written off	536	
Equipment and vehicles	198,096	
Stock at 1 Jan 2004	55,270	
Capital		100,000
Drawings	19,010	
	875,438	875,438

Note: A trial balance which balances is not proof of the complete accuracy of the accounting records; errors not shown by a trial balance include:

- error of omission
- reversal of entries
- mispost/error of commission
- error of principle (here vehicle insurance recorded in the equipment and vehicles account)
- error of original entry (or transcription)
- compensating error

Chapter Summary

- Businesses record financial transactions in order to
  - quantify transactions
  - present the figures in a meaningful way

- The accounting system follows a number of distinct stages
  - prime documents
  - books of prime entry
  - double-entry book-keeping
  - trial balance
  - financial statements

Key Terms

prime documents	sources of accounting information
books of prime entry	day books, journal and cash books where accounting information is gathered and summarised
double-entry book-keeping	recording the dual aspect of accounting transactions in the ledgers of the accounting system
trial balance	arithmetic check of the double-entry book-keeping
financial statements (or final accounts)	comprising profit and loss account and balance sheet (both of which are covered fully at NVQ levels 3 and 4)

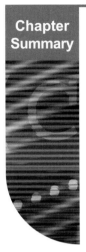

Student Activities

The following background information is common to both Student Activities:

You work as an accounts assistant for 'Fashion Traders'. The company buys 'end-of-line' stocks of clothes for men and women in bulk from manufacturers and sells them on to smaller shops and discount stores. Fashion Traders is registered for VAT.

Your job in the accounts department is principally concerned with the subsidiary purchases and sales ledgers and also with aspects of the main ledger. Main ledger contains purchases ledger and sales ledger control accounts, which form part of the double-entry. Individual accounts of creditors and debtors are kept in subsidiary ledgers.

22.1 Today is 1 October 2004 and you are working on the subsidiary (purchases) ledger and main ledger sections of the accounting system.

Transactions

The following transactions have been entered into the relevant books of prime entry as shown below. No entries have yet been made into the ledger system. The VAT rate is 17.5%.

Purchases Day Book

Date	Details	Invoice No	Total	VAT	Purchases	Stationery
2004			£	£	£	£
1 Oct	Wyvern Clothes	I 4379	1,457	217	1,240	
1 Oct	Jeans-R-Us Ltd	7629	2,820	420	2,400	
1 Oct	One Stop Office	5438	423	63		360
1 Oct	J & S Manufacturing	3941	1,034	154	880	
1 Oct	Wyvern Clothes	I 4385	1,222	182	1,040	
1 Oct	Dalton & Co	A 3691	1,598	238	1,360	
	TOTALS		8,554	1,274	6,920	360

Purchases Returns Day Book						
Date	Details	Credit Note No	Total	VAT	Purchases returns	Stationery returns
2004			£	£	£	£
1 Oct	Jeans-R-Us Ltd	C071	141	21	120	
1 Oct	Dalton & Co	CN764	94	14	80	
1 Oct	One-Stop Office	CN342	47	7		40
	TOTALS		282	42	200	40

CASH BOOK									
Date	Details	Discount allowed	Cash	Bank	Date	Details	Discount received	Cash	Bank
2004		£	£	£	2004		£	£	£
1 Oct	Balances b/d		275	2,054	1 Oct	J & S Manufact.	25		775
1 Oct	Balance c/d			400	1 Oct	Wyvern Clothes	45		1,055
					1 Oct	One-Stop Office			624
					1 Oct	Balance c/d		275	
		–	275	2,454			70	275	2,454
2 Oct	Balance b/d		275		2 Oct	Balance b/d			400

Balances

The following account balances are relevant to you at the start of the day on 1 October 2004:

	£
Credit suppliers:	
Dalton & Co	23,076
Jeans-R-Us Limited	12,120
J & S Manufacturing	13,491
One-Stop Office	9,466
Wyvern Clothes	2,610
Purchases ledger control	60,763
Purchases	428,494
Purchases returns	8,327
Stationery	3,650
Discount received	841
VAT (credit balance)	8,347

You are to:

(a) Enter the opening balances listed above into the following accounts:

Subsidiary (purchases) ledger:	Dalton & Co
	Jeans-R-Us Limited
	J & S Manufacturing
	One-Stop Office
	Wyvern Clothes
Main ledger:	Purchases ledger control
	Purchases
	Purchases returns
	Stationery
	Discount received
	VAT

(b) From the day books and cash book shown on pages 466 and 467, make the relevant entries in the accounts in the subsidiary (purchases) ledger and the main ledger.

(c) Balance the accounts, showing clearly the balance carried down at 1 October 2004 (the closing balance).

(d) Now that you have closed the above accounts, show clearly the balance brought down at 2 October 2004 (the opening balance). Demonstrate a reconciliation of the balance of the purchases ledger control account with the subsidiary accounts.

(e) Prepare a trial balance at the close of business on 1 October 2004 using the balances brought down on the above accounts, cash book, and incorporating the following account balances (on which there have been no transactions on 1 October):

	£
Sales ledger control	100,690
Sales	758,174
Sales returns	12,364
Discount allowed	1,497
General expenses	25,842
Wages and salaries	127,608
Bad debts written off	1,762
Office equipment	7,750
Warehouse equipment	85,250
Stock at 1 Jan 2004	165,940
Bank loan	40,000
Capital	115,324
Drawings	28,600

22.2 Today is 2 October 2004 and you are working on the subsidiary (sales) ledger and main ledger sections of the accounting system.

Transactions

The following transactions have been entered into the relevant books of prime entry as shown below. No entries have yet been made into the ledger system. The VAT rate is 17.5%.

Sales Day Book					
Date	Details	Invoice No	Total	VAT	Net
2004			£	£	£
2 Oct	Bentley Stores Ltd	SI7054	752	112	640
2 Oct	Just Jeans	SI7055	188	28	160
2 Oct	Teme Trading Co	SI7056	329	49	280
2 Oct	Bentley Stores Ltd	SI7057	376	56	320
2 Oct	Southwick Stores	SI7058	470	70	400
2 Oct	Bentley & Co	SI7059	423	63	360
	TOTALS		2,538	378	2,160

Dr SLCA INDIV Cr VAT Cr SALES

Sales Returns Day Book					
Date	Details	Credit Note No	Total	VAT	Net
2004			£	£	£
2 Oct	Teme Trading Co	CN761	94	14	80
2 Oct	Just Jeans	CN762	47	7	40
	TOTALS		141	21	120

Cr SLCA INDIV Dr VAT Dr SALES RET

Dr

CASH BOOK									*CR*
Date	Details	Discount allowed	Cash	Bank	Date	Details	Discount received	Cash	Bank
2004		£	£	£	2004		£	£	£
Oct	Balance b/d		275		2 Oct	Balance b/d			400
2 Oct	Bentley & Co			420	2 Oct	Wages & salaries			1,050
2 Oct	Just Jeans	10		240	2 Oct	Drawings			310
2 Oct	Bentley Stores Ltd	45		1,825	2 Oct	Loan repayment			500
					2 Oct	Balances c/d		275	225
		55	275	2,485			–	275	2,485
3 Oct	Balances b/d		275	225					

Dr DA Cr SLCA *Cr SLCA* *Dr Acc.*

Balances

The following account balances are relevant to you at the start of the day on 2 October 2004:

	£
Credit customers:	
Bentley & Co	31,095
Bentley Stores Limited	21,870
Just Jeans	10,629
Southwick Stores	16,205
Teme Trading Co	20,797
Victoria's Fashions	94
Sales ledger control	100,690
Sales	758,174
Sales returns	12,364
Discount allowed	1,497
VAT (credit balance)	7,115
Wages and salaries	127,608
Bad debts written off	1,762
Bank loan	40,000
Drawings	28,600

Journal entries

The accounts supervisor asks you to make entries in the journal and the double-entry accounts for the following:

- the subsidiary (sales) ledger account balance in the name of Victoria's Fashions is to be written off as a bad debt; you are told that VAT relief is available on this debt
- a cheque for £220 received on 12 September from a debtor, Bentley & Co, has been entered in the account of Bentley Stores Limited, in error; there was no discount allowed on this receipt

You are to:

(a) Enter the opening balances listed above into the following accounts:

Subsidiary (sales) ledger:

Bentley & Co

Bentley Stores Limited

Just Jeans

Southwick Stores

Teme Trading Co

Victoria's Fashions

Main ledger:

Sales ledger control

Sales

Sales returns

Discount allowed

VAT

Wages and salaries

Bad debts written off

Bank loan

Drawings

(b) • From the day books and cash book shown on page 469, make the relevant entries in the accounts in the subsidiary (sales) ledger and the main ledger.

• Record the entries in the journal for the transactions mentioned by the accounts supervisor and then enter the transactions into the relevant accounts.

(c) Balance the accounts, showing clearly the balance carried down at 2 October 2004 (the closing balance).

(d) Now that you have closed the above accounts, show clearly the balance brought down on 3 October 2004 (opening balance). Demonstrate a reconciliation of the balance of sales ledger control account with the subsidiary accounts.

(e) Prepare a trial balance at the close of business on 2 October 2004 using the balances brought down on the above accounts, cash book, and incorporating the following account balances (on which there have been no transactions on 2 October):

	£
Purchases ledger control	66,511
Purchases	435,414
Purchases returns	8,527
Stationery	3,970
Discount received	911
Office equipment	7,750
General expenses	25,842
Warehouse equipment	85,250
Stock at 1 Jan 2004	165,940
Capital	115,324

23 Information for management control

this chapter covers . . .

The accounting system is able to provide information to the managers of a business or organisation to help them in decision-making, planning and control. In this chapter we look at:

- *the information they need from the accounts system*
- *the differences between financial accounting and management accounting*
- *the structure of organisations*
- *costs (materials, labour and expenses) and income*
- *cost centres, profit centres and investment centres*
- *the use of coding for costs and income*

NVQ PERFORMANCE CRITERIA COVERED

unit 4: SUPPLYING INFORMATION FOR MANAGEMENT CONTROL

element 4.1

code and extract information

A *recognise appropriate cost centres and elements of costs*

B *extract income and expenditure details from the relevant sources*

C *code income and expenditure correctly*

D *refer any problems in obtaining the necessary information to the appropriate person*

E *identify and report errors to the appropriate person*

WHO IS A MANAGER?

The word 'manager' these days includes anybody within the business or organisation who is involved in decision-making, planning and control. The concept extends to the 'line manager' (a term which has largely replaced 'supervisor'). Managers can, of course, be male or female. Incidentally the 'man' in manager does not refer to males; instead it comes from the Latin word 'manus' which means 'hand'!

Look at the statements below and decide which of these people are managers:

- The managing director of a bank takes the decision to develop e-banking
- The government's health secretary plans to cut hospital waiting lists
- The finance director is controlling the company's spending to ensure that the bank overdraft limit is not exceeded
- The office manager decides to buy a new Xentra photocopier for use in the office
- The accounts supervisor plans to run the computer payroll program next Tuesday
- The accounts assistant controls the petty cash float

The answer is that all of the above are managers because the statements involve decision-making (managing director of the bank, office manager), planning (health secretary, accounts supervisor), and control (finance director, accounts assistant). We can see, therefore, that management is much more broadly-based than the stereotype image portrayed earlier. In fact, we can go further and say that everybody is responsible for something: making decisions, planning what to do and controlling the progress of work.

Clearly there are different levels of management and it is important to recognise that any information for the use of a manager must be tailored to meet the user's needs. For example, the accounts supervisor will wish to know about a bad debt of £50, but this will be of little or no concern to the managing director (who *would* want to know about a bad debt of £50 million!).

Consider these examples and then relate them to the management of the business where you work, or to an organisation that you know:

Decision-making

- higher level: 'I have taken the decision to close our factory in Wales'
- intermediate level: 'I have decided to buy a new photocopier for the office'
- lower level: 'I will pay this petty cash claim'

Planning

- higher level: 'We need to start planning the firm's expansion programme'
- intermediate level: 'I am planning to increase production of Product Exe next month'
- lower level: 'I plan to extract a trial balance first thing tomorrow'

Control

- higher level: 'Last month's sales were up by ten per cent'
- intermediate level: 'Costs for product Wye were reduced by five per cent last month'
- lower level: 'I have balanced the petty cash book'

The conclusion to be drawn is that we are all managers, but at different levels. For example, within an accounts office, the accounts assistant will be responsible for a different level of management to the supervisor who will, in turn, be responsible for a different level of management to the administration manager.

WHAT INFORMATION DOES A MANAGER NEED?

In order to be able to carry out the functions of decision-making, planning and control, managers need to have relevant management information available to them. Such management information within a business or organisation can take many forms – in this chapter and the next we focus on information available from the accounting records. Such 'known' information is usually the starting point for most management activities.

The Case Study below illustrates how the three themes of management (decision-making, planning and control) relate to the workings of an accounts department. After the Case Study we look in more detail at the accounting information available to management and the purposes to which it is put.

Case Study

MANAGING THE ACCOUNTS DEPARTMENT

situation

You are an accounts assistant at Severnvale Nurseries, a large specialist grower of plants, which supplies garden centres throughout the country. Your experience in the accounts department has been quite varied – you have worked on the subsidiary ledgers for sales and purchases, main ledger, cash book and payroll.

Today the accounts supervisor is off work due to illness and the administration manager asks you to take charge of the accounts department which, as well as yourself, consists of two assistants (one of whom is part-time, working mornings only). In the supervisor's in-tray, you find:

- a number of purchases invoices ready to pay (some of which offer cash discount for prompt settlement)
- changes to the weekly payroll – new employees, tax code changes, pay rate alterations; the payroll needs to be processed today to ensure that the pay will be in employees' bank accounts by the end of the week
- a number of sales invoices to process

The company's bank statement has arrived in the post – it is practice to prepare a bank reconciliation statement on the same day.

The part-time accounts assistant is asking if he should balance the petty cash book and pass it to you for checking – today is the usual day of the week for this to be done.

How will you manage the work of the accounts department?

solution

planning

The first step is to take a few minutes to plan the day's work in order of priority. This would appear to be:

- changes to payroll data to be made
- process the payroll
- take advantage of settlement discounts on purchases invoices
- check the terms of payment to see whether other purchases invoices should be paid today
- processing sales invoices

Balancing the petty cash book and preparing the bank reconciliation statement appear to be lower priority and could be left until tomorrow.

decision-making

You brief the two assistants on your plan for the day.

You ask the full-time assistant to enter the changes to the payroll and then to process the payroll, including preparation of cheques and BACS payments, and also to enter the transactions in the double-entry accounts. The accounts assistant has dealt with payroll before.

The part-time assistant, who has limited accounts experience, will process sales invoices by entering them into the sales day book, subsidiary (sales) ledger and main ledger.

In the meantime you will go through the purchases invoices in order to identify those that offer a cash discount for prompt settlement – they can be paid by cheque or BACS. The details will then be entered in the cash book and subsidiary (purchases) ledger.

control

From time-to-time you check progress on processing the payroll, stressing the need to the accounts assistant to complete the task so that employees will have the pay in their bank accounts by the end of the week. Later on you check the schedule for cheques and BACS payments, together with the entries made in the double-entry accounts. Cheques and the BACS payment schedule have to be signed by an authorised signatory to the company's bank account, so you will need to contact the administration manager to arrange this.

You supervise the work of the part-time assistant and resolve any queries that he may have in processing sales invoices. You check the double-entry transactions (including any entries in sales ledger control account) and, if time permits, ask the assistant to prepare statements of account to be sent out to debtors: this ensures that customers will pay on time.

From the purchases invoices, you select for payment those that offer a settlement discount. You prepare cheques or BACS payments and make the entries in the cash book and subsidiary (purchases) ledger, together with any entries in purchases ledger control account. The administration manager will need to arrange for the cheques and the BACS payment schedule to be signed.

You also check other purchases invoices for the terms of payment – some may be due for payment today, having come to the end of their credit term; for others it might be prudent to pay them as the nursery may want to buy further goods from the suppliers in the near future.

You keep control of the accounts department during the day and, if there is time, you will ask for the petty cash book to be balanced (which you can then check), and for a bank reconciliation statement to be prepared to see if any items are shown that need investigation.

summary

At the end of the day you review progress to see how well your planning, decision-making and control has handled the workload of the department.

With the possibility that the accounts supervisor may not be back to work tomorrow you begin to plan for the next day's work.

ACCOUNTING INFORMATION FOR MANAGERS

The accounting records provide the management of a business or organisation with information to:

- assist with decision-making, for example by giving income from sales, and expenditure costs, of different products or services
- assist with planning, for example by giving details of income and expenditure that can then be estimated for the future
- assist with control, for example by comparing estimates of what was expected to happen with details of what has actually happened

All of these aspects use known information from the accounting records, but some also include estimates of what is likely to happen in the future; such estimates are usually based on what has happened in the past. The accounting records that we have used so far throughout this book are based on actual transactions that have taken place – this type of accounting is referred to as *financial accounting*; taking the actual transactions, looking at them in different ways, and estimating them for the future in order to provide information is referred to as *management accounting*. To use a simple example to illustrate the differences: how much you or a friend *actually* earned last year is financial accounting information; how much you or your friend *expect* to earn next year is management accounting information. In the sections which follow we will look in more detail at the differences between these two types of accounting.

WHAT IS FINANCIAL ACCOUNTING?

Financial accounting is concerned with recording financial transactions that have happened already, and with providing information from the accounting records, for example, in order to prepare VAT returns, and trial balance (the starting point for the preparation of the profit and loss account and balance sheet – covered at NVQ levels 3 and 4).

The main features of financial accounting are that it:

- records transactions that have happened already
- looks backwards to show what has happened in the past
- is accurate to the nearest penny, with no estimated amounts
- is often a legal requirement to keep accounts (in order to prepare VAT returns, and tax returns for the Inland Revenue showing income and expenditure)
- maintains confidentiality of information (eg payroll details, VAT returns)

Case Study

INFORMATION FROM THE FINANCIAL ACCOUNTS

situation

The accounts supervisor at Severnvale Nurseries (see Case Study page 474) is off work for a second day. Again the administration manager asks you to take charge of the accounts department.

The routine work of the accounts department is going well; you receive two queries from other departments of the business.

MEMORANDUM

To	Accounts Supervisor	**Ref**	TS 405
From	Tim Smith, Administration Manager	**Date**	17 May 2004
Subject	Telephone expenses		

Could you please let me have details of the amount spent by the company on telephone expenses last month?

I would appreciate the information as soon as possible. Many thanks.

accounts.dept@severnvalenurseries.co.uk, 17/5/04 10:17 am **1**

To: accounts.dept

From: Jason Miles

I need some information as soon as possible for a meeting of sales staff this afternoon. Please let me know amount of sales commission paid last month.

On another matter, I'd like to have last month's sales figure for our range of conservatory plants. Thanks

Jason Miles, Sales Manager

solution

These two requests are examples of how the accounting records can provide management information to other departments of the business. The information is available from the main ledger accounts of telephone expenses, sales commission and sales: conservatory plants (to provide details of sales for each section or product of the business, separate sales accounts need to be established, eg 'sales: conservatory plants'; 'sales: shrubs', etc). Last month's figures can be calculated by comparing the difference between the opening balance at the beginning of the month with the closing balance at the month-end; for example, with telephone expenses:

balance of account at 30 April 2004	£7,459	(closing balance)
balance of account at 1 April 2004	£6,245	(opening balance)
difference, being amount spent during April 2004	£1,214	

In providing the information to the administration manager and the sales manager, it is important to note that they will want the total only for the month – they will not be interested in individual amounts (if more detailed information is needed, they will make further enquiries of the accounts department).

The replies to the queries are as follows (using example figures):

MEMORANDUM

To	Tim Smith, Administration Manager	**Ref**	AS 309
From	Acting Accounts Supervisor	**Date**	17 May 2004
Subject	Telephone expenses		

Further to your memo of today, the amount spent on telephone expenses during April 2004 was £1,214.

If I can be of further assistance, please do not hesitate to contact me.

JasonMiles@severnvalenurseries.co.uk, 17/5/04 11:54 am 1

To: Jason Miles

From: accounts dept

Further to your e-mail of today, the amounts for April 2004 are as follows:

sales commission paid £2,748

sales of conservatory plants £35,424

If we can be of further assistance, please do not hesitate to contact us.

WHAT IS MANAGEMENT ACCOUNTING?

Management accounting is concerned with looking at actual transactions in different ways from financial accounting. In particular, the costs of each product or service are considered both in the past and the likely costs in the future. In this way, management accounting is able to provide information to help the business or organisation plan for the future.

The main features of management accounting are that it:

- uses accounting information to summarise transactions that have happened already and to make estimates for the future
- looks in detail at the costs – materials, labour and expenses (see below) – and the sales income of products and services
- looks forward to show what is likely to happen in the future

- may use estimates where these are the most useful or suitable form of information
- provides management with reports that are of use in running the business or organisation
- provides management information as frequently as circumstances demand – speed is often vital as information may go out-of-date very quickly
- is not sent to people outside the organisation – it is for internal use
- maintains confidentiality of information (eg payroll details)

HOW THE ORGANISATION IS STRUCTURED

Management information that is available from the accounting records varies according to the structure of the organisation. The diagram below shows how the different types of organisations can be classified between:

- public sector and private sector
- type of industry (note that the term 'industry' includes service providers)

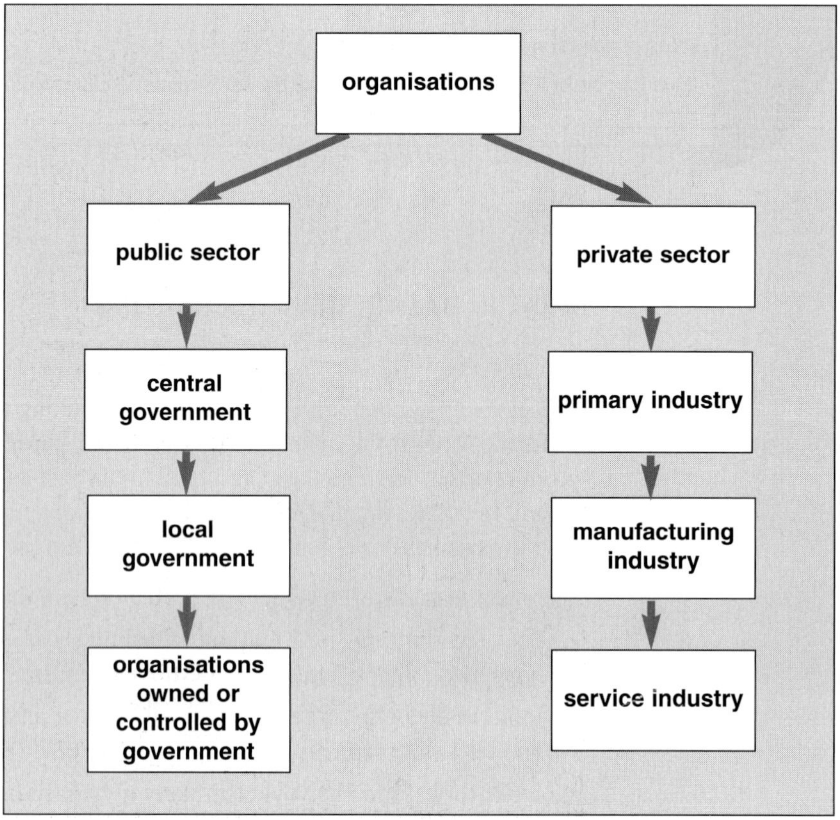

public sector and private sector organisations

Public sector organisations are owned directly or indirectly by central or local government. Examples include the National Health Service and the Post Office.

Private sector organisations are owned by private individuals – as shareholders of a company, owners of partnerships and sole-trader businesses. Examples include well-known names such as Tesco, Marks and Spencer, BT.

types of industry

- primary industries produce the raw materials used by other businesses; examples include oil, gas and agriculture
- manufacturing (secondary) industries manufacture products; examples include the aerospace industry, electronics, pharmaceuticals
- service (tertiary) industries provide services such as transport and tourism

functions within the organisation

The following diagram illustrates the broad functions within most organisations.

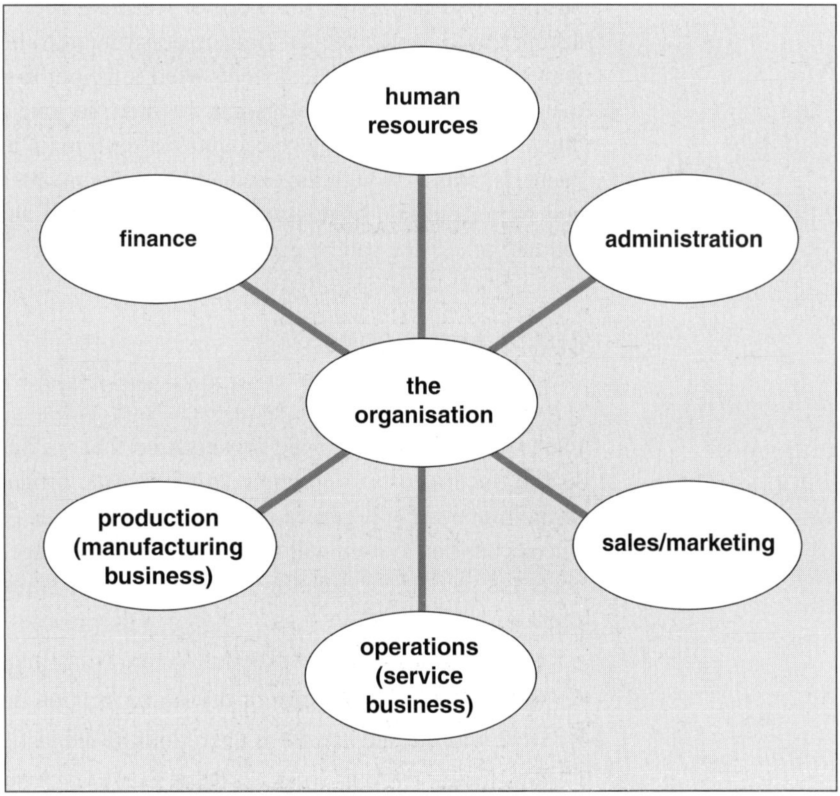

- *finance* – provides financial accounting and management accounting services
- *human resources* – provides the staff to run the business; involved in hiring new staff, laying-off surplus staff, pay and overtime rates, conditions of service
- *administration* – ensures the overall smooth running of the organisation by providing office support
- *sales/marketing* – the promotion and sales of the company's products or services
- *production* – the organisation and operation of the production process in a manufacturing business, including buying materials, incurring labour costs and other expenses and ensuring that production quality and targets are met
- *operations* – the organisation and operation of the provision of services to customers

As businesses grow larger so the functions within the organisation grow more complex. For example, a large manufacturing business may be subdivided into divisions for each product it makes, or even parts of the manufacturing process; a service business may subdivide into different geographical areas. Whatever method is chosen for the organisation of the business will impact on the work of financial accounting and management accounting. In order for the finance department to be able to provide useful management information, systems need to be put in place early on to ensure that information requirements can be met. To give an example, this might mean having separate sales accounts for each main product or service of the business; similarly with the expenditure accounts for costs such as purchases and running costs. In this way the sales income and expenditure for each product or service can be provided readily.

COSTS AND INCOME

Each of the functions of the organisation that we have seen in the previous section incurs costs – eg administration costs, production costs – and some of the functions will generate income, eg from sales of products or services. The accounting system will be able to supply management information about costs and income for each function of the organisation, and answer questions such as:

- what were the sales for products A and B last month?
- what was the payroll cost of the administration department last year?
- what was our income from operations in the last quarter?
- how much was our expenditure on marketing last year?

In order to provide such information we need to consider the main costs and income and then see how it is analysed to the different functions of the business or organisation.

costs

All businesses and organisations, whether they manufacture products or provide services incur costs – these can be broken down into three elements of cost: materials, labour and expenses.

Materials costs include the cost of:

- raw materials and components bought for use by a manufacturing business
- products bought for resale by a shop or a wholesaler
- service items or consumables, such as stationery, bought for use within a business or organisation

Thus materials range from sheet metal and plastics used in a car factory, computer chips and other components bought in by a computer manufacturer, tins of baked beans and other goods bought in by a supermarket, through to photocopying paper used in a college. It is true to say that all business and organisations incur materials costs.

Labour costs refers to the payroll costs of all employees of the business or organisation. Such costs include:

- wages paid to those who work on the production line of a manufacturing business
- wages and salaries paid to those who work for a manufacturing business but are not directly involved in the production line, eg supervisors, maintenance staff, office staff, sales people
- wages and salaries of those who work in the service industry, eg shops, banks, restaurants, accountants
- public sector wages, eg of central and local government employees

Expenses refers to all other running costs of the business or organisation that cannot be included under the headings of materials and labour. Examples include rent, rates, heating, lighting, telephone, advertising, insurance, and so on.

income

The main source of income for the private sector is from the sale of products or services. There may also be other, smaller, amounts of income, eg interest received on bank balances, rental income if a part of the premises is let to a tenant, government grants and allowances for setting up a new business or buying new technology.

For the public sector, the main sources of income for central and local government are from taxes and rates. Government owned or controlled organisations either receive grants and allowances or, in the case of trading businesses in the public sector, such as the Post Office, receive income from the products and services that they supply.

COST CENTRES

In order to provide management with information from the accounting system the costs – materials, labour and expenses – need to be analysed between the different functions, or sections, within the business or organisation. This is achieved by the use of cost centres.

Cost centres are sections of a business to which costs can be charged.

Thus a cost centre can be any function or section of the organisation. In a manufacturing business it can be an entire factory, a department of a factory, or a particular stage in the production process. In a service industry it can be a shop, or group of shops in an area, a teaching department or a resources centre within a college, a ward or operating theatre in a hospital. Any section of a business can be a cost centre – each of the functions within the organisation that we considered earlier (page 481) would be appropriate cost centres. A manager or supervisor will be responsible for each cost centre and it is this person who will be seeking information from the accounts system.

analysis of costs to different cost centres

Once the cost centres of an organisation have been established it is necessary to ensure that the accounts system is able to give information to the manager of each cost centre. In order to do this, separate accounts are established for each cost centre to cover the main cost headings. For example, labour costs can be split between 'wages and salaries: production', 'wages and salaries: administration', 'wages and salaries: human resources', and so on. By analysing costs in this way the accounts system is able to provide the cost centre manager with information about how much has been spent by, or charged to, the centre over the last month, quarter, half-year, or year. Such information will help the manager to:

- plan for the future, eg by using actual costs, will be able to forecast next year's costs
- make decisions, eg by comparing the costs of different products or services, will be helped in deciding whether to increase or decrease output

- control costs, eg by comparing actual costs with budgeted costs (see next chapter), will be able to take steps, where necessary, to reduce costs

Thus the accounts system is able to tell the manager what has happened – at least in terms of financial information.

where does the information come from?

The sources of information to enable the analysis of costs include:

- purchase orders and purchase invoices, for materials and expenses costs
- payroll schedules, for labour costs
- bills and cash receipts, for expenses costs

The amounts of each cost are then analysed to the cost centre which has incurred the cost: the diagram below shows how this process works. A firm's policy manual should give details of which costs are to be charged to which cost centre.

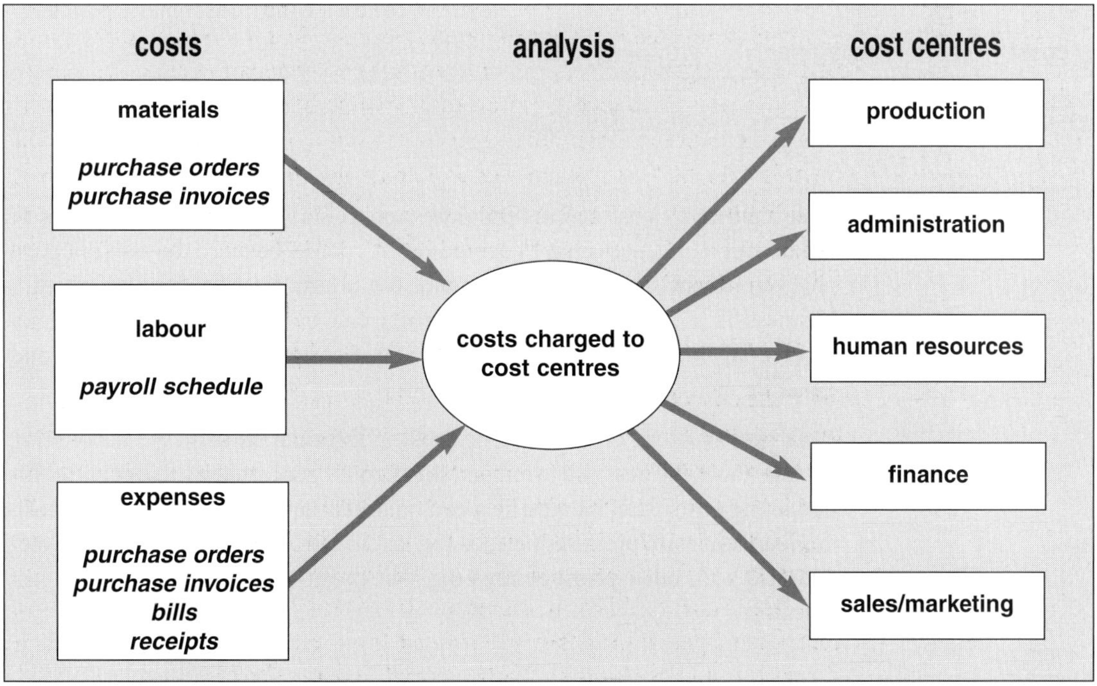

PROFIT CENTRES

For some sections of businesses the cost centre approach of analysing costs is taken to a further level by also analysing sales income to centres. As sales income less costs equals profit, such centres are called profit centres. Note that the source of information on sales comes from sales orders and sales invoices.

Profit centres are sections of a business to which costs can be charged, income can be identified, and profit can be calculated.

From the definition we can see that profit centres have both costs and income. It follows, therefore, that profit centres will be based on sections of the business that make products or services (incur costs) and sell them to customers (receive income from sales). For example, Severnvale Nurseries (see Case Study on page 474) might have conservatory plants as a profit centre as shown in the diagram which follows.

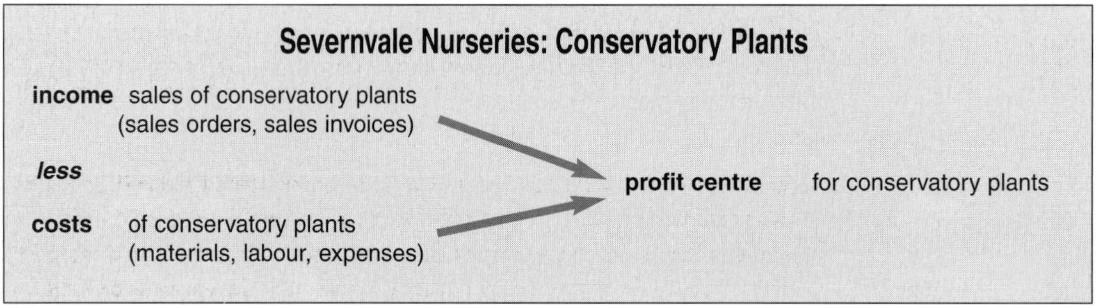

Note that many cost centres provide support services within a business or organisation and, so, cannot become profit centres because they do not have any significant income. For example, the administration department of a business is a cost centre to which costs can be charged, but it does not receive any income. As we have seen profit centres both incur costs and generate income.

Managers of profit centres will be seeking information from the accounting system about the costs incurred and the income generated by their centre. By deducting costs from income they can quantify the profit made and can make comparisons with previous periods (eg last month, last quarter, last year, etc) and also with other profit centres (eg 'our profit was higher than yours last month').

INVESTMENT CENTRES

A further development of profit centres is to consider profit in relation to the amount of money invested in the centre. For *investment centres* the profit of the centre is compared with how much money the business has put in to earn that profit.

Investment centres are sections of a business where profit can be compared with the amount of money invested in the centre.

Profit is usually compared with money invested by means of a percentage as shown in the diagram which follows for Severnvale Nurseries.

Severnvale Nurseries: Conservatory Plants

profit on conservatory plants

divided by

investment in conservatory plants

→ **multiplied by 100*** = **return on investment centre** for conservatory plants

* to express figure as a percentage

Managers of investment centres will wish to make comparisons of the return on investment for the current period with that of previous periods, and also with the other investment centres of the business, eg 'have we done better than last year?', 'how do we compare with the other investment centres?'

Case Study

PROVIDING INFORMATION FOR MANAGEMENT

situation

Once again you are standing in for the accounts supervisor at Severnvale Nurseries (see Case Study on page 474).

The managing director, Charlie Rimmack, has telephoned to ask you for accounting information that is needed for this afternoon. Apparently the managers of two sections of the business – the manager for conservatory plants and the manager for shrubs – have been arguing about which one is doing better. Charlie wants information in order to resolve the dispute; she requests details for each section of costs and income for last year, and the amount of money invested in each section at the end of the year. (She says that all figures can be to the nearest £000.)

solution

You go to accounts which have been set up to show costs, income and money invested for each section, and extract the following information for last year:

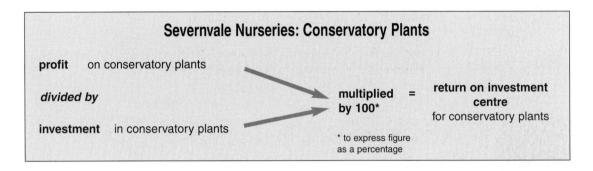

		Conservatory plants	*Shrubs*
		£000s	£000s
Costs:	materials	137	151
	labour	93	134
	expenses	45	70
Sales		425	555
Money invested		300	400

In order to help the managing director you decide to present the management information for each section in the following way:

	Conservatory plants	*Shrubs*
	£000s	£000s
Cost Centre		
Materials	137	151
Labour	93	134
Expenses	45	70
Total	275	355

Here the cost centre for conservatory plants has the lower costs.

Profit Centre		
Income from sales	425	555
less		
Costs (see above)	275	355
Profit	150	200

These figures show that shrubs is the better profit centre.

Investment Centre		
Profit (see above)	150	200
Investment	300	400
Expressed as a percentage (multiplied by 100)	50%	50%

Based on last year's figures both sections of the business, as investment centres, are performing as well as each other.

Conclusion

- The information provided by the accounts supervisor is based on figures taken from the *financial accounting* records. It is taken from the accounts which record the transactions that have happened already.
- The managing director and the managers of the sections will also be interested in using *management accounting* to provide them with information to help with decision-making, planning and control.

ANALYSIS OF COSTS AND INCOME – CODING

what is coding?

Coding is the means by which costs, income and expenditure are analysed to centres (cost centres, profit centres or investment centres). A number is written on each prime document received (eg sales invoices, purchase invoices, receipts, etc) to analyse it to a particular centre, and to indicate the type of cost, income or expenditure, represented by the document. The following code, as an example, is used by Severnvale Nurseries (see Case Study on page 474):

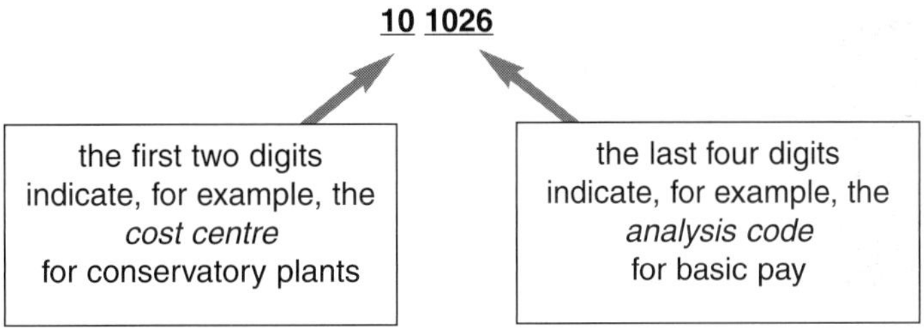

10 1026
the first two digits indicate, for example, the *cost centre* for conservatory plants
the last four digits indicate, for example, the *analysis code* for basic pay

The code 101026 (above) indicates to the book-keeper who is recording items in the accounts that the amount of the prime document is to be debited to 'basic pay – conservatory plants' account. Note that, from the six-digit code used here:

- the first two digits indicate the cost centre
- the last four digits indicate the analysis code

Whilst a six-digit code has been used here, a business can use whatever coding system suits it best – any combination of letters or numbers. For example, Severnvale Nurseries could use letters for the cost centres and numbers for the analysis, so CP 1026 could be used for the conservatory plants (CP) cost centre, with the analysis to basic pay (1026). Whatever system of coding is in use, it must be recorded in the organisation's *policy manual* (the book that states how all operations within the organisation are to be carried out), so that it can be followed, on a consistent basis, by anybody at any time.

A practical point for the establishment of code numbers is that you would not initially use consecutive numbers but would leave plenty of 'gaps' for future development of the system. For example, a business with three cost centres would not code these as 11, 12 and 13; instead it would be more sensible to use 10, 20 and 30 – leaving plenty of space for any new cost centres.

The analysis codes will group together the three main costs of materials, labour and expenses, and the income items, as shown in the example below.

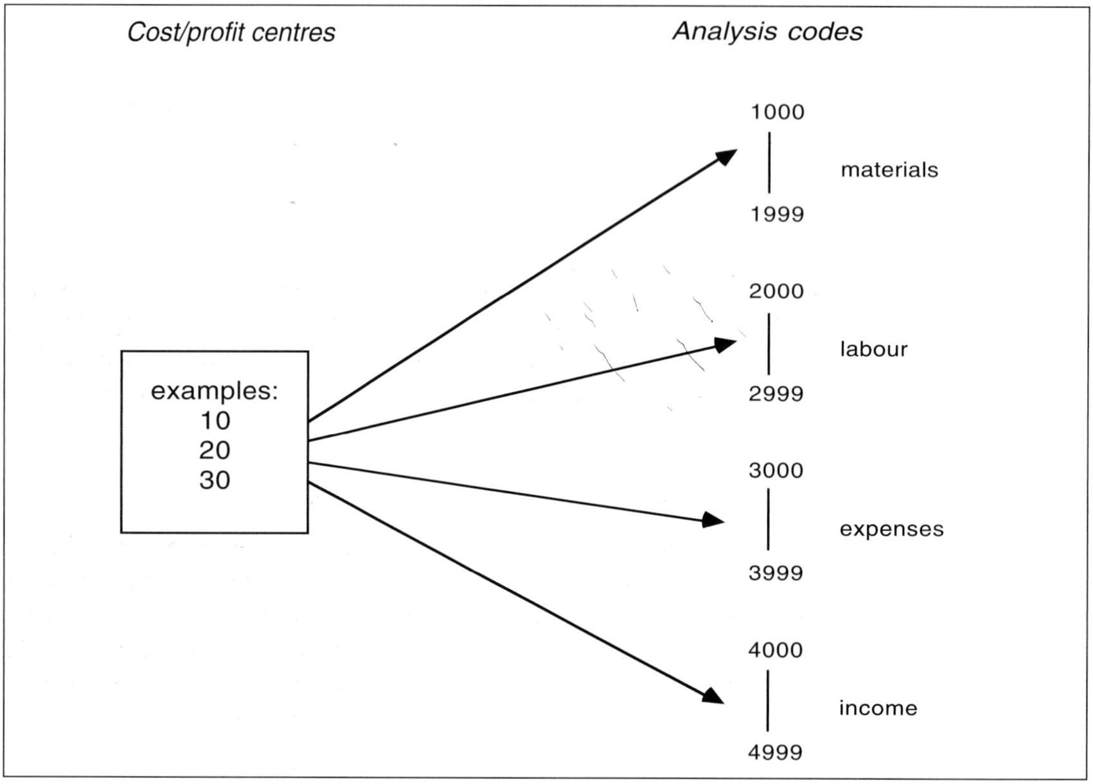

With cost centre numbers in round tens and using a four-digit analysis, the code numbers should not be too difficult to use on a day-to-day basis and will provide the right level of detail. Note that the policy manual will give the full list of codes and this should be referred to as and when necessary.

Within the accounts department of a business or organisation, it is necessary to code prime documents, both received (purchase invoices, receipts) and issued (copies of sales invoices). The person carrying out such coding – the coding clerk – must work to high standards of accuracy – wrong coding of a document will lead to it being posted to the wrong account in the accounts system, which will lead to incorrect information being supplied to the managers, which could in turn lead to wrong decision-making.

The way in which documents are coded varies from one organisation to another. For some, the code number is written on the document and marked clearly; others use a rubber stamp to provide a layout on which can be indicated the code number and the initials of the person entering the code.

For a coding system to work well:

- codes should provide the correct level of detail, ie cost/profit centre code and analysis code
- coding of documents must be accurate
- code numbers must be complete, ie the full code to be indicated, and not just the cost/profit centre or the analysis code
- coding of documents must be carried out at regular intervals within the timescales required by the organisation

The objective of coding is to provide correct analysis so as to give information from the accounts system to managers. By analysing costs and income to cost (and other) centres we can answer questions such as 'how much was the basic pay for my cost centre last month?'; 'how much was overtime?'.

problems and errors with coding

No administration system within an organisation is completely free of problems and 'fool-proof'. With coding the main problem is in deciding the cost centre and the analysis code to be used – the prime document may not be clear as to which centre has incurred the cost and what type of cost it is. The procedures manual may help but, if not, such items will have to be referred to the supervisor (who may need to make further enquiries).

A further difficulty occurs when a bill is received which relates to more than one cost centre (or even all the cost centres of the organisation). For example, an electricity bill is received for the whole business – how is it to be analysed between the cost centres? The answer here (assuming that no cost centres have their own meters and are billed separately) is to *apportion* the cost over all cost centres to which the bill relates. At its most simple, an equal share could be used – if there were ten cost centres then each would be apportioned one-tenth of the bill. However, some cost centres will have used more electricity than others and an appropriate method of apportionment must be found – this could relate to the number of employees in each centre, or the floor area, or other criteria could be used. The accounts assistant who is coding such costs will need guidance on apportionment either from the procedures manual or the accounts supervisor.

As with much of the work of the accounts department, a high level of confidentiality is needed in coding costs and income. In particular, the managers of cost centres and profit centres may seek to influence the coding process in order to reduce their costs and maximise their income. Thus the query from the accounts department 'did your cost centre incur this cost?'

will usually produce a negative response from the cost centre manager; by contrast, the question 'does this income relate to your profit centre?' will invariably be answered with 'yes!' Confidentiality ensures that the accounts department works independently of the other cost (and profit) centres – although some queries may have to be resolved by reference to the centres – and also ensures that management information is accurate.

wrong codes

An error of coding occurs when a wrong code is applied to a prime document. This will lead to the item being posted to the incorrect account in the accounts system. Thus the costs of one cost centre will be overstated whilst those of another will be understated; similarly income will be overstated in one profit centre but will be understated in another.

Wrong coding means that the accounts system is inaccurate for internal management use within the business or organisation. (External suppliers and buyers of goods and services are unaffected as they will still be paid the amounts due to them, or will receive sales invoices for the correct amounts.) Incorrect management information is being supplied, which could lead to wrong estimates for next year (being based on current-year figures), or to wrong decisions being made.

Accuracy of coding is therefore an important step in the provision of accounts information to managers. It is good practice for some codes – particularly for large amounts – to be double-checked. If wrong codes are found on a regular basis, it would be worthwhile to investigate the coding system to see if it can be simplified.

excessive volumes

The coding clerk will also be on the look out for excessive volumes of costs or income. This occurs when the wrong quantity of costs or income is shown on the prime document, and the volume is much greater than the amounts normally seen. Excessive volumes are often caused by a misunderstanding between the buyer and the supplier. For example, you want 30 computer disks for use in the office and fill in a purchase order; the supplier sells disks packed in boxes of 10 and assumes that you mean 30 *boxes* and supplies you with 300 disks!

Clear communication is the best way of avoiding the error of excessive volumes. There should be several checks within the accounts system to avoid the problem, and the coding clerk provides a further line of defence.

other discrepancies in documentation

As well as wrong codes and excessive volumes, the coding clerk will be on the lookout for discrepancies in documentation. These can include invoices addressed to the *wrong organisation* or be for *fictitious expenses*.

- **wrong organisations**

  An error that, in theory, should not slip through the accounts system is where prime documents for costs relate to a different business or organisation. The coding clerk should check carefully that the documents do relate to the organisation, and are not for another business or organisation with a similar name.

- **fictitious expenses**

  The coding clerk must also watch for an unscrupulous business that sends out invoices for fictitious expenses – for example, to cover the cost of an unwanted entry in a trade directory (which may never be published). Because amounts are small and do not raise suspicions, such invoices are often paid by larger businesses and organisations.

Case Study

WYVERN ROYAL HOSPITAL TRUST – CODING THE COSTS

situation

Wyvern Royal Hospital Trust is a National Health Service hospital. You are an assistant in the accounts department and today you are working on the subsidiary (purchases) ledger. For accounting purposes the hospital is divided into a number of cost centres or income centres. The following are the codes for some of the departments which are cost centres:

x-ray department	cost centre code 10
casualty	cost centre code 20
pharmacy	cost centre code 30
physiotherapy	cost centre code 40

The following posting sheet for purchase invoices has been handed to you by the accounts supervisor, Phillippa Farrell, who asks you to complete the coding column for the costs:

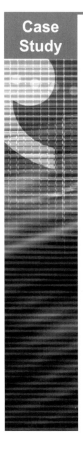

WYVERN ROYAL HOSPITAL TRUST

Posting sheet: purchase invoices

Supplier	Department	Description	Amount	Coding
			£	
Zodak Films	x-ray	x-ray film	4,250.57	
Wye Plaster Co	casualty	fine-grade plaster	754.93	
Beech Drugs plc	pharmacy	drugs	2,941.26	
Tyax Sports Ltd	physiotherapy	rowing machines	3,248.36	
Electro Ltd	x-ray	repairs to scanner	1,495.22	
WR Industries plc	casualty	disposable gloves	472.33	
Country Pie Co	kitchen	pies (various)	528.36	
Wyvern Cleaning Co	casualty	cleaning services	2,871.89	
		Check list total	16,562.92	

Prepared by	*Ginger Waterman*	Date	*17 June 2004*
Checked by	*Lucinda Luz*	Date	*18 June 2004*
Coded by		Date	
Posted by		Date	

The accounts supervisor has given you the coding list which includes the following:

cost	code no
cleaning materials	3200
contract cleaning	3225
dressings and plaster	1100
electricity and gas	1350
exercise equipment	1900
laundry contract	3250
mechanical and electrical repairs	3250
medicines and drugs	1500
uniforms and disposables	1600
x-ray film	1125

You are to complete the coding section of the posting sheet as far as you are able. Any items you are not able to code are to be queried by e-mail to the accounts supervisor asking for the appropriate code(s).

solution

Using the cost centre codes and the cost codes, the posting sheet is coded as follows:

WYVERN ROYAL HOSPITAL TRUST

Posting sheet: purchase invoices

Supplier	Department	Description	Amount	Coding
			£	
Zodak Films	x-ray	x-ray film	4,250.57	101125
Wye Plaster Co	casualty	fine-grade plaster	754.93	201100
Beech Drugs plc	pharmacy	drugs	2,941.26	301500
Tyax Sports Ltd	physiotherapy	rowing machines	3,248.36	401900
Electro Ltd	x-ray	repairs to scanner	1,495.22	103250
WR Industries plc	casualty	disposable gloves	472.33	201600
Country Pie Co	kitchen	pies (various)	528.36	
Wyvern Cleaning Co	casualty	cleaning services	2,871.89	203225
		Check list total	16,562.92	

Prepared by *Ginger Waterman* Date *17 June 2004*

Checked by *Lucinda Luz* Date *18 June 2004*

Coded by ____________ Date ____________

Posted by ____________ Date ____________

As you are unable to complete the coding it is important to be able to describe the problem and refer it to the appropriate person. Accordingly, you send the following e-mail to the accounts supervisor, Phillippa Farrell:

> Phillippa.Farrell@wrht.swest.nhs.uk 20/6/04 10:32.16
> To: Phillippa.Farrell
> From: A.Student
>
> I have been coding the purchases invoices but I don't have a cost centre code and cost code for one of the items. The cost centre is the kitchen and the cost code is for pies (presumably the code will be for food). Can you please advise me?

The accounts supervisor replies by e-mail as follows:

> A.Student@wrht.swest.nhs.uk 20/6/04 11:44.51
> To: A.Student
> From: Phillippa.Farrell
>
> Further to your e-mail this morning, the cost centre code for the kitchen is 60; the cost code for food is 3825.

You are now able to complete the posting sheet with the code 603825. You sign as the person coding it, date it, and pass it on for posting to the subsidiary (purchases) ledger and the purchases ledger control account by the data input clerk.

Chapter Summary

- Managers are those within a business or organisation who are involved in decision-making, planning and control.

- Managers make use of
  - financial accounting to provide reports on past transactions
  - management accounting to provide reports which summarise transactions that have happened in the recent past and to make estimates for the future

- Organisations can be classified between
  - public sector and private sector
  - type of industry (including providers of services)

- The main functions within an organisation include:
  - finance
  - human resources
  - administration
  - sales/marketing
  - production (in a manufacturing business)
  - operations (provision of services to customers)

- The three elements of cost comprise
  - materials, raw materials and components, products bought in for resale, service or consumable items
  - labour, the payroll costs of employees
  - expenses, all other running costs

- Costs are analysed between the different functions or sections of a business or organisation by the use of cost centres.

- Profit centres include an analysis of both costs and income to show the profit (income less costs).

- Investment centres consider profit in relation to the amount of money invested in the centre, and express it as a percentage return on investment.

- Coding is the means by which costs and income are analysed to cost/profit/investment centres.

- Errors in coding and discrepancies in documentation include
  - wrong codes
  - excessive volumes
  - wrong organisations
  - fictitious expenses

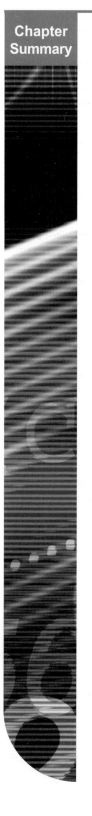

Key Terms

financial accounting	is concerned with recording financial transactions that have happened already, and with providing information from the accounting records
management accounting	uses accounting information to summarise transactions that have happened in the recent past and to make estimates for the future
costs	comprise materials, labour and expenses
income	the sale of products or services
cost centre	section of a business to which costs can be charged
profit centre	a section of a business to which costs can be charged, income can be identified, and profit can be calculated
investment centre	a section of a business where profit can be compared with the amount of money invested in the centre, and can be expressed as a percentage return on investment
coding	a code number written on prime documents to analyse it a particular cost/profit/investment centre and to indicate the type of cost or income

Student Activities

23.1 What are the three main functions of a manager?

23.2 What are the two types of information that the accounting system is able to provide for managers?

23.3 What are the main differences between financial accounting and management accounting?

23.4 'Managers include anybody within the business or organisation who is involved in decision-making, planning and control.'

Using your workplace, or an organisation with which you are familiar, give examples of

- the management functions you undertake
- the management functions undertaken by the managing director or chief executive

Show how each management function relates to the areas of decision-making, planning and control.

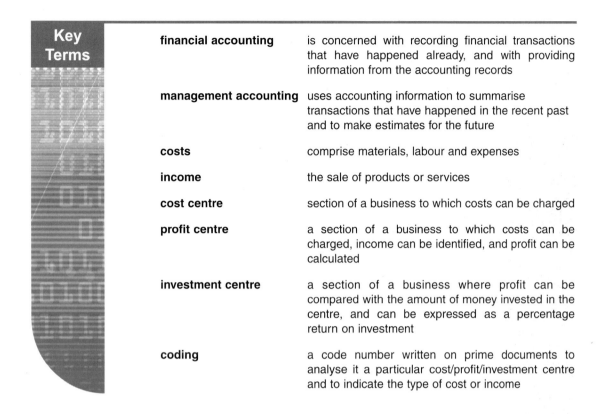

23.5 You work as an accounts assistant at Surestart Training, an organisation funded by central government. It provides skills training to help young people (aged 16-25) who are unemployed following the closure of a major employer in the area.

On return from holiday, you arrive back at work on Monday to find that the accounts supervisor has been off work due to illness all last week and is not expected back for several days. You are asked by the administration manager to take charge of accounts department. There are two assistants working with you today, one of whom is part-time, working mornings only.

The following tasks are waiting:

- cash book wasn't written up last week and the bank statement has arrived in the post this morning
- petty cash book needs to be balanced for last week and the imprest amount restored
- trainers employed by Surestart Training are due to be paid on Friday; there are pay calculations for hourly-paid trainers to be made, together with changes – new employees, tax code changes, etc – before the payroll can be processed
- a number of purchases invoices need to be paid – some are due for payment today at the end of the credit period; others offer cash discount for prompt settlement

Show how you will manage the work of the accounts department in relation to the areas of decision-making, planning and control.

23.6 Study the following accounting activities and decide which of them are financial accounting and which are management accounting:

(a) recording purchases invoices in the subsidiary (purchases) ledger Financial

(b) listing sales invoices in the sales day book Financial

(c) using last year's sales figure to estimate next year's sales Management

(d) reporting last year's cost of materials Financial

(e) analysing costs between different cost centres Management

(f) calculating the return on investment of an investment centre Management

23.7 Using your workplace, or an organisation with which you are familiar, give examples of

- the management accounting information you are asked for
  Estimates of costs Labour, expenses, Materials + Maintenance + Consumables for next yr from last yrs figs
- the management accounting information your supervisor/manager is asked for
  Estimates for improvement projects costs
  Capital expenditure costs for next yr from last yrs figs.

23.8 (a) Explain the difference between

- cost centre *An area of business which incurs costs*
- profit centre *Incurs costs + produces income*
- investment centre *Incurs costs, produces income + is responsible for managing assets + capital*

(b) Suggest likely cost centres for

- a school or a college *Student Centre, Resource Learning Centre, Estate*
- a manufacturing business which makes two product lines

(c) Give examples of cost centres in your workplace, or an organisation with which you are familiar.

Engineering IT
Laboratory
HR

23.9 You work as an accounts assistant at City News and Books, a company which owns a group of shops selling newspapers and magazines, books and stationery. The accounting system has been set up to show costs, income and money invested for each of these three sections of the business: newspapers and magazines, books, stationery.

The finance director has requested details for each section of costs and income for last year, and the amount of money invested in each section at the end of the year. (She says that all figures can be to the nearest £000.)

The accounts supervisor asks you to deal with this request and you go to the accounts and extract the following information for last year:

	Newspapers and magazines	Books	Stationery
	£000s	£000s	£000s
Costs: materials	155	246	122
labour	65	93	58
expenses	27	35	25
Sales	352	544	230
Money invested	420	850	250

The accounts supervisor asks you to present the information for the finance director in the form of a memorandum which shows the costs, profit, and return on investment for each section of the business.

23.10 You are an accounts assistant at Eagle Books, a large publisher of textbooks and novels. The business is split into four divisions: academic textbooks, novels, children's books and sports books. The accounts system is arranged so that each division is a profit centre. There is also a separate cost centre for administration.

An extract from the company's policy manual is as follows:

cost or profit centre number	**cost or profit centre name**
20	academic textbooks
30	novels
40	children's books
50	sports books
60	administration

analysis code	**cost or income**
1050	paper
2100	basic pay
2150	overtime
2200	bonus payments
2300	holiday pay
2400	sick pay
3050	authors' royalties
3100	rates
3150	heating and lighting
3200	telephone
3500	building maintenance
3525	computers and equipment maintenance
3550	vehicle running costs
3700	advertising
4050	sales to bookshops
4250	sales to wholesalers

The following prime documents have been received today (amounts are net of VAT, where applicable):

(a) copy of a sales invoice showing the sale of £14,750 of academic textbooks to Orton Book Wholesalers Limited

(b) printer's bill of £22,740 for paper for printing sports books

(c) payroll summary showing overtime of £840 last month in the children's book section

(d) payment of £1,540 for advertising sports books in the magazine 'Sport Today'

(e) telephone bill of £1,200 to be split equally between all cost and profit centres

(f) royalties of £88,245 paid to children's book authors 40 3050 Exp.

(g) copy of sales invoice showing the sale of £1,890 of novels to the Airport Bookshop
30 4050 Income

You are to code the above transactions using the policy manual extract given.

Your supervisor asks you to provide a summary of the day's costs and income, analysed between materials, labour, expenses, and income. You know that the coding system is split into the following categories:

code numbers	**category**
1000 – 1999	materials
2000 – 2999	labour
3000 – 3999	expenses
4000 – 4999	income

Reply to your supervisor by means of a memorandum or an email.

24 Presenting and comparing management information

this chapter covers . . .

This chapter explains how the information needed by management is collected and presented. This involves:

- *establishing exactly what information is needed and who needs it*
- *appreciating that information can relate to a previous period (eg last year), a corresponding period (eg the same month last year) and a future period (eg forecasts for next year)*
- *working out any differences between forecast data and actual income and costs*
- *identifying the correct format in which to present the data (eg email, report, letter) and appreciating that different formats are used depending on who needs the information and the urgency and confidentiality of the information*

NVQ PERFORMANCE CRITERIA COVERED

unit 4: SUPPLYING INFORMATION FOR MANAGEMENT CONTROL

element 4.2

provide comparisons on costs and income

A *clarify information requirements with the appropriate person*

B *compare information extracted from a particular source with actual results*

C *identify discrepancies*

D *provide comparisons to the appropriate person in the required format*

E *follow organisational requirements for confidentiality strictly*

WHAT INFORMATION DOES THE MANAGER NEED?

what is a manager?

As we saw in the last chapter, the term 'manager' can apply to many different people. A managing director is a manager, so is a supervisor. They are both involved – at different levels of responsibility – in:

- planning what the business does
- making decisions
- controlling business activity

Managers at different levels of the organisation need information so that they can plan, make decisions and run the business more efficiently.

what is management information?

Managers will be interested in financial information for:

- income
- costs

This information comprises:

- a record of transactions that have already taken place and been entered in the accounts of the business – this is part of **financial accounting**
- summaries and analysis of what has happened in the past and estimates of future performance – this is part of **management accounting**

CLARIFYING THE TYPE OF INFORMATION NEEDED

A number of questions need to be asked when gathering data for presenting management information:

1 Who is the **person who needs the information** – is it a supervisor, a departmental manager, or a director?

2 What is the **nature of the information** – does it relate to income (eg sales) or costs (eg wages, expenses)?

3 How is the information to be **presented** – in a standard report form (where you simply have to fill in the figures), an email (quick and brief), a memo, or a letter?

4 How **urgent** is the request? Do you have to give it top priority and do it straightaway, or will later in the week be alright?

5 What **level of detail** is required? Does 'sales for the year' mean the total sales for all products for the year? Does the figure have to be broken down month-by-month and product-by-product?

6 How **accurate** do the figures have to be? The nearest thousand, hundred or an exact figure?

7 How **confidential** is the information? Does it matter if you leave a note of the figures lying around on your desk?

meeting the user's needs

The reason for these questions is that it is important to ensure that you **meet the user's needs** in presenting management information. There is no point in preparing a twenty page memorandum analysing wages figures for different product lines or services on a monthly basis if all the director wanted was the *total* labour cost for this year and last year.

The general principle is that senior managers will want to see information which presents an overview of what is going on so that they can make planning decisions. Departmental managers and supervisors, on the other hand, will be more interested in greater detail so that they can control the day-to-day running of the business. If senior managers want more information they will ask managers and supervisors. Look at the two diagrams which follow. They shows how the finance department provides management information to the two different functions in a business – one relates to income, the other to costs.

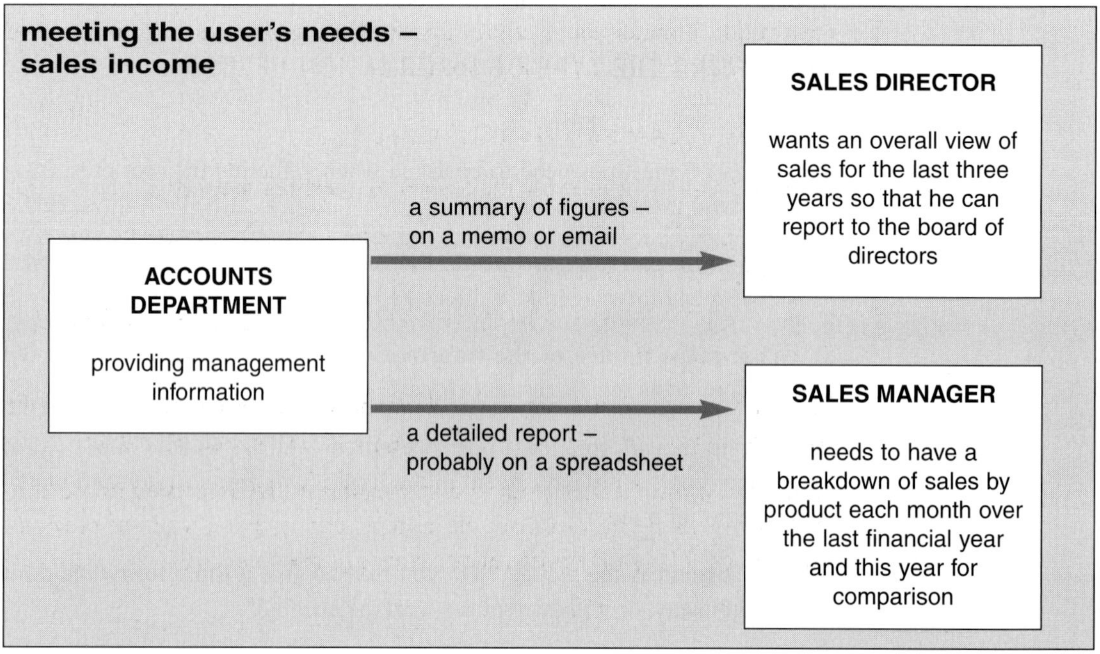
meeting the user's needs –
sales income
SALES DIRECTOR
wants an overall view of sales for the last three years so that he can report to the board of directors
a summary of figures – on a memo or email
ACCOUNTS DEPARTMENT
providing management information
SALES MANAGER
a detailed report – probably on a spreadsheet
needs to have a breakdown of sales by product each month over the last financial year and this year for comparison

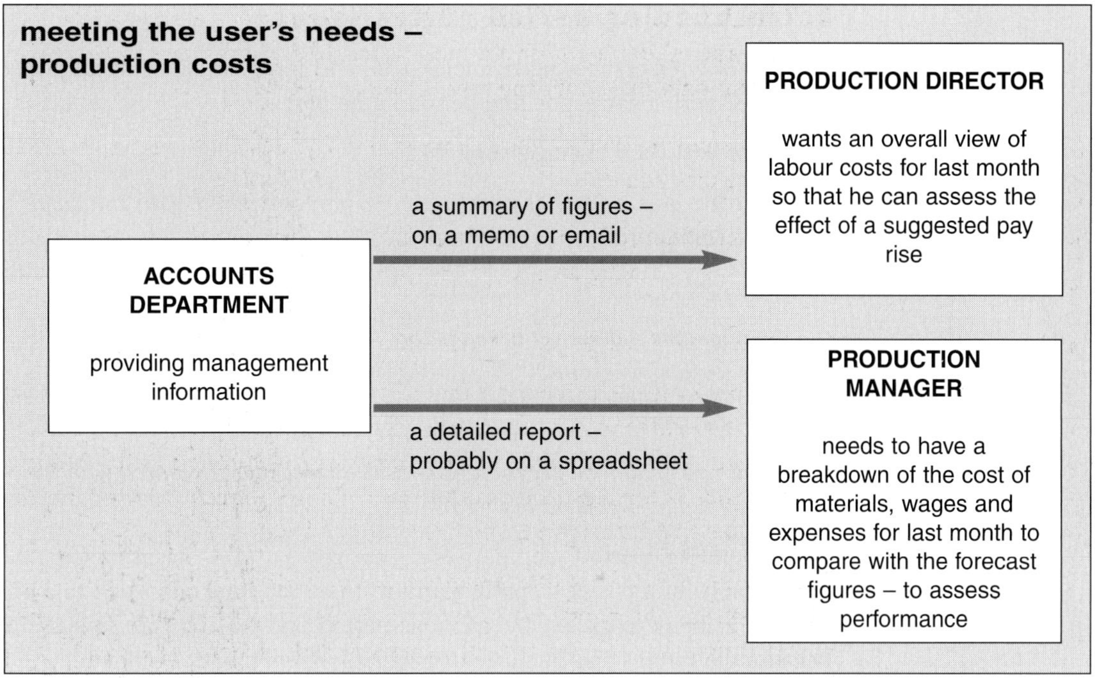
meeting the user's needs – production costs
ACCOUNTS DEPARTMENT
providing management information
a summary of figures – on a memo or email
PRODUCTION DIRECTOR
wants an overall view of labour costs for last month so that he can assess the effect of a suggested pay rise
a detailed report – probably on a spreadsheet
PRODUCTION MANAGER
needs to have a breakdown of the cost of materials, wages and expenses for last month to compare with the forecast figures – to assess performance

COMPARING TIME PERIODS

In the Case Study on page 508 we will look at a number of types of management information and the ways in which it is presented. First, however, it is important to appreciate that management information can be compared over different time periods. . .

previous period comparisons

Managers will want to know the answer to questions such as:

> *'What are the sales for this quarter of the year compared with the figure for the previous quarter?'*
>
> *'How much overtime was paid to production staff this month compared with last month?'*

The data produced will be a **previous period comparison** – a straight comparison between this month or quarter with last month or quarter.

At the end of the financial year the managers are very interested to see how the business has performed over the current year compared with the previous year and are likely to require reports covering sales and costs.

corresponding period comparisons

Another way of comparing financial data is to report on the current period compared with a corresponding period in the past.

For example a shop manager may ask:

> *'What are our sales like this month so far compared with the same period last year?'*

The manager of a theme park, such as Alton Towers, may ask:

> *'What income did we get from visitors this weekend, compared with the figure for last weekend?'*

He may also ask:

> *'What income did we get from visitors this weekend, compared with the corresponding weekend last year?'*

Corresponding period comparisons are very useful in assessing the performance of a business, particularly if it is a seasonal one, such as a gift shop or a theme park, where previous period comparisons are less useful because the figures can fluctuate considerably from month-to-month.

Look at the data in the table below. You can see that corresponding period comparisons can be made between the two years.

Merrie England Theme Park

Monthly income 2002 - 2003

NB Seasonal - compare like with like.

	Jan	Feb	Mar	April	May	June	July	Aug	Sept	Oct	Nov	Dec	TOTAL
	£000	£000	£000	£000	£000	£000	£000	£000	£000	£000	£000	£000	£000
2002	130	140	180	250	360	550	760	700	400	140	120	135	3,865
2003	135	140	160	280	410	600	800	720	380	130	125	130	4,010

cumulative comparisons

Another useful method of comparison used by managers is to calculate **cumulative** financial data over corresponding periods. This is very simple: all you have to do is to add each monthly figure to the previous monthly figure as you go through the year. To get the cumulative figure for February 2002 from the above table you add January's and February's figures together (note that they are quoted in £000s), ie £130,000 plus £140,000 = £270,000. To get March's cumulative you add £180,000 (the March figure) to £270,000 = £450,000. The cumulative income table is shown on the next page.

Merrie England Theme Park

Cumulative monthly income 2002 - 2003

	Jan	Feb	Mar	April	May	June	July	Aug	Sept	Oct	Nov	Dec	TOTAL
	£000	£000	£000	£000	£000	£000	£000	£000	£000	£000	£000	£000	£000
2002	130	270	450	700	1,060	1,610	2,370	3,070	3,470	3,610	3,730	3,865	3,865
2003	135	275	435	715	1,125	1,725	2,525	3,245	3,625	3,755	3,880	4,010	4,010

As you can see from the above table, the corresponding periods from the two years can be compared easily. For example, income for the first six months was £1,610,000 in 2002 and £1,725,000 in 2003 (the figures in the table are quoted in £000s).

comparison of forecast data

So far we have compared data from past periods. Management will often require forecasts which can then be compared with what actually happens – for example a sales forecast. The forecast figures may well already be on a table or a spreadsheet file and you will be required to enter the actual figures so that management can see if the business is on target with the forecast or whether sales are better than forecast, or are below target.

The table below shows the sales forecast for a computer company for the first six months of 2003. The forecast figures are in the left-hand column for each month; the actual figures have been entered for the first three months for comparison purposes in the right-hand column under each month.

Helicon Computing Limited

Sales forecast January-June 2003

Jan		Feb		March		April		May		June	
forecast	actual	forecast	actual	forecast	actual	forecast	actual	forecast	actual	forecast	actual
£000	£000	£000	£000	£000	£000	£000	£000	£000	£000	£000	£000
50	51	60	63	65	69	60		65		70	

actual figures entered for management

Case Study

CLARION CARDS LIMITED – EXTRACTING MANAGEMENT INFORMATION

situation

Clarion Cards Limited is a company which manufactures a wide range of greetings cards and calendars. It employs 50 permanent staff at its factory and also takes on temporary employees in the summer.

You work in the Accounts Department. One of your jobs is to extract and present financial information for the company management. Your supervisor, Ally Gee, gives you these tasks from time-to-time.

The data for the company's income and costs are shown in the tables on the next page. They are presented as quarterly results (figures for three month periods). They show:

- last year's figures
- this year's forecast figures
- the actual figures for the first two quarters of the year (1 January to 30 June)

The date today is 2 July 2003.

Your supervisor has just received the following memos from the Sales Manager, Bartholomew Simpson and the Production Manager, Ramjit Singh.

Ally has asked you to draft reply memos to go out in his name. He points out that the information is needed by the end of the week and that he will need time to check what you have written.

MEMORANDUM

To Ally Gee, Accounts Supervisor **Ref** BS101

From B Simpson, Sales Manager **Date** 30 June 2003

Subject Sales Report

Please can you supply the following figures by 4 July: I need them for a management meeting.

1. Total sales for the last quarter
2. The sales figure for the corresponding quarter last year
3. The forecast sales figure for the last quarter.

Many thanks.

MEMORANDUM

To Ally Gee, Accounts Supervisor **Ref** RS101

From R Singh, Production Manager **Date** 30 June 2003

Subject Costs Report

Please can you supply the following figures by 4 July; I have got a management meeting coming up the following week.

1. Total costs for the last quarter.
2. The costs figure for the corresponding quarter last year.
3. The forecast costs figure for the last quarter.

R.S.

QUARTERLY SALES

	Year 2002 Actual £000s	Year 2003 Forecast £000s	Year 2003 Actual £000s
Jan-Mar	150	160	155
Apr-Jun	160	170	165
Jul-Sep	170	180	
Oct-Dec	250	275	

QUARTERLY COSTS

	Year 2002 Actual £000s	Year 2003 Forecast £000s	Year 2003 Actual £000s
Jan-Mar	100	110	105
Apr-Jun	110	120	115
Jul-Sep	180	190	
Oct-Dec	120	125	

Clarion's sales

Most of Clarion's sales are made in the Autumn when the shops stock up with cards and calendars for Christmas, although it receives a steady income throughout the year for its birthday and 'special occasion' cards.

Clarion's costs

Clarions's costs fall into three main categories:

- materials – the cost of paper and card used in the production process
- labour costs – the wages bill
- expenses – all the other costs, such as advertising, insurance, postage, telephone, rent and rates

Clarion is at its busiest in the summer months when it prints its Christmas stock.

solution

You extract the information from the tables of data (shown on the previous page) and prepare the two memos for your supervisor's signature . . .

MEMORANDUM

To B Simpson, Sales Manager **Ref** AG171

From Ally Gee, Accounts Supervisor **Date** 4 July 2003

Subject Sales Report

Thanks for your memo of 30 June. The figures you requested are:

1.	Total sales for the last quarter (to 30 June)	£165,000
2.	The sales figure for the corresponding quarter last year	£160,000
3.	The forecast sales figure for the last quarter	£170,000

A Gee

MEMORANDUM

To R Singh, Production Manager **Ref** AG172

From Ally Gee, Accounts Supervisor **Date** 4 July 2003

Subject Costs Report

Thanks for your memo of 30 June. The figures you requested are:

1.	Total costs for the last quarter (to 30 June)	£115,000
2.	The costs figure for the corresponding quarter last year	£110,000
3.	The forecast costs figure for the last quarter	£120,000

A Gee

The memos should be passed to your supervisor for checking and signature. You will need to make sure that he gets them in good time so that he can change anything that needs correcting and so that they can reach the appropriate people by 6 July.

As you will see, the memos are brief, clear and to the point. The information they contain is not particularly sensitive. Ally Gee has not asked you to take care over confidentiality, so you can quite safely put your drafts in his in-tray for checking.

Note also that some of the data relates to a past period – this is part of **financial accounting** and will be taken from the ledger accounts. Some of the information is taken from a forecast – this is part of **management accounting** – which involves looking into the future.

IDENTIFYING DIFFERENCES (VARIANCES)

Another function of management accounting is the preparation of financial data so that management can compare actual figures with forecast figures. You will be asked to complete a table of figures – possibly on a computer spreadsheet – and to calculate the difference (also known as a 'variance' or 'discrepancy') between the forecast figures and the actual figures.

income forecasts – differences (variances)

Look at the format shown below. It shows the quarterly sales **income** figures for Clarion Cards. This is how the report would appear at the beginning of July 2003 (the date of the Case Study).

CLARION CARDS – QUARTERLY SALES

	Year 2003 Forecast £	Year 2003 Actual £	Difference + or – £
Jan-Mar	160,000	155,000	– 5,000
Apr-Jun	170,000	165,000	– 5,000
Jul-Sep	180,000	185000	+5000
Oct-Dec	275,000	290,000	+15000
TOTAL	785,000	795,000	+10,000

The difference (variance) figure is shown in this column. It is calculated by deducting forecast sales (the left-hand data column) from actual sales (the middle column):

£155,000 – £160,000 = – £5,000

actual – forecast = difference

Note that a negative figure can be shown either with a minus sign, or in brackets:

– £5,000 *or* (£5,000)

A *negative* difference means that actual sales have not been as good as forecast.

A *positive* difference (a *plus* figure) means that actual sales have been better than forecast.

The actual figures will be filled in at the end of each quarter. The source of the information will be the sales account in the main ledger.

The forecast figures will have been compiled before the start of the year. They will not form part of the accounts (the financial accounting records), but are a future estimate, made as part of the management accounting process. They are totalled to give an estimate of annual sales.

At the end of the year this total will be compared with the total of the actual sales and the difference (variance) for the year will be worked out.

costs forecasts – differences (variances)

The table shown below shows the quarterly **costs** figures for Clarion Cards as it will appear at the beginning of July 2003 (the date of the Case Study). You will see that the format is very similar to the sales forecast. Read the explanations below and note one important change:

- when you work out the difference between forecast and actual **income** (see previous page) you deduct forecast income from actual income:
  actual – forecast = difference
- when you work out the difference between forecast and actual **costs**, the calculation is different – you deduct actual costs from forecast costs:
  forecast – actual = difference

Study the form and the notes and then read the Case Study which follows.

CLARION CARDS – QUARTERLY COSTS

SPENDING

	Year 2003 Forecast £	Year 2003 Actual £	Difference + or – £
Jan-Mar	110,000	105,000	+ 5,000
Apr-Jun	120,000	115,000	+ 5,000
Jul-Sep	190,000		
Oct-Dec	125,000		
TOTAL	545,000		

The difference (variance) figure is shown in this column. It is calculated by deducting actual costs (the middle data column) from the forecast costs (the left-hand column):

£110,000 – £105,000 = + £5,000
forecast – actual = difference (variance)

Note that any *negative* difference would be shown either with a minus sign, or in brackets: – £5,000 *or* (£5,000)

A *positive* difference (as here) means that costs are lower than forecast – which should please the managers.

A *negative* difference means that costs are higher than forecast – which may be a problem for managers to investigate.

The actual figures will be filled in at the end of each quarter. The source of the information will be the costs accounts in the main ledger, eg wages, purchases, expenses.

The forecast figures will have been compiled before the start of the year. They will not form part of the accounts (the financial accounting records), but are a future estimate, made as part of the management accounting process. They are totalled to give an estimate of annual costs.

At the end of the year this total will be compared with the total of the actual costs and the difference (variance) for the year worked out.

Case Study

CLARION CARDS LIMITED – CALCULATING THE DIFFERENCES

This Case Study is a continuation of the Case Study on page 508.

It is now the last week in December and the end of the financial year for Clarion Cards. It is time for the managers to look at the figures for income and costs. These will be available in the financial accounting records of the business and summarised in the trial balance.

The managers will want to compare the actual figures from the accounts with the forecasts made at the beginning of the year. From this they will be able to tell whether the business has done better – or worse – than expected.

It is your job to work out any differences (variances) on the report forms (shown on the previous two pages) and to produce an annual total. The figures for the last two quarters are set out in the tinted table on the right and are shown transferred to the report forms.

CLARION CARDS – QUARTERLY SALES

	Year 2003 Forecast £	Year 2003 Actual £	Difference + or – £
Jan-Mar	160,000	155,000	– 5,000
Apr-Jun	170,000	165,000	– 5,000
Jul-Sep	180,000	185,000	+ 5,000
Oct-Dec	275,000	290,000	+ 15,000
TOTAL	785,000	795,000	+ 10,000

CLARION CARDS QUARTERLY RESULTS

	Jul-Sep £	Oct-Dec £
Sales	185,000	290,000
Costs	195,000	129,000

CLARION CARDS – QUARTERLY COSTS

	Year 2003 Forecast £	Year 2003 Actual £	Difference + or – £
Jan-Mar	110,000	105,000	+ 5,000
Apr-Jun	120,000	115,000	+ 5,000
Jul-Sep	190,000	195,000	– 5,000
Oct-Dec	125,000	129,000	– 4,000
TOTAL	545,000	544,000	+ 1,000

discussion points

What has happened to actual sales and costs for the whole year? Do you think the managers will be pleased or worried?

dealing with differences (variances)

Dealing with differences (variances) is the job of the managers. Your responsibility is to extract and present the information within the given guidelines and to calculate any differences (variances). As we mentioned earlier, you may use a computer spreadsheet, in which case the differences will be calculated automatically. See the Case Study on page 522.

Managers will look at the differences (variances) and decide whether to investigate the cause. Sometimes nothing can be done – for example the wages bill may have gone up because of an increase in the Minimum Wage, or transport costs may have gone up because of a rise in fuel prices. Sometimes managers will be able to take action – for example cutting down on overtime to reduce the wages bill. These are factors which you will examine in detail in your later studies at NVQ levels 3 and 4. For the moment you have to concentrate on presenting data – management information – promptly and accurately in the required format.

THE REQUIRED FORMAT

There is a variety of communication formats you may use when compiling management information. Each format is appropriate to different circumstances. Over the next few pages we will look at examples of these formats to illustrate how they are used in practical business situations.

Routine standard reports, like those in the Case Study earlier in this chapter are used regularly to keep managers informed about the performance of the business so that they can make appropriate decisions. These reports will be set out on pre-printed sheets, or templates on a computer spreadsheet. They include:

- the **standard cost report** which summarises the differences between actual and forecast figures for different types of cost: materials, labour and expenses
- the **budgetary control report** which compares actual and forecast figures over a period of time
- **management accounts** which provide managers with information about specific areas of costs or income, for example sales by product or service

The formats commonly used for 'one-off' situations are:

- **memo** or **email** – used to communicate 'one-off' pieces of information
- **note** – used informally to communicate information for managers
- **letter** – often used to communicate information which is confidential

Now study the use of the formats on the next few pages.

STANDARD COST REPORT

A standard cost report summarises the differences between actual and forecast figures for different types of cost. The format below shows the costs for Zenith, a computer manufacturer, in week 2 of June 2003.

The form is pre-printed and each week (or month in some cases) you will fill in the dates and figures which in the text here have a tinted background.

The financial information you need is the actual cost figures for materials, labour and expenses for the product. The rest is a matter of calculation. Study the form carefully and then read the explanations underneath.

STANDARD COST REPORT – ZENITH COMPUTERS

product desktop computers **date** 16 06 03

period week ending 13 June 03

	forecast cost £000s	actual cost £000s	difference £000s + or –
materials	75	73	+ 2
labour	65	80	– 15
expenses	48	45	+ 3
TOTAL	188	198	–10

this column sets out the types of cost and the total cost for the week; the costs are divided into three categories:

- materials
- labour
- expenses

this column sets out the forecast figures for the types of cost – these figures will already be entered here

you will have to obtain and insert these figures and total them

you will have to calculate the difference figure by deducting the actual cost from the forecast cost

a positive figure has a plus sign and means that costs are lower than forecast

a negative figure has a minus sign and means that costs are higher than forecast

discussion points
What are the managers likely to think about these figures?
How does the report help them to pinpoint any problem?

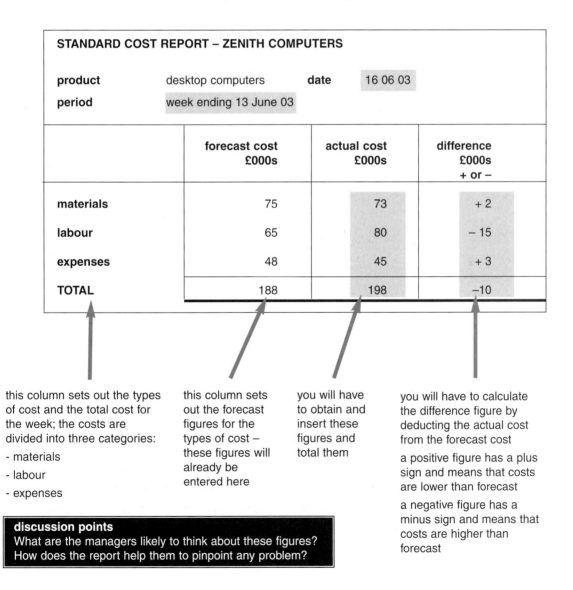

BUDGETARY CONTROL REPORT

During the course of the year, the managers of a business will want to compare the forecast and actual figures for costs and income so that they can take action if problems arise. A budgetary control report focuses on various areas of the business to compare the forecast and actual figures. These reports may cover departments of the business (cost centres) or types of cost and income.

The budgetary control report shown below looks at the sales performance of Zenith Computers each month. You will have to fill in the figures which in the text here have a tinted background.

SALES BUDGETARY CONTROL REPORT – ZENITH COMPUTERS **date** June 2003

	forecast sales (monthly) £000s	**forecast sales (cumulative) £000s**	**actual sales £000s**	**difference + or – £000s**
January	100	100	110	+ 10
February	110	210	115	+ 5
March	110	320	112	+ 2
April	120	440	115	– 5
May	120	560	118	– 2
June	125	685	129	+ 4
July	125	810		
August	130	940		
September	125	1065		
October	125	1190		
November	140	1330		
December	150	1480		
TOTAL	1480	1480	699	+ 14

sales for the year so far compared

this column sets out the forecast sales figures for each month of the year

this column sets out the cumulative forecast sales figures – it shows forecast sales for the year so far

this column sets out the actual sales figures month-by-month

the total at the bottom can be compared with the forecast cumulative total for the year so far

you will have to calculate the difference figure by deducting the forecast sales from the actual sales

a positive figure has a plus sign and means that sales are higher than forecast

MANAGEMENT ACCOUNTS

Managers are likely to need more details from the financial records about aspects of cost or income. You may be asked to provide this information, either on a standard form, or as a 'one off' request made by the manager.

On the next few pages we look at the formats required for 'one-off' situations.

product sales report

You are asked to complete a monthly pre-printed report giving details of sales of individual products.

The example below provides more information about the sales budgetary control report from Zenith Computers shown on the previous page.

The figures you complete are shown with a tinted background. The form may be preprinted, or it may be on a computer spreadsheet file.

PRODUCT SALES REPORT – ZENITH COMPUTERS **date** June 2003

product range	**forecast sales (cumulative) £000s**	**actual sales (cumulative) £000s**	**difference + or – £000s**
Z1276	40	35	– 5
Z2944	210	198	– 12
Z9434	145	164	+ 19
Z9435	85	83	– 2
Z9500	90	94	+ 4
Z9501	115	125	+ 10
TOTAL	685	699	+ 14

product codes for the models of computer produced by Zenith

this column sets out the forecast sales figures for each model

the total at the bottom is the same as the forecast monthly total on the sales budgetary control report

this column sets out the actual sales figures for each model

the total at the bottom is the same as the actual monthly total on the sales budgetary control report

you will have to calculate the difference figure by deducting the forecast sales for each model from the actual sales

a positive figure has a plus sign and means that sales are higher than forecast

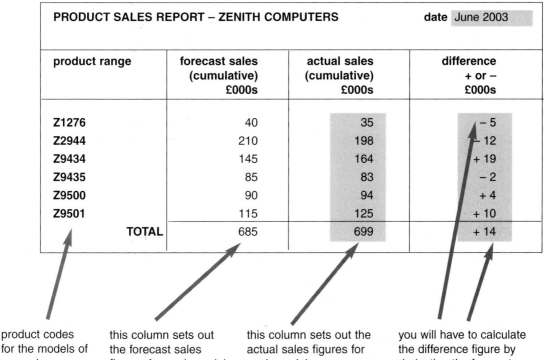

FORMATS FOR 'ONE-OFF' REQUESTS FOR INFORMATION

email and memo (memorandum)

These formats can be used for 'one-off' requests for information by managers.

Emails are used internally if the business has an intranet (a system of computers on-line within the organisation). Memos are used as a traditional paper-based means of communication within the business. Both can be used to send confidential information within the organisation, if required. Emails have the advantage of speed of production and transmission. Also, people also tend to reply to emails more quickly.

The first example below shows how the Production Manager of Zenith Computers is concerned about the labour cost reported for June – it is £15,000 higher than expected (see page 515). He sends an email on the intranet and the Accounts Department replies on the same day.

email request

Zenith Computers Intranet. John Henson. 18 06 03. 10.32. Re: labour costs.

To <Ivor Lewinski. Accounts.003> from <John Henson. Production.002>
18.06.03.10.32.34. Subject: re: labour costs

Hello Ivor

Please send me a breakdown of the labour costs for June, Week 2. I need information about basic pay, overtime and any bonus payments made. As soon as possible please.

Thanks

Regards

John

email reply

Zenith Computers Intranet. Ivor Lewinski. 18 06 03. 14.32. Re: labour costs.

To <John Henson. Production.002> from<Ivor Lewinski. Accounts.003>
18.06.03.16.45.17. Subject: re: labour costs

Hi John

The £80,000 labour costs for June Week 2 comprised £65,100 basic pay and £14,900 overtime. There were no bonus payments.

Regards

Ivor

The same communication could have been done by memorandum, but emails have a number of advantages:

- they take less time to write
- they get to their destination more quickly
- they are likely to be answered more quickly
- they are more informal and 'friendly'

This is clearly why emails are becoming more popular.

If the request for information shown on the previous page was carried out by memorandum, the request and replies would look like this:

memo request

MEMORANDUM

To Ivor Lewinski, Accounts Department **Ref** JH2101

From John Henson, Production Department **Date** 18 June 2003

Subject Labour Costs, June 2003, Week 2

Please send me a breakdown of the labour costs for June, Week 2.

I urgently need information about basic pay, overtime and any bonus payments made.

Many thanks.

John Henson
Production Department

memo reply

MEMORANDUM

To John Henson, Production Department **Ref** IL3411

From Ivor Lewinski, Accounts Department **Date** 19 June 2003

Subject Labour Costs, June 2003, Week 2

Thank you for your memo of 18 June.

The £80,000 labour costs for June Week 2 comprise £65,100 basic pay and £14,900 overtime. There were no bonus payments made in that week.

Ivor Lewinski
Accounts Department

using notes to supply information

Notes can be used if the information is simple and the request is very urgent. For example, the request for a breakdown of labour costs could have been telephoned through to the Accounts Department:

> *'Please send me a breakdown of the labour costs for June, Week 2. Can you make it urgent? I need the figures by the end of tomorrow.'*

The Accounts Department will then extract the information and write it on a note pad and take it or fax it through to the Production Department. The note will look like this:

> **note to**
>
> *John Henson*   *18 June 2003*
>
> *June Week 2 labour costs of £80,000 were made up of:*
>
> *£65,100 basic pay*
>
> *£14,900 overtime*
>
> *No bonuses were involved.*
>
> *Regards*
> *Ivor*

using letters to supply information

Letters are not often used for requesting and supplying internal management information, they are more commonly used for external communications. They could be used, however, for sending information within a large business which operates from a number of sites, although this is more likely to be done by fax, or increasingly, by email.

The one main advantage of letters is that they can be used to send confidential information. A letter addressed to the Accounts Manager and marked 'Confidential' should only be opened by that Manager.

An example letter is shown on the next page. Read it through now.

In this case Mr Lewinski can reply either by a letter marked 'Confidential', enclosing all the information on a schedule, or alternatively he could email the information to the MD's private mailbox. As you will appreciate, if this information got into the wrong hands, the company might have serious labour relations problems. Confidentiality here is very important.

Zenith Computers Limited
Unit 17 Westside Industrial Estate
Mereford MR3 5GV
Tel 01908 287422 Fax 01908 287334 email zenith@zenith.co.uk
VAT Reg UK 38771939

CONFIDENTIAL
Ivor Lewinski, Manager
Accounts Department
Zenith Computers Limited

7 July 2003

Dear Mr Lewinski

Labour costs

I am writing on behalf of the Board of Zenith Computers to advise you that the Directors have decided to cut down on the workforce of the company. Labour costs have been increasing at a steady rate over the last two years and in order to make the business more efficient and profitable we need to cut these costs. This will, I am afraid, inevitably mean reducing the workforce by introducing voluntary redundancy and early retirement schemes.

I shall be grateful therefore if you will provide me with the monthly figures over the last twelve month period for the following:

1. Total labour costs for the company
2. A break-down of labour costs by Department, including a breakdown into basic pay, overtime and any bonuses

Please appreciate that this information is of a highly sensitive nature and should be kept strictly confidential.

I shall be grateful to receive these figures by the end of this week.

Yours sincerely

R Hutton

R Hutton
Managing Director

confidentiality and storage

It is important to realise that information may be confidential. Generally:

- internal management information must not be released to any outside body – particularly competitors!
- some internal management information is for restricted circulation; before you undertake a task you must be clear about who can have access and the format you are to use
- management information must be stored carefully so that it is available only to those who should have access to it

USING 'IT' FOR PRESENTING MANAGEMENT INFORMATION

Organisations employ managers to control resources and to make decisions. In order to make effective decisions, managers need information presented to them in a format that they can easily understand and act upon. **Information technology** ('IT') is vital in enabling managers and their staff to complete their duties to a high professional standard.

Word processing software packages can be used for creating memos, letters and reports. **Spreadsheets** are in effect an electronic worksheet and allow the user to enter text, numbers and calculations. They can be used to record and provide information to managers in a variety of different circumstances, for example:

- petty cash and cash transactions
- details of stock items and the movement of stock
- monitoring and controlling of budgets

We will now look at a Case Study which involves using a spreadsheet and a word processor to present information to a manager.

Case Study

WESTBURY LIMITED – USING 'IT' TO PRESENT INFORMATION

situation

Westbury Ltd is a family-run business, which sells office equipment through two retail outlets – in Huntsville and Yorford. David Westbury is the Accounts/Administration Manager and has overall responsibility for controlling expenditure within the business. He is based at the company's head office in Northford.

Tom McDonald is employed as an accounts assistant and is located in the Accounts Department at Westbury's head office. He is responsible for updating the expenditure budget at the end of the month and providing David Westbury with a summary of this information.

At the top of the next page you will see a copy of the spreadsheet that has to be updated.

the spreadsheet explained

The purpose of the spreadsheet is to record the forecast and actual expenditure for a number of items. It is necessary to hold this information to ensure that costs are controlled.

In cell A1 is the spreadsheet title: WESTBURY LTD – EXPENDITURE BUDGET: APRIL 2003

The content of each column is explained below the spreadsheet illustration.

	A	B	C	D	E	F	G
1	WESTBURY LTD - EXPENDITURE BUDGET: APRIL 2003						
2							
3			Forecast for	Actual for		Difference:	
4	Code	Description	month	month	Difference:	As % of forecast	
5			£	£	£		
6	HU-6000	Wages	5,000.00				
7							
8	HU-6010	Staff Training	500.00				
9							
10	HU-6020	Rent and Rates	750.00				
11							
12	YO-6000	Wages	5,500.00				
13							
14	YO-6010	Staff Training	350.00				
15							
16	YO-6020	Rent and Rates	1,000.00				
17							
18		Totals	13,100.00				
19							

COLUMN	DESCRIPTION OF COLUMN HEADING
A	**Code**. The two letters (HU or YO) at the beginning of the code and the four digits (6000, 6010 or 6020) which follow, indicate the retail outlet and the type of expenditure. For example. HU-6000 is the code for wages at the Huntsville outlet and YO 6010 the code for staff training at Yorford.
B	**Description.** This describes the type of expenditure involved (Wages, Staff Training, Rent and Rates).
C	**Forecast for month.** This is what Westbury Ltd expects to spend on each type of expenditure within the specified outlet.
D	**Actual for month.** This is how much Westbury Ltd actually spends on each type of expenditure within the specified outlet. (These are the values that have to be entered by Tom McDonald).
E	**Difference.** This is the difference between Forecast for month (Column C) and Actual for month (Column D). It is automatically calculated when the actual values are entered into the spreadsheet in Column D.
F	**Difference: As % of forecast.** This calculation expresses the Difference (Column E) as a percentage of the Forecast for month (Column C) and is automatically calculated when the actual values are entered into the spreadsheet.
C, D, E & F	**Totals** Formulae have been entered which automatically calculate the totals of the entries in columns C, D, E and F. Note: the total for column C is £13,100. When Tom updates the spreadsheet, the totals for the other columns will be automatically calculated.

updating the spreadsheet

At the end of each month it is the responsibility of Tom McDonald to update the spreadsheet with the actual expenditure that has been incurred for each type of expense at each of the two outlets. This done as follows . . .

1 At the end of April 2003 the managers of the Huntsville and Yorford outlets will each send Tom an email. These contain details of how much actual expenditure has been incurred by each branch. A summary of this information is shown below:

Huntsville: Actual Expenditure for April 2003	
Wages	£5,500
Staff Training	£480
Rent and Rates	£766

Yorford: Actual Expenditure for April 2003	
Wages	£5,500
Staff Training	£340
Rent and Rates	£980

Tom will use this information to update the Expenditure Budget spreadsheet.

2 Tom will locate and open the Expenditure Budget spreadsheet. It will appear on the screen as shown on the previous page.

3 Tom will enter the actual results into the spreadsheet using the following cell references:

Cell D6	Tom enters £5,500
Cell D8	Tom enters £480
Cell D10	Tom enters £766
Cell D12	Tom enters £5,500
Cell D14	Tom enters £340
Cell D16	Tom enters £980

4 Having entered the actual results, Tom will now save the updated spreadsheet.

5 Tom will prepare a memo regarding the updated expenditure budget for the attention of the Accounts/Administration Manager, David Westbury.

The updated spreadsheet is shown on the top of the next page.

	A	B	C	D	E	F
1	WESTBURY LTD - EXPENDITURE BUDGET: APRIL 2003					
2						
3			Forecast for	Actual for		Difference:
4	Code	Description	month	month	Difference:	As % of forecast
5			£	£	£	
6	HU-6000	Wages	5,000.00	5,500.00	-500.00	-10.00%
7						
8	HU-6010	Staff Training	500.00	480.00	20.00	4.00%
9						
10	HU-6020	Rent and Rates	750.00	766.00	-16.00	-2.13%
11						
12	YO-6000	Wages	5,500.00	5,500.00	0.00	0.00%
13						
14	YO-6010	Staff Training	350.00	340.00	10.00	2.86%
15						
16	YO-6020	Rent and Rates	1,000.00	980.00	20.00	2.00%
17						
18		Totals	13,100.00	13,566.00	-466.00	-3.56%

what does the updated spreadsheet show us?

Using the spreadsheet to automatically produce the figures in columns E and F saves time and effort having to carry out manual calculations. It is also more accurate and the information is immediately available to managers.

For two of the items (HU-6000 and HU-6020) the **Actual for month** has exceeded the **Forecast for month**. This is shown by the negative values in cells E6 and E10 which are present in the **Difference** column. For one item (YO-6000) the **Actual for month** equals the **Forecast for month**. For the remaining items the forecast value is greater than the actual expenditure. This is a positive development and means that the company has spent less money than anticipated.

Calculating **Difference: As % of forecast** indicates the scale of the problem faced by the company if **Actual for month** exceeds **Forecast for month**. Often it is easier to understand financial information if values are presented as percentages. The spreadsheet shows a –10.00% difference for wages at the Huntsville outlet. The manager must identify the reasons for this difference and take action to reduce actual expenditure.

preparing a word processed memo

Having updated the budget expenditure spreadsheet Tom must now prepare a memo for the attention of the Accounts/Administration Manager, David Westbury.

To ensure that the business is run efficiently and effectively, David is required to read and analyse data from a wide variety of sources. Therefore, it is vital that financial information is presented to him in a format that he can easily and quickly understand. Consequently, Tom is required to bring to the attention of David Westbury any differences between actual and forecast expenditure that exceed 3%. The completed word processed memo appears on the screen as shown on the next page.

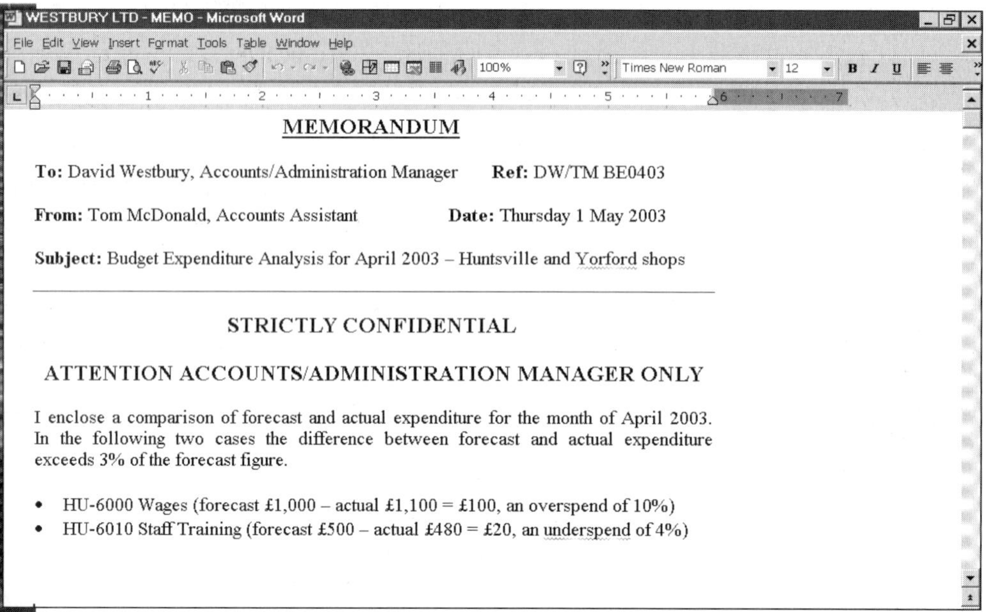

MEMORANDUM

To: David Westbury, Accounts/Administration Manager **Ref:** DW/TM BE0403

From: Tom McDonald, Accounts Assistant **Date:** Thursday 1 May 2003

Subject: Budget Expenditure Analysis for April 2003 – Huntsville and Yorford shops

STRICTLY CONFIDENTIAL

ATTENTION ACCOUNTS/ADMINISTRATION MANAGER ONLY

I enclose a comparison of forecast and actual expenditure for the month of April 2003. In the following two cases the difference between forecast and actual expenditure exceeds 3% of the forecast figure.

- HU-6000 Wages (forecast £1,000 – actual £1,100 = £100, an overspend of 10%)
- HU-6010 Staff Training (forecast £500 – actual £480 = £20, an underspend of 4%)

company house style

To ensure consistency in terms of presenting financial information it is important for organisations to have a 'house style' implemented – ie a standard method of setting out data and communications. The house style will often be kept on computer file as word-processed or spreadsheet templates, eg for letters, memos and standard reports. The elements of the memo prepared by Tom are explained as follows.

MEMORANDUM	This heading is placed at the top of the document and informs the recipient what the document is.
To: and **From:**	The name and job title of the recipient and the sender must be stated.
Ref: DW/TM BE0403	This shows the initials of the recipient and the sender, the subject matter under review (ie 'BE' indicates Budget Expenditure) and the time period involved (0403 indicates April 2003).
Date:	The date on which the memo was prepared.
Subject:	The subject of the memo – in this case the budget analysis.

As far as the content is concerned, Tom has highlighted those items where the difference between actual and forecast expenditure exceeds 3%. Note that the memo is shown as being confidential and is not for the whole staff to read.

David Westbury will digest the information contained within the Expenditure Budget spreadsheet and in the memo prepared by Tom. If he has particular concerns about any of the figures he will contact the managers at the Huntsville and Yorford outlets to discuss what action should be taken to rectify the situation.

Chapter Summary

- Managers need information so that they can carry out the management functions of planning, making decisions and controlling the business.
- Managers need financial information relating to costs and to income.
- Some management information is taken from the ledgers which form part of the financial accounting system – they show a record of actual financial transactions which have taken place in the past.
- Some management information is taken from the summaries and budgets which form part of the management accounting system – they estimate future performance.
- Before gathering financial information, a number of questions have to be asked so that the user's needs can be met:
  - who needs the information?
  - what type of information is it?
  - what level of detail is required?
  - what level of accuracy is required?
  - in what format is it to be presented?
  - when does it have to be presented?
  - how confidential is the information?
- Presenting management information involves comparing financial data:
  - the present period with the previous period – this month and last month
  - the corresponding period – this month with the same month last year
  - comparisons with forecasts – this month's actual results against forecast
- Managers will want to know the differences (variances) between actual and forecast figures so that they can take action if they need to.
- Income differences (variances) are calculated using the formula

  actual figures <u>minus</u> forecast figures <u>equals</u> difference (variance)
- Cost differences (variances) are calculated using the formula

  forecast figures <u>minus</u> actual figures <u>equals</u> difference (variance)

  Remember that this formula varies for income and cost differences.
- It is important to use the appropriate format when presenting management information. Formats include: letter, email, memo, note and standard report forms such as a cost report and a budgetary control report.
- Information technology is a useful tool in processing management information. Spreadsheets can be used for speeding up the 'number crunching' needed in working out the differences between budgeted and actual figures. Word-processing applications can be used for reporting the data, often using a pre-determined house style.

Key Terms

manager — a person whose role it is in an organisation to plan, make decisions, and control business activity

management information — financial information relating to the income and costs of the business

financial accounting — accounting records of transactions which have already taken place

management accounting — summaries of what has happened in the past and estimates of future performance

previous period — a comparison of financial data for the present and the last period – eg this month compared with last month

corresponding period — a comparison of financial data for the present period and the same period in the past, eg this June and last June

cumulative data — results from time periods, eg months, added together as the year progresses to produce 'the year so far' figures

forecast data — financial data which is forecast for budgeting purposes

difference — the difference between actual and forecast figures – also known as the variance

income difference — actual figure *minus* forecast figure

cost difference — forecast figure *minus* actual figure

positive difference — in the case of *income* figures a positive difference means that actual income is *higher* than forecast

in the case of *cost* figures, a positive difference means that actual costs are *lower* than forecast

negative difference — in the case of *income* figures, a negative difference means that actual income is *lower* than forecast

in the case of *cost* figures a negative difference means that actual costs are *higher* than forecast

standard cost report — a summary of differences between forecast and actual figures, broken down into different types of costs – materials, labour and expenses

budgetary control report — a comparison of actual and forecast figures for costs or income over a period of time

management accounts — reports which provide managers with information about specific aspects of cost or income

Student Activities

Note on using IT: *a number of the activities here provide opportunities for using spreadsheets and word-processing programs to produce evidence. Most of the activities require students to prepare the files for themselves. The files for Activity 24.10, however, are available from* www.osbornebooks.co.uk

24.1 Financial accounting aims to provide information for people outside the business. True or false?

TRUE ✓

24.2 Management accounting aims to provide information for people outside the business. True or false?

FALSE ✓

24.3 It is important to meet the user's needs when you are gathering information for managers. List five of the points that you will have to bear in mind when requested to provide information.

BY WHEN | HOW ACCURATE | WHAT FORMAT / HOW DETAILED | CONFIDENTIAL? ✓

24.4 The tables set out below show the quarterly sales and costs for Clarion Cards over two years. Study the tables and answer the questions that follow.

QUARTERLY SALES	Year 2002 Actual £000s	Year 2003 Forecast £000s	Year 2003 Actual £000s
Jan-Mar	300	310	320
Apr-Jun	350	370	375
Jul-Sep	380	400	410
Oct-Dec	400	440	450
	1430	*1520*	*1555*

QUARTERLY COSTS	Year 2002 Actual £000s	Year 2003 Forecast £000s	Year 2003 Actual £000s
Jan-Mar	200	220	225
Apr-Jun	210	240	248
Jul-Sep	230	245	255
Oct-Dec	280	300	320
	920	*1005*	*1048*
		40,000 ✓	

(a) What is the increase in actual sales between the last quarter of 2003 and the previous quarter?

(b) What is the increase in sales between the last quarter of 2003 and the corresponding quarter in 2002? *50,000* ✓

(c) What is the difference between actual and forecast sales in the second quarter of 2003? *+5000*

(d) What is the increase in actual costs between the second quarter of 2003 and the previous quarter? *+23,000* ✓

(e) What is the increase in actual costs between the third quarter of 2003 and the corresponding quarter in 2002? *+25,000* ✓

(f) What is the difference between actual and forecast costs in the fourth quarter of 2003? *-20,000* ✓

(g) You receive the following memo:

MEMORANDUM	
To Ally Gee, Accounts Supervisor	**Ref** BS234
From B Simpson, Sales Manager	**Date** 5 January 2004
Subject Sales and Costs Figures	

Please can you supply the following figures as soon as possible

1. Total sales and costs for 2002
2. Total sales and costs for 2003

How do the actual sales and costs figures for 2003 vary from the forecast sales and costs for that year?

Total up the actual sales and costs for 2002 and 2003 and draw up a table to present the figures, comparing them with the forecasts. A suggested layout is shown below. Write out a suitable memorandum addressed to B Simpson attaching the table and stating how the actual results differ from the forecasts.

***Optional:** use a word-processing program to produce the table and the memorandum.*

	2002 *actual* £000s	2003 *actual* £000s	2003 *forecast* £000s
Total Sales	1430	1555	1520
Total Costs	920	1048	1005

ACTUAL 2003 SALES FIGURES ARE 35000 UP ON FORECAST
COSTS ARE 43,000 UP ON FORECAST

24.5 You work in the Accounts Department of Grampian Plastics and receive the following email from the Sales Manager.

Grampian Plastics Intranet. Iain Mackenzie. 18 01 04. 10.32. Re: Sales figures.

To <Jack Stewart. Accounts.002> from<Iain Mackenzie. Sales.001> 18.01.04.10.32.14. Subject: Re: Sales figures.

Jack

Please fax me the monthly figures for last year's export sales. I need the figures for each month and also the cumulative figures month-by-month. Many thanks.

Iain Mackenzie

You look in your records and extract the monthly sales figures for Grampian Plastics for 2003. They are as follows (quoted in £000s):

January £120, February £130, March £125, April £131, May £139, June £141, July £146,

August £137, September £139, October £143, November £147, December £135.

Draw up a suitable chart (or spreadsheet file and printout) for faxing to the Sales Manager. You are not sure about the format, but your supervisor suggests when you ask her that you run the figures in two vertical columns headed 'Monthly sales' and 'Cumulative sales'.

24.6 Which one of the following formulas shows the calculation for income differences?

A actual figure *minus* forecast figure A ✓

B actual figure *add* forecast figure

C forecast figure *minus* actual figure

D forecast figure *add* actual figure

24.7 Koala Giftware is a business which imports craft products from Australia and sells them to a wide range of UK giftshop outlets. You have just been given the sales and costs figures for the last quarter. They are:

Sales	October-December 2003	£205,000
Costs	October-December 2003	£161,000

You are to complete the sales and costs reports shown below by:

(a) entering the final quarter's figures in the 'Actual' columns

(b) totalling the 'Actual' columns

(c) calculating the differences, adding the plus or minus sign as appropriate

(d) calculating the total (net) differences in the bottom line of each form

Optional: set up the two reports on spreadsheet files to provide evidence.

KOALA GIFTWARE – QUARTERLY SALES

	Year 2003 Forecast	Year 2003 Actual	Difference + or –
Jan-Mar	160,000	165,000	+5,000
Apr-Jun	170,000	175,000	+ 5,000
Jul-Sep	180,000	182,000	+ 2,000
Oct-Dec	195,000	205,000	+10,000
TOTAL	705,000	727,000	+ 22,000

KOALA GIFTWARE – QUARTERLY COSTS

	Year 2003 Forecast	Year 2003 Actual	Difference + or –
Jan-Mar	110,000	105,000	+5,000
Apr-Jun	120,000	115,000	+5,000
Jul-Sep	150,000	149,000	+1,000
Oct-Dec	165,000	161,000	+4,000
TOTAL	545,000	530,000	+15,000

24.8 Tempus Clocks manufactures reproduction antique clocks at its factory in Deddington in Oxfordshire. Your name is R Hand and you work in the Accounts Department. You have been asked to complete the Standard Cost Report for April 2003. The cost figures you have extracted from the accounts are: materials £34,890; labour £17,560; expenses £19,100. You are to enter the figures on the report and calculate the differences, marking them with a minus or plus sign as appropriate. You are also to total the 'actual' figures and find the net difference and enter the figures on the bottom line. You may wish to set up the report on a spreadsheet file.

STANDARD COST REPORT – TEMPUS CLOCKS

product repro clocks **date** 01 05 03

period April 03

	forecast cost	actual cost	difference + or –
materials	35,500	34,890	+ 610
labour	15,800	17,560	– 1760
expenses	18,500	19,100	– 600
TOTAL	69,800	71,550	–1750

The following day you receive this note from the Production Manager:

> **Note to** R Hand, Accounts Dept **date** 2 May 2003
>
> Please can you let me know the breakdown of the April labour figure of £17,560? It seems very high and is well above the forecast figure.
> Thanks
> Tom Gilks, Production Manager

You find from your investigations that the April wages bill consists of £14,040 basic pay and £3,520 overtime. The high overtime figure was due to a machine failure which resulted in production staff having to stay on later than normal to meet production targets.

You are to draft a memorandum to Tom Gilks, providing the figures and explaining the reason for the difference. You may wish to set up the memo on a word-processed file to provide evidence.

24.9 You work in the Accounts Department of a large company and often have to provide financial data to your own boss, and to other Departments. What method of communicating management information would you use in the following cases? Give reasons for your choice of format, stating the level of confidentiality required in each case.

(a) You are asked by your Sales Director to provide the Area Managers throughout the UK with details of the commission paid to their sales representatives.

(b) You are asked by your boss for the last month's sales figures for Products A and B.

(c) You are emailed for sales figures by a sales rep who has a laptop connected to the internet.

24.10 Eastern Ltd is a family-run business, which sells computer supplies through two retail outlets in Todford and Ashville. David Norton is the Accounts/Administration Manager and has overall responsibility for controlling expenditure within the business. He is based at the company's head office in Southbury.

You are employed as an accounts assistant and are located in the Accounts Department at Eastern's head office. You are responsible for updating the expenditure budget spreadsheet at the end of the month and providing David Norton with a summary of this information.

Today's date is 1 May 2003 and the managers of the Todford and Ashville outlets have each sent you an email, which contain details of how much actual expenditure has been incurred by each branch. A summary of this information is shown below:

Todford: Actual Expenditure for April 2003

Wages	£9,700
General expenses	£750
Premises rent	£1,600

Ashville: Actual Expenditure for April 2003

Wages	£12,220
General expenses	£670
Premises rent	£1,300

Note: *for this Activity you will need two computer files*

- *the Excel file 'Eastern Limited spreadsheet.xls' (the screen shown below)*
- *the Word file 'Eastern Limited memo.doc'*

These files can be downloaded from the Student Resources page on www.osbornebooks.co.uk or they may available from your tutor. Alternatively, you may wish to construct the files yourself. Note, however, that the formulas required for the spreadsheet are complex, and you may need help.

File Edit View Insert Format Tools Data Window Help

Arial 10 100%

F23 =

	A	B	C	D	E	F
1	EASTERN LTD - EXPENDITURE BUDGET: APRIL 2003					
2						
3			Forecast for	Actual for		Difference:
4	Code	Description	month	month	Difference:	As % of forecast
5			£	£	£	
6	TO-6000	Wages	10,210.00	9,700-00	+510-00	+5.0
7						
8	T0-6010	General expenses	735.00	750-00	-15-00	-2.0
9						
10	T0-6020	Premises rent	1,600.00	1,600-00	0-00	0.0
11						
12	AS-6000	Wages	11,650.00	12,220-00	-570-00	-4.9
13						
14	AS-6010	General expenses	700.00	670-00	+30-00	+4.3
15						
16	AS-6020	Premises rent	1,275.00	1,300-00	-25-00	-2.0
17						
18		Totals	26,170.00	26,240-00	-70-00	-0.3

You are to:

(a) Load the 'Eastern Limited spreadsheet.xls' on your computer and enter the information shown on the previous page (the data reported from the Todford and Ashville outlets) in the appropriate cells in column D.

As you enter the information you will note how columns E and F are automatically updated.

(b) Save the updated file and print out a copy of the spreadsheet. It should tally with the printout on page 681 of this book.

(c) Prepare a word-processed memo regarding the updated expenditure budget spreadsheet for the attention of the Accounts/Administration Manager, David Norton. The purpose of this memo is to highlight any differences between actual and forecast expenditure that exceed 3%.

If you need guidance on the format and content of the memo, look at the example in the Case Study on page 526 and adopt this as the 'house style'.

A Word file 'Eastern Limited memo.doc' may be downloaded from the Student Resources page on www.osbornebooks.co.uk or you may be able to obtain it from your tutor.

(d) Save the memo file and print out a copy.

Computer Accounting

Practical exercises

This final section of this book contains a series of chapters which take you through the computer accounting requirements of Units 1 to 3. It is recommended that you complete your study of Units 1 to 3 before tackling these chapters and exercises.

The chapters contain text and Case Studies which explain how computer accounting – using Sage software – works in practice. Most chapters conclude with an inputting exercise which enables you to enter accounting data into your computer and print out the evidence you need.

The chapters are written around a single business – Pronto Supplies Limited – which buys and sells computer equipment and software. You will be supplied with a 'Company.25' file which has the company set up on it. All you will have to do is to enter details of invoices, credit notes and payments, as required by your course, and print out various daybooks, documents and reports. These will provide you with the assessment evidence you need for your Portfolio. Details of this evidence is set out at the beginning of this book, on page 3.

If you have any problems obtaining the 'Company.25' file call Osborne Books on 01905 748071.

25 Setting up the computer accounts and ledgers

this chapter covers . . .

This chapter explains how a business – Pronto Supplies Limited – sets up its accounting records on the computer.

It is important that you read the chapter carefully. It explains how the account and ledger structure of the Sage Line 50 software used here relates to the accounts and ledger system you have studied in Units 1 to 3. You will see that there are great similarities, although some of the terminology used is slightly different.

You will not have to input the company details or the customer or supplier accounts – that is all done for you on the files provided by Osborne Books.

This chapter covers:

- *the transfer of data from a manual accounting system to a computer accounting system*
- *the accounts in the Nominal Ledger (another term for the Main Ledger)*
- *the production of a trial balance from the Nominal Ledger*

NVQ PERFORMANCE CRITERIA COVERED

Chapters 25 to 28 cover between them the 'computerised' aspects of the range statement relating to the performance criteria for Units 1, 2 and 3.

Details of the evidence which will be produced by the exercises in Chapters 26, 27, and 28 are set out on page 3 at the beginning of this book. There are no exercises in this introductory chapter, which shows how a computer accounting system can be set up.

technical note

The computer transactions contained in this chapter are contained in a file called 'Company.25' which should be available from your tutor. The software used for this backup is Sage Line 50, version 4, which can be read by any subsequent version of Sage Line 50. The version used for illustrating the text is version 7 of Sage Line 50.

If you have any difficulty in obtaining this file, please call 01905 748071.

WHY SAGE AND WHICH SAGE?

Osborne Books (the publisher of this book) has chosen Sage software for this text for two very good reasons:

1 Sage software is widely used in business and is recognised as a user-friendly and reliable product.

2 Osborne Books has used Sage itself for over ten years and is well used to the way it works.

The Sage software used for illustrating this book is Sage Line 50 Accountant Plus (Version 7) for Windows. The screens displayed in this book are reproduced from this version by kind permission of Sage PLC.

screen illustrations

It should be appreciated that some training centres and businesses may be using older (or newer) versions, and so some of the screens may look slightly different. This does not matter. Using Sage is like driving different models of car – the controls may be located in slightly different places and the dashboard may not look exactly the same, but the controls are still there and they still do the same thing. So if the screens shown here look unfamiliar, examine them carefully and you will see that they contain the same (or very similar) Sage icons and functions as the version you are using.

Case Study

PRONTO SUPPLIES LIMITED: SETTING UP THE COMPANY IN SAGE

the business

Pronto Supplies is a limited company run by Tom Cox who has worked as a computer consultant for over ten years. Pronto Supplies provides local businesses and other organisations with computer hardware, software and all the other computer 'bits and pieces' such as disks and ink cartridges needed in offices. It also provides consultancy for computer set-ups through its proprietor, Tom Cox. Pronto Supplies has eight employees in total. The business is situated on an industrial estate, at Unit 17 Severnvale Estate, Broadwater Road, Mereford, Wyvern, MR1 6TF.

the accounting system

Pronto Supplies Limited started business on 1 January 2001. The business is registered for VAT (ie it charges VAT on its sales) and after a month of using a manual accounting system Tom has decided to transfer the accounts to Sage Line 50 software and sign up for a year's telephone technical support. Tom has also decided to put his payroll onto the computer, but this will be run on a separate Sage program.

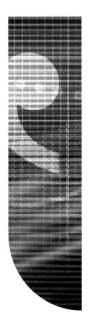

Tom has chosen Sage Line 50 because it will enable him to:

- record the invoices issued to his customers to whom he sells on credit
- pay his suppliers on the due date
- keep a record of his bank receipts and payments
- record his income and expenses, business assets and loans in a main (nominal) ledger

In short he will have a computer accounting package which will enable him to:

- record all his financial transactions
- print out reports
- manage his business finances
- save time (and money) in running his accounting system

TRANSFERRING DATA INTO SAGE

When a business first sets up a computer accounting system a substantial amount of data will need to be transferred onto the computer, even if the business is in its first week of trading.

A summary of this data is shown in the diagram opposite. This transfer is normally done manually, but certain data, eg names and addresses of customers and suppliers might be held already on a different computer program and can be transferred into Sage automatically.

As noted earlier, you will not have to do this data transfer yourself, as it has all been done for you on a file (prepared by Osborne Books) called 'Company.25'. You (or your teaching centre) can install this file on your computer, and this will enable you to get going in Sage and to input the transactions in the next chapter.

The images shown below and in the diagram are the icons on the Sage desktop which represent the different operating areas of the program. As you can see they very much relate to the ledger structure of the manual book-keeping system . . .

from manual records to computer records - an overview

manual records	Sage records
Sales Ledger (accounts of customers who are given credit) - names - addresses - balances (amounts owed)	**Customers** the computerised Sales Ledger
Purchases Ledger (accounts of suppliers who allow credit) - names - addresses - balances (amounts owing)	**Suppliers** the computerised Purchases Ledger
Main Ledger accounts which record: - income - expenses - assets (items owned) - liabilities (loans etc) - capital invested by owner - control accounts	**Nominal** the computerised Nominal (Main) Ledger Note that the bank accounts are listed in Nominal Ledger but are operated through a separate icon
Cash Book accounts which record: - money paid into the bank - money paid out of the bank - petty cash (office cash)	(as Nominal above)

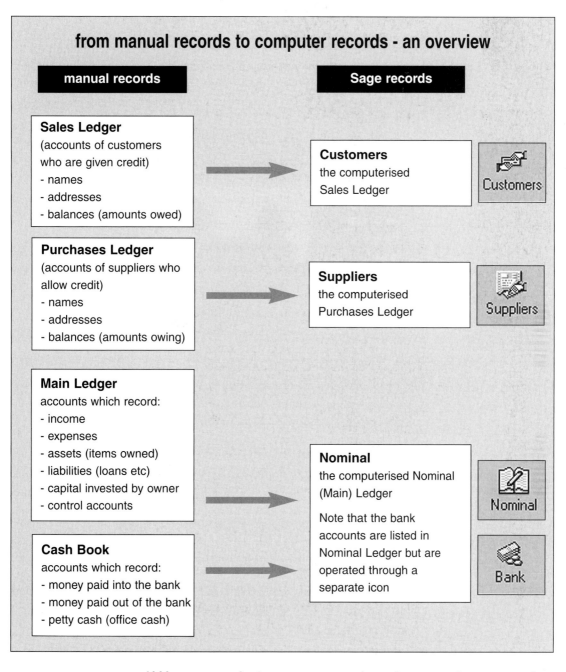

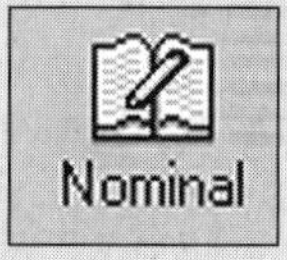

differences between manual and computer records

The main difference to note between the manual and computer accounting records is that the Main Ledger is called the **Nominal Ledger,** a term which is in common use in accounting. In these remaining chapters we will therefore refer to 'nominal accounts' and 'nominal ledger'. When writing in your Exam and Skills Tests, you should use the term 'Main Ledger'.

setting up the organisation details

Setting up a computer accounting system – as seen in the diagram on the previous pages – involves a number of stages. Normally the organisation details are input first: the name, address, telephone, fax, email, and so on. Other details such the VAT registration and financial year-end are also input at this stage.

The screen below shows the details entered for Pronto Supplies Limited.

SETTING UP THE SALES LEDGER

The next step is to input all the details of the customers to whom the business sells on credit. The type of details required include:

- customer name and address
- customer code (a coding reference used on the computer system)
- credit limit
- any discount terms (trade and settlement or cash discounts)
- any analysis code, eg type of customer, region of customer etc
- the balance of the customer's account

Study the input on the 'Customer Record' screen at the top of the next page.

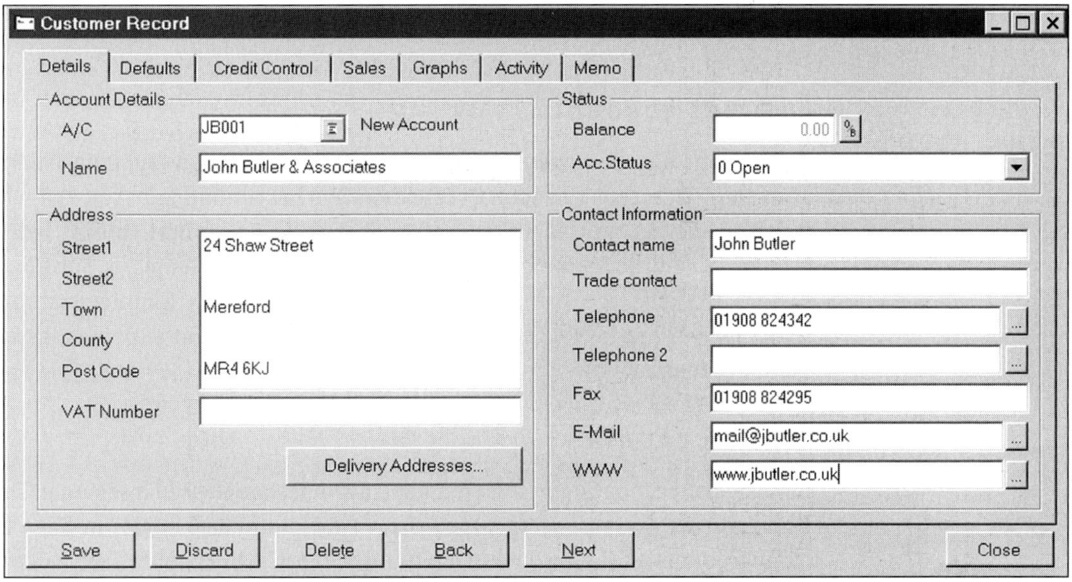

SETTING UP THE PURCHASES LEDGER

The next step is to set up all the supplier accounts, including their opening balances, in the same way:

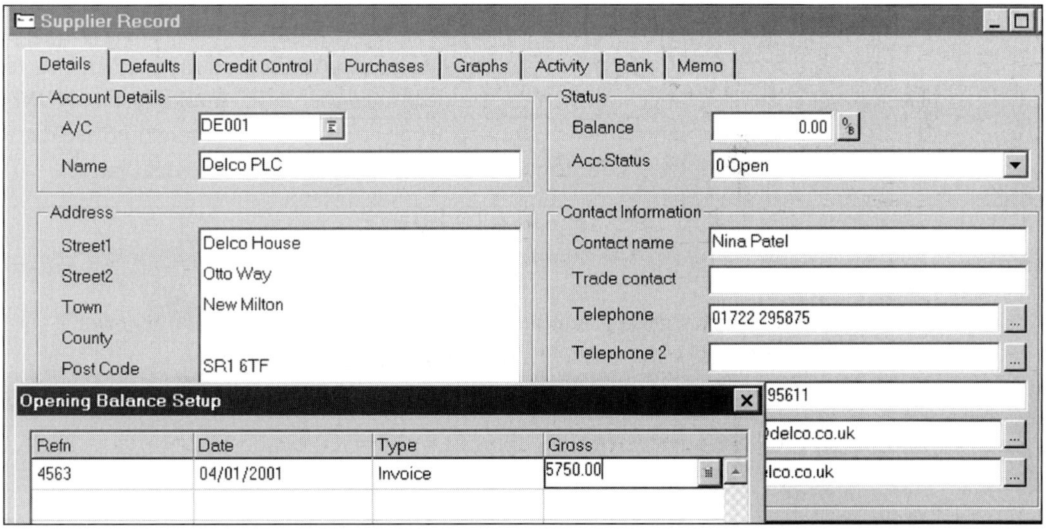

When this data has been input, the Subsidiary Ledgers (Sales and Purchases) – including the balances – will be set up on the system.

The next step will be to set up the Nominal (Main) Ledger.

NOMINAL (MAIN) LEDGER ACCOUNTS

nominal accounts

An account in a computer accounting system works as a 'running balance account' – it records financial transactions and has a running balance of what is left in the account at the end of each day. The **nominal (main) ledger** accounts in any accounting system are the accounts which are not Subsidiary Ledger accounts, ie Customer accounts (Sales ledger) or Supplier accounts (Purchases ledger). Nominal accounts record income and expenses, assets, liabilities and capital.

bank accounts

In a manual accounting system the bank accounts are kept in a separate Cash Book and are not strictly speaking part of the Nominal Ledger. In Sage the bank accounts of the business (including Petty Cash Account) are *listed* in NOMINAL, but they are *operated* from a separate BANK icon, just as in a manual accounting system the bank transactions are recorded in a separate Cash Book.

the default Nominal accounts

When Tom Cox in the Case Study set up his company he chose the set of nominal accounts automatically provided by the Sage program. These 'default' accounts are common to most Sage systems, although they may vary slightly from version to version. If you click on the NOMINAL icon in the Sage opening screen the accounts are to be found in the NOMINAL opening screen (see below). You can scroll down this screen to see the whole list. A typical SAGE nominal list is reproduced on the next page.

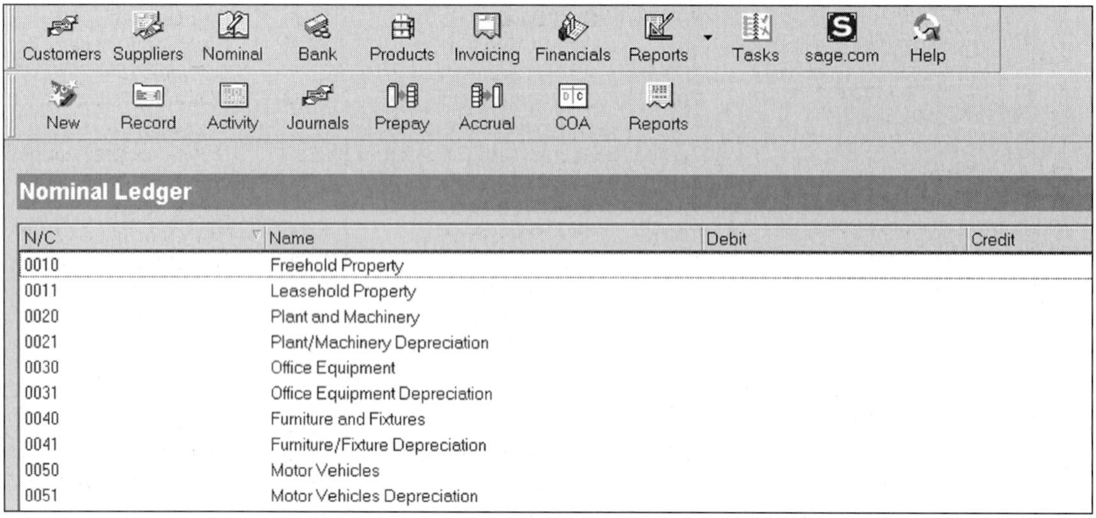

Nominal Account List

0010	Freehold Property
0011	Leasehold Property
0020	Plant and Machinery
0021	Plant/Machinery Depreciation
0030	Office Equipment
0031	Office Equipment Depreciation
0040	Furniture and Fixtures
0041	Furniture/Fixture Depreciation
0050	Motor Vehicles
0051	Motor Vehicles Depreciation
1001	Stock
1002	Work in Progress
1003	Finished Goods
1100	Debtors Control Account
1101	Sundry Debtors
1102	Other Debtors
1103	Prepayments
1200	Bank Current Account
1210	Bank Deposit Account
1220	Building Society Account
1230	Petty Cash
1240	Company Credit Card
1250	Credit Card Receipts
2100	Creditors Control Account
2101	Sundry Creditors
2102	Other Creditors
2109	Accruals
2200	Sales Tax Control Account
2201	Purchase Tax Control Account
2202	VAT Liability
2210	P.A.Y.E.
2211	National Insurance
2220	Net Wages
2230	Pension Fund
2300	Loans
2310	Hire Purchase
2320	Corporation Tax
2330	Mortgages
3000	Ordinary Shares
3010	Preference Shares
3100	Reserves
3101	Undistributed Reserves
3200	Profit and Loss Account
4000	Sales Type A
4001	Sales Type B
4002	Sales Type C
4009	Discounts Allowed
4100	Sales Type D
4101	Sales Type E
4200	Sales of Assets
4400	Credit Charges (Late Payments)
4900	Miscellaneous Income
4901	Royalties Received
4902	Commissions Received
4903	Insurance Claims
4904	Rent Income
4905	Distribution and Carriage
5000	Materials Purchased
5001	Materials Imported
5002	Miscellaneous Purchases
5003	Packaging
5009	Discounts Taken
5100	Carriage
5101	Import Duty
5102	Transport Insurance
5200	Opening Stock
5201	Closing Stock
6000	Productive Labour
6001	Cost of Sales Labour
6002	Sub-Contractors
6100	Sales Commissions
6200	Sales Promotions
6201	Advertising
6202	Gifts and Samples
6203	P.R.(Literature & Brochures)
6900	Miscellaneous Expenses
7000	Gross Wages
7001	Directors Salaries
7002	Directors Remuneration
7003	Staff Salaries
7004	Wages-Regular
7005	Wages-Casual
7006	Employers N.I.
7007	Employers Pensions
7008	Recruitment Expenses
7009	Adjustments
7010	SSP Reclaimed
7011	SMP Reclaimed
7100	Rent
7102	Water Rates
7103	General Rates
7104	Premises Insurance
7200	Electricity
7201	Gas
7202	Oil
7203	Other Heating Costs
7300	Fuel and Oil
7301	Repairs and Servicing
7302	Licences
7303	Vehicle Insurance
7304	Miscellaneous Motor Expenses
7350	Scale Charges
7400	Travelling
7401	Car Hire
7402	Hotels
7403	U.K. Entertainment
7404	Overseas Entertainment
7405	Overseas Travelling
7406	Subsistence
7500	Printing
7501	Postage and Carriage
7502	Telephone
7503	Telex/Telegram/ Facsimile
7504	Office Stationery
7505	Books etc.
7600	Legal Fees
7601	Audit and Accountancy Fees
7602	Consultancy Fees
7603	Professional Fees
7700	Equipment Hire
7701	Office Machine Maintenance
7800	Repairs and Renewals
7801	Cleaning
7802	Laundry
7803	Premises Expenses
7900	Bank Interest Paid
7901	Bank Charges
7902	Currency Charges
7903	Loan Interest Paid
7904	H.P. Interest
7905	Credit Charges
8000	Depreciation
8001	Plant/Machinery Depreciation
8002	Furniture/Fitting Depreciation
8003	Vehicle Depreciation
8004	Office Equipment Depreciation
8100	Bad Debt Write Off
8102	Bad Debt Provision
8200	Donations
8201	Subscriptions
8202	Clothing Costs
8203	Training Costs
8204	Insurance
8205	Refreshments
9998	Suspense Account
9999	Mispostings Account

We will now look at a Case Study showing how Pronto Supplies Limited sets up the nominal accounts and extracts an initial trial balance. As mentioned above, all these transactions have already been input for you on the 'Company.25' file.

Case Study

PRONTO SUPPLIES LIMITED: SETTING UP THE NOMINAL ACCOUNTS

Pronto Supplies Limited was set up in January 2001 and during that month operated a **manual** book-keeping system using hand-written double-entry ledger accounts.

It was a busy month for Tom Cox . . .

financing Tom paid £75,000 into the bank as ordinary share capital (his 'capital') to start up the business.

Tom also raised a £35,000 business loan from the bank.

assets The finance raised enabled Tom to buy:

office machines	£35,000
office equipment & computers	£15,000
furniture for the office	£25,000

purchases Tom bought in a substantial amount of stock during January for £69,100.

All of this stock was for resale by Pronto Supplies Limited.

sales Tom divided his sales into three types:

Computer hardware sales

Computer software sales

Computer consultancy

overheads Tom also had to pay expenses including:

Wages	£16,230
Advertising	£12,400
Rent	£4,500
Rates	£450
Electricity	£150
Telephone	£275
Stationery	£175

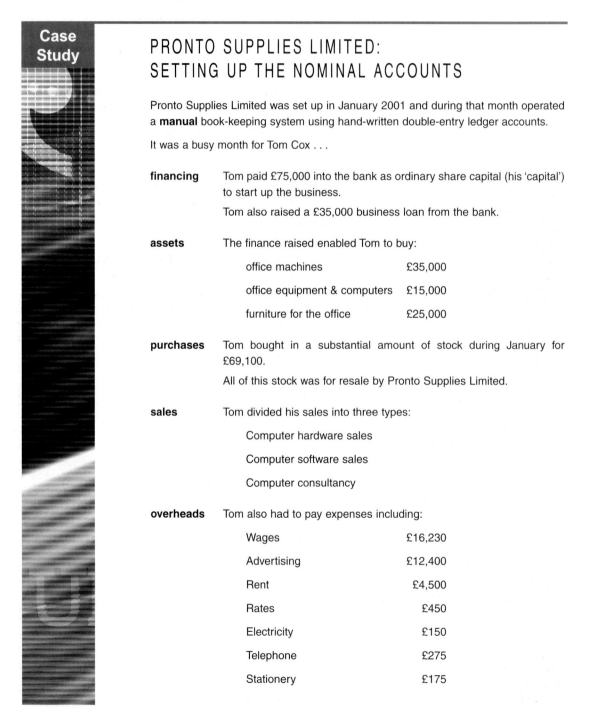

Pronto Supplies Trial Balance

At the end of January, Tom listed all the balances of his accounts in two columns, using a spreadsheet. This is his **trial balance** which will form the basis of the entries to the Sage system.

The columns are headed up Debit (Dr) and Credit (Cr) and they have the same total. In double-entry book-keeping each debit entry in the accounts is mirrored by a credit entry. If the book-keeping is correct, the total of debits should be the same as the total of the credits. The spreadsheet is shown below. Note that:

- The debtors control account (sales ledger control) shows the total amount owed by all Toms' customers; it is a debit balance because it is money owed to the business.
- The creditors control account (purchases ledger control) shows the total amount owed by Tom to his suppliers; it is a credit balance because it is money owed by the business.
- Tom is registered with HM Customs & Excise for Value Added Tax (VAT). This means that he has to quote his registration number on all his documents and also
    - charge VAT on his sales – this is due to HM Customs & Excise and so is a credit balance - Sales tax control account
    - reclaim VAT on what he has bought – this is due from HM Customs & Excise and so is a debit balance - Purchase tax control account

	A	B	C	D	E	F
1		Dr	Cr			
2						
3						
4	Plant and machinery	35000				
5	Office equipment	15000				
6	Furniture and fixtures	25000				
7	Debtors control account	45500				
8	Bank current account	12450				
9	Creditors control account		32510			
10	Sales tax control account		17920			
11	Purchase tax control account	26600				
12	Loans		35000			
13	Ordinary Shares		75000			
14	Hardware sales		85000			
15	Software sales		15000			
16	Computer consultancy		2400			
17	Materials purchased	69100				
18	Advertising	12400				
19	Gross wages	16230				
20	Rent	4500				
21	General rates	450				
22	Electricity	150				
23	Telephone	275				
24	Stationery	175				
25						
26						
27	Total	262830	262830			
28						

inputting the accounts into Sage Nominal

The date is 1 February 2001.

Tom uses his spreadsheet trial balance as the source document for inputting his nominal account balances. The procedure he adopts is:

1 He clicks on the NOMINAL icon on the opening screen and examines the nominal accounts list which appears on the NOMINAL screen. He allocates the accounts in his existing books with computer account numbers as follows:

Plant and machinery	0020
Office equipment (photocopiers, computers)	0030
Furniture and fixtures	0040
Debtors control account	1100
Bank current account	1200
Creditors control account	2100
Sales tax control account	2200
Purchase tax control account	2201
Loans	2300
Ordinary Shares	3000
Computer hardware sales	4000
Computer software sales	4001
Computer consultancy	4002
Materials purchased	5000
Advertising	6201
Gross wages	7000
Rent	7100
General rates	7103
Electricity	7200
Telephone	7502
Stationery	7504

2 Tom scrolls down the screen and clicks on all the accounts that he is going to need – they then show as selected.

But – importantly – he does not click on the following two accounts:

Debtors Control Account (Sales Ledger Control Account)

Creditors Control Account (Purchases Ledger Control Account)

This is because he has already input the debtors' (Customers') and creditors' (Suppliers') balances. If he inputs these totals now they will be entered into the computer twice and cause havoc with the accounting records!

The NOMINAL screen is shown at the top of the next page.

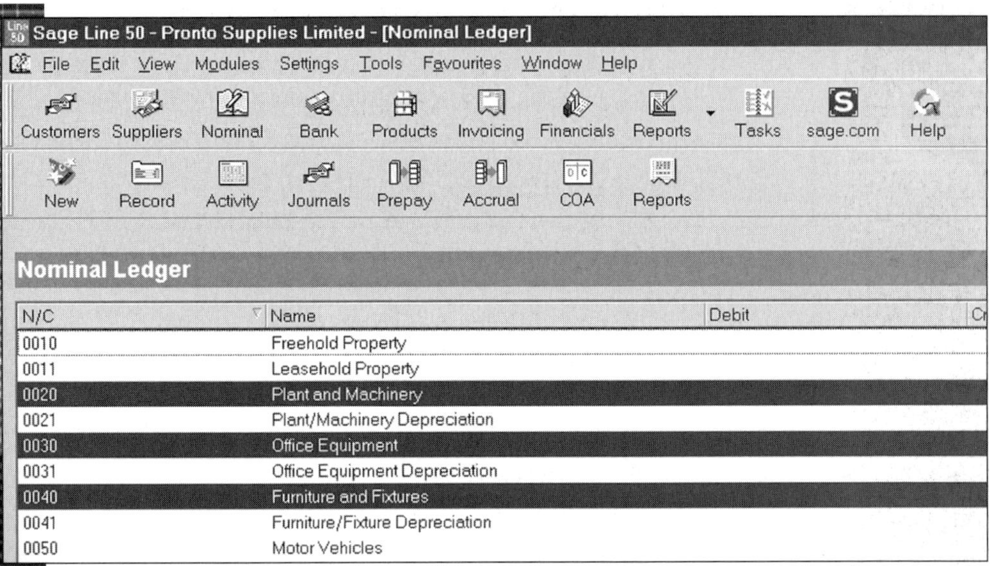

3 Tom is now ready to input the balances of these accounts. To do this he will

- Select the RECORD icon which will bring up a RECORD window.
- Click on O/B (Opening Balance) on the balance box which asks him to enter the date (01/02/2001) and the balance which must go in the correct box: debits on the left, credits on the right. He should ignore the 'ref' box.

The first account entry will look like this;

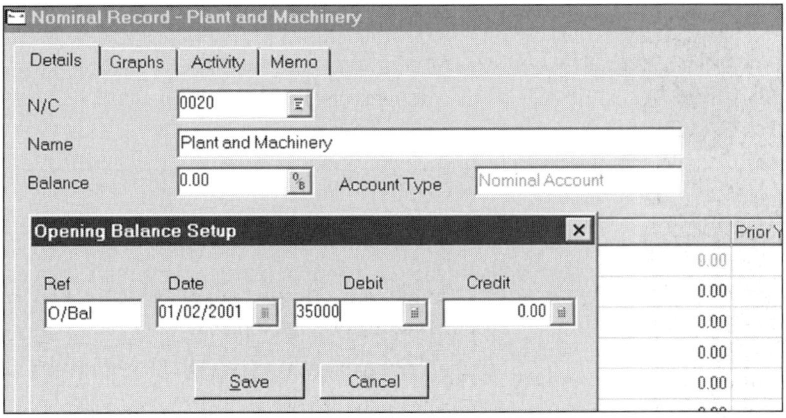

This record should then be saved.

Tom should repeat this for all the selected accounts, making sure that he is saving all the data as he goes along.

checking the input – the trial balance

Tom needs to check that what he has input is accurate. He needs to check his original trial balance (see page 545) – against the computer trial balance.

The trial balance is produced through FINANCIALS by clicking on the TRIAL icon.

The printout produced is shown below.

Pronto Supplies Limited

Period Trial Balance

To Period: Month 12, December 2001

N/C	Name		Debit	Credit
0020	Plant and Machinery		35,000.00	
0030	Office Equipment		15,000.00	
0040	Furniture and Fixtures		25,000.00	
1100	Debtors Control Account		45,500.00	
1200	Bank Current Account		12,450.00	
2100	Creditors Control Account			32,510.00
2200	Sales Tax Control Account			17,920.00
2201	Purchase Tax Control Account		26,600.00	
2300	Loans			35,000.00
3000	Ordinary Shares			75,000.00
4000	Computer hardware sales			85,000.00
4001	Computer software sales			15,000.00
4002	Computer consultancy			2,400.00
5000	Materials Purchased		69,100.00	
6201	Advertising		12,400.00	
7000	Gross Wages		16,230.00	
7100	Rent		4,500.00	
7103	General Rates		450.00	
7200	Electricity		150.00	
7502	Telephone		275.00	
7504	Office Stationery		175.00	
		Totals:	262,830.00	262,830.00

Is the input accurate? Yes, because all the figures agree with the original trial balance figures (see page 545) and they are all in the correct column.

Tom is now ready to input February's transactions – new sales invoices, new purchase invoices and payments in and out of the bank. These will be dealt with in the chapters that follow.

technical note

The stage reached at the end of this Case Study is represented by the data on your 'Company.25' file, which should now be loaded onto your computer. The transactions in the chapters that follow should be input by you and checked by your tutor. You should keep all printouts, as they may be required as assessment evidence.

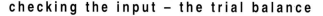

Chapter Summary

- When a business sets up its accounts on a Sage computer accounting package it will have to plan carefully how the data is to be transferred onto the computer.
- The first step in setting up the accounts on a Sage computer accounting package is to input the details of the organisation.
- The next stage will involve the inputting of the Customer and Supplier accounts – the Subsidiary ledgers.
- Lastly, the business will need to set up its Nominal Ledger – in other words, its Main Ledger.
- Account numbers will be allocated to the nominal accounts, adopting the default list of accounts supplied by Sage in its 'chart of accounts' structure.
- If the business has already started trading it should input all its nominal account balances (except for the Debtors and Creditors control accounts).
- The input balances should be checked carefully against the source figures.
- The Sage program can then produce a trial balance which will show the balances that have been input.

Key Terms

nominal ledger — the accounts in the accounting system which are not Customers or Suppliers, eg income, expenses, assets, liabilities – in Sage this is known as 'Nominal'; you will know it from your studies as 'Main Ledger'

trial balance — a list of the accounts of a business divided into two columns:

debits – assets and expenses

credits – income and liabilities

the two columns should have the same total, reflecting the workings of the double-entry book-keeping system

Note

There are no Student Activities in this introductory chapter.
The first set of inputting exercises is in the next chapter.

26 Computer accounting – selling to credit customers

this chapter covers . . .

A business that sells on credit will invoice the goods or services supplied and then receive payment at a later date.

It is essential that details of the invoice are entered in the computer accounting records so that the sale can be recorded and the amount owed by the customer logged into the accounting system.

A credit note is dealt with by a computer accounting program in much the same way as an invoice (in terms of the input screens used.)

This chapter continues the Pronto Supplies Limited Case Study and shows how details of invoices and credit notes are entered into the computer accounting records.

The next chapter looks at how the invoices and credit notes issued by suppliers are dealt with by a computer accounting program.

NVQ PERFORMANCE CRITERIA COVERED

Chapters 25 to 28 cover between them the 'computerised' aspects of the range statement relating to the performance criteria for Units 1, 2 and 3.

Details of the evidence which will be produced by the exercises in Chapters 26, 27, and 28 are set out on page 3 at the beginning of this book.

technical note
The computer transactions contained in this chapter are available on a file called 'Customers.26' which should be available from your tutor. The software used for this backup is Sage Line 50, version 4, which can be read by any subsequent version of Sage Line 50. The version used for illustrating the text is version 7 of Sage Line 50.
If you have any difficullty in obtaining this file, please call 01905 748071.

BACKGROUND TO FINANCIAL DOCUMENTS

When a business sells goods or services it will use a number of different financial documents. A single sales transaction involves both seller and buyer. In this chapter we look at the situation from the point of view of the seller of the goods or services. Documents which are often used in the selling process for goods include:

- **purchase order** which the seller receives from the buyer
- **delivery note** which goes with the goods from the seller to the buyer
- **invoice** which lists the goods and tells the buyer what is owed
- **credit note** which is sent to the buyer if any refund is due
- **statement** sent by the seller to remind the buyer what is owed
- **remittance advice** sent by the buyer with the **cheque** to make payment

You will be familiar from your earlier studies with the way in which the documents 'flow' between buyer and seller.

INVOICES, CREDIT NOTES AND SAGE

the book-keeping background

The totals of invoices and credit notes have to be entered into the accounting records of a business. They record the sales and refunds made to customers who have bought on credit – the **debtors** of the business (known in Sage as Customers).

The amounts from these documents combine to provide the total of the **Sales Ledger**, which is the section of the accounting records which contains all the debtor (Customer) balances. The Sales Ledger is a Subsidiary Ledger. The total of the debtor accounts is recorded in the **Sales Ledger Control Account** (known in Sage as Debtors Control Account). This tells the business how much in total is owing from customers who have bought on credit. The Sales Ledger Control Account is maintained in the Main Ledger, known in Sage as the 'Nominal Ledger'.

methods of recording invoices and credit notes

When a business uses a computer accounting program such as Sage, it will have to make sure that the details of each invoice and credit note issued are entered into the computer accounting records. Businesses using Sage accounting programs have two alternatives: batch entry and computer printed invoices.

batch entry

The business produces the invoices independently of the computer program (ie it types or writes them out) and then enters the invoice details into the computer accounting program on a **batch invoice** screen. A 'batch' is simply a group of items (eg a 'batch' of cakes in the oven). The term is used in this context to describe a group of invoices which are all input at one time. This may not be on the day that each invoice is produced – it may be the end of the week, or even the month.

It is normal practice to add up the totals of all the actual invoices that are being input – the 'batch total' – and check this total against the invoice total calculated by the computer from the actual input. This will pick up any errors.

A batch invoice entry screen with three invoices input is shown below.

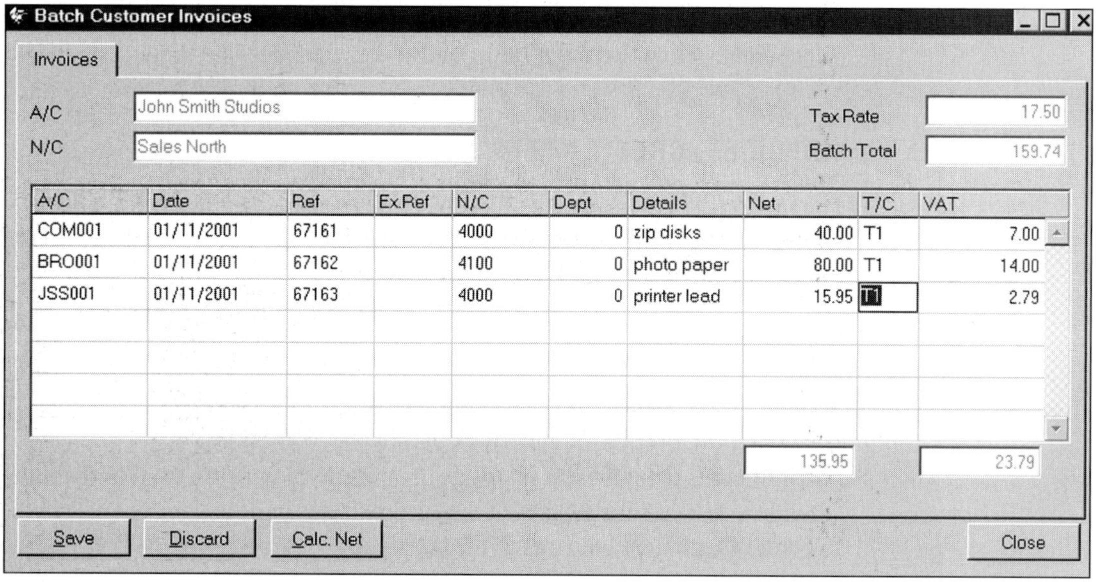

notes on the data entry columns:

- 'A/C' column contains the customer account reference
- 'Date' is the date on which each invoice was issued
- 'Ref' column is the invoice number (note that they are consecutive)
- 'Ex.Ref' is optional – it could be used for the purchase order number
- 'N/C' column is the nominal account code which specifies which type of sale is involved
- 'Dept' is optional and is not used here
- 'Details' describes the goods that have been sold

- 'Net' is the amount of the invoice before VAT is added on
- 'T/C' is the tax code which sets up the VAT rate that applies – here T1 refers to Standard Rate VAT, and is a default rate set up in Sage.
- 'VAT' is calculated automatically

When the operator has completed the input and checked the batch totals with the computer totals, the batched invoices can be saved.

computer printed invoices

Most versions of Sage include an invoicing function which requires the business to input the details of each invoice on screen. The computer system will then print out the invoices on the office printer – exactly as input. The invoices can either be for goods, or for a service provided. If the invoice is for goods, 'product' records with product codes will normally have to be set up in Sage, and the product code used each time stock is invoiced.

Service invoices do not require a product code, because no goods are involved in the transaction. An invoice input screen is shown below.

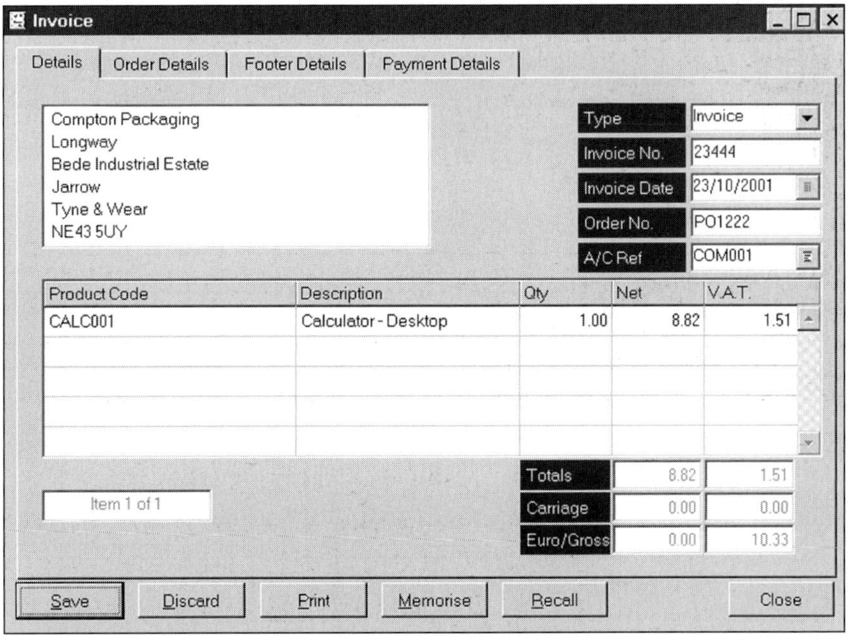

important note: treatment of invoicing in this book

In this book we will concentrate on the batch entry method of recording invoices and credit notes. It is far simpler to operate and is common to all versions of Sage.

Case Study

PRONTO SUPPLIES LIMITED: PROCESSING SALES INVOICES AND CREDIT NOTES

Tom Cox runs Pronto Supplies Limited which provides computer hardware, software and consultancy services. At the beginning of February he input his Nominal accounts and his Customer and Supplier details and balances into his Sage accounting program. He has set up three Sales Accounts in his Nominal Ledger:

Computer hardware sales	Account number 4000
Computer software sales	Account number 4001
Computer consultancy	Account number 4002

It is now 9 February, the end of the first full trading week. Tom needs to input

- the sales invoices he has issued to his customers
- the credit notes he has issued to his customers

He has the documents on file and has collected them in two batches . . .

SALES INVOICES ISSUED

invoice	name	date	details	net amount	VAT
10023	John Butler & Associates	5/02/01	1 x 17" monitor	400.00	70.00
10024	Charisma Design	6/02/01	1 x printer lead	16.00	2.80
10025	Crowmatic Ltd	6/02/01	1 x MacroWorx software	100.00	17.50
10026	Kay Denz	8/02/01	2 hours consultancy	120.00	21.00
Subtotals				636.00	111.30
Batch total					747.30

CREDIT NOTES ISSUED

credit note	name	date	details	net amount	VAT
551	David Boossey	6/02/01	Software returned	200.00	35.00
552	French Emporium	6/02/01	Disks returned (hardware)	40.00	7.00
Subtotals				240.00	42.00
Batch total					282.00

batch invoice entry

Tom will start by opening up the CUSTOMERS screen in Sage and clicking on the INVOICE icon. This will show the screen shown on the next page. He will then

- identify the account references for each of the four customers
- enter each invoice on a new line
- take the data from the invoice: date, invoice no ('Ref'), product details and amounts
- enter the appropriate Sales account number ('N/C') for the type of sale

- enter the T1 tax code for standard rate VAT and check that the VAT amount calculated on screen is the same as on the invoice

When the input is complete Tom should check his original totals (Net, VAT and Batch total) against the computer totals. Once he is happy that his input is correct he should SAVE.

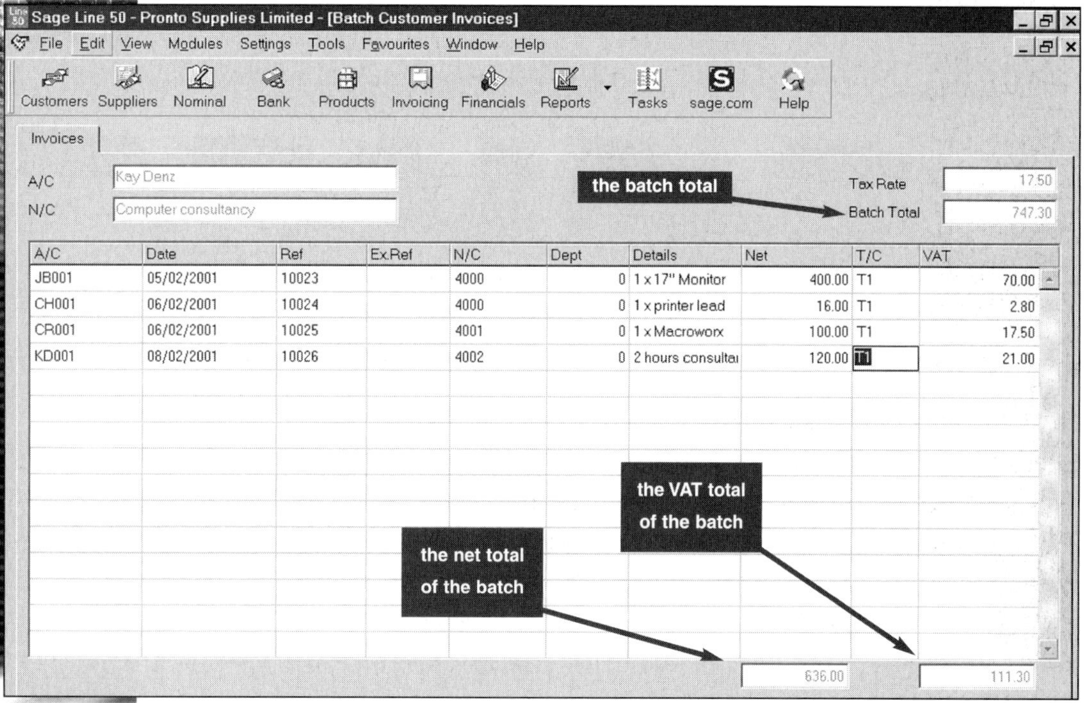

checking the invoices are on the system

As a further check Tom could print out a Day Book Report. This can be obtained through the REPORTS icon on the CUSTOMER menu bar. The title of the report is 'Day Books: Customer Invoices (Summary)'. The report appears as follows:

Date: 01/11/2001 **Pronto Supplies Limited** Page: 1

Time: 14:03:54 **Day Books: Customer Invoices (Summary)**

Date From: 05/02/2001
Date To: 31/12/2019

Transaction From: 1
Transaction To: 99999999

Tran No.	Item	sTp	Date	A/C Ref	Inv Ref	Details	Net Amount	Tax Amount	Gross Amount
54	1	SI	05/02/2001	JB001	10023	1 x 17" Monitor	400.00	70.00	470.00
55	1	SI	06/02/2001	CH001	10024	1 x printer lead	16.00	2.80	18.80
56	1	SI	06/02/2001	CR001	10025	1 x Macroworx	100.00	17.50	117.50
57	1	SI	08/02/2001	KD001	10026	2 hours consultancy	120.00	21.00	141.00
						Totals:	636.00	111.30	747.30

batch credit note entry

Tom will input the details from the two credit notes in much the same way as he processed the invoices. He will start by opening up the CUSTOMERS screen in Sage and clicking on the CREDIT icon. This will show the screen shown below. He will then identify the account references for each of the two customers and the Sales account numbers and input the credit note details as shown on the screen. When the input is complete he should again check his original totals (Net, VAT and Batch total) against the computer totals. Once he is happy that his input is correct he should SAVE.

Batch Customer Credits

Credits

A/C: French Emporium — Tax Rate: 17.50

N/C: Computer hardware sales — Batch Total: 282.00

A/C	Date	Crd.No	Ex.Ref	N/C	Dept	Details	Net	T/C	VAT
DB001	06/02/2001	551		4001	0	Software retur	200.00	T1	35.00
FE001	06/02/2001	552		4000	0	Disks returne	40.00	T1	7.00
							240.00		42.00

Save | Discard | Calc. Net | Close

checking the credit notes are on the system

As a further check Tom could print out a Day Book Report for credit notes. This can be obtained through the REPORTS icon on the CUSTOMER toolbar. The title of the report is 'Day Books: Customer Credits (Summary)'. The report appears as follows:

Date: 01/11/2001 — Time: 14:06:17 — Page: 1

Pronto Supplies Limited

Day Books: Customer Credits (Summary)

Date From: 05/02/2001
Date To: 31/12/2019

Customer From:
Customer To: ZZZZZZZZ

Transaction From: 1
Transaction To: 99999999

Tran No.	Items	Tp	Date	A/C Ref	Inv Ref	Details	Net Amount	Tax Amount	Gross Amount
58	1	SC	06/02/2001	DB001	551	Software return	200.00	35.00	235.00
59	1	SC	06/02/2001	FE001	552	Disks returned	40.00	7.00	47.00
						Totals:	240.00	42.00	282.00

Note: in the examples in this text, computer accounting does not use a separate 'returns' account; instead it automatically debits returns to sales account.

producing statements

The Sage computer accounting system is set up to print out statements of account for customers. This will normally be done at the end of the month, but 'one-off' statements can be issued on any date.

In the example below, one of Tom's customers, David Boossey has asked for a statement of account as at 9 February. Tom selects the STATEMENT icon on the CUSTOMERS screen, follows the on-screen instructions and prints the statement for Customer code DB001 for the defined date range.

He prints onto A4 statement stationery which he has had printed by Sage.

The illustration below shows the text that is printed onto his stationery. The computer also prints a 'tear-off remittance advice which repeats the information shown on the statement. The amount at the bottom shows the total amount due to Pronto Supplies, ie an invoice total of £3,400 minus the credit note for £235 = £3,165.

STATEMENT

Pronto Supplies Limited
Unit 17 Severnvale Estate
Broadwater Road
Mereford
Wyvern
MR1 6TF

David Boossey
17 Harebell Road
Mereford Green
MR6 4NB

DB001

09/02/2001

10/01/01	10016	Opening Balance	3,400.00*	
06/02/01	551	Software returned	*	235.00

-235.00	3,400.00	0.00	0.00	0.00

amount due 3,165.00

Chapter Summary

- Details of invoices and credit notes issued are entered into the accounting records of a business. When a computer program is used the details will be input on screen.
- Computer accounting programs will either print out the invoices and credit notes after input, or will need to have the details of existing invoices and credit notes input, commonly in batches.
- Computer accounting programs will also print out statements of account on demand.
- Organisations often have the stationery for financial documents preprinted. The computer then prints the accounting data on this stationery.

Key Terms

invoice — the financial document issued by the seller which sets out the details of the goods sold or services provided, the amount owing and the date by which the amount is due

credit note — the financial document – issued by the seller when goods are returned – which reduces the amount owing by the customer

batch — a group of documents, eg invoices or credit notes

batch entry — the input of a number of documents in a group

statement — a financial document which is sent to the customer of a business, listing transactions on the account and advising the total amount owed

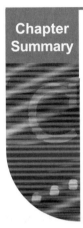

Student Activities

technical note
Before starting these inputting tasks you should ensure that the Sage file 'Company.25' (provided by Osborne Books) is loaded onto your computer.

Task 1

Making sure that you have set the program date to 9 February 2001 (SETTINGS menu), enter the invoice details from the batch sheet below into the computer.

Check your totals before saving and print out a Day Books: Customer Invoices (Summary) Report to confirm the data that you have saved.

BATCH SHEET

SALES INVOICES ISSUED

invoice	name	date	details	net amount	VAT
10023	John Butler & Associates	5/02/01	1 x 17" monitor	400.00	70.00
10024	Charisma Design	6/02/01	1 x printer lead	16.00	2.80
10025	Crowmatic Ltd	6/02/01	1 x MacroWorx software	100.00	17.50
10026	Kay Denz	8/02/01	2 hours consultancy	120.00	21.00
Subtotals				636.00	111.30
Batch total					747.30

Task 2

Enter the following credit note batch details into the computer.

Check your totals before saving and print out a Day Books: Customer Credits (Summary) Report to confirm the data that you have saved.

BATCH SHEET

CREDIT NOTES ISSUED

credit note	name	date	details	net amount	VAT
551	David Boossey	6/02/01	Software returned	200.00	35.00
552	French Emporium	6/02/01	Disks returned (hardware)	40.00	7.00
Subtotals				240.00	42.00
Batch total					282.00

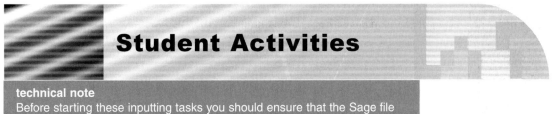

Task 3

It is now a week later and the date is now 16 February 2001. Change your program date setting (SETTINGS menu).

You have a further batch of invoices to process.

Enter the details into the computer. Check your totals before saving and print out a Day Books Summary Report to confirm the data that you have saved.

account	invoice date	number	details	net	VAT
John Butler & Associates	12/02/01	10027	2 hours consultancy	120.00	21.00
David Boossey	13/02/01	10028	1 x EF102 printer	200.00	35.00
French Emporium	14/02/01	10029	1 x QuorkEdit software	400.00	70.00
L Garr & Co	16/02/01	10030	2 x Zap drive	180.00	31.50
Jo Green Systems	16/02/01	10031	1 x Fileperfect software	264.00	46.20
Prism Trading Ltd	16/02/01	10032	1 x 15” monitor	320.00	56.00

Task 4

You also on the same date have two credit notes to process. Enter the details into the computer. Check your totals before saving and print out a Day Books Summary Report to confirm the data that you have saved.

account	date	reference	details	net	VAT
Jo Green Systems	12/02/01	553	1 x printer lead	16.00	2.80
Mendell & Son	13/02/01	554	Zap disks (hardware)	20.00	3.50

Task 5

You have been asked to prepare an Aged Debtors Analysis. Run a debtor analysis report (as at 16 February) from REPORTS in Customers. Print it out.

Task 6

Your customer David Boossey asks you for a statement of account as at 16 February.

Either print out a statement (account DB001) from CUSTOMERS, or email the same data and keep a printed copy.

Task 7

Print out a Trial Balance as at 16 February 2001 to show the balances of the Nominal (Main) Ledger.

The figures should agree with the Trial Balance shown on the next page. If they do, your input is correct. If there are any discrepancies you will need sort them out, or RESTORE from the file ‘Customers.26’ (from Osborne Books) before tackling the inputting exercises in the next chapter.

Reminder! Have you made a backup?

Pronto Supplies, trial balance as at 16 February 2001

Pronto Supplies Limited

Period Trial Balance

To Period: Month 2, February 2001

N/C	Name		Debit	Credit
0020	Plant and Machinery		35,000.00	
0030	Office Equipment		15,000.00	
0040	Furniture and Fixtures		25,000.00	
1100	Debtors Control Account		47,666.70	
1200	Bank Current Account		12,450.00	
2100	Creditors Control Account			32,510.00
2200	Sales Tax Control Account			18,242.70
2201	Purchase Tax Control Account		26,600.00	
2300	Loans			35,000.00
3000	Ordinary Shares			75,000.00
4000	Computer hardware sales			86,040.00
4001	Computer software sales			15,564.00
4002	Computer consultancy			2,640.00
5000	Materials Purchased		69,100.00	
6201	Advertising		12,400.00	
7000	Gross Wages		16,230.00	
7100	Rent		4,500.00	
7103	General Rates		450.00	
7200	Electricity		150.00	
7502	Telephone		275.00	
7504	Office Stationery		175.00	
		Totals:	264,996.70	264,996.70

27 Computer accounting – buying from suppliers

this chapter covers . . .

This chapter should be read in conjunction with the last chapter 'Computer accounting – selling to credit customers' as it represents 'the other side of the coin' – invoices and credit notes as they are dealt with by the purchaser.

A business purchaser that buys on credit will receive an invoice for the goods or services supplied and will then have to pay at a later date.

Details of invoices and any credit notes received are entered by the purchaser into the account of the supplier in the computer accounting records. In this way the credit purchase and any credit due are recorded, and the total amount owing by the purchaser to the supplier logged into the accounting system.

This chapter continues the Pronto Supplies Case Study and shows how details of invoices and credit notes received are entered into supplier accounts in the computer accounting records.

NVQ PERFORMANCE CRITERIA COVERED

Chapters 25 to 28 cover between them the 'computerised' aspects of the range statement relating to the performance criteria for Units 1, 2 and 3.

Details of the evidence which will be produced by the exercises in Chapters 26, 27, and 28 are set out on page 3 at the beginning of this book.

technical note

The computer transactions contained in this chapter are available on a file called 'Suppliers.27' which should be available from your tutor. The software used for this backup is Sage Line 50, version 4, which can be read by any subsequent version of Sage Line 50. The version used for illustrating the text is version 7 of Sage Line 50.

If you have any difficullty in obtaining this file, please call 01905 748071.

THE BOOK-KEEPING BACKGROUND

Details of invoices and credit notes received have to be entered into the accounting records of a business that buys on credit. These documents record the sales and refunds made by suppliers who have sold on credit – the **creditors** of the business, known in Sage as 'Suppliers'.

The amounts from these documents combine to provide the total of the **Purchases Ledger**, which is the section of the accounting records which contains all the supplier accounts and their balances. The total of the **Purchases Ledger** is recorded in the **Purchases Ledger Control Account** (known in Sage as Creditors Control Account). This tells the business how much in total it owes to suppliers.

The documents received from the suppliers – invoices and credit notes – are recorded in the computer accounting system on the **batch** basis illustrated in the Case Study in the last chapter.

PURCHASES AND EXPENSES AND CAPITAL ITEMS

One point that is very important to bear in mind is the difference between **purchases** and **expenses** and **capital items**, as it affects the nominal account codes used when inputting invoices and credit notes on the computer.

Purchases are items a business buys which it expects to turn into a product or sell as part of its day-to-day business. For example:

- a business that makes cheese will buy milk to make the cheese
- a supermarket will buy food and clothes to sell to the public

All these items are bought because they will be sold or turned into a product that will be sold. In Sage these purchases will be recorded in a **purchases account**, normally 5000, or a number in that category.

Expenses, on the other hand, are items which the business pays for which form part of the business running expenses (overheads), eg rent and electricity. Each expense has a separate nominal account number allocated in the Sage accounting system.

Capital items are 'one off' items that the business buys and intends to keep for a number of years, for example office equipment and furniture. These also have separate nominal account numbers in the Sage system.

The important point here is that all of these items may be bought on credit and each will have to be entered into the computer accounting records, **but with the correct nominal account number.**

Case Study

PRONTO SUPPLIES LIMITED: PROCESSING PURCHASES INVOICES AND CREDIT NOTES

It is now February 16 2001. Tom has a number of supplier invoices and supplier credit notes to enter into the computer accounting system.

He has the documents on file and has collected them in two batches.

PURCHASES INVOICES RECEIVED

invoice	name	date	details	net amount	VAT
11365	Delco PLC	9/02/01	Desktop computers	3,600.00	630.00
8576	Electron Supplies	9/02/01	Peripherals	2,000.00	350.00
2947	MacCity	12/02/01	Powerbooks	2,400.00	420.00
34983	Synchromart	14/02/01	Software	1,280.00	224.00
Subtotals				9,280.00	1624.00
Batch total					10,904.00

CREDIT NOTES RECEIVED

credit note	name	date	details	net amount	VAT
7223	Delco PLC	6/02/01	1 x Computer	480.00	84.00
552	MacCity	8/02/01	1 x optical mouse	38.00	6.65
Subtotals				518.00	90.65
Batch total					608.65

batch invoice entry

Tom will start by opening up the SUPPLIERS screen in Sage and clicking on the INVOICE icon. This will show the screen shown on the next page. He will then

- identify the account references for each of the four customers
- enter each invoice on a new line
- take the data from the invoice: date, invoice no ('Ref'), product details and amounts
- enter the Materials Purchased account number 5000 under 'N/C'
- enter the T1 tax code for standard rate VAT and check that the VAT amount calculated on screen is the same as on the invoice – if there is a substantial difference (eg a mistake on the invoice) it should be queried with a higher authority*

When the input is complete Tom should check his original totals (Net, VAT and Batch total) against the computer totals. Once he is happy that his input is correct he can SAVE.

* Sometimes the VAT on the document will vary by a penny from the VAT on the screen. This is because Sage 'rounds' VAT up or down to the nearest penny, whereas the VAT authorities require that VAT is rounded down to the nearest penny. These one penny differences can be altered on the input screen to tally with the document VAT amount – normally without reference to a higher authority.

The batch suppliers' invoice screen will appear like this:

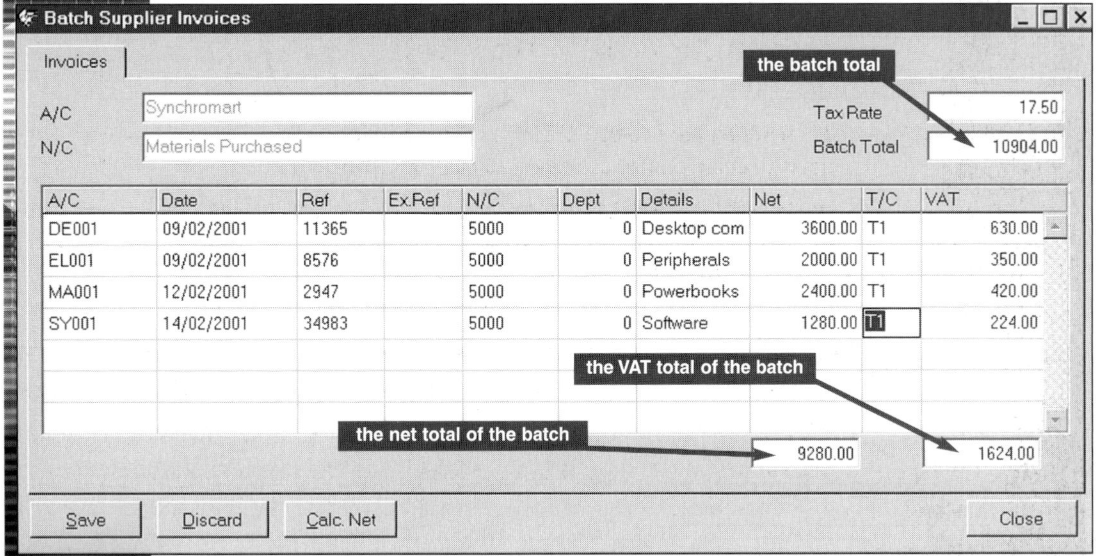

checking the invoices are on the system

As a further check Tom could print out a Day Book Report. This can be obtained through the REPORTS icon on the SUPPLIER menu bar. The title of the report is 'Day Books: Supplier Invoices (Summary)'. The report appears as follows:

Pronto Supplies Limited Page: 1

Day Books: Supplier Invoices (Summary)

Date From: 01/02/2001
Date To: 31/12/2019

Transaction From: 1
Transaction To: 99999999

Tran No.	Item	Tp	Date	A/C Ref	Inv Ref	Details	Net Amount	Tax Amount	Gross Amount
68	1	PI	09/02/2001	DE001	11365	Desktop computers	3,600.00	630.00	4,230.00
69	1	PI	09/02/2001	EL001	8576	Peripherals	2,000.00	350.00	2,350.00
70	1	PI	12/02/2001	MA001	2947	Powerbooks	2,400.00	420.00	2,820.00
71	1	PI	14/02/2001	SY001	34983	Software	1,280.00	224.00	1,504.00
						Totals	9,280.00	1,624.00	10,904.00

batch credit note entry

Tom will input the details from the two credit notes in much the same way as he processed the invoices. He will open up the SUPPLIERS screen in Sage and click on the CREDIT icon. This will show the screen shown on the next page. He will then identify the account references for each of the two customers and input the credit note details as shown on the screen. He will use the Materials Purchased account number 5000. When the input is complete he should again check his original totals (Net, VAT and Batch total) against the computer totals. Once he is happy that his input is correct he should SAVE.

The batch suppliers' credit note screen will appear like this:

	Batch Supplier Credits									_ □ ×

Credits										

| A/C | MacCity | | | | | | Tax Rate | | | 17.50 |
| N/C | Materials Purchased | | | | | | Batch Total | | | 608.65 |

A/C	Date	Cd. No	Ex.Ref	N/C	Dept	Details	Net		T/C	VAT
DE001	06/02/2001	7223		5000	0	1 x computer	480.00		T1	84.00
MA001	08/02/2001	552		5000	0	1 optical mou:	38.00		T1	6.65
							518.00			90.65

Save	Discard	Calc. Net								Close

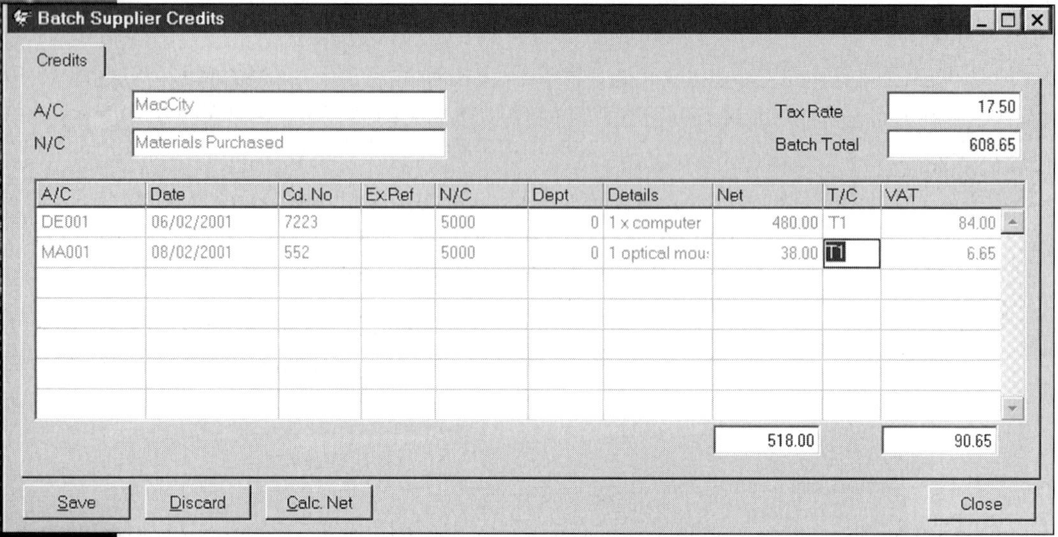

checking the credit notes are on the system

As a further check Tom could print out a Day Book Report for Supplier Credit notes. This can be obtained through the REPORTS icon on the SUPPLIERS toolbar. The title of the report is 'Day Books: Supplier Credits (Summary)'. The report appears as follows:

Date:	05/11/2001		**Pronto Supplies Limited**				Page:	1
Time:	11:01:59		**Day Books: Supplier Credits (Summary)**					

Date From:	01/02/2001				Supplier From:		
Date To:	31/12/2019				Supplier To:	ZZZZZZZZ	

| Transaction From: | 1 | | | | | | |
| Transaction To: | 99999999 | | | | | | |

Tran No.	Item	Tp	Date	A/C Ref	Inv Ref	Details	Net Amount	Tax Amount	Gross Amount
72	1	PC	06/02/2001	DE001	7223	1 x computer	480.00	84.00	564.00
73	1	PC	08/02/2001	MA001	552	1 optical mouse	38.00	6.65	44.65
						Totals	518.00	90.65	608.65

Note: the Sage accounting system does not use a separate 'returns' account for purchases returns; these items are credited to purchases account by the system.

what next?

Tom has now entered into his computer:

• his company details and nominal (Main Ledger) accounts and balances

• customer and supplier details

• customer invoices and credit notes (in the last chapter)

• supplier invoices and credit notes (in this chapter)

The next chapter shows how he enters details of payments made to suppliers and payments received from customers.

Chapter Summary

- When a business buys on credit it will receive invoices and sometimes credit notes from its suppliers as part of the 'flow of documents'.
- The details of invoices and credit notes received must be entered into the accounting records of a business. If a computer program is used the details are input on screen and a report printed out.
- In the case of supplier invoices and credit notes it is important that the correct Nominal account number is used to describe whether the transaction relates to purchases, expenses or capital items.
- It is essential to check the details of invoices and credit notes before input and the details of input by printing out, for example, a day book report.

Key Terms

credit purchase	a purchase made where payment is due at a later date
creditors	suppliers to whom the business owes money
purchases ledger	the part of the accounting system where the suppliers' accounts are kept
purchases	items bought which will be turned into a product or be sold as part of day-to-day-trading
expenses	payments made which relate to the running of the business – also known as overheads
capital items	items bought which the business intends to keep
batch	a group of documents, eg invoices or credit notes

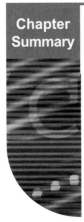

Student Activities

technical note
Before starting these inputting tasks you must ensure either that your input from the last chapter is correct or that the Sage file 'Customers.26' (provided by Osborne Books) is loaded or restored onto your computer.

Task 1

Set the program date to 16 February 2001. Enter the following invoice details into the computer. Check your totals before saving and print out a Day Books: Supplier Invoice (Summary) Report to confirm the data that you have saved.

PURCHASES INVOICES RECEIVED

invoice	name	date	details	net amount	VAT
11365	Delco PLC	9/02/01	Desktop computers	3,600.00	630.00
8576	Electron Supplies	9/02/01	Peripherals	2,000.00	350.00
2947	MacCity	12/02/01	Powerbooks	2,400.00	420.00
34983	Synchromart	14/02/01	Software	1,280.00	224.00
Subtotals				9,280.00	1624.00
Batch total					10,904.00

Task 2

Enter the following credit note details into the computer. Check your totals before saving and print out a Day Books: Supplier Credits (Summary) Report to confirm the data that you have saved.

CREDIT NOTES RECEIVED

credit note	name	date	details	net amount	VAT
7223	Delco PLC	6/02/01	1 x Computer	480.00	84.00
552	MacCity	8/02/01	1 x optical mouse	38.00	6.65
Subtotals				518.00	90.65
Batch total					608.65

Task 3

On the same day Tom receives two further supplier invoices in the post. He wants them to be input straightaway while the computer is up and running. He checks all the documentation and finds that the invoices are both correct. You are to input them, taking care to use the correct nominal code (0030 for Office Equipment). The computer and printer purchased are not for resale to customers but are to be used as office equipment at Pronto Supplies. When the input is complete the totals should be checked and a Day Book Summary Report printed (showing just the last two invoices, if possible).

invoice	name	date	details	net amount	VAT
11377	Delco PLC	14/02/01	Desktop computer	400.00	70.00
8603	Electron Supplies	14/02/01	Laser Printer	360.00	63.00
Subtotals				760.00	133.00
Batch total					893.00

Reminder! Have you made a backup?

Task 4

When you have completed tasks 1 to 3, print out a trial balance dated 16 February 2001.

Also run and print out an Aged Creditors Analysis from Reports in Suppliers to show the position of the Purchases Ledger as at 16 February 2001.

Check your trial balance against the figures shown below. If they agree, your input is correct. If there are any discrepancies you will need sort them out, or RESTORE from the file 'Suppliers.27' (from Osborne Books) before tackling the inputting exercises in the next chapter.

Pronto Supplies, trial balance as at 16 February 2001

Pronto Supplies Limited

Period Trial Balance

To Period: Month 2, February 2001

N/C	Name	Debit	Credit
0020	Plant and Machinery	35,000.00	
0030	Office Equipment	15,760.00	
0040	Furniture and Fixtures	25,000.00	
1100	Debtors Control Account	47,666.70	
1200	Bank Current Account	12,450.00	
2100	Creditors Control Account		43,698.35
2200	Sales Tax Control Account		18,242.70
2201	Purchase Tax Control Account	28,266.35	
2300	Loans		35,000.00
3000	Ordinary Shares		75,000.00
4000	Computer hardware sales		86,040.00
4001	Computer software sales		15,564.00
4002	Computer consultancy		2,640.00
5000	Materials Purchased	77,862.00	
6201	Advertising	12,400.00	
7000	Gross Wages	16,230.00	
7100	Rent	4,500.00	
7103	General Rates	450.00	
7200	Electricity	150.00	
7502	Telephone	275.00	
7504	Office Stationery	175.00	
	Totals:	276,185.05	276,185.05

28 Computer accounting – payments

this chapter covers . . .

So far in this book we have dealt with accounts for customers and suppliers and entered details of financial documents. But we have not covered the way in which the computer accounting system records the payment of money by customers to the business or by the business to suppliers.

The bank account is central to any accounting system as the payment of money is vital to all business transactions.

The bank account is used not only for payments by customers and to suppliers (credit transactions), but also for transactions for which settlement is made straightaway (cash transactions).

The Case Study in this chapter – a continuation of Pronto Supplies Limited – explains how payments made and received are recorded in the computer accounting system.

The chapter concludes by illustrating other aspects of computer accounting payments:

- *dealing with cash payments*
- *the setting up of a petty cash account and a rents receivable account on the computer*
- *journal entries*
- *bank reconciliation statements*

NVQ PERFORMANCE CRITERIA COVERED

Chapters 25 to 28 cover between them the 'computerised' aspects of the range statement relating to the performance criteria for Units 1, 2 and 3.

Details of the evidence which will be produced by the exercises in Chapters 26, 27, and 28 are set out on page 3 at the beginning of this book.

technical note

The computer transactions contained in this chapter are available on a file called 'Payments.28' which should be available from your tutor. The software used for this backup is Sage Line 50, version 4, which can be read by any subsequent version of Sage Line 50. The version used for illustrating the text is version 7 of Sage Line 50.

If you have any difficullty in obtaining this file, please call 01905 748071.

THE BANK ACCOUNTS IN COMPUTER ACCOUNTING

The bank accounts and all the functions associated with them are found in Sage by clicking on the BANK icon in the main menu bar. The BANK screen then appears as shown below.

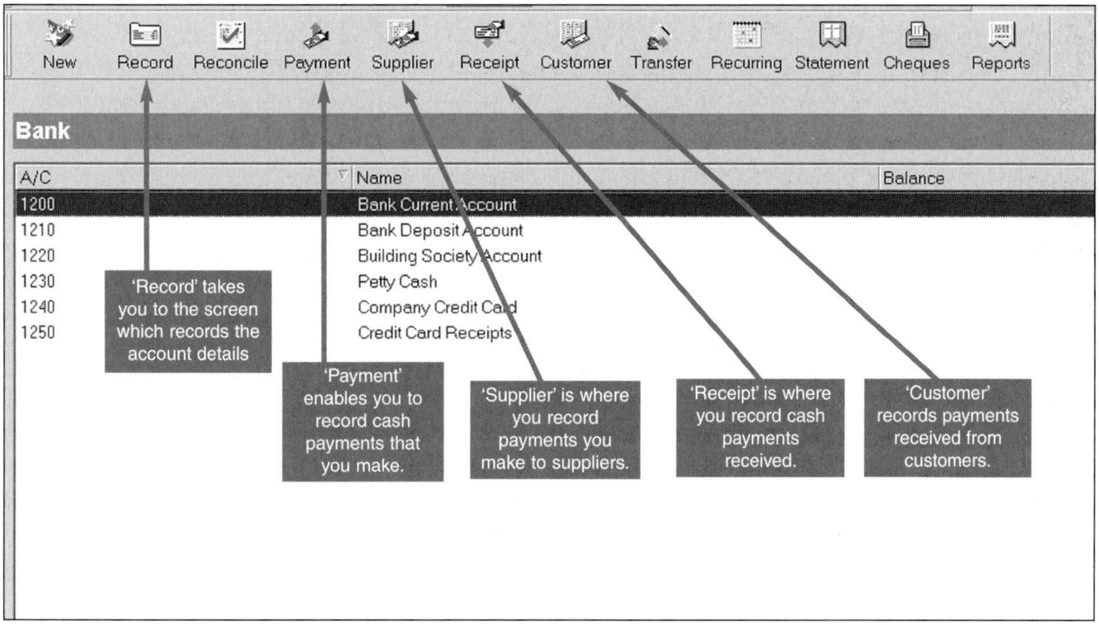

types of bank account

The accounts listed above come from the default list provided by Sage for the Nominal (Main) Ledger. The business does not have to adopt all the bank accounts listed here, but may use some of them if it needs them:

- **bank current account** records all payments in and out of the bank 'cheque' account used for everyday purposes – it is the most commonly used account
- **bank deposit account** and **building society account** can be used if the business maintains interest-paying accounts for savings and for money that is not needed in the short term
- **petty cash account** can be used if the business maintains a petty cash system in the office for small purchases such as stationery and stamps
- **company credit card account** can be used if the business uses credit cards for its employees to pay for expenses
- **credit card receipts account** can be used if the business receives a significant number of credit card payments from its customers

cash or credit payments?

The number of icons on the menu bar record payments which are either:

- **cash payments** – ie made straightaway without the need for invoices or credit notes
- **credit payments** – ie made in settlement of invoices

The problem is, which is which? The rule is:

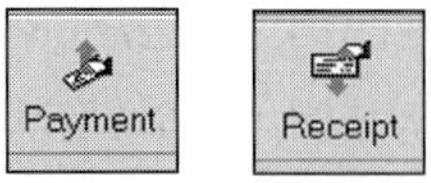

= **cash payments** (not involving credit customers or suppliers)

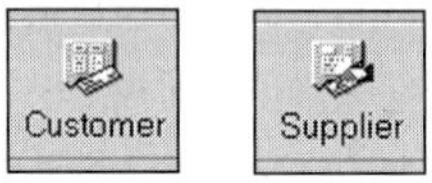

= **credit payments** (payments from customers and to suppliers in settlement of accounts)

bank account details

It must be stressed that if a Sage computer account number is listed on the BANK screen it does not *have* to be used. It is there so that it can be used if the business needs it. The Bank Current Account (here number 1200), for example, is always going to be used, assuming businesses always have bank current accounts!

When a business is setting up its bank accounts it should click on RECORD on the BANK screen to produce the bank account DETAILS screen . . .

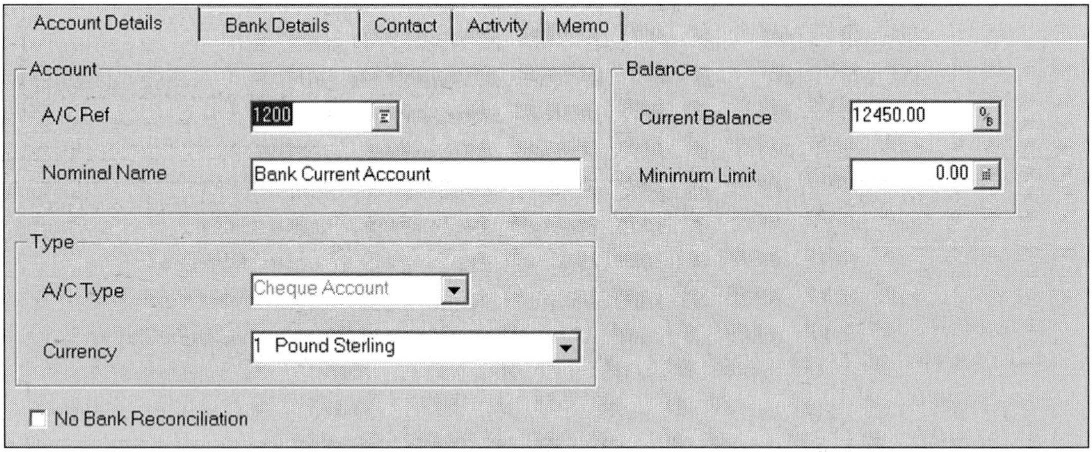

This screen enables the business to input details of the account, the bank and bank contact and to see the activity on the account. The unchecked box at the bottom left in this example shows that the business will use the program to reconcile (tally up) the computer record of the bank account with the bank statement when it is received, to produce a bank reconciliation statement.

RECORDING PAYMENTS FROM CUSTOMERS

how do payments arrive?

When a payment arrives from a customer who has bought on credit it will normally arrive at the business in one of two ways:

- A cheque and **remittance advice**. A remittance advice is a document stating what the payment relates to – eg which invoices and credit notes.
- A remittance advice stating that the money has been sent direct to the business bank account in the form of a **BACS payment** (a BACS [Bankers Automated Clearing Services] payment is a payment sent direct between the banks' computers and does not involve a cheque).

Examples of cheque and BACS remittance advices are shown below:

REMITTANCE ADVICE

TO
A B Supplies Limited
Unit 45 Elgar Estate,
Broadfield, BR7 4ER

FROM
Compsync
4 Friar Street
Broadfield
BR1 3RF
Tel 01908 761234 Fax 01908 761987
VAT REG GB 0745 8383 56

Account 3993 6 November 2003

date	your reference	our reference	payment amount
01 10 03	INVOICE 787923	47609	277.30
10 10 03	CREDIT NOTE 12157	47609	(27.73)
		CHEQUE TOTAL	249.57

BACS REMITTANCE ADVICE

FROM: Excelsior Services
17 Gatley Way
Bristol BS1 9GH

TO
A B Supplies Ltd
Unit 45 Elgar Estate, Broadfield, BR7 4ER

06 12 03

Your ref	Our ref		Amount
788102	3323	BACS TRANSFER	465.00
		TOTAL	465.00

THIS HAS BEEN PAID BY BACS CREDIT TRANSFER DIRECTLY INTO YOUR BANK ACCOUNT AT ALBION BANK NO 11451226 SORT CODE 90 47 17

customer payments and the accounting system

An incoming payment from a customer settling one or more invoices (less any credit notes) needs to be recorded in the accounting system:

- the balance of bank account will increase (a debit in double-entry)
- the balance of the customer's account (and the Sales Ledger Control Account ['Debtors Control Account' in Sage]) will decrease because the customer will owe less (a credit in double-entry accounting)

In computer accounting the payment is input once and the entries will be automatically made from the same screen. Any settlement discount involved will also be entered on the screen and the entries made automatically.

the practicalities

The business will normally input a number (a 'batch') of payments at one time on a regular basis, eg every week, using the remittance advice as the source document. The remittance advice will have all the details on it (date, amount, invoices paid) and in the case of a BACS payment it is the only document from the customer relating to the payment the business will have.

The appropriate bank account should first be selected on the BANK screen and then the CUSTOMER icon selected to access the Customer Receipt input screen:

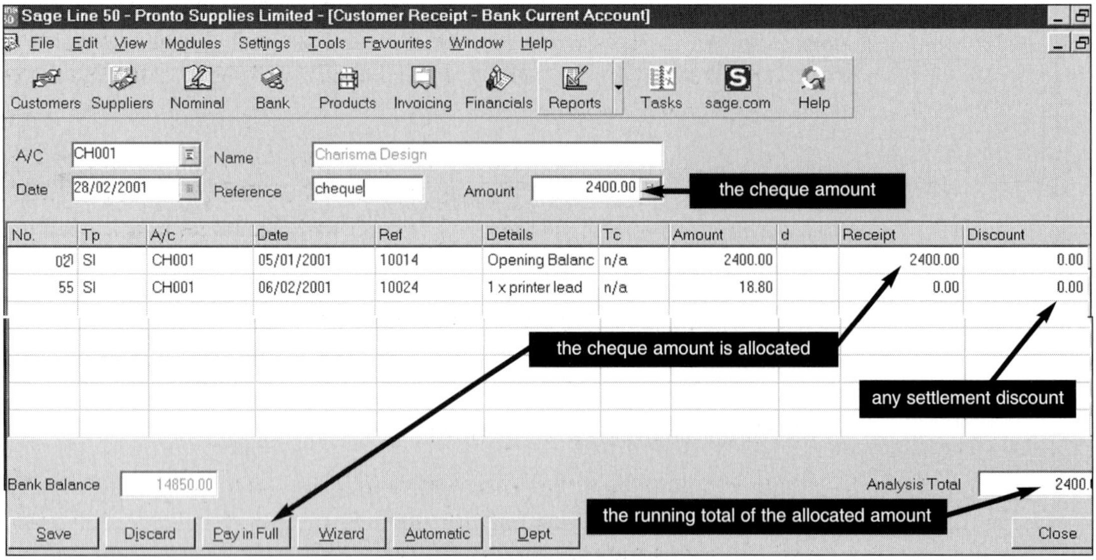

processing the payments received

The procedure for recording the customer payment on this screen is to:

- input the customer account reference – this will bring up on screen the account name and all the outstanding amounts due on invoices

- input a reference if required – for example you might key in 'cheque' or 'BACS' or the numerical reference relating to the payment
- input the amount of the payment in the Amount box
- click on the 'Receipt' box of the invoice that is being paid
- click on the 'Pay in Full' button at the bottom
- if there is more than one invoice being paid click on the items being paid as appropriate; the Analysis Total box at the bottom will shown a running total of the money allocated
- if there is a long list of invoices and a payment to cover them, click on 'Automatic' at the bottom and the computer will allocate the payment down the invoice list until the money amount of the payment runs out
- check that what you have done is correct and SAVE; details to check are:
  - customer, amount, invoices being paid and amount received
  - the amounts in the Amount box and the Analysis Total box should be the same (but see next point)
- if the amount received by way of payment is greater than the amount allocated to outstanding invoices the extra payment will show as a 'Payment on Account' after you have saved
- if the amount received by way of payment is less than the amount of the invoice(s) it is settling, the amount received will be allocated to the appropriate invoice(s) and the unpaid amount will show as outstanding on the Customer's account
- you should print out a Day Books: Customer Receipts (Summary) for these transactions from REPORTS in BANK to check that the total of the cheques (or BACS payments) received equals the total input

RECORDING PAYMENTS TO SUPPLIERS

what documents are involved?

A business pays its suppliers on the invoice due dates or after it receives a **statement** setting out the amounts due from invoices and any deductions made following the issue of credit notes.

Payment is often made by cheque, although some payments may be made by BACS transfer between the banks' computers. Payment is normally made in full, but occasionally a part payment may be made. A typical payment cheque, together with a completed counterfoil (cheque stub) is shown on the next page.

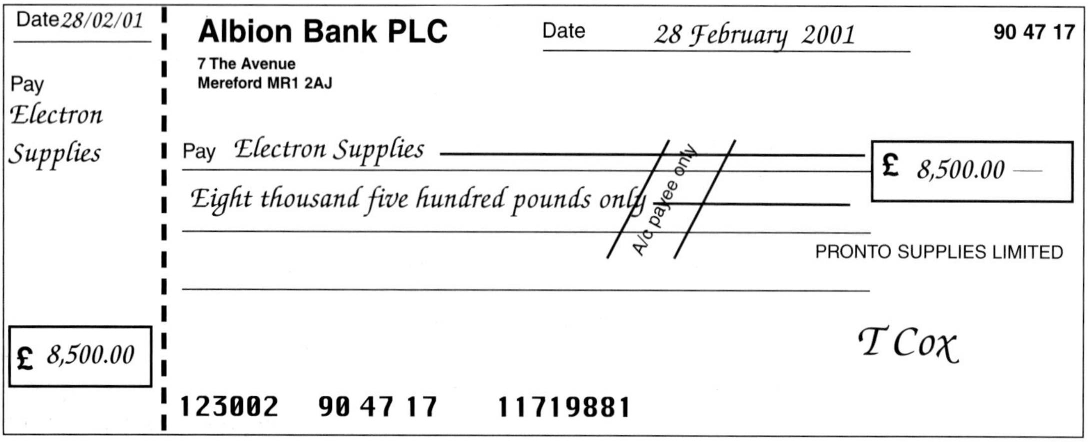

The business will send a **remittance advice** (see page 573) to the supplier with the cheque, or, if a BACS payment is being made, on its own. This, together with the cheque, will often provide the details for the input of the payment details on the computer.

Some programs can print remittance advices on the computer when the payment is processed. If the business decides to do this, the payment details are likely to be taken from the completed cheque and counterfoil. Some computer accounting programs which deal with long 'cheque runs' will also print the cheques themselves on special preprinted cheque stationery.

supplier payments and the accounting system

Payment to a supplier settling one or more invoices (less any credit notes) needs to be recorded in the accounting system:

- the balance of bank account will decrease (a credit in double-entry)
- the balance of the supplier's account (and the Purchases Ledger Control Account ['Creditors Control Account' in Sage]) will decrease because the supplier will be owed less (a debit in double-entry accounting)

In computer accounting the payment is input once and the entries will be automatically made from the same screen. Any settlement discount received will also be entered on the screen and the accounts posted automatically.

processing the payments

As with customer receipts, the business will normally input a number (a 'batch') of payments at one time on a regular basis, for example just after the cheques have been written out or the BACS payment instructions prepared.

The payments are input in Sage from the SUPPLIER icon on the BANK screen – after the appropriate bank account has been selected.

The procedure for recording the supplier payment is to:

- input the supplier reference in the box next to the word 'Payee' on the 'cheque' – this will bring up on screen the account name and all the outstanding amounts due on invoices
- input the cheque number on the cheque and alter the date if the cheque date is different
- input the amount of the payment in the amount box on the cheque; if it is a part payment the same procedure will be followed
- click on the Payment box of the invoice that is being paid – here it is the first one – and click on the 'Pay in full' icon at the bottom; if there is more than one invoice being paid click on the items being paid as appropriate; any part payment will be allocated to the appropriate invoice(s) in the same way
- check that what you have done is correct (ie supplier, amount, invoices being paid), print out a remittance advice if you want one by clicking on REMITTANCE, and SAVE
- print out a Day Books: Customer Payments (Summary) from REPORTS in BANK to check that the total of the cheques (or BACS payments) issued equals the total input on the computer

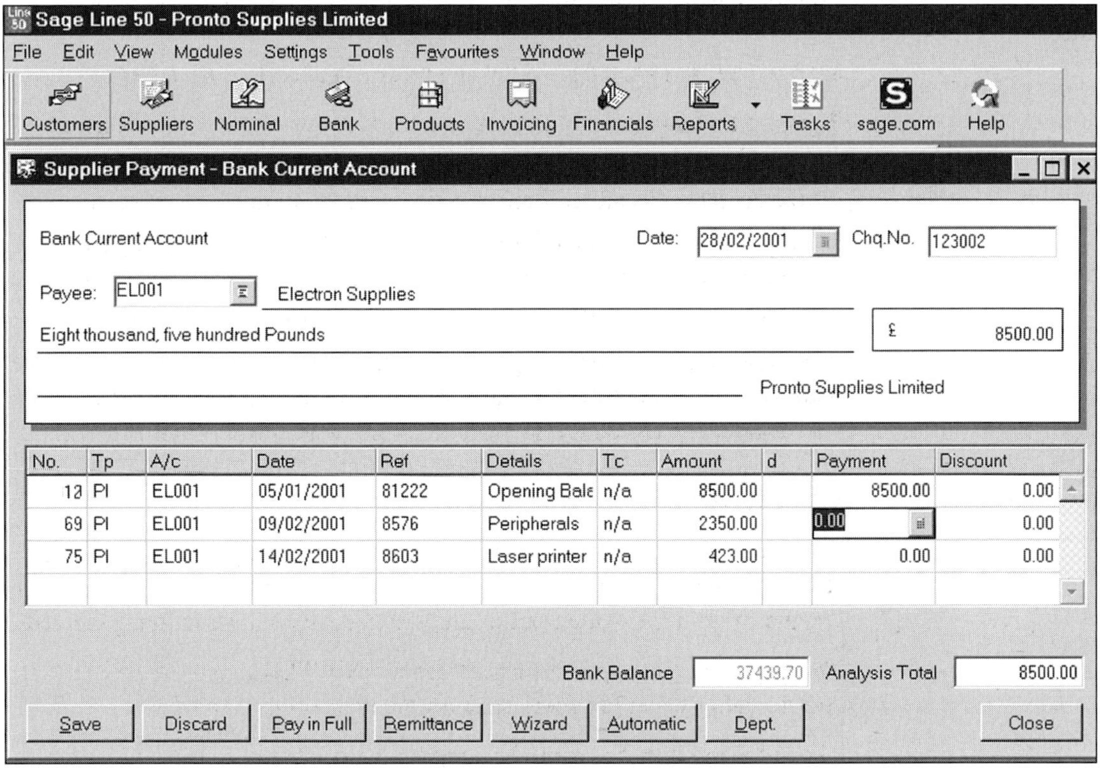

printing remittance advices

As we have already seen, you can print out remittance advices to accompany cheques, or to advise BACS payments to the supplier.

Depending on the version of Sage you are using, the printing may have to be done when you have checked the payment details and before you Save the payment transaction. In Sage Line 50 Version 8 and later you have the facility to print the documents later, from an icon on the BANK toolbar.

In the version of Sage used to illustrate this book (Version 7) you click on the REMITTANCE button at the bottom of the screen. This will bring up a screen for you to select a suitable remittance advice:

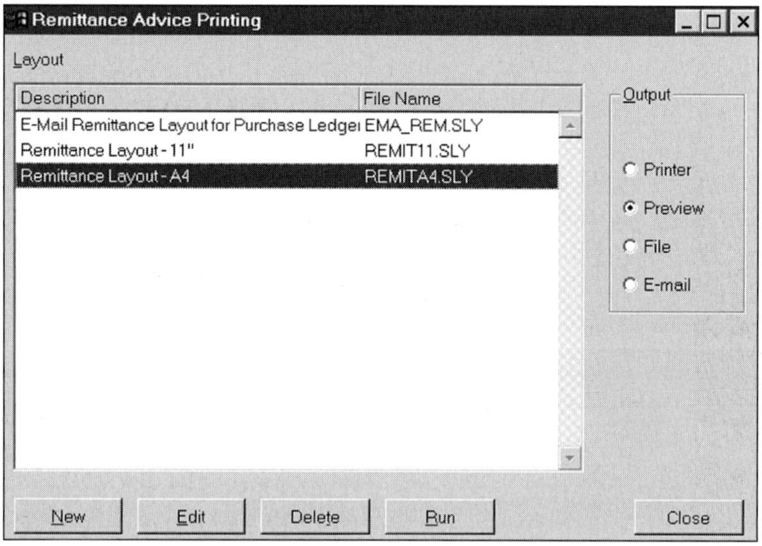

To print the remittance advice click on RUN at the bottom of the screen. A printed remittance advice (extract) is shown below.

Remittance Advice

From:
Pronto Supplies Limited
Unit 17 Severnvale Estate
Broadwater Road
Mereford
Wyvern
MR1 6TF

To:
Electron Supplies
17 Maxim Way
Manchester
M1 5TF

Date: 28/02/2001

Cheque no.

Date	Ref. No.	Details	Debit	Credit
28/02/2001		Payment on Account		8500.00

We will now look at the way in which Tom Cox's business, Pronto Supplies Limited, inputs its payments from customers and payments to suppliers on the computer.

Case Study

PRONTO SUPPLIES LIMITED: PROCESSING PAYMENTS FROM CUSTOMERS AND TO SUPPLIERS

It is February 28 2001. Tom has received a number of cheques (with remittance advices) from his customers in settlement of invoices sent out in January.

Some of the cheques also take into account the credit notes issued by Pronto Supplies.

Tom also has a list of supplier invoices to pay, the money being due at the end of the month.

receipts from customers

The list of cheques received is shown below.

John Butler & Associates	£5,500.00
Charisma Design	£2,400.00
Crowmatic Limited	£3,234.00
David Boossey	£3,165.00
French Emporium	£5,553.00
Jo Green Systems	£3,461.20
L Garr & Co	£8,500.00
Mendell & Son	£4,276.50
Prism Trading Limited	£2,586.00
Batch total of payments received	£38,675.70

These cheques are entered into the computer accounting system under CUSTOMER in the BANK section as shown on the screen shown at the top of the next page. This screen shows the second cheque on the list being input.

Tom then prints out a report 'Day Books: Customer Receipts (Summary)' which shows the transactions he has processed. This is also shown on the next page. He checks the total on the report against the batch total of the cheques (or remittance advices) he has received.

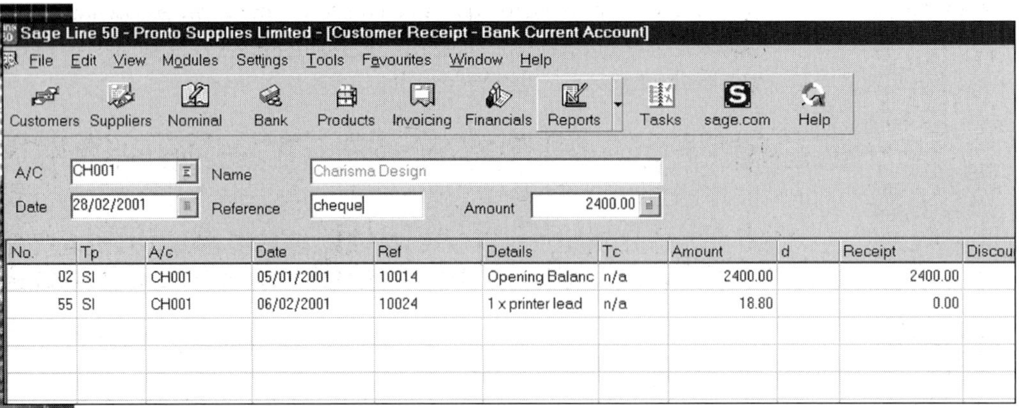

Sage Line 50 - Pronto Supplies Limited - [Customer Receipt - Bank Current Account]

File Edit View Modules Settings Tools Favourites Window Help

Customers Suppliers Nominal Bank Products Invoicing Financials Reports Tasks sage.com Help

A/C: CH001 Name: Charisma Design

Date: 28/02/2001 Reference: cheque Amount: 2400.00

No.	Tp	A/c	Date	Ref	Details	Tc	Amount	d	Receipt	Discou
02	SI	CH001	05/01/2001	10014	Opening Balanc	n/a	2400.00		2400.00	
55	SI	CH001	06/02/2001	10024	1 x printer lead	n/a	18.80		0.00	

Date: 09/11/2001 **Pronto Supplies Limited** Page: 1

Time: 15:01:21 **Day Books: Customer Receipts (Summary)**

Date From: 28/02/2001 **Bank From:**

Date To: 28/02/2001 **Bank To:** 99999999

Transaction From: 1 **Customer From:**

Transaction To: 99999999 **Customer To:** ZZZZZZZZ

No	Tp	Bank	A/C	Date	Refn	Details	Net	Tax	Gross	B
76	SR	1200	JB001	28/02/2001	chq	Sales Receipt	5,500.00	0.00	5,500.00	-
77	SR	1200	CH001	28/02/2001	chq	Sales Receipt	2,400.00	0.00	2,400.00	-
78	SR	1200	CR001	28/02/2001	chq	Sales Receipt	3,234.00	0.00	3,234.00	-
79	SR	1200	DB001	28/02/2001	chq	Sales Receipt	3,165.00	0.00	3,165.00	-
80	SR	1200	FE001	28/02/2001	chq	Sales Receipt	5,553.00	0.00	5,553.00	-
81	SR	1200	JG001	28/02/2001	chq	Sales Receipt	3,461.20	0.00	3,461.20	-
82	SR	1200	LG001	28/02/2001	chq	Sales Receipt	8,500.00	0.00	8,500.00	-
83	SR	1200	ME001	28/02/2001	chq	Sales Receipt	4,276.50	0.00	4,276.50	-
84	SR	1200	PT001	28/02/2001	chq	Sales Receipt	2,586.00	0.00	2,586.00	-
						Totals:	38,675.70	0.00	38,675.70	

payments to suppliers

Tom has made a list of the amounts he owes to his suppliers for goods sent to Pronto Supplies Limited in January.

The documents he has for this are his original purchase orders, invoices received and any credit notes issued by his suppliers.

The payment details are:

Delco PLC	£5,186.00	Cheque 123001
Electron Supplies	£8,500.00	Cheque 123002
MacCity	£4,455.35	Cheque 123003
Synchromart	£7,600.00	Cheque 123004
Tycomp Supplies	£6,160.00	Cheque 123005
Batch total of payments made	£31,901.35	

The cheques are prepared and entered into the computer accounting system under SUPPLIER in the BANK section as shown below. Tom also decides to print out remittance advices as he goes along.

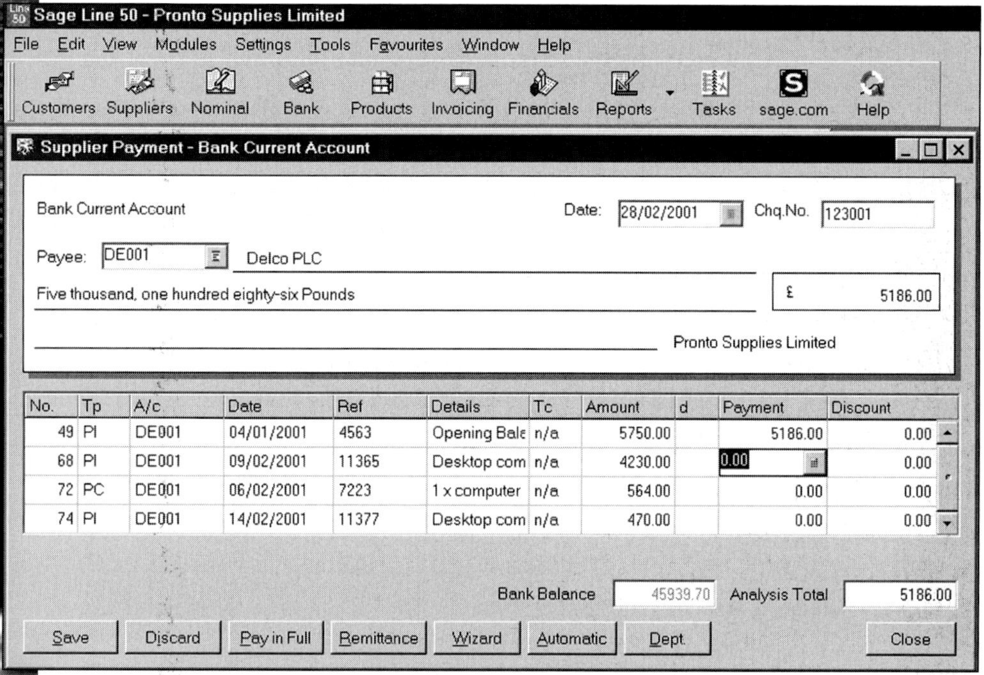

Tom then prints out a report Day Books: Supplier Receipts (Summary) which shows the transactions he has processed. He checks the total on the report against the total of the cheques he has issued.

Date: 09/11/2001
Time: 15:33:36

Pronto Supplies Limited

Day Books: Supplier Payments (Summary)

Page:

Date From: 28/02/2001
DateTo: 28/02/2001

Bank From:
Bank To: 99999999

Transaction From: 1
Transaction To: 99999999

Supplier From:
Supplier To: ZZZZZZZZ

No	Tp	Bank	A/C	Date	Refn	Details	Net	Tax	Gross
85	PP	1200	DE001	28/02/2001	123001	Purchase Payment	5,186.00	0.00	5,186.00
86	PP	1200	EL001	28/02/2001	123002	Purchase Payment	8,500.00	0.00	8,500.00
87	PP	1200	MA001	28/02/2001	123003	Purchase Payment	4,455.35	0.00	4,455.35
88	PP	1200	SY001	28/02/2001	123004	Purchase Payment	7,600.00	0.00	7,600.00
89	PP	1200	TY001	28/02/2001	123005	Purchase Payment	6,160.00	0.00	6,160.00
						Totals:	31,901.35	0.00	31,901.35

DEALING WITH CREDIT NOTES

When inputting payments from customers and to suppliers in a program like Sage, you may encounter the situation where the amount received (or paid out) is not the same as the amount of the invoice being settled.

For example, if a customer is issued with an invoice for £1,000 and then issued with a credit note for £100 because some of the goods are faulty, the customer will only owe – and pay – £900. The computer screen, however, will show this £900 as two separate lines: an invoice for £1,000 and a credit note for £100. If the £900 cheque received is allocated against the £1,000, the computer will think a balance of £100 still needs to be paid against this invoice, even though the account balance is nil!

the solution

The credit note, which is also outstanding on the computer screen needs to be allocated to the balance of the invoice. This is done by:

- clicking on the Receipt box on the credit note line
- clicking on 'Pay in Full' so that the analysis total shows a minus amount
- clicking on the Receipt box on the invoice line and then 'Pay in Full' so that the analysis box shows a nil balance

This tidying up procedure can be carried out before, during or after the payments received routine.

The procedure for allocating supplier credit notes to invoices works on exactly the same principles.

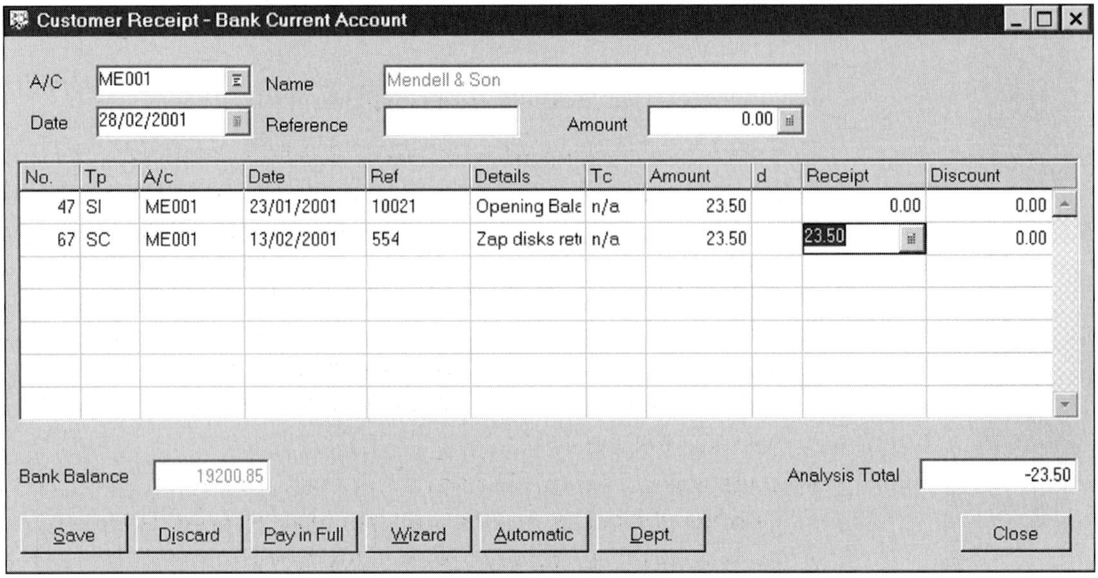

CASH SALES

Cash sales made by a business are usually sales made 'over the counter'.

Cash sales can be made by cash, cheque or debit or credit card – they are not just notes and coins. The important point here is that the business should pay the money into the Bank Current Account as soon as possible – it will be safer in the bank and can be used to meet payments the business may have made.

The input screen for cash sales is reached from the RECEIPT icon on the BANK menu bar. It looks like this:

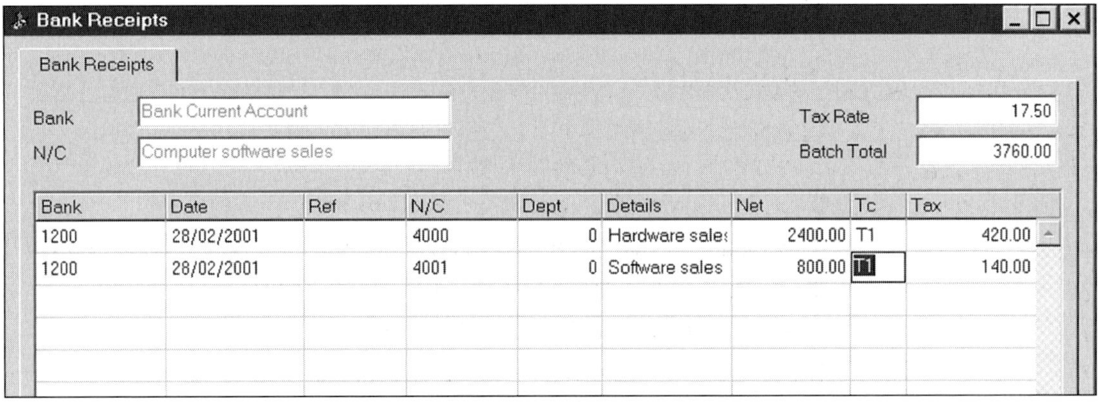

inputting bank receipts

Cash sales paid straight into the bank may be input from the bank paying-in slips recorded in the handwritten business cash book or from a sales listing sheet. These receipts are known in Sage as Bank Receipts and are input as follows:

- input the computer bank account number
- enter the date (usually the date the money is paid into the bank)
- enter a reference (this can be the reference number of the paying-in slip)
- input the appropriate nominal code (N/C) for the type of sales involved
- enter a description of the payment (eg 'hardware sales') under 'Details'
- enter the net amount of the sales (ie the sales amount excluding VAT) and then click on T1 if the goods are standard rated for VAT – the computer will then automatically calculate the VAT amount for you and show it in the right-hand column
- check that the VAT amount shown agrees with your figure and change it on screen if it does not – there may be a rounding difference
- check the input details and totals and then SAVE

CASH PAYMENTS

Most credit payments made by businesses, as we saw in the last chapter, are to suppliers for goods and services provided and paid for on invoice. But businesses also have to make payments on a day-to-day and cash basis (immediate payment) for a wide variety of running costs such as wages and telephone bills.

These payments are input from the screen reached by clicking on the PAYMENT icon on the BANK menu bar. Study the example shown below. Here a telephone bill and wages have been paid from the Bank Current Account.

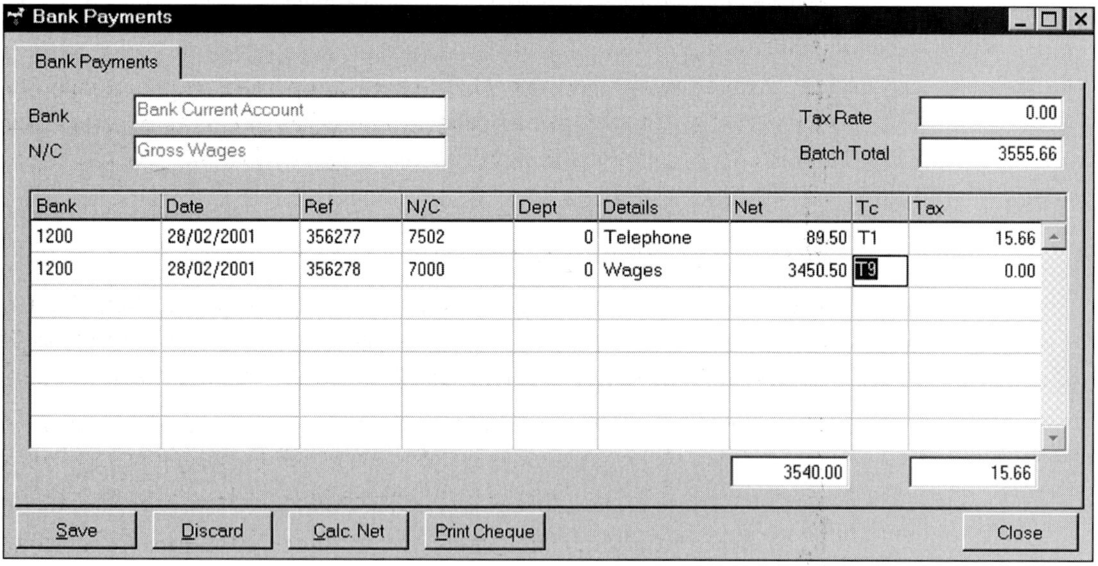

inputting cash payments

Cash payments can be input from the handwritten business **cash book** (if one is used), or from the cheques issued and bills being paid (which should show any VAT element). The procedure for inputting is:

- input the computer bank account number
- enter the date (the date the payment is made)
- enter a reference (normally the cheque number or 'BACS' if the payment is a BACS payment)
- input the appropriate nominal code (N/C) for the type of payment involved
- enter a brief description of the nature of the payment (eg 'Telephone') under 'Details'

- enter the net amount of the payment (ie the amount excluding VAT) and then click on T1 if the product is standard rated for VAT – the computer will then automatically calculate the VAT amount for you and show it in the right-hand column
- check that the VAT amount shown agrees with your figure and change it on screen if it does not – there may be a rounding difference

a note on VAT

The VAT rates used here are:

T1	the telephone bill is standard rated
T9	wages do not involve VAT

The code for a zero-rated item would have been T0. The code for a VAT exempt item would have been T2.

If you do not know what the VAT element of a payment figure is, enter the total figure in the 'Net' column and click on 'Calc.Net' at the bottom of the screen. The computer will then automatically calculate the VAT and adjust the Net figure accordingly.

checking the input data

You will see that the screen on the previous page shows the Net, Tax and Batch totals. These will automatically update as you enter the transactions. It is important to check your input against the source data for your input.

If you are entering the data as a batch of entries you should add up the three totals (Net, VAT and Batch) manually and check them against the screen figures when you have finished your data entry, but before you Save.

As a final check you should print out a Day Book report (see example below) from Reports in BANK and check the entries against your handwritten records (your cash book, for example).

Time: 14:36:46

Day Books: Bank Payments (Summary)

Date From: 01/02/2001
DateTo: 28/02/2001

Bank From:
Bank To: 99999999

Transaction From: 1
Transaction To: 99999999

No	Tp	Bank	Date	Refn	Details	Net	Tax	Gross
96	BP	1200	12/02/2001	122992	Cash purchases	15,500.00	2,712.50	18,212.50
97	BP	1200	14/02/2001	122993	Advert	10,200.00	1,785.00	11,985.00
98	BP	1200	15/02/2001	122994	Furniture	5,000.00	875.00	5,875.00
99	BP	1200	16/02/2001	122995	Rent	4,500.00	787.50	5,287.50
100	BP	1200	19/02/2001	122996	Rates	350.00	0.00	350.00
101	BP	1200	23/02/2001	122997	RPower	158.00	27.65	185.65
102	BP	1200	26/02/2001	122998	ZipTelecom	310.00	54.25	364.25
103	BP	1200	26/02/2001	122999	Stationery	340.00	59.50	399.50
104	BP	1200	28/02/2001	123000	Wages	16,780.00	0.00	16,780.00
					Totals:	53,138.00	6,301.40	59,439.40

Case Study

PRONTO SUPPLIES LIMITED: CASH RECEIPTS AND PAYMENTS

It is February 28 2001 and Tom has completed and checked his input of customer receipts and supplier payments (see pages 579 to 581).

He now has to input the various cash receipts and payments received and made during the month.

cash receipts

Pronto Supplies Limited paid takings of cash sales into the bank current account three times during the month. The amounts recorded in the cash book are shown below. The reference quoted is the paying-in slip reference.

Date	*Details*	*Net amount (£)*	*VAT (£)*	*ref.*
9 Feb 2001	Hardware sales	12,500.00	2187.50	10736
9 Feb 2001	Software sales	4,680.00	819.00	10737
16 Feb 2001	Hardware sales	15,840.00	2,772.00	10738
16 Feb 2001	Software sales	3,680.00	644.00	10739
23 Feb 2001	Hardware sales	17,800.00	3,115.00	10740
23 Feb 2001	Software sales	4,800.00	840.00	10741
	Totals	59,300.00	10,377.50	

These sales receipts are entered into the computer accounting system on the RECEIPTS screen reached from the BANK menu bar. Note that the Bank Current Account and the appropriate nominal sales code (N/C) are used each time.

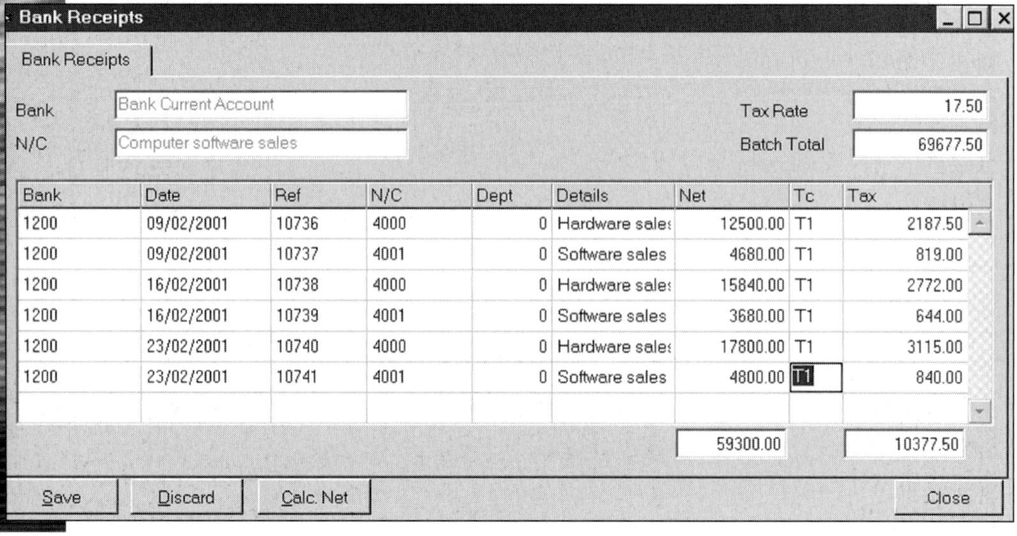

Bank Receipts
Bank Receipts
Bank
Bank Current Account
N/C
Computer software sales
Tax Rate
17.50
Batch Total
69677.50
Bank Date Ref N/C Dept Details Net Tc Tax
1200 09/02/2001 10736 4000 0 Hardware sales 12500.00 T1 2187.50
1200 09/02/2001 10737 4001 0 Software sales 4680.00 T1 819.00
1200 16/02/2001 10738 4000 0 Hardware sales 15840.00 T1 2772.00
1200 16/02/2001 10739 4001 0 Software sales 3680.00 T1 644.00
1200 23/02/2001 10740 4000 0 Hardware sales 17800.00 T1 3115.00
1200 23/02/2001 10741 4001 0 Software sales 4800.00 T1 840.00
59300.00
10377.50
Save
Discard
Calc. Net
Close

Tom then checks his listing totals against the on-screen totals for accuracy and clicks SAVE. He then prints out a report Day Books: Bank Receipts (Summary) as a paper-based record of the transactions he has processed. This is shown below. He again checks the totals on the report against the totals on his original listing.

Pronto Supplies Limited

Day Books: Bank Receipts (Summary)

Date From: 01/02/2001
DateTo: 28/02/2001

Transaction From: 1
Transaction To: 99999999

No	Tp	Bank	Date	Refn	Details	Net	Tax	Gross
90	BR	1200	09/02/2001	10736	Hardware sales	12,500.00	2,187.50	14,687.50
91	BR	1200	09/02/2001	10737	Software sales	4,680.00	819.00	5,499.00
92	BR	1200	16/02/2001	10738	Hardware sales	15,840.00	2,772.00	18,612.00
93	BR	1200	16/02/2001	10739	Software sales	3,680.00	644.00	4,324.00
94	BR	1200	23/02/2001	10740	Hardware sales	17,800.00	3,115.00	20,915.00
95	BR	1200	23/02/2001	10741	Software sales	4,800.00	840.00	5,640.00
					Totals:	59,300.00	10,377.50	69,677.50

cash payments

Tom sees from the company cash book that Pronto Supplies Limited has made a number of cash payments – by cheque – during the month for a variety of purposes. They are listed below. They include:

- normal day-to-day running (revenue) expenses paid on a cash (immediate) basis
- the purchase of furniture (a capital item) for £5,000 on 15 February

Date	*Details*	*Net amount (£)*	*VAT (£)*	*chq no*
12 Feb 2001	Cash purchases	15,500.00	2,712.50	122992
14 Feb 2001	Advertising	10,200.00	1,785.00	122993
15 Feb 2001	Furniture	5,000.00	875.00	122994
16 Feb 2001	Rent	4,500.00	787.50	122995
19 Feb 2001	Rates	350.00	exempt	122996
23 Feb 2001	RPower (Electricity)	158.00	27.65	122997
26 Feb 2001	ZipTelecom (Telephone)	310.00	54.25	122998
26 Feb 2001	Stationery	340.00	59.50	122999
28 Feb 2001	Wages	16,780.00	no VAT	123000
	Totals	53,138.00	6301.40	

These sales payments are entered into the computer accounting system on the PAYMENTS screen reached from the BANK menu bar. Note that the Bank Current Account and the appropriate nominal code (N/C) is used each time. The reference in each case is the relevant cheque number.

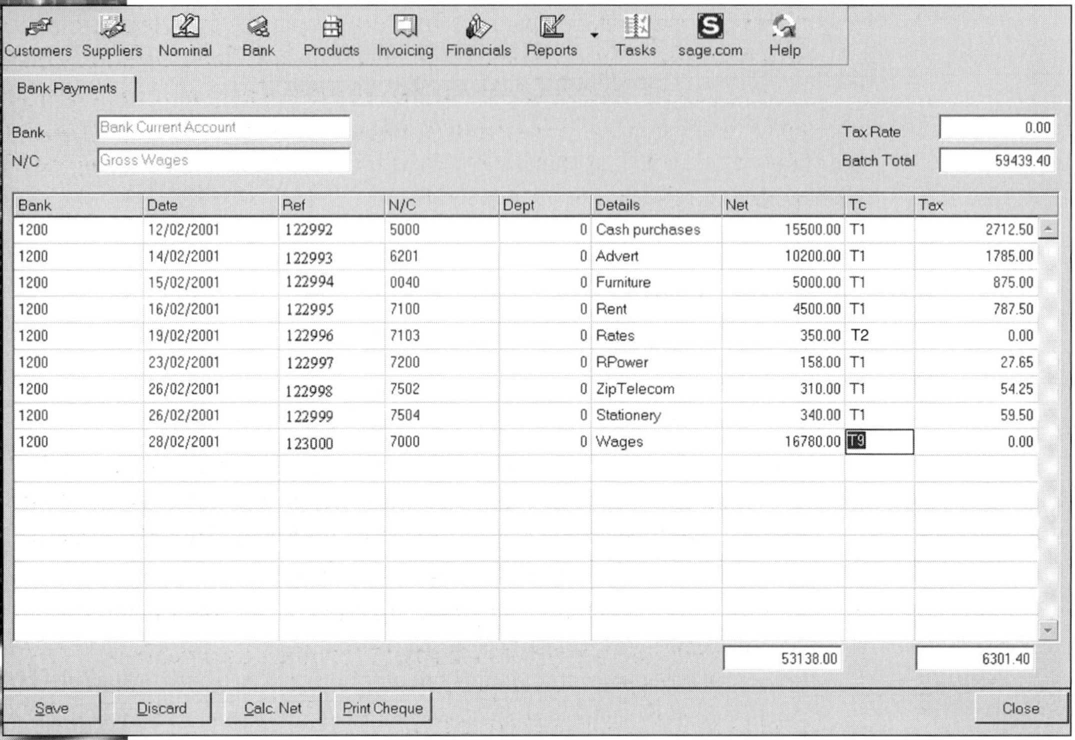

Bank	Date	Ref	N/C	Dept	Details	Net	Tc	Tax
1200	12/02/2001	122992	5000	0	Cash purchases	15500.00	T1	2712.50
1200	14/02/2001	122993	6201	0	Advert	10200.00	T1	1785.00
1200	15/02/2001	122994	0040	0	Furniture	5000.00	T1	875.00
1200	16/02/2001	122995	7100	0	Rent	4500.00	T1	787.50
1200	19/02/2001	122996	7103	0	Rates	350.00	T2	0.00
1200	23/02/2001	122997	7200	0	RPower	158.00	T1	27.65
1200	26/02/2001	122998	7502	0	ZipTelecom	310.00	T1	54.25
1200	26/02/2001	122999	7504	0	Stationery	340.00	T1	59.50
1200	28/02/2001	123000	7000	0	Wages	16780.00	T9	0.00
						53138.00		6301.40

Tom then checks his listing totals against the on-screen totals for accuracy and clicks SAVE. He prints out a report Day Books: Bank Payments (Summary) as a record of the transactions he has processed. This is shown below. He compares the totals on the report against the totals on his original listing as a final check of input accuracy.

Pronto Supplies Limited

Day Books: Bank Payments (Summary)

Date From: 01/02/2001
DateTo: 28/02/2001

Transaction From: 1
Transaction To: 99999999

No	Tp	Bank	Date	Refn	Details	Net	Tax	Gross
96	BP	1200	12/02/2001	122992	Cash purchases	15,500.00	2,712.50	18,212.50
97	BP	1200	14/02/2001	122993	Advert	10,200.00	1,785.00	11,985.00
98	BP	1200	15/02/2001	122994	Furniture	5,000.00	875.00	5,875.00
99	BP	1200	16/02/2001	122995	Rent	4,500.00	787.50	5,287.50
100	BP	1200	19/02/2001	122996	Rates	350.00	0.00	350.00
101	BP	1200	23/02/2001	122997	RPower	158.00	27.65	185.65
102	BP	1200	26/02/2001	122998	ZipTelecom	310.00	54.25	364.25
103	BP	1200	26/02/2001	122999	Stationery	340.00	59.50	399.50
104	BP	1200	28/02/2001	123000	Wages	16,780.00	0.00	16,780.00
					Totals:	53,138.00	6,301.40	59,439.40

USING A 'CASH' ACCOUNT

A business which holds substantial amounts of cash – eg shop 'takings' – may wish to operate a separate Cash Account on the computer, just as it may set up separate 'cash' columns in the manual Cash Book. If this is the case, it will open a separate account in BANK for this purpose. Any transfers to and from the actual bank Current Account will be made using the bank transfer screen. This transfer screen will also be used when making transfers to Petty Cash Account (see below).

PETTY CASH

petty cash and the accounting system

As you will know from your studies, **petty cash** is a fund of money kept in the business in the same way as the bank current account is a fund of money kept in the bank. A 'bank' account will be set up for petty cash on the computer which will handle all the transactions:

- payments of cash into petty cash from the bank current account
- payments out of petty cash to pay for small expense items

payments into petty cash

The Sage computer system has a default Petty Cash Account which it classes as a bank account, although, of course, the money is not in the bank. The computer sees it as a 'money fund'.

When cash is needed to top up the petty cash, the business will normally cash a cheque at the bank and then put the money in the cash tin. The computer program requires the business to input the transaction as a TRANSFER from the BANK menu bar. In the screen below, a business has cashed a £100 cheque at the bank (using cheque 132003) to provide the cash.

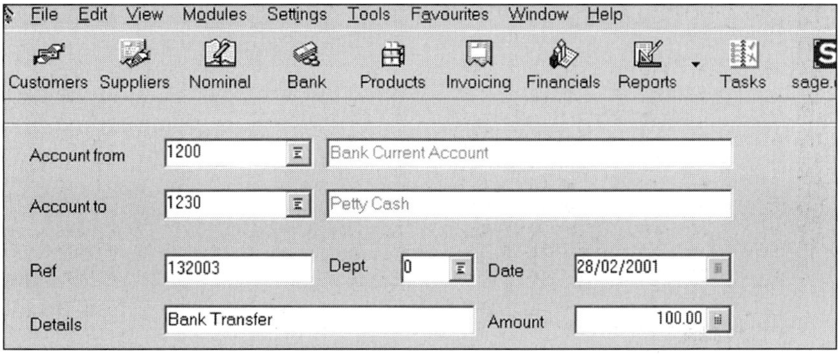

payments out of petty cash

Payments out of Petty Cash Account are handled in exactly the same way on the computer as payments out of Bank Current Account.

The PAYMENTS screen is reached through the BANK menu bar. The details are then input from the petty cash vouchers or the petty cash book in which they are recorded.

The screen below shows a petty cash voucher and the input of the details into the Sage BANK PAYMENTS screen.

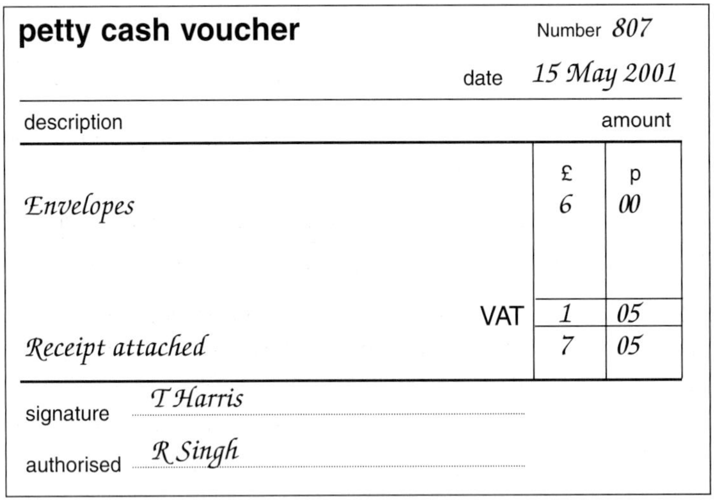

petty cash voucher Number *807*

date *15 May 2001*

description	amount £	p
Envelopes	*6*	*00*
VAT	*1*	*05*
Receipt attached	*7*	*05*

signature *T Harris*

authorised *R Singh*

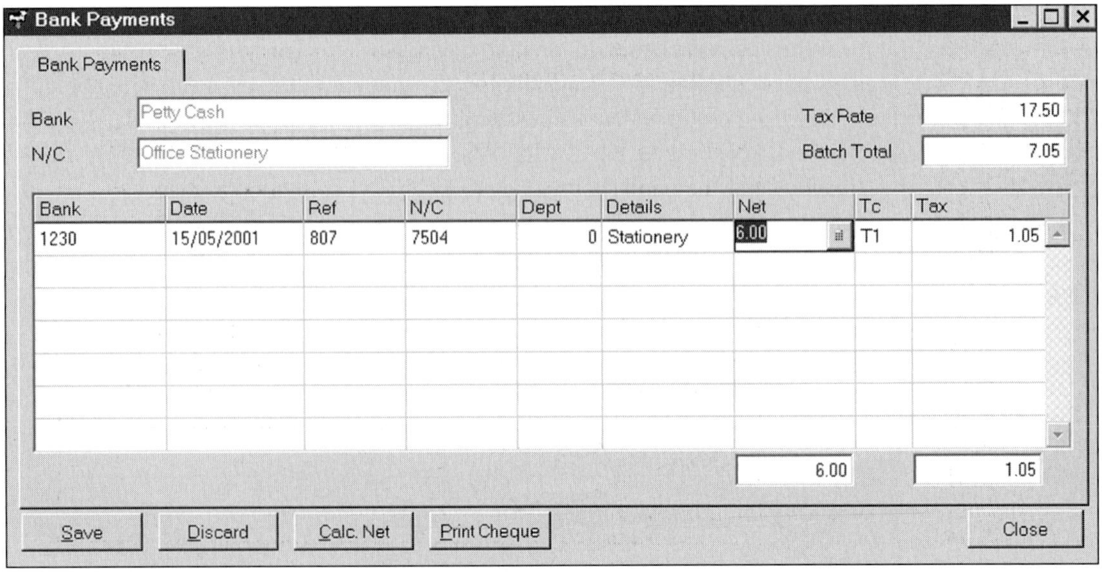

Points to remember are:

- the bank account number used is the Petty Cash Account number
- the reference is the petty cash voucher number
- petty cash vouchers and their receipts will not always show the VAT amount – the VAT and net amount can be calculated on the computer by inputting the full amount under 'Net' and then clicking on 'Calc.Net' at the bottom of the screen (using T1 code to denote standard rate VAT)
- when the details have been checked you should SAVE
- the details can also be checked against a Cash Payments Day Book printout if required (accessed through Reports in BANK)

Case Study

PRONTO SUPPLIES LIMITED: SETTING UP THE PETTY CASH SYSTEM

At the beginning of February Tom Cox set up a petty cash system at Pronto Supplies Limited. The situation at 28 February is as follows:

- Tom notes that he cashed cheque no 122991 for £100 at the bank on 1 February.
- The £100 cash was transferred to the petty cash tin on 1 February.
- The tin contains three vouchers for payments made during the month – these are shown below and on the next page. They are ready for entry in the petty cash book as part of the month-end routine.

  Voucher PC101 shows the VAT included in the total (standard rate: T1)

  Voucher PC102 does not have any VAT in it (postage stamps are exempt:T2)

  Voucher PC103 does not show the VAT included in the total (standard rate: T1) because it was not shown separately on the original receipt.

petty cash voucher

Number *PC101*

date *7 Feb 2001*

description	amount £	p
Stationery	*36*	*00*
VAT	*6*	*30*
Receipt obtained	*42*	*30*

signature *Nick Vellope*

authorised *Tom Cox*

petty cash voucher Number *PC102*

date *14 Feb 2001*

description	amount £	p
Postages	*25*	*00*
VAT		
Receipt obtained	*25*	*00*

signature *R Patel*

authorised *Tom Cox*

petty cash voucher Number *PC103*

date *20 Feb 2001*

description	amount £	p
Stationery		
VAT		
Receipt obtained	*18*	*80*

signature *B Radish*

authorised *Tom Cox*

the transfer to petty cash

Tom Cox first inputs the £100 transfer from the Bank Current Account to the Petty Cash Account. The screen is illustrated below. Note the use of the cheque number as the reference.

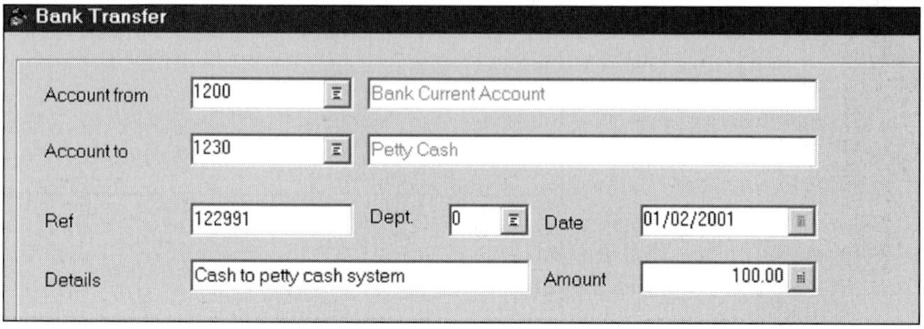

inputting the vouchers

The petty cash payments are entered into the computer accounting system on the PAYMENTS screen reached from the BANK menu bar.

Note that the bank Petty Cash Account number and the appropriate nominal code (N/C) is used each time.

The postages nominal code was taken from the default nominal list.

The reference in each case is the relevant petty cash voucher number.

Postages are VAT exempt. The VAT on the third petty cash voucher was not on the receipt but has been calculated on-screen by inputting the total amount of £18.80 in the 'Net' column and clicking on 'Calc.Net' at the bottom of the screen:

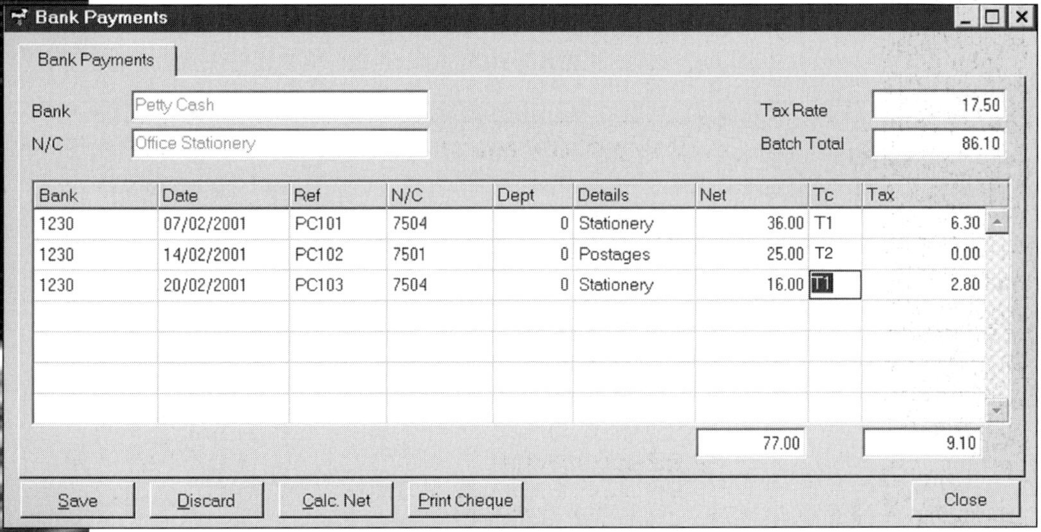

Bank	Date	Ref	N/C	Dept	Details	Net	Tc	Tax
1230	07/02/2001	PC101	7504	0	Stationery	36.00	T1	6.30
1230	14/02/2001	PC102	7501	0	Postages	25.00	T2	0.00
1230	20/02/2001	PC103	7504	0	Stationery	16.00	T1	2.80
						77.00		9.10

Tom then checks the batch total with the total of the vouchers and when he is happy that all the details are correct he will SAVE. The Day Book report will now show the petty cash payments. Note that the transaction code is 'CP' (second column from the left). This stands for 'Cash Payment'. This distinguishes the petty cash payments from payments by cheque (input through the same screen). These cheque payments have the code 'BP' which stands for 'Bank Payment'.

Pronto Supplies Limited

Day Books: Cash Payments (Summary)

Date From: 01/02/2001
Date To: 28/02/2001

Bank From:
Bank To: 99999999

Transaction From: 1
Transaction To: 99999999

No	Tp	Bank	Date	Ref	Details	Net	Tax	Gross
107	CP	1230	07/02/2001	PC101	Stationery	36.00	6.30	42.30
108	CP	1230	14/02/2001	PC102	Postages	25.00	0.00	25.00
109	CP	1230	20/02/2001	PC103	Stationery	16.00	2.80	18.80
					Totals:	77.00	9.10	86.10

JOURNAL ENTRIES

Journal entries enable you to make transfers from one nominal (Main Ledger) account to another. Journal entries are used, for example, when you are completing a VAT return and need to transfer VAT amounts from one VAT account to another. It is also useful if an error needs to be corrected when an entry has been input to the wrong account.

Suppose you are inputting a batch of Bank Payments which include a number of bills that have to be paid. You have written out a cheque for £94 to RPower for a gas bill, but when inputting it you think it is for electricity and so post it to electricity (nominal account 7200) instead of gas (7201). You can correct your mistake using a journal entry. You bring up the screen by clicking on the JOURNALS icon on the NOMINAL menu bar:

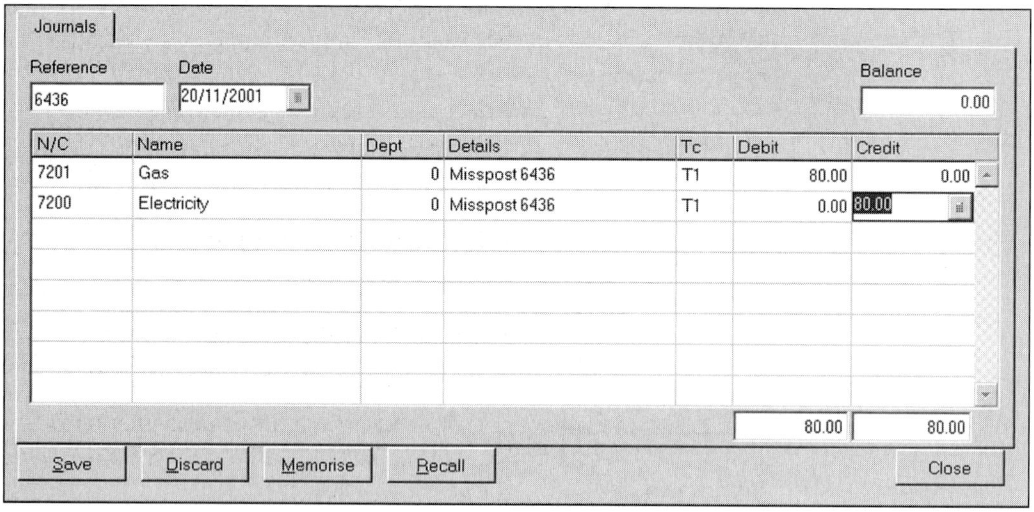

The procedure is:

- enter the reference (this could be the transaction number you can find by opening up the FINANCIALS screen and locating the transaction)
- enter the date
- enter the nominal code of the account to which you are going to post the debit; here it is Gas Account because you are recording an expense
- enter the reason for the transaction – here you are adjusting a mispost
- enter the VAT tax code input on the original (wrong) entry
- enter the net amount in the debit column (ie the amount before VAT has been added on) – here the net amount is £80 and VAT (here at standard rate) is £14 and the total is £94; note that neither the VAT nor the total appear on the screen because you are not adjusting the VAT; *only the net amount* has gone to the wrong account

- enter the nominal code of the account to which you are going to post the credit; here it is Electricity Account because you are effectively refunding the amount to the account – it is an income item and so a credit
- enter the remaining data as you did for the debit, but enter the net amount in the right-hand credit column
- make sure the Balance box reads zero – meaning that the debit equals the credit – and SAVE

BANK RECONCILIATION ON THE COMPUTER

You should already know how to draw up a bank reconciliation statement. If you are not sure what this involves, you should first read pages 386 to 393.

To recap, a bank reconciliation statement forms a link between the balances shown in the bank statement and the Bank Account in the cash book (or its computer equivalent).

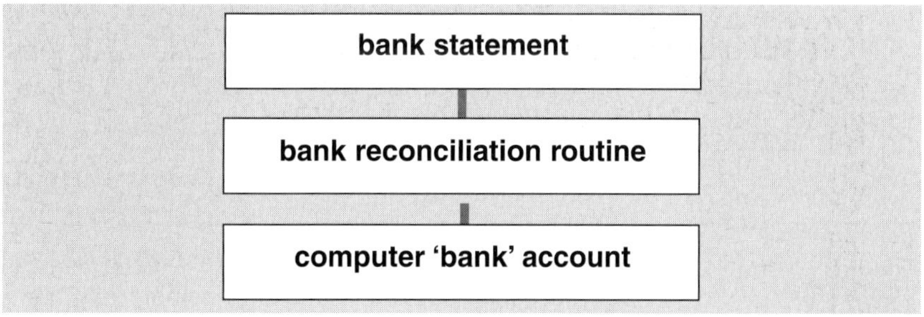

The Sage system allows you to carry out a bank reconciliation. The Bank Reconciliation screen, accessed through RECONCILE in BANK, is shown on the next page. The procedure is as follows:

1. Enter the bank statement date and closing bank statement balance at the top of the screen and check that the opening balance is the same on the computer screen and on the bank statement.
2. Compare the items on the screen with the bank statement – selecting them item by item – and update the computer with any items which appear on the bank statement and not on the computer screen (ie by inputting them, using the Adjustment button).
3. When you have highlighted all the items on screen which are in the bank statement and updated the computer (see **2**), check that the Sage 'Reconcile Balance' matches the bank statement closing balance and the Difference box shows zero. Reconciliation is then complete.
4. Click SAVE – any unselected items (ie items on the computer but not in the bank, eg the £6,160 cheque on the screen on the next page) will appear again when you next carry out this bank reconciliation process.

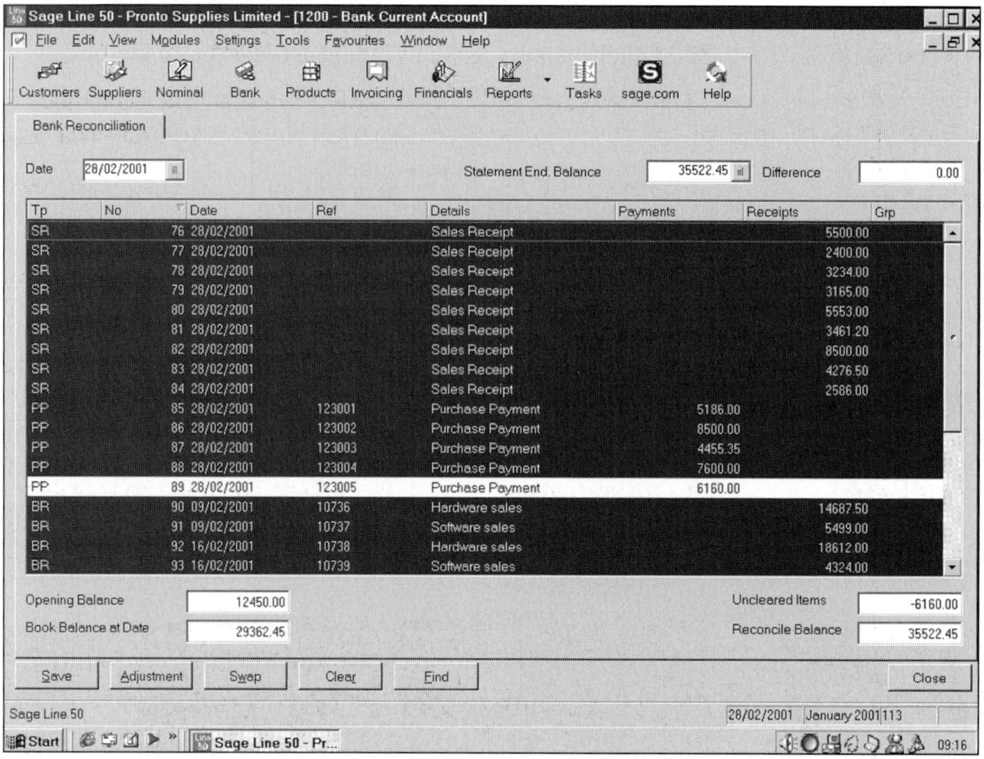

a bank reconciliation screen – see Task 10 of the Student Activities

Chapter Summary

- A business can set up not only the bank current account in the computer accounting system, but also a number of other 'money' accounts. These, which include petty cash account, enable the business to keep track of the processing of money in a variety of forms.

- Payments received from customers who have bought on credit and payments to suppliers from whom the business has bought on credit can be processed through the computer accounting system.

- It is essential to check the input of payments from customers and to suppliers by obtaining a printout – such as a Day Book – from the computer.

- Petty cash transactions are processed on the computer through Petty Cash Account. Cash payments and receipts are either processed on the computer through the Bank Account, or through a special 'Cash' account which is the same as Cash Account in a manual accounting system.

- The computer accounting system also provides the facility for making adjustments with journal entries (eg for correcting errors), and reconciling the bank statement balances with the computer bank account.

Key Terms

cash payments	payments made straightaway
credit payments	payments made at a later date following the issue of an invoice to a customer or by a supplier
remittance advice	a document that tells a business that a payment is being made
petty cash	a float of cash kept in the office for making small purchases
journal	the part of the accounting system which enables you to make transfers from one nominal (main ledger) account to another
bank reconciliation	the 'tallying up' of the bank statement with the bank account in the accounting system and the identification of differences

Student Activities

technical note
Before starting these inputting tasks you must ensure either that your input from the last chapter is correct or that the Sage file 'Suppliers.27' (provided by Osborne Books) is loaded or restored onto your computer.

Task 1

Set the program date to 28 February 2001. Enter the following customer cheques into BANK (CUSTOMER). Use the reference 'cheque'.

Print out a Day Books: Customer Receipts (Summary) Report from REPORTS in BANK. Agree the day book total with the batch total (below) to confirm the accuracy of your input.

John Butler & Associates	£5,500.00
Charisma Design	£2,400.00
Crowmatic Limited	£3,234.00
David Boossey	£3,165.00
French Emporium	£5,553.00
Jo Green Systems	£3,461.20
L Garr & Co	£8,500.00
Mendell & Son	£4,276.50
Prism Trading Limited	£2,586.00
Batch total of payments received	£38,675.70

Task 2

Enter the following cheques Tom is paying to suppliers into the computer (SUPPLIER in BANK). If you are able, print remittance advices for each payment (REMITTANCE button at the bottom of the screen). Print out a Day Books: Supplier Payments (Summary) Report from REPORTS in BANK. Agree the day book total with the batch total (below) to confirm the accuracy of your input. The cheques are dated 28 February.

Delco PLC	£5,186.00	Cheque 123001
Electron Supplies	£8,500.00	Cheque 123002
MacCity	£4,455.35	Cheque 123003
Synchromart	£7,600.00	Cheque 123004
Tycomp Supplies	£6,160.00	Cheque 123005
Batch total of payments made	£31,901.35	

Task 3

If you have not already allocated your credit notes, check through your customer accounts by opening up the Customer Receipts screen for each one. You may find that some of them have a credit note outstanding and an invoice which has not been completely paid. You should in each case allocate the credit note to the appropriate invoice. Ensure in each case that the correct bank account is selected before you make the adjustment.

Task 4

Repeat the procedure in Task 3 by opening up the Supplier Payments screen for each supplier. You should in each case allocate the credit note to the appropriate invoice.

Task 5

Ensure the program date is set at 28 February 2001. Enter the following bank cash receipts into the computer. Check your totals before saving and print out a Day Books: Bank Receipts (Summary) Report to confirm the accuracy of your input. The nominal codes you will need are on the Trial Balance on page 601.

Date	*Details*	*Net amount (£)*	*VAT (£)*	*ref.*
9 Feb 2001	Hardware sales	12,500.00	2187.50	10736
9 Feb 2001	Software sales	4,680.00	819.00	10737
16 Feb 2001	Hardware sales	15,840.00	2,772.00	10738
16 Feb 2001	Software sales	3,680.00	644.00	10739
23 Feb 2001	Hardware sales	17,800.00	3,115.00	10740
23 Feb 2001	Software sales	4,800.00	840.00	10741
	Totals	59,300.00	10,377.50	

Task 6

Keep the program date as 28 February 2001.

Enter the following cash payments into the computer. Take care over the nominal accounts that you choose and the VAT Tax codes used. T1 is the standard rate code, T2 is for exempt items and T9 is the code for transactions which do not involve VAT. You can find the nominal codes on the trial balance on page 601.

Check your totals before saving and print out a Day Books: Bank Payments (Summary) Report

Date	*Details*	*Net amount (£)*	*VAT (£)*	*chq no*
12 Feb 2001	Materials purchased	15,500.00	2,712.50	122992
14 Feb 2001	Advertising	10,200.00	1,785.00	122993
15 Feb 2001	Furniture	5,000.00	875.00	122994
16 Feb 2001	Rent	4,500.00	787.50	122995
19 Feb 2001	Rates	350.00	exempt	122996
23 Feb 2001	Electricity (RPower)	158.00	27.65	122997
26 Feb 2001	Telephone (ZipTelecom)	310.00	54.25	122998
26 Feb 2001	Stationery	340.00	59.50	122999
28 Feb 2001	Wages	16,780.00	no VAT	123000
	Totals	53,138.00	6301.40	

Task 7

Keep the program date as 28 February 2001.

On 1 February Tom cashed cheque 122991 for £100 at his bank to set up a petty cash system.

Carry out a bank transfer from Bank Current Account to Petty Cash Account for this amount.

Task 8

Keep the program date as 28 February 2001. Tom has just authorised two more petty cash vouchers (shown below and on the next page). Input these together with the three petty cash vouchers on pages 591 to 592 into Bank Payments, taking particular care with the VAT element on each one (postages are VAT exempt and stationery is standard-rated).

Print out a Day Books: Cash Payments (Summary) Report to confirm the accuracy of your input of the five vouchers.

Hint: remember to select the Petty Cash Bank account on the screen before running the report.

petty cash voucher Number *PC104*

date *28 Feb 2001*

description	amount £	p
Postage stamps	*5*	*00*
VAT		
Receipt obtained	*5*	*00*

signature *R Cook*

authorised *Tom Cox*

petty cash voucher

Number *PC105*

date *28 Feb 2001*

description	amount £	p
Stationery		
VAT		
Receipt obtained	*4*	*70*

signature *R Patel*

authorised *Tom Cox*

Task 9

Keep the program date as 28 February 2001.

Tom has been talking to his accountant about the categories of expenses which are recorded in his Nominal (Main) Ledger. He finds that a payment of £100, made on 20 January, which appears under advertising (account 6201) was actually for office stationery (account 7504).

The accountant suggests that Tom makes a journal entry to adjust the position, debiting account 7504 and crediting account 6201. Make an appropriate journal entry, using the same VAT code (T1) as on the original transaction. The reference is 0041 and the current date 28 February 2001. The details are 'wrong post 20/01/01'. The JOURNALS screen is accessed through NOMINAL.

Print out a Day Books: Nominal Ledger Report dated 28 February 2001 from REPORTS in NOMINAL and check the details to confirm the accuracy of your input.

Print out a Trial Balance as at 28 February 2001 and check it against the Trial Balance shown opposite.

Task 10

Enter a new program date of 6 March 2001.

Tom has an online facility with his bank and has just printed out his bank statement as at 5 March 2001. He decides to carry out a bank reconciliation on the computer, using the RECONCILE function through BANK.

The starting balance of the bank statement is £12,450, which agrees with the balance of account 1200 'Bank Current Account' on the computer, as shown on the opening trial balance (see page 548). The closing balance of the bank statement is £35,522.45.

All the items on the computer screen are on the bank statement apart from cheque 123005 for £6,160 which has not yet gone through the bank account.

When you have completed the reconciliation process, SAVE and run and print out a 'Bank Report: Reconciled and Un-reconciled' to show the items that have been reconciled and any that have not.

Note that some of the important figures for this Task are shown on the screen illustration on page 596.

Reminder! Have you made a backup?

Task 11

Ensure the program date is still set at 6 March 2001.

Tom has decided to let out two small offices in his building. He wants to set up an account in NOMINAL to record the receipts of rent from the two tenants.

You are to set up a new account called 'Rents Receivable'. The account number allocated will be 4003.

When the account is set up, select account 4003 on the NOMINAL screen and print out a Nominal List Report which will show that you have opened the account.

Pronto Supplies, trial balance as at 28 February 2001

Pronto Supplies Limited

Period Trial Balance

To Period: Month 2, February 2001

N/C	Name		Debit	Credit
0020	Plant and Machinery		35,000.00	
0030	Office Equipment		15,760.00	
0040	Furniture and Fixtures		30,000.00	
1100	Debtors Control Account		8,991.00	
1200	Bank Current Account		29,362.45	
1230	Petty Cash		4.20	
2100	Creditors Control Account			11,797.00
2200	Sales Tax Control Account			28,620.20
2201	Purchase Tax Control Account		34,577.55	
2300	Loans			35,000.00
3000	Ordinary Shares			75,000.00
4000	Computer hardware sales			132,180.00
4001	Computer software sales			28,724.00
4002	Computer consultancy			2,640.00
5000	Materials Purchased		93,362.00	
6201	Advertising		22,500.00	
7000	Gross Wages		33,010.00	
7100	Rent		9,000.00	
7103	General Rates		800.00	
7200	Electricity		308.00	
7501	Postage and Carriage		30.00	
7502	Telephone		585.00	
7504	Office Stationery		671.00	
		Totals:	313,961.20	313,961.20

Answers to student activities

CHAPTER 1: INTRODUCTION TO ACCOUNTING

1.1 (c)

1.2 revenue: (a) (c) (d); capital: (b) (e)

1.3 cash: (a) (b) (d) credit: (c) (e)

1.4 See text, pages 13-14.

1.5 Assets minus liabilities equals capital. See pages 15-16. The capital would increase.

1.6 Advantages: speed (and so cheap to use), accuracy, ability to provide information, integrated function. Disadvantages: expensive to install, staff training needed, danger of failure, security risk (on-line hacking), need for back-up systems.

1.7 See text, page 20.

1.8
(a) Jo's pay packet, income tax and national insurance will be incorrect; if Jo does not check the payslip, the error may go undetected.

(b) The invoice will be incorrect, the customer may exceed the credit limit, the business may lose the customer!

(c) The bank account may go overdrawn, the business may be charged extra interest and fees, cheques may be 'bounced' resulting in the withdrawal of credit by suppliers.

CHAPTER 2: DOCUMENTS FOR GOODS AND SERVICES SUPPLIED

2.1

(a)	delivery note	(b)	returns note	(c)	invoice
(d)	statement	(e)	credit note	(f)	purchase order

2.2

	total	*discount*	*net total*	*VAT*	*invoice total*
	£	£	£	£	£
(a)	160.00	32.00	128.00	22.40	150.40
(b)	400.00	80.00	320.00	56.00	376.00
(c)	40.00	none	40.00	7.00	47.00
(d)	8000.00	1600.00	6400.00	1120.00	7520.00

2.3

	net total	*discount deducted*	*total after cash discount*	*VAT*	*invoice total**
(a)	128.00	3.20	124.80	21.84	149.84
(b)	320.00	8.00	312.00	54.60	374.60
(c)	40.00	1.00	39.00	6.82	46.82
(d)	6400.00	160.00	6240.00	1092.00	7492.00

*Remember that the VAT is normally added to the total before deduction of cash discount.

2.4 Net monthly = payment of net amount one month after the invoice date.

E & OE = Errors and Omissions Excepted (a supplier has the right to correct an invoice after issue).

Carriage paid = Delivery costs paid to the delivery address (contrast with Ex-Works).

2.5 Examples: Purchase order number, delivery note number, invoice number, stock code, account number, credit note number.
The main importance of coding is for accurate cross referencing.

2.6 The problems are the urgency and the need for accuracy. If the wrong goods are sent the problems will be compounded.

Solutions: telephone or e-mail, and fax a copy of the order pointing out the error.

Best and quickest solution - telephone.

Important point – ask for a replacement corrected order to be sent (marked 'confirmation' to avoid duplication), preferably by fax so that a further check can be made. This is to make sure your position is strong, just in case the customer gets it wrong again! This type of problem can be sorted out at assistant level, but should be reported to the supervisor when he/she returns.

2.7 (a) Incorrect discount rate applied (10%), wrong addition for total. Goods total should be £76.00, VAT £13.30 and final total £89.30.

(b) Total before discount should be £250.00. VAT has also been rounded up (should have been rounded down to £35.43). Corrected figures: goods total £225.00 (after deduction of 10% discount), VAT £39.37, final total £264.37.

2.8

	Net amount	*VAT*	*Total*
	£	£	£
(a)	40.00	7.00	47.00
(b)	34,613.60	6,057.38	40,670.98
(c)	34.03	5.95	39.98
(d)	80.00	14.00	94.00
(e)	0.40	0.07	0.47
(f)	1.03	0.17	1.20

2.9 Statement should be dated 31 July 2003 and addressed to Mr Simpson.
The entries are:

		debit £	*credit £*	*balance £*
1 July 2003	Balance /bf	58.75		58.75
4 July	Cheque received		58.75	00.00
8 July	Invoice 10982	340.75		340.75
14 July	Credit note 2378		34.07	306.68
			TOTAL	306.68

CHAPTER 3: ACCOUNTING FOR CREDIT SALES AND SALES RETURNS

3.1 (a)

3.2 (a)

3.3 (a)

- The prime documents for credit sales transactions are sales invoices or copy invoices, that have been checked and authorised.
- The details and amounts of the invoices are entered into sales day book. In the money columns of sales day book is recorded:
  - total column, the final total of each invoice
  - VAT column, the VAT amount shown on each invoice
  - net column, the net ('goods or services total') amount of each invoice
- After sales day book has been written up for the week or month, it is totalled and the information from it is transferred into the double-entry system.
- The book-keeping entries are:
  - the amounts from the total column for each separate transaction are debited to the accounts of the customers in sales (debtors) ledger
  - the total of the VAT column is credited to VAT account in the main (general) ledger
  - the total of the net column is credited to sales account in the main (general) ledger

(b)

- The prime documents for sales returns transactions are credit notes (or copies of credit notes) issued, that have been checked and authorised.
- The details and amounts of the credit notes are entered into sales returns day book. In the money columns of the sales returns day book is recorded:
  - total column, the final total of each credit note
  - VAT column, the VAT amount shown on each credit note
  - net column, the net ('goods or services total') amount of each credit note
- After sales returns day book has been written up for the week or month, it is totalled and the information from it is transferred into the double-entry system.
- The book-keeping entries are:
  - the amounts from the total column for each separate transaction are credited to the accounts of the customers in sales (debtors) ledger
  - the total of the VAT column is debited to VAT account in the main (general) ledger
  - the total of the net column is debited to sales returns account in the main (general) ledger

3.4 (a)

Sales Day Book						SDB 50
Date	Customer	Invoice No	Folio	Total	VAT	Net
2004				£ p	£ p	£ p
2 Apr	Malvern Stores	4578	SL 110	64.62	9.62	55.00
5 Apr	Pershore Retailers	4579	SL 145	76.37	11.37	65.00
7 Apr	E Grainger	4580	SL 55	32.90	4.90	28.00
9 Apr	P Wilson	4581	SL 172	68.15	10.15	58.00
12 Apr	M Kershaw	4582	SL 90	89.30	13.30	76.00
14 Apr	D Lloyd	4583	SL 95	77.55	11.55	66.00
19 Apr	A Cox	4584	SL 32	38.77	5.77	33.00
22 Apr	Dines Stores	4585	SL 48	119.85	17.85	102.00
23 Apr	Malvern Stores	4586	SL 110	55.22	8.22	47.00
26 Apr	P Wilson	4587	SL 172	41.12	6.12	35.00
29 Apr	A Cox	4588	SL 32	96.35	14.35	82.00
30 Apr	Totals for month			760.20	113.20	647.00

(b)

SALES (DEBTORS) LEDGER

Dr **Malvern Stores** (account no 110) Cr

2004			£ p	2004	£ p
2 Apr	Sales	SDB 50	64.62		
23 Apr	Sales	SDB 50	55.22		

Dr **Pershore Retailers** (account no 145) Cr

2004			£ p	2004	£ p
5 Apr	Sales	SDB 50	76.37		

Dr **E Grainger** (account no 55) Cr

2004			£ p	2004	£ p
7 Apr	Sales	SDB 50	32.90		

Dr **P Wilson** (account no 172) Cr

2004			£ p	2004	£ p
9 Apr	Sales	SDB 50	68.15		
26 Apr	Sales	SDB 50	41.12		

Dr **M Kershaw** (account no 90) Cr

2004			£ p	2004	£ p
12 Apr	Sales	SDB 50	89.30		

Dr		**D Lloyd** (account no 95)			Cr
2004		£ p	2004		£ p
14 Apr Sales	SDB 50	77.55			

Dr		**A Cox** (account no 32)			Cr
2004		£ p	2004		£ p
19 Apr Sales	SDB 50	38.77			
29 Apr Sales	SDB 50	96.35			

Dr		**Dines Stores** (account no 48)			Cr
2004		£ p	2004		£ p
22 Apr Sales	SDB 50	119.85			

MAIN (GENERAL) LEDGER

Dr		**Sales Account** (account no 4001)			Cr
2004		£ p	2004		£ p
			30 Apr	Sales Day Book SDB 50	647.00

Dr		**Value Added Tax Account** (account no 2200)			Cr
2004		£ p	2004		£ p
			30 Apr	Sales Day Book SDB 50	113.20

3.5 (a)

Sales Returns Day Book						**SRDB 8**
Date	Customer	Credit Note No	Folio	Total	VAT	Net
2004				£ p	£ p	£ p
8 Apr	Pershore Retailers	CN 572	SL 145	23.50	3.50	20.00
12 Apr	E Grainger	CN 573	SL 55	32.90	4.90	28.00
16 Apr	D Lloyd	CN 574	SL 95	38.77	5.77	33.00
28 Apr	Malvern Stores	CN 575	SL 110	23.50	3.50	20.00
30 Apr	A Cox	CN 576	SL 32	47.00	7.00	40.00
30 Apr	Totals for month			165.67	24.67	141.00

(b)

SALES LEDGER

Dr **Pershore Retailers** (account no 145) Cr

2004			£ p	2004			£ p
5 Apr	Sales	SDB 50	76.37	8 Apr	Sales Returns	SRDB 8	23.50

Dr **E Grainger** (account no 55) Cr

2004			£ p	2004			£ p
7 Apr	Sales	SDB 50	32.90	12 Apr	Sales Returns	SRDB 8	32.90

Dr **D Lloyd** (account no 95) Cr

2004			£ p	2004			£ p
14 Apr	Sales	SDB 50	77.55	16 Apr	Sales Returns	SRDB 8	38.77

Dr **Malvern Stores** (account no 110) Cr

2004			£ p	2004			£ p
2 Apr	Sales	SDB 50	64.62	28 Apr	Sales Returns	SRDB 8	23.50
23 Apr	Sales	SDB 50	55.22				

Dr **A Cox** (account no 32) Cr

2004			£ p	2004			£ p
19 Apr	Sales	SDB 50	38.77	30 Apr	Sales Returns	SRDB 8	47.00
29 Apr	Sales	SDB 50	96.35				

MAIN (GENERAL) LEDGER

Dr **Sales Returns Account** (account no 4010) Cr

2004			£ p	2004			£ p
30 Apr	Sales Returns Day Book	SRDB 8	141.00				

Dr **Value Added Tax Account** (account no 2200) Cr

2004			£ p	2004			£ p
30 Apr	Sales Returns Day Book	SRDB 8	24.67	30 Apr	Sales Day Book	SDB 50	113.20

CHAPTER 4: BALANCING ACCOUNTS AND CONTROL ACCOUNT FOR SALES

4.1

Sales Account

Dr			Cr		
2004		£	2004		£
30 Apr	Balance c/d	17,195	1 Apr	Balance b/d	12,555
			30 Apr	Sales Day Book	4,640
		17,195			17,195
			1 May	Balance b/d	17,195

Sales Returns Account

Dr			Cr		
2004		£	2004		£
1 Apr	Balance b/d	527	30 Apr	Balance c/d	727
30 Apr	Sales Returns Day Book	200			
		727			727
1 May	Balance b/d	727			

Value Added Tax Account

Dr			Cr		
2004		£	2004		£
30 Apr	Sales Returns Day Book	35	1 Apr	Balance b/d	1,233
30 Apr	Balance c/d	2,010	30 Apr	Sales Day Book	812
		2,045			2,045
			1 May	Balance b/d	2,010

T Johnson

Dr			Cr		
2004		£	2004		£
1 Apr	Balance b/d	496	30 Apr	Balance c/d	1,463
5 Apr	Sales	198			
20 Apr	Sales	467			
26 Apr	Sales	302			
		1,463			1,463
1 May	Balance b/d	1,463			

Doyle Traders

Dr			Cr		
2004		£	2004		£
1 Apr	Balance b/d	183	14 Apr	Sales Returns	47
8 Apr	Sales	221	30 Apr	Balance c/d	752
22 Apr	Sales	395			
		799			799
1 May	Balance b/d	752			

4.2 (b)

4.3 *Principles of control accounts*

- Control accounts are 'master' accounts which control a number of subsidiary accounts.
- Control accounts use total figures:
  - total of opening balances
  - total of amounts increasing the balances
  - total of amounts decreasing the balances

  In this way, the total of the closing balances for the subsidiary accounts can be calculated and then checked against a separate listing of the balances of the subsidiary accounts to ensure that the two figures agree.
- Two commonly used control accounts are:
  - sales ledger control account, the total of the subsidiary (sales) ledger
  - purchases ledger control account, the total of the subsidiary (purchases) ledger

Control accounts as an aid to management

- The figures for debtors and creditors are available immediately from the appropriate control account – there is no need to add up the balances of all the individual debtors' or creditors' accounts.
- Control accounts can help in locating errors. The balance of the control account can be checked against the separate listing of balances of the subsidiary accounts to ensure that the two figures agree. However, this only proves the arithmetical accuracy of the control account and subsidiary accounts – there could still be errors within the ledger section.
- Fraud is made more difficult when control accounts are used – this especially applies to a manual accounting system. The reason for this is that any fraudulent transaction to be recorded on the subsidiary account of a debtor or creditor must also be entered in the control account. As the control account will be either maintained by a supervisor, or checked regularly by the manager, the control accounts add another level of security within the accounting system.

Control accounts and book-keeping

- A business must decide how to use control accounts in its book-keeping system; the usual way of doing this is to incorporate the control accounts into double-entry book-keeping.
- The control accounts form part of the double-entry system in the main ledger.
- The individual accounts of debtors and creditors are not part of double-entry but are kept as subsidiary accounts which record how much each debtor owes, and how much is owed to each creditor.
- From time-to-time, the balances of the subsidiary accounts are agreed with the balance of the appropriate control account.

4.4

Dr		**Sales Ledger Control Account**			Cr
2004		£	2004		£
1 Jun	Balance b/d	17,491	30 Jun	Sales returns	1,045
30 Jun	Credit sales	42,591	30 Jun	Payments received from debtors	39,024
			30 Jun	Balance c/d	20,013
		60,082			60,082
1 Jul	Balance b/d	20,013			

4.5 (b) Author's note: Day books are shown before the completed accounts.

Sales Day Book

Date	Customer	Invoice No	Folio	Total	VAT	Net
2004				£ p	£ p	£ p
3 Feb	Arrow Valley Retailers	2731	SL	241.75	36.00	205.75
5 Feb	Mereford Manufact. Co	2732	SL	132.03	19.66	112.37
10 Feb	Wyvern Warehouse Ltd	2733	SL	485.22	72.26	412.96
12 Feb	Redgrove Restorations	2734	SL	303.39	45.18	258.21
19 Apr	B Brick (Builders) Ltd	2735	SL	323.54	48.18	275.36
23 Feb	Redgrove Restorations	2736	SL	240.25	35.78	204.47
29 Feb	Totals for month			1,726.18	257.06	1,469.12

Sales Returns Day Book

Date	Customer	Credit Note No	Folio	Total	VAT	Net
2004				£ p	£ p	£ p
6 Feb	Redgrove Restorations	CN 127	SL	100.93	15.03	85.90
17 Feb	Mereford Manufact. Co	CN 128	SL	53.19	7.92	45.27
27 Feb	B Brick (Builders) Ltd	CN 129	SL	33.37	4.97	28.40
29 Feb	Totals for month			187.49	27.92	159.57

(a) and (c)

MAIN LEDGER

Sales Account

Dr			Cr		
2004		£ p	2004		£ p
29 Feb	Balance c/d	6,566.36	1 Feb	Balance b/d	5,097.24
			29 Feb	Sales Day Book	1,469.12
		6,566.36			6,566.36
			1 Mar	Balance b/d	6,566.36

Sales Returns Account

Dr			Cr		
2004		£ p	2004		£ p
1 Feb	Balance b/d	346.97	29 Feb	Balance c/d	506.54
29 Feb	Sales Returns Day Book	159.57			
		506.54			506.54
1 Mar	Balance b/d	506.54			

Value Added Tax Account

Dr			Cr		
2004		£ p	2004		£ p
29 Feb	Sales Returns Day Book	27.92	1 Feb	Balance b/d	452.31
29 Feb	Balance c/d	681.45	29 Feb	Sales Day Book	257.06
		709.37			709.37
			1 Mar	Balance b/d	681.45

Sales Ledger Control Account

Dr			Cr		
2004		£ p	2004		£ p
1 Feb	Balance b/d	2,012.43	29 Feb	Sales returns	187.49
29 Feb	Credit sales	1,726.18	29 Feb	Balance c/d	3,551.12
		3,738.61			3,738.61
1 Mar	Balance b/d	3,551.12			

SUBSIDIARY (SALES) LEDGER

Arrow Valley Retailers

Dr			Cr		
2004		£ p	2004		£ p
1 Feb	Balance b/d	826.40	29 Feb	Balance c/d	1,068.15
3 Feb	Sales	241.75			
		1,068.15			1,068.15
1 Mar	Balance b/d	1,068.15			

Dr		B Brick (Builders) Limited			Cr
2004		£ p	2004		£ p
1 Feb	Balance b/d	59.28	27 Feb	Sales returns	33.37
19 Feb	Sales	323.54	29 Feb	Balance c/d	349.45
		382.82			382.82
1 Mar	Balance b/d	349.45			

Dr		Mereford Manufacturing Company			Cr
2004		£ p	2004		£ p
1 Feb	Balance b/d	293.49	17 Feb	Sales returns	53.19
5 Feb	Sales	132.03	29 Feb	Balance c/d	372.33
		425.52			425.52
1 Mar	Balance b/d	372.33			

Dr		Redgrove Restorations			Cr
2004		£ p	2004		£ p
1 Feb	Balance b/d	724.86	6 Feb	Sales returns	100.93
12 Feb	Sales	303.39	29 Feb	Balance c/d	1,167.57
23 Feb	Sales	240.25			
		1,268.50			1,268.50
1 Mar	Balance b/d	1,167.57			

Dr		Wyvern Warehouse Limited			Cr
2004		£ p	2004		£ p
1 Feb	Balance b/d	108.40	29 Feb	Balance c/d	593.62
10 Feb	Sales	485.22			
		593.62			593.62
1 Mar	Balance b/d	593.62			

(d) **Reconciliation of sales ledger control account**

	1 February 2004	*29 February 2004*
	£ p	£ p
Arrow Valley Retailers	826.40	1,068.15
B Brick (Builders) Limited	59.28	349.45
Mereford Manufacturing Company	293.49	372.33
Redgrove Restorations	724.86	1,167.57
Wyvern Warehouse Limited	108.40	593.62
Sales ledger control account	2,012.43	3,551.12

CHAPTER 5: RECEIVING AND RECORDING PAYMENTS

5.1

Customer	*Change*	*Notes & coin given in change*
1	£1.50	1 x £1 coin, 1 x 50p coin
2	£6.70	1 x £5 note, 1 x £1 coin, 1 x 50p coin, 1 x 20p coin
3	£2.49	1 x £2 coin, 2 x 20p coins, 1 x 5p coin, 2 x 2p coins
4	£3.21	1 x £2 coin, 1 x £1 coin, 1 x 20p coin, 1 x 1p coin
5	£0.66	1 x 50p coin, 1 x 10p coin, 1 x 5p coin, 1 x 1p coin
6	£3.78	1 x £2 coin, 1 x £1 coin, 1 x 50p coin, 1 x 20p coin, 1 x 5p coin, 1 x 2p coin, 1 x 1p coin
7	£7.24	1 x £5 note, 1 x £2 coin, 1 x 20p coin, 2 x 2p coins
8	£0.58	1 x 50p coin, 1 x 5p coin, 1 x 2p coin, 1 x 1p coin
9	£3.46	1 x £2 coin, 1 x £1 coin, 2 x 20p coins, 1 x 5p coin, 1 x 1p coin
10	£1.92	1 x £1 coin, 1 x 50p coin, 2 x 20p coins, 1 x 2p coin

5.2

	£
cash float at start of day	28.71
plus sales made during the day	46.46
equals amount of cash held at end of day	75.17

5.3 (a) 2 x £13.99 = £27.98; 2 x 85p = £1.70; total £29.68 + VAT £5.19 = £34.87

(b) £149.95 + 99p = £150.94; add VAT of £26.41 = £177.35

(c) 2 x £35.99 = £71.98; add VAT of £12.59 = £84.57

5.4 (a) A & S Systems Ltd (G Brown signs as director – an authorised signatory)

(b) Southern Bank PLC

(c) Electron Games Limited

For explanations see page 92.

5.5 A crossed cheque must be paid into a bank account. A cheque without a crossing – an 'open' cheque – may be cashed by the payee. It is therefore a security risk and is very rare.

5.6 (a) General crossing – the cheque has to be paid into a bank account.

(b) Special crossing – the cheque has to be paid in at Barclays Bank, Hanover Square.

(c) The same as (a) – the phrase '& co' no longer has any significance.

(d) Account payee crossing – the cheque must be paid into the account of the payee.

5.7 The Cheques Act 1992 states that a cheque that is crossed 'account payee' (or similar) is not transferable. The cheque cannot be accepted beacuse the only person who can pay it into a bank account is the payee, Henry Enfield.

5.8 See page 93 of text.

5.9 See page 96 of text.

5.10 See page 99 of text.

5.11 (c)

5.12 False

5.13 (b)

5.14 (d)

5.15 See page 103 of text.

5.16 (a) the bank (both)

(b) large purchase where cash or near cash is required, eg car purchase, house purchase

5.17 Cheques received through the post, cash sales at the counter.

CHAPTER 6: PAYING INTO THE BANK

6.1 See page 115 of text.

6.2 See page 115 of text.

6.3 False. Debtor

6.4 False. Creditor

6.5 (a) ... mortgagor ... mortgagee

(b) ... bailee ... bailor

(c) agent

6.6 (a) Loan account

(b) Overdraft

(c) Deposit account

6.7 (a) 3 days

(b) 24 hours (or as long as first class post takes)

Yes, the business could obtain same day clearance (the two accounts are at the same branch)

6.8 *'Refer to Drawer, Please Represent':* the cheque will be put through the bank clearing system again by the bank, so there is nothing the business can do with the cheque. The business will be alerted, however, to a possible bad debt and will review carefully credit given to the customer in question.

'Refer to Drawer': in this case the cheque will be returned to the business which can then make strenuous efforts to recover the money from the customer. This answer is normally very bad news for a supplier as it normally means the buyer is in serious financial difficulties.

6.9 See page 123 of text.

6.10 See page 126 of text.

6.11 (a) credit (b) debit

6.12

Cheques:	£20.00	Cash:	2 x £20 notes	£40.00
	£18.50		5 x £10 notes	£50.00
	£75.25		8 x £5 notes	£40.00
	£68.95		2 x £1 coins	£2.00
	£182.70		6 x 50p coins	£3.00
			4 x 10p coins	£0.40
			2 x 2p coins	£0.04
				£135.44
Total amount of credit:	£318.14			

6.13 Total of sales vouchers £396.94 less refund voucher £13.50, total of summary £383.44.

CHAPTER 7: CASH BOOK – RECORDING RECEIPTS

7.1 (d)

7.2 *Main responsibilities of the cashier*

- Preparing remittance lists for cheques received in the post
- Recording receipts and payments through the bank and in cash
- Issuing receipts for cash (and sometimes cheques) received
- Making authorised cash payments (except for low-value expenses payments which are paid by the petty cashier)
- Preparing cheques for authorised payments – to be signed by those permitted to sign on behalf of the company
- Paying cash and cheques received into the bank
- Controlling the firm's cash, in a cash till or cash box
- Issuing cash to the petty cashier who operates the firm's petty cash book
- Ensuring that all transactions passing through the cash book are supported by documentary evidence
- Checking the accuracy of the cash and bank balances at regular intervals
- Checking expenses claims and seeking authorisation before making payment
- Liaising with the other accounts staff – accounts clerks and petty cashier

Qualities of a cashier

- Accuracy – in writing up the cash book, in cash handling, and in ensuring that payments are made only against correct documents and appropriate authorisation
- Security – of cash and cheque books, and correct authorisation of payments
- Confidentiality – that all cash/bank transactions, including cash and bank balances, are kept confidential

7.3

Debit		**Cash Book: Receipts**			**CBR 45**
Date	Details	Folio	Discount allowed	Cash	Bank
2004			£	£	£
1 Aug	Balances b/d			276	4,928
3 Aug	Wild & Sons Ltd	SL 843			398
6 Aug	Sales	ML 4001/ 2200		188	
16 Aug	A Lewis Ltd	SL 531	20		1,755
18 Aug	Sales	ML 4001/ 2200		282	
20 Aug	Harvey & Sons Ltd	SL 467			261
23 Aug	Bank loan	ML 2210			750
24 Aug	Sales	ML 4001/ 2200		235	235
26 Aug	Rent received	ML 4951		100	
27 Aug	Wild & Sons Ltd	SL 843	15		595
			35	1,081	8,922

SUBSIDIARY (SALES) LEDGER

Dr		**Wild & Sons Ltd** (account no 843)			Cr
2004	£	2004			£
		3 Aug	Bank	CBR 45	398
		27 Aug	Bank	CBR 45	595
		27 Aug	Discount allowed	ML 6501	15

Dr		**A Lewis Ltd** (account no 531)			Cr
2004	£	2004			£
		16 Aug	Bank	CBR 45	1,755
		16 Aug	Discount allowed	ML 6501	20

Dr				**Harvey & Sons Ltd** (account no 467)			Cr
2004			£	2004			£
				20 Aug	Bank	CBR 45	261

MAIN LEDGER

Dr				**Sales Ledger Control Account** (account no 6001)			Cr
2004			£	2004			£
				31 Aug	Bank	CBR 45	*3,009
				31 Aug	Discount allowed	ML 6501	35

* £398 + £1,755 + £261 + £595

Dr				**Discount Allowed Account** (account no 6501)			Cr
2004			£	2004			£
31 Aug	Cash Book	CBR 45	35				

Dr				**Bank Loan Account** (account no 2210)			Cr
2004			£	2004			£
				23 Aug	Bank	CBR 45	750

Dr				**Rent Received Account** (account no 4951)			Cr
2004			£	2004			£
				26 Aug	Cash	CBR 45	100

Dr				**Sales Account** (account no 4001)			Cr
2004			£	2004			£
				6 Aug	Cash	CBR 45	160
				18 Aug	Cash	CBR 45	240
				24 Aug	Cash	CBR 45	200
				24 Aug	Bank	CBR 45	200

Dr				**Value Added Tax Account** (account no 2200)			Cr
2004			£	2004			£
				6 Aug	Cash	CBR 45	28
				18 Aug	Cash	CBR 45	42
				24 Aug	Cash	CBR 45	35
				24 Aug	Bank	CBR 45	35

7.4

Debit		Cash Book: Receipts			CBR 88
Date	Details	Folio	Discount allowed	VAT	Bank
2004			£	£	£
1 Apr	Balances b/d				718
8 Apr	J Bowen	SL 117	5		85
9 Apr	Sales	ML 4001/ 2200		70	470
12 Apr	Rent received	ML 4951			250
16 Apr	Sales	ML 4001/ 2200		14	94
19 Apr	J Burrows	SL 125	25		575
20 Apr	Sales	ML 4001/ 2200		28	188
26 Apr	Wilson Ltd	SL 855	10		245
			40	112	2,625

SUBSIDIARY (SALES) LEDGER

Dr		**J Bowen** (account no 117)			Cr
2004	£	2004			£
		8 Apr	Bank	CBR 88	85
		8 Apr	Discount allowed	ML 6501	5

Dr		**J Burrows** (account no 125)			Cr
2004	£	2004			£
		19 Apr	Bank	CBR 88	575
		19 Apr	Discount allowed	ML 6501	25

Dr		**Wilson Limited** (account no 855)			Cr
2004	£	2004			£
		26 Apr	Bank	CBR 88	245
		26 Apr	Discount allowed	ML 6501	10

MAIN LEDGER

Dr		**Sales Ledger Control Account** (account no 6001)			Cr
2004	£	2004			£
		30 Apr	Bank	CBR 88	*905
		30 Apr	Discount allowed	ML 6501	40

* £85 + £575 + £245

Dr			Discount Allowed Account (account no 6501)				Cr
2004			£	2004			£
30 Apr	Cash Book	CBR 88	40				

Dr			Rent Received Account (account no 4951)				Cr
2004			£	2004			£
				12 Apr	Bank	CBR 88	250

Dr			Sales Account (account no 4001)				Cr
2004			£	2004			£
				9 Apr	Bank	CBR 88	400
				16 Apr	Bank	CBR 88	80
				20 Apr	Bank	CBR 88	160

Dr			Value Added Tax Account (account no 2200)				Cr
2004			£	2004			£
				30 Apr	Cash Book	CBR 88	112

7.5

Debit				**Cash Book: Receipts**				**CBR 96**
Date	Details	Folio	Bank	Disc allwd	VAT	Sales	Sales ledger	Sundry
2004			£ p	£ p	£ p	£ p	£ p	£ p
17 May	Balances b/d		825.30					
17 May	Sales	ML 4001	534.62		79.62	455.00		
17 May	Rent received	ML 4951	255.50					255.50
18 May	Sales	ML 4001	164.50		24.50	140.00		
18 May	T Jarvis	SL 497	155.00	2.50			155.00	
19 May	Loan: T Lewis	ML 2200	500.00					500.00
19 May	Sales	ML 4001	752.00		112.00	640.00		
20 May	Sales	ML 4001	264.37		39.37	225.00		
21 May	Capital	ML 3005	1,000.00					1,000.00
21 May	Wyvern District Cncl	SL 924	560.45	5.00			560.45	
			5,011.74	7.50	255.49	1,460.00	715.45	1,755.50

SUBSIDIARY (SALES) LEDGER

T Jarvis (account no 497)

Dr				Cr			
2004			£ p	2004			£ p
				18 May	Bank	CBR 96	155.00
				18 May	Discount allowed	ML 6501	2.50

Wyvern District Council (account no 924)

Dr				Cr			
2004			£ p	2004			£ p
				21 May	Bank	CBR 96	560.45
				21 May	Discount allowed	ML 6501	5.00

MAIN LEDGER

Capital Account (account no 3005)

Dr				Cr			
2004			£ p	2004			£ p
				21 May	Bank	CBR 96	1,000.00

Sales Ledger Control Account (account no 6001)

Dr				Cr			
2004			£ p	2004			£ p
				21 May	Cash Book	CBR 96	715.45
				21 May	Discount allowed	ML 6501	7.50

Discount Allowed Account (account no 6501)

Dr				Cr			
2004			£ p	2004			£ p
21 May	Cash Book	CBR 96	7.50				

Loan Account: T Lewis (account no 2220)

Dr				Cr			
2004			£ p	2004			£ p
				19 May	Bank	CBR 96	500.00

Rent Received Account (account no 4951)

Dr				Cr			
2004			£ p	2004			£ p
				17 May	Bank	CBR 96	255.50

Dr			Sales Account (account no 4001)			Cr
2004		£ p	2004			£ p
			21 May	Cash Book	CBR 96	1,460.00

Dr			Value Added Tax Account (account no 2200)			Cr
2004		£ p	2004			£ p
			21 May	Cash Book	CBR 96	255.49

7.6

Dr			Sales Ledger Control Account		Cr
2004		£	2004		£
1 Dec	Balance b/d	38,643	31 Dec	Sales returns	3,210
31 Dec	Credit sales	45,419	31 Dec	Payments received from debtors	43,987
			31 Dec	Discount allowed	695
			31 Dec	Balance c/d	36,170
		84,062			84,062
2005			2005		
1 Jan	Balance b/d	36,170			

CHAPTER 8: COMMUNICATING WITH CUSTOMERS

8.1 The cheque will not be accepted by the bank so it should be returned by post with a request that either a new cheque be issued (best solution) or that the figures changed to £550 and countersigned by the appropriate signatories.

8.2 Fax the invoices through to the customer with a reminder on the fax header sheet that the invoices are now due for payment.

8.3 The memorandum should be correctly headed and addressed. The message should be brief and clear. The memorandum can be signed, although this is not essential. The memorandum should include an 'enc.' (enclosure) marker.

8.4 Examples of different types of chaser are reproduced on pages 167, 169 and 173. The important details to include are invoice amount, number and date (a copy should ideally be enclosed [nb 'enc.' marker]) and terms. The tone should not be too strong – remember that the invoice may even have been lost, or the cheque already be in the post (both common excuses!). The letter should be marked for signature by the Accounts Manager.

8.5 A letter of apology is required here. The error may well be the customer's fault, but on no account should this be suggested in the letter (she is 'a valued customer'). The letter should acknowledge the problem, state what corrective action has been taken and finish on a positive note. The tone should be conciliatory but not 'grovelling' (which sounds insincere). The letter should be correctly addressed and signed off.

CHAPTER 9: BUSINESSES AND THE LAW

9.1 The definition must contain the message that a contract is an agreement that is legally binding and enforceable in a court of law.

9.2 Agreement, bargain, intention to create legal relations. See text on page 177 and following.

9.3 (a) Yes. A contract can be oral. A purchase order is just part of the paperwork confirming the agreement.

(b) Yes. The purchase order and despatch of the goods constitute the agreement, bargain and commercial nature of the transaction.

(c) No. When the job was done there was no intention to create legal relations or to involve consideration (payment) – it was done as a favour. The £10 followed the job and was just incidental.

(d) Yes. The fact that the person is a friend is not relevant. There was an agreement, consideration and an intention to create legal relations.

9.4 The cashier is right. The price on the shelf is just an invitation to treat. The price is agreed at the till.

9.5 No. The stipulation that the goods are received by 4 April amounts to a counter-offer to the supplier's terms and does not constitute an acceptance. It would only be a valid contract if the supplier had agreed to the revised terms.

9.6 17 March. The postal rule applies – as long as the letter is correctly addressed stamped and posted.

9.7 He is wrong. He is liable under the Sale of Goods Act which states that goods sold must be of 'satisfactory quality ... fit for the purpose ... as described.' The purchaser is entitled to a replacement or a refund as long as the problem is reported without delay.

9.8 No. The Trades Descriptions Act states that it is illegal to make false statements about goods offered for sale. The chair is advertised as having an adjustable back; if it does not, you are entitled to your money back. You could also report the matter to Trading Standards Department who can pursue the matter.

9.9 False.

9.10 See page 186.

9.11 C

CHAPTER 10: DOCUMENTS FOR GOODS AND SERVICES RECEIVED

10.1 (a) purchase order
(b) delivery note
(c) goods received note
(d) remittance advice
(e) invoice
(f) returns note

10.2 An unauthorised purchase order cannot be used as the basis for raising an order. The purchase order will have to be returned to the purchaser for signature, or alternatively, if the order is urgent, the purchaser could be contacted and a new order faxed through.

10.3 (d)

10.4 A returns note accompanies any goods returned by the purchaser to the seller; a credit note is issued by the seller when credit has to be given to the purchaser, eg for returned goods. Hence a credit note is usually issued when a returns note is received.

10.5 The buyer would effectively be overcharged. The buyer would request a credit note. Under no circumstances should the invoice be altered.

10.6 The errors are:

(a) the goods were delivered to the wrong address
(b) an incorrect customer discount has been applied (10% instead of 15%)
(c) the wrong goods were sent (product code 4574 instead of 4573)

The total should have been £95 less 15% discount = £80.75 plus VAT of £14.13 = £94.88

The letter should point out these errors and state that the disks are being returned for credit.

10.7 The amount to be paid will be:

£3,650 + £1,200 + £1,945 – £568 = £6,227. The £4,560 invoice will be paid on 12 September.

CHAPTER 11: ACCOUNTING FOR CREDIT PURCHASES AND PURCHASES RETURNS

11.1 (d)

11.2 (a)

- The prime documents for credit purchases transactions are purchases invoices received from suppliers, that have been checked and authorised.
- The details and amounts of the invoices are entered into the purchases day book. In the money columns of purchases day book is recorded:
  - total column, the final total of each invoice
  - VAT column, the VAT amount shown on each invoice
  - net column, the net ('goods or services total') amount of each invoice
- After purchases day book has been written up for the week or month, it is totalled and the information from it is transferred into the double-entry system.
- The book-keeping entries are:
  - the amounts from the total column for each separate transaction are credited to the accounts of the suppliers in purchases (creditors) ledger
  - the total of the VAT column is debited to VAT account in main (general) ledger
  - the total of the net column is debited to purchases account in main (general) ledger

(b)

- The prime documents for purchases returns transactions are credit notes received from suppliers, that have been checked and authorised.
- The details and amounts of the credit notes are entered into purchases returns day book. In the money columns of the purchases returns day book is recorded:
  - total column, the final total of each credit note
  - VAT column, the VAT amount shown on each credit note
  - net column, the net ('goods or services total') amount of each credit note
- After purchases returns day book has been written up for the week or month, it is totalled and the information from it is transferred into the double-entry system.
- The book-keeping entries are:
  - the amounts from the total column for each separate transaction are debited to the accounts of the suppliers in purchases (creditors) ledger
  - the total of the VAT column is credited to VAT account in main (general) ledger
  - the total of the net column is credited to purchases returns account in main (general) ledger

11.3 (a)

Purchases Day Book						PDB 36
Date	Supplier	Invoice No	Folio	Total	VAT	Net
2004				£ p	£ p	£ p
2 Apr	Severn Supplies	6789	PL 721	293.75	43.75	250.00
5 Apr	I Johnstone	A241	PL 604	246.75	36.75	210.00
9 Apr	L Murphy	2456	PL 659	217.37	32.37	185.00
15 Apr	Mercia Manufacturing	X457	PL 627	211.50	31.50	180.00
19 Apr	AMC Enterprises	AMC 456	PL 520	405.37	60.37	345.00
26 Apr	S Green	2846	PL 574	464.12	69.12	395.00
30 Apr	Totals for month			1,838.86	273.86	1,565.00

(b)

PURCHASES (CREDITORS) LEDGER

Dr **Severn Supplies** (account no 721) Cr

2004			£ p	2004			£ p
				2 Apr	Purchases	PDB 36	293.75

Dr **I Johnstone** (account no 604) Cr

2004			£ p	2004			£ p
				5 Apr	Purchases	PDB 36	246.75

Dr **L Murphy** (account no 659) Cr

2004			£ p	2004			£ p
				9 Apr	Purchases	PDB 36	217.37

Dr **Mercia Manufacturing** (account no 627) Cr

2004			£ p	2004			£ p
				15 Apr	Purchases	PDB 36	211.50

Dr **AMC Enterprises** (account no 520) Cr

2004			£ p	2004			£ p
				19 Apr	Purchases	PDB 36	405.37

Dr **S Green** (account no 574) Cr

2004			£ p	2004			£ p
				26 Apr	Purchases	PDB 36	464.12

MAIN (GENERAL) LEDGER

Dr		**Purchases Account** (account no 5001)			Cr
2004		£ p	2004		£ p
30 Apr	Purchases Day Book PDB 36	1,565.00			

Dr		**Value Added Tax Account** (account no 2200)			Cr
2004		£ p	2004		£ p
30 Apr	Purchases Day Book PDB 36	273.86			

11.4 (a)

Purchases Returns Day Book						**PRDB 11**
Date	Supplier	Credit Note No	Folio	Total	VAT	Net
2004				£ p	£ p	£ p
7 Apr	Severn Supplies	CN225	PL 721	58.75	8.75	50.00
14 Apr	L Murphy	X456	PL 659	94.00	14.00	80.00
21 Apr	AMC Enterprises	C3921	PL 520	146.87	21.87	125.00
29 Apr	S Green	CN/SG247	PL 574	79.90	11.90	68.00
30 Apr	Totals for month			379.52	56.52	323.00

(b)

PURCHASES (CREDITORS) LEDGER

Dr		**Severn Supplies** (account no 721)			Cr
2004		£ p	2004		£ p
7 Apr	Purchases Returns PRDB 11	58.75	2 Apr	Purchases PDB 36	293.75

Dr		**L Murphy** (account no 659)			Cr
2004		£ p	2004		£ p
14 Apr	Purchases Returns PRDB 11	94.00	9 Apr	Purchases PDB 36	217.37

Dr		**AMC Enterprises** (account no 520)					Cr
2004			£ p	2004			£ p
21 Apr	Purchases Returns	PRDB 11	146.87	19 Apr	Purchases	PDB 36	405.37

Dr		**S Green** (account no 574)					Cr
2004			£ p	2004			£ p
29 Apr	Purchases Returns	PRDB 11	79.90	26 Apr	Purchases	PDB 36	464.12

MAIN (GENERAL) LEDGER

Dr		**Purchases Returns Account** (account no 5010)					Cr
2004			£ p	2004			£ p
				30 Apr	Purchases Returns Day Book	PRDB 11	323.00

Dr		**Value Added Tax Account** (account no 2200)					Cr
2004			£ p	2004			£ p
30 Apr	Purchases Day Book	PDB 36	273.86	30 Apr	Purchases Returns Day Book	PRDB 11	56.52

11.5

				Purchases Day Book				**PDB 21**
Date	Supplier	Invoice No	Folio	Total	VAT	Net	Furniture	Carpets
2004				£ p	£ p	£ p	£ p	£ p
2 Apr	T Table Ltd	2750		1,465.81	218.31	1,247.50	1,247.50	
7 Apr	Eastern Imports	2751		936.24	139.44	796.80		796.80
9 Apr	Minster Carpets Ltd	2752		2,203.40	328.16	1,875.24		1,875.24
14 Apr	Pegasus Ltd	2753		585.30	87.17	498.13	498.13	
16 Apr	United Carpets Ltd	2754		559.55	83.33	476.22		476.22
21 Apr	Gerrard Furniture	2755		977.00	145.51	831.49	831.49	
23 Apr	T Table Ltd	2756		762.45	113.55	648.90	648.90	
28 Apr	Eastern Imports	2757		1,524.33	227.02	1,297.31		1,297.31
30 Apr	Totals for month			9,014.08	1,342.49	7,671.59	3,226.02	4,445.57

CHAPTER 12: BALANCING ACCOUNTS AND CONTROL ACCOUNT FOR PURCHASES

12.1

Purchases Account

Dr			Cr		
2004		£	2004		£
1 Nov	Balance b/d	64,287	30 Nov	Balance c/d	71,007
30 Nov	Purchases Day Book	6,720			
		71,007			71,007
1 Dec	Balance b/d	71,007			

Purchases Returns Account

Dr			Cr		
2004		£	2004		£
30 Nov	Balance c/d	1,509	1 Nov	Balance b/d	1,349
			30 Nov	Purchases Returns Day Book	160
		1,509			1,509
			1 Dec	Balance b/d	1,509

Value Added Tax Account

Dr			Cr		
2004		£	2004		£
30 Nov	Purchases Day Book	1,176	1 Nov	Balance b/d	644
			30 Nov	Purchases Returns Day Book	28
			30 Nov	Balance c/d	504
		1,176			1,176
1 Dec	Balance b/d	504			

Ryan and Company

Dr			Cr		
2004		£	2004		£
30 Nov	Balance c/d	1,342	1 Nov	Balance b/d	348
			4 Nov	Purchases	427
			19 Nov	Purchases	311
			24 Nov	Purchases	256
		1,342			1,342
			1 Dec	Balance b/d	1,342

Murray Limited

Dr			Cr		
2004		£	2004		£
1 Nov	Balance b/d	15	8 Nov	Purchases	230
11 Nov	Purchases Returns	42	16 Nov	Purchases	315
30 Nov	Balance c/d	659	24 Nov	Purchases	171
		716			716
			1 Dec	Balance b/d	659

12.2 (c)

12.3

Dr	Purchases Ledger Control Account				Cr
2004		£	2004		£
30 Apr	Purchases returns	653	1 Apr	Balance b/d	14,275
30 Apr	Payments made to creditors	31,074	30 Apr	Credit purchases	36,592
30 Apr	Set-off: sales ledger	597			
30 Apr	Balance c/d	18,543			
		50,867			50,867
			1 May	Balance b/d	18,543

12.4 (b) Author's note: Day books are shown before the completed accounts.

Purchases Day Book

Date	Supplier	Invoice No	Folio	Total	VAT	Net
2004				£ p	£ p	£ p
3 Feb	Apple Supplies Ltd	6434	PL	1,207.87	179.89	1,027.98
5 Feb	Beatty Brothers	6435	PL	177.04	26.36	150.68
6 Feb	J Johnson	6436	PL	385.65	57.43	328.22
14 Feb	W Wright	6437	PL	559.74	83.36	476.38
24 Feb	Apple Supplies Ltd	6438	PL	997.99	148.63	849.36
29 Feb	Totals for month			3,328.29	495.67	2,832.62

Purchases Returns Day Book

Date	Supplier	Credit Note No	Folio	Total	VAT	Net
2004				£ p	£ p	£ p
10 Feb	Apple Supplies Ltd	CN145	PL	184.71	27.51	157.20
17 Feb	Newtown Equipment Ltd	CN146	PL	124.17	18.49	105.68
29 Feb	Totals for month			308.88	46.00	262.88

(a) and (c)

MAIN LEDGER

Purchases Account

Dr			Cr		
2004		£ p	2004		£ p
1 Feb	Balance b/d	4,397.21	29 Feb	Balance c/d	7,229.83
29 Feb	Purchases Day Book	2,832.62			
		7,229.83			7,229.83
1 Mar	Balance b/d	7,229.83			

Purchases Returns Account

Dr			Cr		
2004		£ p	2004		£ p
29 Feb	Balance c/d	719.17	1 Feb	Balance b/d	456.29
			29 Feb	Purchases Returns Day Book	262.88
		719.17			719.17
			1 Mar	Balance b/d	719.17

Value Added Tax Account

Dr			Cr		
2004		£ p	2004		£ p
29 Feb	Purchases Day Book	495.67	1 Feb	Balance b/d	524.86
29 Feb	Balance c/d	75.19	29 Feb	Purchases Returns Day Book	46.00
		570.86			570.86
			1 Mar	Balance b/d	75.19

Purchases Ledger Control Account

Dr			Cr		
2004		£ p	2004		£ p
			1 Feb	Balance b/d	4,617.48
27 Feb	Set off: sales ledger	154.27	29 Feb	Credit purchases	3,328.29
29 Feb	Purchases returns	308.88			
29 Feb	Balance c/d	7,482.62			
		7,945.77			7,945.77
			1 Mar	Balance b/d	7,482.62

SUBSIDIARY (PURCHASES) LEDGER

Apple Supplies Limited

Dr 2004		£ p	Cr 2004		£ p
10 Feb	Purchases returns	184.71	1 Feb	Balance b/d	1,843.22
29 Feb	Balance c/d	3,864.37	3 Feb	Purchases	1,207.87
			24 Feb	Purchases	997.99
		4,049.08			4,049.08
			1 Mar	Balance b/d	3,864.37

Beatty Brothers

Dr 2004		£ p	Cr 2004		£ p
1 Feb	Balance b/d	51.47	5 Feb	Purchases	177.04
29 Feb	Balance c/d	125.57			
		177.04			177.04
			1 Mar	Balance b/d	125.57

J Johnson

Dr 2004		£ p	Cr 2004		£ p
29 Feb	Balance c/d	1,061.03	1 Feb	Balance b/d	675.38
			6 Feb	Purchases	385.65
		1,061.03			1,061.03
			1 Mar	Balance b/d	1,061.03

Myford Limited

Dr 2004		£ p	Cr 2004		£ p
27 Feb	Set-off: sales ledger	154.27	1 Feb	Balance b/d	478.29
29 Feb	Balance c/d	324.02			
		478.29			478.29
			1 Mar	Balance b/d	324.02

Newtown Equipment Limited

Dr 2004		£ p	Cr 2004		£ p
17 Feb	Purchases returns	124.17	1 Feb	Balance b/d	684.86
29 Feb	Balance c/d	560.69			
		684.86			684.86
			1 Mar	Balance b/d	560.69

Dr		W Wright			Cr
2004		£ p	2004		£ p
29 Feb	Balance c/d	1,546.94	1 Feb	Balance b/d	987.20
			14 Feb	Purchases	559.74
		1,546.94			1,546.94
			1 Mar	Balance b/d	1,546.94

(d) **Reconciliation of purchases ledger control account**

	1 February 2004	*29 February 2004*
	£ p	£ p
Apple Supplies Limited	1,843.22	3,864.37
Beatty Brothers	*(51.47)	125.57
J Johnson	675.38	1,061.03
Myford Limited	478.29	324.02
Newtown Equipment Limited	684.86	560.69
W Wright	987.20	1,546.94
Purchases ledger control account	4,617.48	7,482.62

* debit balance

CHAPTER 13: MAKING PAYMENTS

13.1 False. No cheque is involved in a BACS payment.

13.2 For security reasons: to prevent fraudulent alterations.

13.3 (d)

13.4 To establish the legal relationship between the bank and the business. The bank has to know *who* can sign cheques, and for what amounts. It also needs specimen signatures so that it can verify written instructions, eg cheque signatures and other payment instructions.

13.5 (a) See text pages 250 and 253. (b) Standing order (c) Direct debit

13.6 (a) Bank draft (b) CHAPS

13.7 (a) He/she doesn't have to rely on carrying his/her own money; or he/she doesn't have to pay!

(b) Monitoring of expenditure, or control of expenditure.

13.8 Note that the cash discount is not available – the period has expired. Total £15,255.34.

13.9 Total £4,083.05

13.10 The most normal methods are:

(a) BACS
(b) bank giro credit
(c) bank draft
(d) company credit card
(e) CHAPS

13.11 standing order

(a) Standing order completed as shown below.

(b) The form will be sent to the National Bank, as they will set up the payments.

(c) The standing order will have to be signed by an authorised signatory (or two) within the business. It should also be noted that details of the due payments will be passed to the person in charge of entering up the cash book as the payments will form part of the double-entry book-keeping of the company.

STANDING ORDER MANDATE

To NATIONAL Bank

Address 10 CATHEDRAL STREET MEREFORD MR1 5DE

PLEASE PAY TO

Bank BARCLAYS Branch EVESHORE Sort code 30 98 15

Beneficiary Account number 72627161

The sum of £ 350 Amount in words THREE HUNDRED AND FIFTY POUNDS

Date of first payment 15 MAY 2003 Frequency of payment MONTHLY

Until 15 APRIL 2004 Reference BE/6637

Account to be debited NIMROD DRAINAGE LTD Account number 12034875

SIGNATURE(S) ....

.... date..........

direct debit

(a) Direct debit form completed as shown below (standing order form above).

(b) The form will be sent to Tradesure Insurance, as they will set up the payments.

(c) The direct debit will have to be signed by an authorised signatory (or two) within the business. It should also be noted that details of the due payments are normally advised by the originator of the direct debit (here the insurance company). These will be passed to the person in charge of entering up the cash book as the payments will form part of the double-entry book-keeping of the company.

direct debit instruction

Tradesure Insurance Company
PO Box 134, Helliford, HL9 6TY

Originator's Identification Number 914208

Reference(tobecompletedbyTradesureInsurance)....03924540234....

Please complete the details and return this form to Tradesure Insurance

name and address of bank/building society

NATIONAL BANK
10 CATHEDRAL STREET
MEREFORD
MR1 5DE

instructions to bank/building society

- I instruct you to pay direct debits from my account at the request of Tradesure Insurance Company
- The amounts are variable and may be debited on various dates
- I understand that Tradesure Insurance Company may change the amounts and dates only after giving me prior notice
- I will inform the bank/building society if I wish to cancel this instruction
- I understand that if any direct debit is paid which breaks the terms of this instruction, the bank/building society will make a refund.

account name

NIMROD DRAINAGE LIMITED

account number	sort code	signature(s)	date
12034875	35.09.75		

CHAPTER 14: PAYROLL PAYMENTS

14.1 (a) gross pay = pay before deductions, net pay = pay after deductions

(b) overtime = time worked outside normal hours, shift allowance is paid for normal work in unsocial hours

(c) bonus payment extra to normal pay, often based on percentage of sales; piece rate is related to number of items produced

(d) time book = signing in book kept on premises; time sheet records hours worked off premises

(e) clock card = cardboard card inserted in mechanical clock machine; swipe card = plastic card 'swiped' through electronic reader

14.2 (a) £125; (b) £180; (c) £220; (d) £130; (e) £150

14.3 (a) £210; (b) £240 + £18 = £258; (c) £240 + £72 = £312; (d) £240 + £90 = £330; (e) £234

14.4 (a) £138.50 (b) £1,169.50 (c) £1,829.50 (d) £2,509.50 (e) £4,689.50 (f) £8,428.80 (g) £16,428.80

14.5 (a) to (d) see chapter text; (e) the entry is likely to be zero because there is no loan to repay; (f) employer's National Insurance Contributions

14.6

employee	*employer's contribution (£)*	*employee's contribution (£)*
(a)	0	0
(b)	0.77	0.66
(c)	20.61	17.71
(d)	78.21	55.66 + 1.05 = 56.71
(e)	103.81	55.66 + 3.05 = 58.71

14.7 Payslips set out as per guide in the chapter.

14.8 Income tax £848.25; National Insurance £997.10; total £1,845.35.

14.9	total	£50	£20	£10	£5	£2	£1	50p	20p	10p	5p	2p	1p
W Rowberry	£211.56	2	5	1			1	1			1		1
M Richardson	£189.74	2	4		1	2		1	1			2	
D Stanbury	£206.83	2	5		1		1	1	1	1		1	1
D Payne	£196.75	2	4	1	1		1	1	1		1		
K Peters	£178.89	2	3	1	1	1	1	1	1	1	1	2	
O Robinson	£183.69	2	4			1	1	1		1	1	2	
number		12	25	3	4	4	5	6	4	3	4	7	2
totals (£)	1167.46	600	500	30	20	8	5	3	0.80	0.30	0.20	0.14	0.02

14.10 (a) BACS – supply of data direct to BACS by employer

(b) automated credit system through the employer's bank (routed via BACS)

(c) cash

14.11 (d)

14.12 (c)

14.13 (a)

14.14 (a) £119,150

(b) £40,510

(c) £71,140

(d)

account	*debit (£)*		*credit (£)*	
Wages & Salaries	Wages & Salaries Control	119,150		
Bank			Wages & Salaries Control	71,140
Inland Revenue			Wages & Salaries Control	40,510
Pension Fund			Wages & Salaries Control	7,500
Wages & Salaries Control	Bank	71,140	Wages & Salaries	119,150
	Inland Revenue	40,510		
	Pension Fund	7,500		

14.15 (a) £56,110

(b) £21,105

(c) £2,200

(d) £32,805

(e)

account	*debit (£)*		*credit (£)*	
Wages & Salaries	Wages & Salaries Control	56,110		
Bank			Wages & Salaries Control	32,805
Inland Revenue			Wages & Salaries Control	21,105
Pension Fund			Wages & Salaries Control	2,200
Wages & Salaries Control	Bank	32,805	Wages & Salaries	56,110
	Inland Revenue	21,105		
	Pension Fund	2,200		

CHAPTER 15: CASH BOOK– RECORDING PAYMENTS

15.1 (d)

15.2

Credit			Cash Book: Payments			CBP 22
Date	Details		Folio	Discount received	Cash	Bank
				£	£	£
2004						
3 Feb	G Wheaton	101359	PL			195
5 Feb	A Aznar	101360	PL	10		390
10 Feb	Wages		ML		370	
12 Feb	Singh Limited	101361	PL	15		570
17 Feb	Telephone		ML		155	
19 Feb	Farr and Company	101362	PL	10		220
27 Feb	Rent	SO	ML			160
				35	525	1,535

15.3

Credit		Cash Book: Payments			CBP 45
Date	Details	Folio	Discount received	Cash	Bank
2004			£	£	£
2 Aug	Purchases	ML 5001/ 2200		94	
5 Aug	T Hall Ltd	PL 451	24		541
9 Aug	Wages	ML 7750		254	
17 Aug	F Jarvis	PL 510			457
18 Aug	Drawings	ML 7005		200	
19 Aug	Rent paid	ML 6950			275
20 Aug	Wages	ML 7750		436	
24 Aug	J Jones	ML 643	33		628
27 Aug	Purchases	ML 5001/ 2200			235
27 Aug	Salaries	ML 7750			2,043
30 Aug	Telephone	ML 6212/ 2200			282
30 Aug	Office equipment	ML 750/ 2200			705
			57	984	5,166

SUBSIDIARY (PURCHASES) LEDGER

Dr			**T Hall Limited** (account no 451)		Cr
2004			£	2004	£
5 Aug	Bank	CBP 45	541		
5 Aug	Discount received	ML 6502	24		

Dr			**F Jarvis** (account no 510)		Cr
2004			£	2004	£
17 Aug	Bank	CBP 45	457		

Dr			**J Jones** (account no 643)		Cr
2004			£	2004	£
24 Aug	Bank	CBP 45	628		
24 Aug	Discount received	ML 6502	33		

MAIN LEDGER

Dr			**Purchases Ledger Control Account** (account no 6002)		Cr
2004			£	2004	£
31 Aug	Bank	CBP 45	*1,626		
31 Aug	Discount received	ML 6502	57		

* £541 + £457 + £628

Dr				**Discount Received Account** (account no 6502)		Cr
2004		£	2004			£
			31 Aug	Cash Book	CBP 45	57

Dr				**Drawings Account** (account no 7005)		Cr
2004		£	2004			£
18 Aug	Cash CBP 45	200				

Dr				**Office Equipment Account** (account no 750)		Cr
2004		£	2004			£
30 Aug	Bank CBP 45	600				

Dr				**Purchases Account** (account no 5001)		Cr
2004		£	2004			£
2 Aug	Cash CBP 45	80				
27 Aug	Bank CBP 45	200				

Dr				**Rent Paid Account** (account no 6950)		Cr
2004		£	2004			£
19 Aug	Bank CBP 45	275				

Dr				**Telephone Expenses Account** (account no 6212)		Cr
2004		£	2004			£
30 Aug	Bank CBP 45	240				

Dr				**Value Added Tax Account** (account no 2200)		Cr
2004		£	2004			£
2 Aug	Cash CBP 45	14				
27 Aug	Bank CBP 45	35				
30 Aug	Bank CBP 45	42				
30 Aug	Bank CBP 45	105				

Dr				**Wages and Salaries Account** (account no 7750)		Cr
2004		£	2004			£
9 Aug	Cash CBP 45	254				
20 Aug	Cash CBP 45	436				
27 Aug	Bank CBP 45	2,043				

15.4

Credit		**Cash Book: Payments**			**CBP 88**
Date	Details	Folio	Discount received	VAT	Bank
2004			£	£	£
2 Apr	Purchases	ML 5001/2200		7	47
2 Apr	Travelling expenses	ML 6330			65
5 Apr	Telephone	ML 6212/2200		35	235
6 Apr	ABC Bank: loan	ML 2250			500
9 Apr	Drawings	ML 7005			600
13 Apr	M Hughes	PL 498	10		180
15 Apr	Office stationery	ML 6384/2200		14	94
16 Apr	Purchases	ML 5001/2200		14	94
19 Apr	Office equipment	ML 750/2200		70	470
26 Apr	Wilson Ltd	PL 752	10		245
27 Apr	Purchases	ML 5001/2200		21	141
29 Apr	Wages	ML 7750			350
30 Apr	L Luz	PL 601	20		560
			40	161	3,581

SUBSIDIARY (PURCHASES) LEDGER

Dr				**M Hughes** (account no 498)			Cr
2004			£	2004			£
13 Apr	Bank	CBP 88	180				
13 Apr	Discount received	ML 6502	10				

Dr				**Wilson Limited** (account no 752)			Cr
2004			£	2004			£
26 Apr	Bank	CBP 88	245				
26 Apr	Discount received	ML 6502	10				

Dr				**Lucinda Luz** (account no 601)			Cr
2004			£	2004			£
30 Apr	Bank	CBP 88	560				
30 Apr	Discount received	ML 6502	20				

MAIN LEDGER

Dr				**Purchases Ledger Control Account** (account no 6002)			Cr
2004			£	2004			£
30 Apr	Bank	CBP 88	*985				
30 Apr	Discount received	ML 6502	40				

* £180 + £245 + £560

Dr				**Discount Received Account** (account no 6502)			Cr
2004			£	2004			£
				30 Apr	Cash Book	CBP 88	40

Dr			**Drawings Account** (account no 7005)		Cr
2004			£	2004	£
9 Apr	Bank	CBP 88	600		

Dr			**Loan Account: ABC Bank** (account no 2250)		Cr
2004			£	2004	£
6 Apr	Bank	CBP 88	500		

Dr			**Office Equipment Account** (account no 750)		Cr
2004			£	2004	£
19 Apr	Bank	CBP 88	400		

Dr			**Office Stationery Account** (account no 6384)		Cr
2004			£	2004	£
15 Apr	Bank	CBP 88	80		

Dr			**Purchases Account** (account no 5001)		Cr
2004			£	2004	£
2 Apr	Bank	CBP 88	40		
16 Apr	Bank	CBP 88	80		
27 Apr	Bank	CBP 88	120		

Dr			**Telephone Expenses Account** (account no 6212)		Cr
2004			£	2004	£
5 Apr	Bank	CBP 88	200		

Dr			**Travelling Expenses Account** (account no 6330)		Cr
2004			£	2004	£
2 Apr	Bank	CBP 88	65		

Dr			**Value Added Tax Account** (account no 2200)		Cr
2004			£	2004	£
30 Apr	Cash Book	CBP 88	161		

Dr			**Wages and Salaries Account** (account no 7750)		Cr
2004			£	2004	£
29 Apr	Bank	CBP 88	350		

15.5

Credit		**Cash Book: Payments**						**CBP 96**
Date	Details	Folio	Bank	Disc recvd	VAT	Purchases	Purchases ledger	Sundry
2004			£ p	£ p	£ p	£ p	£ p	£ p
17 May	Purchases	ML 5001/ 2200	88.94		13.24	75.70		
17 May	Telephone	ML 6212/ 2200	238.90		35.58			203.32
18 May	Wyvern Finance:loan	ML 2270	250.00					250.00
18 May	Shop rent	ML 6345	255.50					255.50
19 May	Purchases	ML 5001/ 2200	100.00		14.89	85.11		
19 May	Terry Carpets Ltd	PL 721	363.55	4.65			363.55	
19 May	Stationery	ML 6382/ 2200	28.20		4.20			24.00
20 May	Drawings	ML 7005	100.00					100.00
20 May	Shop fittings	ML 740/ 2200	311.37		46.37			265.00
21 May	Longlife Carpets Ltd	PL 624	291.50	4.30			291.50	
21 May	Wages	ML 7750	314.20					314.20
21 May	Trade Supplies	PL 784	145.50	3.50			145.50	
			2,487.66	12.45	114.28	160.81	800.55	1,412.02

SUBSIDIARY (PURCHASES) LEDGER

Dr	**Terry Carpets Limited** (account no 721)				Cr
2004			£ p	2004	£ p
19 May	Bank	CBP 96	363.55		
19 May	Discount received	ML 6502	4.65		

Dr	**Longlife Carpets Limited** (account no 624)				Cr
2004			£ p	2004	£ p
21 May	Bank	CBP 96	291.50		
21 May	Discount received	ML 6502	4.30		

Dr	**Trade Supplies** (account no 784)				Cr
2004			£ p	2004	£ p
21 May	Bank	CBP 96	145.50		
21 May	Discount received	ML 6502	3.50		

MAIN LEDGER

Dr **Purchases Ledger Control Account** (account no 6002) Cr

2004			£ p	2004			£ p
21 May	Cash Book	CBP 96	800.55				
21 May	Discount received	CBP 96	12.45				

Dr **Discount Received Account** (account no 6502) Cr

2004			£ p	2004			£ p
				21 May	Cash Book	CBP 96	12.45

Dr **Drawings Account** (account no 7005) Cr

2004			£ p	2004			£ p
20 May	Bank	CBP 96	100.00				

Dr **Loan Account: Wyvern Finance** (account no 2270) Cr

2004			£ p	2004			£ p
18 May	Bank	CBP 96	250.00				

Dr **Purchases Account** (account no 5001) Cr

2004			£ p	2004			£ p
21 May	Cash Book	CBP 96	160.81				

Dr **Shop Fittings Account** (account no 740) Cr

2004			£ p	2004			£ p
20 May	Bank	CBP 96	265.00				

Dr **Shop Rent Account** (account no 6345) Cr

2004			£ p	2004			£ p
18 May	Bank	CBP 96	255.50				

Dr **Stationery Account** (account no 6382) Cr

2004			£ p	2004			£ p
19 May	Bank	CBP 96	24.00				

Dr **Telephone Expenses Account** (account no 6212) Cr

2004			£ p	2004			£ p
17 May	Bank	CBP 96	203.32				

Dr **Value Added Tax Account** (account no 2200) Cr

2004			£ p	2004			£ p
21 May	Cash Book	CBP 96	114.28				

Dr **Wages and Salaries Account** (account no 7750) Cr

2004			£ p	2004			£ p
21 May	Bank	CBP 96	314.20				

15.6

Dr		Purchases Ledger Control Account			Cr
2004		£	2004		£
30 Apr	Purchases returns	653	1 Apr	Balance b/d	14,275
30 Apr	Payments made to creditors	31,074	30 Apr	Credit purchases	36,592
30 Apr	Discount received	1,048			
30 Apr	Set-off: sales ledger	597			
30 Apr	Balance c/d	17,495			
		50,867			50,867
			1 May	Balance b/d	17,495

CHAPTER 16: PETTY CASH BOOK

16.1 (d)

16.2 *Allow:* (a), (b), (f), (g), (h), (j) – all supported by an appropriate receipt being attached to the petty cash voucher.

Refer:

- (c) travel to work – not normally a business expense, except for emergency call-outs
- (d) donation to charity – subject to authorisation by supervisor
- (e) staff tea and coffee – check if it is company policy to pay for this personal expense of the office staff
- (i) shelving for the office – this expense is above the authorisation limit of the petty cashier; the item should be referred to the accounts supervisor, who may authorise it for payment through the main cash book.

16.3

petty cash voucher No. 851

date *today*

description	amount (£)	
Postage on urgent parcel of spare parts to Evelode Supplies Ltd	4	45
	4	45
VAT		
	4	45

signature *Jayne Smith*

authorised *A Student*

Documentation will be a Post Office receipt for £4.45.

petty cash voucher No. 852

date *today*

description	amount (£)	
Airmail envelopes	2	00
	2	00
VAT	0	35
	2	35

signature *Tanya Howard*

authorised *A Student*

Documentation will be a till receipt from the stationery shop for £2.35.

petty cash voucher		No. 853
		date *today*
description	amount (£)	
Taxi fare re visit to Jasper Ltd	7	32
	7	32
VAT	1	28
	8	60
signature *Josh Delabole*		
authorised *A Student*		

Documentation will be a receipt from the taxi company for £8.60.

16.4

	Expense (excluding VAT)	*VAT*	*Total*
	£	£	£
(a)	8.00	1.40	9.40
(b)	4.00	0.70	4.70
(c)	2.00	0.35	2.35
(d)	2.09	0.36	2.45
(e)	4.77	0.83	5.60
(f)	2.96	0.51	3.47
(g)	7.45	1.30	8.75
(h)	0.80	0.14	0.94
(i)	0.85	0.14	0.99
(j)	8.01	1.40	9.41

16.5

Petty Cash Book

Receipts	Date	Details	Voucher No	Total Payment	Analysis columns				
					VAT	Postages	Travel	Meals	Office Sundries
£	2004			£	£	£	£	£	£
75.00	1 Aug	Balance b/d							
	4 Aug	Postages	223	7.20		7.20			
	6 Aug	Travel expenses	224	4.50			4.50		
	9 Aug	Postages	225	2.54		2.54			
	12 Aug	Envelopes	226	4.70	0.70				4.00
	13 Aug	Window cleaning	227	7.05	1.05				6.00
	17 Aug	Taxi fare	228	7.52	1.12		6.40		
	20 Aug	Postages	229	8.56		8.56			
	23 Aug	Meals	230	6.35				6.35	
	27 Aug	Envelopes	231	6.58	0.98				5.60
				55.00	3.85	18.30	10.90	6.35	15.60
55.00	31 Aug	Cash received							
	31 Aug	Balance c/d		75.00					
130.00				130.00					
75.00	1 Sep	Balance b/d							

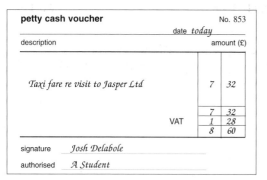

16.6 **Petty Cash Book** **PCB 42**

Receipts	Date	Details	Voucher No	Total Payment	VAT	Travel	Postages	Stationery	Meals	Misc
					Analysis columns					
£	2004			£	£	£	£	£	£	£
75.00	1 Aug	Balance b/d								
	4 Aug	Taxi fare	39	3.80	0.56	3.24				
	6 Aug	Parcel post	40	2.35			2.35			
	9 Aug	Pencils	41	1.26	0.18			1.08		
	11 Aug	Travel expenses	42	5.46		5.46				
	12 Aug	Window cleaner	43	8.50						8.50
	16 Aug	Envelopes	44	2.45	0.36			2.09		
	18 Aug	Donation	45	5.00						5.00
	19 Aug	Rail fare/meal allow	46	10.60		5.60			5.00	
	20 Aug	Postage	47	0.75			0.75			
	23 Aug	Tape	48	1.50	0.22			1.28		
	25 Aug	Postage	49	0.55			0.55			
	27 Aug	Taxi fare	50	5.40	0.80	4.60				
				47.62	2.12	18.90	3.65	4.45	5.00	13.50
47.62	31 Aug	Cash received								
	31 Aug	Balance c/d		75.00						
122.62				122.62						
75.00	1 Sep	Balance b/d								

CARR TRADING

Posting sheet: petty cash

account name	account number	debit	credit	reference
		£	£	
VAT	ML	2.12		PCB 42
Travel	ML	18.90		PCB 42
Postages	ML	3.65		PCB 42
Stationery	ML	4.45		PCB 42
Meals	ML	5.00		PCB 42
Miscellaneous	ML	13.50		PCB 42
Bank	CBP		47.62	PCB 42
TOTAL		47.62	47.62	

Prepared by *A Student* Date *31 August 2004*

Checked by ______________ Date ______________

Posted by ______________ Date ______________

16.7 **Petty Cash Book** **PCB 18**

Receipts	Date	Details	Voucher No	Total Payment	VAT	Postages	Travel	Meals	Sundry Office
					Analysis columns				
£	2004			£	£	£	£	£	£
100.00	7 Jun	Balance b/d							
	7 Jun	Postages	123	6.35		6.35			
	8 Jun	Travel expenses	124	3.25			3.25		
	8 Jun	Postages	125	1.28		1.28			
	9 Jun	Envelopes	126	4.54	0.67				3.87
	9 Jun	Window cleaning	127	5.50	0.81				4.69
	10 Jun	Taxi fare/meals	128	15.41	2.29		3.88	9.24	
	10 Jun	Post/packing	129	11.81	0.48	8.56			2.77
	10 Jun	Taxi fare/meals	130	11.95	1.77		3.83	6.35	
	11 Jun	Pens/envelopes	131	6.35	0.94				5.41
				66.44	6.96	16.19	10.96	15.59	16.74
66.44	11 Jun	Cash received							
	11 Jun	Balance c/d		100.00					
166.44				166.44					
100.00	11 Jun	Balance b/d							

TYAX SYSTEMS LIMITED

Posting sheet: petty cash

account name	account number	debit	credit	reference
		£	£	
VAT	ML	6.96		PCB 18
Postages	ML	16.19		PCB 18
Travel	ML	10.96		PCB 18
Meals	ML	15.59		PCB 18
Sundry office	ML	16.74		PCB 18
Bank	CBP		66.44	PCB 18
TOTAL		66.44	66.44	

Prepared by *A Student* Date *11 June 2004*

Checked by __________ Date __________

Posted by __________ Date __________

CHAPTER 17: FURTHER ASPECTS OF DOUBLE-ENTRY ACCOUNTS

17.1 (c) **17.2** (b)

17.3 Computer

- The double-entry book-keeping transaction for the purchase of a computer is:
  - *debit* computer account
  - *credit* cash account or bank account

  (This assumes that the computer has been bought as a fixed asset, ie for use in the business, and that it has been paid for either in cash or by cheque.)
- Thus, the computer account records an asset, while cash/bank account has given value.
- The computer, being an asset, is recorded in the accounts by a debit transaction; the method of paying for it is recorded in cash/bank account by a credit transaction.

Capital

- The double-entry book-keeping transaction for the introduction of capital into a business is:
  - *debit* cash account or bank account
  - *credit* capital account

  (This assumes that the capital was in the form of money rather than other assets.)
- Thus, the cash/bank account has gained value, while capital account records a liability to the owner. It is a liability that is unlikely to be repaid immediately as the business would then be unable to operate.

17.4

JAMES ANDERSON

Capital Account

Dr		£	Cr		£
2004		£	2004		£
			1 Mar	Bank	7,500

Computer Account

Dr		£	Cr		£
2004		£	2004		£
5 Mar	Bank	2,000			

Rent Paid Account

Dr		£	Cr		£
2004		£	2004		£
8 Mar	Bank	500			

Wages Account

Dr		£	Cr		£
2004		£	2004		£
12 Mar	Bank	425			
26 Mar	Bank	380			

Bank Loan Account

Dr		£	Cr		£
2004		£	2004		£
			15 Mar	Bank	2,500

Commission Received Account

Dr		£	Cr		£
2004		£	2004		£
			19 Mar	Bank	120

Dr		Drawings Account			Cr
2004		£	2004		£
23 Mar	Bank	200			

Dr		Van Account			Cr
2004		£	2004		£
29 Mar	Bank	5,000			

Dr		Value Added Tax Account			Cr
2004		£	2004		£
5 Mar	Bank (computer)	350	19 Mar	Bank (commission received)	21
29 Mar	Bank (van)	875			

17.5 **TONY LONG**

Debit	Cash Book: Receipts			CBR
Date	Details	Folio	Discount allowed	Bank
2004			£	£
3 May	Capital			6,000
13 May	L Warner: loan			1,000
18 May	Commission received			188

Credit	Cash Book: Payments			CBP
Date	Details	Folio	Discount received	Bank
2004			£	£
4 May	Machine			2,350
7 May	Office equipment			2,820
10 May	Rent			350
14 May	Wages			250
21 May	Drawings			85
28 May	Wages			135

Dr		Capital Account			Cr
2004		£	2004		£
			3 May	Bank	6,000

Dr		Machinery Account			Cr
2004		£	2004		£
4 May	Bank	2,000			

Dr		Office Equipment Account			Cr
2004		£	2004		£
7 May	Bank	2,400			

Dr		Rent Paid Account			Cr
2004		£	2004		£
10 May	Bank	350			

Dr		Lucy Warner: Loan Account			Cr
2004		£	2004		£
			13 May	Bank	1,000

Dr		Wages Account			Cr
2004		£	2004		£
14 May	Bank	250			
28 May	Bank	135			

Dr		Commission Received Account			Cr
2004		£	2004		£
			18 May	Bank	160

Dr		Drawings Account			Cr
2004		£	2004		£
21 May	Bank	85			

Dr		Value Added Tax Account			Cr
2004		£	2004		£
4 May	Bank (machinery)	350	18 May	Bank (commission received)	28
7 May	Bank (office equipment)	420			

17.6 **JEAN LACEY**

Debit	Cash Book: Receipts			CBR
Date	Details	Folio	Discount allowed	Bank
2004			£	£
2 Aug	Capital			5,000
10 Aug	Commission received			
16 Aug	S Orton: loan			1,000
20 Aug	Office fittings			282
24 Aug	Commission received			188

Credit		Cash Book: Payments		CBP
Date	Details	Folio	Discount received	Bank
2004			£	£
3 Aug	Computer			2,115
6 Aug	Rent paid			100
13 Aug	Office fittings			2,350
17 Aug	Drawings			100
27 Aug	S Orton: loan			150

Capital Account

Dr					Cr
2004		£	2004		£
			2 Aug	Bank	5,000

Computer Account

Dr					Cr
2004		£	2004		£
3 Aug	Bank	1,800			

Rent Paid Account

Dr					Cr
2004		£	2004		£
6 Aug	Bank	100			

Commission Received Account

Dr					Cr
2004		£	2004		£
			10 Aug	Bank	200
			24 Aug	Bank	160

Office Fittings Account

Dr					Cr
2004		£	2004		£
13 Aug	Bank	2,000	20 Aug	Bank	240

Sally Orton: Loan Account

Dr					Cr
2004		£	2004		£
27 Aug	Bank	150	16 Aug	Bank	1,000

Drawings Account

Dr					Cr
2004		£	2004		£
17 Aug	Bank	100			

Value Added Tax Account

Dr					Cr
2004		£	2004		£
3 Aug	Bank (computer)	315	10 Aug	Bank (commission recvd)	35
13 Aug	Bank (office fittings)	350	20 Aug	Bank (office fittings)	42
			24 Aug	Bank (commission recvd)	28

17.7

Date	Details	Folio	Dr	Cr
2004			£	£
29 Nov	Bad debts written off account	ML	80	
	Value Added Tax account	ML	14	
	Sales ledger control account	ML		94
			94	94
	Balance of subsidiary (sales) ledger account of Dailey Trading Company written off as a bad debt, as per memo from accounts supervisor dated 29 November 2004			

SUBSIDIARY (SALES) LEDGER

Dr	**Dailey Trading Company** (account no 754)				Cr
2004		£	2004		£
15 Jan	Sales	94	29 Nov	Bad debts written off	80
			29 Nov	Value Added Tax	14
		94			94

MAIN LEDGER

Dr	**Bad Debts Written Off Account**				Cr
2004		£	2004		£
29 Nov	Dailey Trading Co	80			

Dr	**Value Added Tax Account**				Cr
2004		£	2004		£
29 Nov	Dailey Trading Co	14			

Dr	**Sales Ledger Control Account**				Cr
2004		£	2004		£
			29 Nov	Bad debts written off	80
			29 Nov	Value Added Tax	14

17.8

		capital expenditure	**revenue expenditure**
(a)	purchase of vehicles	✓	
(b)	rent paid on premises		✓
(c)	wages and salaries		✓
(d)	legal fees relating to the purchase of property	✓	
(e)	redecoration of office		✓
(f)	installation of air-conditioning in office	✓	
(g)	wages of own employees used to build extension to the stockroom	✓	
(h)	installation and setting up of a new machine	✓	

CHAPTER 18: COMMUNICATING WITH SUPPLIERS

18.1 Something like: 'Hello. This is J Smith calling from Omnisupplies Limited at (give time and day). We recently received your invoice 24622 but notice that the five luxury chairs we ordered under code 2982B have been invoiced under code 2982GL. As a result we have been overcharged. Please can you investigate this and call me back on 01908 287416. Thank you.'

18.2 The email should point out the omissions and ask for a new invoice to be issued as soon as possible. The new net total should be £400, which would then attract cash discount of £10. VAT is charged on the lower amount but the invoice final total does not include the cash discount.

18.3 Fax the credit note through to Mordern Stationery with a message on the fax sheet that the credit note has been received and should appear on the statement. The total due on the statement as it stands is £345 higher than it should be.

18.4 The letter should be addressed to the Accounts Manager at Regal Supplies, be dated and headed with a description such as 'Trade Discount'. The letter should point out politely but firmly that the normal level of trade discount is 20% and in view of the level of business passed through Regal Supplies, you would expect this level yourselves. It would not be appropriate at this stage to threaten taking the business elsewhere. This could be done later if Regal Supplies does not comply with the request. The letter should be signed by the Omnisupplies Accounts Manager.

CHAPTER 19: BALANCING THE CASH BOOK AND BANK RECONCILIATION

19.1

Dr				CASH BOOK							Cr
Date	Details	Folio	Discount allowed	Cash	Bank	Date	Details	Folio	Discount received	Cash	Bank
2004			£	£	£	2004			£	£	£
1 Aug	Balances b/d			325	925	6 Aug	Crane & Co		35		845
4 Aug	S Quesne		2		98	12 Aug	Wages			275	
17 Aug	J Ahmed		4	76		16 Aug	T Lewis		15		285
23 Aug	D Lloyd		3		45	27 Aug	S Ford		5	70	
31 Aug	Balance c/d				62	31 Aug	Balance c/d			56	
			9	401	1,130				55	401	1,130
1 Sep	Balance b/d			56		1 Sep	Balance b/d				62

19.2 (a)

19.3 (c)

19.4

TOM REID
BANK RECONCILIATION STATEMENT AS AT 31 DECEMBER 2004

	£
Balance at bank as per bank statement	207
Less: unpresented cheque:	
B Kay (cheque no 345126)	20
	187
Add: outstanding lodgement:	
J Hill	13
Balance at bank as per cash book	200

19.5 (a)

2004	*Receipts*		£	2004	*Payments*		£
1 Jan	Balance b/d		800.50	2 Jan	A Arthur Ltd	001351	100.00
6 Jan	J Baker		495.60	9 Jan	C Curtis	001352	398.50
30 Jan	G Shotton Ltd		335.75	13 Jan	Donald & Co	001353	229.70
13 Jan	*TK Supplies*	*BACS*	*716.50*	14 Jan	Bryant & Sons	001354	312.00
				23 Jan	P Reid	001355	176.50
				23 Jan	*Omni Finance*	*DD*	*207.95*
				31 Jan	*Balance c/d*		*923.70*
			2,348.35				*2,348.35*
1 Feb	*Balance b/d*		*923.70*				

(b)

P GERRARD

BANK RECONCILIATION STATEMENT AS AT 31 JANUARY 2004

		£	£
Balance at bank as per bank statement			1,076.45
Less:	unpresented cheques:		
	Bryant & Sons (001354)	312.00	
	P Reid (001355)	176.50	
			488.50
			587.95
Add:	outstanding lodgement:		
	G Shotton Limited		335.75
Balance at bank as per cash book			923.70

19.6 (a)

Dr **Cash Book** (bank columns) Cr

2004		£	2004			£
1 May	Balance b/d	300	3 May	P Stone	867714	28
7 May	Cash	162	14 May	Alpha Ltd	867715	50
17 May	C Brewster	89	28 May	E Deakin	867716	110
24 May	Cash	60	*17 May*	*Standing order: A-Z Insurance*		*25*
28 May	Cash	40	*31 May*	*Bank charges*		*10*
			31 May	*Balance c/d*		*428*
		651				*651*
1 Jun	*Balance b/d*	*428*				

(b)

JANE DOYLE

BANK RECONCILIATION STATEMENT AS AT 31 MAY 2004

		£
Balance at bank as per bank statement		498
Less:	unpresented cheque:	
	E Deakin (867716)	110
		388
Add:	outstanding lodgement:	
	cash	40
Balance at bank as per cash book		428

19.7 (a) - (c)

CASH BOOK

Date	Details	Bank	Date	Cheque no	Details	Bank
2004		£	2004			£
1 May	Balance b/f	3,652	4 May	451762	Smith and Company	751
26 May	J Ackland	832	4 May	451763	Bryant Limited	268
28 May	Stamp Limited	1,119	7 May	451764	Curtis Cars	1,895
14 May	*Perran Taxis*	*2,596*	7 May	451765	Parts Supplies	1,045
			18 May		*Wyvern Council*	*198*
			20 May		*A1 Insurance*	*1,005*
			25 May		*Okaro and Company*	*254*
			25 May		*Bank charges*	*20*
			31 May		*Balance c/d*	*2,763*
		8,199				*8,199*
1 Jun	*Balance b/d*	*2,763*				

(d)

MILESTONE MOTORS

Bank Reconciliation Statement as at 31 May 2004

		£	£
Balance at bank as per bank statement			2,707
Less:	unpresented cheque no 451764		1,895
			812
Add:	outstanding lodgements		
	J Ackland	832	
	Stamp Limited	1,119	
			1,951
Balance at bank as per cash book			2,763

CHAPTER 20: USING THE JOURNAL AND RECONCILING CONTROL ACCOUNTS

20.1 (b)

20.2

business transaction	*book of prime entry*
credit sale of a fixed asset	journal
credit purchase of goods from a supplier	purchases day book
returned credit purchases to the supplier	purchases returns day book
customer returns goods sold on credit	sales returns day book
cheque received from a debtor	cash book
credit sale of goods to a customer	sales day book
expense paid out of petty cash	petty cash book

20.3

	book of prime entry	*debit*	*credit*
(a)	purchases day book	purchases a/c	purchases ledger control a/c
(b)	sales day book	sales ledger control a/c	sales a/c
(c)	journal	office equipment a/c	purchases ledger control a/c
(d)	sales returns day book	sales returns a/c	sales ledger control a/c
(e)	cash book	bank a/c	sales ledger control a/c
(f)	cash book	cash a/c	sales a/c
(g)	cash book	drawings a/c	cash a/c
(h)	cash book	purchases ledger control a/c	bank a/c
(i)	journal	bad debts written off a/c	sales ledger control a/c
(j)	purchases returns day book	purchases ledger control a/c	purchases returns a/c

Notes:

- Where control accounts are used, transactions will need to be recorded in the appropriate subsidiary ledger accounts.
- An alternative for (c) is to open a main ledger account for the creditor, A-Z Computers Limited – this will avoid confusion with trade creditors in the subsidiary (purchases) ledger.

20.4 (a)

Sales Ledger Control Account

Dr		£		Cr	£
2004		£	2004		£
1 Mar	Balance b/d	142,830	31 Mar	Bank	97,247
31 Mar	Sales	105,350	31 Mar	Discount allowed	840
			31 Mar	Sales returns	2,890
			31 Mar	Bad debt written off	250
			31 Mar	Balance c/d	146,953
		248,180			248,180
1 Apr	Balance b/d	146,953			

(b)

	£
Sales ledger control account balance as at 31 March 2004	146,953
Total of subsidiary (sales) ledger accounts as at 31 March 2004	147,203
Difference	250

(c) The bad debt of £250 may not have been written off in the subsidiary (sales) ledger, and could relate to the account of Portreath Home and Garden.

20.5 (a)

Dr **Purchases Ledger Control Account** Cr

2004		£	2004		£
31 Oct	Bank	28,070	1 Oct	Balance b/d	35,105
31 Oct	Discount received	430	31 Oct	Purchases	23,294
31 Oct	Purchases returns	1,270			
31 Oct	Balance c/d	28,629			
		58,399			58,399
			1 Nov	Balance b/d	28,629

(b)

	£
Purchases ledger control account balance as at 31 October 2004	28,629
Total of subsidiary (purchases) ledger accounts as at 31 October 2004	27,929
Difference	700

(c) There may have been a posting error and the debit balance of Hawke Supplies may in fact be a credit balance.

20.6 (a)

Dr **Petty Cash Control Account** Cr

2004		£	2004		£
1 Apr	Balance b/d	250	30 Apr	Petty cash book	176
30 Apr	Cash book	176	30 Apr	Balance c/d	250
		426			426
1 May	Balance b/d	250			

(b) Carry out a physical check of the amount of cash in the petty cash box.

20.7

Dr **Cash Book** (bank columns) Cr

2004		£	2004		£
6 Apr	Archibald and Company	250	30 Apr	Balance c/d	1,850
23 Apr	Marshall and Perry	700			
26 Apr	Okara and Associates	200			
28 Apr	Archibald and Company	500			
30 Apr	Okara and Associates	200			
		1,850			1,850
1 May	Balance b/d	1,850			

MAIN LEDGER

Dr **Rent Receivable Control Account** Cr

2004		£	2004		£
1 Apr	Balance b/d	250	30 Apr	Cash book	1,850
22 Apr	Rent receivable	2,000	30 Apr	Balance c/d	400
		2,250			2,250
1 May	Balance b/d	400			

SUBSIDIARY (NON-TRADE DEBTORS) LEDGER

Dr **Archibald and Company** Cr

2004		£	2004		£
1 Apr	Balance b/d	250	6 Apr	Cash book	250
22 Apr	Rent receivable	800	28 Apr	Cash book	500
			30 Apr	Balance c/d	300
		1,050			1,050
1 May	Balance b/d	300			

Dr **Marshall and Perry** Cr

2004		£	2004		£
22 Apr	Rent receivable	700	23 Apr	Cash book	700

Dr **Okara and Associates** Cr

2004		£	2004		£
22 Apr	Rent receivable	500	26 Apr	Cash book	200
			30 Apr	Cash book	200
			30 Apr	Balance c/d	100
		500			500
1 May	Balance b/d	100			

20.8 (a)

MAIN LEDGER

Dr **Rent Receivable Control Account** Cr

2004		£	2004		£
1 Oct	Balance b/d	350	31 Oct	Cash book	2,300
31 Oct	Rent receivable	2,400	31 Oct	Journal	150
			31 Oct	Balance c/d	300
		2,750			2,750
1 Nov	Balance b/d	300			

(b)

	£
Rent receivable control account balance as at 31 October 2004	300
Total of subsidiary (non-trade debtors) ledger accounts as at 31 October 2004	450
Difference	150

(c) The journal entry of £150 in the rent receivable control account may not have been entered in the subsidiary (non-trade debtors) ledger, and could relate to the account of Zelah Limited.

CHAPTER 21: INITIAL TRIAL BALANCE AND CORRECTION OF ERRORS

21.1 (b)

21.2 (c)

21.3 (a)

Dr				CASH BOOK					Cr
Date	Details	Folio	Discount allowed	Bank	Date	Details	Folio	Discount received	Bank
2004			£	£	2004			£	£
1 Apr	Capital			1,000	2 Apr	Purchases			255
7 Apr	Sales			195	5 Apr	Advertising			60
9 Apr	Sales			248	8 Apr	Rent paid			125
16 Apr	J Couchman: loan			1,000	12 Apr	Drawings			100
19 Apr	Sales			220	14 Apr	Purchases			240
28 Apr	Sales			312	21 Apr	Shop fittings			1,250
					23 Apr	Purchases			180
					26 Apr	Advertising			90
					29 Apr	Rent			125
					30 Apr	Drawings			125
					30 Apr	Balance c/d			425
			–	2,975				–	2,975
1 May	Balance b/d		–	425					

(b) and (c)

MAIN LEDGER

Dr		Capital Account			Cr
2004		£	2004		£
			1 Apr	Bank	1,000

Dr		Purchases Account			Cr
2004		£	2004		£
2 Apr	Bank	255	30 Apr	Balance c/d	675
14 Apr	Bank	240			
23 Apr	Bank	180			
		675			675
1 May	Balance b/d	675			

Dr		Advertising Account			Cr
2004		£	2004		£
5 Apr	Bank	60	30 Apr	Balance c/d	150
26 Apr	Bank	90			
		150			150
1 May	Balance b/d	150			

Sales Account

Dr 2004		£	Cr 2004		£
30 Apr	Balance c/d	975	7 Apr	Bank	195
			9 Apr	Bank	248
			19 Apr	Bank	220
			28 Apr	Bank	312
		975			975
			1 May	Balance b/d	975

Rent Paid Account

Dr 2004		£	Cr 2004		£
8 Apr	Bank	125	30 Apr	Balance c/d	250
29 Apr	Bank	125			
		250			250
1 May	Balance b/d	250			

Drawings Account

Dr 2004		£	Cr 2004		£
12 Apr	Bank	100	30 Apr	Balance c/d	225
30 Apr	Bank	125			
		225			225
1 May	Balance b/d	225			

J Couchman: Loan Account

Dr 2004		£	Cr 2004		£
			16 Apr	Bank	1,000

Shop Fittings Account

Dr 2004		£	Cr 2004		£
21 Apr	Bank	1,250			

(d) **Trial balance of Andrew Jarvis as at 30 April 2004**

Name of account	Dr £	Cr £
Bank	425	
Capital		1,000
Purchases	675	
Advertising	150	
Sales		975
Rent paid	250	
Drawings	225	
J Couchman: Loan		1,000
Shop fittings	1,250	
	2,975	2,975

21.4 **Trial balance of Jane Greenwell as at 29 February 2004**

Name of account	Dr £	Cr £
Bank		1,250
Purchases	850	
Cash	48	
Sales		1,940
Purchases returns		144
Creditors		1,442
Equipment	2,704	
Van	3,200	
Stock at 1 Jan 2004	1,210	
Sales returns	90	
Debtors	1,174	
Wages	1,500	
Capital *(missing figure)*		6,000
	10,776	10,776

21.5 (a) will cause an imbalance in the trial balance

(b) will not cause an imbalance in the trial balance

(c) will not cause an imbalance in the trial balance

(d) will not cause an imbalance in the trial balance

21.6 (d)

21.7 (a)

21.8

Date	Details	Folio	Dr	Cr
			£	£
(a)	Rates		100	
	Rent paid			100
(b)	Sales ledger control		96	
	Sales returns			96
	Sales returns		69	
	Sales ledger control			69
			165	165
(c)	Bad debts written off		200	
	Value Added Tax		35	
	Sales ledger control			235
			235	235

Date	Details	Folio	Dr	Cr
			£	£
(d)	Purchases ledger control		175	
	Purchases returns			175
	Purchases ledger control		175	
	Purchases returns			175
			350	350
(e)	Vehicle running expenses		45	
	Vehicles			45

21.9 (a) *error of omission*

Date	Details	Folio	Dr	Cr
			£	£
	Sales ledger control	ML	150	
	Sales	ML		150
	Sales invoice no .... omitted from the accounts: in the subsidiary (sales) ledger – debit J Rigby £150			

(b) *mispost/error of commission*

Date	Details	Folio	Dr	Cr
			£	£
	Purchases ledger control	ML	125	
	Purchases ledger control	ML		125
	Correction of mispost – cheque no .....: in the subsidiary (purchases) ledger – debit H Price Limited – credit H Prince			

(c) *error of principle*

Date	Details	Folio	Dr	Cr
			£	£
	Delivery van	ML	10,000	
	Vehicle expenses	ML		10,000
	Correction of error – vehicle no .... invoice no			

(d) *reversal of entries*

Date	Details	Folio	Dr	Cr
			£	£
	Postages	ML	55	
	Bank	CBP		55
	Postages	ML	55	
	Bank	CBP		55
			110	110
	Correction of reversal of entries on			

(e) *compensating error*

Date	Details	Folio	Dr	Cr
			£	£
	Purchases	ML	100	
	Purchases returns	ML		100
	Correction of under-cast on purchases account and purchases returns account on ....(date).......			

(f) *error of original entry*

Date	Details	Folio	Dr	Cr
			£	£
	Sales ledger control	ML	98	
	Bank	CBP		98
	Bank	CBR	89	
	Sales ledger control	ML		89
			187	187
	Correction of error – cheque for £89 received on ....(date)....: in the subsidiary (sales) ledger *– debit L Johnson £98* *– credit L Johnson £89*			

21.10

Date	Details	Folio	Dr	Cr
			£	£
(a)	Office expenses	ML	85	
	Suspense	ML		85
	Omission of entry in office expenses account – payment made by cheque no .... on ....(date)			
(b)	Suspense	ML	78	
	Photocopying	ML		78
	Photocopying	ML	87	
	Suspense	ML		87
			165	165
	Payment for photocopying £87 (cheque no .... on ....) entered in photocopying account as £78 in error			
(c)	Suspense	ML	100	
	Sales returns	ML		100
	Overcast on ...(date)... now corrected			
(d)	Commission received	ML	25	
	Suspense	ML		25
	Commission received on .... entered twice in commission received account, now corrected			

Suspense Account

Dr		£		Cr	£
2004		£	2004		£
30 Sep	Trial balance difference	19	(a)	Office expenses	85
(b)	Photocopying	78	(b)	Photocopying	87
(c)	Sales returns	100	(d)	Commission received	25
		197			197

21.11

Date	Details	Folio	Dr	Cr
			£	£
(a)	Sales		100	
	Suspense			100
(b)	Suspense		205	
	Rent paid			205
(c)	Suspense		65	
	Telephone expenses			65
	Telephone expenses		56	
	Suspense			56
			121	121
(d)	Heating and lighting		160	
	Suspense			160

Dr		Suspense Account			Cr
2004		£	2004		£
29 Feb	Trial balance difference	46		Sales	100
	Rent paid	205		Telephone expenses	56
	Telephone expenses	65		Heating and lighting	160
		316			316

Note: the net difference on telephone expenses is a £9 debit to suspense account.

Trial balance as at 29 February 2004
after correction of errors

	Dr	Cr
	£	£
Purchases	122,500	
Sales		239,750
Rent paid	5,015	
Wages	96,310	
Office equipment	6,000	
Machinery	12,000	
Heating and lighting	3,670	
Telephone expenses	2,045	
Stock at 1 March 2003	24,740	
Bank	8,230	
Sales ledger control	22,840	
Purchases ledger control		15,680
Value Added Tax		5,320
Capital		58,500
Drawings	15,900	
Suspense	–	
	319,250	319,250

CHAPTER 22: USING THE TRIAL BALANCE

22.1 **SUBSIDIARY (PURCHASES) LEDGER**

Dalton & Co

Date	Details	Amount	Date	Details	Amount
2004		£	2004		£
1 Oct	Purchases returns	94	1 Oct	Balance b/d	23,076
1 Oct	Balance c/d	24,580	1 Oct	Purchases	1,598
		24,674			24,674
			2 Oct	Balance b/d	24,580

Jeans-R-Us Limited

Date	Details	Amount	Date	Details	Amount
2004		£	2004		£
1 Oct	Purchases returns	141	1 Oct	Balance b/d	12,120
1 Oct	Balance c/d	14,799	1 Oct	Purchases	2,820
		14,940			14,940
			2 Oct	Balance b/d	14,799

J & S Manufacturing

Date	Details	Amount	Date	Details	Amount
2004		£	2004		£
1 Oct	Bank	775	1 Oct	Balance b/d	13,491
1 Oct	Discount received	25	1 Oct	Purchases	1,034
1 Oct	Balance c/d	13,725			
		14,525			14,525
			2 Oct	Balance b/d	13,725

One-Stop Office

Date	Details	Amount	Date	Details	Amount
2004		£	2004		£
1 Oct	Stationery returns	47	1 Oct	Balance b/d	9,466
1 Oct	Bank	624	1 Oct	Stationery	423
1 Oct	Balance c/d	9,218			
		9,889			9,889
			2 Oct	Balance b/d	9,218

Wyvern Clothes

Date	Details	Amount	Date	Details	Amount
2004		£	2004		£
1 Oct	Bank	1,055	1 Oct	Balance b/d	2,610
1 Oct	Discount received	45	1 Oct	Purchases	1,457
1 Oct	Balance c/d	4,189	1 Oct	Purchases	1,222
		5,289			5,289
			2 Oct	Balance b/d	4,189

Reconciliation of purchases ledger control account

	1 Oct 2004	2 Oct 2004
	£	£
Dalton & Co	23,076	24,580
Jeans-R-Us Limited	12,120	14,799
J & S Manufacturing	13,491	13,725
One-Stop Office	9,466	9,218
Wyvern Clothes	2,610	4,189
Purchases ledger control account (see below)	60,763	66,511

MAIN LEDGER

Purchases Ledger Control Account

Date	Details	Amount	Date	Details	Amount
2004		£	2004		£
1 Oct	Purchases Returns Day Book	282	1 Oct	Balance b/d	60,763
1 Oct	Bank	*2,454	1 Oct	Purchases Day Book	8,554
1 Oct	Discount received	70			
1 Oct	Balance c/d	66,511			
		69,317			69,317
			2 Oct	Balance b/d	66,511

* £775 + £1,055 + £624

Purchases Account

Date	Details	Amount	Date	Details	Amount
2004		£	2004		£
1 Oct	Balance b/d	428,494	1 Oct	Balance b/d	435,414
1 Oct	Purchases Day Book	6,920			
		435,414			435,414
2 Oct	Balance b/d	435,414			

Purchases Returns Account

Date	Details	Amount	Date	Details	Amount
2004		£	2004		£
1 Oct	Balance c/d	8,527	1 Oct	Balance b/d	8,327
			1 Oct	Purchases Returns Day Book	200
		8,527			8,527
			2 Oct	Balance b/d	8,527

Stationery Account

Date	Details	Amount	Date	Details	Amount
2004		£	2004		£
1 Oct	Balance b/d	3,650	1 Oct	Purchases Returns Day	
1 Oct	Purchases Day Book	360		Book	40
			1 Oct	Balance c/d	3,970
		4,010			4,010
2 Oct	Balance b/d	3,970			

Discount Received Account

Date	Details	Amount	Date	Details	Amount
2004		£	2004		£
1 Oct	Balance c/d	911	1 Oct	Balance b/d	841
			1 Oct	Cash Book	70
		911			911
			2 Oct	Balance b/d	911

Value Added Tax Account

Date	Details	Amount	Date	Details	Amount
2004		£	2004		£
1 Oct	Purchases Day Book	1,274	1 Oct	Balance b/d	8,347
1 Oct	Balance c/d	7,115	1 Oct	Purchases Returns Day	
				Book	42
		8,389			8,389
			2 Oct	Balance b/d	7,115

Fashion Traders

Trial balance as at 1 October 2004

	Dr	Cr
Name of account	£	£
Purchases ledger control		66,511
Purchases	435,414	
Purchases returns		8,527
Stationery	3,970	
Discount received		911
Value Added Tax		7,115
Cash	275	
Bank		400
Sales ledger control	100,690	
Sales		758,174

continued on next page

Sales returns	12,364	
Discount allowed	1,497	
General expenses	25,842	
Wages and salaries	127,608	
Bad debts written off	1,762	
Office equipment	7,750	
Warehouse equipment	85,250	
Stock at 1 Jan 2004	165,940	
Bank loan		40,000
Capital		115,324
Drawings	28,600	
	996,962	996,962

22.2 **JOURNAL**

Date	Details	Debit	Credit
2004		£	£
2 Oct	Bad debts written off account	80	
	Value Added Tax account	14	
	Sales ledger control account		94
		94	94
	Balance of subsidiary (sales) ledger account of Victoria's Fashions written off as a bad debt on instructions of the accounts supervisor		
2 Oct	Sales ledger control account	220	
	Sales ledger control account		220
	Correction of mispost on 12 September; in the subsidiary (sales) ledger:		
	– debit Bentley Stores Limited		
	– credit Bentley & Co		

SUBSIDIARY (SALES) LEDGER

Bentley & Co

Date	Details	Amount	Date	Details	Amount
2004		£	2004		£
2 Oct	Balance b/d	31,095	2 Oct	Bank	420
2 Oct	Sales	423	2 Oct	Bentley Stores	220
			2 Oct	Balance c/d	30,878
		31,518			31,518
3 Oct	Balance b/d	30,878			

Bentley Stores Limited

Date	Details	Amount	Date	Details	Amount
2004		£	2004		£
2 Oct	Balance b/d	21,870	2 Oct	Bank	1,825
2 Oct	Sales	752	2 Oct	Discount allowed	45
2 Oct	Sales	376	2 Oct	Balance c/d	21,348
2 Oct	Bentley & Co	220			
		23,218			23,218
3 Oct	Balance b/d	21,348			

Just Jeans

Date	Details	Amount	Date	Details	Amount
2004		£	2004		£
2 Oct	Balance b/d	10,629	2 Oct	Sales returns	47
2 Oct	Sales	188	2 Oct	Bank	240
			2 Oct	Discount allowed	10
			2 Oct	Balance c/d	10,520
		10,817			10,817
3 Oct	Balance b/d	10,520			

Southwick Stores

Date	Details	Amount	Date	Details	Amount
2004		£	2004		£
2 Oct	Balance b/d	16,205	2 Oct	Balance c/d	16,675
2 Oct	Sales	470			
		16,675			16,675
3 Oct	Balance b/d	16,675			

Teme Trading Co

Date	Details	Amount	Date	Details	Amount
2004		£	2004		£
2 Oct	Balance b/d	20,797	2 Oct	Sales returns	94
2 Oct	Sales	329	2 Oct	Balance c/d	21,032
		21,126			21,126
3 Oct	Balance b/d	21,032			

Victoria's Fashions

Date	Details	Amount	Date	Details	Amount
2004		£	2004		£
2 Oct	Balance b/d	94	2 Oct	Bad debts written off	80
			2 Oct	Value Added Tax	14
		94			94

Reconciliation of sales ledger control account

	2 Oct 2004	3 Oct 2004
	£	£
Bentley & Co	31,095	30,878
Bentley Stores Limited	21,870	21,348
Just Jeans	10,629	10,520
Southwick Stores	16,205	16,675
Teme Trading Co	20,797	21,032
Victoria's Fashions	94	–
Sales ledger control account (see below)	100,690	100,453

MAIN LEDGER

Sales Ledger Control Account

Date	Details	Amount	Date	Details	Amount
2004		£	2004		£
2 Oct	Balance b/d	100,690	2 Oct	Sales Returns Day Book	141
2 Oct	Sales Day Book	2,538	2 Oct	Bank	*2,485
			2 Oct	Discount allowed	55
			2 Oct	Bad debt written off	80
			2 Oct	Value Added Tax	14
			2 Oct	Balance c/d	100,453
		103,228			103,228
3 Oct	Balance b/d	100,453			

* £420 + £240 + £1,825

Sales Account

Date	Details	Amount	Date	Details	Amount
2004		£	2004		£
2 Oct	Balance c/d	760,334	2 Oct	Balance b/d	758,174
			2 Oct	Sales Day Book	2,160
		760,334			760,334
			3 Oct	Balance b/d	760,334

Sales Returns Account

Date	Details	Amount	Date	Details	Amount
2004		£	2004		£
2 Oct	Balance b/d	12,364	2 Oct	Balance c/d	12,484
2 Oct	Sales Returns Day Book	120			
		12,484			12,484
3 Oct	Balance b/d	12,484			

Discount Allowed Account

Date	Details	Amount	Date	Details	Amount
2004		£	2004		£
2 Oct	Balance b/d	1,497	2 Oct	Balance c/d	1,552
2 Oct	Cash Book	55			
		1,552			1,552
3 Oct	Balance b/d	1,552			

Value Added Tax Account

Date	Details	Amount	Date	Details	Amount
2004		£	2004		£
2 Oct	Sales Returns Day Book	21	2 Oct	Balance b/d	7,115
2 Oct	Victoria's Fashions	14	2 Oct	Sales Day Book	378
2 Oct	Balance c/d	7,458			
		7,493			7,493
			3 Oct	Balance b/d	7,458

Wages and Salaries Account

Date	Details	Amount	Date	Details	Amount
2004		£	2004		£
2 Oct	Balance b/d	127,608	2 Oct	Balance c/d	128,658
2 Oct	Bank	1,050			
		128,658			128,658
3 Oct	Balance b/d	128,658			

Bad Debts Written Off Account

Date	Details	Amount	Date	Details	Amount
2004		£	2004		£
2 Oct	Balance b/d	1,762	2 Oct	Balance c/d	1,842
2 Oct	Victoria's Fashions	80			
		1,842			1,842
3 Oct	Balance b/d	1,842			

Bank Loan Account

Date	Details	Amount	Date	Details	Amount
2004		£	2004		£
2 Oct	Bank	500	2 Oct	Balance b/d	40,000
2 Oct	Balance c/d	39,500			
		40,000			40,000
			3 Oct	Balance b/d	39,500

Drawings Account

Date	Details	Amount	Date	Details	Amount
2004		£	2004		£
2 Oct	Balance b/d	28,600	2 Oct	Balance c/d	28,910
2 Oct	Bank	310			
		28,910			28,910
3 Oct	Balance b/d	28,910			

Fashion Traders

Trial balance as at 2 October 2004

	Dr	Cr
	£	£
Name of account		
Purchases ledger control		66,511
Purchases	435,414	
Purchases returns		8,527
Stationery	3,970	
Discount received		911
Value Added Tax		7,458
Cash	275	
Bank	225	
Sales ledger control	100,453	
Sales		760,334
Sales returns	12,484	
Discount allowed	1,552	
General expenses	25,842	
Wages and salaries	128,658	
Bad debts written off	1,842	
Office equipment	7,750	
Warehouse equipment	85,250	
Stock at 1 Jan 2004	165,940	
Bank loan		39,500
Capital		115,324
Drawings	28,910	
	998,565	998,565

CHAPTER 23: INFORMATION FOR MANAGEMENT CONTROL

23.1
- *decision-making* – deciding what action to take, eg production, new products
- *planning* – for the future of the business or organisation
- *control* – comparing actual results with forecasts and seeking reasons for discrepancies

23.2
- *costs* – materials, labour and expenses
- *income* – mainly from the sale of products or services

23.3 *Financial accounting*

- records transactions that have happened already
- looks backwards to show what has happened in the past
- is accurate to the nearest penny, with no estimated amounts
- is often a legal requirement to keep accounts (eg for VAT and Inland Revenue purposes)
- maintains confidentiality of information (eg payroll details, VAT returns, sales figures)

Management accounting

- uses accounting information to summarise transactions that have happened already and to make estimates for the future
- looks in detail at costs – materials, labour and expenses – and income
- looks forward to show what is likely to happen in the future
- may use estimates where these are the most useful or suitable form of information
- provides management with reports that are of use in running the business or organisation
- provides management information as frequently as circumstances demand – speed is often vital as information may go out-of-date very quickly
- is not sent to people outside the organisation – it is for internal use
- maintains confidentiality of information (eg payroll details)

23.4
- A discussion question which focuses on the management functions of decision-making, planning and control.
- The student is likely to undertake tasks such as balancing the petty cash book, reconciling control accounts with subsidiary ledgers, dealing with queries and correcting errors, preparing a bank reconciliation statement.
- The managing director or chief executive will undertake tasks of a strategic nature, such as deciding whether the business is to expand, which new products are to be developed, reviewing the cost and income figures for last month, monitoring the overall performance of the business or organisation.

23.5 *planning*

The first step is to take a few minutes to plan the day's work in order of priority. This would appear to be:

- changes to payroll data to be made
- process the payroll
- take advantage of settlement discounts on purchases invoices
- check the terms of payment to see whether other purchases invoices should be paid today
- write the cash book up-to-date

Preparing the bank reconciliation statement and balancing the petty cash book (and restoring the imprest amount) appear to be lower priority.

decision-making

The two accounts assistants are briefed on your plan for the day. You ask the full-time assistant to enter the changes to the payroll and then to process the payroll, including preparation of cheques and BACS payments, and also to enter the transactions in the double-entry accounts.

The part-time assistant is to process payments for those purchases invoices at the end of their credit period.

You will go through the other purchases invoices to identify those that offer a cash discount for prompt settlement – you will take the decision as to whether or not the cash discount is worth taking. The part-time assistant will then process the payments for those that you decide to pay.

control

Progress on processing the payroll needs to be checked from time-to-time – the task needs to be completed so that the employees of Surestart Training can be paid on Friday. Later on you check the schedule for cheques and BACS payments, together with the entries made in the double-entry accounts. Cheques and the BACS payment schedule have to be signed by an authorised signatory to the company's bank account, so you will need to contact the administration manager to arrange this.

You supervise the work of the part-time assistant and resolve any queries in the processing of payments to creditors. You check the double-entry transactions in the subsidiary (purchases) ledger and cash book together with the cheques or BACS payments. The administration manager will need to arrange for the cheques and the BACS payment schedule to be signed.

If time permits you will ask for the cash book to be written up last week and balanced (which you can then check). You can then examine the bank statement for unpresented cheques and outstanding lodgements – from which a bank reconciliation statement can be prepared. Also, petty cash book can be balanced (which you can check) and the imprest amount can be restored.

summary

At the end of the day you can review progress to see how well your planning, decision-making and control has handled the workload of the accounts department. As the accounts supervisor will not be back for some days, you can plan for the next day's work ...

23.6 (a) financial accounting

(b) financial accounting

(c) management accounting

(d) financial accounting

(e) management accounting (using financial accounting information)

(f) management accounting

23.7

- A discussion question which focuses on the different levels of management accounting information.
- The student is likely to be asked for analysis of costs or income to date, cost centre information, comparisons between actual and estimated figures, estimates for next year of costs for which he or she is responsible.
- The supervisor/manager is likely to be asked for an analysis of costs and/or income for particular products or services, a comparison of actual costs and/or income with forecasts and the reasons for differences, estimated future costs and/or income for the section of the business or organisation for which the manager is responsible.

23.8 (a)
- cost centres – section of a business to which costs can be charged
- profit centre – section of a business to which costs can be charged, income can be identified, and profit can be calculated
- investment centre – section of a business where profit can be compared with the amount of money invested in the centre

(b)
- school or college – teaching departments, eg languages, science; also administrative departments, eg human resources, library, educational technology
- manufacturing business – by product, eg product A, product B, or by factory, eg Birmingham, Coventry

(c) A discussion topic which draws on the student's own experience

23.9

MEMORANDUM

To: Finance Director
From: A Student, Accounts Assistant
Subject: Costs and income for last year

Ref: AS
Date: today

I refer to your request for details of the costs and income for last year of each section of the business. Details are as follows:

	Newspapers and magazines	*Books*	*Stationery*
Cost Centre	£000s	£000s	£000s
• materials	155	246	122
• labour	65	93	58
• expenses	27	35	25
• total	247	374	205
Profit Centre			
Income from sales	352	544	230
less Costs (see above)	247	374	205
Profit	105	170	25
Investment Centre			
Profit (see above)	105	170	25
Investment	420	850	250
Expressed as a percentage	25%	20%	10%

If I can be of further assistance, please do not hesitate to contact me.

23.10 (a) 204250

(b) 501050

(c) 402150

(d) 503700

(e) £240 to each centre: 203200, 303200, 403200, 503200, 603200

(f) 403050

(g) 304050

MEMORANDUM

To: Supervisor **Ref:** AS
From: A Student **Date:** today
Subject: Today's costs and income

As requested, I give details of today's costs and income that I have coded:

	£
• materials (code numbers 1000–1999)	22,740
• labour (code numbers 2000–2999)	840
• expenses (code numbers 3000–3999)	90,985
• income (code numbers 4000–4999)	16,640

Please let me know if I can be of further assistance.

CHAPTER 24: PRESENTING AND COMPARING MANAGEMENT INFORMATION

24.1 True.

24.2 False.

24.3 See text pages 503 to 504.

24.4 (a) £40,000 (b) £50,000 (c) £5,000 (d) £23,000 (e) £25,000 (f) £20,000

(g)

	2002 *actual* £000s	2003 *actual* £000s	2003 *forecast* £000s
Total Sales	1,430	1,555	1,520
Total Costs	920	1,048	1,005

The memo should point out that the difference between actual and forecast figures for 2003 is: Sales £35,000 higher than forecast, Costs £43,000 higher than forecast.

24.5 Monthly sales as per question (suggested left-hand column). Cumulative monthly sales (suggested right-hand column) quoted in £000s:

January £120, February £250, March £375, April £506, May £645, June £786, July £932, August £1,069, September £1,208, October £1,351, November £1,498, December £1,633.

24.6 (a)

24.7 (b) Sales total £727,000; costs £530,000

(c/d) Sales differences; +£5,000, +£5,000, +£2,000, +£10,000, total +£22,000

Cost differences; +£5,000, +£5,000, +£1,000, +£4,000, total +£15,000

24.8 Differences: materials +£610, labour –£1,760, expenses –£600, total –£1,750. The memo should point out the reason for the labour costs, ie machine failure and added overtime.

24.9 (a) This is highly confidential information which could be communicated by letter, or by e-mail if the managers have restricted access mailboxes.

(b) This is not confidential and could be openly e-mailed or written on a note.

(c) The figures will not be confidential and can readily be e-mailed

24.10 (b)

	A	B	C	D	E	F
1	**EASTERN LTD - EXPENDITURE BUDGET: APRIL 2003**					
2						
3			**Forecast for**	**Actual for**		**Difference:**
4	**Code**	**Description**	**month**	**month**	**Difference:**	**As % of forecast**
5			**£**	**£**	**£**	
6	**TO-6000**	**Wages**	10,210.00	9,700.00	510.00	5.00%
7						
8	**T0-6010**	**General expenses**	735.00	750.00	-15.00	-2.04%
9						
10	**T0-6020**	**Premises rent**	1,600.00	1,600.00	0.00	0.00%
11						
12	**AS-6000**	**Wages**	11,650.00	12,220.00	-570.00	-4.89%
13						
14	**AS-6010**	**General expenses**	700.00	670.00	30.00	4.29%
15						
16	**AS-6020**	**Premises rent**	1,275.00	1,300.00	-25.00	-1.96%
17						
18		**Totals**	26,170.00	26,240.00	-70.00	-0.27%

(d)

MEMORANDUM

To: David Norton, Accounts/Administration Manager — Ref: DN/AS BE0403

From: A Student, Accounts Assistant — Date: 1 May 2003

Subject: Budget Expenditure Analysis for April 2003 – Todford and Ashville

STRICTLY CONFIDENTIAL:

FAO ACCOUNTS/ADMINISTRATION MANAGER ONLY

I enclose a comparison of forecast and actual expenditure for the month of April 2003 for the Todford and Ashville outlets. In the following two cases the difference between forecast and actual expenditure exceeds 3% of the forecast figure.

- TO-6000 Wages (forecast £10,210 – actual £9,700 – an underspend of 5%)
- AS-6010 Wages (forecast £11,650 – actual £12,220 – an overspend of 4.89%)
- AS-6010 General expenses (forecast £700 – actual £670 – an underspend of 4.29%)

Index